THE END
OF THE
AMERICAN
CENTURY

THE END OF THE AMERICAN CENTURY

STEVEN SCHLOSSSTEIN

CONGDON & WEED, INC.
New York • Chicago

Library of Congress Cataloging-in-Publication Data
Schlossstein, Steven.
    The end of the American century / Steven Schlossstein.
      p.   cm.
    Includes bibliographical references.
    ISBN 0-86553-201-0 : $22.95
    1. United States—Politics and government—1989-   2. United
States—Politics and government—1981–1989.   3. United States—
Economic policy—1981-   4. Education—United States.   5. United
States—Social policy—1980-   I. Title.
E881.S35   1989
973.92—dc20   89-38064
                                                          CIP

Copyright © 1989 by Steven Schlossstein
International Standard Book Number: 0-86553-201-0
                            0-8092-0201-0Z (Contemporary Books, Inc.)
Published by Congdon & Weed, Inc.
A subsidiary of Contemporary Books, Inc.
298 Fifth Avenue, New York, New York 10001
Distributed by Contemporary Books, Inc.
180 North Michigan Avenue, Chicago, Illinois 60601

Published simultaneously in Canada by Beaverbooks, Ltd.
195 Allstate Parkway, Valleywood Business Park
Markham, Ontario L3R 4T8 Canada

COPYRIGHT ACKNOWLEDGMENTS

Grateful acknowledgment is made for permission to use material from the following. *Beyond American Hegemony*, by David Calleo. *The Closing of the American
Mind*, by Allan Bloom; copyright © 1987 by Allan Bloom; reprinted by permission
of Simon & Schuster, Inc. *Cultural Literacy*, by E. D. Hirsch; copyright © 1987
by Houghton Mifflin Company; reprinted by permission of Houghton Mifflin
Company. *Japan as Number One* and "Pax Nipponica?," by Ezra Vogel. *Losing
Ground: American Social Policy, 1950–1980*, by Charles Murray; copyright © 1984
by Charles Murray; reprinted by permission of Basic Books, Inc., Publishers. *MITI
and the Japanese Miracle*, "The End of American Hegemony and the Future of
Japanese-American Relations," "MITI, MPT, and the Telecom Wars: How Japan

For Claire and Peter
Born in Asia
Reared in America
Heirs to America's Pacific Century

CONTENTS

INTRODUCTION

This book is about America, a nation uncompromisingly committed to freedom and liberty and open markets. Yet it is a nation that has seen its standard of living decline, its level of industrial dominance threatened by foreign competition, its political system infected by the narrowness (and money) of special interests, its public education systems plagued by low achievement, its families and children seared by the emotional trauma of single parenthood and divorce, its society ripped apart by drugs, its national defense weakened by fraud and mismanagement, and its position of global leadership increasingly open to challenge—all in less than a generation's time.

But this book is also about Asia; inevitably, Japan and the Little Dragons—Korea, Taiwan, Hong Kong, and Singapore—whose dramatic rates of economic growth, soaring personal incomes, and aggressive trade and investment strategies are forcing America to rethink its own free-market ideology. That these Asian nations are setting new international standards for product quality and manufacturing excellence is by now well known. But these nations are also establishing new barometers for measuring the effectiveness of government-business cooperation, dramatic rates of savings and capital formation, social cohesiveness through inherently stable families, higher standards of achievement in public education, and the unparalleled development of human resources as national priorities.

A century ago, on the eve of the industrial age, America was blessed with the twin benefits of historical accident and circumstance: it possessed the most abundant natural resources in the world and was beginning to develop an industrial system to take advantage of them. Today, at the dawn of an emerging information age, Japan and the nations of East Asia are blessed with both historical accident and circumstance: they possess the most keenly developed human resources in the world and are creating the technological systems necessary to employ them.

In the past hundred years our nation outstripped all rivals in productive capability. We used to set every standard against which the world measured its achievement and progress. We gradually became accustomed to a world that we could dominate without fear of competition. But America is just now beginning to learn that a nation's competitiveness is not limited to what happens on the factory floor; it is organically related to the quality of its public education systems and the emotional stability of its families and the courage and ability of its political leadership to lead.

Consequently, when we talk about the end of the American century, we mean the *old* American century is coming to an end. The transition is proving to be abrupt and painful, its outcome by no means assured. In place of the old could be a new American century, an America reinvigorated by this prodding, competitive spur from East Asia. But if the next century too is to be an American century, it will have its taproots across the Pacific, not across the Atlantic. Much depends on how we respond to the Asian challenge, on making some hard choices in the years ahead, on learning how to live within our means rather than beyond them, on finding ways to balance our political commitment to freedom with our duties and responsibilities as a nation. We must continue to find new and innovative ways to regenerate the energy and vitality and entrepreneurial genius that are the essence of America.

So this book is about revitalization too, about a nation whose future remains very much in its own hands. The notion of America's decline has struck a popular chord in recent years, and many have come to accept a pessimism that says America's greatness is behind it. That the United States will follow other great powers before it on the downhill path to obscurity. That America's position of global leadership will in time be eclipsed by a Japan that is already the world's richest nation and is seeking political power commensurate with its economic strength.

The Japanese, in particular, view America's perceived decline with a strange mixture of satisfaction and concern. In the course of the past two years, several books that became bestsellers in Tokyo have warned Japanese readers about the consequences of an America no longer able to lead the world and have naturally (if not arrogantly) assumed that Japan will rise while America falls. *Pax Japonica* by University of Tokyo physicist Toshiyasu Kunii predicts a Japan atop an "information empire" based on its strengths in education, electronics, and high technology. *Pax Consortis* by Sophia University professor Kuniko Inoguchi foresees a world governed by a consortium of more pluralistic powers as America's unilateral power wanes.

Jun Etoh's *Nichibei Senso wa Owatteinai (The War Between Japan and America Is Not Over)*, perhaps the most sensational of the lot, projects a continued "war of protraction" between the two countries based on a hard-fought struggle for global leadership in the strategic, high-technology industries of the future. And Sha Seiki's *America no Choraku (America's Decline)* describes an America weakened by poor public education, a business leadership preoccupied with asset-shuffling, a debased currency, a hollowed-out manufacturing sector, and fiscal irresponsibility, suggesting in all this that not just America but the entire West, too, is experiencing an irreversible decline and that East Asia—led, of course, by its "top runner," Japan—will rise to rule the future. All these books share the single theme that the United States clearly represents the past and Japan the future; not one of them even *hints* at the possibility of a revitalized America.

But *The End of the American Century* is not about the pessimism of America's decline; it is about the optimism of an American renewal. In an era of cumulative trade and federal deficits, the debate about federal spending—how much, for what purposes, to what end—continues. Yet reliance on spending alone is no longer a practical policy response in any case; America cannot afford it even if it were. Rather, the nation needs to look increasingly at the thoughtful use of *incentives* to help restore its competitive greatness: incentives that will strengthen its strategic manufacturing sectors and enhance its technological leadership; incentives to revive its system of representative democracy; *massive* incentives to boost the rate of domestic savings and capital formation to curb its dependence on foreign capital and to prevent the nation's future from being held hostage by foreign powers; incentives to give Americans greater competition and choice in public education and restore the nation's previously high standards of achievement; incentives to revitalize the family by increasing the level of personal tax deductions, putting child-care decisions in the hands of parents, not the state, and thereby further reinforcing the freedom of individual choice; incentives to provide more flexibility between employer and employee, to ensure that America continues to get its very best and brightest into the work force and yet enables them, mothers and fathers alike, to perform their vital roles as custodians of the nation's future— as parents of America's children; and incentives to make America's military-industrial sector more productive, reliable, and cost-effective.

The use of thoughtful incentives that are both positive and practical, that can strengthen these vital institutions in American life, is a more innovative attempt to solve American problems the *American* way. Over the years, any number of proposals have been made that emulate Asian techniques, from creating a new federal bureaucracy cloned from Japan's famed Ministry of International Trade and Industry (MITI) to developing a national industrial policy that would put Washington in charge of guiding and directing the nation's economic future. But while these methods may suit a more homogeneous (and authoritarian) East Asian culture well, they cannot be employed productively in a pluralistic, ethnically diverse, multiracial nation like America.

Incentives can. America has a long history of using incentives to reinforce the behavior of its individual citizens in desired directions. Whereas the nations of East Asia can often rely on historical traditions— because they are perhaps more permanently ingrained in the cultural fabric—a younger nation like America must often look to public policy as a means of influencing the course of its future. And tax policy is one of the most powerful tactical tools the nation can use. Unfortunately, many thoughtful incentives were eliminated in the 1986 tax reform legislation—such as deductible individual retirement accounts (IRAs) that encouraged citizens to save and the Investment Tax Credit (ITC) that encouraged manufacturers to invest. They need to be restored, and new ones need to be devised (and implemented), to ensure that America enters the new century in a position of strength, able to provide the kind of global leadership necessary for the new age. As with trade and investment policy, so with education and social policy: emulation of Asian systems is not the answer; the application of incentives is.

America is at its strongest and most competitive when it is open, vigorous, and hopeful about the future; its legacy is the legacy of ordinary people working together to achieve extraordinary things. Americans are a beneficent people; but, short of a crisis, they would just as soon be left alone, as they would leave others alone. War should not, however, be the only crisis capable of galvanizing the nation's consciousness; the threat to American leadership in the strategic, high-technology industries, principally from Japan, ought to generate a comparable competitive response.

For the primary challenge to this nation in the last decade of the twentieth century may come not from the military and ideological threat posed by Soviet Russia, as in the recent past, but from the technological supremacy and political ideology of an increasingly adversarial Japan. Protectionism is not the answer to this challenge; adaptation is. America's leaders must learn to distinguish between being tough with the Japanese and being negative toward them, a distinction that is not yet fully understood. America has too frequently blamed Japan for its own policy failures and competitive shortcomings. Japan, for its part, has been skilled (if not ruthless) in defending its own national interests, but far less adept at helping to maintain the harmony a global system requires.

America must remain the world's preeminent power as a *primus inter pares* in a more pluralistic age so that the global system can continue to be driven by its values of freedom, liberty, and justice. The alternatives to Pax Americana may either be chaos and instability on the one hand or Pax Nipponica on the other, symbolized by a politically more powerful Japan whose controlling values are conformity, loyalty, hierarchy, obedience, and duty—values that resonate in a culturally homogeneous nation but command no wider outside audience. Ever shrewd in its strategy, always aggressive in its tactics, Japan could move quickly to fill the global political vacuum created by the failed ideology of communism. This means potentially more, not less, conflict between America and its most important Pacific partner. That Tokyo, and not Moscow, may represent the primary challenge to American global leadership in the waning years of this century has profound implications for American policy formulation and response.

Finally, for busy businesspeople and public policy officials, some suggestions for navigating this lengthy material in a more targeted manner, as alternatives to proceeding from beginning to end.

The book is divided into five distinct, stand-alone sections, each treating a separate theme: trade, investment, and economic policy in Part I; government and political affairs in Part II; public education in Part III; social policy and the family in Part IV; and national security in Part V. The prologue sets the scene by taking a futuristic look at some hypothetical (but by no means unrealistic) events through the remainder of the twentieth century, and the epilogue pulls all these thematic threads together in looking at the reinvigoration of Pax Americana for the new century.

Generally speaking, the first two chapters of each section treat contemporary developments in East Asia, showing how the competitive pressure on America is emerging. The final two chapters in each section then deal principally with an American perspective on these themes, beginning with the problems America is experiencing and then concluding with a look at the kinds of incentives that might be considered to help solve them.

Those who may be put off by the book's somewhat daunting length may also wish to consider that it comprises a useful one-volume source of valuable material on five of the most important issues that will continue to concern our nation for the rest of this century. Its end notes and its bibliographic citations may be especially helpful for those who are looking for a convenient collection of the best and most recent related references, whether for further analysis, for public speaking purposes, or for assistance in the preparation of internal working memoranda. In the spirit of this book, these may represent a few additional incentives to help beat the competitive challenge to America in an American way.

The overriding thrust of the book—competitiveness—necessarily involves more than just trade policy, investment incentives, or what happens solely on the factory floor. It requires a more responsive political system, a much more productive and achievement-driven public education system, more durable families, and emotionally healthy children, in addition to a necessary system of national defense. These themes all contribute to a concept of comprehensive national security that must be regarded in broader terms than just the military.

In a word, the five themes of this book that together comprise a more complete view of the nation's competitiveness are *organically* interrelated, which is why public policy attempts to deal just with trade and investment problems without addressing the other related issues will fail, and, too, why consideration of just one individual theme (or section) by the reader is but a one-dimensional view of the whole. It matters little if America equips its factories with sophisticated, state-of-the-art manufacturing equipment, unless America's workers are also the products of a better public education system that enables them to manage this more complex environment. Yet without the emotional stability of strong families, our nation's children cannot achieve their full potential. And a system of representative democracy that remains unresponsive, failing to create new and innovative incentives but protected by a massive defense establishment appropriate to another age, could prove to be as precarious as a castle constructed on sand.

THE END
OF THE
AMERICAN
CENTURY

"*Nations do not have permanent enemies; Nor do they have permanent friends. They have only permanent interests.*"

Henry John Temple,
Lord Palmerston
(1784–1865)

"*To win a hundred victories in a hundred battles is not the acme of skill; to defeat the enemy* without fighting *is the acme of skill.*"

Sun–tzu,
The Art of War
Fourth Century B.C.

PROLOGUE

1

LOOKING BACK FROM THE YEAR 2001: RESOLUTIONS FOR THE NEXT CENTURY

It's December 31, 2000, and you're a little worried.

You're trying to come up with a reasonable list of New Year's resolutions for the first day of the first month of the first year of the new century. You sit and stare out your living room window at the mounting drifts of fresh winter snow.

You cast back in your mind to a time when life seemed easier, when things were simple. Hard to believe that as recently as 1980 America was still number one in practically everything, from tons of steel made to numbers of cars produced to the quality of high-technology products in the workplace. But today—on the threshold of the twenty-first century—most of the country's basic sheet steel is imported from Korea, one out of every two cars sold in America is Japanese, the nation's entire consumer electronics sector is based in Taiwan, and virtually all American computer software is created in Singapore or Hong Kong— the latter then a British crown colony, now a fragile capitalist protectorate of a Communist province of the People's Republic of China, a shadow of its former self. Things aren't so simple anymore. What happened?

The marker year was 1980.

That was the year an ideology called Reaganomics decreed that you could have a dollar's worth of government for only seventy-five cents. A bargain. The patron saints of this new ideology were neoclassical economists, theologians who stood common sense on its head and declared that America would undergo a spiritual revolution in its financial accounts, that Adam Smith's "invisible hand of the market" would perform magic, that lower taxes would generate both economic growth and social equity. They were right, of course, but they couldn't bring

3

off the other half of the equation: to control the exponential growth of federal spending by a fiscally irresponsible Congress that routinely pronounced the administration's budgets dead on arrival.

That was the last year America ran a global surplus in its foreign trade account, when the bilateral deficit with Japan was only $10 billion. But by 1987 America's global deficit soared to more than $160 billion, more than half of which was with East Asia: the deficit with Japan alone was then more than $60 billion, with Taiwan nearly $20 billion, and with Korea almost $10 billion. Every year from 1895 to 1980, America had sold more goods and services abroad than it had bought in return. In seven short years the nation had undone what it had taken three generations to accomplish.

East Asia had begun to control America's destiny.

Prior to 1980 America's trade across the Atlantic—with Europe—had dominated its foreign economic relations. But by 1980 America's Pacific trade already equaled its Atlantic trade. By 1986 its Pacific trade was 125 percent of its Atlantic trade, by 1993 nearly double. Why three East Asian countries—Japan, Korea, and Taiwan—had the world's highest real economic growth rates, the highest savings and investment rates, and the highest rates of manufacturing productivity and how two others, Singapore and Hong Kong, had become virtual reexport and value-added service centers was no longer a mystery. They were all outward-looking, dynamic, and powered by a radically different concept in capitalist developmental economics.

By 1987 Japan alone accounted for nearly 80 percent of the East Asian GNP, making it a global economic superpower second only to the United States in size and influence. Its high-technology industries had outstripped those of America, supported by economic policies built on an entirely new premise of government-business cooperation—strategic industrial policies that became in effect a "visible hand of the market." Free trade had become de facto managed trade, with nearly three-quarters of Japan's exports subject to quota, restraint, or orderly marketing agreement. Its aggressive external commercial strategies had worked brilliantly, exactly according to plan: competition, then domination, then elimination.

America's cumulative trade deficit had already reached $550 billion in 1987 and went past the $1 trillion mark in 1992—nearly 20 percent of current GNP. Despite warnings that these deficit levels were unsustainable, unpredictable, and risky, the nation suffered from political gridlock: it could neither increase its anemic savings rate to finance a higher level of investment and make its industrial structure more competitive nor devise a system of innovative taxation to generate the necessary revenues to unwind its cumulative federal deficit, now nearing $3 trillion.

By 1988 America's net foreign capital position (what it owed minus what others owed it) had reached a negative $500 billion, too. In the space of eight years, as a result of the budget deficits and inadequate domestic private savings, the nation had wasted half a trillion dollars selling foreign assets and borrowing extensively from foreigners. These numbers dwarfed the recycled petrodollars stemming from oil shocks in 1973 and 1979 and made Third World borrowers like Mexico and Brazil look frugal by comparison. America's total foreign debt was approaching Germany's reparations burden following World War I. The United States had become the world's number one debtor nation.

By 1987 Japan had already become the world's number one creditor, with total overseas assets exceeding $500 billion. By 1991 Japan had completed a three-year series of strategic acquisitions in America, giving it control of key American industries. Honda Motor, already the largest foreign automaker in America with its Ohio factory, acquired the Buick-Oldsmobile-Cadillac Group of General Motors, sending shock waves through the industry. Nippon Electric Corporation, which had already acquired Honeywell Computer in 1986, took over the assets of the failing Zenith Company, America's last remaining competitor in consumer electronics. And in a major coup, the *Nihon Keizai Shimbun (Nikkei)*, Japan's leading business publisher, acquired Dow Jones and with it the *Wall Street Journal*; Nikkei now controlled the world's largest financial database.

By 1991 Japan had become the number one contributor to the World Bank and the International Monetary Fund, replacing the United States. Since its inception in the early 1960s, the Asian Development Bank, headquartered in Manila, had had a Japanese president. By 1991 Japan was underwriting virtually its entire soft loan portfolio—America could afford no further capital. In 1993 Japan became the largest shareholder of the ADB and took control; the U.S. was bumped to second place.

Between 1979 and 1987 America had tripled the size of its national debt to more than $2 trillion, and total federal spending was nearly a quarter of GNP. Individual prosperity, national misery, your friends liked to say: you seemed to be doing all right, but the country as a whole was not prospering. Its future was being buried under a mountain of public and private debt, mortgaged to its children's paychecks. The old Keynesian motto, "tax and spend," had been replaced with a new one: "borrow and spend."

Total consumer installment debt had soared to an all-time high of $600 billion by 1988; even without the accounting gimmickry of home equity loans, it had risen from 12 percent of personal income in 1982 to 17 percent by 1988. Federal interest payments on the national debt were now costing American taxpayers almost $150 billion a year, nearly 3 percent of GNP, about equal to the total savings originally projected in the 1981 tax cut.

By 1988 America's savings rate as a percentage of net disposable income had dropped to below 5 percent, the lowest in the industrialized world. Japan's savings rate, despite domestic tax reforms, was still 17 percent, Korea's more than 20 percent, and Taiwan's more than 30 percent. The political logjam in Washington prevented the nation from creating necessary incentives to boost its savings rate, so America's productivity, capital formation, and relative standard of living all continued to suffer.

By 1987 Japan and Western Europe held $179 billion worth of U.S. Treasury bonds, plus another $250 billion in America's common stocks and corporate bonds. In 1979 Germany had refused to go along with U.S. monetary policy, giving Washington no recourse but to raise interest rates, which jumped to all-time highs by spring of 1980. In late 1987 Germany again refused to play "chicken" and raised its domestic interest rates to stabilize the deutsche mark, forcing America to devalue the dollar even further. Washington's threat threw the specter of dollar free-fall over the world's financial markets. The Japanese reacted by selling their dollar bonds aggressively. They precipitated a crisis and spread panic the following day on Wall Street. The result was Black Monday and market meltdown.

When the stock market crashed on October 19, 1987, the Dow Jones Industrial Average plunged 508 points, or 22.6 percent, the largest single-day drop in history. More than $1 trillion in stock value vanished overnight. Professionals quickly pointed out that 1987 was not another 1929; back then, most stocks were bought on 70 percent margin, whereas now the margin was only 50 percent and not nearly so heavily used. But the lower stock margins had really masked other means of

borrowing to buy stocks—principally from home equity loans, which
had soared in value to nearly $200 billion.

Worse was what had happened to the nation's currency, once the
strongest in the world. For years it had been out of alignment, in part
because of macroeconomic fundamentals, in part because American
political leadership had believed in the theological sanctity of free markets, forgetting all the while that markets were, in fact, man-made. So
in 1985, the Group of Five—America, Great Britain, West Germany,
Japan, and Canada—weakened the dollar against the yen and the mark.
The dollar fell from ¥240-to-1 in September 1985 to nearly ¥130-to-1
by October 1987, when almost a third of the nation's stock value disappeared overnight. The crunch came in 1991, when the dollar touched
¥100-to-1, the last psychological threshold. Once it broke through that
barrier, it went into free-fall. Dollar interest rates soared, rekindling
double-digit inflation and creating the deepest recession in postwar
history.

Everyone had wanted to call the recession of 1991–95 a depression,
but the politicians didn't dare. True, it had been without the grim
breadlines of the 1930s because of the government's safety net—individual bank accounts insured to $100,000, brokerage accounts insured
to $500,000, the Social Security system. But by 1993 Social Security
was taking nearly 25 percent of the American worker's paycheck, up
from 13.2 percent in 1988, forcing you to borrow more simply to
maintain your standard of living. You had no choice. The nation was
now borrowing the equivalent of 3 percent of its GNP every year.
That made you very nervous.

It made foreign lenders very nervous, too. So the Japanese finally
poured salt into America's wounds. In 1993, holding more than two-
thirds of Washington's total foreign debt, Tokyo refused to take another
IOU from Uncle Sam and boycotted new Treasury bond issues. The
world's financial markets went into total panic and unloaded dollar
assets. Black Monday of 1987 looked tame by comparison. For the first
time in over 200 years of its organized history, the full faith and credit
of the U.S. government came into doubt.

Late in 1995 America had been hit by a third oil crisis, pushing the
country's dependence on imported oil back up to 60 percent, nearly
double the rate a decade earlier. OPEC had pulled off another tactical
political move and doubled the price of oil from $18 a barrel to $35,
as the Israeli-Palestinian conflict continued to fester. But Indonesia

broke ranks and withdrew from OPEC, aligning itself economically with East Asia rather than politically with the Arabs. Together with Thailand and Malaysia, Indonesia was industrializing rapidly now, to become one of Asia's three new dragons.

The major economies of East Asia—Japan, Korea, and Taiwan—took the latest oil price increases in stride, having long since implemented stringent policies on energy pricing, consumption, and alternative sourcing. They also had surplus domestic savings ample to cushion the shock. Alone among the major industrial nations, America had steadfastly refused to develop its own strategic energy policy, preferring to let domestic energy politics dictate through the market. The price of a gallon of gasoline rose to $2.35, still cheaper in inflation-adjusted terms in 1995 than the 35¢ fuel of forty years earlier, yet 50 percent lower than average pump prices around the world. Déjà vu gas lines appeared again, and sales of large American cars, so popular a decade earlier, plummeted. Private American savings were insufficient to ride out the storm, and additional borrowing was out of the question, so the economy stayed on the skids and unemployment soared.

In 1995, in response to the escalation of hostilities in the Middle East and the persistent inability of American foreign policy to defuse geopolitical tensions, Japanese naval destroyers appeared in the Persian Gulf for the first time to protect East Asian commercial shipping on the long supply routes back to the Far East. "Black 202s" from Tokyo, crack counterterrorist teams modeled after the Tokugawa's ninja, maneuvered behind the scenes in Baghdad and Tehran, using political infiltration tactics to defuse the crisis.

The sight of the Rising Sun flag so far from Japan had raised eyebrows, of course, and Washington had responded with angry retorts about the reemergence of Japanese militarism. Washington's objections, in fact, had been ironic. For years successive American governments had pressured Japan to spend more on defense, to dampen the criticism that Japan was "free-riding" at American expense. Already by 1989 Japan had the free world's second-highest defense budget in absolute terms, spending nearly $30 billion a year. Japan's traditional 1 percent-of–GNP threshold had been breached long before, in 1986; its military expenditures had risen to nearly 2 percent of GNP by 1993, or about $70 billion. Washington had pushed Tokyo too far. Under the terms of the U.S.–Japan bilateral Security Treaty, Japan had given America the requisite one-year notice that it would not renew the treaty after 1995. It would now take responsibility for its own defense.

Conservative Japanese political leaders had long chafed under a political constitution written hastily and forced on it by the American occupation at a time when Japan had no sovereignty. In 1980 an *Asahi Shimbun* newspaper poll surveyed members of Japan's ruling party, the Liberal Democrats, and found that more than two-thirds favored revision of the Constitution. After long years of domestic debate, revision was finally achieved in 1993. Key among the revised provisions were renunciation of the controversial Article 9, which prohibited Japan from maintaining offensive military forces, and abrogation of its three non-nuclear principles (not to build, possess, or permit entry of nuclear weapons). It was called the Jiyu Kempo. The Free Constitution.

So by 1995 Japan had joined the nuclear club and had become a full-fledged political and military superpower. The timing had seemed propitious.

Earlier that year a Philippine military junta had taken power, forcing America to vacate Clark Air Base and Subic Bay Naval Station just as negotiations to renew the base agreements had gotten under way in Manila. The United States had refused to be blackmailed by the Aquino government—which had held out for $1 billion a year, more than triple the previous compensation—and was threatening to withhold all economic aid to the Philippines.

The Aquino administration had been powerless to resist. Philippine population growth, at 3 percent a year already one of the highest rates in the world, kept two-thirds of its people in poverty and forced the government to increase its foreign debt, now well over $50 billion. The country would go bankrupt without American aid.

But a new generation of Philippine leaders, educated and trained in Japan instead of the United States, knew that the Philippines' main problem was economic overdependence on its American colonizer. That dependence had to be broken, so they used the army to bring about a coup to force America's hand. The poorly trained Philippine military would have been no match for the superior American forces at Clark and Subic unless the Filipinos had a more powerful ally. So the Young Turks turned again to Tokyo.

When that fleet of destroyers flying the Rising Sun flag sailed into Manila Bay in late 1995 for the first time in over fifty years, the Japanese ironically were hailed as liberators from the American colonialists. They stayed only temporarily, as a show of power, but brought Washington and Tokyo to the brink of hostility. Washington wisely backed down. On the heels of a wrenching depression, America no longer had the financial resources or the clear technological superiority in advanced weaponry to challenge the Japanese. America withdrew from Clark and Subic to a smaller presence on Guam.

The American people would realize only later how fortuitous that decision had been. Beginning in 1993, Manila had requested military advisers from Washington to help contain the expanding Communist threat. By 1995 America had nearly 50,000 "advisers" in the Philippines, spread over seven of the country's 7,000 islands, and domestic political opposition to another potential Vietnam had become more strident as news of each dead American soldier hit home.

As America was being forced out, the Japanese moved in to fill the security vacuum. America no longer called the shots.

The Soviet Union, still preoccupied predominantly with Europe, had become anxious at the display of Japanese military power in the Philippines and began concentrating armed troops and attack aircraft on the disputed Kurile Islands. Ceded by Japan to the USSR at the end of World War II, the Kuriles had remained a central source of conflict between Japan and the Soviet Union for half a century.

But when the Soviets moved to shore up their forces on the Kuriles, Japan moved resolutely and promptly to annihilate them. Highly skilled Japanese pilots of the Air Self-Defense Forces flew under Soviet radar at Mach 3 in downsized attack fighters developed by Mitsubishi Heavy Industries to knock out Soviet airfields before their outdated MiG-23s could become airborne. The Japanese navy surrounded the islands with a chain of satellites with sophisticated electronic technology that rendered a Soviet response meaningless. The Soviet Union could not risk a nuclear attack, given Japan's own nuclear capability, so it withdrew. For the second time in the twentieth century Japan had defeated the USSR in a major military encounter. Moscow returned the Kuriles to Japan under the new Treaty of Peace and Friendship that brought Pacific Siberia needed development capital and guaranteed vital natural resources to Japan.

The defeat had been doubly galling for Moscow. Earlier its efforts at economic reform through *perestroika* had failed, too. Mikhail Gorbachev and his loyalists had been purged in 1992 and sent to the Siberian camps. The dreaded KGB took control of the Politburo, restored power to the central bureaucracy, and sealed off Russia's borders again. Moscow then turned to the Japanese economic model for emulation. But as the only means of distracting its population from domestic failure, the Red Army had marched into Warsaw to occupy Poland, which had threatened to leave the Eastern Bloc. Refugees flooded Western Europe again, and the Continent pulsed with instability.

In 1995 Mexico finally defaulted on its more than $100 billion of global debt. The Japanese government stepped in with a massive financial aid program from the nation's ample reserves and tied its assistance to a systematic, conditional, institutional reorganization of the Mexican government based on Japan's industrial policy model. Technocrats from Tokyo worked side by side with their Mexican counterparts to create a disciplined bureaucracy, devised financial incentives to increase domestic savings and investment, erected tariff walls to constrain imports, implemented subsidies to stimulate higher value-added exports, and created policies to target high technology. Mexico would become the first major showcase of capitalist developmental economics outside East Asia, with dazzling results.

The technocrats instituted new social planning goals too, with aggressive financial incentives for families to limit population growth and to spur massive investment in education. Local universities became national technical institutes devoted to developmental economics and engineering. The Mexican political process became much more authoritarian to ensure the stability necessary for rapid economic growth. Elections were suspended until economic performance justified their resumption. Loyalty replaced liberty as the nation's underlying political value. A national identity card system was introduced. The penalty for possession or sale of drugs was death.

By early 1999 preliminary results indicated a stunning turnaround in Mexico's fortunes. Its external debt had been restructured and stretched out, not a new tactic in developmental economics, but successful this time because Japan had brought about a shift in Mexico's industrial structure from natural resource–intensive industries and handicrafts to human resource–intensive industries, such as state-of-the-art manufacturing plants in the *maquiladoras* and high-tech engineering services to complement them, supplemented by a more efficient, corruption-free bureaucracy. Foreign capital began to pour into Mexico City. The potential ripple effect on Third World economies was now a perceived reality, as the benefits of Japan's superior capitalist developmental system became demonstrably apparent.

Mexico proved that the model was not applicable only to Confucian cultures in Asia, as many had predicted. It could be exported and transplanted halfway around the world. Brazil, with its indigenous population of nearly 1 million Portuguese-speaking Japanese, would be next to emulate the Mexican example, with hopes for equally impressive results.

By the mid-1990s the world had evolved into three distinct economic and trading blocs: North and South America, with New York as the commercial center; Europe, Africa, and the Middle East, centered not in London but in Frankfurt; and East Asia and the Pacific, based of course in Tokyo.

The Pacific Zone, as it came to be known, experimented with some innovative intraregional tariff adjustments, at Japan's initiative: trade duties, quotas, and tariffs were eliminated for all countries within the region, making it the world's first comprehensive regional free-trade zone. This innovation further accelerated the world's fastest economic growth rates and spawned a new era of technology sharing among the advanced Asian economies. These dynamic developments gave birth to a new "USA": the United States of Asia.

As a result, three more nations in East Asia emerged as newly industrializing countries and came to be known as the NICs of the nineties. Thailand, Malaysia, and Indonesia made the necessary adjustments to their economies effected by Korea, Taiwan, and Singapore a decade earlier and based on the Japanese model. They implemented strategic industrial policies to spur export growth, targeted high technology to strengthen the value-added and higher-productivity manufacturing sectors, boosted domestic savings through massive financial incentives, and pushed higher educational standards as a national priority. As lower value-added industries became uncompetitive, capital investment from the "old" NICs poured into the "new" NICs, creating a dynamic cycle of growth and opportunity.

In 1996 the world's first hypersonic jet aircraft, made in Japan, had initiated its inaugural flight from Tokyo to New York with great fanfare. It took off from the new Tokyo Bay International Airport, which had been built on reclaimed land and was linked to downtown Tokyo by a new high-speed levitation railway. The flight over the North Pacific and arctic Canada took less than three hours of elapsed time.

A decade in the making, the Taiheiyo Tokkyu, or Orient Express, became an instant success with commercial travelers, dramatically shrinking the distance between America and the Pacific Zone. Subsequent nonstop flights were announced linking San Francisco and Singapore, Tokyo and Sydney, and Los Angeles and Beijing. Japanese industrial policy planners and aerospace engineers had been ecstatic: their goal of becoming a world-class competitor in commercial jet aviation had been reached. No export was more highly prized.

American politicians and business leaders were chagrined and embarrassed at having been outmaneuvered yet again by Japan, but they had been politically handcuffed. Constrained by continued federal budget deficits and inadequate private capital formation, America had simply been unable to underwrite a major new development in commercial aviation technology. U.S. leaders were also angered by Japan's continued practice of targeting strategic industries, through which new developments in industrial ceramics, semiconductor technology, high-definition TV, superconductivity, biotechnology, and avionics had been achieved. Yet America continued to license its own technology to Japan; it had no one but itself to blame.

By 1996 Japan had also replaced the United States as the major contributor to the United Nations, in effect now underwriting the UN's operating budget. Tokyo had worked long and hard to cultivate close relations with the individually small but collectively influential countries in black Africa, eventually achieving consensus on Japanese leadership for economic issues. The showcase model under way in Mexico was becoming a dramatic example of what Third World nations could potentially achieve themselves. Rather than writing them off as politically insignificant, as America had often done, Japan recognized their value as a group and organized them accordingly. Their support had been crucial in obtaining the necessary votes in the General Assembly to elect Japan as a permanent member of the Security Council, displacing France.

And so, in 1996, a year before Hong Kong reverted to China, the headquarters of the United Nations moved to Tokyo. The year before, the Japanese government had relocated its major bureaucracies to newly reclaimed land in Tokyo Bay. The new UN headquarters was located nearby, within minutes of key Japanese government offices and less than half an hour from Parliament by high-speed levitation rail. All of

Asia, with nearly two-thirds of the world's population, reacted pre-dictably to this prestigious development.

By July 1, 1997, when Hong Kong became a captive of the People's Republic of China under the dubious "one country, two systems" con-cept, a tidal wave of well-educated, highly skilled professionals had swept across the Pacific, emigrating to Australia, Singapore, Taiwan, Canada, and America. This trend had begun years earlier, when China refused to grant the people of Hong Kong fundamental voting rights under its Basic Law. The concept was a sham, and Hong Kong lost nearly a quarter of its population.

In the first six months of 1997 alone a million people left. China had no alternative but to send the Red Army into Kowloon to seal off Kai Tak airport, erecting a human "Berlin Wall of Asia." Those forced to remain were the less skilled, but eventually many of them too fled by sea and became the boat people of the 1990s. Manufacturers relo-cated to Singapore and Taiwan. Financiers reappeared in Tokyo, the region's financial center. Traders went to America, to strengthen its entrepreneurial class. Hong Kong became a ghost town in a country increasingly in turmoil. Communism, a failed ideology, was dead, and Hong Kong had become its coffin.

What had seemed, a decade earlier, to be the beginnings of China's new industrialization program, under former premier Deng Xiaoping's famous Four Modernizations, had instead turned into political quick-sand. Back in 1986 China had set out to triple its per-capita income of $400 by the turn of the century, with the goal of having its 1.3 billion people join the ranks of the newly industrializing countries. But the Communist planners failed to realize that rapid industrialization would outstrip the ability of Chinese society and its inexperienced institutions to cope.

Inflation had become rampant, causing prices to skyrocket. Huge bottlenecks developed in China's primitive distribution system. People deserted the rural areas for the cities, doubling the country's urban population and resulting in unforeseen social unrest, overcrowding, and disease. Air and water pollution threatened countless lives. Illegitimate births exploded, putting renewed pressure on China's already swelling population. Corruption had become pervasive again. The students and the workers were clamoring for democracy. China was out of control.

Already by late 1989 the party traditionalists had had no alternative but to take political control again, repeating a pattern whose roots went back centuries in Chinese history. The army reasserted itself, and its highest-ranking officers assumed key posts in the Central Committee to prevent both a counterrevolution and another civil war. China was ashamed to admit that its experiments with liberalization and modernization had failed. Beijing sent discreet feelers to Tokyo to explore versions of Japan's capitalist developmental model for China. Pride could be swallowed in the name of domestic stability. Thus were the seeds of China's own industrial policies sown for the twenty-first century.

When Kim Il-sung, premier of North Korea, died in late 1997, his son Kim Chong-il assumed power. Based on the failure of China's Four Modernizations and the demonstration effect of Japan's showcase economic model in Mexico, young Kim recognized straight away the futility of continuing a Communist system. He sent a team of trusted aides to Beijing to request their assistance in acting as intermediaries between Pyongyang and Tokyo. At the same time, he approached Seoul through Beijing on the sensitive issue of reunification.

About a year later, in 1998, Pyongyang and Seoul issued a joint proclamation abolishing the Demilitarized Zone that had separated their countries since 1945. This could not have been achieved without the tacit consent of Moscow and Washington, which were each preoccupied with domestic economic problems. But a mutual reduction of forces on the Korean Peninsula represented a golden opportunity to cut the expense of their own regional defense burdens in East Asia. America shifted its two remaining divisions from Korea to Guam and San Diego.

The integration of the two Korean economies followed a pattern of harmony now instead of conflict. Coal, iron ore, and petrochemicals flowed into the South from the resource-rich North. Automobiles, semiconductors, and advanced machine tools were shipped from technology-rich Seoul to Pyongyang. Mail, telephone, and telex lines were opened, and a common currency was devised.

Ultimately, North and South Korea would succeed where China and Hong Kong had failed. Their own "one country, two systems" format bridged the economic and industrial gap that existed between North and South. Technocrats from Seoul worked side by side with their counterparts in Pyongyang to develop the strategic industrial policies that would lead them confidently into the twenty-first century as one country, the Republic of Unified Korea.

For the first time since 1908 a unified Korea would send a united delegation to the Beijing Olympiad in September 2004. The first Olympics of the new century would be held, also for the first time, in the capital city of the largest country in the world. The International Olympic Committee had withheld its commitment pending resolution of the Hong Kong problem and, with Japan's help, restoration of economic and political stability. But the IOC had finally selected Beijing over the alternative sites, Caracas and Seattle.

Buoyed by the Korean example, and watching developments in China and Hong Kong closely, the independence movement gathered unmistakable momentum in Taiwan. Its political leadership convened in late 1997 to proclaim the formation of an independent Republic of Taiwan. A new national flag was designed and a new national anthem composed to reflect the emotional ebullience of this nation, nearly 90 percent of whose population were native to the island of Taiwan, not China. China would still be viewed as the primary source of Taiwan's cultural heritage, much as Americans still looked to England and Europe for theirs. But the thought of reunification paled in comparison with Taiwan's new spirit of independence and its outstanding economic achievements, especially after Hong Kong had been so rudely absorbed into the Communist system.

So it was with great fanfare on January 1, 1998, that the democratically elected premier of the new republic of Taiwan stood before the General Assembly of the United Nations in Tokyo to deliver her carefully rehearsed speech. To tumultuous applause, Taiwan became the 160th member of the UN. Shortly thereafter, it rejoined the IMF, the World Bank, and the General Agreement on Tariffs and Trade (GATT). Taiwan had the second-highest foreign exchange reserves in the world, after Japan; its export economy remained outward-looking and accounted for 80 percent of GNP, with a world-class manufacturing base competitive in leading-edge technology.

You frown as you watch the snow come down harder now, and your thoughts turn back to home. You were divorced in 1995, when you turned forty-three and your elder daughter was graduating from high school; you remember that feeling of helplessness tinged with fear. Your father is a healthy man in his early seventies. But America's own age composition in 1999 had become what it was in Florida in 1987. By the time your dad turns eighty, more Americans will be eighty or older than were sixty-five or older back then. Nearly two-thirds of the

American government's entitlement benefits, not means-tested, were now going to about 15 percent of the population, the elderly.

In 1986, 56 percent of all federal entitlement benefits went to the elderly, then just 12 percent of the population. America's population of senior citizens was projected to more than double by the year 2040, while its working-age population would grow by only 15 percent. The elderly of Japan, Korea, and Taiwan were projected to grow at comparable rates. The difference was that those countries had the invested savings to support them. In 1986 the salaries of more than three active workers supported each American retiree, but now, at the turn of the new century, barely two did.

By 1991 illegitimate teenage births in America had exploded to the highest rate in the industrial world. Nearly two-thirds of the recorded births in Washington, D.C., alone were to unmarried teenage mothers, and half of these were second or third children. The nation's dwindling tax revenues and anemic private savings could no longer underwrite that burden. The increase in low-value service jobs paralleled these demographic developments: the fastest-growing job sectors in America were janitors, fast-food workers, and clerks in retail sales. The growth in higher value-added manufacturing jobs was not in America, but in East Asia, and the higher value-added service jobs went with them.

Despite the widespread call for reform of America's public education system, nothing much seemed to happen. Teachers' salaries had increased nominally throughout the 1990s, but their blue-collar unions stood in the way of white-collar respect: incompetent teachers still couldn't be fired, accountability was a major problem, and merit pay for superior teaching was resisted strongly by the unions. Lip service was paid to the importance of improving rigor in the curriculum, but only the political rhetoric seemed to improve.

Scores on international achievement tests continued to decline; by 1999 American middle and high school students were placing dead last among all industrialized countries. School dropout rates rose; America was graduating fewer than 70 percent of its students from high school despite a shorter school year of only 185 days. Japan, Singapore, Korea, and Taiwan continued to graduate more than 90 percent of their high school students, with a rigorous school year averaging 225 days. New international standards in public education were now being set not by America but by Japan.

American education somehow seemed institutionally immune to reform; you wondered if a nation wedded to a century-old school system
dominated by local politics could find a way to restore that "vital triangle" that linked parent with teacher with child. America's public
schools would have to become more responsive to their markets—students and their parents—rather than remain captives of political control
symbolized by local school boards. The role models were there, but
they were America's private schools, rich and poor alike, with strong
leadership, leaner organizations, teacher accountability, higher standards, and an exit option parents could exercise if performance lagged.
Could the public schools possibly shed their vertical, rigidly bureaucratic structures to become more horizontal, flexible, and responsive?
Could parents be given greater freedom of choice? If America could
develop its human resources with as much dedication and skill as the
nations of East Asia had shown, it could survive with pride in a more
intensely competitive age.

The American family remained unstable and insecure at the turn of
the century, too. In 1988 half of American marriages still ended in
divorce, and more than half of all American women with children under
one were in the work force. But by 1995 over a third of America's
children were living with a single parent, most of them with their
mothers, and nearly two-thirds of all American women with young
children worked full-time. Child poverty had increased exponentially,
and there were still no comprehensive, national child-care tax credits
or parental leave policies. Could a nation whose families had disintegrated, whose children were insecure, and whose schools were substandard hope to retain the mantle of global leadership?

America's political system remained structurally unresponsive in
1999. Special interest groups were still the dominant influence and
PACs their dominant source of funding. Had the country's two-party
system become irrelevant—with Republicans dominating the White
House and Democrats controlling Congress—such that political gridlock was inevitable? Was this what the Founding Fathers had in mind
when they created America's unique and lasting political system?

You realize now as you never had before that America's days of
unbridled consumption and adversarial political behavior were over.
You had been uncomfortable knowing America seemed to be losing
control of its destiny, subject to the whims of foreign governments that
controlled ever-larger amounts of the nation's debt and held its future

hostage—foreign governments that didn't share America's commitment to freedom, liberty, or justice.

You realize too that the American century came to an end not in 2000 but in 1987, with market meltdown, or perhaps even earlier, in 1973, with the first oil crisis. America's festering federal deficits said volumes about its inability to respond to any crisis short of war. And its burgeoning trade deficits showed it was incapable of coming to grips with the growing economic challenge from Japan and East Asia.

A century ago, endowed with unlimited natural resources, America had been favored by accident if not by historical circumstance to succeed in the industrial era. Its brilliant entrepreneurial system, forged on the anvil of competitive individualism, had become a powerful beacon for the world. Now, a century later, Japan and East Asia seem equally endowed with unparalleled *human* resources, favored by accident if not by historical circumstance to succeed in the information age. Their durable social systems, innovative economic policies, and rigorous educational standards, all perfected through the dynamics of small group cooperation, had become the world's new emulation models.

But you're optimistic about the future, confident in the country's ability to meet this global challenge head-on, provided America could create the incentives to strengthen its competitive systems. Will the twenty-first century be the Pacific century, under a Pax Nipponica dominated by an authoritarian Japan, or can America revitalize itself to retain global leadership and extend the American century into the new millennium? As long as the international system is dominated by one superpower, hegemonic theorists argue, it doesn't really matter—England in the nineteenth century, via Pax Britannica, America in this century, via Pax Americana, perhaps Japan in the next. But historically, in the absence of one dominant power, the world has seen only stagnant or declining economic growth and ultimately instability, chaos, or war.

America's great contribution to global stability has been achieved through its primary principles of freedom, liberty, and justice. Japan is driven by a different value system, one that stresses loyalty, conformity, hierarchy, duty, and obedience. A global system dominated by those values, despite the inherent economic efficiencies, would be radically different. While the Third World might welcome a global hierarchy dominated by Japan, it is not at all clear that the industrialized world would. Least of all, America.

The story of America is the story of ordinary people working together to achieve extraordinary things. But in order to lead the twenty-first century, America needs to recover its competitive spirit. It must create new strategic policies—commercial, industrial, political, educational, and social—to retain global leadership in the new era. Those strategic policies must be the nation's resolutions for the next century.

You realize now that the key to America's competitive survival is not just in America's factories; it is in America's families and in America's classrooms and in the way America organizes itself politically. The process is not static, but organic.

You shake your head.

Why, then, did it take American leadership a full generation to wake up to the Asian challenge, risking another major war in the process, losing technological superiority in the balance, and putting national survival irrevocably on the line, when the facts had been known so long ago?

PART I
THE VISIBLE HAND OF THE MARKET: POLICIES AND INCENTIVES FOR GROWTH

2

TURBOCHARGED CAPITALISM: THE DYNAMICS OF JAPANESE ECONOMIC DEVELOPMENT

In 1945, when the Japanese surrendered to British troops in Singapore, their downcast leader commented to the victorious commanding general, as he handed across his sword, "We have lost only the first battle in the hundred years' war. There are still ninety-six years to go."

In a 1985 meeting with a senior Japanese official from MITI, a European trade minister said, "Japan's aggressive commercial tactics could lead to a trade war with my country." His Japanese counterpart replied, "This is war, Mr. Minister, and if you're not reading Clausewitz, you're not doing your job."

Trade deficits, and the negative political rhetoric that accompanies them, are in a sense standard fare for Americans today. Rare is the day when you can pick up your morning paper and *not* read another story about how Japanese computer chips are being "dumped" in the American market at unfair prices, or how Korea is aggressively selling Hyundai Excels and Samsung VCRs to grab a secure position on the first rung of the market share ladder, or how Taiwan is making practically anything and everything American customers want, from transistors to television sets to toys.

In fact, you have to go back pretty far to find a time when this was not the case. In 1960 America's trade across the Pacific was merely half the value of its trade across the Atlantic, and the total GNP of the Asia-Pacific region was a mere 29 percent of that of Western Europe. It was the time of Jean-Jacques Servan-Schreiber's apocalyptic best-seller, *The American Challenge*, in which the author documented the strategic American penetration of Europe and the growing European fear of America's dominant organizational system, the multinational corporation.

But by 1980 all this had changed. America's Pacific trade had exploded to 110 percent of the value of its Atlantic trade, and the Asia-Pacific GNP was now nearly two-thirds that of Western Europe. Conservative growth estimates indicated that by the year 2000 the Asia-Pacific GNP would equal that of America and Europe *combined*. Today about three-fourths of California's exports alone go to the Pacific region, and over 85 percent of its imports come from there.

In 1980 America's trade deficit with Japan was "only" about $10 billion, out of a total U.S. trade deficit that year of around $36 billion. But by 1987 not only had America's worldwide trade deficit increased almost fivefold, but the portion with Japan had jumped to nearly 40 percent of the total from just over 25 percent in 1980. Add in a deficit with Taiwan of nearly $20 billion, and with Korea of close to $10 billion, and more than 50 percent of America's global trade deficit in 1987 was with three East Asian countries, primarily in manufactured goods.

In 1945 Japan lay in ruins, its government humiliated by military defeat, its economy shattered. But by 1950 Japan had already recovered to its prewar peak of industrial production. By 1980 its per-capita GNP was nearly 80 percent of America's and was second in size only to that of the United States. By 1988 Japan's per-capita income was the highest in the world. Its economy was growing at an annual rate nearly twice that of the U.S. Taiwan's rate of economic growth was faster than Japan's, and Korea's was even faster than that; in fact, Korea in the 1970s and 1980s was expanding at the highest rate in the world.

Clearly, America and Europe weren't standing still. What was going on? How were these Asian countries able to come so far so fast?

JAPAN: EAST ASIA'S ECONOMIC GIANT

So much has been written about Japan in the past decade that Americans have begun to suffer from "Japan daze": an overabundance of information, analysis, hyperbole, insight, and deduction, all of which purports to explain the invincibility of Asia's economic giant and leave Americans feeling either captivated and impressed or disbelieving and angry.

Japan, critics say, subsidizes exports and keeps its own market closed to imports, so no wonder its export growth is so high. Or, Japan cheats by engaging in insidious, subversive, or questionable practices such as industrial policy and sectoral targeting and infant industry protectionism, all of which would either be illegal or represent serious antitrust violations in the West. Or, Japan grinds its students into the ground and subjects them to relentless competitive examinations, which turns them, uncreative and docile, into hardworking cogs for the national economic machine. Or, Japan steals technology from the West, employs nontariff barriers to keep foreign products out, manipulates the yen, and engages in unfair trade practices overseas, such as dumping, to exploit competitive advantage for its manufactured goods.

Or, obversely, isolated and vulnerable, Japan saves and invests a much higher percentage of disposable income. It rejects Adam Smith's neoclassical economic ideology and his invisible hand of the market, preferring to implement a hybrid economic ideology that becomes a visible hand of the market and creating new forms of government-business interaction. Or, totally void of natural resources and raw materials, Japan has no option but to develop its human resources to the fullest extent possible. Or, knowing that foreign trade is the commercial equivalent of national security, Japan plays hardball and uses aggressive export strategies, including predatory pricing tactics, to penetrate foreign markets, viewing its global economic role in strategic terms.

The failure of the West to understand, let alone to study, Japan's strategic orientation toward trade and economic policy stems in part from the irrational but widely held belief that the policy roots of Japan's economic growth lie entirely in the postwar recovery period and in part from an equally irrational but as widely held belief that Japan would forever and always remain an underdeveloped country.

From the earliest days of Japan's opening to the West in the mid–nineteenth century, when no volunteers welcomed Commodore Perry's Black Ships at Shimoda, its political and economic leadership during the Meiji era (1868–1912) was committed to two basic principles: (1) preventing from happening to Japan what had happened to China and thereby protecting Japan's national identity and (2) establishing a concept of strategic industries that would enable Japan to compete with the West in economic terms, catching up with and ultimately beating the West.

The responses of Japan and China to the Western threat couldn't have been more different. The unpatriotic attitude of the Manchu dynasty was reflected in the traditional aphorism "It is better to make a present to friendly states than to give it to your domestic slaves." The more hostile Japanese attitude stemmed from the thinking of an eighteenth-century Tokugawa philosopher named Rimei Honda, who noted that the wealth and power of Western nations depended fundamentally on foreign trade, on shipping, and above all, on manufacturing. His aphorism captured the very essence of an emerging Japanese mercantilism: "Foreign trade is a war in that each party seeks to extract wealth from the other."

So from the beginning Japan relied on a philosophy that reflected not only a need to keep the West out but also a burning desire to beat the West at its own game, trade. It is a philosophy with deep roots, as we shall see, and one that remains very much alive today.

Herbert Norman, a Canadian born in Japan of missionary parents in the early years of this century, became a prominent Japanese historian, interested primarily in how feudal influences of the Tokugawa era would affect Japan's new relationships with the outside world. He did postgraduate work at Harvard and wrote an insightful account of the late–nineteenth century Japanese policy formation process, called *Origins of the Modern Japanese State.*

"The special attention paid from the first to the strategic importance of modernization," Norman wrote in 1940, "in turn arose from the political necessity of throwing up a rampart of defense around Japan to ward off the danger of attack which had been hanging over the country ever since the beginning of the 19th century, while at the same time guarding against internal disturbances which might arise from the excessive burdens laid upon the population in paying for this modernization. The keenest political minds were concerned with such questions as the creation of trade and industry, not for their own sake, but rather to establish those industries one might call *strategic* [italics added]. So from the first, the military and the export industries were favored, and were soon on a level with the most advanced Western countries."

Briefly, to put the sequence of emphasis in logical order, the Japanese oligarchs thought somewhat as follows: What do we need most to save us from the fate of China? A modern army and navy. And on what do the creation and maintenance of modern armed forces depend? Chiefly on heavy industries: engineering, mining, shipbuilding, steel. In a word, strategic industries.

In Norman's interpretation Japan's formative years of industrial development following three centuries of cultural isolation were characterized by a unique feature of Japanese industrialization: state control of strategic industries. These industries were considered strategic either because of their connection with naval and military defense or because of their importance in export industries intended to compete against foreign products and hence requiring subsidy or protection.

What Norman clearly shows is that the concept of industrial policy in Japan is neither postwar nor prewar but *premodern*. It gave rise to popular slogans of the time, such as *sonno jo-i* (revere the emperor and expel the barbarians) and *wakon yosai* (Western science with Japanese spirit). Not to understand this highly nationalistic sentiment is to miss a deep and vital component of the Japanese psyche.

The results of Japan's industrial policy, as analysts never cease telling us, not only have been impressive but outstrip any accomplishments in the West over a comparable period. When we look at Japan's prewar military accomplishments, we see significant victories in every decade but one. And if we look at Japan's postwar economic achievements, we find they are telling indeed. The free world's leading steel maker. The number one producer of automobiles. Until recently displaced by Korea, the world's leading shipbuilder. Manufacturer, *par excellence*, of cameras and consumer electronics and office equipment, through companies whose names alone symbolize a new standard of quality and over the years have become *American* household words: Sony, Honda, Canon, Nissan, Hitachi, Sharp, Mitsubishi, Toyota, Toshiba, NEC. Dominant in semiconductor technology, biotechnology, communications technology, space technology, the technology of miniaturization. On and on the list goes, seemingly endless, with achievement after unparalleled achievement in industry after advanced industry.

Somehow the Japanese developed powerful additives for their economic fuel that were unknown, or undiscovered, in the West. They devised a hybrid system called *capitalist developmental economics*, a term coined by Chalmers Johnson of the University of California. For lack of a more cryptic name, I call the system "turbocharged capitalism."

Years ago Johnson wrote *Japan's Public Policy Companies*, which analyzed the more than one hundred public corporations that comprise the operating arms of Japan's industrial policy, control nearly half the national budget, and alone account for 5 percent of GNP. Then, in 1982, he published a brilliant and highly acclaimed work called *MITI and the*

Japanese Miracle, which tracked the development of Japan's industrial policy over half a century, from 1925 to 1975, under the skillful and strategic leadership of the Ministry of International Trade and Industry.

Johnson's creative analysis demonstrated that Japan's accomplishments are neither as mysterious nor as nefarious as many in the West believed, and he focused on Japanese public policies that were based on five rather simple strategic concepts: (1) instituting new forms of government-business interaction, based on cooperation rather than confrontation, that link long-term incentives to the maintenance of domestic competition while encouraging a cooperative internal stance against all foreigners; (2) making a commitment to export-oriented growth, which looks outward in search of global standards against which to measure product prices, product quality, and performance; (3) encouraging extremely high rates of savings and investment through massive strategic incentives from the Ministry of Finance, which lead to a primacy of production over consumption; (4) establishing an equitable system of income distribution across all industries and classes and egalitarian access to high-quality education as a national priority; and (5) emphasizing small, frequent, *incremental* enhancements in R&D technology, which the Japanese call *kaizen* and which leads to thousands of technological innovations but few basic inventions, as opposed to the heavier, expensive, more time-consuming, all-or-nothing "breakthrough" process of R&D common in the West, which wins Nobel prizes but tends to lose market share.

In most forms of Western capitalism, Johnson held, the state took the role of regulating private economic activities. Not so in Japan. "In nations that were late to industrialize," he wrote, "the state itself led the industrialization drive and took on *developmental* functions." A regulatory state concerns itself with the rules of competition, but not with substantive matters. The American government may issue antitrust regulations regarding firm size, for example, but does not concern itself strategically with which industries ought to, or ought not to, exist. The developmental state, by contrast, has as its dominant feature precisely the setting of such strategic economic goals.

In classical capitalist development the starting point is light industry, and the process moves on to the production of more capital-intensive goods. Heavy industries did not assume importance in the British economy until the end of the eighteenth century, with the invention of the lathe. But this normal order of transition was simply reversed in Japan.

This means that, in a capitalist developmental state like Japan (and Korea, for that matter), government gives priority attention to industrial policy; namely, it will concern itself with the structure of domestic industry and with promoting the structure that enhances the nation's international competitiveness. The very existence of an industrial policy implies a strategic, or goal-oriented, approach.

So regulatory states, like America, set rules and regulations for the economy that may be simple or complex but operate both internally and externally on the classical economic principles of Adam Smith, the eighteenth-century theorist who devised the famous "invisible hand of the market" as the means by which economies, experiencing imbalances of production or distribution, would correct themselves.

Needless to say, the Japanese do not subscribe to Adam Smith and never have. A popular joke, which one hears frequently in Tokyo these days, captures the essence of what the Japanese consider to be Adam Smith's shortcomings: How many neoclassical economists does it take to change a light bulb? The answer: None; they simply sit and wait for the invisible hand of the market to do it for them.

Johnson tracked the development of Japan's industrial policy through its primary life-giving force, MITI, and showed how it developed not as a policy directive handed down by the political leadership, but organically, evolving over time in response to external environmental circumstances. One influential prewar MITI bureaucrat was Shinji Yoshino, who discovered that despite the huge power of Japan's *zaibatsu* (the industrial conglomerates), it was the small and medium-sized enterprises that accounted for the lion's share of jobs in the economy. He also found that the *zaibatsu* produced principally for the domestic market, whereas the smaller firms were the country's major exporters. So in 1925 he and his colleagues pushed the ministry to sponsor two new laws. One helped the smaller companies create cooperative export unions along specific product lines. The other attempted to restrain excessive competition by organizing cartellike arrangements whereby member firms agreed to specified production volumes.

By 1927 the global financial panic had hit Japan, and the Depression was on its way. Banks collapsed, smaller firms found it harder to get loans, and the *zaibatsu* took advantage of circumstances by attempting to increase their power and control. Yoshino and his colleagues responded by setting up a Commerce and Industry Deliberation Council within the ministry that brought everybody together to talk about all the negative things that were happening in the economy. Not just the *zaibatsu*, but small firms, exporters, importers, academics, other government agencies, trade associations, manufacturers, the press, *everybody*. In time, the council persuaded the ministry to sharpen its compilation of industrial statistics, orchestrate mergers where excessive competition could be eliminated, make more loan funds available to smaller companies, and improve the quality of trade data.

For the first time the term *industrial rationalization—sangyo gorika* in Japanese—came into use, and it has remained to this day. Industrial rationalization meant the adoption of new techniques of production, investment in new equipment and facilities, quality control, cost reduction, adoption of new management techniques, and the perfection of managerial control. It meant the rationalization of the environment of enterprises, including land and water transportation and industrial location. It created a framework for all enterprises in one industry in which each could compete fairly or in which they could cooperate in a cartellike arrangement of mutual assistance. And it rationalized the industrial structure of the economy itself in order to meet international competitive standards.

Yoshino began to see that excessive competition ought to be replaced by cooperation and that the purpose of business activities should be an attempt to lower costs, not to make profits. "Modern industries attained their present development primarily through free competition," he wrote in an internal memo. "But various evils of the capitalist order are gradually becoming apparent. Holding to absolute freedom will not rescue the industrial world from its present disturbances. Industry needs both a plan of comprehensive development *and* a measure of control. Concerning control, there are many complex explanations of it in terms of logical principles, but all one really needs to understand it is common sense."

Yoshino went out of his way to make sure people understood what he meant by "a measure of control." He most certainly was *not* talking about bureaucratic supervision of industry. He was referring to the creation of what he called "industrial order," the same kind of order and control that had characterized Japanese society for centuries. Order and hierarchy were uniquely Japanese and had their roots in the country's feudal past, principally during the Tokugawa era, when Japan had been closed to the outside world for nearly three hundred years.

Here was the continuation of Norman's emphasis on strategic industries as the core of its industrial policy formulation: the need to promote exports, the importance of a keen competitive ability in foreign trade, and the overwhelming necessity to rationalize industry to take advantage of economies of scale. Most of the elite who helped create the *postwar* economic miracle in Japan were the same individuals who had guided Japan's industrial policy throughout the entire *prewar* era. The civilian bureaucracy was characterized by nothing if not by continuity.

This historical continuity, as Chalmers Johnson points out, is evidence that Japan's industrial policy is rooted in its conscious institutional innovation: economic crisis gave birth to industrial policy. That the Japanese solved their problems more effectively during the postwar period than during the 1930s is greater testimony to their ability to profit from experience than to any fundamental change in the situation they faced.

Johnson's concept of the developmental state clearly distinguishes him from two other schools of thought that may be said to represent opposing views of Japanese economic development. One school, called the *projectionists*, consists of those who "project" onto the Japanese Western concepts, values, and norms of economic behavior. (Japan, they say, does the same things Western economies do, only better.) The other, called the *socioeconomic school*, says Japan's accomplishments are a result of the "unique" Japanese character or structural functions, such as their capacity to cooperate. So Johnson's efforts represent a new approach to interpreting Japan's success. Having read and admired his works over the years, and corresponded with him at times, I sought him out at a recent meeting of the Association for Asian Studies to talk about his work.

"I think the burden of proof is now on the neoclassical economists," he was saying one afternoon. Soft-spoken but by no means shy, he has a clear baritone voice that belies a talent for tactical understatement. "There is more than enough evidence in to make a sufficient case for industrial policy, but nowhere in Washington do you find proponents willing to put any innovative policy proposals forward—either for financial incentives or for R&D or for trade. In a sense our policymakers have become rather like theologians, who see only the validity of their own beliefs."

Part of the problem, Johnson said, stems from what he thinks has become virtually an American academic scandal. In almost every economics department in the U.S. there is systematic discrimination against the strategic study of the Japanese economy. American economists prefer to study theory and avoid applied empirical research, since the latter might reveal the anomalies that have developed in American neoclassical theory over the years.

What are these anomalies? "Well," Johnson replied, "they include the inability of the main schools of economic theory to explain Japan's achievements. Or the failure of macroeconomic theory to show how, three years after the Plaza Accord has revalued the yen by almost 50 percent, America's trade deficit remains almost totally unaffected. Or the failure of neoclassical theory to recognize that pure competition and perfect information never occur in advanced market economies, which must have rules—as well as rights and institutions—in order to function. So political economists have begun to show how economic theory and strategy may be actualized through these institutions."

American students of the Japanese economy have missed this dimension of Japan's achievement because the study of institutions has been slighted in Western scholarship, Johnson said. Research on Japanese economic institutions must unavoidably include analysis of their history. For example, the scholar Andrew Gordon had to go back to the 1850s to show how contemporary Japanese labor relations had evolved. And in order to understand the origins of Japan's postwar economic bureaucracy, Johnson himself had to go back to the prewar era (and beyond) to develop the concept of the capitalist developmental state.

Japanese economic policymakers, by and large, would agree with Johnson's assessment of industrial policy, his concept of the developmental state, and the historical role played by MITI. Chief among these policymakers was, until his recent retirement, a senior MITI official by the name of Naohiro Amaya, who entered the Ministry of Commerce and Industry, MITI's predecessor, in 1948. (MITI had been created in the Meiji era as the Ministry of Commerce and Agriculture and was spun off separately following the rice riots of 1918. During the war it became the Ministry of Munitions.)

During his thirty-five-year MITI career, Amaya served as director of the important International Economic Affairs Department of the International Trade Policy Bureau and subsequently as director general of the Agency for Natural Resources and Energy. In 1962, as assistant chief of the General Affairs Section, he wrote the first of several internal papers that would lead to his becoming known as MITI's "house theorist." It was called *What Do the Times Require of Us?* and argued strongly in favor of continued public-private cooperation, a policy line that favored further conversion of Japan's industrial structure from heavy industries to higher value-added, technology-intensive manufacturing. But since his superiors thought him a bit pushy, they sent him overseas to MITI's Sydney office for a while to cool down.

After he returned to Tokyo, in 1969, he wrote another paper, *Basic Direction of the New International Trade and Industry Policy*, known as the "second Amaya thesis." In it he argued that the ministry should answer the public, who were calling for less high-speed growth-for-growth's-sake. Amaya felt Japan was already shifting from an industrial-mechanical age to an information-intensive era and would therefore require changes in policy direction every bit as monumental as those that had begun a shift away from heavy industries years before.

This new transition, Amaya argued, would emphasize robot-operated factories, "verticalize" Japanese companies engaged in high-tech assembly operations, revolutionize industrial technology, and coax Japan into the emerging "knowledge-intensive" industries: semiconductor technology, computers, biotechnology, commercial jet aviation, and space technology. (This was in 1969, remember.) MITI had already taken steps to organize a new Information and Industrial Machinery Division, based on the distressing news that Japan would soon have a shortage of skilled labor and needed to devise ways of solving the problem without creating a host of social problems, as the Western economies had done by importing foreign guest workers. Amaya set the wheels in motion for the ultimate adoption of industrial robots and numerically controlled machine tools, which in turn led to Japan's dominance of a new factory format known as *flexible manufacturing systems*.

Early in 1980 Amaya was promoted to vice minister for international affairs, a post directly under the minister and the highest position to which a career bureaucrat at MITI could aspire. I first met him that year, in the aftermath of negotiations that ultimately set in motion a series of restraints on Japanese automobile exports, and have stayed in periodic contact with him since. He is now executive director of the Dentsu Institute for Human Studies, a private Japanese think tank, and

has been published widely; most recently, a best-seller in Tokyo called
Where Is Japan Going?

I saw Amaya again in early 1988 at his Dentsu office in downtown
Tokyo, in the Ginza, the most expensive commercial real estate district
in the world. Offices and showrooms of many of Japan's major corporations are located here—the Sony Building is nearby, not far from
Nissan's headquarters building—and the area is a popular entertainment
district at night.

We talked at length, in Japanese, about recent economic developments, and I asked him about industrial targeting, a tactical tool of
MITI policy that had been used with considerable success and had been
criticized increasingly as "insidious, pernicious, and unfair" by many
Western observers.

Amaya laughed.

"How can you hunt without a target?" he asked, breaking into a
wide grin. He has a quick and thoughtful sense of humor and a cherubic
face highlighted by prematurely white hair that he keeps neatly combed,
straight back from his forehead, creating a soft halo effect.

"When you go hunting, you have to shoot at a target," he said. "But
your neoclassical school of economics says you can fire in all directions
at once and the 'market' will ensure you hit the target. Well, we don't
accept that line of reasoning, and our economic model will probably
be stronger in the future, and have a greater demonstration effect for
developing countries, than either the American model, which has become weak and less relevant, or the Soviet central-command model,
which will probably cease to exist as a practical alternative early in the
twenty-first century, if not before. American politicians, preoccupied
with political affairs, take a high public profile and spend too much
time criticizing Japanese industrial policy practices. In Japan we tend
to be too preoccupied with economic matters, and our politicians prefer
a much lower public profile."

I asked Amaya whether Japan's concept of strategic industries, as
part of its comprehensive industrial policy, had the potential for wider
applicability, even in America.

He shrugged his shoulders slightly.

"America's self-confidence has slipped," he said. "Just look at the
current political dialogue. American politicians seem unable to take up
key issues and tend to ignore the country's strategic problems. Since
there is no overriding national agenda in your country there is a focus

only on self-interest, whether political or corporate. And there is no strategy for domestic investment, which has fallen dramatically in recent years, so you put all your faith in a devalued currency, believing the cheaper dollar alone will make things better again. But there is a real need for belt-tightening now, to help solve the huge budget and trade deficits, which American politicians seem unable to grasp. So a big problem has emerged in the Congress, where there appears to be more interest in criticizing the behavior of successful foreign countries, especially Asian countries, than in taking strategic steps to improve America's own competitive position. With an inability to set policy objectives, the real question then becomes how quickly America will be able to recover. American leadership is older now, perhaps not as courageous or as firm as before."

He paused, collected his thoughts, and took a sip of tea.

"Two hundred years ago," he went on, "James Watt invented the steam engine and created the Industrial Revolution. The first half of this industrial age was dominated by England, and coal was the power that fueled it. By the late nineteenth century oil and electricity had replaced coal, and America became dominant. But by 1973 this era was finished. Why did it stop? I think there were five distinct reasons."

He ticked them off crisply on his fingers.

"One, there was a decline in new technology suited to the age.

"Two, important frontiers to explore had become much too narrow.

"Three, resources previously thought to be unlimited, like oil, were now considered finite.

"Four, previous emphasis had been on development of technology for hardware, such as the automobile and industrial machinery, neglecting the development of software—namely, the human resources necessary to run the hardware. Consequently, the real question has now become, how can we improve our social systems, which are the all-important software of tomorrow?

"And five, as the process of oil and natural resources exploitation bumped into the question of finiteness, it did not affect Japan as much because of our ability to manage our way out of problems that hit America and Europe so hard. People tend to think Japan is vulnerable because it is isolated and lacks natural resources, but natural resources are the software of the past and are becoming less relevant, especially in an information-intensive age that depends more on knowledge than on raw materials for progress and development. So if human resources are tomorrow's software, then countries like America, which are rich in natural resources but have less developed human resources, may be at a disadvantage in comparison with countries like Japan, which have put a greater priority on development of human resources, through education. The world is on the verge of a metamorphosis from the industrial age to the electronic era. Like a caterpillar changing into a butterfly, those who can make the transition will succeed; those who cannot may be left behind."

He took another sip of tea and then brought our conversation full circle.

"It is a mistake to think that Japan is still in the industrial age," he said. "America had the baton of industrial leadership, then passed it to Japan. We ran for a while and then passed the baton to the NICs— newly industrializing countries like Korea and Taiwan. They are just on the threshold of the electronic age, but still in the hardware age. In time they in turn will pass the baton on to China, to Africa, to Latin America, which are developing more slowly. With the commitment Japan has made to developing human resources during the past century, the challenge now is to develop our political leadership and bring it up to the level of our economic leadership. That will be a great challenge."

Japanese public policy officials learn to speak with foreigners, and with the public, in a somewhat contrived way, called *tatemae*, which conveys a convenient pretense or principle, as opposed to *honne*, its opposite, which is one's real intention or true motive but is revealed only in private. Consequently, when foreigners speak with Japanese officials or read their public comments, it is important to distinguish between what, for public relations purposes, may be construed as pretense and what is true. Rarely will a foreigner be exposed to the real, underlying feelings of a Japanese, and then only if they have known each other for a long time, allowing a sense of trust and intimacy to develop. While my conversation with Amaya was a mixture of both, it seemed to me, there was a sense in which *honne* prevailed; his comments about the new era and Japan's place in it were, I felt, genuine, although statements about political leadership, whether American or Japanese, seemed more like an "official line."

Outside, with the traffic backed up, I decided against taking a cab to the Bank of Japan, Japan's central bank, where I was to lunch with Akira Nambara, director general of its statistical research department, and where I would hear considerably more *tatemae* than *honne*. Instead

I walked a few short blocks to the Tokyo metropolitan subway, whose underground stations downtown are now completely air-conditioned, and rode in a brand-new, whisper-quiet car of the Ginza line, with its distinctive yellow exterior. A small sign at the end of the car testified, in Japanese characters, or *kanji* (using the imperial dating system still customary in Japan), to its youth. It said "Showa 61," which meant the sixty-first year of the reign of former emperor Hirohito, the Era of Peace and Harmony, which began in 1926, making it 1987 when that car rolled off the Kawasaki Heavy Industries assembly line in Yokohama. In less than ten minutes I exited at Mitsukoshi-Mae, in Nihonbashi, around the corner from the Bank of Japan—the BOJ, as it is known.

While I did not know Nambara personally, I had known many of his colleagues over the years. His department publishes a widely read and highly useful statistical summary of both domestic Japanese economic developments and international trends, called *Chosa Geppo*.

After brief pleasantries in his office at the fortresslike BOJ, we lunched informally at a small Western restaurant nearby. Our conversation covered the full range of current economic issues, from America's decline to Japan's greater responsibility in the international economic system. On the subject of American competitiveness, Nambara cited statistics that indicated that U.S. unit labor costs were getting lower, which suggested its industries were becoming more competitive (but he conveniently omitted a companion statistic that shows that the American labor component as a percentage of total input is still high by international standards).

On the anemic American savings rate, he suggested that it would rise more or less automatically as the baby boomers moved into prime saving age, but he said nothing about the massive financial incentives that the Ministry of Finance had created to boost Japan's own savings rate over the years. Questioned on this, he politely brushed my objections aside, saying, "It is impossible to adjust your savings rate by policy." On the inability of America's trade deficit with Japan to improve, he said merely, "It takes time." (Other, more caustic, observers have called this adjustment process the slowest J-curve in history.)

On the growing competitive hostility between Japan and America, Nambara preferred instead a concept called the *Nichibei* economy, which has gained theoretical currency in recent years and foresees an interdependent, combined, "borderless" economy consisting of America *plus* Japan rather than two independent and antagonistic competitors.

"The U.S. and Japan are separated not by borders, but simply by a large ocean," he said. (While that concept has been popular in some academic circles, it lacks a sense of geopolitical reality.)

On the subject of deregulation, Nambara remarked that Adam Smith opposed the concept of deregulation of banks and interest rates. "It's on page 323 of *The Wealth of Nations*," he said. Recent deregulation of Japanese financial markets had basically favored domestic Japanese financial institutions in sectors like trust banking, foreign currency swaps, and impact loans and given them superior market shares. Although the foreign business community had welcomed the opening of Tokyo's equities market, the jury was withholding judgment on the final results. Japanese investment banks, notably the Big Four, still control more than three-fourths of the securities markets in Tokyo, which is now the world's largest stock exchange; Osaka, Japan's number two, today has a market capitalization even larger than New York. And on the subject of tax reform, Nambara suggested that since both taxes and allowable deductions have been lowered, American consumption will slow down, and its savings rate should rise over time.

The course of our discussion demonstrated the mesmerizing effects of *tatemae*, which American businessmen, politicians, and policymakers hear *ad infinitum* when they visit Japan. This pretense deflects attention away from discussions of the more substantive strategic aspects of policy formulation, which are much needed but which Americans basically don't understand, to the more market-oriented aspects, which strike a more familiar chord but have become increasingly irrelevant.

Amaya's focus was reflected in a meeting I had in late 1988 with Haruo Mayekawa, former governor of the Bank of Japan and now, well into his seventies, chairman of Kokusai Denshin Denwa (KDD), the company that owns and maintains Japan's international telegraph and telephone transmission lines. If Japan were still an oligarchy, Mayekawa would be one of the nation's ruling oligarchs. In 1985 he had been asked by former prime minister Nakasone to head a commission whose task was to examine whether (and how) Japan could shift from an export-led economy back to being domestically demand-driven. In April 1986 the commission published its conclusions, known as the Mayekawa Report, which contained numerous recommendations to stimulate domestic demand, reduce exports, and expand fiscal spending. The surprise was not that the Japanese economy shifted, but that it was able to shift so quickly.

"What is impressive is not the magnitude, but the speed," Mayekawa told me. "Still, restructuring cannot be accomplished overnight and will take another five years. Imports of finished goods and growth in the housing market both seem to be on target. But our overall price index, although flat and stable, must be brought down, as prices in Japan are the highest in the world now. If we don't do this, our cost structure will eventually shut us out of world markets."

Japan's industrial successes have created a rich storehouse of anecdotal lore (both pretentious and true) about the country's hard-earned economic power, unquestionably world-class now. Not long ago, when President Reagan was on a state visit to the Vatican, he spent considerable time, one-on-one, with the pope when he noticed a gold telephone on the papal desk and asked what it was for.

Pope John Paul II told him it was his hot line to Heaven.

"I must talk with Him five or six times a day," he said.

Intrigued, Reagan asked if he could give it a try.

"Of course," said the pope. "It's a direct dial, and we can arrange a call immediately. But I should warn you, it costs $10,000 for the first three minutes."

Reagan's eyebrows shot up.

"Since Americans have such strong feelings about the separation of church and state," the president said, "I had best decline. I could get myself into real trouble spending the taxpayers' money on a phone call to God."

The president concluded his visit to Rome and proceeded to Asia, where his first stop was Tokyo, for a meeting with then prime minister Yasuhiro Nakasone to defuse the growing economic friction. The president noticed a gold telephone on Nakasone's desk, too, and asked him about it. He told Reagan it was his hot line to Heaven.

"Our rapid economic growth has created international problems that only God can solve," the prime minister said. "I must talk with Him five or six times a day."

Intrigued, President Reagan asked if he could give it a try.

"But of course," Nakasone said. "It's a direct dial, and we can arrange a call immediately. The nice thing is, it's only fifty yen for the first three minutes."

"Only fifty yen!" the president exclaimed. "Why, from the Vatican it costs $10,000."

"Yes, Mr. President," said the PM softly. "But from Japan it's just a local call."

Japan's industrial successes have also created an unprecedented amount of resentment, jealousy, and mistrust among Western nations, inspiring, in the words of one observer, an uncomfortable combination of awe and admiration mixed with fear and loathing. In a recent poll, 59 percent of the American electorate said economic competitors like Japan pose more of a threat to national security than our traditional military adversaries like the Soviet Union. "For the first time since World War II," the report concluded, "the American people no longer assume their position as the number one economic power in the world can be taken for granted." By better than a two-to-one margin the public acknowledged that improving the efficiency and productivity of U.S. industries, rather than forcing other countries to adopt fairer trade practices, may be a better way to reduce the trade deficit.

But administration after administration in Washington has focused its attention not on improving the efficiency and productivity of U.S. industries, but on trying to force other countries—primarily Japan—to adopt "fairer" trade practices. Because Japan's trade and investment policies have been so aggressive, fully two-thirds of all Japanese exports today are covered by some form of voluntary export restraint, a euphemism for export quotas and orderly marketing agreements negotiated by Washington with Tokyo. Since 1982 the value of Japanese exports subject to quota has *tripled*, yet despite these restraints, America still runs a structural trade deficit with Japan in excess of $50 billion a year.

The success of Japanese industrial policy has meant that there is hardly a factory in Japan that has not been built, rebuilt, or refurbished since the late 1970s, with every Japanese worker supported by more than twice the value of plant and equipment that supports his American counterpart. The story of Japanese dominance in automobiles and electronics is now familiar to even the most casual observer of Japan's rise to industrial preeminence; less so, perhaps, is the story on machine tools (where Japan now controls more than 50 percent of the U.S. market for numerically controlled equipment) or computer chips (Japan now makes virtually all the 64K memory chips in the world and controls about 80 percent of 256K production). America may dominate the defense applications of automation, but Japan controls its commercial use. And the same industrial policy is being applied to the strategic industries of the future: industrial ceramics, supercomputers, telecommunications, high-definition TV, biotechnology, superconductivity, and commercial jet aviation.

Several trends have developed as a result of Washington's emphasis on other-directed rather than inner-directed trade and investment policy, in addition to the process of negotiating ever more comprehensive export restraints.

One is a focus on "market access" in Japan, to secure more favorable market penetration for American products. Another is the prevalence of "trade politics" over trade policy, whereby politically influential special interest groups, notably agricultural lobbies such as American beef growers and tobacco companies, gain primacy in the development of trade policy, despite the fact that they do not constitute a strategic manufacturing sector and the value of exported farm products barely makes a dent in the trade deficit. (Japan is America's number one customer, taking about $6 billion worth of farm goods a year.)

A third trend is the tendency to let exchange rates dictate trade and investment policy, by depreciating the dollar to unprecedented levels. A fourth is the neglect of important domestic savings and investment incentives that are vital to the strengthening of America's manufacturing sector. And a fifth is America's inability to exploit more aggressively the concept of complementary strategic alliances, both domestically and internationally, combined with a failure to develop a more strategic manufacturing sector.

The limitations of American policy have become increasingly apparent. Japan has been developing its strategic industrial policies in response to external environmental conditions for more than a century now, and the institutional patterns for the sustenance and continued evolution of those policies are well established. It is irrational to believe they can be delayed, altered, or stopped. "Market access" is not so much a question of the competitiveness of American exports as it is a question of American strategy *in* the Japanese market, as manufacturers, not as exporters. The resolution of the bilateral trade deficit with Japan ultimately becomes less a question of exchange rate and other macroeconomic considerations than of American political leadership, because a key to solving the structural trade problem is not through the further application of neoclassical economic theory, but through the adoption of incentives based on a more innovative, strategic policy orientation.

Most observers now agree American efforts to cope with Japan's more aggressive strategic policies have, on the whole, been unsuccessful. Attempts to issue "ultimatums" to the Japanese have proved fruitless, as have the umbrellalike export quotas and market-opening measures tried by successive American administrations. The French had better success with a more strategic policy that blunted Japanese exports of videocassette recorders, which had been swamping the French market some years back. Paris ordered the Japanese to clear their VCRs through customs in Poitiers, a small inland town some distance from Le Havre, and have each machine inspected individually rather than having them cleared by container, as was previously done at the port city. The subsequent delays, hassles, and bureaucratic red tape sent Japan the kind of message that no ultimatum could ever deliver, and before long Tokyo was negotiating seriously with Paris on outstanding bilateral issues.

A similar strategic policy response occurred in early 1987 when Washington proceeded to impose $300 million worth of tariffs on Japanese electronics exports in retaliation for dumping by Japanese semiconductor companies in both the U.S. and third-country markets. Sharply focused measures such as these, which were one-time successes amid a history of failures, force Tokyo to change its operating tactics in ways not otherwise possible, but they have to be *strategically* derived and deal with a strict *quid pro quo*.

There is a sense in which a more strategic orientation to American trade policy may be emerging, however, as reflected in the 1988 Trade Act passed by Congress. The legislation strengthened Section 301, which permits an industry to file a trade complaint with the U.S. Trade Representative and request a presidential review. The new section has become known as "Super 301" because of its enhanced powers, which mandated a specific schedule for USTR compliance.

So in April 1989 USTR issued its *National Trade Estimates Report on Foreign Trade Barriers*, and the section on Japan alone comprised eighteen pages (the longest), citing major issues such as certification and standards, government procurement practices, and barriers to distribution for critical high-technology products like satellites, telecommunications equipment, and supercomputers. By the end of May, on schedule, Japan was one of three nations (the other two were Brazil and India) cited as priority countries (aka "unfair traders"), and the reaction from Tokyo (mostly *tatemae*) was predictable.

Critics contend that the legislation is protectionist, that it will prompt more "Japan bashing" as well as invite retaliation, and that it represents unwarranted congressional meddling in affairs of the executive branch. But if the president's men had been doing a tougher job to begin with, Congress may not have felt it necessary to intervene. And the process has finally caught Japan's attention like nothing else the U.S. has done in recent years, creating the likelihood of more significant bilateral negotiations. It showed how to be tough with Japan without being negative.

As a Japanese friend well up in the hierarchy at MITI recently told me, "So long as America stays wedded to its free-market, free-trade ideology, Japan will win, hands down. But if Washington keeps developing a more strategic orientation to its policy initiatives, the outcome is by no means clear. In that case the competition will become very tough indeed."

Japan, by the sheer size of its $3 trillion GNP alone, accounts for about three-quarters of the entire Asia-Pacific GNP, so if Japan were the *only* Asian country capable of these economic achievements, the competitive challenge to America might somehow seem more manageable. But, as we shall see, Korea and Taiwan have both cloned their economic systems from the successful Japanese model, and Singapore too has emulated some of the adaptive aspects of Japan's capitalist developmental state (though without the mercenary aspects of its mercantilist policies), creating a powerful demonstration effect for turbocharged capitalism throughout East Asia.

The implications for further economic modeling in the lesser developed countries of the world—in Latin America, for example, or in Africa—may be no less stunning, and the need for a complete rethinking of American trade and investment policy in more strategic terms has probably never been more urgent, for an electronic age dominated by East Asia will be much more intensely competitive than any America has seen before in its history. The information revolution, which is being created in part by a transition from the advantageous exploitation of natural resources to the superior utilization of human resources, is the first revolution America has had to experience that is being accelerated and advanced by influences *outside its direct control*. For America not to respond strategically to this external challenge could mean the nation may have to abdicate not only its present position of global economic and technological leadership, which it is already in the process of losing, but its future claims to world political leadership as well.

3

CLONES OF THE CAPITALIST DEVELOPMENTAL STATE: KOREA, TAIWAN, SINGAPORE, AND HONG KONG

Our future is what we make of it, and we will use to best advantage the factors in our favor. First, the strategic. As long as the balance of geopolitical forces in Southeast and East Asia remain as they are, then Singapore's strategic value will continue undiminished. Second, our contribution to world trading, shipping, and servicing will continue to grow and expand while we add an ever bigger industrial sector to our economic base. Third, and most important, the ability and industry of our young people, willing and eager to learn, prepared to work hard and pay their way in the world, finding pride and pleasure in constructive endeavor. But in any case, they are disciplined and determined to defend what their ingenuity and effort have created.

There is no law of nature which provides that life will get better next year. We have to work to make it better.

Lee Kuan Yew, prime minister of Singapore

During the past several years, a new phenomenon called the *newly industrializing country*, or *NIC*, has emerged, distinguishing the more advanced and faster-growing economies from a previous category called the *lesser developed country*, or *LDC*. It should come as no surprise that *all* the world's NICs are located in East Asia, from Korea and Taiwan in the northeast to Hong Kong and Singapore farther south.

These four countries are known collectively as the "Little Dragons," nations whose economic systems have been cloned, to a greater or lesser extent, from the highly successful Japanese model, with stunning results. The hyper-growth machine called turbocharged capitalism gives rise to the thought (if not the fear) that the Organization of Economic Cooperation and Development (OECD), once an exclusive Western

44

club of the advanced European economies plus America and now including Japan, will soon have to open its doors to include other members too, all of whom are Asian.

KOREA: THE LAND OF THE ALMOST-PERFECT

"The facts are not in serious dispute," Chalmers Johnson wrote, "even if their explanation and interpretation are among the most controversial issues in the field of comparative political economy today." In 1950 Korea had a per-capita GNP of $146, way behind the per-capita income "leaders" of the day.

By 1980, thirty years later, Korea's per-capita GNP had risen to $1,553. The "leaders" had moved moderately ahead, with Brazil at $1,780, Mexico at $1,640, and Argentina at $2,230. But by 1987, with a per-capita GNP of nearly $3,000, Korea had moved ahead of them all, and it was still only *fifth* in Asia after Japan, Singapore, Hong Kong, and Taiwan.

In twenty-five years, between 1962 and 1987, Korea's GNP increased more than ten times, from $12 billion to nearly $120 billion, and the country's hardworking population of 40 million people had accomplished more, in a shorter period of time, than Brazil with its 130 million or Mexico with 75 million. The two Latin economies had also enjoyed better access, and for longer periods, to the paternalistic American market; both of them had also patterned their economic systems after the free-enterprise, free-market, neoclassical American model. And neither had experienced the devastating effects of civil war, which further delayed Korea's start.

Content for centuries to be the Middle Kingdom, known as the Land of the Morning Calm, Korea occupies the strategic peninsula that juts into the Sea of Japan (or the Sea of Korea, depending on whose textbooks you read) between China and Japan. In 1592 and 1597 the Japanese warlord Toyotomi Hideyoshi unsuccessfully tried to lead his invading forces through Korea to Manchuria, and in 1627 the Manchus pushed down into the peninsula after the Koreans had barely recovered from repelling Hideyoshi's forces.

In 1882, imbued with new military power after nearly three centuries of isolation, Japan signed a treaty that opened the Korean ports of Pusan and Inchon. From then until Japan gained custody of Korea under a treaty with a China it defeated in 1895, the Japanese assassinated Queen Min, put down a coup, repelled a Chinese invasion, quelled the Tonghak rebellion of Korean farmers, and then attacked China and won. No sooner had they begun to enjoy the spoils of war than the Soviets, who will be Soviets, stirred up trouble next by expanding into the Korean Peninsula, losing a major naval confrontation with Japan in 1905.

In 1910 Japan took complete control of Korea by forced annexation, and for the next thirty-five years Korea was run as a Japanese colony. Its national language, *hangul*, was banned both at home and in school. Every Korean was required to adopt a Japanese name, and hundreds of thousands of Korean laborers were forced to work in Japanese coal mines and steel mills. At the end of the Pacific war, in 1945, the country was liberated and divided by the superpowers at the thirty-eighth parallel, with the Soviet Union occupying the northern half and the Allies holding the South.

Since the Japanese ran the country while they occupied it, it took even longer for Korea to get organized economically. But the Korean reputation for toughness and ruthless determination enabled the Koreans to persevere with such discipline that, by comparison and by their own proud admission, they made the Japanese look lazy. The cycle of invasions, but especially the colonization by Japan, left a legacy of hostility and hatred toward Japan that still lingers and that, by various accounts, fuels a powerful competitive drive in the Koreans to best the Japanese at whatever they try to do.

It wasn't until a young army major by the name of Park Chung-hee, taking advantage of traditional student protest against President Syngman Rhee's economic inaction, executed a coup d'état in 1961, toppled the Rhee regime with the backing of the armed forces, and set the country's economic forces in gear under the watchful eye of a more authoritarian government, that the economy acquired a sound footing. Initially, to keep watch on dissidents and to enforce his rule, Park created his own CIA, which, by most accounts, was financed by skimming proceeds from foreign currency loans (and which, in due course, became his undoing: he was assassinated by the CIA head, Kim Chae-kyu, in 1979). His successor, Choi Kyu-hah, was unable to cope with the resulting chaos, so another army major, Chun Doo-hwan, took control in 1980 and ruled, with an even stronger authoritarian hand, until the pressure of political liberalization after nearly three decades of dazzling economic growth forced him to step down following a new constitution and presidential elections in 1987.

Between 1945 and 1978 Korea received some $13 billion in American aid, of which $6 billion was economic and the rest military. In the 1950s U.S. aid accounted for more than 50 percent of Korean imports and about 15 percent of the Korean GNP. The Korean landlord class, which had been weakened during Japanese colonial rule, was further eroded by the Korean War, but new land reform legislation ended the power of the old rural elite by imposing limits of one hectare (about 2.5 acres) per capita. This thorough land reform program established a base of small, owner-operated farms, eliminated an important source of political instability in the countryside, and laid the foundation of an egalitarian society. No other strategic move would prove as significant.

Still, it wasn't until the late 1960s that Korea, well ahead of Latin America, embarked on a program of aggressive export-led growth, combined with impressive financial incentives to encourage extremely high rates of savings and investment, higher even than in Japan. While the Japanese, during their decades of high-speed growth, generated a savings rate averaging well over 20 percent of net disposable income, the Koreans, during their decades of growth, achieved an average rate of more than 30 percent. Korea moved through similar stages in its economic development, from petrochemicals and steel to automobiles and consumer electronics, up the ladder of higher value-added manufacturing, rung by rung.

As Hagen Koo, an experienced observer of the Korean economy, described it in his 1987 article, "The Interplay of State, Social Class, and World System in East Asian Development," "The Korean government regulates the flow of capital through its control of the banks, controls the level and use of foreign loans, and has the power to screen and monitor the activities of multinational corporations and other foreign investors. It even interferes with enterprise-level decisions concerning investment, production, and pricing. What really distinguishes South Korea from other, less successful developing countries is not so much the level of the state's involvement as its ability to implement its economic policies." Tactical tools of strategic economic development that would make Adam Smith quite ill at ease.

The government took the lead, primarily through credit allocation, in helping to form Korea's big business conglomerates, called *chaebol*, the top thirty of which, including such giants as Samsung, Hyundai, and Lucky Goldstar, comprise about two-thirds of Korea's GNP of nearly $120 billion. Korea has also developed a bureaucratic elite, which is well trained, efficient, and comparatively uncorrupt.

In the fifteen years since I started visiting this dynamic country, Seoul has progressed from a noisy, dusty, crowded town to a world-class city. It is bright and modern now, awash at night with colorful neon signs that blaze atop tall buildings downtown, flashing and blinking their testimonials in digital rainbows: Daewoo, Saemaul, Hyundai. All-new Hyundai and Daewoo city buses, in gleaming stainless steel and glass, purr silently through traffic, replacing the old mud-encrusted, diesel-belching Hino models that were used far beyond their depreciable lives.

For verifiable evidence of Korea's famed toughness, you need only wait for a taxi at the airport. On my last arrival, from Taipei late at night, as some seventy people queued for a cab, the line moved almost imperceptibly. When several taxis approached at once, three Koreans behind me broke from the queue and piled into one of them. Three *other* Koreans broke ranks and pulled the interlopers out, and not gently. Such a sight would never be seen in Japan, where the pressure to conform is so great, or in America, where even the words *taxi queue* constitute a contemporary oxymoron.

Anyone walking the streets of Seoul in early 1988, as I often did, would have found a strange mixture of both confidence and caution in the air—as well as tear gas, which stings the eyes long after rowdy student demonstrations are dispersed. Korean riot police often use a more caustic variety called *pepper gas*; when canisters hit the pavement, tiny chemical granules become embedded in the concrete grooves, and the pungent effects tend to linger. Still, student riots have been a common feature of Korean life since well back in the Yi dynasty, except during the Japanese occupation. Most Western observers, and nearly all Western press accounts of recent political unrest, fail to make mention of the historical role students have played as harbingers of change, violent though they may be. Their demonstrations are treated as the criminal exception rather than the political rule.

On one visit, holding a handkerchief over my nose to block out the nauseating effects of the pepper gas, which hung in the air after a recent riot, I went to see S. H. Jang, president of a strategic consulting firm that bears his name. Jang is a trained chemist who spent his early career in the pharmaceutical industry. He is also the author of a rather popular book called *The Key to Successful Business in Korea*.

"Koreans are driven by the future and by an ineradicable desire to outcompete the Japanese," he was telling me. "We export to China, manufacture in China, sell to Russia, to Iran, to Iraq. We don't see a difference between ideologies as far as markets are concerned. We make more than a million and a half cars a year now and expect to produce 4.5 million annually by 1995. Since we absorb less than a million a year in the domestic market, you know where the rest will go—overseas. The same is true of our other high-quality consumer products—color TVs, VCRs, camcorders. Koreans adapt very quickly to changing global conditions, adopt Western technology easily, and invest for the future."

"I don't think we should underestimate the Koreans one bit," Roger Mathus, general manager of Texas Instruments in Seoul, said to me the next evening. Mathus has been in Seoul continuously since 1980, speaks Korean, and reads *hangul*, but more importantly understands the culture and what makes Koreans tick. He is very knowledgeable about Korean geography, too, having hiked more than 3,000 miles there. He is also very knowledgeable about Korean competition.

"Take electronics," he said. "The Koreans identified it as a strategic industry. The Economic Planning Board and the Ministry of Trade and Industry looked at the domestic infrastructure—potential manufacturers, suppliers, support industries, education—and realized they couldn't be world-class players overnight. So they set up long-term objectives, *targeted* the sector, and showered it with financial incentives. They even set up their own wafer fabrication facility at Seoul National University. In response, under pressure from special interest lobbying groups, Washington pushes the Koreans to smoke American cigarettes. The Koreans know they're overdependent on the U.S. market, with nearly half their exports going there now, so they're diversifying, looking to Southeast Asia for food and to Europe for military equipment, so whatever Washington thinks they may gain by declines in Korean exports, they'll ultimately lose in American exports too. What's really interesting is the emergence of triangular relationships. We're seeing American technology being put together with Korean manufacturing processes using mainland Chinese labor. The Koreans are aggressive. Twenty-five percent of the U.S. market for VCRs is now theirs. They're willing to take a chance and bet. Americans are too conservative."

We were sitting in a restaurant on one of the craggy hilltops overlooking Seoul, with the colorful neon pulsating below. We talked about the Japanese drive to dominate technology so as to maintain global leadership, and I asked Roger what drove the Koreans.

"They want to be number one, too," he said. "In their own niche sectors. Intermediate manufactured goods. Mass-market consumer electronics. Small cars. Their export product quality is superb, but it's not perfect. Japan's *is*. That's one reason the Koreans keep competing so hard. You have to be careful, though, when you license, or Korean products using your own technology may come back to bite you at home."

Indeed. Texas Instruments had just settled a patent infringement suit with eight Japanese semiconductor manufacturers and Samsung, the leading Korean fabricator, for about $100 million.

"The Koreans know that labor demands will be in excess of what the market can absorb," Mathus said, "since they want to make up for lost time. They figure the GNP has to grow at 7 to 8 percent, or productivity and employment will both suffer. And U.S. pressure to open the domestic market here will continue."

A similar point was made by Suh Sang-mok, vice president of the Korean Development Institute, a Korean think tank that is said to have more analysts with PhDs than the Brookings Institution in Washington. In a recent interview he talked about industrial restructuring in Korea and the government policy responses that would be necessary. Suh predicted growing trade friction between Asia and America and continued technological innovation as Korea's driving economic force. Despite occasional storm clouds, Korea would be well positioned for future growth, Suh said, based on favorable demographics (due to the war, its population is still relatively young), a commitment to technological development, and its high domestic savings rate.

His analysts had calculated a growth rate for the Korean manufacturing sector of about 10 percent through 1991 and over 7 percent through the end of the century, with double-digit growth in electronics. Korea may experience problems in the financial sector, however, because Korean banks tend to be undercapitalized (weak ones are kept afloat by government credit) and because Korean firms generate inadequate profits. But in time, the government would legislate needed reforms to recapitalize the banks and give them more autonomy.

Western critics often argue that countries like Korea, which depend on export markets for growth, can no longer sustain their export-led performance. But Japan shifted impressively and effortlessly in 1986, following delayed currency revaluations, to domestic-led demand in underutilized sectors such as infrastructure development and housing. (Japan remains a huge market unto itself, with a population of 125 million and a $3 trillion GNP.) Still, Korea has shown, and continues to demonstrate, an impressive ability to diversify both its export and import markets. It will continue to run a sizable trade surplus with the U.S. every year for the foreseeable future, because it must pay close attention to its structural trade deficit with Japan (the source of most of its advanced technology) and to its foreign debt, which, at just under $40 billion, is still high and being paid off by earnings from exports of manufactures to America. Its currency, the won, has appreciated less than other Asian currencies and certainly less than Washington wants, but it has strengthened to below W800-to-1 and should continue to rise. Yet Korea's GNP is a mere 4 percent of Japan's and barely 2 percent of America's, so those who fear Korea will become another Japan need to look more carefully at the differentials.

And Korea's critics may also be wrong again. In a global economy that is growing less rapidly (say 2 percent, more or less), or in a world increasingly subject to protectionist pressures, outward-looking economies such as Korea's may still grow marginally faster because they tie labor demands to rigorous increases in manufacturing productivity, they measure product quality against *global* standards, and they maintain that the only meaningful prices are world prices.

TAIWAN: LAND OF THE ORDER TAKER

When Sun Yat-sen proclaimed his Three Principles of the People and created the Republic of China in 1911, as the Ch'ing dynasty wobbled on its last legs and lost the Mandate of Heaven, little did he know that his chief antagonist would be an ambitious tinhorn general named Chiang Kai-shek, who would later become president of the republic. Chiang's claim to fame, as is part of the folklore now, was his incompetence as a military commander. He fought two losing battles (three, if you include his inability to retake the mainland) in his lifetime, one against the invading Japanese in the 1930s, the other against Mao Zedong and the Chinese Communists in the 1940s. So in 1947 he and his Nationalist Chinese Party, the Kuomintang, fled to the offshore island of Taiwan to proclaim the Republic of China as representative of all China.

Japan had colonized Taiwan, too, which was a plum that fell into its hands as victor in the Sino-Japanese War of 1895. The Japanese proved, however, to be more tolerant colonialists on Taiwan than in Korea. They developed the local infrastructure and trained native Taiwanese to run the bureaucracy, even though the Taiwanese were also forced to learn Japanese.

As was true in Korea, politics and national security were Taiwan's preoccupation in the 1950s, with the United States giving a large chunk of military aid to Taiwan, estimated at about $6 billion from 1949 to 1978. To put this amount in perspective, during that time all of Latin America and all of Africa received only $3.2 billion from America, and Soviet economic aid to *all* LDCs was just over $7 billion.

Foreign savings, mostly from U.S. economic aid, constituted 40 percent of Taiwan's gross domestic capital formation during the 1950s, which was low compared to Korea. Per-capita economic aid from America to Taiwan was estimated at around $425 per annum during the 1950s, a considerable portion of the Taiwanese's total annual income.

Two events jump-started the Taiwanese economy. In 1953, under American pressure, the Land-to-the-Tiller Act was passed, which completed a staggered three-year land reform program causing the landlord class virtually to vanish and establishing the groundwork for an egalitarian society of small owner-operators in the dominant agricultural sector. The Chinese Nationalists who had fled from the mainland had no landholdings on Taiwan, so there were no vested interests to protect—interests that had seriously undermined previous land reform efforts in China.

Taiwan's land reform program has been called a showcase model because of its stunning results: typical real net family income practically doubled in a short time. Even before the farmers experienced yield increases, their increases in income were widespread. More money soon meant more schools and higher literacy. Urban and regional industry grew more quickly, driven by an increasingly prosperous countryside. With higher food productivity and better health care came better nutrition and a lower infant mortality rate. Famine and rural violence were reduced, as was unemployment. Over time, the average Taiwan farmer also *doubled* his productivity in rice.

Then, in 1963, came the second event: Taiwan created an economic planning agency, called the Council on International Economic Cooperation and Development (CIECD), the strategic model for which was Korea's Economic Planning Board. There was nothing magical about 1963, but the U.S. announced it was terminating economic aid

that year, so Taiwan was on its own. Chiang Ching-kuo, the generalissimo's son, took charge of CIECD, looked to Japan for inspiration,
and proved to be a very adept planner.

CIECD unleashed the full power of Taiwan's export-led economic
strategy in the 1960s through a familiar process of financial incentives
to stimulate savings and investment, strategic industrial targeting, and
close business-government cooperation. Taiwan's historical savings rate
of 35 percent is arguably the highest in the world. If the close business-
government relationship in Japan is like an equal partnership, then the
relationship in Korea is a senior partnership, with the government as
dominant partner, and in Taiwan a silent partnership. Unlike in Korea,
where a handful of large conglomerates, the *chaebol*, comprise about
two-thirds of the GNP, the concentration of economic power in Taiwan
is distributed more evenly among smaller and more entrepreneurial
firms. It takes the 500 largest corporations in Taiwan to generate, say,
a third of Taiwan's total GNP.

While Taiwan's CIECD emulated the Korean model, strategic ideas
came primarily from Japan. Chiang had studied an earlier Japanese
economist by the name of Kaname Akamatsu, who described his famous
product-cycle theory in terms of a "flying geese" model, showing how
industrial development in follower countries tends to form a pattern,
like wild geese flying in ranks. In textiles, steel, automobiles, and electronics, the cycle of origin, rise, apogee, and decline was not only
marked, but mastered, in Japan. In each life cycle, Akamatsu argued,
there is an appropriate jumping-off place, a point at which it pays to
let others make the product or provide the labor. Chiang and his colleagues at CIECD tried to calculate appropriate jumping-off places for
Taiwan in various industrial sectors, and one would have to say they
did pretty well.

Since the 1960s Taiwan has virtually flooded foreign markets, starting
with plastics and toys and eventually moving into more sophisticated
electronic products, intermediate manufactured goods, and industrial
equipment, right up the value-added ladder. By 1987 this crucible of
turbocharged capitalism had become so successful it was generating a
trade surplus of nearly $20 billion with the United States (the largest
in East Asia after Japan) and had amassed the world's third-largest
absolute level of foreign exchange reserves behind Japan and West
Germany, about $100 billion. It had also created its own trade frictions
in Washington, culminating in a healthy revaluation of the New Taiwan

dollar from a postwar norm of NT$40-to-1 to NT$28-to-1, an appreciation of over 25 percent. By 1987 half of Taiwan's total exports were going to the United States, with foreign trade accounting for more than 80 percent of its GNP. Today 20 million Taiwanese produce a GNP of close to $75 billion, giving them a per-capita income of nearly $4,000, *with virtually no foreign debt*. Not bad for a generation's work.

Taiwan's attention to exports is reflected in many practical ways. In most cities, when you check into a hotel, you find a host of helpful publications in your room, from city maps to local entertainment guides to cultural attractions, including a copy of the Gideon Bible (generally accompanied, in Asia, by the sayings of Buddha). In Taipei's hotels, you find a ten-pound, 925-page, three-inch-thick telephone book of yellow classified pages listing virtually every product that can be made by virtually every manufacturer in Taiwan, from abrasives to zippers. In the electronics section, Chinese names typically connoting good fortune fairly fly off the page: Auspicious Electrical, Brilliant Electronics, Wonderful Wire & Cable, Taiwan Prosperity Electronics, King Gold Enterprises. This cornucopia of entrepreneurial talent in Taiwan has earned the country a new nickname: "Land of the Order Taker."

On a recent visit to Taipei with a group of industrial clients, I met with Jim Klein, the mustachioed general manager of General Instruments Corporation in Taiwan, who is one of the most knowledgeable Americans about the country. We talked about the value-added process of shifting from cheap plastics to more sophisticated electronics.

"General Instruments has been able to shift over 50 percent of its manufacturing costs from the U.S. to Taiwan without having to raise prices, all through productivity enhancement, automation, and implementation of advanced process technology," he said during a working breakfast. "We source nearly 90 percent of our purchases from Taiwanese vendors, and you can achieve close cooperation *if* you have quality suppliers. We also pay top salaries for top talent, and we've found more and more American-educated Taiwanese engineers want to come back home, so we can pick up a crackerjack engineer here for about half of what that position costs in the States. The really low-cost labor you read about these days is in China, or India, or Sri Lanka, but the real benefit in Taiwan is the ability to get excellent *manufacturing* people at reasonable cost—engineering, software development, executive management, production, operations, you name it. There is still an incredibly strong work ethic in Taiwan."

That incredibly strong work ethic is personally symbolized by Morris Chang, an American-educated native Taiwanese who worked as an electrical engineer for Texas Instruments for many years and ultimately rose to become senior vice president responsible for TI's worldwide semiconductor manufacturing business. In 1987, at the pinnacle of his career with TI and nearing retirement, Chang returned to Taiwan from Texas at the urging of late president Chiang Ching-kuo to help make the nation a force in the global computer chip industry. He is president of Taiwan's Industrial Technology Research Institute (ITRI), which coordinates the national effort, and concurrently chairman of the new manufacturing facility that has been established with Philips N.V. of the Netherlands as technical partner and shareholder. In his mid-sixties, Chang has twice the energy level of an average high-achiever; his concentration and attention are similarly focused.

"We had to be careful in our selection of a partner," he said to me during an informal lunch in his office at ITRI. "We may have had to sacrifice too much had we joined forces with one of the big Japanese merchant chip makers, given our embryonic size, but we need access to state-of-the-art technology in order to survive. There is no question that we have the human resources now, especially since more of our engineers are coming back home from the States, and there is also no doubt in my mind that we have to develop the technological capabilities to be competitive in the information age."

The taxi that took me across town next to the Ministry of Finance was a locally made Yue Loong, a small, peppy, four-passenger sedan manufactured with Mitsubishi technology that could well follow Korea's Hyundai into the American market. City traffic in Asia generally reflects the local culture, and Taipei is no exception. More individualistic than the more group-oriented Japanese or Koreans, the Chinese tend to drive that way too, and my driver dodged recklessly from lane to lane, darting endlessly in and out of traffic. Packs of motorbikes and scooters crisscrossed at random, coughing blue clouds of exhaust. At stoplights the motorbikes huddled together in small clusters, their tiny engines clattering like a chorus of chain saws, and when the signal changed, they quickly scattered, revving to the highest gear, like a swarm of angry bees.

In Taiwan there is neither the fanatic attention to detail nor the fetish for cleanliness that exists in Japan; rapid industrial growth has made Taipei one of Asia's least clean cities. Sewage and water treatment facilities are severely overtaxed. Rainwater sits in large puddles near clogged gutters long after a storm blows through, and drinking water always seems to contain more than an acceptable level of microorganisms, as measured by the gradual effects on one's gastrointestinal system. The Taiwan government has spent billions of its well-earned foreign exchange dollars in improving and expanding the modern expressway that connects Taipei and its port city, Keelung, in the north, with the major export processing zone of Kaohsiung, to the south. By popular consensus, the next target for modernization would seem to be pollution-control equipment.

"It *is* a priority, you see. We have plans to build more schools, hospitals, sewers, water-treatment stations, smokestack scrubbers. We even have plans for a Taipei subway to control this awful traffic. We know we need to improve our quality of life."

Vice Minister Y. T. Chang sipped from a jade teacup as we sat in a large conference room at the Ministry of Finance discussing Taiwan's strategic economic incentives. Like most government officials, Chang was educated in America. After graduating from Taiwan National University, he studied law at SMU and entered the MOF on his return.

"You see," he said, "in the past we needed capital formation for investment, to build factories and to develop export industries, so we implemented a tax law that makes earned income from interest or dividends on a principal amount of up to 11,000 U.S. dollars a year tax-exempt. We also created incentives for strategic industries, including a five-year tax holiday and a low standard corporate tax of only 25 percent. Thirty percent of investment income can be used to reduce tax liability, dollar for dollar, in the strategic sectors. Exports are taxed at a zero rate. All business taxes paid are refunded back to the exporter, a value-added tax in accordance with GATT, but nonstrategic sectors bear the full brunt of taxes."

Taiwan has four export processing zones, or free trade zones, in which both domestic and foreign investors can manufacture products for export. No taxes are paid, either on the imported parts and components used in the manufacturing process or on the exported goods themselves. In a sense, the whole island of Taiwan is an export processing zone.

It seems improving the quality of life, and using the country's mountain of foreign exchange reserves to pay for it, is on everyone's mind, not least Shirley W. Y. Kuo, then deputy governor of the central bank, now minister of finance.

"We have major infrastructure plans in progress," she told me. "Hospitals, schools, power stations, sewers, especially pollution-abatement equipment, all on a major scale. It's time."

Mrs. Kuo was trained as an economist and taught for many years at Taiwan National University. Attractive, extraordinarily bright, and very articulate, she spent her elementary school years in Taiwan during the Japanese occupation and is trilingual. We conversed in a combination of Japanese and English.

"The disposition of our foreign exchange reserves is an obvious priority," she said. "We have issued certificates of deposit and savings bonds to absorb the rapid growth of our money supply as exports have grown so fast. And we let importers borrow dollars up to expected import liabilities to cushion the impact of further local currency appreciation. Most of our reserves are invested in U.S. Treasury bills, as our principal objectives are safety and liquidity. But our trade surplus— or your trade deficit, I should say—occurs primarily because America consumes so much more than it saves, in both its public and private sectors. America has never really developed a foreign trade strategy, because trade is such a small percentage of that huge economy. Taiwan *has* to pay attention to trade if we want to survive and grow."

SINGAPORE: THE LION CITY

In the thirteenth century, when the colorful Malay ruler of Palembang, Sri Tri Buana, landed on a small island at the southern tip of the Malay Peninsula to seek shelter from a severe storm, he saw an animal that he took to be a lion and established a settlement he called "Singapura," or Lion City. For several hundred years Singapore was caught in a vortex of conflict for control of the peninsula. By the early nineteenth century Singapore's strategic location became obvious even to the British, who dispatched Sir Thomas Stamford Raffles to establish a trading station there. Singapore's status as a British possession was formalized in 1824 by treaty with the Dutch. Two years later Singapore became part of the Straits Settlements, together with Penang and Malacca, and after the invention of the steamship the British found Singapore's deep-water harbor and strategic position ideal as a main stopping point between Europe and the Far East. The opening of the Suez Canal further bolstered Singapore's major port status, and in 1867 the Straits Settlements became a crown colony.

In 1946, following Japan's defeat in the Pacific war, Singapore became a separate crown colony, while Penang and Malacca joined the Federation of Malaya. Throughout the 1950s Britain fought the Communists in Malaya, and Singapore was practically torn apart by Communist-led agitation and riots. In 1959 Singapore became internally self-governing, and in 1963 it achieved independence as part of the new state of Malaysia. But assimilation with Malaysia did not work; in 1965 the Lion City became a totally independent and sovereign state, headed by a man about whom we will hear more later, its first (and only) prime minister, Lee Kuan Yew.

Singapore turned early, and with enthusiasm, to exports, such that by 1988 its 2 million people were exporting as much as China's 1.2 billion. The architect of Singapore's version of the capitalist developmental state was Malaccan-born Goh Keng Swee, an economist educated at Raffles College (predecessor to the National University of Singapore) and the London School of Economics. Goh knew that Singapore's fortunes would be tied to two factors—its people and its location—and that its economy would be linked inextricably to three regions: the OECD for markets, ASEAN (the Association of Southeast Asian Nations) for raw materials, and Singapore itself for capital formation and productivity.

From the beginning, Goh had no delusions about neoclassical free-market economics for Singapore. The government was the primary player, buying and clearing tracts of land for national housing developments, where 85 percent of Singapore's people live today and where light industries are given incentives to site smaller manufacturing or assembly plants.

In the early days Singapore's economy was dependent on its role as an *entrepôt*, refining oil from Indonesia or shipping tin and rubber from Malaysia, until Goh pushed the Lion City upmarket into shipbuilding and direct manufacturing. Huge industrial estates were created from swampland, like Jurong, which was initially known as "Goh's Folly" but later became the launching pad for Singapore's impressive export success. Goh helped create two of the nation's most important policy institutions, the Monetary Authority of Singapore, on whose board he still sits, and the Economic Development Board, which implements Singapore's version of industrial policy and became known as the "invisible hand of Adam Goh."

Multinational corporations were attracted to Singapore by its well-educated, efficient, and hardworking people, but also by tax holidays and incentives for expansion. Foreign banks were encouraged to use Singapore as a regional financial center, so that by the early 1970s Singapore had become the focal point of the fast-growing Asian dollar market. Goh's dealings with foreign banks were strict and unapologetic. He said that regulation of bankers was like frying fish: they must not be overdone.

Singapore's annual GNP growth rate averaged a healthy 11.4 percent in the ten-year period from 1977 through 1986, including a serious hiccup in 1985. Confronted with a severe economic recession that year (the economy contracted by some 4 percent), the government decided to cut business costs drastically to regain its international competitiveness. This meant holding down wages and reducing contributions to the Central Provident Fund—in effect, an across-the-board pay cut. Singapore's union leaders understood the gravity of the situation and backed the government's policy fully. Growth rebounded by about 2 percent the following year and was back to the robust average of 11 percent by 1988. Such close cooperation is more difficult to achieve in Western societies, which exalt rights over responsibilities and put individual liberties ahead of the claims of society.

On a recent visit to the Economic Development Board I met with Daniel Selvaratnam, a young Tamil who is director of planning there. The EDB's offices are located high atop the Raffles City Tower, one of the many new skyscrapers prominent in the downtown financial district. We talked about the system of incentives the EDB used to attract and keep companies in Singapore.

"We don't have the kind of integrated industrial policy Japan has," he told me. "But we do maintain a system of incentives for investment and expansion, and we will withhold tax incentives if the projects impact the economy negatively. We also make a distinction between the kind of business services that are more important to Singapore's growth and development as an information economy, like engineering and financial services, and those that are not, like fast foods. We make the tax holiday available to all qualified businesses for five years initially and then let the market decide who stays and who goes. We are presently considering future incentives for the knowledge-intensive, high value-added industries and are putting a new emphasis on training. We have set up new research centers for artificial intelligence, for robotics, for flexible manufacturing systems, and for computer-aided design. We have also created a science park, attached to the national university. Sony has taken advantage of our incentive scheme, as well as our superior communication facilities, to set up an engineering center here to service its own subsidiaries in the region. In fact, the Japanese are now the largest single source of foreign investment in Singapore and have been since 1986."

Development of Singapore's human resources is a theme to which most government officials often return, and for good reason. Totally bereft of natural resources, the Lion City has no choice but to rely on its tiny population of 2.5 million people as the primary source of productivity growth.

This point was emphasized a number of times when I met with Dr. Richard Hu, Singapore's minister of finance. Hu did undergraduate work in chemistry at Berkeley and earned his doctorate in England. He joined Shell in 1960, became chairman of Shell (Singapore) in 1982, and was appointed minister of finance in 1985.

"We are basically dealing with a limitation on numbers in Singapore," he said. "With our small population, we have to compete on quality and build a more skilled work force to provide superior support services in key areas such as telecommunications, financial services, and all these 'brainpower' industries. We've become the financial center for the region, which is encouraging, and we have an obvious lead in the knowledge industries, which we want to maintain. We can adapt and adjust rather quickly; we also keep taxes to a minimum."

Singapore's currency, the Singapore dollar, has appreciated nearly 50 percent during the past decade, to S$2-to-1. The Monetary Authority of Singapore, the MAS as it is known, is the equivalent of its central bank. I visited Dr. Teh Kok Peng, its director of economic development, to talk about savings.

"Our high savings rate is part cultural, part incentive," Dr. Teh said. "And maybe partly demographic. Unlike Western economies, it is our younger people who save more. No matter how you look at it, America is geared to consumption. This point stuck vividly in my mind when I worked for the World Bank in Washington some time back. But there are no taxes on capital gains or dividends in Singapore. If your tax structure favored investment over consumption, that would certainly turn things around."

Singapore's vaunted savings rate was the product of the Central Provident Fund, which administers the system's various incentives. Funds deposited into an individual's CPF account accumulate tax-free. They help Singaporeans save for retirement, buy their own homes (or housing flats), and provide for their own health care. It is called a forced-savings system, since it is involuntary. Each month, salaried employees contribute 25 percent of their gross wages to their individual CPF account, and their employers match that amount up to the first S$6,000 of income. At age fifty-five, individual account holders may withdraw everything down to a base balance, at once or in annuities, tax-free; looked at in this way, the system represents a kind of turbocharged IRA. At the end of 1986 CPF account holders held a total of S$29.4 billion, proceeds from which were actively invested by the government in either approved securities or local development projects that yielded an attractive return, like Singapore's new rapid transit.

Standing at the mouth of the Singapore River today, where the old hotel bearing his name has become a high-rise tower of glass and steel, Sir Thomas Stamford Raffles would rub his eyes in astonishment. Given the physical constraints of geography, Singapore has to grow up, into the air, or down, into the ground, as its infrastructure expands. The most recent addition to its impressive array of developments is the mass rapid transit system (MRTS), a S$5 billion project begun in 1983 and completed, two years *ahead* of schedule, in early 1988. (Japanese engineering firms did the construction.) An old friend and former colleague, Fock Siew-wah, was chairman of the MRTS Corporation. With over thirty-five miles of underground track, the rapid transit system carries more than three-quarters of a million people every day, 30 percent of whom live within walking distance of one of the system's thirty-five stations. The MRT is quiet, clean, and efficient, characteristic of just about everything Singapore does.

I took the train downtown, from its Orchard Road station near the Goodwood Park, where I always stay when I visit the Lion City, to the Tanjong Pagar station near Shenton Way, a short walk from Fock's office, to give him a firsthand report on the system and to ask how he was able to finish the project so quickly.

"In Singapore," he said with a smile, "we're like chopsticks. Individually, we might snap quite easily. But when we work together, we're strong and virtually unbreakable."

HONG KONG: THE FRAGRANT HARBOR

Hong Kong is perhaps more familiar to more Americans than Singapore, not only because it is geographically closer than the Lion City, but also because it is a popular site for American tourist junkets and a veritable mecca for shoppers as the K mart of the Far East.

Most Americans are also more familiar with the story of Hong Kong's creation in the mid–nineteenth century. First the island of Hong Kong and then Kowloon were ceded to Britain under treaties never truly accepted by China, following defeat in the opium wars. In 1898, realizing that defense of Hong Kong's deep-water harbor depended on control of the land surrounding it, Britain signed a convention with Peking leasing the New Territories from China for a period of ninety-nine years, to June 30, 1997, the political significance of which date we will explore later.

The colony has retained more of its British influence than Singapore, too, perhaps because it still *is* a colony and because its climate is considerably cooler. It also has a larger population, nearly 5.5 million people, more than twice Singapore's, and its colonial government has a reputation for being quintessentially *laissez-faire*.

That reputation, though, is more superficial than real. It is true that Hong Kong's corporate (and personal) tax rate of 17.5 percent qualifies the colony for virtual tax haven status. But the government extends, *either directly or indirectly*, a number of financial and investment incentives that qualify as ingredients for some pretty impressive turbocharged capitalism, colonial-style.

In fact, the low income tax rate itself qualifies as a major investment incentive, as does the local currency, the Hong Kong dollar, which is kept artificially weak, at HK$7.8-to-1, and linked to the U.S. dollar. But Hong Kong also has a generous industrial estate program, which leases manufacturing sites to corporations in preferred industry sectors under highly favorable terms—terms that comprise a fairly healthy industrial policy. Hong Kong has two industrial estates currently in operation, Tai Po, consisting of some sixty-nine hectares, and Yuen Long, sixty-seven hectares in size; a third, Tseung Kwan, roughly the same size as the other two, will become operational in 1990.

Francis Leung, manager of Tai Po, explained to me how the system functions.

"The Hong Kong Industrial Estates Corporation decides the conditions under which a lessee may build," he said. "These conditions include factory size, setback requirements, effluent control, emission guidelines, rates of electricity and water consumption, and the financial terms and conditions of the lease. This may be the most significant factor, since the corporation essentially develops the land for the estate at zero cost to itself and then leases the factory sites at rates that are about a third as cheap as land can be purchased or leased outside the estates."

Tai Po is located a half hour from downtown Hong Kong and borders a craggy body of water called Tolo Harbor. Tai Po currently has forty-eight factories in operation, about two-thirds of which are Japanese-owned, the balance American; another forty have been approved and are under construction. Leung was Hong Kong–born and –educated. He is an articulate and enthusiastic supporter of the system.

"Our depreciation benefits are also quite generous," he continued, "allowing a lessee company to recoup two-thirds of its plant and equipment costs during the first year of operation. We also help companies recruit employees, put them in touch with local labor offices, get permission for notices to be posted in the housing estates nearby, and provide ready access to the Labor Department. Our location on a landfill site close to the housing estates is no accident; it eliminates transportation worries for the workers. And we don't impose taxes on dividends any lessee companies may repatriate to their parent companies."

The overall effects of Hong Kong's industrial (estate) policy help the colony stay competitive with other countries in East Asia that also provide incentives for their higher value-added manufacturing industries. In practical terms, this means the R&D and advanced technology from America or Japan, or Korea or Taiwan, can be applied in the industrial estates at a lower overall cost. This trend is being accelerated now that the Shenzhen special export zone has been established in China, just over the border from the New Territories, where Hong Kong capital combines with ultracheap Chinese labor to churn out even cheaper products.

Tony Miller, deputy director of Hong Kong's Department of Trade, explained in concrete terms what development of the Shenzhen export processing zone meant for both Hong Kong and China as we sat in his waterfront office overlooking the active, picturesque harbor.

"There are now 2 million people from Canton working in Shenzhen for Hong Kong joint ventures," he told me. "Chinese firms are increasingly active in Hong Kong, too, learning to be capitalists. China is now Hong Kong's third-largest investor after America and Japan."

He gestured out the window toward the harbor.

"Hong Kong is now the world's second-largest port, after Rotterdam," he said. "We're way ahead of New York now in total tonnage. More than 14,000 oceangoing vessels enter and leave this harbor every year. And we have the world's largest air cargo terminal at Kai Tak, which flies out 500,000 tons of cargo a year."

The cumulative effect of Hong Kong's various incentives, in numerical terms, is impressive. By 1987 more than half the world's toys, with an export value exceeding $5 billion, were manufactured or assembled in Hong Kong. More watches are now made in Hong Kong than anywhere else in the world, including Japan and Switzerland. Forty percent of Hong Kong's total exports of nearly $50 billion consist of textile goods and clothing. Fifteen percent are toys, sporting goods, and games. And most of these manufactured goods, nearly half of Hong Kong's total exports, head for the U.S. market, for sale to America's insatiable consumers.

THE PHILIPPINES: ODD MAN OUT

In 1950, when Korea had a measly per-capita income of $146 and Taiwan $224, Filipinos were sitting pretty with an annual income of over $600, making the Philippines a "wealthy" country by Asian standards.

By 1980 the Philippines was the *only* country in East Asia to experience a real decline in per-capita income, *despite* its abundant natural resources, its head start, and an American-style democracy. More accurately, it had become Asia's economic basket case perhaps *because* of those factors.

The Negritos, the people of the Philippines, settled the archipelago's 7,000 islands nearly 30,000 years ago. In 1521 Ferdinand Magellan claimed the country for Spain, converted it to Catholicism, and established an oligarchic system of Spanish colonial rule that lasted for four centuries. The United States defeated Spain in 1898, during the Spanish-American War, and won the Philippines as a prize. President McKinley made his now-famous prayer to God, asking whether America should keep it as a protectorate or let the Filipinos have it back. On one of those many occasions when God ought to have kept quiet, He answered.

America colonized the Philippines, bringing flush toilets to Manila, one-room schoolhouses to the barrios, and democratic politics to the government. Despite a generous American foreign aid program, which contributed more than $5 billion to the Philippines between 1946 and 1978, the sparks never caught fire as they had in Korea and Taiwan. America's Philippine preoccupation was strategic, not economic. Put bluntly, manufacturing never had a chance; the oligarchs permitted agriculture to dominate the economy, which protected their elevated status, and failed to implement a land reform program, which would have threatened it.

Failure to come to grips with meaningful land reform has practically destroyed the Philippines.

Agriculture accounts for about a third of the Philippine gross national product, employs over half the total labor force, and generates a third of the country's export earnings. Two crops, sugarcane and coconut, comprise nearly half of total agricultural production and over a third of total land harvested. Nearly two-thirds of Filipino farmers cultivate farms of less than three hectares yet own only 24 percent of the land, compared with 5 percent of the farmers who own more than ten hectares—the *haciendas*—and control 34 percent of the land.

Overreliance on agriculture has resulted in poor national health and lagging education. Philippine population growth, exploding at a rate of more than 3 percent a year courtesy of Spain's gift of Catholicism, has outstripped economic growth. A population of nearly 60 million creates a total GNP of little more than $30 billion today—a per-capita income of barely $500.

By 1985 the top 10 percent of the population had more than fifteen times the income of the poorest 10 percent, and more than half of the country's 56 million people lived in poverty. Today roughly 70 percent of all poor families live in rural areas, most of them small farmers characterized by large families and low levels of education. More than a third have not completed elementary school, and 10 percent have never attended school at all. The infant mortality rate is the highest in Asia. The average Filipino gets less than 90 percent of the calories necessary for adequate nutrition, while the nation exports an average of 800 calories per capita per day via coconut oil alone. Added to all this is a foreign debt of nearly $30 billion, one of the largest in the world.

How can this be?

In a country with rich volcanic soil, abundant rainfall, deep mineral deposits, well-endowed fishing fields, natural topographic conditions conducive to the growth of corn and sugarcane, and the International Rice Research Institute (IRRI) which created the green revolution called "miracle rice" that has produced dramatic yields and incomparable prosperity for every other Asian country, how could things go so wrong?

Land reform.

No American knows more about land reform than Roy Prosterman, an agricultural economist at the University of Washington in Seattle. Several years ago he wrote a book with Jeffrey Riediger of Princeton called *Land Reform and Democratic Development* in which he discussed the importance of resolving the land tenure problem as a precondition for economic takeoff.

"Based on our analysis," he wrote, "we would predict a substantial danger of major revolution for any country twenty-five percent or more of whose population consisted of landless peasants. No social group is more conservative than a landowning peasantry, and none is more revolutionary than a peasantry which owns too little land or pays too high a rental."

Prosterman documents the dramatic results of the three nonviolent postwar land reform revolutions in Japan, Korea, and Taiwan. He shows that landless populations have constituted a quarter or more of the total population in twenty-two countries in the world. Of these, fifteen have experienced revolution or protracted conflict. Five others have not dealt with their land tenure problem in any significant way. Two have yet to deal with land tenure problems at all: the Philippines and Guatemala.

Prosterman uses a birth-and-death-based Modernization Index, which gives equal weight to the relative infant mortality rates and crude birth rates as a means of rating the relative advancement of countries. Not surprisingly, Japan tops the scale with a score of ninety-seven, followed closely by the U.S. with ninety-two. The Philippines has the lowest score, sixty-four.

On his scale of agricultural productivity per hectare, the Netherlands ranks highest, followed by Japan and Korea; the Philippines, again, is dead last. In rice production alone, Japan again ranks at the top. Between 1947 and 1982 Japan doubled its productivity in rice, Korea more than tripled its rice output, and Taiwan increased its output 2.7 times.

The Philippines is a classic case of frustration in a series of failed land reform efforts. Using successively lower nonzero ceilings for tenant farmers called *retention limits*, 300 hectares was set in 1955, and the ceiling was lowered to seventy-five hectares in 1963, twenty-four in 1971, and seven (Ferdinand Marcos's lucky number) in 1972. Each time, most of the land "evaporated," so fewer than 20 percent of Filipino corn and rice tenants have become landowners. Cheating is facilitated by inadequate public land records and by widespread corruption and cronyism, characteristics that predate Marcos. (They continue under Aquino. In June 1989 she had to sack her agrarian reform secretary, Philip Juico, and twenty officers of his department in the wake of the worst scandal of her administration: unproductive land was being bought by the government for as much as twenty times its real value.)

Both Japanese and Taiwanese land reform programs had substantial and credible penalties for landlords who cheated and were found out. So nonzero retention limits became possible if retained land was restricted to the village in which the landlord resided, if there were accurate land records against which landlord claims could be kept, and if credible penalties were imposed for noncompliance.

Political feasibility for land reform includes three key independent variables, Prosterman says. One is the degree of compensation to affected landowners, a second is the degree to which the country has a centralized political authority with power to implement the reforms, and a third is the degree to which effective village organizations can support the land reform measures. Unfortunately for the Philippines, none of these variables exists, so political feasibility is dead on arrival.

During a recent visit to Manila I saw the secretary of agriculture, Carlos "Sonny" Dominguez, who has a reputation as a youthful, energetic, "reform-minded" government official.

When you arrive at the Manila airport, you quickly realize that the Philippines does not belong to hyper-growth Asia but to the stagnant Third World. The baggage claim area is a mass of bodies slick with sweat from the tropical heat. Customs inspectors stand sluggishly, half-asleep. In an era of electronic circuitry, foreign currency desks are manned by clerks operating hand-cranked calculators and old manual typewriters.

Outside, sweltering in a taxi that sputtered down Roxas Boulevard, I watched the familiar Latin jeepneys—half-jeep, half-van, their exteriors trimmed in chrome and pastel, passengers jammed in like sardines on their way from nowhere to nowhere—chug by. Each jeepney had its name on a small placard above the windshield, some with fringe, others with plastic sequins that glitter in the sunlight: Sex Pistols, Money Honey, Thank God, Praise the Lord. Diversions from reality.

Roxas Boulevard, lined on both sides by large banyan trees and bordering the bay, passes through a nondescript part of town en route to downtown Manila. Josephine's Coffee Shop and a McDonald's sit sandwiched between corrugated-tin-roofed squatter shacks and crumbling concrete office buildings, unfinished and vacant, their cocoonlike shapes testimony to a stillborn economy. At stoplights blind beggars led by young, undernourished children emerge and limp from car to car, arms extended for a handout. They are pursued by the skeletal bodies of young hawkers selling everything from plastic purses to rotting fruit.

As I drove out to the Agriculture Ministry in Quezon City, I was struck by another contrast. One cannot visit Singapore or Seoul, or Taipei or even Tokyo, and not be impressed by how much the modern landscape changes from year to year. In Manila one is impressed by how *little* things change. Philippine government offices, their corridors piled high with unused desks and chairs, remind me of India, except that in New Delhi stray cows instead of dilapidated motorbikes crowd the entryways.

Sonny Dominguez, known to friends as "Smurfy" because of his diminutive size, led me into a spacious office where we talked about land reform and economic development for several hours. In his early forties, handsome, and fit, he ran a bamboo business in Davao years ago. He studied advanced management at Stanford and spent several years at the Bank of the Philippine Islands. When Cory Aquino swept into power in early 1986, she recruited him as assistant secretary of agriculture. He moved up when his boss entered the Senate in 1987.

"After Marcos, we killed four monopolies," he was telling me proudly as we sat across from a whining air conditioner, "copra, sugar, coconut, and fertilizer. We spent $100 million liberalizing fertilizer imports. Under Marcos four importers monopolized the market, forcing farmers to pay nearly 300 pesos per fifty-kilogram bag. This fell to a hundred pesos a bag after we let more importers compete. There are now fifteen, after the shakeout, and many complain that they can't make money—to which we say, 'Look, we didn't tell you to get into the business, you did it on your own. So either compete or do something else.' "

I referred to a recent memo by Prosterman that updated the current progress, or lack of it, on land reform. Dominguez sighed.

"I think land reform is something we better do now, on our own, and by ourselves," he said, "or somebody will do it for us. It can't be done in the future—our population is growing too fast. Critics say that other countries in Asia are *consolidating* farms now, but they all went through land reform two generations ago."

He pulled out a small cigar and puffed it alive.

"There are four parts to the land reform problem here," he went on, exhaling heavily. "First, we have to complete the rice and corn programs under laws that have been on our books for thirty years. Next, we have to distribute lands that were turned over to the government voluntarily by absentee landowners. Then we have the *very* controversial problem of acquiring privately owned farmland: how much to pay, over how long a period, and what the retention limits are to be. Finally, we have to distribute the government land.

"The hard part is the controversial part, which Congress is dickering over now. Most members of Congress are from the landed wealth, so you can guess how long *that's* going to take. There are four bills pending, two in the House and two in the Senate, out of twenty-three originally drafted. If we passed a comprehensive land reform bill today, there would be a mountain of short-term adjustment and enforcement problems, but longer-term, we could get on with our economic restructuring, which is so important. But we can't even decide the basic issue, which is the nonzero retention limit."

I asked him if the Philippines was sitting on a time bomb.

There was a long delay. He took a deep breath, sighed again, and stared out the window.

"I don't know."

American officials at the embassy in Manila, not surprisingly, view the economic situation in typically free-market terms.

"There is nothing inherently wrong with the Philippine economy that more foreign investment can't solve," the embassy's senior economic officer told me. "There is a consumer-led recovery; it's just not sustainable. Commodities prices are up, but government pump-priming is down, so more foreign investment is needed. Unemployment is below 10 percent for the first time in four years."

I asked him about land reform. He shrugged his shoulders.

"It's trapped in congressional committees," he said. "Even if some watered-down legislation passes, it will get bogged down in implementation. There's really no rush on this. It'll be years before they get around to anything."

Other friends in Manila say that what the embassy says is precisely what Washington wants to hear. They call it "bottled sunshine."

The Philippines is the only country in East Asia that has modeled its economic structure, its educational system, and its form of government on the United States, and it is the only country in East Asia that has failed to improve either the income or the standard of living of its people during the postwar period of unprecedented economic growth. It is the only country in East Asia whose currency, like the dollar, has been debased and devalued. Only in the Philippines have the seeds of American democracy and free-market economics been planted; as a demonstration effect, it is a crop failure.

The United States remains committed to the Philippines for two simple reasons. One is the political benefits of propaganda, to advertise a working model of American democracy to the Third World. The other has to do with the strategic aspects of military security, given the significance of American bases at Clark Air Base and Subic Bay Naval Station.

But neither the political benefits of propaganda nor the strategic aspects of regional security can continue to support an inefficient Philippine political system and its corrupt oligarchy. In the probable absence of comprehensive land reform the likely consequence, and soon, may be revolution—violent revolution, not the suburban coming-out party held by Cory Aquino and her friends in 1986. That could also be a devastating setback for the American political and economic model, not just in the Philippines but elsewhere in the Third World as well.

4
WHY AMERICAN POLICY MECHANISMS HAVE FAILED

The concept of free access of every country to every market, the gradual reduction of trade barriers, and the openness of capital markets have served us very well, given our internal political and economic structure and given our position in the world from 1945 on.

But one observes the way in which Japan has organized itself, with a certain unity of purpose, which can easily be exaggerated but nonetheless at the same time should not be overlooked. One looks at the way in which state enterprises are being used somewhat *by the other advanced industrial countries and now by the developing countries in very considerable degree. Observing these various forms of interference with the operation of market mechanisms, I find myself constantly pushed back to the question of whether we have to opt for a set of institutional relationships and principles that reflect a second-best world from our point of view. We have to somehow organize ourselves.*

Professor Raymond Vernon, Harvard University

I was standing recently in the spacious lobby of the American Institute in Taiwan, an organization that anywhere else would have comprised the United States embassy, but in Taiwan it had to be designated a nonprofit cultural institution. In 1977 America had finally recognized the People's Republic as the legitimate government of China, and shortly thereafter Washington and Beijing exchanged embassies. As a result the American embassy in Taipei became the American Institute in Taiwan, and the former Nationalist Chinese Embassy in Washington became the Coordination Council for North American Affairs. Relationships had become "unofficially" official.

I was leading a group of senior American executives on a fact-finding mission to Taipei at the time, and we were waiting to see the institute's

71

senior commercial officers, who were, for the moment, busy upstairs. As we waited in the lobby, we found ourselves in the midst of a demonstration by Land O Lakes, Inc., a Minnesota-based dairy products firm that was touting the benefits of American turkey to a small group of somewhat curious Chinese onlookers. The backdrop was a familiar effort to increase American agricultural exports to Taiwan.

On a large table sat platters overflowing with turkey products: roast turkey, turkey bologna, turkey sandwiches, turkey *mousse*. There was not a chopstick in sight. An American official from the AIT welcomed the Chinese guests in passable Chinese and then proceeded to demonstrate the superiority of America's agricultural products by reaching into a microwave oven behind him and sampling a forkful of roasted turkey, which nearly convulsed the Chinese with laughter and brought a rather wide grin to my face.

The irony of the moment, which the Chinese had captured instantly, was that, although the turkey was American, the microwave was a product of Tatung, Taiwan's largest manufacturer of consumer electronics products. Here was a snapshot, in brief, of America's basic trade problem with Asia: Taiwan was sending the U.S. shipload after shipload of high value-added, top-quality manufactured products, and the United States was responding by trying to get Taiwan to buy more farm goods. It was a pattern typical of a traditional colonial relationship, only in reverse: America had become the colony, shipping the low value-added produce to Taiwan.

American policy responses to the Pacific challenge have been on the whole singularly ineffective in dealing with what can only be called East Asia's systematic effort to wrest global commercial and technological leadership away from the United States. The fact that the effort has been relatively successful can be measured in any one of about three ways, which, taken together, represent a reasonably comprehensive view of the problem.

The first is an external score-keeping mechanism, the balance of trade. The second is an internal score-keeping mechanism, which we might call market share dominance, which has been strong especially for Japan's strategic industries, helped by more effective market-protecting strategies in the domestic Japanese market and by better market-penetrating strategies overseas. The third is a manifestation of America's commitment to neoclassical economic theory—"free trade" and a historical attitude of benign neglect toward its exchange rate, which was bound to fail sooner or later and thus leave Washington with no alternative but to shift the entire burden of the trade deficit onto the exchange rate.

Regarding the external mechanism, American trade policy (to the extent that Washington has a policy) has been cut from the same neo-classical mold of free-market economics, which means that if America is behaving according to free-market principles and others aren't, then it is up to the others to change. Consequently the political thrust has been to label the trade practices of Japan, Korea, and Taiwan as mercantilistic, insidious, or unfair and to get these nations to change their behavior.

But America tends to forget that, as the eminent MIT economist Charles Kindleberger has said so eloquently, free trade is the hypocrisy of the export interest, the clever device of the climber who kicks the ladder away when he has attained the summit of greatness. As the only country to survive the Second World War with its economic and industrial infrastructure intact, it was only reasonable that the United States use its considerable power to help restore the economies of Japan and West Germany, since both countries were key to America's strategic interests in East Asia and Western Europe, respectively, and reasonable that America, as the clever climber with the strongest economy, support free trade.

As exports of computer chips or VCRs from Japan, automobiles from Korea, and consumer electronic goods from Taiwan to the United States have exploded in recent years, Washington has criticized both the aggressive export policies of these countries and the domestic industrial policies that have made their strategic sectors so much more competitive, rather than formulating its *own* strategic policies as to how America's manufacturing sector might be strengthened and made more competitive. America has failed to measure up to other industrialized nations in improving its economic position in the world during the past twenty years. Worker productivity, trade performance, capital formation, and investment in competitive plant and equipment have all lagged far behind East Asia.

The flip side of the criticize-what-they-do policy is an equally flawed approach that says, if you're going to sell America so much, then you ought to at least buy more from America. This is where the lobbying strength of Washington's special interest groups infects American trade policy with domestic politics. National associations for meat exporters, citrus growers, and the tobacco companies, combined with the power of their corporate members and representatives in Congress, all bring concerted influence to bear to put meat, fruit, and cigarettes in the vanguard of American trade policy in Asia.

The expected result is an escalation of both emotional and political undertones in bilateral trade negotiations, which has led to serious outbreaks of anti-American sentiment in Asia. No three industries seem to get more political attention in Washington than meat, oranges, and tobacco as far as America's external trade is concerned, but no three industries are less critical in strategic terms.

Asian analysts in turn criticize Washington as having an abundance of "trade politics" but no concerted, comprehensive "trade policy," and one must admit they have a point. Asian attitudes toward imports of American agricultural products are also highly emotional, closely tied to their own staple product, rice, which has evolved into an issue of national security rather than just trade, especially in Japan. It is important to remember that in *any* country agriculture is an extension of domestic politics before it becomes a factor in external trade.

When I visited Taiwan in early 1988, a large team of American negotiators had arrived in Taipei almost simultaneously, to resume bilateral negotiations with their Chinese counterparts on reducing the Taiwanese trade surplus, second-largest in Asia after Japan. The focus was, not unexpectedly, agricultural products.

I glanced through several local press accounts, which centered on Washington's demands that Taiwan increase its imports of American agricultural goods, as my cab inched through traffic from the airport into Taipei. The night was cool and drizzly, typical of late spring weather in Taiwan. Earlier that day nearly 8,000 political prisoners had been released by the government, creating huge traffic jams throughout Taipei. It was long past midnight by the time I arrived at the Grand Hotel, exhausted by both the long week in Tokyo and the long ride into town.

The next morning the streets of Taipei were clogged again, not with people this time but with pigs, and my cab snaked through a small army of Taiwanese farmers, more than 200 of whom had brought truckloads of their favorite animals into Taipei as a protest against Washington's demands that Taiwan import more American turkey, peanuts, and tobacco. They wanted to be sure both their own government and the American trade representatives in town got the message. As my cab crept through this squeaking mass of live bacon, I thought the Chinese might do better if they invited some of those American turkeys from the land of lakes to negotiate directly with the Taiwanese pigs.

Companies and their industries can become more competitive, but countries cannot, though countries can change the policies that influence the productivity and total output of companies and industries, through taxes, expenditures, incentives, subsidies, and laws.

It is primarily through policies and incentives that East Asian competitors have succeeded where American firms have failed, which raises the second comparative barometer of performance, the internal score-keeping mechanism called *market share dominance*.

As a percentage of GNP, the U.S. spends more on research and development, both relatively and absolutely, than any other country in the world. But when federal funds (principally from the Pentagon) are excluded, America spends less on *commercial* R&D—only about 1.8 percent of GNP—than Japan, which spends nearly 3 percent. Capital spending by Japanese semiconductor firms also outstrips the American effort, by a factor of about three to one. In 1986 Japanese companies spent $2.6 billion investing in new equipment, or about 22 percent of sales; American semiconductor makers spent $990 million, or about 9 percent of sales. In private sector R&D, spending on chips by the two countries is nearly equal. In 1986 Japanese firms spent $1.3 billion, or 15 percent of total sales, versus about $1.5 billion by U.S. firms, also about 15 percent of sales.

In the highly competitive sector of dynamic random-access memory chip production, market share dominance has completely reversed in a decade. In 1976 the U.S. had an 84 percent global share of memory chip production; Japan only 16 percent. By 1986, however, Japan had a global share of 78 percent, the U.S. 16 percent, Asian NICs 3 percent, and Europe 3 percent. In total semiconductor production (which includes microprocessors and custom-designed chips), the U.S. had a global market share of about 62 percent in 1976, compared with 24 percent for Japan. By 1986 Japan's share had increased to 45 percent, and America's had fallen to 42 percent. In 1970 America had 52 percent of the global electronic end-equipment market (such as computers, printers, and telephone systems), and Japan only 16 percent. But by 1986 America's share had dropped to 45 percent and Japan's had increased by half, to 24 percent. (In 1988 all Japanese companies outspent their U.S. counterparts on new plant and capital equipment investments by more than $10 billion, even though Japan's economy is just over half the size of America's—a two-to-one per-capita advantage.)

These turnarounds in market share are also reflected in America's balance of trade in electronics equipment. In 1980 the U.S. had a trade surplus of $11 billion in high-tech equipment, which by 1986 had become a *deficit* of nearly $8 billion. Import penetration of foreign computers had risen from a share of less than 4 percent in 1980 to more than 30 percent by 1987; the market share of foreign communications equipment alone doubled during the same period. The share of foreign durable goods rose from less than 15 percent in 1970 to nearly 35 percent in 1986, and foreign cars from about 16 percent of the American market in 1970 to nearly 30 percent in 1986. It was these shifts in *manufacturing* trade that led, over time, to the burgeoning American trade deficit of more than $160 billion in 1987.

American policy responses to these dramatic reversals in market share dominance over the past twenty years have tended to focus externally on what Washington has perceived to be unfair Asian (primarily Japanese) trade practices, unacceptable firm behavior, and closed domestic markets. An eternal emphasis on changing what essentially cannot be changed—the foundations of capitalist developmental economics or the hyper-growth machines of turbocharged capitalism—and a lack of attention to what can be changed, namely, domestic American policies, incentives, and laws, laid the groundwork for cumulatively greater frustration between Washington and Tokyo (and Seoul and Taipei). This process culminated in one senior American official's insistence that in order for any progress to be made Japan would, in his view, "simply have to change its culture." The language of trade politics in Washington in turn became increasingly hostile, calling for outrageous tariffs on Korean automobiles and taking sledgehammers to Japanese electronics products. More civilized behavior has been thought to have occurred in banana republics, though one can sympathize with the growing frustration of American policymakers. (Super 301 will likely achieve better results, because America can be tough without being negative.)

The fuel for this peculiar policy engine is also derived from the American love affair with neoclassical economics, which posits the premise of free markets and free competition and tends to ignore institutional behavior. Author and critic Robert Kuttner caught the essence of this unique romance in a recent *Atlantic* article called "The Poverty of Economics."

"In economics, deduction drives out empiricism," Kuttner wrote. "Those who have real empirical curiosity about the workings of banks, corporations, production technologies, trade unions, or individual behavior are dismissed as casual empiricists or sociologists, and marginalized within the profession. In their place departments of economics are graduating a generation of *idiots savants*, brilliant at esoteric mathematics yet innocent of actual economic life."

Esoteric mathematics postulates a theory of perfect markets and creates complicated econometric models, leading at least one practitioner to proclaim that "if the world is not like the model, so much the worse for the world." One of America's outstanding economists, Harvard professor and 1973 Nobel laureate Wassily Leontief, did an analysis of articles in *The American Economic Review* and found only one article in five years that was based on empirical research, and it was about the utility maximization of pigeons.

So it matters, Kuttner wrote, that American economists are trained to view the world the way they do: *almost all public policy questions are economic ones.* The key concerns of an empirical, strategic, capitalist developmental type are missing from the American approach. How do technological and institutional changes influence economic growth? he asked. What institutional circumstances merit public intervention? What are the links between economic performance and cultural and political values? *Which* markets behave like the textbook market?

Kuttner concluded his insightful analysis by quoting the well-known economist Robert Heilbroner, author of *The Worldly Philosophers.* "There is a profound weakness at the core of neo-classical economics," Heilbroner said. "It can't answer the most basic questions. What is a price? What killed full employment? It has become like medieval theology." The most frequently repeated wisdom is that a paradigm cannot be displaced by evidence, only by another paradigm. So economists have become the least worldly of social scientists.

If the contemporary theologians, America's neoclassical economists, have control over the formulation of trade, investment, and other public policy, little wonder their concentration becomes external—trying to persuade Japan, Korea, and Taiwan to stop doing what they do so well—rather than internal, trying to create new domestic savings and investment incentives with a strategic orientation. The theology, by definition, tolerates no other religion.

A new school of economic analysis, still in its infancy, suggests that trade policies based on neoclassical theory no longer reflect the world in which we live. One member of this school is Paul Krugman, who teaches at MIT and recently wrote a book called *Strategic Trade Policy and the New International Economics*. He argues that there are reasons to believe that in concentrated industries trade policy could usefully take on a more active role in promoting the interests of domestic firms against foreign competitors and that America should at least be concerned about the *possibility* that other governments might use trade policies to promote their own firms in these industries.

"The reasons for the massive two-way trade in products in which countries have no underlying comparative advantage are not particularly hard to find," Krugman wrote. "They lie in the advantages of large-scale production, which lead to a random division of labor among countries; in the cumulative advantages of experience, which sometimes perpetuate accidental initial advantages; and in the temporary advantages conveyed by innovation. What is important is that the conventional economic analysis of trade policy is based on a theory of trade that does not allow for these kinds of motives. Traditional conclusions about trade policy may therefore not be right for the kind of world we live in, where these motives are as important in explaining trade as the better-understood forces of comparative advantage."

Traditional trade analysis and the new wave share certain important features, such as that trade is not necessarily a zero-sum game. But the new analysis considers the crucial point that industries within a country compete with each other for limited supplies of labor and capital as well as compete with those in other countries for markets. This means that an attempt to promote or protect some particular sector domestically means promoting or protecting that sector at the expense of other sectors. This is true whether foreign competition is viewed as fair or unfair, whether it comes from underlying comparative advantage or is a result of government-encouraged advantages, like incentives or subsidies.

The new analysts, like Krugman, ask whether foreign trade policies might cause some sectors of the American economy to contract and others to expand and, if so, whether this might lower national income. And they ask whether the United States can raise income by actively favoring certain key sectors.

"The answers to these questions," Krugman wrote, "depend on whether it is possible to identify sectors that at the margin are more valuable than others. Are there strategic sectors in the economy, where labor and capital either directly receive a higher return or generate special benefits for the rest of the economy? This is the question on which old and new thinking about trade differs. The conventional view argues that there are no strategic sectors. The new approaches open up the possibility that there may be strategic sectors, after all."

In sum, the new school says that America's traditional free trade position based on the perfect market model may have become outdated and untenable. America may have more to gain than it has to lose by embracing tactical tools that can be used in formulating more aggressive strategic policies.

"Can we identify strategic sectors?" Krugman asked. "Can we successfully pursue a strategic trade policy? Can we trust ourselves to use the new ideas wisely? How will other governments respond? It has become clear that a good deal of nationalistic trade and industrial policy is going on anyway, some of it at the expense of U.S. interests. What would happen if the U.S. were, on the basis of these new theories, to become more willing to adopt activist trade or industrial policies? Some argue that the result would be to undermine what cooperation there is, and lead us into a world of beggar-my-neighbor trade policies. Others argue that U.S. bargaining power would be strengthened and that the United States could be more effective at persuading other countries to abandon policies that hurt our interests."

Like pushing agricultural products or criticizing Japan and the Little Dragons for having "closed" markets. Many observers have acknowledged that the traditional factors that comprise a "closed" domestic market—protectionist tariffs, explicit quotas, bureaucratic red tape, tougher safety or quality standards, different technical specifications, onerous inspection of imports, regulatory constraints, and government procurement requirements—and that receive the lion's share of political attention account for a relatively modest proportion of the total trade imbalance. In the case of Japan, some private economists have estimated the cumulative effect of these constraints as being from about $2 billion annually, based on complicated econometric models, to around $5 billion, based on differences in macroeconomic fundamentals. The Department of Commerce's own estimate—somewhat higher because of perceived political necessity—is about $10 billion, based on a presumed

American share of the Japanese market equivalent to its average share of other foreign markets. But the total *annual* trade deficit with Japan is more than $50 billion.

This question of "market access" to East Asian "closed" markets has been a staple feature of American trade politics for twenty years. Critics have argued—persuasively, it seems to me—that trade politics based on scapegoating, "Japan bashing," and political ultimatums are doomed to fail because they do not come to grips with the underlying strategic issues. In recent years Washington trade officials have attempted to gain "market access" for American firms in the Japanese market by pressing Tokyo for improved access of American agricultural goods, construction project management skills, and computer chips, forest products, pharmaceuticals, medical equipment, and telecommunications, the last product groups having been driven by a new tactic called *MOSS*, an acronym for *market-opening, sector-specific*, which quickly became known as "more of the same stuff." The results, not surprisingly, were relatively insignificant, although proponents would argue that without this approach the Japanese market would have remained frustratingly inaccessible. It still is.

"Our negotiations should always be for results," former Department of Commerce official Clyde Prestowitz wrote in his recent book, *Trading Places*. "To negotiate over the procedures of a foreign culture in hopes of obtaining an undefined 'open' market is to court failure and frustration. We can negotiate to alter a revision in a law. We can negotiate to prevent a law from passing. We can negotiate a market share or a specific amount of sales or a sliding scale. But we cannot negotiate philosophy or perceptions and should not try to do so."

Daniel Okimoto, a specialist in the Japanese political economy at Stanford, asked if there might be a limit on what these bilateral negotiations can achieve. Were there other factors, possibly institutional, possibly *structural*, that could impede the flow of foreign manufactures into Japan? Okimoto offered some answers in a thoughtful article in the *Journal of Japanese Studies* in 1987 called "Outsider Trading: Coping with Japanese Industrial Organization."

Even the most casual observer of Japan must now be familiar with the Japanese *keiretsu*, large conglomerates with household names such as Mitsubishi, Sumitomo, and Mitsui, which are based on a strong combination of banking, trading, and industrial skills. This combination has been called a "banking-industrial complex" and has contributed to

Japan's competitiveness as an exporter of high value-added products and to its relative resistance, as a market, to the import of foreign goods.

"The capacity of Japanese firms to forsake short-term profits in favor of long-term market share," Okimoto wrote, "which is often cited as Japan's biggest competitive advantage, can also be attributed to such institutional characteristics as the interlocking pattern of intercorporate stockholders. In a variety of crucial ways, the distinctive features of Japanese industrial organization have helped to make Japan's economy a dynamic force in world markets. It has permitted companies to make heavy and continuous capital investments, reduce production costs, slash prices, and even sustain short-term losses in order to secure and expand large shares of domestic and overseas markets. Thus, Japan's export prowess—indeed, its international competitiveness—can be traced directly (though not exclusively) to the strengths of its industrial organization."

American firms (and, not surprisingly, American consumers) tend to focus on price—a market function—as the predominant factor in determining the viability of a transaction and downplay, or ignore outright, nonprice factors inherent in organizational relationships.

Looking at the semiconductor market in Japan, Okimoto showed how important those nonprice factors become.

In selecting the vendors from which to purchase semiconductor components, Japanese end-user companies (that is, those that purchase semiconductors to install in computers, cars, and other end products) take a variety of factors into account in addition to price: the volume of supplies from in-house production, technical functions, product quality, delivery schedules, after-sales service, historical business ties, and vertical or horizontal linkages (such as equity share ownership). Any foreign firm that lacks a manufacturing base in Japan, as many do, automatically eliminates itself from these nonmarket, nonprice, relationship-oriented mechanisms.

Consequently, Okimoto asked, "do structures of corporate interdependence, subcontracting networks, and long-term, reciprocal relationships raise significant barriers to foreign producers trying to break into the Japanese market? The answer is yes; having to break into a labyrinth of intertwined networks is much harder than selling into a less structured market like America's, which functions more on the basis of spot transactions."

The consequences of Japan's having a different organizational structure are many and tend to frustrate American firms because of their
inherent belief that foreign markets should operate on the same principles as the American market—which they don't. In Japan, the largest
single market outside the United States, and the fastest-growing, this
unique institutional structure incubates a host of nonmarket factors that
become impediments to the penetration of foreign products and act to
sustain America's bilateral trade deficit with Japan (as well as efforts
to reduce it).

These factors are a fiercely competitive domestic environment; the
emphasis of long-term market share growth over short-term profits;
ongoing product cost reductions through high production volume; constant upgrading of plant and equipment, made possible by aggressive
financial and public policy incentives; production engineering and process technology as corporate priorities over financial accounting; the
capacity to fill new market niches quickly and efficiently; close working
interrelationships between buyer and seller; a focus on quality over
price; the power to pressure subcontractors to share costs and margins
when external conditions demand it; financing flexibility through large
(and often shareholding) banks rather than dependence on the more
volatile capital and equity markets; long-term relationships based on
reciprocity rather than short-term transactions based on price; close
business-government relationships in pursuit of common national-in-
terest goals; close communication among dominant producers in any
given industry (which would raise serious antitrust considerations in
other countries); and extensive countercyclical flexibility, enabling
buyer and seller to reap rewards in good years and to share the burden
in bad.

Japanese firms have also used many of these institutional or organizational factors to compete more successfully in *overseas* markets as
well as in their own, in effect making nonmarket or nonprice mechanisms function to their advantage in markets (such as America) where
the price mechanism is supposedly all-powerful. In industry after industry in the U.S. market, Japanese competitors have produced impressive empirical evidence of the benefits of this strategic approach
to organization. They have adapted their domestic government-business
relationships to come up with an American version, investing heavily
in the Washington-based lobbyists who are the most influential and
have the most extensive experience. (And they spend up to an estimated

$100 million a year doing this.) Critics complain about a "Japan lobby," but the Japanese are simply using American organizations to help them find American solutions to their American problems.

The Japanese have also implemented a policy of playing off one American state against another in their effort to seek the most competitive conditions under which to establish a manufacturing presence, most notably in the nonunion Southeast and Midwest, almost to the point of securing more favorable terms and conditions than their domestic American competitors. During 1987 governors from forty-three states made eighty-seven overseas trips to solicit foreign business; not surprisingly, their most frequent destinations were Japan (thirty-six stops), Korea (nineteen), and Taiwan (seventeen).

So all of America's institutional features—an "open" market, transactions determined primarily by price, short-term financial priorities, and no strategic orientation—work equally to Japan's advantage in the American market. Unfortunately, the obverse does not hold true: *none* of Japan's institutional characteristics—a web of tight, interlocking relationships, a complex industrial structure, and a strategic orientation toward doing business—work to America's advantage in the Japanese market. It this somehow *unfair?*

Sun-tzu, the Chinese military strategist, was a genius who lived nearly 3,000 years ago. In the fourth century B.C. he wrote *The Art of War*, a brilliant and comprehensive account of the nature of military conflict. Sun-tzu knew that war demanded study and analysis, and he was convinced that careful planning based on sound information and intelligence about the enemy would contribute more toward victory than either men or matériel. "Numbers alone," he wrote, "confer no advantage."

Napoléon read Sun-tzu. So did Mao Zedong. And so do most Japanese managers.

Sun-tzu believed that the skillful strategist should be able to subdue the enemy's army without laying siege to it. "To win a hundred victories in a hundred battles is not the acme of skill," he wrote. "To defeat the enemy without fighting is the acme of skill." He put great emphasis on developing superior information about the enemy. "Know your enemy better than he knows you" was one of his favorite maxims. "One spy in the enemy camp is worth more than ten thousand footsoldiers," read another, "because an army without secret agents is like a man without eyes or ears." So the emphasis on strategy becomes all-encompassing, whether in warfare or in trade.

With the failure of American public policy to deal effectively with either the external score-keeping mechanism (the balance of trade) or the more strategic, internal score-keeping mechanism (market share dominance), only one other policy option has remained for Washington to pursue, and that is the arena of exchange rate relationships. America's inability to develop more strategic, less market-oriented policies has strongly prejudiced its efforts to deal with the dollar. True to its neoclassical macroeconomic ideology, Washington has recently had to emphasize monetary policy, putting almost the entire burden of realigning the trade imbalance onto the exchange rate, after having treated the dollar with virtual neglect for years.

A brief look just at the yen shows the shortsightedness of this approach. The yen peaked at about ¥175-to-1 in 1978, having strengthened from its postwar norm of ¥360 in the early 1970s. With the deterioration of the Bretton Woods system of fixed foreign exchange rates, and its replacement by the current system of floating rates, the traditional determinants of the value of a nation's currency, such as inflation, interest rates, a trade surplus (or deficit), unemployment, and capital flows, became much less significant than the supply of (and demand for) that currency in global foreign exchange markets.

When Washington put new tax cuts into effect in 1981, and the American economy shortly thereafter began to expand, foreign imports flooded into the market at unprecedented levels, creating an overabundance of dollars in the exchange markets, which should have had the effect of weakening the price of the dollar. But the dollar remained overvalued. A spendthrift Congress failed to implement the other half of the administration's economic plan—cutbacks in federal spending— and as a consequence the U.S. budget deficit began to mount. Then the Treasury Department had to pay higher rates of interest to borrow the necessary shortfalls in revenue, creating a demand for dollars from foreign lenders since domestic American savings alone were insufficient. The undervalued yen weakened substantially during this period, from ¥198.70 in 1981 to ¥263.65 in 1985.

Washington officials had typically adopted a policy of benign neglect with regard to exchange rates, and their arguments rang with theological sanctity. "Let the market decide," was their response, and the market did. Overwhelmingly, in fact, against the dollar. The federal budget deficits required so much foreign borrowing that by late 1985 it had become clear that the administration had to take a stand on the currency and push for a stronger yen. (The Japanese share of Treasury borrowings was about 50 percent, and the trade deficit with Japan alone was stuck at about $50 billion a year.) So the Group of Five—the United States, Japan, West Germany, England, and Canada—met, in September, at the Plaza Hotel in New York and agreed to monitor exchange rates to establish more realistic values. That agreement became known as the Plaza Accord.

The results should not have been hard to predict. By early 1986 the yen had broken through its first "psychological threshold" of ¥200, rose steadily throughout that year to a peak of ¥152, continued its ascent through 1987 to the ¥130 level, until it had reached a temporary stabilization point of about ¥125-to-1, near where it is today. By mid-1986 Japan had replaced America as the world's number one creditor, the U.S. had replaced Brazil as the world's leading debtor, and it was now almost cheaper to buy a new suit before leaving home than to have one dry-cleaned during a business trip to Tokyo.

But exchange markets have a way of overshooting: my own calculations, based on purchasing power parity (and admittedly contrarian) pegged a more realistic yen–dollar rate of about ¥150-to-1, which interestingly enough matched similar calculations made by *The Economist* of London, although the magazine used a somewhat different formula. Its formula also indicated the yen was overvalued against the dollar by nearly 20 percent, and a more accurate exchange rate would be, well, ¥150.

So with liquidity in global markets strong, and credit easily available, the hottest game in town became betting against the dollar. Foreign exchange traders at major multinational corporations and banks bolstered their institutional profits considerably. Efforts of the central banks—the Federal Reserve or the Bank of Japan—to slow the process met with limited success, simply because of the magnitudes involved. While they might buy a couple of billion dollars a day to smooth out rates, their capabilities were swamped by a global foreign exchange market estimated at a volatile $600 billion a day.

Now, the reasoning of America's neoclassical theologians seems to have been, if the Japanese are so successful selling their goods at an artificially weak yen rate, they will encounter difficulty if the yen is stronger—so much stronger that they will either have to sustain insurmountable pressure on profit margins or raise dollar prices to protect those margins to the extent that American goods will once again become price-competitive. At the same time, export prices of American products will become cheaper again and enable American manufacturers to sell more abroad.

But the sole emphasis on price as a means of determining product competitiveness can be misplaced, as Stanford's Okimoto has shown, since price is only one of more than a dozen *nonmarket* factors affecting a firm's ability to penetrate a market. Using the external score-keeping mechanism of the trade balance as a barometer, with intended exchange rate effects now in place the American trade deficit with Japan should have begun to show some improvement. It did not. It *worsened*, from a bilateral deficit of nearly $50 billion in 1985, to more than $60 billion in 1986, and to more than $50 billion in each of 1987 and 1988. Normally about a year is necessary to effect a turnaround in trade balances after exchange realignment. In this case, more than *three* years after the event, the figures were for all intents and purposes unimproved.

Fred Bergsten, executive director of the Institute for International Economics in Washington, and his colleague, William Cline, are two economists representative of the macroeconomic approach to solving trade deficits. Neither reads Japanese, and neither has studied the Japanese strategic approach to trade and investment in detail. Yet they wrote an analysis of the bilateral trade deficit called *The United States–Japan Economic Problem* in which they concluded that the rise in the U.S.–Japanese trade deficit from 1980 to 1984 could be explained fully by changes in the exchange rates and rates of economic growth.

"In 1981," they wrote, "U.S. imports rose briskly as the result of substantial appreciation in the real value of the dollar relative to the yen. In 1982, the further real appreciation of the dollar relative to the yen would have meant a major increase in imports if nothing else had happened. By 1983 and especially 1984, however, the ongoing import pressure from dollar appreciation was augmented by a boost to import demand from U.S. domestic growth. Although there was a moderating effect on U.S. imports in 1984 from Japan's own cyclical recovery, the strong expansion of Japan's industrial capacity more than offset this influence."

GNP growth was accelerating faster in America than in Japan in the 1981–84 period. But after 1985, Japanese economic growth rates outstripped America's, as Japan shifted away from exports to domestic-led growth, and the bilateral trade figures *still* did not adjust. The reasons for that were relatively easy to understand, provided you understood the dynamics of capitalist developmental economics or the hyper-growth machine called turbocharged capitalism.

First, major Japanese exporters had built up sizable profit reserves after many years of a weak yen, giving them a significant cushion against the yen's subsequent appreciation. Second, major Japanese firms accelerated plans to shift the manufacture of lower value-added components offshore, to countries with more favorable labor rates and currencies that were *not* appreciating against the dollar, such as Hong Kong, Taiwan, and Thailand. Third, major Japanese manufacturers put pressure on their domestic subcontractors to share the burden of the currency rise. Fourth, Japanese firms developed a "crisis mentality" and relentlessly put productivity-enhancing measures in place. And fifth, they purposely delayed dollar price increases in the American market to protect, or even increase, market share, a strategy also later criticized by Washington as "unfair." Long before the yen–dollar rate plunged to ¥125-to-1, major Japanese competitors were formulating external strategies based on an eventual exchange rate of ¥100-to-1.

Playing games with exchange rates is a dangerous business, as Secretary of the Treasury James Baker learned in the fall of 1987, when he waged verbal war on the deutsche mark to get it to strengthen further. The Germans, generally more experienced at this kind of thing, called Baker's bluff. Then the Japanese flinched and sold Treasury bonds. The ensuing panic created a wave of frantic selling on all the world's stock markets.

Playing games with exchange rates is also a two-edged sword. In the process of forcing the markets toward a weaker dollar, Washington automatically gave the Japanese fifty-cent dollars with which to fund their corporate acquisitions in America. As with all other aspects of business, the Japanese moved strategically throughout 1986 and 1987, making key acquisitions in commercial metropolitan real estate (buying prime properties in New York and Los Angeles), basic industries (purchasing Firestone Tire & Rubber), foods (acquiring Knorr), high technology (acquiring Siltec, one of the last two independent U.S. manufacturers of semiconductor wafers), and financial services (gaining strategic shares of Goldman, Sachs and Shearson Lehman Hutton). *Caveat divestor.*

With the yen twice as dear as in 1985, operating costs for American firms in Japan, in dollar terms, now were twice as high, driving up the cost of doing business in Tokyo, already one of the world's highest-priced cities. For American companies not already present in Japan, which could not use yen revenues to offset yen expenses, the costs of starting up there or expanding overseas operations to include Japan became prohibitive.

So nonmarket factors affecting competitiveness have not been given much attention by American policymakers. And the results of U.S. policy, judged by any one of the three score-keeping mechanisms, have not been impressive, even though some modest—one deigns to call them marginal—signs of improvement were noted in America's global trade deficit for 1988, from an annual deficit of more than $160 billion in 1987 to an annual deficit of just under $140 billion for the following year. Far from signifying a turnaround, however, these numbers may simply suggest a slower rate of continued deterioration. The gross trade figures still hide a continuing monthly deficit in *manufactured goods*, so while agricultural exports and receipts from financial services may be up, the fundamental category—manufacturing—remains weak.

"I do not think it an exaggeration to say that the unspoken concern on Wall Street is that the United States, for the first time in its history, is not in charge of its destiny," Robert Heilbroner wrote in a recent *New Yorker* article called "Hard Times." "Without question, the cause of this anxiety is our catastrophic failure to balance our international books. It is clear that we grew up in the immense assurance that the United States was marked by nature and history to supply the world with the commodities it wanted: timber in our earliest days; then cotton from the South and steel from the Midwest; thereafter, automobiles from Detroit and high tech from Massachusetts and California; and, always, wheat, corn, and soybeans from the great American breadbasket. In virtually every year, from 1896 through 1981, we sold more goods and services abroad than we bought in return. But in the decade from 1978, the merchandise we bought from other nations will amount to al-most a half-trillion dollars more than what we have been able to sell."

The cumulative effects of this turnaround are quite astonishing.

"How much, exactly, do we owe the rest of the world?" former secretary of commerce Peter Peterson asked in his recent *Atlantic* article. "Officially, our net position at the end of 1986 was a negative $264 billion. By the end of 1988, we will be closing in on a negative

$500 billion. The incredible speed of America's transformation from creditor to debtor can hardly be exaggerated. Only six years ago, the United States had achieved its all-time apogee as a net creditor, with an official position of a positive $141 billion. America has burned up more than $500 billion, net, by liquidating foreign assets and borrowing from abroad. That's an immense flow of capital; it dwarfed the fabled bank recycling of OPEC surpluses after the oil price hikes of 1973 and 1979, and was twice the size of foreign interest payments by all the less-developed debtor nations."

It is practically inevitable, Peterson wrote, that America's net debt will reach the $1 trillion mark by the early 1990s. To turn this deficit around, some analysts suggest a real annual growth rate of 10 percent in American manufactured goods exports will be necessary over the next decade. In this decade American manufactured exports have declined in real terms, yet over the coming decade we will aim for a higher export growth rate than we have ever achieved in the twentieth century? Such an achievement would be unprecedented. Not only would we have to break our earlier record, but we would have to do it with a lower average level of domestic business investment, a complete ban on imports, and steadily declining standards of living. Rarely have an economy's large size, its world-class currency, and its open capital markets enabled it to borrow immense sums solely for the purpose of consumption and without regard to productive return.

Overlaid against this foreign deficit is, of course, the U.S. federal budget deficit, which has tripled during the past eight years, from just under $700 billion in 1979 to nearly $3 trillion in 1989, increasing at anywhere between $100 billion and $150 billion a year. "Fifteen years ago," Peterson wrote, "if the United States had borrowed the equivalent of 3.5 percent of its GNP from abroad, it would have created a national emergency, with Churchillian warnings and wartime austerity measures." Today that's a figure you can read about in the business section of any newspaper.

Frustration with aggressive East Asian trade and investment policies has pushed America to its political wit's end. The increasing danger of protectionism as an emotional backlash looms ugly in the background. The problem, however, is not one of protection *from* competition, which results in isolationist policies, scapegoating, and external criticism, but of adjustment *to* competition, which should result in creative incentives, adaptive policies, heightened awareness, and innovation.

"No country has an entitlement to prosperity," the Scandinavian economist Staffan Burenstam Linder wrote in 1986 in a thoughtful book called *The Pacific Century*. "No region has special privileges. Historically inspired feelings of superiority cause misunderstandings, and the ensuing inflexibilities are not affordable. Asian-Pacific competition now underscores this reality. It demonstrates that staleness is not tolerable. The virtue of the demonstration effect of Pacific dynamism is that it exposes the need for vitality and the necessity to look for what can be achieved rather than for what can be maintained."

These various developments suggest that neither adversarial trade nor managed trade but *strategic* trade is becoming the trend (certainly with Japan), and like it or not, American policy will somehow have to adapt and adjust. That this adaptation and adjustment must focus more on America's strategic manufacturing skills is being recognized by an increasing number of American leaders in the private sector, but America's public sector leadership appears to lag considerably behind. Rather than looking over the stern at the disappearing wake and mourning the erosion of the postwar free trade system and America's once-dominant position in it, the political captains might be better advised to stand watch over the bow and guide the ship more effectively through the uncharted waters that lie ahead.

5
AMERICA'S RETURN TO WORLD-CLASS MANUFACTURING

If management is successful in improving the culture of the organization, the company will be more productive, more competitive, and more profitable in the long run. But the full impact of the effort to improve the culture will not be felt until years later. If managers are concerned primarily with immediate profit, they will be reluctant to spend time and effort improving the culture, and over the long run the organization may fail to become more competitive. Thus, when Western managers try to improve productivity, they usually try to do so without hurting short-term profitability. On the other hand, when Japanese managers take measures to improve the corporate culture, they often do so with the knowledge that they risk hurting short-term profitability in order to pursue the longer-term goal of creating a more competitive organization.

Masaaki Imai, *Kaizen*

"Nothing is ever accomplished by a reasonable man."

This sign, in plain lettering, hangs over the desk of Mark Shepherd, Jr., the sixty-five-year-old former chairman of Texas Instruments. We were sitting in his office at the company's headquarters in Dallas talking about trade, talking about government policy, talking about the importance of America's regaining competitiveness in manufacturing.

Atypical of American senior management but typical of Texas Instruments, Shepherd was trained as an electrical engineer at SMU and earned his graduate degree in double-E, as they call it, at the University of Illinois. He joined Texas Instruments in 1948, was promoted to general manager of its semiconductor components division in 1954 following the invention of the silicon chip by TI's Jack Kilby, and became chief operating officer in 1961, CEO in 1969, and chairman of the board in 1976.

"The indisputable fact is that foreign companies have learned to sell to the American market," he was saying, "and Americans have learned to like foreign goods. For that reason, we need strategies to enhance our manufacturing competitiveness. Although government can help provide a healthy environment for manufacturing innovation, implementing new manufacturing strategies is up to industry."

Shepherd pushed a hand through his thinning hair and smiled.

"Productivity has been the real key to America's competitive advantage," he said in his soft Texas drawl. "Over the long period from the Civil War to World War II, America's gain in productivity far outstripped the rest of the world. By 1950 U.S. industry dominated the world. But our current problems stem from the fact that since 1960 Japan's productivity gains in manufacturing have increased sixfold relative to the U.S., and Europe's increases have exceeded the U.S. by a factor of two.

"Throughout history, technological progress has been the driving force behind most of the productivity gains made in this country. It can be so again. New technical developments have given America the potential to boost manufacturing productivity sharply. But the private sector has to adapt this new technology, particularly information technology, into the manufacturing process. The goal has to be to improve manufacturing efficiency, reduce costs, and improve quality all at the same time."

Texas Instruments was once the world's largest manufacturer of semiconductors, the tiny memory chips used as building blocks in virtually every manufactured product from automobiles to telephones to computers. TI invented the basic chip in the 1950s and patented it in the early 1960s. Just as the Japanese have taken on America, TI, then a tiny company, took on GE and Westinghouse, the established giants, and won, operating on the same basic principles that drive Japanese firms. Texas Instruments has always been and is lean; the firm is committed to quality, innovation, and growth, with very high outlays for R&D; it is aggressive, looking to the future rather than to its past; it recruits, hires, and retains quality talent; and it does not squander money on nonessentials.

Like offices, including the chairman's. The best way to describe TI's corporate offices is to say they are comfortable but practical; they are by no means luxurious. Shepherd's office has a linoleum floor and simple, unadorned furnishings. Covering one wall is a bookshelf holding some familiar titles: *The Emerging Japanese Superstate,* by the late futurist Herman Kahn, and *The Zero-Sum Solution,* by MIT economist Lester Thurow, among others.

TI is a $5 billion company now, with leading-edge technology in sophisticated defense equipment, artificial intelligence, and manufacturing systems in addition to its basic semiconductor business. The company spends, on average, about 8 percent of sales on research and development, which is high for any company, American or Japanese; more typical averages are around 5 percent. In 1985 TI's bipolar semiconductor plant in Japan won the coveted Deming Prize, named after the *American* quality control expert D. Edwards Deming, which is Japan's most prestigious award for quality and is normally won by a Japanese company.

We talked about manufacturing systems for a while.

"All this talk about a postindustrial society is pure hogwash," Shepherd said. "If we don't regain a position of world-class leadership in basic manufacturing, our standard of living will continue to decline. Why?"

He pulled forward and leaned across his plain wooden desk, ticking the points off his fingers.

"First, despite its low growth relative to Japan, American manufacturing productivity has still grown at roughly three-and-a-half times the rate in the service sector. Second, the rate of inflation in manufacturing is less than two-thirds the rate of inflation in services. Third, strong manufacturing generates ripple effects in services, like trucking, accounting, banking, and data processing. Fourth, if we don't have a competitive manufacturing sector, we can't generate the export income we need to pay for imports—agriculture and services aren't big enough to carry that load. And fifth, manufacturing is vital to our national security, both as a foundation for future economic growth and as the source of military equipment for defense."

I mentioned Japan's greater commitment to commercial R&D. Shepherd leaned back and nodded.

"The Japanese devote nearly two-thirds of their R&D to process technology, on getting an idea from the design board to market. Too often, manufacturing is a stepchild in American companies, where strategic planning focuses on the numbers, profitability, and basic research. This is why TI stresses manufacturing as an *integrated* process, making it an equal partner with R&D and marketing as an integral part of our total business strategy. We call this 'computer-integrated manufacturing'—CIM for short. What CIM does is pull computing power out of the data processing room and put it to work on the factory floor. Our distributed computing power can bring a problem, the information needed to solve it, and the mechanism for solving it together at the same workstation."

That was fine, I suggested, provided you had college-educated specialists at every workstation. But how could the average high school graduate handle that degree of sophisticated detail on the factory floor?

"Minds, money, and motivation," he said with a tight smile. "Hell, for the first time in history our schools are producing high school graduates who are less educated than their predecessors. That's one of our biggest problems, and we don't know how to solve it yet. And we haven't done a good enough job to get more of those graduates into science and engineering. But where the Japanese and the rest of the folks in Asia are beating the pants off us is on the factory floor. We've tended to let manufacturing be our backwater. I think there has to be a stronger manufacturing culture in our boardrooms and in senior executive offices. All these things are going to take a long time to fix. It just boils down to leadership."

Many of the same points were made by Stephen Cohen and John Zysman, directors of the Berkeley Roundtable on International Economy at the University of California, in a recent book called *Manufacturing Matters.*

Manufacturing matters, they wrote, because it is critical to our economic health: lose manufacturing and you lose high-wage service jobs. Changes in international competition, coupled with the mass application of new microelectronics-based technologies, are revolutionizing production, yet America has not adjusted well to these changes. Weaknesses in production have eroded our competitive position. Manufacturing capabilities are crucial to the competitiveness of industrial firms, they said; over time, you can't control what you don't produce.

The authors showed that manufacturing and services are linked directly and that the higher the value added in manufacturing, the higher the value added in services. Hence a postindustrial society based entirely on services is a myth. Their concept is one of linkage rather than succession. So if the trend is toward manufacturing offshore in lower-wage countries like Korea, Taiwan, and Thailand, service jobs like data processing and construction and banking will ultimately gravitate toward those countries, too.

In some market segments, like construction engineering and banking, American services used to be second to none. That is no longer the case now that international competition is much more intense. In construction, Bechtel, Brown & Root, and Westinghouse once had the lion's share of global engineering contracts; they now face relentless competition from world-class firms like Chiyoda Engineering and Kumagai Gumi of Japan, Korea's Hyundai and Lucky Goldstar, and Bouyges of France. Foreign financial institutions have emerged to compete fiercely with American multinationals, such that the top ten international banks, measured by total assets, are now Japanese. Seven of California's ten largest banks are now Japanese-owned; foreign banks dominate nearly 40 percent of America's commercial and industrial loan market. Japan dominates the general trading business worldwide as well; its top ten trading companies handle about two-thirds of Japan's total external trade and alone account for nearly 15 percent of America's.

All these high value-added service functions—engineering, finance, and trading—are linked directly to manufacturing strengths, which is why so many of the firms in these specialized categories are Japanese. The service functions in turn become strategic industry sectors if the industries they service are strategic—which is why they are hard to penetrate at home and tough to compete with abroad.

The Bureau of Labor Statistics recently compiled a list showing where the new jobs in America will be between now and the turn of the century. Most of them are service jobs, which is not surprising, but very few of them are in *manufacturing-related* service jobs, a fact that stuns. Of the top ten job categories, those with the largest *absolute* growth include, in descending order, retail sales clerks, waiters and waitresses, nurses, janitors, food counter workers, and cashiers. Job categories with the fastest *rates* of growth are paralegal assistants, medical assistants, physical therapists, physical therapy aides, home health aides, and medical records technicians. These are comparatively low value-added jobs.

This means that jobs at McDonald's and Burger King and K mart and Sears, along with jobs at local clothing boutiques and quick-copy shops and bed-and-bath stores, are those with the largest absolute growth. It also means that jobs at Massachusetts General Hospital, Shearman & Sterling, and Hoosick Nursing Home are those with the fastest rates of growth. Demographers will tell you this is so because of America's rapidly aging population.

The seeds of the future are contained in the present, and the present is but an extension of the immediate past. Between 1955 and 1980 the American economy generated about 40 million jobs, but only one out of ten was in manufacturing, and all *net* new jobs in manufacturing were created prior to 1973. The total number of service jobs has grown from 47 million in 1970 to more than 78 million today.

The loss of manufacturing jobs that pay better than service jobs has two unfortunate side effects. First, a high proportion of the best-paying new service jobs require far more education and training than the jobs that disappear. Second, many of the best-paying service jobs normally pay less than those lost in manufacturing. This is why today's employment statistics are misleading: when you read in the business section of your newspaper that American jobs are up and unemployment is down, you have to look at the quality of the jobs being created. Nearly half of the 6 million new jobs created between 1975 and 1980 were in two specific service sectors: retail trade and health services.

Measured in each of seven different ways, American industry confronts a severe problem of competitiveness it has never known before, Cohen and Zysman concluded. Whether measured by unprecedented trade deficits in manufactured goods, by declining shares of world markets for exports, by lagging rates of productivity increases, by eroding profit margins, by declining real wages, by the increasing price elasticities of imports, or by an eroding position in world high-technology markets, America is in danger of becoming a second-class industrial power.

The Office of Technology Assessment of the U.S. Congress reached a similar conclusion in its own report, called *International Competition in Services.*

"Not only does domestic production of services greatly exceed exports and imports of services," the OTA said, "but U.S.–based service firms do more overseas business through foreign affiliates than through direct exporting. Investment abroad means jobs in foreign countries. Almost certainly, services embodied in U.S. goods exports contribute more to U.S. employment than do exports of services alone."

The OTA saw foreign competition rapidly narrowing the gap in services based on manufacturing, especially from Japan. As in many manufacturing industries, the report concluded, many of the future competitive threats in the service sector will come from Japanese firms. Japan has already proven its competitive ability in computer hardware and in telecommunications equipment. Improvements in services ranging from software products to computers and communications networks will follow. This thrust into information-based services promises to boost Japan's international competitiveness even further in manufacturing.

The project director for the OTA report was a young scientist named John Alic, a mechanical engineer by training who is as comfortable discussing disaggregated tax incentives as he is analyzing trade and investment data. Tall and lean, with angular features and a thick, full beard, he looks very much like a youthful Abe Lincoln.

"There is no choice to be made between a manufacturing economy and a service economy," he was saying over lunch in early 1988. "Basically, our work shows that the services cannot, in any simple sense, replace manufacturing in the U.S. economy. Nor can exports of services compensate for our huge current deficits in merchandise trade."

I asked him about the impact of technology on competitiveness in manufacturing.

"Our assessments have shown again and again that technical expertise is a vital ingredient in competitive success," he said. "High-technology products embody a high service content in the sense of knowledge and expertise. American manufacturing companies depend on knowledge-based services, so the service sector and the manufacturing sector will either prosper together or decline together, both at home and abroad."

I asked him whether he saw signs that American firms were strengthening their competitive positions in the domestic market.

"In manufacturing," he said soberly, "international competition has forced American companies to take a series of interrelated steps to cut much of the domestic labor content from their output. They have redesigned products so they are cheaper to make, and they have automated their production processes, but mostly they have moved production overseas, to Mexico or to Taiwan, where labor rates are lower. So when value-added manufacturing moves overseas, the services that depend on manufacturing move overseas as well. And if the manufacturing base shrinks, demand for services will also shrink. It has to."

Manufacturing jobs, as a percentage of total employment, have shrunk from 30 percent in 1950 to around 18 percent in 1988. Manufacturing firms employed about 19 million people in 1988, a decline of 1.2 million from 1980 and almost 2 million fewer than the peak in 1979.

The primary source of any nation's economic growth is improved production techniques that allow increased amounts of output to be produced from given amounts of capital and labor; in short, enhanced productivity. Between 1973 and 1984 manufacturing productivity exceeded that of all other sectors by nearly 3 percent in the United States, by more than 5 percent in Japan, and by almost 3 percent in Europe. Countries like Japan that specialize in making products where productivity rises rapidly are likely to enjoy more rapid growth and higher real incomes than those where productivity is stagnant.

A report commissioned in 1988 by the Eastman Kodak Company and written by economists at MIT and Harvard, called "The Case for Manufacturing in America's Future," focused attention on domestic American tax policies that have benefited investment in nonmanufacturing sectors in unintended ways and showed how these tax policies have influenced the flow of available investment in the economy.

Businesspeople in any country in the world that practices capitalist economics will be most concerned with one thing: the return on their investment in the business. If they make money, they stay in business; if they lose money, they go out of business. It's a fairly simple concept, in principle. But in order to make money businesspeople have to spend money, investing in the infrastructure—plant and machinery and equipment—to make their products if they are manufacturers or investing in real estate—buying or renting floor space—to sell their products if they are in services. And in order to make necessary investments businesspeople will be singularly concerned with one more thing.

Incentives.

Incentives normally come in a variety of sizes. There is a tax on profits; is it high or low? There is depreciation; is the schedule aggressive, or is the useful life too long? There can be an investment tax credit, known as ITC, which defines specific incentives a government may grant to invest in specific machinery or equipment or industry sectors. (This is called "targeting" in Japan.) There may be taxes on dividends (are after-tax profits taxed twice, once at the firm and again when they are paid to the shareholder?) and taxes on capital gains (if outside investors make an investment in a firm's equity, will a tax be imposed on the profits they make when they sell those shares?). There are also credits for specific-purpose expenses, like research and development; are R&D outlays tax-deductible in the year they are incurred, or must they be amortized over the life of the product they funded? And so on. You get the idea.

The United States utilizes an *aggregated* business tax system, so incentives to invest in expensive semiconductor manufacturing equipment may not differ substantially from incentives to invest in a small retail sales outlet. The tax on corporate profits in both businesses is the same, depreciation schedules are about the same, an investment tax credit may or may not apply to either, the tax on dividends will be the same, the capital gains tax will be the same (perhaps adjusted for required holding periods, long or short), and credits for specific-purpose expenses will be the same.

Normally, it is fair to say, investments in the manufacturing sector are more expensive than investments in the service sector, since investments by manufacturing firms naturally tend to be more equipment-intensive. Figures for 1986 indicate that American manufacturing firms used about $30,000 of equipment per worker, compared with only half that amount per worker in services. Therefore, to the extent the federal government does not create incentives designed specifically to stimulate investment in manufacturing, investment may tend to gravitate toward the nonmanufacturing sector because the amounts required are smaller. And if federal incentives discriminate further in favor of real property, investment will tend to gravitate even *faster* toward the nonmanufacturing sector because of the attractiveness of real estate as an investment *over and above* factors stemming from an aggregated tax system that already favors nonmanufacturing.

In countries like Japan and Korea that utilize *disaggregated* business tax systems, incentives to invest in expensive semiconductor manufacturing equipment differ substantially from incentives to invest in, say, retail sales, because semiconductor manufacturing is a *strategic* sector and is targeted. While overall rates of corporate taxation between the two may be the same, depreciation incentives heavily favor strategic investments, and more aggressive ITC and R&D benefits also apply. In a system like Japan's, in which incentives are designed to favor strategic industries, those sectors can grow faster and more productively, rather like a lawn that has been fertilized compared to one that has not.

The Eastman Kodak report examined the American tax system in the light of the 1986 Tax Reform Act. "To restore the competitiveness of American manufacturers," it said, "it is necessary to provide more adequate incentives for plant and equipment investment. The Act is particularly unfortunate in this regard. Equipment investments are especially hard hit because of the abolition of the investment tax credit, which previously provided a 10 percent reduction in the effective purchase price of new equipment."

The total tax burden on corporate investment depends principally on three features: the statutory tax rate, the generosity of tax depreciation, and the investment tax credit.

But the new tax law undoes the old law's increased investment incentives. While it slightly reduces the effective tax rate on structures, the increased tax burden on equipment is likely to discourage investment in precisely those asset categories that reflect the greatest amount of technological progress. The fundamental basis of recent tax reform is flawed, therefore, because it reduces the incentive for new investment while providing a windfall to the owners of existing capital. For the five-year period through 1991, increased taxes on new investment nearly *double*, to 188.4 percent of their level prior to 1986.

During my long interview with TI's Mark Shepherd in Dallas, I asked him about depreciation, taxes, and other investment incentives for American manufacturers.

"Somehow, we need a better mechanism to drive the businesses we really want to succeed," he said, "and I realize I may be getting into indicative planning here. But if war is too important to be left to generals, then maybe this is too important to be left to politicians inside the Beltway. The old ITC was better than none, and a flat ITC set at a high figure at least solves a lot of the problems we're worried about, because the Burger Kings and the McDonald's don't buy enough of the big-ticket items to qualify anyway. But the *real* problem is to distinguish between the semiconductor business and the buggywhip business, and we need policies that will enhance and drive our future businesses, not just subsidize industries of the past."

Analysts talk about "orders of magnitude" when it comes to investments in a complex, high-technology business like semiconductors. Where $1 million might have purchased the equipment necessary to manufacture early generations of the computer chip, multiples of that amount became necessary to make the one-megabit chip now coming onstream, on the "order of magnitude" of hundreds of millions of dollars.

"We need to find ways to fine-tune the process better, to get more capital formation into those sectors that are key to our long-term industrial survival," Shepherd said. "Depletion laws for the oil patch and depreciation for real property were not economically or rationally driven; they were politically driven, because oil drillers and real estate developers were better organized. Manufacturers don't have the same cohesive, political clout. But how do we get people who are objective enough to set this fine-tuning mechanism? If politics is called 'the art of the possible,' this may not be possible."

More emphasis on manufacturing ultimately means more emphasis on *process* technology, on getting a product from prototype stage to full-scale production to market faster, more cheaply, and more productively. If a nation develops incentives that stimulate investment in one desired industry sector, like manufacturing, over another, like retail trade, it would follow that those incentives will also stimulate investment in sectors dependent on manufacturers for their survival, like companies that make the equipment the manufacturers use those incentives to buy.

This is more or less what happened in Japan in the late 1960s when senior officials at MITI took a look at demographic trends and decided that the flow of labor from the agricultural sector to urban manufacturing centers would soon dry up. The country would either have to devise ways to enhance manufacturing productivity with fewer workers or else import foreign labor, as West Germany had done. As a homogeneous culture, Japan would not be best served, MITI concluded, by importing inferior labor from Southeast Asia. So MITI created a new division called the Information and Industrial Machinery Bureau, which studied the relationship of information to machines and invested a lot of money (and incentives) in researching the development of "smart equipment." The result, as must now be obvious to the most casual observer today, was robotics. Japan quickly became the world leader in industrial robots: automatic machines that bend, weld, assemble, move, and handle manufactured work in process. By 1986 Japan had a total "population" of nearly 100,000 industrial robots at work, far ahead of second-place America, which had only 20,000 in place.

Industrial robots clearly play a role in accelerating the development of process technology. So do machine tools, which in effect help machines "make" machines—a whole range of tool-and-die equipment, lathes, metal cutters, components- and parts-stampers, process control equipment, and inventory management devices. Advanced machine tools, called *computer numerically controlled*, or *CNC* for short, are programmable machines that can be "instructed" to do any number of tasks. MITI's Information and Industrial Machinery Bureau targeted CNC machines and encouraged developers with generous incentives, including some questionable funding from bicycle racing and speedboat gambling revenues, controlled in part by the Japanese underworld, to help Japanese manufacturers become leading-edge producers of state-of-the-art equipment as quickly as possible.

(The questionable funding ultimately became a serious point of contention between Tokyo and Washington, which criticized the gambling subsidies as insidious and unfair. This earned the Japanese a somewhat disreputable image, which critics call *zurui*, a Japanese word that means "cunning" or "clever," as in "too clever for your own good." That the Mafia might have such a keen sense of the national interest in America, however, does defy the imagination. But Atlantic City and Las Vegas are only two of the more obvious sources of additional revenue in these deficit-ridden times.)

It would be only a matter of time before leading Japanese machine tool manufacturers like Okuma Seisakusho and Mori Seiki came to dominate overseas export markets. By 1986 Japanese CNC machines controlled more than 50 percent of the American market. Gradually CNC machines were combined to form units called *flexible manufacturing systems*. These are unmanned machining centers turning out, automatically, large industrial housings, crankcases, and other standard components used in the assembly of larger pieces of equipment such as automobiles and trucks.

In the last five years Japan has outspent the United States by two to one in automation. During that time more than half the machine tools introduced in Japan were CNC machines, key components of the flexible manufacturing systems. In the U.S. the figure was only 18 percent. Of all these machines installed worldwide since 1975, more than 40 percent are in Japan. Over two-thirds of the CNC machines in Japan went to small and medium-sized companies.

Ramchandran Jaikumar of the Harvard Business School spent three years studying thirty-five flexible manufacturing systems, or FMSs, in the United States and sixty in Japan. He visited machine tool competitors in both countries. The systems were comparable in size and complexity and used similar numbers of tools and precision parts. American systems had an average of seven CNC machines, the Japanese six. But there the similarities ended.

"The average number of parts made by an FMS in the U.S. was ten; in Japan the average was ninety-three, almost ten times greater," Jaikumar wrote in a recent *Harvard Business Review* article. "The U.S. companies were using FMSs the wrong way—for high-volume production of a few parts rather than for high-variety production of many parts at low unit cost. For every new part introduced into an American system, twenty-two parts were introduced in Japan."

Because software development lies at the heart of this increasingly information-intensive manufacturing process, Jaikumar concluded, the technological literacy of a company's workers becomes critical. In the Japanese companies he visited, nearly half the work force was made up of college-educated engineers, and all had been trained in the use of CNC machines. In the American firms only 8 percent of the workers were engineers and fewer than 25 percent had been trained on CNC machines. Training to upgrade skills was three times longer in Japan, and Japanese factories had four times as many engineers trained to use the machines.

The implications for process technology are, in the light of Jaikumar's findings, rather clear. A company that can conceive, develop, install, and get these flexible manufacturing systems up to speed faster than its competitors will gain added advantage in the marketplace. On average, the Japanese take about one-fourth fewer man-hours and about half the time to do this than their American counterparts, which helps explain why Toyota or Honda can bring a new car model from design stage to market in about half the time required by General Motors or Ford. For Japan, which educates, trains, and hires twice as many engineers per capita as America does, the advantages are obvious; for an America seeking to recapture its competitive position, the lessons are both daunting and painful.

This pattern often replicates itself in even the smallest of companies. Not long ago I visited a tiny manufacturer of metal office equipment in Japan, just outside Osaka. While its more advanced products were off-limits and could not be viewed, I spent half a day watching the production of simple lockers and filing cabinets, translating the process for a group of American industry executives.

The company employed fewer than 200 workers and made about 40,000 lockers and cabinets a month, on a one-shift, six-day week. It had a computer-controlled Amada turret press, press brakes with numerically controlled backstops, and a state-of-the-art EDM machine with a video display, *in color,* that outlined the complex electrodeposition machining process taking place on a die.

Sheet metal lines on the factory floor, completely unmanned, were fed by a computer-controlled cut-to-length line that used coil-steel stock. A trio of standard punch presses was tied together with automatic transfer devices, also completely untended. These clusters of machines with highly automated interfaces are typical of Japanese manufacturing where load-unload functions are automatic and help keep direct labor costs to an absolute minimum. (Average direct labor costs in Japan are now below 20 percent of total manufacturing costs, while the average in America is around 25 percent, and at larger companies, like General Motors, closer to 30 percent.)

Most of the production took place in large batches, and most of the welding was done by automatic robot. Cabinets entering a paint booth passed by an electronic gate with sophisticated sensing devices; these sensors determined the size and shape of the product about to enter. The painting was then done with robotically controlled paint heads that sprayed the exact contours of both flat and formed surfaces.

The company's workers on the plant floor, where they were present, were alert and appeared highly skilled. They tended to cluster in small groups, or teams, to collaborate, keep each other informed, and share necessary information, rather than stand alone at individual workstations, which is more common in the West.

Some of the success Japanese companies have enjoyed at the expense of their American competitors comes from a radically different way of organizing their corporate culture and their approach to research and development. This is partly incentive-driven, but also partly culturally derived, from an emphasis on small group interaction rather than on individual performance. In flexible manufacturing the focus is on small teams of well-educated, very competent, highly trained engineers interacting together rather than working individually at their tasks.

Nowhere is this difference revealed more strikingly than in an analysis by the Japanese management specialist Masaaki Imai in his book *Kaizen. Kaizen* is a Japanese word that, literally translated, means "improvement," and Imai uses it to describe a management system that is deeply ingrained in world-class Japanese firms, symbolizing their approach to everything from inventory management to research.

The essence of *kaizen* is captured in the Japanese definition of innovation, which implies long-term and long-lasting but more "evolutionary" effects on product and process technology, compared with the Western emphasis on invention, which stresses shorter-term but much more dramatic "breakthrough" effects.

The pace of *kaizen* is slower, too, with smaller steps; the time frame is continuous and incremental; change is gradual and constant. Everyone in the corporation is involved; the delivery mechanism is the small group or the interactive system. The spark is conventional know-how adapted from state-of-the-art technology, with a focus on *incremental* innovation and constant tinkering. The mode is constant maintenance and improvement. The practical requirements involve relatively lower financial investment but greater personal effort. And the evaluation criteria focus on process and continued effort for better results, regardless of how well the company has done, rather than on profits.

In most Western organizations the pace is faster, with bigger steps; the time frame is intermittent and nonincremental; change tends to be abrupt and volatile. Only a few select "champions" are involved in the process; the delivery mechanism is the "rugged individual." The spark is infrequent technological breakthrough, with a focus on new inventions and new theories. The mode is scrap and rebuild. Practical requirements involve a preference for large financial investment but comparatively little effort to maintain it. And the evaluation criteria focus on earnings.

"Total improvement is not limited to product quality alone," Imai wrote. "The aim is to improve *everything* the company does."

Kaizen is essentially a customer-driven strategy for improvement, ideally suited to a global environment characterized by sharp increases in the cost of materials, energy, and labor, by overcapacity of production facilities, by increased competition, by more exacting consumer preferences, *by a need to introduce new products more quickly,* and by a need to lower break-even points for profitability.

"In the West," Imai noted, "cross-functional problems are usually seen in terms of conflict resolution. Kaizen strategy enables Japanese management to take a systematic, open, and *collaborative* approach to cross-functional problem solving. Since kaizen is process-oriented, it requires everyone's personal efforts. It advances inch-by-inch on the strength of many small, combined steps. In a slow-growth economy charaterized by high costs of labor and materials, overcapacity, and stagnant markets, this strategy will often have a better payoff than the breakthrough strategy more common in the West."

American firms that have taken the Japanese competitive challenge seriously, like IBM, Texas Instruments, and Ford, have begun to see the wisdom of a *kaizen*like strategy. IBM, long the established industry leader in mainframe computers, has adopted a total-quality approach that permeates its entire organization and now has one of the world's most advanced flexible manufacturing systems at its personal computer plant in Florida. Texas Instruments has put new stress on both internal and external collaboration, having moved away from its more independent, shoot-from-the-hip style of earlier years, with a positive impact on both customers and suppliers. And the senior management of Ford, on the verge of scrapping one of its least productive automotive plants, went directly to production workers on the factory floor and asked *them* how *they* would redesign the plant and the production process if they were allowed to work together to do it. The workers responded with unprecedented enthusiasm, and the Flat Rock, Michigan, plant became one of the most productive facilities in Ford's system prior to its sale to Mazda.

Richard Schonberger, a manufacturing specialist, senses a determined effort to improve on the part of American firms today, because they are increasingly aware of the immense gap in manufacturing technology between Japan and America and because more intense competition brings on self-examination and change. He wrote a thoughtful comparison of Japanese and American manufacturing in a recent book called *Japanese Manufacturing Techniques* in which he isolated nine hidden lessons in simplicity.

"In visiting Japanese industrial companies," Schonberger observed, "one is struck as much by the lack of sophisticated staff journeymen as by the productivity of the line organization. In the face of this evidence, there is all the more reason to question the effectiveness of business school education in the U.S., which emphasizes sophisticated techniques and supplies industry with accountants, systems analysts, financial managers, lawyers, and market researchers, all peddling high-cost programs. This emphasis on staff has added layers of complexity. The kinds of highly effective, simple systems of enhancing quality and productivity that we can borrow from the Japanese do not fit in easily with such an environment."

Schonberger's conclusion: simplify and reduce, simplify and integrate, simplify and expect results.

Ichak Adizes would agree.

Adizes is an Israeli-born, Columbia-educated management consultant who recently wrote a perceptive book about American corporate problems called *How to Solve the Mismanagement Crisis*. He presently heads the Adizes Institute in California. Not much over five feet tall but intensely energetic, Adizes explodes like a firecracker when he works with business groups. He is best known as a process specialist.

Adizes divides management into four classes, which he says all organizations have and all organizations need in order to function effectively.

There is the producer, who works for results, who is both aggressive and a workaholic, usually the first to arrive and the last to leave. He (or she) is highly individualistic and compulsive and hates to delegate because he thinks there is no one competent to delegate to. This is the Lone Ranger, and only Tontos work for him.

Next there is the administrator, the manager who organizes a company so that things get done in the right order. He manages by the book, usually a policy manual, and is most concerned about efficiency. This is the Bureaucrat, who is most comfortable in a bank, an insurance company, or an accounting firm. He would rather be precisely wrong than approximately correct.

Third is the entrepreneur, the manager who has no agendas, hates meetings, generates scores of new ideas, and makes things happen in unpredictable ways. The worst situation for him is a three-hour plane ride, because he can think up too many new ideas to swamp his subordinates with. This is the Arsonist, someone who is constantly anticipating and planning, who puts a premium on both creativity and a willingness to risk.

Finally, there is the consensus-seeker, someone who is sensitive to direction, finds the destination everyone wants to reach, and tries to take them there. He has a good political nose and keeps his eyes focused well ahead and his ear to the ground. This is the Integrator, the consummate team player, most concerned about organic integration across functional boundaries. He is like a hand, which coordinates the movements and functions of all five fingers.

"Management theory describes a manager only in theory, which is why he exists only in textbooks," Adizes was saying to me on one of his recent trips to New York. "There is such a thing as a perfect manager, but you need a management *team*, so you want different people with all these various skills who can work together as a complementary group. That's one reason the Japanese have been so successful. They have created an organic system, which is too intense, too difficult, and too strong to be penetrated by individuals working alone. Their management model is the Boston Celtics, not the Lone Ranger. One of America's problems as a culture is its glorification of the individual. We desperately need to learn how to work better together in teams."

Adizes believes that all four management types are indispensable to the effective functioning of a good organization. A company needs the results-oriented focus of the producer, the organizational ability of the administrator, the creativity of the entrepreneur, and the orchestrating ability of a consensus-seeker to make management work well. It is when any one of these skills is lacking that organizations experience serious problems and begin to flounder. It is also when one of these skills is lacking that internal conflict escalates.

"Conflict is necessary and indispensable for good management," Adizes said. "Management education is basically learning how to take more conflict. Unfortunately, most of our conflict is internal, between individuals or divisions, which occurs in destructive ways rather than in a supportive environment based on trust and respect. The point is not *whether* you have conflict, but how you handle it. There is no growth without it, so the trick is to make it functional. The Japanese have done well in part because they have learned how to structure their organizations better than we have and how to make conflict work to their advantage. Good organizations should be structured by geniuses so that idiots can run them. Unfortunately, most American organizations are structured by idiots so that it takes a genius to run them."

In addition to incentives for strengthening American manufacturing competitiveness and improving American management skills, a focus on strategy is key to developing effective alliances in manufacturing. In the old days, when direct foreign investment was not permitted in Japan or Korea and wholly owned subsidiaries were not allowed in those markets, strategic alliances were simply called "joint ventures," fifty-fifty tie-ups between, say, a Japanese and an American company.

Today competitors are taking a different look at strategic alliances, given the structural difficulties of penetrating the Japanese market. Ideally a strong strategic alliance will be complementary in nature, meaning that it works best when the strengths of one partner can be leveraged against the weaknesses of another. For example, about twenty-five years ago Caterpillar Inc. allied itself with Mitsubishi Heavy Industries to manufacture earth-moving equipment directly in Japan so it could compete more effectively as Cat-Mitsubishi against its primary international competitor, Komatsu. Mitsubishi was not in the bulldozer business, so the alliance merged Cat's product strengths with MHI's distribution and network strengths. Similarly, Sumitomo-3M was a strategic tie-up among 3M, Sumitomo Electric, and NEC, one of Japan's largest electronics firms, leveraging the distribution network of the Sumitomo group against 3M's new product development strengths. In a more recent transaction Merck Pharmaceutical acquired 51 percent of Banyu Seiyaku to create a strategic alliance that merged Banyu's weak R&D (but superior distribution strengths in Japan) with Merck's strong product research (but weak marketing and distribution).

As an alternative to exporting, strategic manufacturing alliances are considered essential to competing effectively in the tougher Japanese market. American firms need to be in these structurally complex East Asian markets—especially Japan—to stay close to the product cycles, monitor what the competition is doing, and follow developments in technology, quality, and price. Today a foreign investor owns at least 25 percent of the equity in more than 1,500 companies in Japan.

In surveying successful foreign ventures in Japan, Stanford's Daniel Okimoto has found that an interesting pattern develops. Most of the foreign successes are in consumer nondurables—products like disposable razors, instant coffee, fast foods, and facial tissues. It is therefore no surprise that foreign firms that have carved out sizable market shares for these products sell directly to the Japanese consumer, not to Japanese corporate customers, because of the greater difficulty in penetrating Japan's industrial structure.

According to Okimoto's analysis, and confirmed by my own experience, many more joint ventures have failed in Japan than have succeeded. This is attributable to underlying strategies that may have been ill conceived, perhaps between partners who did not know each other well enough. Smaller American companies, which are often technology-rich but cash-poor, frequently find themselves in a position of licensing their technology to a Japanese company, since the Japanese typically want immediate access to the most advanced technology they can find.

American firms too often lose their competitive technological edge this way.

"An analysis of foreign direct investments thus suggests," Okimoto wrote in his "Outsider Trading" article, "that the difficulty of establishing a strong, physical presence in Japan is not only a reflection of, but also a contributing factor to, the difficulties of exporting to Japan. The impediments to foreign direct investment come from the reciprocal, long-term nature of Japanese industrial organization. The underdeveloped infrastructure of direct foreign investment, particularly in intermediate products, diminishes the capacity of foreign producers to tailor their organizations, product lines, marketing efforts, and service to the specific needs and circumstances of the Japanese market."

C. K. Prahalad, who teaches in the business school at the University of Michigan, reached a similar conclusion in an article called "Strategic Partnerships: The Challenge of Competitive Collaboration."

"It is no coincidence that the partners with the intent to gain global leadership are mostly Japanese," he wrote. "Partnerships are but one more step in the strategy of global dominance by a few Japanese groups."

Prahalad is representative of a growing number of critics of strategic alliances who believe these tie-ups may actually serve to strengthen Japan's competitive edge and weaken America's. Prahalad concentrates on three key factors—strategic intent, relative contributions, and relative power in a partnership—and believes Western firms should take a cautious attitude toward developing strategic alliances with the Japanese.

"Partnerships with Japan are a second best solution," he concluded. "They should be entered into carefully and limited to situations where they are clearly needed. Strategic intent matters more than initial starting position. If one partner's intent is to use the alliance merely as a springboard to capture global leadership in the industry, it will attempt to steadily erode the partner's advantage, appropriate its skills, and ultimately dispose of its contributions."

Just such dangers as these are inherent in Boeing's alliance with a consortium of Japanese firms in the aerospace industry that are cooperating as subcontractors on Boeing's 757 and 767 commercial jet aircraft projects. Estimates indicate that nearly half of the sophisticated components of these advanced aircraft, such as radar systems, cockpit controls, and avionics, are designed, manufactured, and assembled in Japan. Some observers have criticized Boeing's decision to allocate such sensitive technological componentry to the Japanese, because Japan has targeted commercial jet aviation as a strategic industry of its own for the 1990s and one in which it intends to be a global player.

(Indications persist that Boeing may have had no choice; the Japanese government is strongly rumored to have said that if Boeing wanted to sell subsequent generations of aircraft to Japanese airlines, and to other national airlines in Asia, most of which are government-controlled and over which the Japanese government has considerable influence through its foreign aid programs, then Boeing would have to agree to the strategic alliance, which it ultimately did. For its part, Boeing has indicated that Japanese companies supply only a limited part of the structural hardware for these aircraft and that the Japanese government had never brought pressure to bear with regard to the bidding process. Boeing views the current threat from Europe's Airbus as much more significant than any potential or future threat from Japan.)

Other critics of strategic alliances acknowledge that while foreign products need to be "Japanized" or "Koreanized" in order to appeal to local consumers, whether individual or corporate, there is no substitute for a long-term commitment to these markets, as IBM, Texas Instruments, Hewlett-Packard, and other American firms have demonstrated. Time and money are still the most necessary tactical tools of a broad market-penetrating strategy in Japan, and strategic alliances with suppliers and end users are often necessary to implement that strategy.

But Japanese penetration of the American market cannot be stopped unless that competition is met head-on here. A refocused priority on manufacturing, spurred by the right policy incentives, could do more than anything to help American products compete, quality for quality and price for price, against the Japanese competition.

Another dimension of the manufacturing approach is to forge strategic alliances between American and non-Japanese Asian firms, to marry superior American R&D and product development strengths, say, with state-of-the-art manufacturing techniques in Korea or Taiwan and use the products of those alliances to compete more effectively against Japanese products in the U.S. market.

Based on my own consulting experience, several American multinationals are engaged in doing just that. One such venture, an alliance between the medical equipment division of a large American company and a major Korean electronics manufacturer, is manufacturing medical equipment in Korea, exporting it to the United States, and giving its main Japanese competitor, in the words of its American manager in Seoul, "fits." But unless these Korean-American alliances are monitored closely, and the technology contribution is strictly controlled, the

American partners may be in danger of providing their Korean competitors with exactly the kind of technological advantages for the 1990s that they gave to their Japanese competitors ten and twenty years ago. (Protection of intellectual property rights has become a major concern. Texas Instruments recently won a major patent infringement case against eight Japanese and one Korean manufacturer of semiconductors.)

A third dimension of the manufacturing approach is to forge strategic alliances solely between domestic American companies *in* the domestic American market, leveraging strength with strength where necessary to make the combined entity a stronger competitor against Japan or merging strength with weakness to enable important but weaker partners to survive. However, outdated American antitrust considerations still make some domestic tie-ups dangerous, if not illegal, so a substantial amount of criticism is leveled at IBM for consistently engaging in strategic alliances with its domestic suppliers and customers. U.S. antitrust laws now must reflect global markets and competitors, not just those in domestic America.

While regulations have been relaxed somewhat to permit a sharing of limited research and development between and among American firms, more can probably be done. The formation of the Microelectronics Computer Corporation, a research consortium of American competitors in the domestic computer business, based in Austin, Texas, is one example; the recent creation of Sematech, also based in Austin, formed to pool R&D in semiconductor manufacturing technology, is another. A third is the recent formation of the National Center for Manufacturing Sciences, in Ann Arbor, Michigan, with seed funding from the Pentagon to sponsor research on basic problems of American manufacturing.

One serious impediment to successful cross-industry alliances is the overwhelming American emphasis on maximizing shareholder value. This encourages leveraged buyouts rather than strategic alliances, although most of the LBOs have been concentrated in nonstrategic sectors. But the time, money, and attention lavished on these financial restructurings add little to America's competitive position.

Growth of LBOs and takeovers during the past decade has been explosive—*$1.2 trillion* worth in the ten years ending December 31, 1988. A recent Salomon Brothers study indicates that over the four-year period 1985–88 there were twenty-eight LBOs of more than $500 million each, totaling $65 billion in value and utilizing $25 billion worth of junk (non-investment-grade) bonds. In early 1989, when RJR Nabisco went private for $25 billion, it became the single largest LBO ever.

Though there have clearly been gains in financial performance by some of the firms bought out, they tend to be overshadowed by the costs as well as by the risks of this speculative junk financing. In contested bids about half of the 80 percent premiums being paid are financed by junk bonds, and restructured companies are now covering their interest charges by no more than about one-to-one. For the five years ending December 31, 1988, the economist Henry Kaufman estimates that the debt of nonfinancial U.S. corporations has soared by $840 billion, compared to the value of corporate shareholder equity, which has dropped by nearly $300 billion over the same period. (In Japan, these trends are just the reverse.)

Once again, current incentives in the tax code favor debt over equity, because interest on borrowed money is deductible for tax purposes while dividends are double-, and in some cases triple-, taxed. Some recent proposals have called for restrictions on deductibility of interest, disallowing it for these huge LBOs; while it might be worthwhile to consider limiting deductibility to nonstrategic transactions, a much more significant step would be to eliminate the unequal treatment accorded equity by allowing our corporations to deduct dividends from pretax income. It should be possible to permit equal deduction of both interest and dividends (or a deduction of neither), though in the interest of competitiveness the tax code ought to be jiggled to favor equity and be linked to a reduction of taxes on capital gains.

A fourth dimension of strategic alliances is the business-government partnership, an area in which American firms have far to go compared with their Asian competitors. The Defense Advanced Research Projects Agency (DARPA) at the Pentagon is one strategic funnel for the application of government funds to significant American research efforts, but DARPA's mandate is focused more on defense needs than on the ultimate commercialization of products in research. DARPA has no delusions about the relevance of neoclassical ideology; it is America's most significant pocket of strategic policy.

A fifth and final dimension of the strategic alliance concept is an extension of the advantages of complementarity, focusing more on size and industry concentration. Some have called this "tiering." Strategic alliances between two dominant and leading competitors in their industry, such as the recent alliance between Texas Instruments and Hitachi in semiconductors or between Boeing and Mitsubishi Heavy Industries in aerospace, may fail because of the ability of the Japanese partner to exploit, to its advantage, the technology that is its object of the alliance.

But alliances between firms in different industry tiers—a first-tier American competitor allied with, say, a second-tier Japanese competitor, in different industries—may not be so strategically disadvantaged, particularly if the focus of the alliance is the Japanese market and not technology. Second-tier Japanese companies are ruthlessly motivated to move up in the fiercely competitive hierarchy of their domestic market and will do just about anything to enhance their competitive position, even if it means tying up with a foreign firm.

The ability of American manufacturers to meet the competition from East Asia head-on in the domestic American market is also a function of two other related factors: one is public policy coordination, and the other is a concerted defense against Japanese acquisitions of American companies in the strategic industries. Recent legislation requiring acquisitions by foreign firms that could affect America's national interests to be referred to the Treasury Department for screening is a step in the right direction.

Numerous proposals have been made, from establishing an industrial policy council that would coordinate national economic policy to creating a department of international trade and industry that would merge the trade and investment skills of the Department of Commerce with the Office of the U.S. Trade Representative to create a stronger combined approach. Should individual states be allowed to compete *against* each other for foreign business, with no policy coordination effort in Washington to adjudicate the national interest? Until and unless American public policy officials understand how the business objectives of East Asian competitors are strategically driven, and as long as private shareholders continue to sell American companies to Asian competitors for financially driven reasons only, America will find itself at an even larger competitive disadvantage. At some point a "national clearinghouse" may have to be created to coordinate public policy among conflicting agencies for foreign investment and trade. Such coordination will be essential to America's competing more effectively against Japan. But let us be realistic: it is not a bigger bureaucracy but more strategically targeted incentives that more accurately reflect the American way.

Manufacturing is the key to growth in services, as we have seen, whether in international trade or in the domestic economy. It is also the key to blunting the prowess of Asian products in the American market. Complementary strategic alliances, crafted carefully, driven strategically, and controlled closely, can be a useful tactical tool in strengthening American manufacturing capabilities. But in the absence of specific government incentives that direct available investment in strategically desirable directions, manufacturing may continue to be American industry's backwater, and a once-proud America will find itself increasingly dominated by manufactured products either made in Asia and exported to America or made in America but by Asian firms, with profound implications for the nation's employment, wealth creation, and standard of living.

PART II
EAST ASIA'S AUTHORITARIAN SYSTEMS AND THE FUTURE OF REPRESENTATIVE DEMOCRACY

6
AUTHORITARIANISM ON THE SOFT SHELL

There is the fiction that Japan is a sovereign state like any other, with central organs of government which can recognize what is good for the country and bear ultimate responsibility for national decision-making. This illusion is very difficult to dispel.

In fact, statecraft in Japan is quite different. The most powerful components of the Japanese System are certain groups of bureaucrats, some political cliques, and clusters of industrialists. These semiautonomous components, each endowed with great discretionary powers, are not represented in one central ruling body. It is crucial to distinguish Japan from other nations with governments that are besieged by special interest groups. We are not dealing with lobbies but with a structural phenomenon not encompassed by the categories of accepted political theory. A hierarchy, or rather a complex of overlapping hierarchies, is maintained, but it has no top. There is no supreme institution with jurisdiction over the others. Thus there is no place where, as Harry Truman would say, the buck stops. The buck keeps circulating.

Karel van Wolferen, "The Japan Problem"

Over the years, I have, not without difficulty, established a number of close personal friendships in Japan, sufficiently close and sufficiently few to force me to regard with suspicion any foreigner who brags about how many friends he has there. If American society is like a loose-leaf notebook, Japanese society is like an onion; peel off one layer, and there's another layer just behind it. Peel off *that* layer, and there's another one behind it. It's hard enough for the Japanese themselves to penetrate this multilayered sphere, let alone a dreaded foreigner. If you find you can't seem to get anywhere, it often doesn't do much good to ask; foreigners are outside the frame of reference anyway.

So it takes an enormous amount of time and an enormous amount of effort to develop personal relationships with the Japanese, but once established, they last. Close friendships in Japan are quite different from the more disposable American variety because Japanese relationships invariably involve another factor, which is a large dose of mutual obligation. It is called *on-giri*, which is variously translated as "duty and obligation" or "kindness and gratitude." No act is ever an isolated event; every favor bestowed must eventually be repaid in kind, so over time a kind of unwritten ledger of IOUs develops.

One Japanese in particular, a man who is my godfather, has been especially close. He is many years my senior—older enough, in fact, to qualify him as *oyabun*, or "mentor," were we to work within the same company. He is president of a large Japanese firm that is a member of one of those industrial conglomerates called *keiretsu*. When my first book was published some years ago, he was singularly responsible for the creation of my Japanese literary name, Shikibu Shiroishi, a combination of the *kanji* for my German surname and a pun on Shikibu Murasaki, the famous female author of the historical *Genji monogatari*, Japan's earliest, most renowed novel (and the world's first). My godfather was also responsible for introducing me to the world of Japanese politics.

"The key to understanding the Japanese political system," he said to me many years ago, over sushi, "is realizing that it is a blend of authority, power, and influence. You have to consider those three elements together, *organically*, because individually they are like legs of a stool: put all the weight on one leg, and the stool collapses; take one leg away, and it collapses too."

Chalmers Johnson has written widely about Japanese politics. In a *Journal of Japanese Studies* article called "Japan: Who Governs?" he carried my godfather's three-legged stool concept a step or two further and analyzed the organic interdependence of authority, power, and influence based on historical Japanese artifacts of the shrine, representing authority; the official, having power; and the *ronin*, or swordless samurai, symbolizing influence.

From Meiji through the prewar years, Johnson noted, the Japanese Parliament (the Diet) represented authority, the official bureaucracy was power, and the masses of common people became the *ronin*. The common people demonstrated often, and not without violence, to bring influence to bear on the other two forces. After the war Japan's dominant political party, the Liberal Democratic Party, or LDP, came to represent authority, the bureaucracy still held power, but the press came to symbolize influence.

In recent years other Japanese scholars have substituted different symbols for influence—such as big business or consumer protest groups—but the first two legs of the stool, the LDP and the bureaucracy, everyone agrees, remain unquestioned. (One political scientist, Kenzo Kono, regards politicians, bureaucrats, and businessmen as functional equivalents of the popular children's game of paper, scissors, and rock.)

Consensus would suggest that, more than the press or consumer interest groups, influence is wielded today by Japanese business—the *zaikai*—represented by its professional association, Keidanren, the Federation of Economic Organizations. (Thus the derivation, some years ago, of the popular concept, Japan, Inc., to characterize the Japanese government-business complex.)

"The relationship between Japan's political system and its economic achievements," Johnson wrote, "is perhaps the most fundamental controversy within the field of Japanese political economy. In Japan, the politicians reign but do not rule; the actual decision-makers are an elite bureaucracy of economic technocrats; the system works by serving those interests that are necessary to perpetuate it."

Failure to understand that political *power* in Japan is wielded by entrenched, well-trained, highly competent bureaucrats, while political *authority* is legitimized, through the Diet, by the factional leadership of the LDP, is to miss a fundamental aspect of political reality in Japan. During the 1950s and 1960s, for example, legislation was introduced into the Diet only after consensus had been reached among the appropriate bureaucracies—notably the Ministry of Finance, as the most powerful, and MITI—and the LDP. About two-thirds of all legislation introduced came about in this way.

Failure to understand this distinction between Japanese power and authority has also led to serious bilateral friction in the past and probably will in the future. Senator John Danforth, Republican of Missouri, once publicly complained that, as a result of the dominant power of the official bureaucracy, bilateral negotiations were not easily conducted because "behind every door there is another door." And Senator Robert Dole, Republican of Kansas, when he was told of the power of Japan's entrenched bureaucracy, said he could not imagine a political system in which the elected representatives couldn't get something done if it was sufficiently important.

When American occupying powers took control over the administrative functions of the Japanese government in 1945, they purged the military and the wartime *zaibatsu* of their senior officers, but they left the bureaucracy pretty much intact. This made it even easier, especially for the economic planners in MITI, to pick up where they had left off and to build on the strong ties to industrial continuity going back to the prewar efforts of Shinji Yoshino. This also made it easier for the bureaucracy to say one thing to MacArthur's staff but turn around and do another, reflecting a popular Japanese saying, *menjuu fukuhai*, which means "false obedience": saying one thing to a person's face, but literally "turning it around in the belly" and doing another.

"Japan's burcaucratic structure was one aspect of Japanese life General MacArthur failed to reform," the *Japan Times*, Tokyo's largest English-language daily, once noted. "Instead of chopping away at the base of the bureaucratic pyramid, he simply chopped off the apex by purging a few key Government officials. In due course, the pyramid grew a new apex, and the bureaucracy continued unchanged from its prewar days."

Most Western observers start with the assumption that Japan is a genuine democracy. Therefore, they proceed with the notion that, since power in Western forms of democratic government is synonymous with the legislative bodies of freely elected representatives, or with the most powerful person who heads those governments, the same must be true in Japan. It is not.

Karel van Wolferen, East Asia correspondent for the Dutch daily *NRC Handelsblad*, has lived in Japan continuously since the early 1960s. He is the author of *The Enigma of Japanese Power*, a book about contemporary Japanese politics, and he wrote a rather controversial article called "The Japan Problem," which appeared not long ago in *Foreign Affairs* and a portion of which was quoted to open this chapter.

"What makes conflict between Japan and the United States so menacing," he wrote, "is that the two countries do not know how to cope with each other. America does not understand the nature of the Japanese political economy, and thus cannot accept the way it behaves, and Japan is largely unaware of the threat posed by America's unwillingness to accept it for what it is. The bureaucracy had been left almost entirely intact during the Occupation to administer the policy of unlimited industrial expansion. Japan's de facto one-party system, dominated by the LDP, guaranteed that there would be no disturbing confusion from messy parliamentary processes. A political mechanism to change the priority of unlimited industrial expansion does not exist. The bureaucrats tinker with the economy by making adjustments that enable its further growth. Even though the Diet technically controls the national budget, most of the time the politicians keep out of the bureaucrats' way. So the industrialists carry on expanding their market shares, enter new markets with the help of the bureaucrats, and are kept in line by their peers. Looked at from an international perspective, however, the system is an anachronism, for its finely meshed all-Japanese components are glaringly deficient in providing the country with an effective foreign policy."

I met with van Wolferen on a recent trip to Japan and asked if he saw this triangular structure changing in any way.

"Well, the anthropomorphic analogy is dead," he was saying over an exorbitantly expensive lunch, made all the more so by dollars that bought only half as much yen. "It simply doesn't make sense to talk about a nation as if it knows what is good or bad for it. That Japan has created these dysfunctional trade surpluses, which are potentially destabilizing and need to be brought into balance, is well recognized, but the bureaucratic machine keeps on humming, unable to be constrained by the politicians."

Rudderless momentum was the phrase I had often heard used to describe this state of affairs.

"The Japanese people have no power," van Wolferen admitted. "Japan is a functional democracy in name only. Power is monopolized by the bureaucrats, who through the system of *amakudari* occupy positions of tremendous influence in the business world as well."

Amakudari is a Japanese term that literally means "descent from heaven." It refers to the process by which retiring bureaucrats take up senior positions in Japanese companies, in Tokyo think tanks, or in many of the quasi-public agencies, as chief executives or board members. Only a very few powerful ex-ministers have eschewed the *amakudari* process. One was Shigeru Sahashi, a former vice minister of MITI, the highest rank a career bureaucrat can attain, who once said, "Bureaucrats are officials of the various ministries first, and only second are they servants of the nation."

Most of Japan's postwar prime ministers have been former bureaucrats themselves. By the early 1970s nearly one-fourth of the House of Representatives (the lower house) and almost 40 percent of the House of Councillors (the upper house) were former bureaucrats who belonged to the LDP. By the early 1980s the numbers for the lower house were closer to one-third.

Did van Wolferen think the bureaucrats were aware of the problem?

"Some are, but they are powerless to act," he said. "The system is out of their control. They realize the uncertainties and risks of continuing as is, but they feel powerless to stop it. And all their younger colleagues in the bureaucracy are dependent on their continued support as mentors. They would like to overthrow the current system, but nobody is really willing to listen to them or take them very seriously. *Deru kugi,* you know. And why should the Japanese people support such a position when they have basically benefited from the way things are?"

The Japanese expression van Wolferen used, *deru kugi,* was from an old Japanese proverb, *deru kugi wa utareru.* It is perhaps the expression most frequently used to describe how Japanese society really functions. Literally translated, it means, "the nail standing up gets hammered down." Functionally applied, it means a person better not get out of line. If he does, peer pressure will be applied ruthlessly to make him conform. If he doesn't, humiliation and ostracism will be the result.

I thought about van Wolferen's comments as I took the train across town to my next destination, to meet with one of Japan's most senior politicians, Motoo Shiina, an elder statesman within the LDP and vice chairman of its influential Policy Research Council, the Seichokai. His father, Etsusaburo Shiina, had been a vice minister of MITI during the war and had returned, following his purge during the Allied occupation, to become minister of MITI (twice) and foreign minister (once) in the postwar years.

Age is always a difficult matter to gauge with a Japanese, but I knew Shiina was in his late fifties, although he did not look it. He had entered politics just a decade ago, following a successful business career. When I saw him, he was currently in his fourth term as an LDP representative, looking very fit and smoking a small pipe at his book-lined office in Nagata-cho behind the Diet buildings.

We talked about foreign perceptions of the Japanese political system and whether a "perception gap," as many Japanese were calling it, had come to characterize how America believes the system works.

"The real perception gap," Shiina was telling me, "is that America needs some serious belt-tightening efforts itself over the coming years. If you overeat and overdrink, then you have to take measures to lose weight and slim down. Not in a crash program, overnight, but gradually, with discipline. Because if it took you ten years to get fat, then it will take you a long time to get lean and healthy again. So it seems to me Americans would be better advised to put their own house in order before criticizing the Japanese system."

I asked Shiina if bureaucratic domination of the Japanese political process would continue or if he saw it in decline.

He smiled politely.

"The only thing in decline is America's competitive position vis-à-vis the 1950s," he said. "Americans view that era as their heyday and glory, but we view it as an unusual, abnormal, extraordinary age. Those days will never come back, and we should not expect them to, but America seems to be creating economic and trade policies *as if* that era still existed, instead of adjusting and adapting to the reality of a more pluralistic world. Our fear is that it could lead to an age of techno-nationalism in which protectionism insulates not just products but their underlying technology. American politicians, it seems to me, have to bear responsibility for their inability to lead the American people, but the American people are also responsible for continuing to live in a dream world of the past."

Japanese bureaucrats live in anything but a dream world, being more attuned to the future than they are to the past. From the beginning the bureaucracy has drawn its talent from the country's leading universities, the elite almost always graduates of Tokyo University. The process has created not only a highly educated cadre of civil servants but also a network of school ties that permeates the leadership of the LDP as well as the bureaucracy. It is analogous to the close relationships that exist in England, whose elite come from Oxford and Cambridge, or in France, whose able bureaucrats in the Ecole Nationale d'Administration matriculate from the Instituts d'Etudes Politiques.

This pattern has been quite consistent in Japan, as a look at the university backgrounds of successful candidates for higher civil service examinations shows. Throughout the 1960s and 1970s a minimum of about one-fourth and a maximum of around 40 percent of the bureaucracy's new entrants came from Tokyo University alone; the proportion is closer to 50 percent when Kyoto University, Japan's second-ranking institution, is included.

During the entire postwar period the ratio of all applicants to successful candidates for the type A higher civil service exam, the highest level, has never fallen below ten to one, and in recent years the ratio has been closer to *thirty* to one. Not surprisingly, the Ministry of Finance and MITI, in that order, are the top two ministries of choice for the best of the best, reflecting their positions of power in the bureaucratic hierarchy.

In America no such elite sourcing exists, with arguable effect on administrative quality. In a recent survey of career civil servants holding the rank of GS-14 or higher, no more than 3 percent came from any one university (George Washington University, in fact), and only in the foreign service did Ivy League universities contribute a larger share, though Harvard, Princeton, and Yale supplied only 14 percent of the total.

The Japanese bureaucracy places a very high priority on training its analysts thoroughly in the subjects of American politics, economics, security affairs, social policy, and trade. In Washington, by comparison, whether at State, Commerce, Defense, or Treasury, executive branch departments will be lucky to have *one* Japan specialist out of twenty Asian experts, since the weighting is so heavily skewed toward China and the Soviet Union. What's worse, with every change of administration more than *3,000* middle- and upper-level political appointees rotate out of the capital.

Westerners are often critical of the Japanese inability to speak English well, but this is tantamount to the pot calling the kettle black. Japan's national educational curriculum requires written English for all students beginning in the seventh grade, so three years of middle school, plus three years of high school, plus four years of university work give Japanese bureaucrats a strong reading skill in the English language, though their conversation ability may be deceptively less impressive.

Despite an increasing number of Americans now studying Japanese at the university level, the Soviet Embassy in Tokyo has more Japanese-speaking staff than the U.S. Embassy there does. In Washington Japanese firms use more than a hundred private lobbyists; one out of five registered foreign agents now works on behalf of Japan. Overall, with about a thirteen-to-one personnel advantage in every respect, Tokyo has a tremendous "bureaucratic edge" over Washington, which makes the job quite tough for American negotiators. One of them, a Japanese-speaking veteran of many years in Japan, a participant in key bilateral trade negotiations, compared this lopsided Tokyo-Washington matchup to the San Francisco 49ers playing a weekend touch-football team.

"With regard to the future," Chalmers Johnson noted in his article, "all of the envisaged solutions to the problems facing Japan and comparable societies are likely to entail an enlargement of official bureaucracy. Given its experience with bureaucracy and its alertness to the political problems of bureaucracy, Japan may adjust to the consequences better than some other open societies. The Japanese bureaucracy does not rule in a vacuum, but it does hold an ascendant position, and is likely to continue to do so."

Intramural power in the bureaucracy is wielded by the Ministry of Finance, through its control of the purse strings. MOF administers the all-important fiscal and investment loan program (FILP), an off-budget account that invests the massive funds taken in through Japan's postal savings system. If private, it would be the single largest bank in the world, with assets of more than $1 trillion—larger than the twelve biggest U.S. banks combined.

In 1979, when the Japanese government was financing a third of its general account expenditures through national bond issues and devoting nearly 12 percent of the budget to debt service, MOF realized it had to put a program of fiscal austerity into place. But fiscal cutbacks meant that growth in the Japanese economy would have to be orchestrated through monetary policy, which meant lower interest rates and a weaker yen. Meanwhile, in Washington a spendthrift Congress began legislating enormous budget deficits to stimulate the American economy, which put the burden of fighting inflation on monetary policy and resulted in *higher* U.S. interest rates and a stronger dollar.

By 1984, when Washington got around to pressing Tokyo to liberalize its financial markets and deregulate domestic interest rates (which MOF sets by fiat), MOF was hardly in a receptive mood. It was preoccupied by its fiscal austerity program and by increasing interministerial conflict with MITI.

Unfortunately for American policymakers, by the time many of them realize the extent to which MOF and MITI wield power within the Japanese bureaucratic hierarchy, interministerial conflict can generate a Tokyo version of turf war. In recent years these territorial disputes, called *nawabari arasoi*, have probably been caused more by technological change (and much of it Japan's own making) than by external pressure. But the results have spawned some new entrants into the contest for traditional MOF–MITI domination of the bureaucracy.

Throughout the 1970s MITI maintained its position of power atop the economic bureaucracy, having benefited from two international oil crises, from its efforts to guide R&D in high technology (which led to Japanese global dominance in semiconductors and machine tools), and from trade wars with the U.S., which led to MITI's control over various voluntary export restraints beginning in 1980.

Since then, given the general global trends toward deregulation and privatization, MITI's position of control has been increasingly contested. Worldwide developments in telecommunications and biotechnology, in particular, have necessitated the creation of new strategic policies within the Japanese government. This has led one high-ranking MITI bureaucrat to pine rather wistfully (though not without a touch of *tatemae*) that "MITI has three roles now: to say hello to new technology, to say good-bye to vanishing industries, and to write white papers."

Japanese policymakers do not accept the concept of a "postindustrial" age, as Americans fondly do. They believe it is backward-looking, so they prefer to speak of a "knowledge-intensive" era, which is more forward-looking. They firmly believe the information revolution that is now occurring will favor natural resource–poor countries with highly developed human resources, like Japan, over natural resource–rich countries with less developed human resources, like the United States.

So when a complex industry like telecommunications experiences exponential growth, as it has in the 1980s, the primary policy question becomes, is it a computer business with linkage to telephone networks, or is it primarily a telephone business with linkage to computers? As MITI bureaucrats express it, "A computer without software is only a box, and a computer with software is still only a computer. But a computer connected to a telephone circuit is something else again: it is a telecommunications network." Computers are clearly within MITI's jurisdiction; telephone circuits, unfortunately, are not. They are controlled by the Ministry of Posts and Telecommunications (MPT).

MITI bureaucrats have always held MPT in rather low regard, considering it a third-rate bureaucracy. Still, MPT was a key stepping-stone to political influence in Japan. After MOF and MITI, being minister of MPT was the third most common career step to assuming the prime ministership in postwar Japan. MPT was the single *largest*

Japanese bureacracy, with all its postal carriers, and its responsibility for the strategic location of post offices became a valuable political asset: they were conduits for the nation's massive and highly successful postal savings system.

In recent years this exponential growth in telecommunications technology, privatization of Nippon Telegraph and Telephone, external pressure from Washington to "open" the "closed" Japanese market, and internal pressure to restore MPT to its previous "prestige" rank all combined to set the scene for some rather dramatic turf wars between MITI and MPT. These ultimately became known as the "telecom wars."

With MPT trying to outflank MITI on one side, the Ministry of Health and Welfare (MHW) tried to outflank MITI on the other as equally important developments in biotechnology began to flow. MITI had earlier targeted biotechnology as a strategic industry, but MHW had domestic regulatory control over Japanese pharmaceutical companies, product licensing and approvals, and social welfare, so the stage was set for another turf war, this time between MITI and MHW.

This interministerial conflict continues in Tokyo today, still dominated by MITI and MOF but with other ministries now flexing their muscles. MPT has fought with MOF over financial affairs, since MPT has control over the postal savings system, but MOF regulates interest rates and the commercial banks. MITI and the Ministry of Foreign Affairs clash over control of foreign policy.

MITI and the Ministry of Education are fighting over the application of technology to the classroom, since education reform is a priority. And the Ministry of Education and MHW are battling over which should have responsibility for new research in biotechnology. All of these conflicts have some rather profound implications for American policy, both public and private, as the bureaucratic landscape shifts away from its formerly monolithic state under the dominance of MITI and MOF.

These turf wars have led to new developments within the dominant Liberal Democratic Party, too, which brings us back full circle to politics. Conservative lawmakers with similar (or overlapping) functional interests and expertise have established what are known as *zoku*. These are groups (literally, "tribes") of policy-making politicians who feel that, as war is too important to be left to the generals, public policy is too important to be left entirely to the bureaucrats. So the *zoku* began a trend toward preemptory control over public policy formulation by the LDP.

The *zoku* were controlled not by ex-bureaucrats but by pure politicians who had little or no prior experience in functional areas such as agriculture, foreign policy, or national security. The head of each *zoku* is called a *bosu*, or boss, an underworld term that reflects the kind of vertical, hierarchical structure implicit throughout Japanese society, including the very core of the LDP, its factions.

Membership in a political party means loyalty to an individual, not to an institution or an ideology. Among the LDP politicians there is no systematic organization, but only temporary obedience to a few very powerful leaders.

In 1945, when the right to vote was extended to both women and men twenty years of age or older, the number of eligible voters increased 2.5 times. For a decade, *sixteen* conservative parties competed with each other for power until the Liberal and Democratic parties merged in 1955 to shut out all the others. Since 1955 there has been no opposition party in Japan with the faintest chance of challenging the LDP. Etsusaburo Shiina called the socialists a "cat who would never catch the mouse."

The LDP became known as "the party that will rule for half an eternity." The fact that it has dominated Japanese politics for more than thirty years has given Japan a de facto one-party political system, a development that in any other country would clearly be authoritarian, if not totalitarian. In Japan the party has traditionally been obscured by the bureaucracy, which has wielded the power, and by big business, which has the economic clout, so the LDP's authority has effectively been concealed beneath a very thin veneer of democracy.

Factions, called *habatsu*, are the primary mechanism through which political power in the party is achieved. The LDP chooses its party leader through its factions, which raise and distribute necessary operating funds, determine influential party posts, supply campaign contributions to individual candidates at election time, and provide psychological support by satisfying their members' need for companionship and for valuable political allies.

The faction is feudal in nature and goes all the way back to the twelfth century, when *han*, or clans, were formed to provide allegiance and loyalty to their lords, the *daimyo* who controlled regions of the country (which later became Japan's modern prefectures). The clans fought bitterly against each other through fierce domestic rivalries in attempts to expand areas under their control, a process that bears a striking resemblance to the bureaucratic turf wars of today.

Loyalty, hierarchy, conformity, obedience, and duty are the operative values of the faction, which puts great premium on school ties, personal friends, relatives, and business contacts in determining a faction's internal hierarchical order and its funding sources. Japanese politicians, like members of society at large, like to move in groups, and the larger the group, the better. The LDP party president, Japan's prime minister, is elected by its factions, not by the people.

As Japanese politicians move up the ladder of experience, they want ultimate control over their own factions, and they can't become prime minister unless they do achieve that. Kakuei Tanaka, who was deposed as prime minister by the Lockheed scandal in the 1970s, not only remained an elected representative and in charge of his own faction afterward; he was able to *increase* the size of his faction and his intra-party influence. Former prime minister Yasuhiro Nakasone depended on the Tanaka faction for his rise to power, and his successor, former prime minister Noboru Takeshita, ultimately took over the Tanaka faction in his own name.

Because of the massive amounts of cash contributions to the factions, nasty political scandals in Japan erupt on the average of about once a decade. Thirty years ago there was the Black Mist scandal, centering on Japan's shipbuilding industry; fifteen years ago, Lockheed's payments to high-ranking officials. More recently, in 1987–88, the Recruit Cosmos scandal implicated several senior LDP politicians in Takeshita's cabinet, including the ministers of finance and justice, who resigned when they admitted receiving political contributions in the form of unlisted shares in a Recruit subsidiary and then selling them, at striking profits, when the company went public. There is a fine line between seeking favors and buying influence in Japan; it has been called "institutional corruption."

By late spring 1989, Prime Minister Takeshita had succumbed to intense public pressure in order to take responsibility for the LDP's serious errors of misjudgment and was himself forced to resign in late April. The pervasiveness of institutional corruption made it nearly impossible to find a successor, because practically every other ranking party member was tainted by the Recruit scandal. (Imagine President Bush and his entire cabinet being forced out of office, and you have a close parallel.) Masayoshi Ito, a septuagenarian party elder, declined the post because the LDP refused to implement far-reaching reforms he had proposed in order to eliminate the corrupting influence of money (even though the Recruit scandal *itself* had occurred despite earlier reforms, such as ceilings on contributions and disclosure of contributors, put in place following the disastrous Lockheed scandal of 1973–74).

Finally, after several weeks of paralyzing indecisiveness, Foreign Minister Sosuke Uno was chosen by LDP leaders as party president and then elected Japan's eighteenth postwar prime minister in June, since he was about the only senior Japanese politician still considered relatively "clean." Uno was widely viewed as a caretaker leader, however; he would have to guide the LDP through Upper House elections in August and implement some nominal reforms, so if the party suffered severe losses or stonewalled the reforms, he would face the possibility of being asked to step down to make way for one of the party's senior faction leaders (such as former foreign and MITI minister Shintaro Abe) to take charge.

Uno's future was also clouded by the fact that he was a member of former prime minister Nakasone's own faction, though he nominally resigned his factional membership after becoming prime minister. For his part, Nakasone, who had led the nation from 1981 to 1987, was forced to resign his own LDP party membership because the Recruit scandal had emerged during his watch, although he retained his seat in the Diet. Like former prime minister Kakuei Tanaka, however, whose control over and influence in the party expanded greatly *after* the Lockheed scandal forced him from office and from the party (he came to dominate the LDP's largest faction), Nakasone too may see his own power grow, and Takeshita himself could conceivably rise to prominence again after the shock waves from the most recent scandal have dissipated. In fact, six of Prime Minister Uno's twenty-two new cabinet members were chosen from Takeshita's own faction within the LDP, including the powerful position of LDP secretary general, so Takeshita will probably continue to exert primary influence behind the scenes; his career appears to be far from over.

When the LDP did lose its majority in the Upper House as a result of the August elections, Uno of course resigned, and a new face emerged as Japan's nineteenth postwar prime minister. Toshiki Kaifu, a protégé of former prime minister Takeo Miki, who followed Kakuei Tanaka and became known as Mr. Clean, was relatively unknown, having held only one previous cabinet post, as education minister. But the preoccupation by the Western press with party politics, and its infatuation with Takako Doi, the leader of the Socialist Party, meant that the substance of policy making in Japan—the bureaucracy—was being overlooked if not ignored.

Arguably the best analysis of Japanese political values was written more than thirty years ago by Robert Bellah in a book called *Tokugawa Religion*, which focused on the evolution of values during the preindustrial period of Japan's development. Bellah understood Japanese society to be characterized by values that were concerned with goal attainment and with power. He reasoned that since Japan's process of industrialization was government-sponsored or, in some cases, government-controlled, Japan was able to accept rapid industrialization *because* it possessed strong central political values.

"Whatever specific form they take," Bellah wrote, "political values and a strong polity would seem to be a great advantage and perhaps even a prerequisite for industrialization in the 'backward' areas of today's world. Unfortunately, any strongly goal-oriented society is perilously close to totalitarianism, if we take that term to define the situation in which political considerations tend to override all others."

The Japanese political faction too, Bellah showed, had its origins in these strong central political values.

"From the earliest period of Japanese history," he wrote, "we have evidence of a very high regard for personal loyalty. It was a disgrace to live if one's lord died in battle. A samurai was to give his life for his lord, if need be, in return for all that he had received from him. When claims of the lord clashed with those of the kindred, duty to the lord came first. The resulting emphasis on filial piety, an important influence of Confucian thinking, helped rationalize the Japanese idea of the family in terms of 'political' values without at the same time making familistic values as central as in China. It seems clear that a great deal of the motivation for modernization in Japan was political rather than economic, concerned with the increase of power, for which the increase of wealth was but a means."

The dominance of the bureaucracy, the recent turf wars, the *zoku*, and the LDP's factional alliances all contribute to a sense of political unaccountability within the Japanese system, a shifting center of power.

"The political center in any pluralistic society is always shifting," George Packard, dean of the School of Advanced International Studies at Johns Hopkins University, said to me recently. "In Washington, one day it's on the Hill, the next day in the White House, another day shared," he said. "In Tokyo there is no single document, speech, or mechanism that announces new or major policy shifts, but rather a synthesis of ideas generated behind closed doors, then proposed, turned over, analyzed, reviewed, and put forth. Therefore, the *process* becomes the political center. It's almost imperceptible. It uses code words most foreign observers don't understand, and it moves with the speed of a glacier."

Packard had himself recently written an article in *Foreign Affairs* in which he called for the creation of a permanent wise man's commission that would serve to mediate the many bilateral problems that festered between Tokyo and Washington. Unfortunately, presidential commissions in the U.S. tend to be rather narrowly defined and poorly staffed; politically they are weightless. Japanese commissions, on the other hand, are more powerful and have broader constituent participation, since they are drawn from the same pool of retired bureaucrats, businessmen, and political *zoku*—all mentors of the younger elite who run the country.

Thus the "commission" idea tends to favor the Japanese side over the American, leading some critics to chastise Packard, among other academicians, as having "sold out" to Japanese interests, a charge that, needless to say, he denies. Still, former prime minister Nakasone's faction has endowed a chair in international studies at Johns Hopkins, in addition to his receiving an honorary doctorate from the university; Japanese institutions are aggressively funding academic chairs at many other American universities, which raises potential questions of propriety, since objectivity in both research and teaching could conceivably become compromised.

In a recent *Washington Post* article called "Co-Opting America's Objectivity on Japan," I raised this question of propriety following a review of Karel van Wolferen's book, *The Enigma of Japanese Power*, by Nathaniel Thayer, who occupies the Nakasone chair at SAIS. No disclosure was made by the reviewer of his institutional relationship with either Nakasone or the LDP. When he suggested that the book "in its totality, fails," he expressed his fear that some Americans might somehow find it easier to bash Japan, having a new book to use as justification that Japan is, in fact, no democracy.

At a minimum, when America's leading academics or Japan specialists go public with their views, the public deserves to know who is paying which piper for what particular tune. Knowing the extent to which an expert's support stems from the Japanese establishment, they could more ably judge for themselves whether objectivity had been co-opted. This becomes critically important when much of America's knowledge about Japan must come from many experts who are, in effect, partly compensated by those very institutions they are responsible for analyzing and whose policies they must interpret or judge.

(These Americans, whose livelihoods have come to depend on Japanese funding and whose positions often support official Japanese policy, are known informally as members of the "Chrysanthemum Club," in honor of the traditional symbol of Japan's imperial family. Japanese members of Parliament wear their chrysanthemum lapel pins, in gold with maroon velvet petals, proudly. It has been suggested that American members of the club ought to do the same.)

In a *Journal of Japanese Studies* article called "The Future of Japanese Nationality," Kenneth Pyle, a political scientist at the University of Washington, summarized these various political developments and transposed them into four schools that crystallize recent trends rather nicely.

One group, which Pyle calls the Progressives, spans a broad middle-class spectrum and is distrustful of traditional state power. The "siege mentality" that has confronted Japan from outside in recent years has shown that the Progressives' ideal, a new world order based on peace and idealism, was not coming to pass and that Japan's national interests were being held hostage to superpower politics.

A second school, the Realists, opposes an unarmed, neutral Japan and sees Japan's national interests linked to direct defense relationships with liberal Western democracies. The Realists hold that Japan must accept more international responsibility commensurate with its growing economic influence in the world.

The Mercantilists, on the other hand, a third school, argue that Japan has been and always will be a merchant-middleman, taking advantage of commercial relationships and avoiding international politics—essentially what Japan has been doing for the past forty years—and that Japan should in effect become the world's supermerchant. If, as a merchant country, Japan cannot guarantee its own security, then the time will have come for it to become a samurai nation, joining America and the Soviet Union.

The Neo-Nationalists, the fourth school, hold that in the end Japan can rely only on Japan and the Japanese, that national interest is the only way to make sense of international anarchy. They embrace the economic nationalism of the Mercantilist school but argue that Japan should amend its peace constitution and exercise the nuclear option. Because military power is intimately commensurate with economic power, other nations would finally show Japan the respect it is due.

Critics, however, openly say that Neo-Nationalist policies will lead to the same fate that ultimately befell imperial Japan; namely, total defeat.

A common thread runs through all four Japanese schools of thought: that Japan should play a much more dominant role on the world stage than it has heretofore, an emerging role that most critics agree will be characteristic of a Japan that is both economically *and* politically self-confident.

The process has already begun. In 1988 Japan and the U.S. fought to become the dominant shareholding country in the Asian Development Bank, a regional institution in which they have traditionally held identical shares but for which Japan supplies the chief executive and virtually all the money for the soft loan program. During the Toronto summit that summer, when Japan flexed its diplomatic muscles to propose a new international debt plan, it deftly used the IMF as an intermediary as an end run around the U.S. Washington was caught off-guard, defensive and unprepared, a role it is clearly not accustomed to playing. Japan is lobbying hard to become the second-largest IMF shareholder.

In the Middle East and Central America, Japan has taken positions diametrically opposed to those of the U.S., siding more with Palestinian interests than with Israel (because of Japan's overwhelming dependence on imported oil, mostly from Arabian countries) and taking economic rather than political views on issues concerning the Americas.

One of Japan's most influential daily newspapers, the *Asahi Shimbun*, in a recent editorial titled "Let Go of America's Apron Strings," suggested that the "big tree called America" was now in decay and that Japan should strive to take a more independent tack. Lord Palmerston said it succinctly himself more than a century ago: a nation has neither permanent allies nor permanent enemies, but only permanent interests.

America's leadership in the postwar era has been characterized alternatively as decisive, individualistic, active, confrontational, loud, abrasive, contentious, ideological, Christian, results-oriented, and nothing if not direct. Japan's leadership is often characterized as passive, nonconfrontational, quiet, consensus-seeking, slow, persistent, thoughtful, persevering, nonideological but strongly self-centered, process-oriented, and nothing if not indirect.

This dichotomy was captured by a Tokyo taxi driver who ferried me back to my hotel one night at the end of a very long day. Japanese newspapers that evening were full of front-page stories that told, in not very friendly language, of American pressure on Japan to increase its defense spending and to eliminate its ban on the import of rice.

I asked my driver, in Japanese, as I nearly always do, what his background was. He said he was a retired chauffeur from a small Japanese securities company.

I asked him if he had seen the evening edition of the *Nihon Keizai Shimbun,* Japan's *Wall Street Journal,* which appears twice a day, Monday through Saturday, and once on Sunday.

He said he had. We talked about the front-page stories, and he had an informed comment to make about each of them, making for a discussion that would be difficult to replicate with a taxi driver in New York or Los Angeles.

I asked him what he thought of Washington's demands.

He looked at me in the rearview mirror.

"Onbu ni dakko ni kataguruma," he said with a wry smile. "Give them an inch, and they'll take a mile."

His point, of course, was that national roles were becoming reversed. An increasingly self-confident Japan would now be less willing to tolerate the willful demands of a declining America. That an ordinary Japanese cabdriver thought so was a sign perhaps that decay in the big tree called America was even more widespread than commonly believed.

SINGAPORE: THE MAN AND THE ISLAND

In virtually every country of the world you are required to complete a disembarkation card to facilitate clearance through immigration and customs. Singapore is no exception. Moments before arrival at Changi Airport, you will be handed a landing card that looks quite standard. It is white with black print.

On the back side, however, is a statement in bold, all-capital lettering in blood-red ink:

WARNING:

DEATH TO DRUG TRAFFICKERS

UNDER SINGAPORE LAW

Those eight words say more about Singapore than a month's worth of editorial columns and news articles. In short, Singapore *works,* and the reason it works has much to do with its authoritarian system of government, an impressive system that has been much maligned in the West but that has given its citizens the highest standard of living in Asia outside Japan, one of the cleanest capital cities in the world (both visually and as measured by the absence of corruption), and a virtually crime-free, drug-free environment.

Singapore, the Lion City, is almost inseparable from Singapore, the Man, and that man is Lee Kuan Yew, the nation's first prime minister, still in office. Known simply as "the PM," Lee was the third generation of his family to be born in Singapore, in 1923. The Lee family is of Hakka stock, northern Chinese known for their aggressiveness, their toughness, their courage. These traits give the PM both his reputation and his enemies.

In his time, Lee Kuan Yew was the most brilliant scholar in Singapore. Upon graduation from the Raffles Institution, principal source of the nation's elite leaders, he won a prize to enter Raffles College, forerunner of the National University of Singapore, where he studied economics when the outbreak of war prevented him from proceeding to England. He later attended Cambridge, where he was a brilliant student in law. "I speak to Harold Macmillan as an equal," he was fond of saying. "At Cambridge, I got two firsts and a star for distinction. Macmillan did not."

Lee Kuan Yew is an intellectual, a careful thinker, intense, often aloof, a hard worker, intolerant of sloppy work, occasionally arrogant, a brilliant orator, ruthless, and tough. About five feet ten inches tall and 160 pounds, the PM seldom reads for distraction, suffers no fools, believes in the greatest good for the greatest number, cleans his own shoes, and possesses a keen sense of history. He has attracted the best brains into government, believes that not everyone can make the grade but that everyone must make the effort, and hates poverty. He does not think the best way to provide for the poor is through charity, and he once said, "Give a man a gold coin, and he will spend it and ask for more." By his own admission, he would rather be respected than loved.

Local Singaporeans like to recount a popular story. When Lee Kuan Yew knocked at the gate of Heaven, St. Peter said, "Creation's purpose will not be fulfilled until Hell is transformed. Since you have put a God-forsaken place like Singapore right, you might try your hand with Hell." Lee did not hesitate and set off for the netherworld. Twenty-four hours later, Lucifer was knocking frantically at the Pearly Gates, panting and sweating profusely, begging St. Peter for refuge. "Where's Lee?" St. Peter asked. "My God!" Lucifer exclaimed. "Yesterday you sent him down, and he just took over. Now he expects even *me* to work!"

From a young age, Lee never saw himself in anything but a position of authority. But it was the Japanese, and indirectly the British, who pushed Lee Kuan Yew into politics. "They made me, and a whole generation like me, determined to work for freedom," he once said. "I decided that we should not be the pawns and playthings of foreign powers."

In his book *Lee Kuan Yew*, Alex Josey, British author and sometime biographer, wrote, "Lee is an emphatic realist. Some things are possible, others are not. He believes deeply in democratic methods, and his philosophy is built around the sanctity of law and the free will of the people: but there are times when he is reluctantly forced to take strict, even non-democratic measures against a minority of thugs, secret society gansters, and political opportunists—those who have placed themselves outside the rules."

Lee created the People's Action Party (PAP) in 1954, when Singapore was still a British colony. The PAP has been the ruling party since 1959, when Singapore achieved internal self-government, prior to joining the Federation of Malaya in 1963. It became a fully independent and sovereign state in 1965. The ruling party won all seats in all four general elections after 1968, and an opposition party member was elected for the first time in a by-election in 1981.

Typically the PAP generates between two-thirds and three-quarters of all votes cast, despite twenty opposition parties officially registered, under a British-style system whereby voting is secret and compulsory. Singapore's Parliament is unicameral, with seventy-nine members; it elects a president, a largely ceremonial role, who in turn appoints the PM and members of the cabinet (on the PM's advice).

Like Japan, Singapore is a single-party state, and the resulting political system is similarly authoritarian. This fact prompts much (and frequent) criticism from the (mostly) liberal Western press. But Western observers tend to forget that Singapore was born in a crucible of violent strikes, riots, and insurgency following the war, when the British empire was crumbling. Considerable efforts were made by the Communists, based in Malaya, to subvert Singapore and bring it under totalitarian rule. Initially they allied themselves with Lee in their opposition to British rule, but he turned increasingly against them as he realized their goals, not to mention their tactics, were incompatible with the kind of future he had in mind for Singapore.

"I remember, as a kid growing up here, there were strikes every day," Goh Geok Ling was telling me on a recent visit. "The bus drivers' union would strike one day, the postal workers the next, then the ship workers, the dockworkers, teachers, street cleaners, taxi drivers, police. *Every day.* It was total chaos. Lee Kuan Yew negotiated coolly with them, but he was tough and did a first-class job. Singapore wouldn't be where it is today without him."

Goh Geok Ling is a young Singaporean in his mid-forties, vice president for Asia-Pacific at Texas Instruments. He was educated at Raffles and then, as an engineer, in Sydney.

"The Western press often acts rather childishly," he said in response to a question about criticism from abroad. "The *Asian Wall Street Journal* was flat wrong about Sesdaq—our equivalent of your Nasdaq—being a dumping ground for losing companies. But they refused to print the PM's rebuttal. *Time* magazine said maybe they would print it, but six months later, so he slammed the door on them. Moral of the story: they should know better than to play games with him."

There are seven daily newspapers in Singapore, two that publish in English, three in Chinese, one each in Malay and Tamil. Nearly one hundred accredited correspondents representing more than sixty foreign news agencies, magazines, newspapers, and broadcasting companies are there. Despite all the brouhaha about the foreign press, publications critical of Singapore can be bought freely there, including biographies of the PM that are not altogether favorable.

In the early 1970s Lee shut down three newspapers that he accused of glamorizing Communism and stirring up communal and chauvinistic sentiments over language and culture. One of them, the *Singapore Herald,* was thought to have CIA backing and had been financed by the Chase Manhattan Bank. The PM forced the bank to call its loan, and when the paper kept going, he revoked its printing and publishing license.

"We will not tolerate the efforts of foreign agents to use local proxies to set up or buy into newspapers, not to make money but to make political gain by shaping opinions and attitudes," he said at the time. "Freedom of the press must be subordinate to the overriding needs of the integrity of Singapore and to the primacy of purpose of an elected government."

There is a fine line in any democratic country between freedom and responsibility, between individual rights and collective duty. Because of Singapore's origins in violence and chaos, and because of its efforts to create a truly multiracial society, the Lion City's leaders have staunchly defended the republic against tyranny and subversion from the outside. Authoritarianism, they said, could be blended with a benevolent, paternal Confucianism to achieve the goals of economic development desired by all.

The focus on authority, and on Lee Kuan Yew's ruthless determination to protect Singapore's hard-earned status as a democratic high-achiever, naturally leads skeptical Western observers to conclude that when the PM retires Singapore will collapse. But such criticism, it seems to me, fails to take into account Singapore's past history of violence and uncertainty, the overwhelming competence of the next generation of Singapore's leadership, or the nation's bright future based on that outstanding leadership.

The PM, at sixty-six, today plays what he calls a "goalkeeper" role, having delegated primary political responsibility to younger party leaders, including Deputy Prime Minister Goh Chok Tong and the PM's son, Brigadier-General Lee Hsien Loong (known as "BG"), minister for trade and industry and second minister for defense, to run the day-to-day affairs of state. They are foreign-educated, for the most part in England, extremely bright, and highly capable individuals. Singapore has bench strength of considerable talent.

Most people I spoke with on a recent visit, from taxi drivers to hotel clerks to foreign diplomats, felt that Deputy Prime Minister Goh would be next in line for succession. Born in 1941, an alumnus of Raffles and the National University of Singapore, Goh did graduate work in economics at Williams College. He drafted the national budget in 1979 and presented it to Parliament, coordinated the Second Industrial Revolution to upgrade the work force for high technology, and became deputy PM after the 1984 elections.

Both Lee Kuan Yew and Goh Chok Tong were out of the country during my last visit—the PM was attending Chiang Ching-kuo's funeral in Taiwan, the only head of a foreign government to do so, and his deputy was on a state visit to Indonesia—but I did see Lee's son in his spacious office high atop the Treasury Building overlooking Singapore harbor, the world's busiest port in terms of shipping tonnage, fourth-largest as a container handler, and third-largest oil refining center. I told him I had been impressed with what I had seen after an absence of ten years, especially the people's confidence in its next generation of highly educated, competent, and capable leadership.

"America has a large number of highly intelligent, well-educated, very capable university graduates, too," he said to me, "but they are mostly interested in doing their own thing. There appears to be a lack of leadership in the United States, which can lead to stasis. The system itself tends to undermine the country's will, by virtue of its preoccupation with the present, whether in business, as with quarterly results, or in politics, by virtue of elections every other year."

Born in 1952, Lee attended Cambridge, where he graduated with first-class honors in 1974, and holds a master's degree in public administration from Harvard. He has had a career described as spectacular. He is a quick thinker, articulate, and self-confident. He has the same high-cut forehead and wiry hair as the PM, a similar clipped British accent. He speaks authoritatively and confidently but also with precision. He is strong on facts, also not unlike his father. (Critics contend that his initials, BG, stand for "Baby God.")

"Singapore and the other NICs have a symbolic role to play in their greater group orientation, social harmony, and ability to work together toward common goals," he said. "America lacks this ability now and needs to find some way of developing it. Thirty years ago the U.S. would simply brush Asian comments aside, with the retort that 'America is the greatest country in the world.' You can't do that anymore. In 1947 the United States had 45 percent of the world's output; now it is below 25 percent and falling. Japan is increasing its share aggressively and pushing hard. Times have changed, and American leadership lags in perceiving that change."

Lee expanded on this theme when I saw him again in Washington in late spring 1989.

"Singapore's concern is that the U.S. may eventually tire of its role in the Asia-Pacific region," he was saying, "either for lack of resources or because of more pressing priorities elsewhere. Other colonial powers have come and gone—the French in Indochina, the Dutch in Indonesia, and the British in Malaysia and Singapore. Each of these colonial powers in its time appeared eternal and unshakable, yet eventually each had to leave as its national vitality ebbed and it could no longer sustain far-flung obligations. But unlike the French, the Dutch, or the British, U.S. strength does not derive from an empire; therefore, its presence should not be transient."

A similar perspective emerged from my conversation with Foreign Minister Wong Kan Seng in Singapore in early 1988. In his early forties, he was a manager with Hewlett-Packard for several years prior to being appointed minister of community development in 1985.

"We do not prioritize our relationships with foreign countries," he said to me. "We see all of them as important. We have diversified our trade, for example, so that about 12 percent is with Europe, 14 percent with Japan, and 19 percent with America. We don't want to have all our eggs in one basket."

Singapore has long viewed itself as the Switzerland of Asia. I asked him about America's slowness in perceiving its competitive decline.

"We can't hold ourselves up as an example for the United States, because we have learned many things from America, particularly technology, foreign assistance, and so on. We won't dare to say there are things you can learn from us. I think we should be judged by our actions and not be penalized just because we succeed. We are very small, and America is very large. Our cultures are totally different. But I don't think it is appropriate to say that the American system is best for all countries, including Singapore."

I later met with a British foreign service officer, a young man whose clear blue eyes and penetrating look reminded me very much of Robert Redford and who had characterized Singapore's influence as being much greater than its size would indicate. He felt the second-generation leaders were capable technocrats but lacked political finesse because they hadn't yet been seasoned. His view seemed to be based on an aura of past British dominance in Asia, an attitude that made it difficult to accept Asians on equal terms today.

A more typically Asian view was expressed when I met with Dr. Kernial Sandhu, executive director of Southeast Asia's leading think tank, the Institute of Southeast Asian Studies (ISEAS), in early 1988. The feelings of pride and respect—not only for past accomplishments but also for future possibilities—were unmistakably strong.

"Singapore's past history is colonial history," Sandhu told me as we sat in his office in Pasir Panjang. "Now Singapore and Malaysia are awake and no longer slumbering. Look what we can do when we're not under colonial control! The younger brother does even better when not propped up by his older sibling. Capitalism against Communism is a war of ideas, which is why the PM was right to appeal to man's reason and his logic, not just his emotions. Economic development is no longer just a Western club."

In early 1988 twenty-two people were arrested under the Internal Security Act for participating in an alleged Marxist conspiracy. Shortly after their arrest, twenty-one of them were released and then rearrested for having recanted statements that they had not been maltreated in jail. Some of them were being detained without trial.

In writing up the affair, the *Far Eastern Economic Review*, a weekly magazine based in Hong Kong, was accused by the Singapore government of not checking its sources and failing to confirm the accuracy of its account. (At least one of its stories contained statements by a "witness" who had not been physically present at a key meeting, so the government's accusations were not without basis in fact.) Instead of printing a correction, the *Review* took on Lee Kuan Yew. It should have known better. The PM moved to restrict the magazine's circulation, and it later decided to pull out; the conflict between Lee and the magazine drags on.

Not long afterward, an American diplomat, E. Mason Hendrickson, a first secretary at the U.S. Embassy, was accused by the government of meddling in Singapore's internal affairs by encouraging the lawyer for the detainees, fifty-nine-year-old Francis Seow, to run as an opposition candidate against the PAP. Hendrickson, who denied the accusations, was nonetheless expelled from the country, and the U.S. retaliated by removing a Singaporean diplomat from Washington. For his involvement with Hendrickson, Seow was detained for seventy-two days, fined, and released.

Westerners unfamiliar with the details of Singapore's history fail to appreciate, as Goh Geok Ling knows only too well, how covert subversion can quickly lead to violence. Singapore has never accepted the American definition of a "free and unrestricted press," which in Washington means a press free to publish or not publish what it chooses, however irresponsible or biased the press's actions may seem to be.

The Singapore government has always maintained a right of rebuttal to irresponsible or biased reporting, because when reporting has been left to the marketplace to determine its accuracy, it has frequently led to civil unrest and riots. Given Singapore's impressive political achievements and outstanding economic performance over the past thirty years, my own sense is that Lee Kuan Yew and the new generation of competent leaders behind him are more capable of judging what is in the Lion City's best interests than newspaper and magazine editors sitting half a world away. After all, Singapore is no continental power, insulated on both sides by the world's largest oceans.

"Consumed by fear," one Western account of the incidents read, "the PM has become like an enraged father devouring his brightest children." Highly overdrawn, I thought, but typical of a Western press that enjoys criticizing this island republic, taunting its capable political leadership, ignoring its economic achievements, and painting a rather distorted picture of emotional repression. Vigilance and restraint have been essential ingredients in Singapore's success, and those who refuse to take note of these factors are either calculating or underinformed.

The issues of individual rights versus collective duty tugged at my consciousness as I waited, at midday, near the national university, in the peak of lunch hour traffic, for a taxi to take me back downtown. Even in early February the tropical heat and humidity were oppressive, and there was a paucity of empty cabs.

At the next red light, embarrassingly late and moving quickly between stopped cars, I approached a taxi with passenger and tapped lightly on the window.

The driver rolled the window down, and I hurriedly explained my predicament. He motioned for me to get in.

Apologizing, I introduced myself to the passenger, who said he was Singaporean, a middle-aged importer of metals and ores. He brushed my apology aside with a wave of his hand, and we spoke for a few minutes about our respective business interests.

"I've lived in Australia, and I've traveled in Europe and America," he said to me, looking out the window. "Two generations ago, the yellow peril was Chinese, then a generation ago it became the 'Dirty Jap' or the 'Dirty Nip.' Now 60 percent of Australian trade is with Japan, and they've become simply 'the Japanese,' all in less than thirty years. I've watched it happen."

He turned and eyed me carefully.

"Maybe the white man does it because he's afraid," he said. "He is, after all, in the minority. In my younger years, with all the violence here, I was tempted to move away. But no longer. This is my home. We have created something from nothing."

I noticed the cabdriver nodding as the passenger spoke. The National Trade Union Congress sign attached to his visor boasted of the driver's

"3-s" productivity plan: social responsibility, service, and skill—Singapore's motto in microcosm.

For all its accomplishments, it seemed to me, Singapore deserved better in terms of the esteem in which it was held by the outside world. It has been maligned as a technocracy, an uptight fiefdom, and a nation without a soul. My sense was that its influence would, in time, extend well beyond its size, that the second generation of political leaders who were poised, waiting to take Singapore into the twenty-first century, had a better grasp of the challenges to their future than they were being given credit for.

Southeast Asia's own stability, its economic growth, and its future are significantly linked to Singapore, one of America's staunchest allies in the global battle to protect freedom, liberty, and justice from continuing attack by the forces of totalitarianism. The Lion City is a beacon of brightness in a sea of shifting political uncertainty.

Singaporeans are survivors. That their discipline, their energy, and the authoritarian political system that anchors their achievements are not better appreciated in the West says volumes about the inability of Westerners to understand Asia.

7

THE DELICATE SEEDS OF DEMOCRACY

Until this century, the vast communities of Asia were communities of want and ignorance. The great majority of its people were illiterate and lived in poverty. Throughout their history, they had never known democracy or dreamed of civil liberties. The masses knew government only as taxes and police. Even the educated had no word for "liberty" in Chinese [or for "freedom" or "justice" in Japanese]. Hence the peculiar difficulties of Eastern peoples today. What they are seeking to change, or are being forced to change, is not merely a form of government, but a whole way of life.

Herbert Muller, *The Loom of History*

Based on the evidence, it seems safe to say that the traditional one-party political systems of Japan and Singapore have been relatively insulated from the cultural shocks that other East Asian countries have, almost without exception, experienced during the past few years. The power of Japan's bureaucracy and the deep strengths of Singapore's national leadership have given these two nations a pervasive sense of stability and a vigilant self-assurance that, with their "softer" authoritarian heritage, have helped buffer them from these external shocks.

Not so Hong Kong, Korea, Taiwan, or the Philippines. In Britain's last overseas colony all eyes have turned to 1997 and Hong Kong's reversion to China. In Korea, labor unrest and student riots in 1987 unseated one government, changed the nature of its successor, and put continued pressure on the process of policy formulation. Following the death in early 1988 of Premier Chiang Ching-kuo, the generalissimo's son and the Nationalists' last link to the mainland, Taiwan's political system has undergone dramatic liberalization under Lee Teng-hui, the first native Taiwanese to head his country. And in early 1986 Ferdinand

Marcos was overthrown in Manila by the now-famous Yellow Revolution of Corazon Aquino, widow of martyred husband Ninoy, an event that should perhaps be viewed not as a revolution but as the restoration of the old order.

The world was witnessing the emergence of new forms of democratic expression in East Asia. Were the foundations of economic success now strong enough to permit them? Or was the very basis of East Asia's stunning economic growth now coming under attack, with potentially grave consequences for the vaunted demonstration effect of turbo-charged capitalism?

HONG KONG: ONE COUNTRY, TWO SYSTEMS

On September 26, 1984, Prime Minister Margaret Thatcher of the United Kingdom and Premier Deng Xiaoping of the People's Republic of China signed a detailed, forty-six-page agreement spelling out the terms and conditions under which Britain's last overseas colony would revert to China on July 1, 1997. The Sino-British Accord turned Hong Kong into a special administrative region (SAR), ensuring, on paper at least, the preservation of Hong Kong's territorial status as a capitalist enclave for a period of fifty years following reversion.

In a place where only former Chinese emperors are allowed to congregate, Mao Zedong must have rubbed his hands in glee. After more than a century of occupation by the dreaded barbarians, Hong Kong, Kowloon, and the New Territories would revert to their rightful owners, the Chinese people, from whom they had been stolen unlawfully.

The basic concept under which the joint accord was conceived had been formulated years earlier by Deng Xiaoping in a moment of thoughtful reflection: devise a plan whereby two competing economic systems, Communist and capitalist, could coexist with one overarching framework of Chinese politics. His selection of terms for this phenomenon: one country, two systems.

Britain knew it would sooner or later have to hand the colony back to China, because after 1982, land leases in Hong Kong, the standard length of which was fifteen years, began to nibble into the post-1997 period, so the basic problem was how to make reversion palatable to London. Deng's solution paved the way. But while there may have been acceptance followed by euphoria in Whitehall, nobody stopped to ask the 5.5 million people of Hong Kong what *they* thought about the prospects of living in a tiny capitalist enclave controlled by an enormous

Communist country. Well, they weren't terribly keen about the idea. For those who had fled the mainland to get out from under a Communist system to begin with, the thought of being brought back under the control of that system again was not especially pleasant.

Britain also knew the preservation of Hong Kong's independent status would be a problem, so Margaret Thatcher's emissaries persuaded the Chinese to permit a high degree of autonomy for Hong Kong, guaranteed under a "Basic Law" (in essence, a constitution) and protected by its own government and legislature.

In a concluding annex to the accord, the Chinese government elaborated on its basic policies regarding Hong Kong. They confirmed that socialist policies applicable to the rest of China would not be extended to Hong Kong and pledged that Hong Kong's capitalist system and lifestyle would be unchanged for fifty years. The British flag would come down, and the Chinese flag would go up, but Hong Kong could still fly its own flag, if it so desired, and join international organizations under the name "Hong Kong, China." The Chinese also agreed that the new Hong Kong government and legislature would consist of local inhabitants, that the governing officials would be selected by election or through local consultations under appointment by Beijing, and that the local legislature "will be elected."

If ever there were a loose thread that could cause the whole fabric of the joint accord to unravel, it was elections. The British, with a 300-year history of parliamentary democracy, came away with one perception, and the Chinese, with a view of elections determined by whether one happens to be on the Central Committee of the Communist party of China, came away with quite another. And the people of Hong Kong, who had spent the better part of their lives building their economic livelihood with the help of incentives created by an authoritarian colonial government in which they had had very little say, came away with still another, based more on the British model than the Chinese. Otherwise, how could the assurances written into the accord be guaranteed?

A brief visit to a small, out-of-the-way office at 6 Shelter Street in Causeway Bay would have provided the answer. This is where any resident of Hong Kong must come to receive a "Certificate of No Criminal Conviction," a small slip of paper required by some forty-five countries that regularly receive requests for permanent visas. The wealthy of Hong Kong, those with high levels of education, experience, and net worth, had always believed in a strong sense of geographical diversification, investing in real estate overseas, opening bank accounts, and establishing alternate residences. Prior to execution of the joint accord in 1984, applications for the Certificate of No Criminal Conviction ran about 20,000 a year. In 1985 nearly 30,000 were issued. In 1986 there were more than 35,000. In 1987 the total was more than 50,000. Now the ordinary people of Hong Kong were voting, all right, but their ballot was an exit permit.

Because the wealthy weren't the people forming long lines in Causeway Bay. Those in the queues were office clerks, bank tellers, accountants, lawyers, civil servants, financial analysts, and teachers—for the first time Hong Kong was experiencing an exodus of its well-trained professional elite. Their assets were modest. They would not be boat people when they moved overseas; they would be solid contributors to the broad middle class. Any country would be lucky to have them, and America was getting its fair share.

Within the structure of the Hong Kong government, one man is known as "Mr. 1997." His name is Barrie Wiggham, and he is a career civil servant with the title of secretary for general duties, a rank equal to that of other senior posts (such as finance or education). He is responsible for coordinating all official input from Hong Kong to London and Beijing, and I met with him on my last visit to the colony. A sincere man, and severely overtaxed, he impressed me as trying to do his best in a situation that had become somewhat awkward.

"If we have elections, then Britain is perceived to be in control," he was saying to me. "But if no elections are held, then China appears to be in control. Our own surveys show people are not that interested in elections. There is so much else going on, whatever else you read—we are setting up district boards, financial liaison groups, landlord-tenant committees, a land use council, and a new legislative council, two-thirds of whose members are already selected through indirect elections and the rest appointed by the governor."

Hong Kong's 5.5 million people are governed principally by an executive council, which is comprised of the chief secretary, the commander of British forces, the financial secretary, and the attorney general, plus the governor himself, who is, of course, appointed by the queen. The Legislative Council (known as Legco), all of whose fifty-six members were previously appointed by the governor, has as its primary function the passage of legislation, which becomes law if the governor so consents. It has twenty-two appointed members, twenty-four members "elected" indirectly by functional constituencies (such as professional groups), and ten permanent members, including the governor.

"The joint declaration says that the legislature shall be determined by elections," Wiggham went on, "though it doesn't specify whether direct or indirect, and there are strong differences of opinion between London and Beijing as to interpretation and timing."

The surveys to which Wiggham referred had been criticized in the local press for having questions either formulated unclearly or stated in too complex and ambiguous a manner. A single, simple, uncomplicated question about elections was never posed. Confusion contributed to the resulting uncertainty and low response rate, which prompted the government to interpret the questionnaire results as showing a lack of interest.

The Basic Law, which will be Hong Kong's mini-constitution, is currently under negotiation by a drafting committee of fifty-nine people, twenty-three of whom are from Hong Kong. Unlike the joint accord, which had an authorized version in both English and Chinese, the Basic Law will have an official version in Chinese only, when it is completed in 1990, even though the official language of Hong Kong is English. (The dialect spoken in Beijing is Mandarin; in Hong Kong it is Cantonese. The two are not compatible.)

Martin Lee, a Hong Kong lawyer, member of Legco, and on the Basic Law drafting committee, was not in the colony on my last visit in early 1988. I managed to catch up with him some weeks later in San Francisco, where he presented a paper at a conference I was attending.

Lee had visited London earlier as leader of a group called the Delegation for Democracy in Hong Kong, to persuade members of Parliament to introduce direct elections for the Legislative Council as soon as possible. His argument was based on the premise that the sooner Legco had direct elections, the greater would be Hong Kong's opportunity to develop a more workable democratic process by 1997. He engaged in a lengthy debate with Britain's foreign minister, Sir Geoffrey Howe, accusing the British government of trying to sell the joint accord *without* elections. (In a white paper issued early in 1988 the Hong Kong government ducked the issue, postponing elections to 1991 on the grounds that the drafting committee had to complete the Basic Law first.)

"The choice was whether to introduce elections in 1988," Lee was telling me during a break in the conference proceedings, "which we felt the people of Hong Kong preferred, or in 1991, which the Chinese would prefer. By introducing elections sooner, it would not only give Hong Kong more practice in representative government, and in developing more seasoned political leadership, it would also have a positive influence on the drafting of the Basic Law."

By 1991, of course, the Basic Law will have been drafted and approved, and elections could be meaningless if that law creates a truncated legislature. Everything comes back full circle to the definition of elections. The Chinese, who have said they are not opposed to elections, and mentioned them specifically in their annex to the joint accord, are thinking like a good Central Committee, not like parliamentarians in Whitehall.

"Many who are not familiar with Hong Kong," Lee went on, "have asked why the people of Hong Kong, which has never been democratic in its 140-year existence, should care about democracy now. That is very simple. It is not the Hong Kong colonial government that has protected the freedom of the people; it is the democratically elected *British* government that has done so. But with such a momentous change coming in 1997, can we still entrust the protection of our freedom and rights to a political system that operates under the control of the Communist party?"

To many, especially the increasing numbers of professional people who are voting with their visas, this question raises the real specter of a ghost town a decade from now. The British can leave with a clear conscience, having dotted their *i*s and crossed their *t*s, as they were taught to do at Oxford and Cambridge, and having handed the Chinese a deep-water harbor but none of the skilled professional talent they will need to continue the capitalist miracle or to maintain the system from which China has historically gleaned nearly half its foreign exchange earnings.

"Well, the British can certainly benefit from all the flak Martin Lee is raising," Frank Ching said to me over coffee one morning when I was last in Hong Kong. "At least he'll serve the purpose of raising consciousness on both sides, British and Chinese."

Frank Ching is American-educated and the author of a recent book on China. A resident of Hong Kong now, and writing for an Australian paper, he has worked in Beijing and helped draft the position paper for the Delegation for Democracy.

"According to China, Britain's responsibility is to *administer* Hong Kong up to 1997, not institute or engineer political reforms," he explained. "When the issue of elections was debated in Parliament in late 1984, and there were no objections from China, everybody thought the issue was only a question of time."

By virtue of remaining silent on the concept, China had contributed to the perception, regardless of the facts, that it did not object. In politics, Mark Twain once said, perception is everything.

"What is more to the point is that all those who have been playing the game should now ask why they have done so and why they have accepted the joint accord," wrote Margaret Ng, a columnist for the *South China Morning Post,* one of Hong Kong's major English dailies. "If the reason was because they believed this was the best way to protect the interests of Hong Kong, they must acknowledge that they were mistaken. They have trusted where they should have been mistrustful, and cooperated where they should have opposed."

George Hicks is a native Australian businessman and a longtime resident of Hong Kong. He looks at Hong Kong's emerging political problems from the perspective of a trained economist and comes away with an equally pessimistic view.

"The threat ordinary businessmen sense is a heavy-handed intrusion by the Chinese in the day-to-day affairs of their business," he told me one evening during dinner. "So despite the best intentions of Beijing to let Hong Kong function as an autonomous, independent entity—a special administrative region in the language of the joint accord—reality would hold that no such thing is possible."

A similar point was made by a Hong Kong–born Chinese general manager of a U.S. manufacturing plant in the Yuen Long industrial estate.

"After 1997," he said to me, "the real problem will be in the way business is done here. There will be more red tape, the pace will be considerably less brisk, corruption will increase, there will be more vagueness and indirection, and the process can't help but be more cumbersome because the bureaucracy will be heavier. After 1997 you won't be able to come here with a blank check, the way I did, and set up a business practically overnight."

T. L. Tsim would agree. Young and energetic, he is director of the Chinese University Press in Hong Kong.

"The Hong Kong government is trying to sell us down the river," he was telling me. "They forget that most of Hong Kong was built by refugees who came out of China in the late forties and early fifties. *We*, the people of Hong Kong, the cream of Chinese society, made this place what it is. So the Hong Kong government, and their peers in London, have to paint a rosy picture of the future in order to sell the package."

We talked for a while about China and its intentions for Hong Kong.

Tsim smiled, an easy but serious smile.

"China is like Errol Flynn," he said. "You always know where you stand, because he will always let you down. There are certain innate cultural factors about China you have to keep in mind: it is antidevelopmental, antichange, antiprogress, *anti*–everything Hong Kong stands for."

In the early fifties, Tsim recounted, there were the three antis in China—antibureaucracy, anticorruption, antirightism—followed by the Great Leap Forward, then the Hundred Flowers Campaign, then the Cultural Revolution, and now the Four Modernizations. A century ago, in the 1860s, during the T'ung-chih Restoration, in the late Manchu dynasty, there was the Self-Strengthening Movement, at the time Japan had embarked on the Meiji Restoration. Japan succeeded where China has failed.

In the 1980s, of course, calls for more democracy from below have been met with antidemocracy responses from those in power above. In 1979 free expression was labeled "unstabilizing" and was repressed; in 1983 it was called "spiritual pollution"; and in 1987, as posters went up on Democracy Wall in Beijing, it was denounced as "bourgeois liberalism" and again snuffed out. China's top leadership has always somehow seemed cynical and distrustful, blind to change.

Still, many American specialists were arguing that China had more to lose than to gain by not permitting Hong Kong to remain autonomous and independent. China would not only lose foreign exchange but also a key intelligence center, a valuable window on the world.

Tsim shook his head.

"Your State Department people do not view problems in isolation," he said. "Hong Kong is just a part of Asia, and America's Asian policy is driven by the Soviets and the Chinese. The cornerstone of Soviet policy is to keep China Communist and to keep the Chinese weak, to protect the Soviets' own flank and prevent China from becoming more of a threat than it is. Therefore, U.S. policy stems from a contrarian view, to strengthen China, make the Chinese more open, and encourage their efforts at modernization, to counter the Russians. Hong Kong is simply a pawn in this whole process. One country, two systems? No way."

James So disagreed. So is secretary of transport in the Hong Kong government and one of its highest-ranking officials. He ticked off a laundry list of statistics in an attempt to show that China had more to lose than to gain by choking off Hong Kong.

"China has to be practical and pragmatic, it seems to me," he said, drawing on a small pipe. "What does Beijing have to gain by strangling this place? Ideologically, they might gain 5½ million adherents to Communism, but what would they lose? The whole professional class, which is already nervous and uncertain, their foreign exchange earnings, their major entrepôt for trade, access to new technology and new ideas, a primary listening post—Hong Kong is the spy capital of Asia. How will they replace all that?"

Some reports suggest Shanghai might become the Hong Kong of China's future if China really closes the door here.

"Shanghai can't even come close," he said with a chuckle. "They have a perennial problem with silt from the Yangtze River floods. That's why Beijing is investing so heavily here. The new Bank of China building, the proposed Eastern Harbor Tunnel Crossing, Tait's Cairn Tunnel. Anything can happen, of course, but the best way to perpetuate your self-interest is not to strangle the golden goose. That would hurt China far more than it would the rest of the world. One country, two systems? They'll make it work."

If China did cut off its nose to spite its face, it wouldn't be the first time. The argument that China will continue to learn from Hong Kong and use it to strengthen its international presence in the world was weakened, it seemed to me, by other evidence of the recent past. The Bank of China, China's central bank and the second-largest financial institution in Hong Kong after the Hong Kong and Shanghai Banking Corporation, is distinctly down-market. Its service is cumbersome and of lower quality, its attitude toward customers is, in the words of one longtime account holder, "abysmal," and it places far more emphasis on bureaucratic form than on business substance.

"Local pop songs and soap operas are already beginning to appear with the 1997 theme in their lyrics," Leo Goodstadt was telling me as we walked along the harbor near the Star Ferry. "And the theme is consistently a sad one, pining about the loss of freedom and constraints on travel, which are sure to come."

Goodstadt had been deputy editor of the *Far Eastern Economic Review* years earlier, when I lived in Hong Kong, and was now the host of a popular TV talk show. We had kept in touch over the years, and his insights into the Chinese mind had always been perceptive and thoughtful.

"I look at China's future role here in terms of the Chinese potential for interference," he said, rubbing a palm over his balding head. "Beijing claims that Hong Kong will welcome its 'liberation from colonialism' and will be grateful for China's 'interference.' But since Beijing's definitions of freedom and liberty and democracy are obviously different from traditional Western concepts, what constitutes interference to us is of course not interference to them; it's merely the normal functioning of their government. But make no mistake, the 'one country, two systems' concept is impossible. In addition to their multilayered bureaucracy, the poor customer service, the lack of responsiveness, and all the red tape, the Chinese will also want to restructure the schools and reteach Chinese history. Things will be very different here."

One is staggered by the potential for change by the Chinese once they take over. Streets will have to be renamed, for a start. Queen's Road Central, Connaught Road, and Lower Albert don't quite stir Chinese emotions. New stamps will have to be issued. A new flag will have to be designed. Eventually a new passport will have to come into being.

"Well, I'm staying," a Chinese friend told me over dim sum in Kowloon. "I've been offered a teaching position in the United States, but I declined. This is my home. I love it here. I have two children, seven and five, and this is their home, too. My wife is actively involved in the Presbyterian Church, and we are very happy here. Many of my professional friends are leaving, but I plan to stay. We Hong Kong Chinese are nothing if not adaptable. We've done it before, and we'll do it again."

I asked him about perception in politics, and he smiled.

"The fact is, it's more than perception," he said. "The Hong Kong people feel cheated by their government, and by the British, who promised a measure of direct representation in the legislature here *before* 1997. It now looks as if that promise will not be fulfilled. So you see more and more professionals leaving the colony, because they know from past experience that China will be unable to keep its hands off. Beijing simply doesn't understand what makes this place tick. In its view, Hong Kong will become a part of China—the reunification part— so why should the Chinese treat Hong Kong any differently from the way they treat the rest of China?"

The taxi driver, a young woman who lived in the New Territories, divorced with one child in elementary school, downshifted and accelerated as we exited the jammed Cross-Harbor Tunnel en route to Kai Tak airport for my flight to Seoul.

"I have no passport," she said, looking at me through narrowed eyes in her rearview mirror. "Only a Hong Kong Identity Card, which says I belong here. And my brother is coming back. He went to Manila last year to open a retail business there, but he says it's terrible. He misses Hong Kong."

We passed by the outskirts of the Tsim Sha Tsui district, its new hotels towering majestically over the roadway, then through the tight streets of neighboring To Kwa Wan, where the small vans and lorries were picking up load after load of clothing and toys from packed warehouses. I was reminded of the insight by Richard Hughes in *Hong Kong: Borrowed Place, Borrowed Time.*

"If Hong Kong lives out its legal term as a colony," he wrote nearly thirty years ago, "the world of that distant era will have been so transformed that Hong Kong's fate and influence will be of even less importance than it is today. There will be no ghost city of rusting skyscrapers, no vacant tenements, no matter whether the East Wind is prevailing over the West Wind or the other way about. Even if capital is progressively and furtively withdrawn there will always be traffic congestion inside that Hong Kong harbour tunnel."

Perhaps. But I couldn't help thinking that Hong Kong's present system of benevolent authoritarianism is being jiggled, and nobody really knows what the outcome will be. Somehow a ghost town seems more likely than continued traffic congestion.

It was not until late spring 1989 that democracy's coals were really stoked in Hong Kong. While previous public demonstrations for democratic elections in the colony drew perhaps a few hundred active participants, *half a million*—nearly 10 percent of the population—

jammed Hong Kong's central business district in support of democracy when a million clamoring demonstrators clogged Tiananmen Square in Beijing calling for more political freedom in China. The local Hang Seng stock index lost 22 percent of its value in a single day as a result.

"If they won't listen to the wishes of their own people now," Martin Lee said, referring to the Chinese Communist political elite, "they certainly won't listen to the wishes of Hong Kong's people in 1997." There has been amazingly little focus in the outside world on this unfolding drama, which could soon lead to a massive exodus of highly talented, experienced, and well-educated people by the planeload. America, if it is smart, will open its doors to them. They will be America's pioneers of the twenty-first century, as they settle in, with their professional skills and Confucian discipline, to train their offspring in the new traditions of the information age. America will need them. All of them.

KOREA AND TAIWAN: "HARD" AUTHORITARIANISM

Back in December 1987, when Korea held its last presidential election, a high-ranking official in the Ministry of Foreign Affairs confided to me that, whatever the outcome, there was the potential for still more unrest. "If Roh Tae-woo wins," he said with a sigh, "the students will revolt. If Kim Young-sam wins, business will revolt. And if Kim Dae-jung wins, the army will revolt. It's almost a no-win situation."

As it turned out, Roh Tae-woo, the candidate of the government's Democratic Justice Party, won the presidency, and, true to form, students took to the streets to protest the usual litany of ballot-box stuffing and voter registration fraud. But President Roh's primary advantage had been the failure of the opposition to unite behind a single candidate. Both Kim Dae-jung, who had spent many years in exile in the U.S. and under house arrest in his own country, and Kim Young-sam, who rose to a position of leadership in the Reunification Democratic Party in Kim Dae-jung's absence, fought throughout 1987 to take control of the RDP but never achieved unity of purpose. So Kim Dae-jung split off and formed his own Party for Peace and Democracy, virtually assuring Roh of victory.

The election itself was a precedent. For the first time in postwar history Korea's political succession had been determined democratically and, the street demonstrations and tear gas notwithstanding, relatively peacefully.

In 1986 and 1987, two major events, one positive and one negative, planted the seeds of rapid political development in Korea and spawned a more definitive process of democratization.

The positive event was the selection of Seoul as the site for the 1988 Olympics, creating a "window of opportunity" for protest against continuation of the tough, authoritarian political system. Korea could risk losing the Olympics if an internationally embarrassing event, such as the government's violent suppression of democratic protest, occurred.

The negative event was former president Chun's callous decision to postpone a national referendum on Korea's Constitution until after the Olympics. This produced the unintentional effect of opening that window of opportunity, with highly publicized violent protest. For the first time middle-class merchants and striking workers from the big *chaebol* joined with the traditionally protest-prone students and took to the streets. More tear gas reportedly was used by Korean police during the month of June 1987 than in the previous twelve months combined.

Roh Tae-woo wisely acceded to the opposition's demands for resumption of the constitutional referendum before the Olympics, eliminated police surveillance of opposition candidates, and promised an investigation of public grievances, most of which dealt with harsh police treatment of student demonstrators during the Kwangju uprising in 1980. His tactics were a stunning success. The revolts and the labor unrest subsided, the constitutional referendum was held on schedule, in November, and the presidential elections took place the following month.

By the spring of 1988, when I next visited Seoul, elections for the National Assembly, Korea's legislature, were scheduled, and the same cynical predictions of government manipulation could be heard in idle conversation with businessmen and read in the daily press. In fact, the day before the elections, the government-owned Mutual Broadcasting Company, MBC-TV, announced computer-simulated results of the election, showing the Democratic Justice Party victorious with a majority of the votes cast, adding fuel to the cynical fire and prompting critical outbursts from the opposition.

The actual results of the National Assembly elections, however, confounded the cynics and surprised everyone, not least the government party itself, whose candidates did *not* win a majority but only 125 of the 299 seats contested. Kim Dae-jung's Party for Peace and Democracy won seventy seats, Kim Young-sam's Reunification Democratic Party won fifty-nine, and the New Republican Democratic Party under Kim Jong-pil won thirty-five.

"You see, we just *love* democracy," B. S. Kang was telling me as we sat in a quiet, out-of-the-way Seoul restaurant not long after the National Assembly elections. Kang is managing director of the Korean Press Center and an unusually thoughtful observer of the Korean political scene. A lean, trim man in his late forties, he was educated at Waseda University, one of Japan's elite private schools, and spent many years at the Korean Embassy in Tokyo. His Japanese is flawless, which creates a great demand for his talents as an official translator when Japan's VIPs visit Seoul.

"We're back to regionalism now," he said, flashing his wry smile. "This is a cultural problem, which goes way back in Korean history. The Cholla, Koryo, and Yi dynasties were all characterized by a strong sense of regionalism. It dominates Korean politics the way factionalism dominates politics in Japan."

I asked him which of the major parties represented Korea's national interests.

He smiled and shook his head.

"That's a good question," he said. "None of them does, really. Since they all work on behalf of their regions, this poses a potential problem. And since our bureaucracy is not as strong as Japan's, it can't march so easily to its own drummer, so cabinet politics may be the name of the game, given the outcome of the elections."

This point was confirmed in a subsequent discussion I had with a senior Western diplomat in Seoul, who agreed with the conventional assessment that Korea seemed to be heading toward a more mature process of democratization.

"Issues that could have been sacrificed in the past by the Korean government, with little pain, may now have to be surrendered with significant pain in the future," he told me. "The new political process will mean that much will have to be done in public now that was done secretly earlier, behind closed doors, and that could not only slow things down, but also render the government an even bigger target for anti-American sentiment."

There are perhaps two key points to remember in assessing Korean political developments over the past thirty years. First, Korea has essentially been governed by martial law throughout the entire period, but with its leaders dressed in mufti rather than in uniform. Second,

Korea could never have cloned its capitalist developmental state and achieved the rates of economic hyper-growth that ultimately legitimized its government *without* the enforced stability provided by its authoritarian regime.

Korea's disproportionate focus on economic growth, which was unavoidable given its stagnation in the 1950s, meant that the nation's other developmental goals—social and political—had to be secondary, and remain relatively neglected, unlike the broader social and political gains arguably made by Japan in its softer system.

Korean politics, it seemed to me, being less developed and consequently less mature than Korean business, would in all likelihood become comparatively unpredictable in the future; certainly, the state of tension between the two would become more apparent. President Roh, being more moderate than his unpopular and more militaristic predecessor, Chun, does not appear to be as forceful or as decisive as previous leaders. But he cannot afford to be as forceful and decisive, since he has to take into account a broader array of more pluralistic issues and be responsive to a larger constituency, now that Korea has gone beyond economic catch-up and achieved its stunning economic success.

But while a return, for any extended period of time, to the harder, more rigid authoritarian forms of the past appears unlikely, Roh is more vulnerable than his predecessors, especially with less than majority control of the National Assembly. Indications for the short term, based on a precarious harmony among the three major parties, appear for the time being to be good, although that harmony could unravel if external pressures on the system prove to be too much, either from the North, in terms of irrational, stepped-up terrorist tactics, or from the U.S., in terms of untimely (and unwise) efforts to push Korea to open its markets further.

Washington's market-opening efforts have so far not only failed to achieve substantive results; they have also fanned the flames of considerable anti-American sentiment in Korea, stemming from the continued presence of nearly 50,000 American troops there. Korea's progress toward political liberalization has been prompted by internal developments—primarily the discontent of two minorities, students and labor, which have pressed, to date successfully, for less rigidity in the system.

Western observers have been quick to suggest that democratization in Korea is a direct consequence of economic growth. One experienced analyst noted that "economic growth *promotes* democracy," and the *Wall Street Journal* commented that "you can't sustain economic growth over the long run without relaxing political restrictions." But these views assume a cause-effect relationship that is by no means so obvious. Continued external pressure from the Americans, in their attempts to prevent Korea from becoming another Japan, could well sow the seeds of serious domestic unrest that could conceivably undermine the fragile foundation of the country's new political process and prompt the military to enter again to resume authoritarian control.

In Korea there is clearly more concern now for equity, and not just growth, reflected in four major areas: regional equity, whereby other regions, and not just Seoul, benefit from subsequent economic growth; credit equity, meaning access to financial resources by small and medium-sized businesses; gender equity, to advance the gains of women in the society; and social service equity, through which broader social gains such as insurance and old-age pensions can be achieved.

Tension is likely to increase, also in four sectors, as a practical consequence of this wider concern for equity. There will be tension between the process of centralization in Seoul and that of decentralization in the regions; tension between the *chaebol* and government, as the big conglomerates seek to maintain their privileged position; tension between the military and the civilian sectors, depending on how well the public process of political problem solving ensues; and tension between internal policies, such as those for social development, and those that respond to external pressures, such as foreign affairs and defense. The political parties, because of the changing nature of Korean political power, will likely play a more active role in policy formulation, too, in competition with the bureaucracy.

Students, especially those who are prone to demonstrate at the drop of a hat, and especially those among them who comprise the radical core, are likely to remain a major problem for Korea. Their violent activism, as we know, has deep roots in Korean history. Having settled the immediate issues of the constitutional referendum and elections, the radical leadership next pressed the issue of reunification, taking to the streets with hard hats and firebombs in an attempt to march to the thirty-eighth parallel. (One Korean friend remarked to me, informally, that she felt the students were in danger of becoming professional rioters.)

Korea has achieved its highest rates of economic growth during periods of rigid, or "hard," authoritarian political rule. The economy can probably continue to grow faster than its Western rivals (and possibly faster than Japan), even if it has to sacrifice a few points on the hypergrowth scale while it yields to the various issues of equity during the process of democratization. But as Chalmers Johnson recently said to me, "the inability of the opposition to unite behind principles rather than personalities, and the extreme regionalism displayed in the elections, suggest that democracy may only be a slogan for them. If the Korean National Assembly, like the Japanese Diet, is unable to hold Korea's formidable bureaucracy accountable, Korean democracy may prove to be only formal and empty. The best thing going for democracy there is that the people themselves were involved in its creation and have a stake in its survival."

Such has not been the case in Taiwan, where the decision to liberalize was made solely by the authoritarian regime itself, beginning in July 1987 with the lifting of martial law by the late premier Chiang Ching-kuo, the head of Taiwan's only officially recognized political party, the Kuomintang (KMT). That was a decision of no mean consequence. I have vivid memories, from my earliest visits to Taipei in the late 1960s, of armed soldiers standing on virtually every street corner.

The Chinese are nothing if not practical, so there are a number of reasons why the government would unilaterally choose to liberalize. First, commercial trade between Taiwan and China had been taking place, unofficially, for years, expanding until it had reached the equivalent of nearly $2 billion by 1987. (It was always an open secret that freshwater fish and vegetables in Taipei's best restaurants came directly from the mainland, via Hong Kong.) Second, with the signing of the Shanghai Communiqué between President Nixon and Mao Zedong in 1972 and establishment of formal diplomatic relations between Washington and Beijing in 1979, followed by a downgrading of the U.S.–Taiwan relationship to "unofficial status," the geopolitical landscape had shifted significantly. And third, economic growth in Taiwan had been accompanied all along by greater equity in social development, given the much broader entrepreneurial business base in the country compared to Korea. Too, Chiang's decision to lift martial law may have reflected the old truism that the Taiwanese are far more interested in profits than in politics.

But thirty-eight years under continuous martial law is a long time—nearly two generations—which is one reason Taiwan also became known as a "hard" authoritarian state and one reason the country, like Korea, was able to focus its primary attention on economic growth. Still, unlike his father, Chiang Ching-kuo seemed to have no desire to pass political leadership on to his son and instead chose a sixty-five-year-old American-educated native Taiwanese, Lee Teng-hui, as vice president, to succeed him. Not long after Chiang's public announcement, he died, in January 1988, at the age of seventy-seven. On the night of his death several senior Kuomintang party members met at his residence in Taipei to argue for the reimposition of martial law. President Lee, together with the nation's premier, Harvard-educated Yu Kuo-hwa, agreed to impose a thirty-day ban on demonstrations, as a compromise, but decided against bringing martial law back. The external political environment was unquestionably a factor in their decision; they were not keen to repeat the mistakes, made earlier in Manila and in Seoul, that had created such high levels of social and political unrest.

The National Assembly, which meets every six years to elect the president and vice president, gathered to confirm Lee Teng-hui but left the post of vice president open until 1990. This deliberative body had last conducted elections in 1947, with a membership of 2,961 mainland Chinese. By 1987 death had reduced this number to 972. The number continues to decline, at the rate of about one death a week; local Taiwanese call them *rou zou*, the walking dead.

Taiwan's Legislative Yuan, whose responsibilities conform to those of a Western-style parliament, had a membership forty years ago of 760 but has only slightly more than 300 today. The average age in the Legislative Yuan is over eighty, and many members are reportedly infirm, which has prompted *The Economist* of London to call it "a parliament pickled in formaldehyde." A third group, the Control Yuan, an appointed body of supervisors, manages state security and controls the secret police organizations, of which there are estimated to be about a dozen in Taiwan and without which no Chinese government has ever been able to hold power.

One opposition party, the Democratic Progressives, was formed several years ago but is still technically illegal because the enabling legislation permitting it to form has yet to be passed. The fact that it could proceed in 1986 to file a slate of candidates and then have twelve of them elected is further evidence of the primacy of form over substance in Chinese society. As of 1989 a dozen "illegal" opposition parties were in existence.

I discussed these remarkable developments one evening during a recent visit to Taipei with Nicholas Kristof, a foreign correspondent for the *New York Times,* who was spending a year in Taiwan studying Mandarin prior to his new assignment in Beijing. Kristof attended Harvard and had been a Rhodes Scholar at Oxford.

"There are thirty-one Chinese-language dailies now in circulation here," he was telling me over a dinner of *mabudofu* and *kung p'ao* chicken at a local restaurant. "The press is now unfettered, digging and reporting on things they could never report on before, including some rather unflattering stories on Premier Yu Kuo-hwa and Madame Chiang Kai-shek, who may be either eighty-seven or ninety-two, depending on which stories you read. *Time* and *Newsweek* both circulate freely now, and it's been more than a year, I think, since any paragraphs have been blacked out. The two leading newspaper publishers—the United Daily News and the China Times—are members of the KMT Central Committee and control 80 percent of the circulation, and the three television stations are run, either directly or indirectly, by the government, but with everybody permitted to print twenty-four pages now instead of just twelve, there's more information, more depth, and much more accuracy."

I asked him about the leadership transition.

"The fact that Lee Teng-hui, a native Taiwanese, could be selected as Chiang's successor," he said, "is almost unprecedented in Chinese dynastic politics. He is a remarkable man—he has a doctorate in agricultural economics from Cornell and implemented some of the land reform policy in the 1950s—not only because he is not Chinese-born, but because he delivered his New Year's message both in Mandarin and in the Taiwanese dialect, the first time that has ever been done here. It was a very moving experience. Taiwan has a larger number of American-educated officials than any government in Asia. The leadership is very bright and very capable, including Yao Chia-wen, the head of the opposition Democratic Progressive Party. He was educated at Berkeley. When he set up the DPP, Chiang basically told the cops to leave him alone. They have an image problem, though. They're pugilistic and prone to fistfights in the Legislative Yuan."

On February 28, 1947, the Kuomintang killed thousands of Taiwanese in a local uprising that turned into a very nasty affair and later became known as the "2-28 incident." Lee Teng-hui made reference to the episode shortly after his inauguration, saying it should be put to rest. In 1979 the *dangwai*—the outsiders who formed the DPP illegally—held a mass rally in Kaohsiung urging independence for Taiwan and soliciting support for their radical magazine, *Formosa*. They were suppressed brutally by the police, with several killed, and their leaders, including Yao Chia-wen, were arrested and kept locked up for seven years. Then, in 1981, a Carnegie-Mellon professor named Chen mysteriously fell to his death while being interrogated by the Garrison Command about his supposed pro-independence activities in America. Three years after that, Henry Liu, who had written a critical biography of Chiang Ching-kuo, was assassinated near his home in California by Taiwanese gangsters. Under pressure from Washington the perpetrators were eventually tried and punished. But with liberalization, by all accounts, the violence and suppression are not likely to resurface.

Officially, Taiwan's policy toward the mainland is the Three Nos—no contact, no negotiation, no compromise—but friends in Taipei tell me it's now considered to be the Three Maybes. References in the local press to the People's Republic of China have to be either in quotation marks or prefaced with the qualifier *so-called*. Taiwan's new political leaders, being realistic, now recognize the gray areas and understand that the Republic of China flag, which has flown over Taiwan for the past forty years, will probably never fly over the mainland again.

The response of local Taiwanese to the government's policy of allowing visits to the motherland has been overwhelmingly positive: more than 20,000 trips a month have been recorded since November 1987, when the policy was first announced. Still, Taiwan stamps can't be used for mail to the mainland, so the Red Cross has to courier letters to Hong Kong on a regular basis and post them from there.

Books containing references to the PRC can now be shipped into Taipei, and you find them in local bookstores; years ago they would have been confiscated or destroyed. There is still some mild concern about the PRC's military threat to the island, but it is important to see how *much* things are changing. The younger generation of Taiwanese leaders do not appear to have quite the visceral hostility to the Communists their predecessors had.

There is an interesting parallel between what is happening in Taiwan now and what happened in the seventeenth century, according to other Taiwanese friends. In 1644, when the Ming dynasty was overthrown, supporters of the Ming fled to southern China, to Canton, and across the straits of Formosa to Taiwan, vowing to retake the mainland. They persisted for just about forty years, until they finally admitted they couldn't realistically do so. In 1949 there was another change in dynasties when Mao Zedong captured Beijing and the KMT fled to Taiwan, vowing to recapture the mainland. It has become clear now, after forty years, that this strategy is unlikely to work. What is not clear is whether these developments will eventually lead to independence for Taiwan—still a subject that cannot be written about in the local press and a very dangerous one for advocates of independence, who can be arrested for and easily convicted of sedition.

But independence carries with it still another interesting historical parallel. In 1871 the Manchu government stated to Japan that Taiwan was "outside its jurisdiction" and China could thus not be held responsible for what the Taiwanese had done to Japanese nationals in Taiwan. Not until 1887 did the Manchu government proclaim Taiwan a province of China. But less than a decade later, in 1895, China ceded Taiwan to Japan, following its defeat in the Sino-Japanese War. Even if the island was Chinese territory during the nineteenth century, Taiwan is still separable from China: nearly one hundred nations today were the territories of other nations in the last century.

One interpretation of international law holds that a nation can acquire sovereignty over a territory through continuous and undisturbed exercise of sovereignty over it for a sufficient period of time, even though other states may file disputes, protests, and conflicting claims. In 1971 Washington declared that sovereignty over Taiwan was an unsettled question, subject to future international resolution. The Shanghai Communiqué, in 1972, *acknowledged*, but did not recognize, the Chinese claim that Taiwan was a part of China.

Following execution of the Sino-British Accord in 1984, Deng Xiaoping suggested that the "one country, two systems" concept might also be suitable for Taiwan, although the Taiwanese treated that suggestion with about as much enthusiasm as did the people of Hong Kong. Their reaction was understandable, given the extreme disparities in per-capita income and standards of living between China and Taiwan today. In 1985 the *dangwai* of Taiwan's opposition parties stipulated in their campaign platforms that "the future of Taiwan should be determined by the people of Taiwan." Today only twenty-two countries extend diplomatic recognition to Taiwan, even though, with a population of nearly 20 million, it has more people than 123 of the 159 members of the United Nations.

Taiwan's educational achievement is so high that a plebiscite could be the most effective way of determining the nation's future. But because China's influence in the UN is so strong, such a vote probably could not be supervised internationally. The U.S. has already said it would not extend diplomatic recognition to an independent republic of Taiwan, but the Presbyterian Church in Taiwan has urged the KMT to be realistic and start thinking about measures that would bring about independence. Over time, China's attitude could change, too, and it might either abandon its claims to the island or, as the Mauchu government did more than a hundred years ago, state that the territory is outside its jurisdiction.

"The PRC would never allow another system to function under the same leadership," Thomas Lee was telling me as we sat in his office at the Society for Strategic Studies of Tamkang University in Taipei. A graduate of Taiwan National University, Dr. Lee earned his PhD at St. John's University in New York and taught in the U.S. for many years.

"Peking is using the same old tactics to isolate us in the international community," he continued. "In the Olympics we now have to compete using the name 'Chinese Taipei', and in the Asian Development Bank, where we have returned after an absence of two years, we sit under the name 'Taipei, China.' But the Hong Kong formula is doomed. We think the PRC will use it merely as a stepping-stone to capture Taiwan, and they will gradually tighten the noose around Hong Kong's neck. They will not keep Hong Kong free; Hong Kong is too vulnerable, it depends on China for all its food and water to begin with, and besides, what can the West do? They're helpless."

I asked him about the brain drain from Hong Kong.

"I think a massive outflow of refugees will result in the next few years," he said, "and we ought to take as many of them as we can. With our population we could easily absorb a half million more people, and these are the people we *should* be taking, because they have the capital, the education, the entrepreneurial talent, the energy, and the business skills to be successful here and to influence our economy in a positive way. They are quick, aggressive, practical, and above all, adaptable. If your country is smart, you'll open your doors to them, too, because American businessmen cannot fight their trade wars in Asia alone. They need allies—Asian allies."

As I drove back out to the airport late on a cool, drizzly day, through mile after mile of small factories separated by equally small rice paddies, it seemed to me that Taiwan, not unlike America, had become a country without a soul. Like America, its culture is its market, and beyond the daily activity of commerce, while lip service may be paid to art and music and literature and poetry and drama, intellectual activity finds its most pronounced forms in the marketplace.

It also seemed that the relationship between China and Taiwan was becoming more like that between Britain and America, two countries that share a common language but are separated by a large body of water. Today, after nearly a century of separation from the mainland, first under Japanese occupation and then under the repressive Kuomintang, Taiwan in many ways seems no more Chinese than America is British. I had the strong feeling that the great depth and historical genius of China, as reflected in the Confucian tradition, seem much shallower today than many Americans, lured by the magic and mystery of the mainland, are prepared to believe, and while conventional wisdom holds much promise for Deng Xiaoping's reforms, I was unconvinced.

For forty years Taiwan's *raison d'être,* which had formed the basis for its "hard" authoritarian system of martial law, had been the mystical recapture of the mainland. Now, as power was being transferred to a new generation of highly capable, well-educated native Taiwanese, a quiet political transition was taking place.

While the future portended uncertainty, and a lot of it, this enlightened leadership, based on the progress of the past several years, had much going for it. The likelihood that Taiwan would eventually seek independence from China and forge its own successful way in the world, just as America fought to free itself from Britain two centuries ago, seemed to be not merely hypothetical, but real.

Taiwan, too, was benefiting from the exodus of Hong Kong's well-educated, highly skilled, and experienced class of professionals. Young Taiwanese men and women who had completed their graduate studies in America in a host of scientific and technical specialties were now returning to Taiwan in a massive "reverse brain drain," like Morris

Chang before them, ready to position Taiwan even more competitively in the knowledge-intensive age.

THE PHILIPPINES:
AN ISLAND OF FAILURE IN A SEA OF SUCCESS

If the Southeast Asian country endowed most abundantly with natural resources is unable to turn that bounty into a competitive advantage, can one support a claim that its democratic political system is inherently more advantageous than the more authoritarian forms of government that have brought their people greater economic prosperity?

More defensible, it seems to me, based on the East Asian experience, is the position that capitalist economic growth flows from the political stability provided by an authoritarian system *rather than* that democracy is a natural outcome of economic growth. In any case, the Philippines has neither economic prosperity nor an effective democratic system, despite all the publicity to the contrary.

In the two decades following independence in 1946, Philippine politics, seasoned observer Robert Shaplen wrote in *A Turning Wheel*, "had always been a wild, rollicking Wild West kind of performance, in which guns and goons played a major role and the press was a flagrantly reckless chorus of vaudevillian proportions." When I last spoke with Shaplen, shortly before his death from thyroid cancer in early 1988 at the age of seventy-one, he was not optimistic about the future of this country he had come to know, and to love, better than any of the others he wrote so often and so knowledgeably about.

He told me he was personally disappointed in and deeply concerned about the inability of the Aquino government to come to grips with the many problems confronting the country, both political and economic, not least those of its own making. Two-thirds of its population still lived in what by any standard was poverty, he acknowledged, and the violence and recklessness of the pre-Marcos years seemed to have returned.

When I first visited the Philippines in 1971, I was startled more by the lack of order than by the prevalence of poverty, a condition that, at that time, one could see elsewhere, of course, in India or Indonesia. But it seemed as if there were no *rules* by which Philippine society functioned. Manila was a loose, lawless, unstructured city where handguns were as visible as pocketbooks and where hand-lettered signs posted in public places reminded patrons to check their firearms at the door. It was Abilene, Kansas, a century ago, stuck in time. Worse, despite the nation's twenty-five-year experience with "democracy" since independence in 1946, *nobody seemed to be in charge.*

A similar thought must have occurred to Ferdinand Marcos, who had first been elected president in 1965 and returned to office in 1969 for a second four-year term, when, in September 1972, he unilaterally declared a state of martial law. The American system of politics, he reckoned, which had been grafted onto the laid-back Philippine culture, was proving insufficient to deal with the country's massive economic problems. Past presidents—such as Magsaysay, García, and Macapagal— had shown, through a constantly declining standard of living and a constantly escalating level of violence, their inability to govern. So Marcos suspended the legislature, eliminated elections, put the Constitution on hold, packed the judiciary with his friends, forcibly collected all firearms (which proved numerous enough to supply a *large* army and included a privately owned Belgian half-track), and subsequently ruled through a system of presidential decrees. It was to be a period of constitutional authoritarianism, in which economic growth and political stability would finally take root.

Marcos had unwittingly stumbled onto one of the three important legs that provided the foundation on which a capitalist developmental state could be built. Unfortunately, both for Marcos and for his country, the other two legs were nonexistent: the Philippines had neither a well-trained, highly educated, technocratic elite in the form of a controlling bureaucracy nor a strategically driven, historically rooted, nationalistic business leadership managing a higher value-added industrial structure. So his system of constitutional authoritarianism was doomed to failure from the outset, because the only strategic alliance he could forge was with the oligarchy and its inbred cult of corruption.

That alliance would eventually be his undoing. During the next fifteen years he would increase the country's international debt from $2 billion to nearly $30 billion; alienate his people as well as his primary overseas supporter, the United States; unconscionably enrich himself and his wife, Imelda, in the process; and sow the seeds of his own destruction. Marcos had neglected to read the famous letter from John Emerich Edward Dalberg-Acton, Lord Acton, to Bishop Mandell Creighton: "Power tends to corrupt and absolute power corrupts absolutely."

In December 1985 Marcos felt confident enough to permit elections for the first time in seventeen years. Having eliminated his primary opposition, Benigno (Ninoy) Aquino, in a bloody assassination as Aquino stepped off the plane on his return from exile in August 1983, Marcos felt unbeatable. It was a monumental error in judgment; Cory Aquino, Ninoy's widow, became his opponent and attracted great popular support, overwhelming him in the election. When Marcos announced his own victory, having manipulated the ballot count, people took to the streets *en masse* in a peaceful revolt, which later became known as the Yellow Revolution, in support of Cory Aquino. Marcos was forced to flee the country, and in March 1986 Aquino took power. Her yellow dress and bright smile captivated millions (yellow was the Aquino family color, from a sugar mill her husband had once painted that color), and her People's Power "revolution" held out great hope.

Aquino's assumption of power meant a return to pre-Marcos normalcy, which meant continuation of control by the oligarchy beneath a veneer of democracy. Politics was still a hobby of the rich, a kind of leisure game for the wealthy underemployed. The Philippine political system was patterned on the American system, with all of its defects and none of its strengths.

"Because previous changes of government have meant so little to the Philippines, it is hard to believe that replacing Marcos with Aquino, desirable as it doubtless is, will do much besides stanching the flow of crony profits out of the country," James Fallows wrote in an *Atlantic* article, "A Damaged Culture." In the absence of more courageous national leadership, economic gains cannot and will not come to the Philippines unless either a thorough, painful land reform program is implemented or a real revolution occurs, with real bloodshed, to overthrow the corrupt oligarchic elite.

Philippine political parties are coalitions of powerful families. The ascension of Cory Aquino's government raised hopes for the prospects of a more democratic political system in the post-Marcos era. The emerging reality, however, is different. The results of the May 1987 elections show that 130 out of 200 candidates elected to the House of Representatives belonged to traditional political families (such as Romualdez, Osmeña, Lopez, Aquino, Laurel, and Cojuangco), while another thirty-nine were relatives of these families. Of the 169 representatives from the traditional political clans, 102 were identified with the pre-1986 anti-Marcos forces and sixty-seven with pro-Marcos clans. Of the twenty-four elected senators, the overwhelming majority were from the traditional clans that were prominent in the pre–martial law period. Many Filipinos offer a simple reason for the continued political dominance of a few old families: society itself has not changed very much. What all these families have in common is their ability to transform the electoral process into an ideological ritual to justify their domination.

Cory Aquino is reluctant to exercise power. She is also a devout Catholic in a Catholic country, a living symbol of the Virgin Mary, which has a mesmerizing effect on the massive illiterate segment of the population.

"A politician," said Father Edicio (Ed) de la Torre, who spent many years in jail as an alleged Communist and who was released at the order of Cory Aquino, "must make up his mind whom to accommodate and whom to represent. Cory tries to accommodate everybody and represents nobody."

"She has been slow to address such basic questions as land reform," Seth Mydans, Manila correspondent for the *New York Times,* has observed, "or to check the spread of corruption. She has failed to give firm direction to local governments or to lead a forceful effort to check a growing Communist insurgency. And she has tolerated an escalation of lawlessness and violence in the countryside and the cities."

Aquino has admitted that her country needs forceful, aggressive leadership, but it is becoming more doubtful that this need can be filled by a person whose character is not defined by forcefulness and whose hero—Gandhi—was a passive proponent of nonviolent change. The persistent challenge to her legitimacy comes from the military, which sees her as incapable of meeting the threat posed by the Communist-led New People's Army.

"Not a single official from the Marcos era has been put in jail," another of my Filipino friends was telling me as we sat in his cramped office in downtown Manila one hot and sticky February day. "And it's now two years after the event. What is the lady waiting for? I sometimes think we would benefit most by a Noah's ark solution to our problems. Let the islands be completely flooded and start over with one boy and one girl. I've reached the depressing conclusion that something is wrong with us. We are an imitative culture. Leaders need to lead, not follow."

I asked him about the growing insurgency.

He shook his head.

"Flies and mosquitoes," he said, "thrive in dirty places."

A similar point was made by another longtime Filipino friend, one of the country's ruling elite. His comments in early 1988 were understandably more guarded but equally revealing.

"Having completed the three stages of democratic restoration, Mrs. Aquino is not tottering," he said emphatically. "But the problem is not just Cory; it is also her relatives. Her sister-in-law was defeated in Quezon City. In Tarlac, home of both her family, the Cojuangcos, and her husband's family, the Aquinos, two relatives were soundly defeated by Jovito Salonga, president of the Senate and Cory's most probable challenger in 1992. He also crushed her mother's candidates, the Sulumongs, in Rizal Province, so she is getting the message: stuff the ballot box or lose. Johnny Enrile barely squeaked into the Senate. He had to challenge the election results in his province when the candidate from Cory's clique had 160 percent of the votes cast. Cory has to maneuver through all this in order to avoid the charges of corruption that are being made against her as she seeks to replace Marcos's cronies and those of his wife, Imelda, and her family, the Romualdez clan. You see, blood is thicker than marriage, and family allegiance is stronger than any political party."

He paused, then shrugged his shoulders.

"And throughout all the elections," he went on, "the killings resumed. For us a return to democracy means a return to violence, not unlike your westward expansion, when violence ruled and you killed off the Indians."

"The problem is the colonial overlay," another old friend, with connections in high places in the Aquino government, lamented. "First the Spanish, then the Americans, then the Japanese military occupation, then the oligarchy of landed wealth that has dominated Philippine politics for generations. Cory is no different; sure, cronyism is down, but the oligarchic, dynastic group remains. *Nothing has changed.* Even Marcos, when he was first elected, was viewed in the same light as Cory is today."

With all the disaffection, I asked how she was able to stay in power.

"Cory is able to stay in power for much the same reason Marcos was," he said. "She uses her family clique and wealth as allies and keeps shuffling her cabinet to keep the opposition off-base. Expectations were so high that they can't possibly be fulfilled. She should have used her full power ruthlessly on day one to sack the Marcos cronies and execute the blatant architects of his corruption schemes in order to establish a strong central authority."

Unlike Japan, which probably has the deepest bench strength of bureaucratic talent in the world, or Singapore, in which a well-trained cadre of highly educated and experienced second-generation leaders is poised to take over, the Philippines doesn't even have a *first* generation of trained technocrats to do the job. Jaime Ongpin, who helped to restructure the country's bloated foreign debt as governor of the Central Bank of the Philippines early in Aquino's administration, became so disillusioned, discouraged, and depressed by the continuation of politics as usual that he committed suicide in November 1987.

"On a bright morning in July, 1946, the people of the Philippines entered upon their existence as an independent nation, filled with dreams of prosperity and economic well-being for themselves and their children," the columnist Rodolfo Romero wrote early last year in the *Manila Bulletin*. "Today, nearly forty-two years later, those dreams remain unfulfilled for the great majority of Filipinos, and the economic life of this country continues to be characterized by inefficiency, weakness, and instability."

Everybody in the Philippines has a nickname. Corazon Aquino is Cory. Her husband's nickname was Ninoy, and her former personal secretary is Joker Arroyo. Former minister of defense Juan Ponce-Enrile is Johnny. Marcos's elder son was called Bong-Bong. Rolando Tinio, a columnist for the *Manila Daily Globe*, is known to his friends as Rollie.

On a recent visit to Manila I contacted Rollie, who had been a Marcos supporter in his early years, to talk about the oligarchy and Philippine politics. Was there perhaps something abnormal in the Filipino toleration of poverty, the acceptance of what normal people found so repulsive?

"Poverty," soft-spoken, burr-headed Rollie Tinio said as we sat in the lobby of the Manila Hotel one afternoon, "is based on the Western concept that money equals wealth. But that idea is not indigenous to the Philippines. It is only the civilized who are repelled by poverty."

He glanced over his shoulder and then leaned forward.

"And who can say that the Philippine oligarchy is civilized? Did you know that there have been more human rights violations recorded under Aquino than there were under Marcos? Marcos loyalists have neither been arrested, jailed, nor convicted. Nothing has changed."

Blas Ople was minister of labor in the final Marcos years, helped Washington monitor and engineer his exile to Hawaii, and then became a member of Cory Aquino's Constitutional Commission. He is currently chairman of the Institute for Public Policy, a Manila think tank, and a member of the Economic Board of *Asiaweek*.

I met him in the Makati Intercontinental's coffee shop, the Jeepney, where on most mornings most politicians, in or out of power, can be found conducting *kapi han*, or coffee hours.

On the signboard in the lobby was an announcement for a luncheon meeting in celebration of the recent appointment of Fidel Ramos as defense minister and de Villa as chief of staff of the Philippine Armed Forces. The notice for their wives, "Hail and Farewell for Monetta de Villa and Camelia Ramos, Solysombra Room," was sandwiched between a Max Factor sales conference and a Spiritual Life Ministries seminar. Such are the priorities of political life in Manila.

"I personally believe the Constitutional Commission should have opted for a parliamentary system of government," Blas Ople was telling me, "which makes the ruling party and the opposition stand together and share responsibility. But we chose to defer to prevailing public opinion, which prefers the American presidential system. Still, that is no excuse for national leadership to pull apart when they should be working together."

Ople is a balding man, whom I gauged to be in his late fifties. His middle-aged paunch partially obscured a fancy belt buckle, he wore soft Italian loafers, and his left arm seemed incapable of movement, weighed down by an enormous gold Rolex. He was affable during our conversation, with an easy smile.

"The existing congressional setup, especially in the Senate," he went on, "puts a premium on individual celebrity, not on collective responsibility. In the House, a substantial share of the agenda consists of local bills renaming schools, parks, and hospitals. These are manifestations of a weak political ego rather than a strong public conscience."

I asked him whether a more authoritarian system might be more relevant to the Philippines than either the British or American forms of democratic government.

He smiled.

"Cory's husband liked to say that an authoritarian government here could at least have justified itself by creating an economic miracle, like some of our neighbors in Northeast Asia. But that statement can now be turned on its head. The president's popular support will amount to nothing unless it is translated effectively into a major economic performance. But in the way we think, Filipinos reflect the constraints of a subsistence economy. The original East Asian economic miracle happened in Japan, yet it is simply amazing to me how our leaders have been the *least* disposed among the elite of Southeast Asia to study the Japanese model of economic development. We have the fewest scholars in Japan, but the largest contingent of barmaids."

My interview with Ople delayed my return to the Manila Hotel, where I had been told Senator Johnny Enrile, former minister of defense under both the Marcos and Aquino administrations, would be holding forth in a *kapi han* of his own. I managed to arrive just as Enrile was leaving, his readily identifiable aviator glasses and Hollywood style unmistakable. "I'm speaking in the Senate this afternoon," he said. "Why don't you come over?"

The Philippine Senate is housed on the top floor of a stark stone building with imitation-Greek columns, not five minutes by cab from the Manila Hotel. When I took my seat in the press gallery on the Senate floor, Enrile was already in debate on another current topic of irrelevance: whether to expand Manila's administrative authority into a broader Metro Manila concept, including large neighboring communities like Quezon City, where the House of Representatives and many government ministries were headquartered.

Johnny Enrile had generated his wealth as chairman of the Philippine coconut monopoly, the United Coconut Oil Mills (Unicom), which Marcos had created in 1977, and as chairman of the United Coconut Planters Bank, which obtained its funds from fees levied on producers. The Unicom monopoly conspired to fix coconut oil prices at unrealistic highs, since the Philippines produced 70 percent of the world supply and nearly all American imports. But the scam came unhinged when world prices collapsed in 1979, and Unicom found itself the target of a Justice Department antitrust investigation.

Enrile was strutting behind his microphone like a proud cock, wearing a tailored mohair jacket, flared worsted trousers, and a pair of Gucci loafers that shone under the bright Senate ceiling lights. On a distant wall was a sign printed in capital letters: NO FIREARMS ALLOWED.

". . . And I would like to be corrected by my esteemed colleague," Enrile purred in an articulate delivery that must have come as part of his training at Harvard Law School, ". . . to establish a Metro Manila Authority with four cities and thirteen towns."

"We're not creating another political subdivision, your honor," the opposition intoned.

"But isn't the political subdivision of Metro Manila under the authority of the president of the Philippines?" Enrile asked, turning to the visitors' gallery packed with his admirers. He smiled. He was onstage now. The microphone was his.

"Yes, your honor."

"And isn't it unfair, your honor, that the government of Manila will represent the largest number of voters but will have only one vote in the Metro Manila council?"

Turn. Smile. Beam at the fans.

"That's a fair point, your honor, and we are open to amendments."

The process went on for more than an hour. I must admit, I was not alone in being unable to follow the proceedings with interest. Beside me, reporters from the Philippine press dozed off in boredom. Other senators couldn't be bothered to pay attention. Some huddled around individual desks, joking and laughing. Others read newspapers, spoke on the phone, or slept. The sense of national purpose seemed nowhere in sight, the crisis born of economic urgency nowhere near the seat of government.

When it was over, the reporters snapped to attention and followed Enrile out of the chambers, swirling around his heels like dust kittens, into the hallway for the obligatory interviews and the thirty-second sound bites for Philippine TV.

"The democratic institutions restored by President Aquino are functioning well," David Lambertson, deputy assistant secretary for East Asian and Pacific affairs, said in December 1987 in a statement to the Foreign Affairs Committee of the U.S. House of Representatives in Washington. "The new Congress is fully operating as the legislative body it was designed to be. The institutional revival of a free and independent legislative branch after the absence of such a body for fifteen years represents a major accomplishment."

Bottled sunshine.

Economic deterioration, political disintegration. Two highly flammable ingredients for revolution. That the Philippines is able to teeter on is even greater evidence of the American security relationship, for the American "father image" has much to do with the inability of the Philippines to mature into an independent country.

Democratic politics, as currently practiced in the Philippines, seems irrelevant, both to the nation's pressing economic problems and to its need for political change. Only a full-scale, bloody revolution, from the bottom up, may be able to accomplish the necessary land reforms, eliminate the stranglehold of the landowning oligarchy, and restructure the nation's political economy, which is still somewhere back in the seventeenth century. The Yellow Revolution of Cory Aquino can in no way, and under no circumstances, be called a real revolution, because no far-reaching reforms, economic or political, have been accomplished, although it was certainly yellow in that no one was called upon to die for a higher cause.

The Philippines missed its chance in an earlier shift, under Marcos, to constitutional authoritarianism. Now, if the country does not find a way to borrow some of the more readily available political, economic, and tactical policy tools from the Little Dragons, it may be relegated to the bottom of the heap as the information age accelerates into the next century.

8

FLAWS IN THE AMERICAN POLITICAL MODEL

The least productive enterprise Americans can engage in, though it is virtually second nature, is trying to place the blame for what has happened to our economy in the 1980s on one political party or ideology. Blame is beside the point, for it is something we all share.

Today we hear every politician complaining about the lack of vision in America. The reason we feel adrift is that we are waking up to the fact that blind and self-indulgent gusto is not vision at all, but denial. True vision requires the forging of a farsighted and realistic connection between our present and our future. It means recognizing in today's choices the sacrifices all of us must make for posterity. America's unfettered individualism has endowed our people with enormous energy and great aspirations. It has not, however, given us license to do anything we please so long as we do it with conviction.

Peter Peterson, "The Morning After"

Individual prosperity, national misery.

Those were the words the Japanese sociologist Takeshi Ishida used to describe America's national malaise, which has become the mirror image of Japan's. In less than a decade America has managed to undo what it had taken generations to accomplish, losing status as the world's leading creditor nation and becoming the number one debtor, with cumulative debt of more than $500 billion, reflecting year upon year of red ink in the national trade accounts. In the same period America more than tripled its federal debt to the point where interest payments are now the fastest-growing component of the federal budget.

Yet unemployment is at a postwar low, personal incomes have risen, individual taxes are lower, and credit is, in the jargon of Wall Street, a "no-brainer." Still, the quality of jobs America has created is suspect; *net* disposable income has declined, in real terms, reflecting America's deteriorating living standard relative to other OECD countries; lower taxes have meant less money available to maintain or upgrade an aging infrastructure; and incentives to spend have put the American consumer over his head in personal debt.

A question that might reasonably be posed is what difference it makes. If America can keep its GNP growing by borrowing from the future in order to enrich the present, why is this wrong? Why should Americans abandon the very policies that have made them so rich individually, even if the nation as a whole may be less well off?

Because national economic failure could mean the end of American hegemony. In the absence of a renewed and upgraded infrastructure, or rates of capital formation that can sustain future investments, or tax incentives to create the savings and guide the investments into desired sectors, all devised, funded, and implemented in a more prudent fashion, the American political economy could continue to suffer the inevitable consequences of systemic gridlock.

Nothing is perhaps more symbolic of how America organizes itself politically than the ways in which Americans agree to tax themselves— the institutional process by which the federal budget is prepared, debated, and passed every year by Congress. The "Me Generation" of the 1960s and 1970s produced a "give me" government, with dramatic increases in demands for federal spending across the board.

That sentiment was produced, by and large, by a change in the way federal budgets were legislated. Federal spending used to be discretionary and nonindexed, with amounts decided every year under the prudent proviso that commitments should be funded from actual tax revenues; that is, governments should try to live within their means. Big federal deficits were, practically speaking, difficult to achieve, and though they were necessary during the Korean and Vietnam wars, their size, relative to present deficits in a period of peacetime prosperity, was small.

But as Pete Peterson wrote in his thoughtful *Atlantic* article, "The spending rule was eliminated in the early 1970s by our decision to transform most non-poverty benefit programs into untouchable and inflation-proof entitlements. Then the taxing rule was eliminated in the early 1980s by the jihad prayers of supply-side economists. Our deficit has thus become no one's responsibility. It is subject to 'projection' but no longer to control."

The traditional Keynesian demand-side approach to fiscal management was replaced by a new supply-side philosophy. Throughout the process none of the underlying *incentives* was changed, either to reflect a more strategic orientation to policy formulation or to replace the old aggregated formula for taxation and investment by a disaggregated one. And the process was exacerbated by a spendthrift Congress that strongly resisted spending cuts proposed by the administration.

"The outlines of the problem appear," James Fallows wrote in his award-winning book *National Defense*, "when the American economy is divided into its three essential spheres: consumption, investment, and government. Consumption is food, travel, everything that people buy and use; investment is expansion of productive capacity, financed by money that someone has saved rather than consumed; government is the cost of the state, federal, and local bureaucracies. An increase in the size of any one share—especially the government's—means an immediate decrease in the other two. This is not to say that government spending serves no purpose; only that all government efforts come at a price."

When well-intentioned budget-cutters talk about "slashing federal spending," it is helpful to keep in mind just what can and what cannot be cut. To begin with, more than 60 percent of the federal budget goes to groups that no politician can afford to ignore: Social Security payments to the retired head the list, along with interest on the federal debt, Medicare payments to the elderly, and price support payments to farmers. These four groups alone comprise nearly *half* of all non-means-tested entitlement payments. Support for the poor represents only about 5 percent of the total budget, or barely 10 percent of total entitlements.

In addition to entitlements is, of course, the defense budget, which comprises about 30 percent of total federal spending. "Everything else the government does," Fallows wrote, "*everything*, comes out of the remaining ten percent," which is discretionary: trips to the moon, interstate highways, federal salaries, the Congress and its staff, foreign aid, the Peace Corps, drug enforcement, the IRS, the Library of Congress, national forests and parks, environmental protection, alternative energy developments, federal aid to education, the CIA, occupational safety programs, the FBI, federal deposit insurance, the National Endowment for the Arts and Humanities, and the salaries of the president and the vice president of the United States.

Budget-cutting efforts can only go so far, because entitlement benefits have been politically untouchable. By 1986 discretionary nondefense expenditures had been reduced to about 4 percent of GNP, their lowest level since 1961. One reason America is not developing leading-edge technology in transportation is that Washington has chosen not to fund it. And net real investment in public works has dropped by 75 percent over the past two decades. The collapse of the Schooharie Bridge on the New York State Thruway in the summer of 1987, and the closing of the Williamsburg Bridge, a major artery connecting Manhattan with Brooklyn, in early 1988, both due to erosion of steel beam supports resulting from lack of proper maintenance and repair, were but two examples of America's deteriorating infrastructure.

Between 1980 and 1986 federal spending on natural resources declined by more than 20 percent, nondefense R&D by 25 percent, public investment in sewers and water by 25 percent, and aid to education by nearly 15 percent. Such investments represent priorities for the future, not for the present, but the future has no constituency and cannot vote.

If all these entitlement benefits went just to the poor, as many erroneously believe, there would be cause for concern. Only about 10 percent of the total was paid to welfare recipients; the balance represented income transfers from "nonpoor taxpayers" to "nonpoor beneficiaries," including foreign holders of the federal debt, which received more than half. Social Security is the single largest component of entitlement benefits. Elderly beneficiaries now have the lowest poverty rate of any age group, their benefits tend to be regressive (the higher the income, the higher the payments), and their cohorts are the fastest-growing age group in America.

More than half of all federal benefits now go to that segment of the American population (about 12 percent) aged sixty-five or older, averaging just under $10,000 a year per capita. The burden of payments to the elderly is projected to increase dramatically in the decades ahead, for one simple reason: while America's working-age population is projected to grow by a maximum of about 18 percent during the next fifty years, the population of America's elderly will more than double.

Budget priorities bring us full circle back to incentives, and when you look at the overall impact of the budget, it is important to understand the impact of those incentives on society and how the American political system has deteriorated to the point of putting special interests ahead of the national interest.

Through the tax and incentive process of the budget, 12 million new jobs have been created in the past decade, primarily in four major categories: services to wealth, such as finance, insurance, and real estate; welfare society services, such as health, education, social services, and government; retail trade and related services; and construction, trucking, and wholesale trade.

Employees in retail trade and personal services make, on the average, less than half the average earnings in American manufacturing. Illegal immigrants are also concentrated in this category, particularly in restaurant and janitorial jobs. Services to wealth are the highest-paying jobs of the four categories; about one-fourth of all people employed in finance, insurance, and real estate are "executives," but the rest are in sales and administrative jobs (such as back office work). Services to wealth also have the lowest proportion of black and Hispanic workers of any job category, with the exception of mining.

Nearly two-thirds of the new jobs in construction, trucking, and wholesale trade (officially referred to as "precision production occupations") have been in the construction industry. These jobs are mostly for men, they are dangerous, and nearly half the workers are black or Hispanic. The expansion of jobs in trucking epitomizes the impact of budget policy incentives: trucks now account for nearly half of all motor fuel consumption, compared to less than 30 percent in 1974, and America uses about a third more energy for transportation alone than Japan uses for *all* purposes combined.

The federal budget is allocated the way it is, and the incentives contained in the budget create jobs the way they do, for a very good reason. It is fairly straightforward and simple to explain: the American political system has degenerated to the point where its elected representatives are no longer accountable to their traditional constituents, but to the special interest groups that finance their elections.

In the major federal budget category of non–means-tested entitlements, recall that four groups account for nearly half of all benefits paid: Social Security beneficiaries, Medicare recipients, farmers receiving price support payments, and coupon-clippers who hold Treasury notes, bills, and bonds. One of the most powerful lobbies in America, the American Association of Retired Persons, now represents interests of the retired and the elderly better than either of the traditional political parties.

Japanese institutions, which account for about half the total federal debt held by foreigners, now spend about $100 million a year to hire the top lawyers and lobbyists in Washington to represent their interests. Farmers have the National Farmers Union and the American Farm Bureau Federation. Teachers have the National Education Association, whose *raison d'être* has clearly become more political than educational. Government workers have the National Association of Government Employees, the American Federation of Government Employees, and the National Association of Municipal Employees. Everybody, it seems, except ordinary citizens without collective economic power, has a national association to represent his or her specific interests.

America's political parties have been replaced by special interest groups that dominate the system through their political action committees—the PACs. Elizabeth Drew, Washington correspondent for *The New Yorker*, recently wrote an insightful analysis of the problems created by PACs, called "Politics and Money." In it she recounted one of the most spectacular examples of special interest group legislation when, in 1982, used-car dealers successfully persuaded the House and Senate to eliminate a regulation of the Federal Trade Commission that required known defects of an automobile to be listed for the buyer's benefit. Of the 286 House members who voted to kill the legislation, 242 had received contributions from the auto dealers. "Of course it was money," one legislator said afterward. "Why else would they vote for used-car dealers?"

The growth of business PACs is related directly to the growth of government regulation of business. The 1981 tax cut for independent oil producers was a case in point: the industry was less interested in what it could contribute to energy policy than in what it could contribute to politicians by way of defeating the troublesome ones. PACs demand, and get, access; that is the name of the game. Members of Congress find it hard to say no to people who give them money. As a result, politicians are forced to spend less and less time with their constituents and more and more time with their contributors.

"It is the role of money," Drew contended, "that has given us, increasingly, politicians who are exhausted, who can't think clearly, who don't think about broad questions—don't have the time, even if they have the inclination, to do so. The role of money has delivered us into the special-interest state. What results is a corrosion of the system and a new kind of squalor. As the public cynicism gets deeper, the political system gets worse."

The National Education Association has the third-largest PAC in the country, behind the National Association of Realtors and the American Medical Association. Phil Stern, who wrote *The Best Congress Money Can Buy*, estimated that members of the House of Representatives must raise, on average, $15,000 every month during their two-year terms just to finance their election campaigns. Senators are even worse; with the average cost of running a successful Senate campaign now more than $3 million, they have to raise $10,000 *a week* during the six years they are in office.

As a consequence, American politicians defend the system by saying it is the escalating cost of campaigns that drives the need for money. But the need for money, Drew argued, creates its own momentum, what she calls the domestic equivalent of the arms race. A potential candidate has to make the rounds of all the key special interest groups, assuring them that he (or she) supports their legislative agenda. He thus becomes their prisoner and is thereafter incapable of independent judgment, of thinking in terms of the broader national interest. He has to measure every action he takes in terms of the financial consequences to him personally. What is the difference between that and corruption?

"It is clear that the politicians' anxiety about having access to enough money corrodes, and even corrupts, the political system," Drew went on. "The effect on them is degrading and distracting at best. At the least, politicians increasingly consider how their votes will affect their own—and their opponents'—ability to raise money. At worst, votes are actually traded for money. It is clear that we are at some distance from the way the democratic process is supposed to work."

The danger is that special interest groups threaten to replace the traditional committee system through which legislation has historically originated. The effect is that they already have. Special interest groups draft legislation, discuss it, amend it, get the necessary co-sponsors to push it, and the congressional committee becomes irrelevant.

"Until the problem of money is dealt with, it is unrealistic to expect the political process to improve in any other respect," Drew concluded. "The issue is not how much is spent on elections, but the way the money is obtained. The argument made by some that the amount spent on campaigns is not particularly bothersome because it is less than what is spent on advertising cola or purchasing hair-care products misses the point stunningly. The point is what *raising* money, not simply spending it, does to the political process. It is not just that the legislative product is bent or stymied. It is not just that citizens without organized economic power pay the bill for the successes of those with organized economic power. It is not even relevant which interests happen to be winning. What is relevant is what the whole thing is doing to the democratic process. What is at stake is the idea of representative government, the soul of this country."

Public financing for both congressional and presidential election campaigns has been suggested as one possible reform. But one wonders whether the power of money can be curbed so easily. It was earlier reforms, after all, that created the PACs by limiting individual contributions. Money still erodes the influence of the average citizen who has nothing else to offer a politician but his or her vote.

As special interest groups replace congressional committees as the originating focus of legislation, the entire *process* is shifting from the committee to the floor. In the last three decades the number of House members offering amendments has more than doubled, the total number of proposed amendments to legislation has tripled, and the percentage of legislation subject to amendment has quadrupled. During the same period the number of subcommittees has exploded to more than 150. Electronic voting, introduced in 1973, stripped away the political cover of anonymous voting and enhanced the influence of outsiders, such as special interest groups. This process has led to more frequent interaction among members on the floor, but a decline in depth and richness. Consequently, as personal relationships have weakened, they have been supplanted by members' relationships with the financially more important interest groups, which increasingly characterize the changing institutional context of Congress.

Congress is the most heavily staffed lawmaking body in the world. Its 451 members now have more than 30,000 unelected employees, a tenfold increase in the past thirty years. The 650 members of England's House of Commons, by comparison, employ fewer than 1,000. Senators and congressmen no longer write their own speeches, draft their own press releases, research the issues, or answer mail. As a result, fewer members of Congress are experts on the legislation they are either sponsoring or drafting. During the first six months of 1988 the Senate voted to limit debate twenty-six times—a number greater than the *total* of such votes between 1919 and 1960. Substance thus becomes mired in political quicksand.

Congress has become an institution of individuals rather than a community of common concern. It now operates out of a dozen buildings on Capitol Hill. Legislators have voted to exempt themselves from practically every regulatory law: they do not have to comply with the Civil Rights Act or the Equal Pay Act, and when they leave the congressional service they are not bound by the Ethics in Government Act. When controversial issues, like a pay raise, are considered, they are relegated to powerless commissions.

Part of the problem has to do with the fact that one party, the Democrats, has controlled the House for the past thirty-five years. During that time America has had seven presidents and four different changes of party in the White House. In 1986, when ten of thirty-four Senate seats and fourteen of thirty-three governorships changed parties, 98 percent of the 393 House members seeking reelection were successful. The average swing between parties has declined from an average of forty-five seats per election during the 1950s to fewer than twenty today.

Columnist David Broder of the *Washington Post* has calculated that during the last decade the number of bills reported by House committees has dropped by nearly 40 percent. In the last Congress, the House passed more than 300 bills that had never moved through committee. Under the effective control of one party, the House has become the federal institution most immune to change, but the Founding Fathers intended it to be the most sensitive to shifts in political sentiment. Incumbency has come to mean lifetime employment: in the first three months of 1988 House incumbents had already raised more than $75 million for the November elections, compared to less than $10 million for the challengers. *The Economist* was moved to comment that the House has fallen under a party hegemony whose duration is rivaled hardly anywhere outside the Communist world.

If America had the kind of meritocratic bureaucracy that functions so effectively in Japan or in Singapore, this process would be of comparatively less concern. But the American government does not have a bureaucratic elite. It has a career civil service that employs mediocre talent, compensates them at mediocre rates of pay, and provides more desirable pension and retirement benefits than the private sector. More and more responsibility has been shifted from career civil servants to political appointees.

Turnover is a systemic problem. With every change of administration in Washington more than 3,000 jobs held by political appointees change hands, with a corresponding lack of continuity and momentum, not to mention experience and judgment. These political appointees also don't stay very long: their average tenure is now barely two years. Graduates of American institutions that were originally created to prepare young people for careers in government service now gravitate to the private sector, where, as consultants and investment bankers, they earn multiples of the salaries earned by the career government officials they are soliciting or advising.

Given a spendthrift Congress increasingly unable, if not unwilling, to reduce the federal budget deficit and curtail spending; a political system increasingly corrupted by money, stalled by legislative gridlock, and dominated by special interest groups; a mediocre career bureaucracy increasingly frustrated by its loss of power and responsibility; and a cynical public increasingly aloof and detached, a troubling question emerges: how can America continue to assume the role of global political leadership on the threshold of the twenty-first century, an era that will be more competitive, by orders of magnitude, than any prior period in its history?

I put this question to Mark Shepherd, Jr., the former chairman of Texas Instruments.

"The thing that's incomprehensible to me," he said, shaking his head somewhat wistfully, "is that when you go to Washington and talk to these politicians, most of them seem to be pretty conscientious. A few are pretty smart, and a lot of them are pretty dumb, but collectively they're absolutely incapable of acting responsible *as a group*. I think we have a crisis of government on our hands, I really do, and we've got to figure out a way to do things differently, or we're going to continue this downhill slide."

I asked him whether doing things differently meant new ways of organizing ourselves politically.

"I'd give the president six years, and out," he said in his soft drawl. "Representation in the House ought to be changed so that members have four-year terms, with a maximum of two consecutive terms, period. For the Senate we need a term of eight, maybe ten years, and I'm not sure I'd let them stay more than one term. Like a CEO of any good organization, when a man's done his job, he ought to step aside and let people who are younger and hungrier and more energetic do the work."

His thoughts about the budget process were not optimistic.

"You know," he said, "that goddamn continuing resolution on the budget was a disgrace. Congress just cannot make a budget any longer—it's that simple. All the hoo-rah about cutting expenditures—hell, we don't have to *cut* them, we just have to stop increasing them. But one thing's for sure: this country's first order of business has to be a return to fiscal discipline."

We talked for a while about PACs—national PACs and local PACs and industry PACs. The American beer industry had long had a political action committee called the Six-PAC, and business had created a BI-PAC—a Business and Industry Political Action Committee.

"I don't know about PACs," Shepherd said with a frown. "Labor unions like the AFL-CIO and the UAW have always been able to pour all the money they wanted to into the political process. I guess I believe the PACs don't have all that much impact on what goes on at the polls, but they sure as hell influence what happens after a guy gets elected."

At Shepherd's invitation, I walked down the hall to see Vladi Catto, TI's Italian-born, American-educated chief economist, whom I had known for some years, to talk about his perspective on the budget numbers. His idea, he told me, was to freeze the nonentitlement, non-defense portion of the budget called discretionary spending, about 10 percent of the total. Catto's calculations showed total federal spending in 1988 was taking 23.3 percent of GNP. Freezing discretionary spending, holding defense expenditures to a constant 6 percent of GNP, allowing entitlements to grow by inflation (4 percent) and population growth (estimated at 0.8 percent through the year 2000), and projecting nominal GNP growth at 6.5 percent a year (2.5 percent real and 4.0 percent inflation) would put the budget in surplus by 1997 and reduce government spending to around 19 percent of GNP, the 1960–87 average.

But those estimates, it seemed to me, while reasonable and by no means aggressive, contravened one basic business belief: beware the permanent trend. Economies, as we know, do not expand arithmetically; sooner or later a recession intervenes to deflate them, and America's GNP growth during the longest postwar recovery period of 1982–88 averaged only slightly more than 2 percent anyway.

Not everybody believes the federal deficit is a problem of critical magnitude. One of those who does not is Robert Eisner, former president of the American Economic Association and professor of economics at Northwestern University, who wrote a contrarian book called *How Real Is the Federal Deficit?* In it he contended that there has always been a certain amount of hysteria concerning the federal debt and the annual budget deficits. He argued that the effects of inflation have pretty much been ignored throughout the whole budget debate process, but that they are significant. Why? Because as inflation erodes the value of money, it also erodes the value of debt, so the cumulative deficit should be adjusted for the effects of inflation. He also suggested reducing the deficit by privatizing more federal activities and by selling off some federal property, such as the government's gold reserves, certain loan portfolios, or national land. And he strongly urged dividing the budget into two accounts, one for long-term capital spending, which represents investment, and one for current operations, to reflect consumption.

But everybody knows that a dollar is a dollar, and even if 1980 debts must be repaid in 1990 dollars, no sophisticated accounting games can ease the burden of raising the necessary funds, unless, of course, the debt is cheapened by the effects of higher inflation. But nobody is arguing for a return to the double-digit inflation of the Carter years simply because it will make debt repayment easier. The Federal Reserve has already moved interest rates up to choke off an early inflationary surge.

A number of approaches need to be considered in any serious attempt to reduce the cumulative budget deficit and restore a process of fiscal discipline to America's national accounts. Virtually *all* of them will be unpopular, which is why America's elected representatives must uncouple themselves from the financial life-support systems called special interest groups and initiate the process of building a broad consensus on issues of national interest. The sacrifices that have to be made in the decade ahead, to help pay for the excesses of the past and to invest more productively for the future, need to be shared by all Americans. Broadly, these proposals come under the three rubrics of taxes, incentives, and innovations.

The federal budget deficits cannot be reduced entirely without considering an increase in some taxes; growth alone is not enough. People normally recoil from taxes because they think only in terms of individual *income* taxes. But the 1986 reduction of personal income taxes need not be changed; most evidence clearly shows the negative impact on GNP growth and unemployment resulting from higher personal taxes. Rather, a series of thoughtful user taxes, examined carefully, applied broadly, and phased in gradually, could contribute enormously.

Chief among these is a tax on oil, already widely debated and dismissed as regressive, but without question the single most useful source of potential revenues. The retail price of gasoline today, at a dollar and change a gallon, is, *inflation-adjusted,* cheaper than gasoline at 35¢ a gallon in 1955. For every penny of tax on a gallon of gasoline, the federal government raises $1 billion. Think about that for a minute: increasing the pump price of a gallon of gasoline by $1 a gallon will raise $100 billion. A tax of 50¢ a gallon could be set initially, most economists agree, with little negative impact on the economy. And a gasoline tax has more going for it than just additional government revenues: it serves as an incentive to develop an energy policy with domestic pricing more in line with global standards—the average price of fuel in OECD countries is about three times as high as it is in America—and it serves as a *dis*incentive to consume energy wastefully. Tied to conservation efforts, since the world price of oil has declined in the past two years, the net effect of a gasoline tax should not be inflationary.

Similarly, higher excise taxes on tobacco and alcohol, called "sin" taxes, ought to be given thorough consideration. Conservative estimates by Steve Roach, an economist at Morgan Stanley in New York, indicate that additional federal revenues of between $10 billion and $20 billion a year could be generated this way. Restoring federal liquor taxes to 1951 real levels and equalizing the tax on wine and beer would raise $20 billion annually. And that's just the tax side, the incentive. Conservation, represented by a declining use of cigarettes and liquor, could also result. But the House is especially captive of special interest groups here, particularly the American Tobacco Institute, which dictates not only domestic policy but trade policy as well. Sin taxes could also arrest other disturbing trends by cutting cigarette and alcohol consumption among America's teenagers. (For every four drunk drivers who kill themselves, statistics tell us, three innocent victims die.)

Other taxes also need to be given serious thought, such as a luxury tax that would penalize consumption of unnecessary luxury goods. Finally, a national sales or value-added tax deserves full study. Most

OECD nations use them, and they work in progressive stages as a levy on each step in the production and distribution process. They can also be deducted from the selling price of goods for export, which helps promote external trade. The rough formula is that for every 1 percent of VAT, the federal government would raise about $15 billion a year, so a 3 percent national sales tax could generate nearly $50 billion in new revenues.

The ball is clearly in Congress's court; the risk is that its elected representatives will use increased tax revenues to increase spending, not to reduce the deficit. And to the extent that the cost of higher federal spending outweighs the benefits of higher revenues, the exercise will have been in vain. Ideally, if the economy can be enticed to grow faster, as the turbocharged economies of Japan and Korea and Taiwan have shown, the need for higher taxes will be eliminated. But in the absence of federal incentives to accelerate growth in the strategic sectors, some increase in taxes may be unavoidable.

Beyond taxes, however, new incentives to save, rather than to spend, need even more urgent consideration.

The rate of personal savings in America is at an all-time low—now down to about 4 percent of net disposable income (up insignificantly from 3.8 percent to 4.2 percent as of early 1989), well below the historical average of about 6 percent and stunningly behind the savings rates in more productive economies abroad: 15 percent in West Germany, 20 percent in Japan, 30 percent in Korea, 35 percent in Taiwan. As a share of GNP, America's savings fell from 17 percent in 1981 to about 12 percent in 1987.

To generate higher savings in the United States, interest, dividends, and capital gains must be exempt from tax. Congress will have to consider some rather draconian measures, such as exempting from tax all interest on savings and money market accounts with a principal amount of up to $100,000, for instance, or exempting earned interest of $5,000 per person. Reinvested interest should be exempt from tax; interest withdrawn for consumption should be taxable. Dividends should be totally tax-free to the recipient; they are currently subject to double taxation as it is, since they are paid out of after-tax corporate income.

The Treasury has conducted studies showing that an optimum tax rate on capital gains is about 15 percent, and the Bush administration has proposed reducing capital gains taxes to that level. Today capital gains are taxed as ordinary income, at 28 percent (or 33 percent for higher-income taxpayers), currently the highest rate of tax on capital gains in the industrialized world, except for Britain. Rates in Western Europe are uniformly below 20 percent, and the capitalist developmental states of East Asia impose *no* tax on long-term capital gains at all.

The Treasury also calculates that total accumulation of unrealized capital gains at year-end 1987 was about $4 trillion (that's *trillion,* not billion). If gains from the sale of private residences (which are sheltered from tax by rollover provisions and a one-time $125,000 exclusion) are excluded from this figure, the total pool of realizable capital gains is still about $2 trillion. And the year-to-year increase in this accumulation, which Treasury thinks is a good guide to potential long-term realizations, is estimated to be about $350 billion a year and growing, even excluding personal residences.

"While low [personal income] tax rates were an enormous step forward," a February 1989 Treasury report concluded, "the Tax Reform Act of 1986 also raised the rate of tax on capital gains. In this area, our major competitors now have the upper hand: none of them taxes long-term capital gains in full. Restoring a tax differential for capital gains will solidify the favorable tax position of the United States relative to the major industrial nations of the world."

Under current tax law, investors are not only taxed on capital gains at the same rate as for ordinary personal income; they are also taxed the same whether they hold an asset for three months or for three years. So reducing the tax on capital gains to 15 percent would not only encourage greater savings, as more funds would flow to sources of income with lower tax rates; it would also enhance federal revenues by increasing the total amount of income subject to tax. And by staggering the capital gains rate to favor long-term assets over short-term, the nation would benefit by encouraging investment oriented toward long-run growth rather than short-swing speculation.

Eighty percent of America's savings is traditionally generated by about 20 percent of the taxpayers. The 1979 capital gains tax reduction from 35 percent to 28 percent produced an additional $15 billion in tax revenues through 1985, because the lower tax acted as an incentive for people to invest: higher returns, even though taxed at a lower rate, produced greater tax revenues. Similar results were achieved when the rate was reduced further, from 28 percent to 20 percent, in 1981. And the tax could be staggered: the longer the holding period, the lower the tax, falling to zero after three years.

Since federal borrowing (dissaving) has taken about three-fourths of net private savings by all American families and business *combined*, there is insufficient savings available to finance the necessary investment in new and more productive plant and equipment. The first order of business for American economic policy must be to allow private savings to determine the country's level of investment, and thereby its economic growth, which is another way of saying that the federal deficit has to be eliminated so that private savings can then accomplish that.

"The openness of opportunity, the social mobility, and the continuous striving for excellence that have traditionally distinguished America," Harvard economist Benjamin Friedman wrote recently in the *National Review*, "have been able to sustain the ideal of forward progress for over two centuries [because] Americans' standard of living has roughly doubled once per generation throughout this time. Without the fact of forward progress, our willingness to work to make reality conform to our democratic ideals would probably wither, and America would succumb to the social rigidity and acceptance of mediocrity that are characteristic of economically stagnant societies elsewhere."

By far the hardest part of the process, politically, is eliminating cost of living adjustments (COLAs) and reestablishing some sort of means testing for entitlements benefits. Some politicians have said that any candidate for president who suggests tinkering with the Social Security system is also a "candidate for a frontal lobotomy." But Social Security is the second-fastest-growing component of the national budget, after interest on the federal debt, and has practically doubled in the last decade, from $118 billion to $220 billion. Wealthy or well-to-do recipients do not need the money. Somehow the principle of need has to be restored. With the generation of baby boomers—the 78 million Americans born between 1946 and 1964—now moving into middle age, demands on the Social Security system will be greater than for any earlier generation.

Social Security is a vital source of income for Americans who are members of "double jeopardy" groups, those characterized by any two of the following: older than seventy-five, widowed, single, divorced, in poor health, with no private pension, or nonwhite. For the large number of middle- and upper-middle-class recipients, however, taxing those benefits, or eliminating them altogether, may be critical to saving the system as well as reducing the deficit. And finding ways for America's elderly, who are the best protected from inflation and poverty today, to share the necessary sacrifices with America's children, who are not, will be no easy task for the American political process.

In 1983 the Grace Commission, chaired by the well-known businessman Peter Grace, produced 2,478 recommendations to reduce the federal deficit by $400 billion over three years and make government more efficient by emulating private-sector business practices. Of those 2,478 suggestions, the rhetorical question was: how many were implemented? The not-so-obvious answer: none of them. The most significant savings, representing more than $50 billion, or 14 percent of the total, was a single recommendation to cut federal pensions, both civilian and military.

In the civil service, Pete Peterson has noted, the pension level is so high (averaging 56 percent of preretirement pay), the retirement age is so young (fifty-five after thirty years of service), and the disability criteria are so easy to meet (one-quarter of all civil service pensioners are "disabled") that benefits far exceed contributions. In 1987, $47 billion was spent by Washington on the two most generous pension systems in America. The *average* pension for retired government workers is now $35,000. Unlike any private pension, however, civil service pensions are fully indexed to the consumer price index, with the result that retirees often earn more than their successors in office.

Military pensions are the ultimate bonanza. When a serviceman reaches age forty-one and has completed twenty years of service, he can receive a minimum of 50 percent and a maximum of 75 percent of base pay, fully indexed annually, for life. Only a quarter of America's military pensioners are older than sixty-five, all are eligible for Social Security, and many continue in second careers to earn additional income and qualify for a "triple-dip" private pension. As with Social Security, the issue is equity.

Medicare and Medicaid costs—not to mention the newly approved costs of catastrophic illness coverage—are worth a chapter themselves, if not a separate book. Medicare expenditures more than doubled, from $32 billion in 1980 to $66 billion in 1985. They will cost $78 billion in 1988 and an estimated $84 billion in 1989; they represent about 25 percent of *all* federal benefit spending. The rate of inflation for medical care in America now averages twice the CPI. Indexation—the source of COLAs—is another sacred cow overdue for killing. In the late 1960s only 6 percent of all federal benefits were indexed, but by 1988 nearly 80 percent were. This practice insulates recipients from the consequences of inflation and higher living costs but does nothing to encourage either thrift or conservation. It also removes larger portions of the budget from congressional control.

"The government of the United States was not fashioned out of self-evident truths," Pat Moynihan wrote in *Came the Revolution*, "but rather was the work of scholar-statesmen who had studied hard, learned much, and believed they had come upon some principles in human behavior which made possible the reintroduction of republican government nearly two millennia after Caesar had ended the experiment. Today we are short on Madisons and Hamiltons and Jays."

Columnist George Will commented recently on the lessons America ought to be learning from recent experience. "We need to come to grips with the mismatch between the readiness of national governments to spend money and the reluctance of those governments to tax sufficiently to pay for their bills."

Well, America has two mismatches, not just one: a cumulative and expanding trade deficit and a cumulative and expanding budget deficit. To continue with a business-as-usual approach is to invite real trouble. Policy difficulties inherent in turning the trade deficit around are mirrored by the political difficulties inherent in eliminating the budget deficit. This is not to say that change is impossible, only that it will be extraordinarily difficult. Citizens in a democracy, however, tend to want to be left alone, except in cases of extreme crisis, such as war. The question for America's citizens, then, is how much further the nation's political process has to deteriorate before they respond to the crisis.

To move a nation from consumption addiction to investment cure will be no easy task, requiring the wisdom of both liberal and conservative. These are *national* issues. America's addiction to consumption over the years has created, in the words of MIT economist Emma Rothschild, a teenaged python, which must be fed increasingly large amounts of foreign capital to satisfy its craving for consumer goods. In 1982 America borrowed from foreigners the equivalent of half of Iceland's GNP; in 1983 all of New Zealand's; in 1984 Norway's; in 1985 Switzerland's; and in 1986 Sweden's. By 1987 America was borrowing the equivalent of the GNP of the entire continent of Africa, and Japan alone held half the Treasury bonds owned by foreigners.

As foreigners hold a larger and larger share of America's debt, the opportunity to hold the United States hostage to opposing foreign policy or national interest objectives looms larger and larger, too. Just as Washington waged war on sterling in 1956, during the Suez crisis, Tokyo could well wage war on the dollar during a Pacific crisis, to further Japan's own future hegemonic aims, thereby shifting the geopolitical center of gravity even more dramatically from West to East. To wean itself away from foreign capital dependence, America must begin generating a dramatically higher share of its own domestic savings. This implies consensus, which will inevitably involve sacrifice.

"Hard times will come," economist Robert Heilbroner wrote in *The New Yorker* recently, "and indeed are already here, because the establishment of a strong but not hegemonic American economic role requires the most extraordinary exercise of political foresight and economic pragmatism. These are not qualities that have been abundantly evident in recent years. Both political and economic decisions must play critical roles in determining our future. Insofar as such decisions place our destiny within our grasp in a manner that a surrender to the market does not, the future has never been more firmly entrusted to our own devices. What remains to be seen is the use we will make of this onerous privilege."

The *Economic Report of the President* makes explicit mention of America's "proven market-oriented policies" being adopted as a blueprint for progress by more and more countries throughout the world. But America's policies, one European observer has noted, "remind me of Christopher Columbus's travels. He didn't know where he was when he got there. And he didn't know where he'd been when he got back. All he knew for sure was that the whole trip had been financed with foreign money."

Recently I was sitting in the New York office of Japan's former consul general, Ambassador Hidetoshi Ukawa, a very polished representative of Tokyo's elite foreign ministry. "I think it's rather a question of mentality," he said to me. "Can your private sector recapture its work ethic and the puritan values your country used to have? Tax incentives and public policy can go only so far. There has to be a will on the part of the people."

Ambassador Ukawa's own country has shown, as we have seen, that the formulation of strategic policies and the relevance of targeted incentives can create that will. What's missing in America today is the effective leadership to design the incentives that will help generate the national will.

"The dangers of America's decline are already evident," James Chace wrote in his thoughtful book, *Solvency: The Price of Survival.* "Continuing trade and budget deficits mount as we spend ourselves into insolvency, as we refuse to consume less and produce more until our capital is exhausted and with it the world we have known. There is a limit to how long a great nation can allow itself to be governed by those who lack the capacity to lead. For a time its failures can be covered up, but the danger is that when the crisis can no longer be hidden there may be no providential statesmen to reinvigorate a society in peril."

Can America presume to lead a more competitive world into the twenty-first century if it can't revitalize its political system, reinvigorate its arsenal of economic incentives, and reverse the process of decline?

9

REINVIGORATING AMERICAN DEMOCRACY

No other nation has a political system whose basic character has remained unchanged for so long as the United States. We have been holding presidential and congressional elections for 200 years now, and in that time just 41 men have held our highest office. The senior senator from New Hampshire still sits at Daniel Webster's desk; the ink-well is kept filled and sand is provided for blotting. Our political parties, though not mentioned in the Constitution, are nearly as old. The Democratic Party was formed in the early 1830s, under Andrew Jackson's aegis, by that master politician Martin Van Buren; the Republican Party sprung up almost spontaneously in reaction to Stephen Douglas's Kansas-Nebraska Act of 1854 and won the congressional elections that year. The two have remained our major parties ever since.

Michael Barone and Grant Ujifusa,
The Almanac of American Politics

Two decades ago, when the British comedy team Beyond the Fringe was in vogue, there was a brief but very telling dialogue among the actors (and authors), Alan Bennett, Peter Cook, Dudley Moore, and Jonathan Miller, about American politics. Moore was on his way to America for the first time and was practicing singing the national anthem, not always on key.

"I thought I'd brush up on my 'Star-Spangled Banner' before I go," he said.

"Well, you have to do that," Bennett said. "Otherwise, they won't give you a visa. They're very sticky about that. Toscanini waited for years and years."

"I understand the whole dilemma of the American Constitution,"

Moore said, "is that there is no royal family. I mean, their president is rather like our queen and prime minister rolled into one."

"Yes, and the first thing you'll notice about Americans," Jonathan Miller interjected, "is that they're not English."

"Another thing you'll notice about America," Peter Cook added, "is that it is a very young country. Rather like Ghana in that respect."

"Except for the fact that the Americans have inherited our two-party system," Miller corrected.

"Oh?" Moore asked. "How does that work?"

"Well, you see, they have the Republican party, which is the equivalent of our Conservative party," he explained. "And they have the Democratic party, which is the equivalent of our Conservative party."

"Are the liberals Democrats or Republicans?"

"Yes. As is convenient for them."

In an age of politics dominated by special interest groups, it comes as no surprise that the traditional political parties no longer represent the American people. The difficulty comes in trying to assess which came first: the rise of the special interest group, which gradually replaced the party as a focal point for political concerns, or the demise of the political party, creating a vacuum that was filled by the special interest group. My sense is, probably the latter.

Gradually, almost imperceptibly, the power and influence of the smoke-filled halls in America's big cities gave way to a more transparent, though arguably less efficient, political system dominated by national television. Political machines withered and then died as the bosses themselves passed away, and the broad middle class that had been their traditional political base moved out of the city and into the suburbs. As America's demographic center of gravity shifted westward, the city, once the barometer of American politics, became its coffin.

And as contemporary life became more complex, special interest groups rose to prominence with a narrow focus based on a narrow specialty. Whether a politician was a Democrat or a Republican became irrelevant; relevance was translated into votes on legislation, and if you voted in favor of the issue being sponsored by one interest group or another, you got that group's backing and money, regardless of your party affiliation. In a sense, the rise of special interest groups could be called the homogenizing of American politics.

"The American political system, which in its original form was the greatest contribution to modern civilization," Edward Vrdolyak wrote recently in the *Wall Street Journal*, "has evolved from a system in which great men debated important issues to a sport in which a lot of people debate mostly trivial issues. Where the founding fathers were admired for their intellect, and *what* they knew, now politicians are just as often admired for their connections, or *whom* they know." In the sixteenth century Niccolò Machiavelli told future politicians to stay close to the people they were ruling. Today Washington is the real home for American politicians; their true constituents are lobbyists, special interest groups, journalists, and PACS.

America's two-party system is as familiar as, well, the arbitrary division of twenty-four hours into daytime and nighttime. But it hasn't always been so. There was a succession of minor parties in the early nineteenth century, the most significant of which were the Whigs and the Mugwumps. Today it is fair to say that there are two minority parties in America, the smaller of which is the Republican.

Traditionally, Republicans stood for prudence in fiscal management and tried to slow down the spendthrift Democrats, until Reagan conservatives took power on the strength of their ability to win the blue-collar vote away from the Democrats. But Americans have tended to favor Republicans in the White House (they have won seven of the ten presidential elections since 1952), preferring to put Democrats in control of Congress. If the presidency is a tone-setting institution, as some have observed, then Republicans have done a better job of articulating a vision for America; but just to be on the safe side, Americans hedge their bets by returning Democrats to power in the House and Senate. By 1980 Americans decided they no longer wanted "big government" and voted into power a man whose administration promised to reduce its size. As we have seen, thwarted by a spendthrift Congress, it could do no such thing. All that was reduced was the willingness of Americans to pay for the level of government many pollsters said they no longer wanted.

Who would have ever suspected that Republican administrations would wind up generating a higher rate of budget deficits (and a larger absolute deficit) than traditional Democratic administrations had proved capable of doing? (Well, a fiscally imprudent Congress, for one.) And who would have guessed that, despite deregulation of AT&T, the airlines, and a host of other highly regulated industries, the process of deregulation would trigger only superficial change? It was Richard Nixon, a Republican president who, in 1971, proudly pronounced himself a Keynesian; the most popular candidate ever, he received the highest absolute number of votes in American history.

Many Republicans, one observer has noted, are either businesspeople, economists, or lawyers. American businesspeople believe they live in a highly ordered world of competition that is defined primarily by a huge domestic market and only secondarily (if at all) by global markets. They tend to be rational. Economists, as we have seen, live in a world of models and formulas and are always trying to make reality fit the model. They too are rational, but they are mostly irrelevant. Lawyers are trained to view the world in contentious terms. They thrive on dispute, drawn to adversity like vultures to a cadaver. Nations, however, are neither naturally rational nor inherently disputatious.

"Growth of government," Pat Moynihan has said, "is a natural, inevitable product of the political bargaining process among interest groups that favor government outlays that benefit them." Republicans are no different in this regard. In fact, the "dirty little secret" of the Republican party is that 80 percent of House Republicans and 90 percent of Senate Republicans have voted for *all* major expansions of the American welfare state during the postwar political era. Despite their claims to the contrary, the irritation of Americans with government has less to do with its size than with its intrusiveness.

"The irritant is the increased intrusiveness of government," George Will wrote in *The New Season*, "an intrusiveness perceived as irrational, arrogant, and bullying. Millions of Americans found intolerable such government actions as forced busing to achieve racial balance, mandatory reverse discrimination, including hiring and firing quotas that overrode seniority claims, the minute supervision of businesses by bureaucratic administrators of occupational safety and health regulations, the overturning of fifty state judgments concerning the regulation of abortion, the banning of voluntary prayer in public schools, and on and on. The nation began a realignment, not so much from Democrat to Republican as from 'liberal' to 'conservative.' Conservatives value continuity and disvalue change; liberals love change, and the more, the better."

As to political choice, there was once a story about a mountain climber perched precariously near the top of a dangerous ledge. As he inched forward, his footing gave way, and he grabbed the branch of a tree nearby, holding on for dear life. When he looked down, he could see the water crashing onto the rocks 500 feet below.

He looked up and yelled, "Help! Is anybody up there?"

"Have faith!" a voice thundered from Heaven. "Trust in the Lord, let yourself go, and you will float softly down until you are wrapped in the welcoming arms of the sea."

He looked up again and swallowed.

"Is anybody else up there?"

For Americans choice implies one of two, Republican or Democrat. America has no "opposition" parties, as in parliamentary political systems, nor is there a "ruling" party that has dominated for generations, as with the Liberal Democrats in Japan or the People's Action Party in Singapore. Dean Acheson, once the wise old man of the Democratic party, was told by a friend, "You are intelligent and experienced, yet you are a Democrat. How can this be?" Acheson said he thought all intelligent people were Democrats and tended to believe that, while not all conservatives were stupid, all stupid people were conservative.

In nine presidential elections from 1952 to 1984, thirty-nine states, representing 441 electoral votes (171 more than the 270 needed to win), have voted Republican at least five times; thirty-three states, with 322 electoral votes, voted Republican six times; seventeen, with 143 votes, went Republican eight times, producing, in the words of political analyst Horace Busby, an "electoral college lock" for Republicans. Democrats have nowhere near this stable a political base. Their presidential candidates in 1980 and 1984, Jimmy Carter and Walter Mondale, won fewer electoral votes in two elections (sixty-two) than any candidate in American history. Part of the Democratic party's problem is identification: the average American voter is typically "unyoung, unpoor, and unblack," but the Democratic party has become identified in voters' minds as the party of the poor, the black, and government workers.

As the Democratic party rotates through its nominating process, it has become more and more liberal, causing it to lose its more conservative members to the Republicans. And as candidates compete for the Democratic nomination in the now-transparent primary campaigns, by appealing for votes from remaining Democrats who form an increasingly liberal party base, internal consensus for the candidate has not translated successfully into a broader national mandate. In the 1988 campaign Michael Dukakis dodged the liberal label for weeks. In 1984 Democrats thought vice presidential candidate Geraldine Ferraro would have broad national appeal because she was a woman, a Catholic, an Italian-American, and from Queens. (She carried the women's vote, Catholics, Italian-Americans, and the borough of Queens.)

If, as some observers believe, Americans are inherently optimistic and hopeful, then they will vote for the candidate who inspires the most optimism and hope. Change therefore has to be perceived as beneficial and positive, rather than constraining. In the 1860s, under Abraham Lincoln, the new Republican party ended slavery, setting loose a generation of positive change, from industrialization and westward expansion to immigration and dramatic growth of the nation's railroads. Between 1860 and 1932 the Democrats elected only *two* presidents, until FDR. But FDR capitalized on major shocks to the economic system to enable Democrats to be perceived as the party of positive change. The New Deal was the result. Republican victories since 1952 can be viewed as opportunistic, since they occurred at times when the Democratic party appeared to be stagnating and in disarray.

The Democratic party had come to be identified as the principal foe of the greatest evil of the twentieth century, totalitarianism. While the American political system has welcomed the Cold War thaw, neither Republican nor Democratic leaders have yet come to grips with the realistic consequences of a Soviet Union in decline. In the meantime, Democrats have embraced protectionism as a potential springboard to their political future, perhaps without realizing that, as a result, they may spring themselves even further into the past.

Not long ago I was invited to give a speech on Asia to the annual meeting of the Construction Industry Manufacturers Association. As I was drafting my speech, which focused on the dynamics of Japan's economic development and its aggressive external orientation to trade, I learned that I would be followed by George Will. I spoke briefly with him following his own talk.

I voiced surprise that neither the Republicans nor the Democrats had targeted the baby boom generation as a natural constituency.

George Will smiled behind his familiar glasses.

"The first rule of understanding politics," he said, "is that demographics is destiny. A significant proportion of the 78 million baby boomers are the new-collar workers of America, neither white-collar nor blue-. The youngest are almost twenty-four, the oldest forty-two, and the 25 million new-collar workers comprise 15 percent of the vote. They are very family-centered, but with equally strong priorities on their work. They know they aren't as well off as their parents, so economic issues tend to predominate. They tend toward political activism, but they haven't gravitated toward either party."

I asked him whether traditional distinctions between Republican and Democrat were blurring faster now, and he said, "Both parties are facing intellectual exhaustion. Three things have changed in the past decade: tax revenues are lower, the tax code has been indexed, and marginal tax rates have been reduced. Fifteen percent of American households now spend more than half of their net disposable income on debt service, not unlike their federal government. And that exemplifies what is wrong with the country."

Would gasoline and sin taxes help?

Will grinned. He has a patentable, boyish grin.

"Washington can generate nearly $50 billion with a 50¢ tax on a gallon of gasoline," he said crisply. "And in 1984, when an 8¢ tax was added to tobacco, 2 million smokers stopped smoking and a half million young ones never started. One in every five Americans dies from tobacco or liquor, so you can draw some easy conclusions. But leadership is the ability to inflict pain and get away with it, the ability to say 'No, we've had enough.' That, I think, is the real challenge facing America's political leaders today."

Demographics is destiny.

Through a circuitous path I contacted Paul Hewitt, the young executive director of a nonprofit, nonpartisan public policy group in Washington called Americans for Generational Equity, with the rather interesting acronym AGE. Hewitt, trained as an economist at Berkeley, was a former staff member of the Advisory Commission on Intergovernmental Relations when he became aware of the growing inequity between the federal government's spending on the elderly, who symbolized the present, and its spending on the young, who represented the future. Wanting to educate and inform the public on the political and social implications of the nation's aging population, he formed AGE, as he put it, "with a finger in the wind." We met to talk about the relationship between demographics and politics and how it affects the issue of generational equity.

"In 1983," he said, massaging the ends of his sandy moustache, "half of all Americans polled by the advisory commission said that interest groups represented them better than their political party did. This indicated to me a distinct shift from backrooms and traditional machine politics to media campaigns. Remember, in 1968 the median age of

Americans was just twenty-eight, but by 1988 it was thirty-three and rising. Those under eighteen can't vote, and those between eighteen and forty—baby boomers, for the most part—don't yet vote with a purpose, swinging distinct political influence disproportionately to the elderly. We know that voter participation rises with age. After 1996 the baby boom generation moves into prime voting and institution-control age."

But hadn't the baby boomers become a selfish, inward-looking generation, symbolized by young urban professionals?

Hewitt shook his head.

"The yuppie was a big misnomer," he said. "Compared to the yuppie, baby boomers have less money, are more family-centered, have more children, and are far more numerous. Baby boomers have stood for a number of healthy issues over the years: environmentalism, good government, consumerism, education reform, and so on. The Me Generation was not the baby boomers, but their parents. Still, when they look ahead at their future retirement, they see some pretty frightening things. Middle and upper middle classes are reproducing at a rate of about 1.4 children per woman of childbearing age—you need a 2.1 rate for zero population growth—while blacks and Hispanics are reproducing at a rate nearly double that, about 2.8 children per woman of childbearing age. What that means is that today you have 18 percent of American children, and 23 percent of all children of preschool age, living in poverty. Demographers now project that Caucasians will be in the minority in America as a whole by the year 2050, at these rates."

Paul Hewitt explained what he thought were the implications of these demographic trends.

"What this means is that not only will Social Security be affected," he went on, "but so will our schools, the job markets, drug use, and so on. The underclass may be expanding beyond the ability of the federal government to provide for it. This is especially cause for concern with regard to education, because it means that the class of youngsters that is growing the fastest is the class we have not successfully been able to educate. Think of the implications for the job market, for America's international competitiveness, for the nation's future standard of living."

I asked him how he related these demographic trends to issues like savings and investment or retirement.

"As long as the U.S. savings rate is low," Hewitt said, "the opportunity for productive enhancements is not good. Therefore, America will likely lurch from crisis to crisis, with no great sense of political stewardship. The intergenerational burden is now beginning to shift from the elderly to the young. We see a coming confrontation between young and old, which will produce a process of atomization within organizations like AARP and which will cause it to split off into several separate entities, each representing specific segments, by age."

He then explained how these intergenerational issues would filter into the political process.

"America's political process has become a media-based politics of homogenized, thirty-second slogans—the sound bite," he said. "So there is less of a sense of loyalty and community in belonging to a party. If the constituency of a politician is media-based, it gives the opposition a better opportunity to promote negative images. For example, in 1960 TV network news was only fifteen minutes. Now you can spend practically half an evening watching news and news commentary and half a *day* on Sunday. Therefore, what has happened as a result of expansion of the media is enhanced influence of interest groups—the strong get stronger. Politically, in the old days, it was easier to generate consensus: LBJ, Sam Rayburn, and Mike Mansfield, say, would get together, hammer out a compromise, then announce, 'This is where we want to take the country.' Today the special interest groups play divide-and-conquer politics, driven by a very short-term philosophy: we don't buy green bananas. These interest groups can focus tremendous attention on the welfare of some (such as age-based entitlements, for example), and others, like our children and the young, lose out. It's like a political teeter-totter. Proposition 13, in California, a decade ago, was a good example. A group of older, childless, empty-nest voters wanted to lower the property tax, and it took years for the state to raise revenues from other sources so that education and the needs of children—the state's future—would not suffer."

Hewitt then brought the argument full circle.

"We have to ask ourselves," he said, "why are these special interest groups so effective? That's the key. Since our political parties no longer stand for anything, there is now a massive center, with an ideological left and an ideological right, like a flock of sheep with a pair of sheepdogs keeping them in the center. There is tremendous consensus in America, I feel, but over irrelevant or trivial issues, because the issues have become controlled by interest groups. Neither party is willing to take on the antitax or pro-benefits crowd, for instance, whereas if you really had an effective two-party system, you'd line up support on both sides and begin to hammer out compromises. American politicians today are dealing primarily with unreality, and not with real trade-offs, in order to give in to the interest groups. The result is political stagnation."

The outlook, it seemed to me, hardly augured well for optimism. There didn't appear to be any effective ways of jolting the system back to reality.

"America tends to respond best to a sense of crisis," Hewitt said, nodding. "The generations that experienced the Depression, World War II, the Marshall Plan, even *Sputnik,* shared a sense of community, of common effort, of mission. If we experience a severe national crisis in the 1990s, such as a prolonged recession, for example, we could potentially sober up, but ex that, there appears to be no possibility for a general renewal. The energy crisis in the early 1970s was the last great test, and even that didn't do it. In the 1990s we may become obsessed with savings, not only because of international pressure on our government to do so, but also because the growing number of aging baby boomers will realize that their own retirement will be impossible without it. So our decline may also bring with it the possibility of renewal."

Had the time come to create a new, results-oriented political party in America, using the baby boom generation as its power base to generate that renewal? A constitutional party, for instance, that would be pro-incentive, pro-growth, pro-strategy, pro-results, pro-future. Could it short-circuit the special interest groups by preempting, as its base, the single largest group of political constituents in America, the baby boom generation?

Hewitt smiled and raised an eyebrow.

"Very interesting," he said. "Of course the Republicans started back in the 1850s, and Abraham Lincoln, their first president, rose to prominence on the issue of slavery. But the process had been building for a long time before that. You could conceive of a third party forming from within both the Republican and Democratic parties, I guess. But the problem with basing them on the baby boomers is that they're not a homogeneous group. Stewardship is the issue. For your constitutionalists, the galvanizing issue could be entitlements. It will be very interesting to see."

A brief look at demographics shows the potential power inherent within the baby boom generation's grasp. Baby boomers are the pig in America's population python. Increases in life expectancy, through advances in medical technology, combined with decreases in the overall American birth rate from the baby bust generation following behind, means the baby boomers, as they age, will dominate the graying of America.

According to the Census Bureau, about 11 percent of America's population was sixty-five or over in 1980; by the year 2030 this segment will double, to more than 21 percent. In 1900 only 4 percent of America's population was eighty-five or older; in 1980, 9 percent; by 2030, the very-old population will nearly double again. America has just begun to come to grips with the social and political implications of these population trends, which are especially pronounced in medical and health care services. Researchers indicate that a new 220-bed nursing home will be opened every day between now and the year 2000 just to keep even with demand, and this is before the baby boomers reach old age.

Fully 90 percent of all baby boomers are now in the work force. But this trend will reverse itself as the baby boomers reach retirement. In 1985 there were 4.9 working Americans paying benefits for every retiree over age sixty-five. By 2030 the Census Bureau projects this ratio could fall to 2.2 to one. Today every fortieth American is eighty or over; by 2050, one in twelve will be. Unable to depend on population growth to finance their old age benefits, the baby boomers have an unavoidable need to accumulate assets from which they can draw later income. The average retirement age today is sixty-two, while average life expectancy for men is seventy-seven and for women eighty-two. The combination of a larger number of workers plus a decrease in America's rate of productive investment (i.e., lower savings) has created the decline in productivity, lower-quality jobs, and falling real wages.

So the downward spiral continues. In 1949 the average thirty-year-old who bought the median American house needed only 14 percent of take-home pay to meet the mortgage. By 1983 the combination of inflation in real estate and falling real wages meant the average thirty-year-old was paying 44 percent of his or her income to meet housing costs. The same year, two-thirds of all first-time home buyers needed two paychecks to meet monthly expenses. Home equity is an important traditional source of American wealth and economic security. More than 70 percent of America's elderly own their own homes today, but barely half of all Americans aged thirty to thirty-four do, and less than forty percent of those aged twenty-five to twenty-nine.

These 78 million Americans are moving, year by year, into middle age, into the realm of high voter participation. The future of the nation rests increasingly in their hands. Issues have begun to crystallize now. America could well be on the verge of creating, during the 1990s, a restructured political process that might have as one of its results a new party or as another an amended constitution, brought about by a more results-oriented political system responding to socially critical issues of numerically superior baby boomers.

Someone once said that there wasn't enough caffeine to keep America awake through the presidential campaign of 1988, and he was right. The campaign seemed magnetized by the pledge of allegiance and prisoner furloughs. Before the elections, in Cambridge, I was speaking to a group of Harvard alumni on the concept of a Pacific century, an era in which the world's standards and values and principles (and the rules for international public goods) might be dominated by Asia rather than by America. We talked about the strategic approach to public policy formulation in East Asia, and someone asked which of the two presidential candidates might be most inclined to implement these kinds of strategic policies for America, if elected. Neither, I said, because the strategy has to be built on the concept of a national consensus, on what matters for the future of a nation, not on the narrow, parochial concern of special interests. Because, by default, America's political system is driven by these special interests, it cannot achieve that national consensus.

But a national agenda that America might embrace as a means of setting a new course for the future based on the kinds of incentives we have stressed has begun to jell, and there seems to be a growing consensus among mainstream Americans. For starters, new tax revenues could be derived from use taxes, such as a gasoline tax, staggered over time to allow American energy prices to rise to world levels. There could be increased excise taxes on liquor and cigarettes and a luxury tax to penalize the consumption of nonstrategic goods. And over time a phased-in national sales tax or VAT.

The distinction between user taxes and income taxes must be drawn clearly; Americans already pay personal taxes at one of the highest rates of any industrialized country in the world. As the economy expands, a case should be made for further reductions in personal tax rates as an incentive for growth. Nor should Congress be permitted to increase spending by using increased tax revenues to do so. The revenues must be mandated to reduce the federal deficit and to make the effect of incentives more powerful in the private sector.

To boost private savings, an aggressive program of strategic financial incentives will be needed, to exempt from tax all interest earned on principal amounts invested in approved money market accounts and savings bonds of up to, say, $50,000 per person. Savings earmarked for the college education of America's children should be exempt from both federal and local tax, as an incentive to involve more qualified youngsters in higher education. Federal taxes on dividends should be eliminated, and capital gains taxes reduced to 15 percent, assuming a minimum holding period of one year and reducing the tax to zero after a holding period of three years. Short-term gains could continue to be taxed at ordinary income rates.

To enhance investment in strategic industries and to spur their growth, higher depreciation benefits should be available for the more advanced technology sectors, along with an investment tax credit, disaggregated to favor strategic priorities. Aggressive deductions for higher research and development expenses should be permitted, front-loading them into the year they are expensed rather than staggering them over product cycles. Investments in new technology, in new productive plant and equipment, in higher value-added manufacturing, and in exports would also receive favorable, disaggregated tax and depreciation benefits. Investments in unproductive (or consumption) sectors, such as real estate, retail sales, and fast foods, would receive none.

The market could then move in the direction of higher value-added jobs, with higher real wages for more Americans, making America a nation of producers again. Yet the shift from consumption to production may generate an unavoidable recession; there will be a need to dilute the harsher side effects of unemployment and dislocation through worker retraining for higher value-added jobs, not conditionless unemployment insurance.

An increase in the personal deduction for married couples and children to $5,000 per person would shelter a higher threshold of the median American family income from federal tax. The amount would reflect in inflation-adjusted terms the $600 exemption that was created in 1948, when American tax policy strongly favored families. Over time, means testing for federal entitlements would be reinstated, indexation adjusted, and cost of living adjustments now locked into federal benefits reduced. Federal civil service retirement benefits could be set on a common basis with average private sector benefits.

The Constitution, last amended by the Twenty-sixth Amendment in 1971 setting the right to vote at age eighteen, may need to be amended again. At issue are the term of America's elected representatives and the funding of national elections. If members of the House were elected for one six-year term, and a maximum of two consecutive terms were permitted, then much of the wasteful churning in America's political system might be eliminated. At the same time, consideration should be given to mandating a single six-year term for the presidency, putting all of America's elected representatives on the same basis.

At the same time, perhaps in the process of constitutional review, consideration could be given to eliminating all personal and corporate contributions to candidates running for any national office and establishing, by constitutional amendment, public financing for national elections. Ways will have to be found to wean the electoral process away from television and to force politicians back into personal contact with their traditional constituencies, to bring the American voter closer to the historical concept of the citizen-legislator.

We are asking of ourselves today no less than the Founding Fathers asked two centuries ago: duty, sacrifice, commitment, and a patriotism that finds expression by taking part and pitching in. Public money alone, in the form of increased federal spending, cannot and will not solve our problems. Already by the early 1970s, if not the late 1960s, it had become clear that federal programs were costing too much, making the national government too intrusive in the lives of its people, deflating morale and offending ordinary virtues and values.

A nation that cannot govern its own appetite for consumption may prove to be incapable of self-government. People need empowerment, yet that should not be dependent on the state but should come from their own personal associations. The individual citizen is the agent of change, the federal government a summoned midwife; it works best by getting out of the way. America is on the threshold of a revolution in policy. Washington can help create the incentives, but it should not pave the path to justice. Michael Novak of the American Enterprise Institute put it best when he said that to feed the sparrows by feeding horses is inefficient.

The focus of any national agenda should be on *incentives,* to guide and direct the market and the behavior of the nation's citizens in the desired direction. This may well mean, as Charles Murray has argued so brilliantly in *Losing Ground,* that the entire federal welfare system has to be scrapped, to leave the working-age person with no recourse except the job market, family, and friends. But with the proper incentives, a more productive job market can expand through faster growth in the strategic, externally driven manufacturing sectors. Using tax policy to fine-tune the process is one of the most powerful tactical tools America has.

A revitalized American political system could work wonders in eliminating the tendency of a spendthrift Congress to step on the funding accelerator as a solution to every problem. As it has responded effectively to crises in the past, America must now find a way to do again what it does so well—reinforcing the investment of an individual in *himself.* The federal government should not stage-manage the nation's strategic investment decisions, but help set the incentives and then get out of the nation's way as it makes those decisions on its own. Unlike the homogeneous cultures of East Asia, America will never be 250 million hearts beating as one. Its federal system thrives on decentralization, yet the nation has somehow gotten its priorities reversed: it tries to centralize human welfare needs, for example, which are better administered at the local level, and often leaves vital investment decisions to the states, enabling foreign governments to play them off against each other.

At risk is not only the way Americans govern themselves, but also the survival of American democracy. America must look to the greatness of its future, not be constrained by the brilliance of its past. The nation may have the world's oldest unchanged political system, but that system may be threatened unless America shows itself capable of responding more creatively to the challenges being imposed both from outside, by the aggressive, externally oriented capitalist developmental states of East Asia, and from within, by a younger generation that sees itself closed out of the political process by special interest groups.

"When the war of independence was terminated, and the foundations of the new government were to be laid down," Alexis de Tocqueville wrote more than a century ago in *Democracy in America,* "the nation was divided between two opinions—two opinions which are as old as the world, and which are perpetually to be met with, under different forms and various names, in all free communities—the one tending to limit, the other to extend indefinitely, the power of the people. Great political parties are not to be met with in the United States at the present time. In the absence of great parties, the United States swarms with lesser controversies; and public opinion is divided into a thousand minute shades of difference upon questions of detail."

America today still swarms with lesser controversies, a process termed "the trivialization of democracy." In the absence of great parties, and in a vacuum of enlightened leadership, political gridlock has resulted. Individual prosperity, national misery. America can achieve a better balance.

Many Japanese are dismayed and disappointed at what has happened to this once-proud country.

"What has become of your mighty America?" Noboru Makino, chairman of the Mitsubishi Research Institute and author of *Decline and Prosperity,* asked me recently. "We hope that its frontier spirit will be rekindled and that it will establish a new image for the next century." For Makino, the keys to America's future are its political leadership and its institutional cooperation.

"The United States is unlike other major nations, in that it did not evolve, it was created," Naohiro Amaya wrote in his recent best-seller, *Where Is Japan Going?* "Japan, China, France, Britain, all evolved naturally, over time, into their present forms. No one crafted or designed them from the outset by plan. But America is different. It was created, by design, on the principles of freedom, democracy, justice, and equality. These principles are the essence of the American political bible."

America has been experiencing the unmistakable signs of decline. But as the world's greatest living experiment in democracy, it also stands on the threshold of regeneration and renewal. There's a strong national agenda, for the most part already existing, that needs some fairly prompt attention, to fine-tune the process and bring it more sharply into focus. But America's political leadership has not shown much capacity for addressing it.

"America is being fibbed to by its leaders," George Will wrote in *The New Season.* "In the United States, the public is not being brought face-to-face with its needs and appetites, of the bill that will come due down the road, if the costs are not paid responsibly. The political class has not been telling the public the truth. The electorate is in no mood for amateur hour in Washington. It craves competence."

Someone, somewhere, once said, "Never bet against the New York Yankees, Notre Dame, or the United States." George Steinbrenner has turned the Yankees into perennial losers, and I don't know about Notre Dame, but I sure wouldn't sell America short. The story of this country is none other than the story of ordinary people working together to achieve extraordinary things. The will to win, and the will to excel, are the things that endure.

"How do you get the focus back on the common good?" former Arizona governor Bruce Babbitt asked me during an interview in Phoenix after his defeat in the 1988 presidential primaries. He was repeating the question I had just asked him. "I guess that can only happen when the political system focuses on individual citizens as an integral part of the process. And it happens in times of crisis, but not in normalcy."

There is perhaps no place more important to begin the process of political restructuring, of regenerating the concept of citizen-legislator, than with America's vertically layered, politically driven, and rigidly bureaucratic public education system. Americans need to understand how East Asia's education systems have effectively redefined the global standards against which educational excellence is now measured. America must respond to those changed and higher standards not by emulating Asian practices, but by finding approaches unique to its own culture to meet the tougher educational challenges being posed for the next century.

It is to those critical challenges that we turn next.

PART III
THE LEGACY OF CONFUCIUS: FORGING EDUCATIONAL EXCELLENCE

10
COOPERATIVE LEARNING IN JAPAN: PARENTS, TEACHERS, AND CHILDREN AS THE VITAL TRIANGLE

Japan possesses one of the most advanced state and private educational systems in the world today. The attendance rate in public primary schools is more than 99 percent, the literacy rate more than 98 percent. Education in Japan is, and has been for many decades, a serious business, in fact one of the most competitive areas of Japanese life. This is in part a legacy from the attitudes toward learning popularized by the Confucian mentors of the 17th and 18th centuries, but it is also a product of the everyday world in which the Japanese have had to compete for social status and economic opportunity.

Even in the prewar years, Japanese education was remarkably efficient in doing what had been asked of it. A literacy rate that was the highest in Asia and comparable to those of the most advanced Western countries, a citizenry intelligent in its behavior and educated to high standards in lawful conduct and personal hygiene, farmers willing to profit from the results of scientific experimentation, businessmen able to adjust their policies to world market conditions . . . these were just some of the remarkable achievements of the Japanese educational system.

John Whitney Hall,
Education and Modern National Development

Conventional wisdom in America about public education in Japan revolves around several negative, if not overstated, themes. More than just competitive, Japanese education is stressful, the argument goes, and students spend long hours every night grinding away on homework. The Japanese system emphasizes rote memorization and strict factual recall, to the detriment of innovation and creativity in the classroom. Teachers in Japan move whole classes forward at the same rate, unable to distinguish individual achievement or reward innate ability in students.

Classes are large, about twice as large, on average, as in American schools, which further discourages individual attention, critics assert. Students are motivated solely by a system of intensive national examinations that determine who gets into which prestigious universities. Cram schools thrive on the intensity produced by this "examination hell" and generate additional psychological stress.

The long school year in Japan, which begins April 1 every year and ends March 31, means about 225 total school days, including half-days on Saturday, compared to about 185 days in America, so Japanese students have no time for social life or personal interests and are therefore developmentally deprived, it is said. Discipline, order, and regimentation characterize the Japanese school, to the detriment of vitality, diversity, and uniqueness. In short, critics say, the Japanese educational system offers little America would want to learn from or borrow.

Much of this conventional wisdom may stem, at least in part, from what Americans *want* to believe about Japanese education. By focusing on the negative, Americans can heave a huge sigh of relief and say, "Thank God we don't have that kind of uncreative, group-centered education in this country, or we'd never be where we are today. After all, Japan doesn't win the Nobel Prizes. America does." By focusing on the negative, Americans are also prevented from seeing many of the positive aspects of Japanese education, which in the long run may outweigh the negative and could, in any case, be positioning Japan for an even greater competitive advantage in the next century.

So it is the positive features we want to take a brief look at here. They include a focus on cooperative learning through small subgroups, or teams, within the classroom, called *han*, which begins in the earliest years, and an incredibly strong sense of parental involvement in the education process, which enhances academic performance and percolates upward into a strong sense of national commitment. The educational system's standards of achievement, like Japanese excellence in product quality, are arguably the highest in the world and consistently reward effort over ability. Those standards and the team structure in turn produce among Japan's industrial workers levels of individual competence and the capability to cooperate that are without doubt the highest in the world. Finally, the Japanese system incorporates a process of reform that is consensus-based and committed to making Japanese education more flexible and responsive to the needs of the emerging information age.

Most Western observers are astonished to learn that by the middle of the nineteenth century one-quarter of Japan's population was already literate, an achievement that gave Japan a ranking equal to that of any of the advanced European countries of the time. Prior to modernization, Japan was ruled, of course, by the *samurai,* and Tokugawa-era education was organized in the fiefs around temple schools, called *terakoya,* one-room private schools with students of mixed age and ability who studied reading, writing, arithmetic (through the use of the abacus), and calligraphy. By the end of the feudal period 14,000 *terakoya* existed in Japan.

Education was based not on the premise that knowledge was discovery, but rather on the idea that truth was known and could be taught through the Confucian classics, by mastering the wisdom of the ages. Correct conduct was important, as were correct relations and hierarchy respect for the teacher, and loyalty; the subordinate's obedience to the superior was the highest moral virtue—all this stemmed from the Confucian tradition. The practical virtues of persistence, perseverance, equanimity, frugality, and hard work were all taught culturally and were well absorbed by the beginning of the Meiji era, when Japan embarked on its impressive program of modernization and nation-building, borrowing organizational techniques from the West but never abandoning its own Confucian heritage.

By the early twentieth century universal compulsory education had become the norm, as in the West, and from the beginning great emphasis had been placed on early education. If you would form a tree, an old Japanese proverb went, do so while it is very young.

Today Japan is the only industrialized nation in the world in which a majority of children younger than age five are enrolled in an organized preschool program. Two types of formal preschool programs exist in Japan. One is the *yochien,* early kindergarten or preschool, of which there are about 15,000 and two-thirds of which are run privately on a half-day basis, six days a week, supervised by the Ministry of Education. The other is the *hoikuen,* day care or nursery school, of which there are about 20,000 and two-thirds of which are run publicly on a full-day basis, six days a week, primarily for the benefit of working mothers, supervised by the Ministry of Health and Welfare. The curricula are for all intents and purposes the same.

Nearly 40 percent of Japanese three-year-olds, two-thirds of all Japanese four-year-olds, and virtually all Japanese five-year-olds are enrolled in one or the other. Formal Japanese public education begins with first grade, not with kindergarten, as in the U.S. Comparable American attendance ratios for toddlers are about half those in Japan; only about 20 percent of American three-year-olds and a third of American four-year-olds attend preschool.

One of the first things that strikes a foreigner visiting a Japanese preschool is the very large class size. Classes averaging forty young children are typical, and even larger classes are not unusual. Put another way, the profile of adult authority is very low. Competition for a teacher's attention (and resources) is symptomatic of students in any classroom in any school in the world, so the Japanese have developed a system for reducing this competition by substituting attention to cooperative learning and interpersonal behavior. Large groups of young people are unmanageable, so they are divided into smaller subgroups or teams (the *han*) of about six to eight children each, which become the basic units for chores, learning projects, lunch, and informal play. Teachers determine the composition of these teams based on friendship (children who play well together, for example, may be on the same team) or ability, such as leadership, social skills, or artistic ability, trying to distribute these attributes equitably among the teams so the composition is complementary. Once a team is formed, it tends to keep its constituency, with minor changes, for the duration of the school year.

Japanese teachers consciously arrange activities for the preschool teams that stress cooperation and interdependence. For example, oversized wooden blocks used in most Japanese preschools are too large for any one young child to lift or move alone, so cooperation between two or more youngsters is imperative (and automatic) when the children build their imaginary castles and playhouses.

Classroom supplies are also distributed in ways that encourage give-and-take. A teacher may provide one team with fewer bottles of paint than it has members, which stimulates a spirit of sharing or, more creatively, of mixing colors. Another teacher may distribute fewer paintbrushes or toys, which enhances the process of taking turns. Or a teacher might spontaneously withdraw toys as children become older to help them learn the benefits of cooperative play. Teachers tend to view scarce resources as a pedagogical advantage. As with the nation's natural resources, so with children's classroom resources: scarcity breeds both conservation and cooperation.

Large class sizes can, of course, lead to aggressive behavior, but teachers seem less interested in direct intervention than in developing the children's own ability to stop aggression. In the end it is the children, not the teachers, who are inconvenienced by disruptive behavior. One Japanese teacher, who simply stood by and watched one five-year-old push another onto the floor during a formal dance session, said she had not intervened because the child who had been pushed had not been dancing seriously and deserved the appropriate feedback from a peer.

"When I see kids fighting," one teacher observed, "I tell them to go where there are mats. Of course, if they're completely out of control, I stop it. But if children can solve fights on their own without people getting hurt, I let them do it themselves. Kids start out rooting for the weak kid if the teacher stays out of it. So if I can, I let them solve it. We try to plan things so there *may* be more fighting, like reducing the number of toys. We try to get kids to take responsibility for each other's quarrels and encourage them to look when someone's crying, to talk about what that child is feeling and thinking."

Westerners generally fear that the Japanese emphasis on the dynamics of small group interaction snuffs out individual initiative and stifles creative ability. But that's not what John Dewey found when he observed Japanese students in 1919. "They have a great deal of freedom," he remarked, "and instead of the children imitating and showing no individuality—which seems to be the proper thing to say—I never saw so much variety in drawings and other handwork, to say nothing of its quality being much better than the average of ours. The children were under no visible discipline, but were good as well as happy."

The distinction between adult intervention and peer sanctions is like the difference between force and persuasion, an old Aesop fable about the winter wind and the summer sun. The wind had bet the sun it was stronger, so they had a contest. Aggressively confident, the wind blew and blew, forcing a man to clutch his clothes tightly. Then it howled in anger, so the man sought refuge behind a tree. Then the sun took over, shining warmly on all below. The man emerged, removed his scarf, then his overcoat and jacket, as the sun rose higher in the sky, flush with victory.

Cathy Lewis is an educational psychologist at the University of California, fluent in Japanese, and an experienced observer of Japanese early education. When I met with her, she talked about some of the differences that characterize Japanese attitudes toward children and why they may be important.

"There are a lot of positive psychological consequences of having kids' behavior regulated by other kids, rather than by adults," she said. "Peer feedback is more natural and is communicated more effectively than adult intervention, and it shapes kids' behavior more naturally, because their own sanctions or criticisms tend to be more gentle than those of adults, whose reactions for a young child can often be devastating. Also, when kids regulate their own behavior, adults can take a more Olympian attitude and be more detached."

Research on young peer behavior in the U.S. tends to confirm this; American adults intervene too much when children misbehave, behavioral psychologists suggest, which not only reinforces the process of intervention (i.e., children learn early how to attract adults' attention and hold it) but also precludes children's learning for themselves how to resolve conflict creatively.

"That's why the use of small subgroups in Japan has so much potential," she went on. "Kids stay together in these teams for a long time; they play together, eat lunch together, and do their chores as a unit—cleaning the classrooms, sweeping, dusting—it all adds to the cooperative process. Japanese children are given many more chances, and earlier, for responsibility and authority than in America."

Leadership and responsibility are taught through the *toban*, a system of rotating classroom monitors, which begins in preschool and continues until high school. Every day (or week) a different child will call the class to order, assign each *han* the order of play, and rotate the order of lunch and dismissal. The *toban* will also search for missing children at assembly time and give individual permission to play after lunch. Since the position rotates regularly, every child, quick or slow, strong or weak, is given an opportunity to lead.

Great pomp is often attached to the role, with a song or ceremony to celebrate the occasion, along with a badge the monitor wears as his or her identifying mark. Parents often say they cannot keep their children home if they happen to be sick and it is their turn. As one teacher put it, "*Toban* grows naturally out of children's helping. It allows even a child who can't normally be a leader a chance to lead. Children who are least able to lead others in daily encounters are often the ones who work the most carefully when they are *toban*. They think up the jobs that need to be done, then decide who will do them. You understand how hard people can make it for you and how much better it is to have help."

Much of the Japanese emphasis on small group cooperation and shared leadership comes from their fundamental attitude toward children. Many traditional Japanese proverbs underscore cultural beliefs about the inherent goodness of children and how special childhood is in life. *Ko ni sugitara takara nashi,* the Japanese say, which means "There is no treasure that surpasses a child." Another saying goes, *Nanatsu made wa kami no uchi de aru,* or "Until the age of seven, children are with the gods."

Japanese teachers do not accuse young students of being bad when they misbehave, nor do they punish undesirable behavior; rather, they say that children have not yet learned the correct or appropriate behavior. The emphasis is thus placed on understanding. Japanese teachers seem to grasp intuitively the importance of positive reinforcement, or praise, as a reward for desired behavior, rather than singling out bad behavior for punishment or blame.

While techniques of behavioral modification are increasingly being taught to American teachers of young children, they are by no means yet representative of general practice. And the Japanese practice is more a traditional or intuitive one than one that is formally learned. Peer punishment (or negative feedback) for unacceptable behavior is still the preferred norm, giving teachers the opportunity to reward children by praising them for behaving in ways considered to be acceptable.

One incident I recall as typical and thus noteworthy. A young Japanese boy, who was having problems adjusting to the dynamics of his team, found himself shouting at the teachers and constantly squabbling with the other children, almost to the point of their ostracizing him from the group. But during a picture identification drill later that day, he was the only child on his team who correctly identified an electric rice cooker, so his teacher singled him out for special praise. She asked him to come to the front of the class, put her arm around him, and said, "You are very smart. Most older children don't know a word as difficult as that. See how well he has done, everyone? Let's all clap for him. He's done so well today." When asked about this afterward, the teacher said she needed to find something to praise him for every day, to keep his classmates from giving up on him. He was getting all the negative feedback about his unacceptable behavior that he needed from his peers.

The process of teaching cooperation through small teams, enhancing leadership skills through the *toban,* letting children (in their own way) criticize unacceptable peer behavior, and having teachers praise positive or desired behavior leads ultimately to a strong sense of socialization, of group cohesiveness, and, not least, of peer pressure to conform. The worst conceivable punishment is not criticism, but shame; humiliation means not poor individual performance, but disloyalty to and exclusion from the group.

As a result, achievement is often evaluated more in terms of how the team performs than with respect to the individual child. Thus you will often hear teachers say things like "Groups one and four were ready to begin every lesson today, but groups two and three need to try harder," or "Group one did beautifully, which made me very happy, but group three made a mess. Group four came up with a wonderful idea; let's ask them about it."

The seeds of cooperative behavior, so strong in Japanese industrial organizations, are sown at the ages of three, four, and five. Success or failure is translated into how well the group does. The group's goals—for the school, for the class, and for the team—are displayed prominently on the walls in phonetic script, a process that is often repeated, later in life, in both government and corporate offices. I recall the experience, years ago, of a Japanese friend, a division manager for a foreign affiliate in Tokyo, who won a company sales contest sponsored by his American boss—a round-trip ticket to Hawaii. But he declined, saying he could not have met his targets without the close help and cooperation of his colleagues; victory belonged not to him, but to his division. Such concepts are not easy for Westerners to comprehend.

Sarane Boocock teaches sociology at Rutgers University. Fluent in Japanese, she has studied Japanese early education for many years, with a particular focus on nursery school. When we met recently, she talked about the process of socialization and the Japanese focus on effort, as opposed to innate ability, as a motivating factor for children.

"Socialization, both at home and in school, emphasizes doing one's best and doing things correctly," she said. "Differences in behavior and achievement are viewed not from the perspective of differences in natural talent, but rather from differences in effort. The Confucian model taught that there is a correct way to carry out any task and that if the student is taught the correct way, he or she will do it freely, without external constraints. In the preschools I have observed, a good deal of time is spent teaching children the 'correct' way to do many things—how to sit in a chair with correct posture, how to hold chopsticks the right way, how to arrange one's backpack, and so on."

Most Japanese teachers accordingly spend the first several weeks at the beginning of each school year teaching procedural skills, she said, emphasizing how and why they are important and building on the skills learned at home. Procedures are also important in helping to create a constructive classroom atmosphere. Teachers say they want to develop children who instinctively know what to do, who learn to judge things for themselves.

"But what also tends to distinguish Japanese preschools from Western nursery schools," Boocock went on, "is the portion of classroom content dedicated to daily activities that require concentration and attention to detail for long periods of time. Hideki Yukawa, one of Japan's Nobel Prize winners, is often singled out as a role model for Japanese schoolchildren because of his comment that success in any endeavor comes through continuous repetitive practice until one masters every detail. This attitude is conveyed, too, through the Japanese belief that children learn better through observation and imitation than they do solely through abstract verbal instruction. This is also the basis for the Suzuki method of music instruction."

Critics who hastily scold the Japanese educational system for stifling individual initiative and creativity ("... the way a landscape gardener treats a hedge: protruding bits of the personality are regularly snipped off...," said one) ought rather to look critically at the broader social system. For it is the unremitting pressure to conform that is so strong at all levels of Japanese society and that inescapably permeates the schools as well as large industrial organizations and the bureaucracy. And yet Japanese creativity—through *kaizen*, as we have seen—takes its cues not from an Andy Warhol but from a Thomas Edison, who said that innovation is 99 percent perspiration and only 1 percent inspiration.

For all the criticism that Japanese public education, in later years, is so intense, stressful, and competitive, the evidence, in the early years, tends to indicate otherwise. The content of Japanese preschool education is remarkably nonacademic for a system that, later on, revs up academics to such a high degree. Outside personal interests and individual hobbies are developed during late preschool years, with a majority of both boys and girls taking swimming, piano, and calligraphy lessons. Gymnastics, art, and ballet are also popular. Group activities that center on play and cooperative interaction form the core school focus of these early years; American research also confirms that children who are subject to a process that stresses socioemotional behavior and group interaction possess stronger concentration skills in later years and don't give up as easily.

By the time most Japanese children enter the first grade they are already able to read and write the forty-eight basic Japanese phonetic symbols. This fact relates to the role Japanese mothers play in providing informal learning opportunities for their children during the preschool years, such as drawing, painting, and playing familiar games related to reading and counting skills. Mothers stimulate their children's interests in reading through traditional letter recognition and phonetic games and by using activity books.

Mothers also provide their children with desks at an early age; 98 percent of all Japanese six-year-olds have their own study desks at home, compared with fewer than half that number in America. Research in both countries has shown that academic achievement is directly correlated. (Most desks are, for the most part, fairly simple, with a comfortable, ergonomically sound chair for proper posture. The more devoted can buy desks with built-in pencil sharpeners, calculators, scratch pads, and alarm clocks.)

Despite the fact that women comprise nearly half the work force in Japan, mothers take primary responsibility for their children's education, a phenomenon that has become known in the extreme as *kyoiku mama*—education mother—symbolizing her role as tutor, motivator, and cheerleader all rolled into one. Japanese families are inherently more stable, too, with the lowest divorce rate in the industrialized world, only about one-fourth that of the U.S., the world's highest. Families headed by single parents comprise only 6 percent of the total in Japan, less than a third of the comparable American rate.

There is no role confusion about child rearing in Japan. Even mothers who work are expected to be the primary caretaker and place children at the top of their list of priorities, and they worry constantly about the quality of job they are doing. The quality of their performance as mothers stems in part from historical Confucian tradition, in part from the fact that Japanese fathers work long hours, and in part from strong "peer pressure" that applies to mothers as a group. Traditionally fathers were more involved in a child's upbringing, but their influence has lessened, given Japan's workaholic culture. An old Japanese proverb holds that the four most feared things in life are *jishin, kaji, kaminari, oyaji:* earthquakes, fires, thunder, and fathers.

Japanese mothers form close and important working relationships with their children's teachers. Every day, the child carries a notebook back and forth to school, in which mother and teacher alternately write notes regarding the child's health, mood, and activities both at home and at school. Twice a month, on average, the mothers meet at the school as a group, and they hold frequent meetings of committees that are responsible for special projects such as maintaining the school garden or preparing the school's hot lunches.

It is axiomatic that a child's first and most influential teachers are his parents. Research in America as well as in Japan indicates that students whose parents are involved with them throughout their years in school consistently receive better marks, achieve higher test scores, and have a more complete sense of self than those whose parents are not. Japanese mothers also often buy extra copies of their children's textbooks so they can follow the lessons and provide tutoring if necessary. (In some American communities with large contingents of Japanese families, school districts often run short of textbooks because Japanese students take two—one for themselves and one for their mothers.) And in later years many Japanese mothers actually attend classes and take notes when their children are sick so the students will not fall behind.

Japanese teachers form the third link in this strategic alliance with parents and children, and public teaching has always been a respected profession in status terms. Average teaching salaries in Japan are higher than those of any other public employees and compare favorably with salaries of white-collar professionals in the private sector. Japanese teaching salaries average 2.4 times the nation's per-capita income; in America the comparable figure is about 1.7.

By 1984 the beginning salary of a Japanese high school teacher with a B.A. degree was 15 percent higher than the starting salary of a white-collar employee with an equivalent degree in a private company and 12 percent higher than the starting salary of an engineer with a comparable degree. In America average professional salaries in the private sector, such as accounting or law, are about twice as high as those for teachers.

Teaching is considered an elite career in Japan; for every vacancy in the public school system there are five applicants competing to fill it. Men are also more prominent in the profession, especially in the later years. While more than 90 percent of preschool teachers in Japan are women, only about half of the elementary-level teachers, one-third of the middle school teachers, and 15 percent of high school teachers are women. Minimum requirements for certification are specified by national law, but prefectural (similar to counties in the U.S.) school boards may stiffen them further. All applicants must take formal prefectural examinations consisting of written tests in both general and specialized fields of education followed by extensive oral interviews.

Japanese teachers are represented by the Japanese Teachers Union (Nikkyoso), which has strong historical links to the Socialist party and has fairly liberal views, even though it is quite conservative when it comes to a preference for orderly schools. The JTU acts as a kind of counterweight to the conservative Ministry of Education and regularly pushes for decentralized control, school autonomy, teacher participation in curriculum development, and greater freedom to choose textbooks.

While Japanese schools are administered by a principal, who is compensated only marginally more than his teaching peers, the schools' daily life is directed by a head teacher who combines teaching with the implementation of policy, curriculum coordination, and special projects. At the elementary level teachers teach a different grade every year, gaining broad experience with the entire curriculum. Specialties emerge at the middle and high school levels.

By American standards Japanese schools are spartan. They would never win an award for architectural design, but the lack of interior decoration and luxurious accommodations—such as indoor/outdoor carpeting or air-conditioning and heating—helps build character and enables the children to concentrate, without distraction, on learning, a process in which students lose interest, the Japanese believe, if physical surroundings are too comfortable. The cultural concepts of *sabi* and *wabi*, simplicity and starkness, are still highly valued in Japan, a heritage of the nation's strong *samurai* ethic.

School buildings are generally multistory, drab concrete structures, L-shaped or U-shaped, which open onto a large courtyard where all outdoor play, assemblies, and group activities are held. But what the Japanese save on form they spend on content: Japanese schools have

well-equipped libraries, science labs, music and art rooms, athletic facilities (more than 75 percent of them with swimming pools), and
playgrounds.

Uniforms are typical at Japanese public schools, as throughout East
Asia. In primary school they may consist of merely the same-colored
blouse and skirt for girls or shirt and pants for boys, but by middle
school the boys wear a militarylike tunic, in regimental black, complete
with cap, and the girls a sailor blouse with a navy skirt. Critics of public
school uniforms often single out the Japanese custom, saying it retards
choice, as if the American practice, which finds adolescent boys wearing
old army fatigues and girls dressed in designer clothes, is somehow
superior. Private schools in America find uniforms a net plus, enhancing
both commitment and self-esteem.

A content-rich curriculum and the much longer school year mean
that Japanese students move through their subjects at a considerably
faster pace than their American counterparts. Double-column addition
is normally taught in the third grade in the U.S.; Japanese kids learn
it in the first grade. Multiplication tables are introduced in the third
grade in Japan, but not until the fourth grade in America. Fractions are
introduced in the fourth grade in Japan, the fifth grade in American
schools, while calculation of percentages is learned in the fifth grade
in Japan but not until the sixth or seventh grade in the U.S. Serious
homework begins in Japan in the first grade and increases as the students
move through the system.

On average, two-thirds of all Japanese students spend more than five
hours a week on homework, not a particularly heavy load; but by contrast, fewer than one-fifth of American students spend that much time
studying out of class. By high school the best Japanese students spend
several hours on homework each evening and on Saturday afternoons
as well. The top 5 percent of American high school students do less
homework than the average Japanese. The point is not homework *per
se*, but total out-of-school study, which takes up much more time in
Japan than in the U.S.

If Japanese students go to school about forty days a year more than
American students, this means they get about two months' more education every year. By extrapolation, at the end of twelve years of
elementary and secondary education, Japanese students will have received the cumulative equivalent of between one and two years' more
schooling than their American counterparts. (One expert has gone so

far as to equate an average high school education in Japan with the average *college* education in America.)

Japanese eighth-graders now consistently get the highest scores in the world on international math tests; America's eighth-graders placed thirteenth out of fifteen countries recently taking the exams. In algebra and calculus the top 5 percent of Japan's twelfth-graders are in first place, too, compared to the top 5 percent of twelfth-graders from a dozen industrialized countries; in this elite group America's top 5 percent scored dead last.

"Are we not witnessing in all of this something highly indicative of the Japanese national character?" Thomas Rohlen wrote in *Japan's High Schools*. "Many important virtues—diligence, sacrifice, mastery of detailed information, endurance over the many preparatory years, willingness to postpone gratification, and competitive spirit—are tied together at a formative period and are motivated largely by a rather selfish individual desire to get ahead (or, as many put it, not to fall behind). We are discussing an educational system in which the crucial difference affecting achievement has been seen traditionally as ability and effort. Ability is innate and cannot be changed; only effort makes a difference. Exam preparation is viewed as essentially hard work. Those willing, able, and encouraged in the effort are the ones who succeed."

This educational achievement, however, is not without its cost, and the price is paid increasingly in later years, by the time the Japanese students enter high school. Attendance in cram schools, called *juku*, starts during elementary years and intensifies during middle school, so students who are on the upper track can take competitive examinations for entry into the most prestigious private secondary schools in Japan. But the *juku* serve a second purpose, in addition to allowing cramming for exams; since Japanese students are moved along uniformly by class throughout their nine years of compulsory education, there is always the problem of what to do with gifted children and how to handle the slow learners and those with learning disabilities. The *juku* do both.

In a sense the *juku* free up the schools to concentrate on the fat part of the bell curve and take the 10 percent at either end for more advanced work, on the one hand, or remedial and special education, on the other. During the elementary years, when the *han* function so well, much need for special education is eliminated through peer teaching, since the faster students pair off to tutor the slower ones, helping their team compete successfully against the others. Peer tutors also learn more, and sometimes faster, than students who do not tutor, a fact also confirmed by American research about a process not used widely in American schools.

As Japanese students progress through the higher grades, especially in the transition from middle to high school, the *han* system gives way to more emphasis on individual performance, so much so that one's former colleagues and teammates often become one's rivals. Critics tend to focus on the "hypertrophy of examinations," a process that causes other learning experiences—sports, leisure activities, dating, art—to atrophy and delays the formation of more well-rounded personalities. Also, by this time in a student's life school has become so rank-conscious, so hierarchically ordered in terms of achievement, that the choice of a school or subjects has less to do with a child's own interest and more to do with his or her level of performance on the all-important examinations, many of which are administered as "mock" exams years before the real ones are scheduled.

I thought about these factors—the group cohesiveness, the strong curriculum, the fierce competitiveness in examinations—when I visited Hibiya High School. It is located in central Tokyo, a short walk from the famous entertainment district in Akasaka. The National Diet building in Kasumigaseki, Japan's parliament, can be seen from the school's athletic field.

Hibiya is and has always been one of Tokyo's leading public secondary schools. Until 1967 it drew students from all over Tokyo (it serves a smaller district now), and of its average graduating class of 400 about half went to Tokyo University (Todai). Today the senior class is a bit larger, around 420, of whom only ten will now enter Todai, but another hundred will attend one of Japan's other elite national institutions, such as Kyoto University, and another eighty will go to a private university, such as Keio or Waseda, so about half of all Hibiya graduates ultimately attend a prestigious university. The rest, who fail entry on their first try, can, of course, attend a second-tier university, but most become *ronin*, "swordless samurai," and continue their preparations to take the entrance exams again a year later. (The most famous private high school in Japan, Nada, in Kobe, regularly sends half of its graduating class of 400 each year to Tokyo University; the statistical chances of the average high school student attending Todai are one in 440, but at Nada they are one in two.)

Hibiya is unique, not only in the number of graduates it sends to elite universities, but also in the fact that it does not have a statue of Sontoku Ninomiya. Most Japanese schools do. Ninomiya is a model of scholarly perseverance and dates from the Tokugawa era. An orphan, he lived with his uncle, a stingy man who forced him to spend long hours tilling the family ricefields. Ninomiya was determined to rise above manual labor and stayed up late, night after night, reading the Confucian classics. When his uncle complained that he was depleting their precious supply of lamp oil, Ninomiya grew rapeweed and pressed his own. He learned how to reclaim wasteland, grew more crops, and then sold them to buy his freedom. He is usually shown doubled over with a load of firewood on his back, walking forward and reading—a singular symbol in Japan for the power of effort, diligently applied.

I asked Akio Yoshimine, Hibiya's head teacher, about the curriculum and daily schedule as we toured the school.

"Classes start at 8:30 each morning and run until 4:00," he said. "On Saturdays we meet from 8:30 to 12:30. Generally the students stay in the same room, and the teachers move. Our national curriculum emphasizes five core subjects: Japanese, of course, English, math, science, and social studies. It is fairly intensive. Our ratio of required courses to electives is much higher than yours, yet the students have a wide range of choice—music, art, drama, history, economics, and so on. But they are required to have three full years each in the five basic subjects."

We stopped by a science lab. The familiar sight of Bunsen burners, goosenecked faucets, Erlenmeyer flasks, and glass beakers brought back memories of my own science-intensive years in high school, during the *Sputnik* era. This Japanese lab was as well equipped as any one would find in a good high school in America.

We talked for a while about group activities, raising our voices as we climbed the stairs. Many students were practicing music, and the noise level had escalated considerably.

"The students clean their own classrooms every day, of course," he said, "but our janitors keep the entryway and halls clean. Once a month everybody—the entire student body—participates in *ohsohji*, when we clean the whole school and sweep the grounds outside. This is *our* school, and when everybody participates, it helps maintain a sense of collective responsibility."

We walked up to the library, and I paused when I saw a few pink scribbles, called *rakugaki*, on an otherwise all-white wall. I asked Yoshimine whether graffiti was a problem.

"Occasional scribblings," he said, gesturing toward the scrawl, "but not much more. There was a period, maybe four or five years ago, when *rakugaki* was a fad, but then it passed. Certainly it was never as bad as the graffiti on subway cars in New York, although Kawasaki is now exporting special stainless-steel cars to America that can't be marked up."

Ijime, the bullying of shy or slower-track students, coupled with a rash of vandalism and hostility, had recently become problematic in the lower secondary or middle schools, prompting the creation of special commissions and more intensive teacher-parent communication. *Ijime* is an outgrowth of negative peer feedback experienced from preschool on, and individual students are tormented because they do not conform to the group, either because they are outsiders (as with Koreans and the *eta,* Japan's outcasts) or because they do not pursue their studies with sufficient seriousness of purpose.

Still, in some recent statistics I had seen, the total number of reported instances of hostility and vandalism in Japanese schools overall for a full year *nationwide* was less than reported in the first three months of that year for New York City alone.

"This business of bullying," he suggested, "which you read about, is not a problem here, although it is in many of our elementary and middle schools. It is quite worrisome."

We stopped in the library. It was clean and quiet, the shelves fully stocked. Students ran the library, too, and several girls were clustered around the checkout counter, giggling as they watched the foreign guest poke around. I stopped at the counter and chatted informally with them, in Japanese, about whether they were studying diligently for their exams. That seemed to extinguish the giggles. Yoshimine took me by the arm and showed me the study carrels toward the back. They were not all arranged as individual cubicles, as we would find in American schools, but also in circular clusters of five and six, to facilitate work on group projects. One team sat huddled together, collaborating on a joint report, impervious to our presence.

"We have a couple of incidents a year involving tobacco," he said as we walked back downstairs, "which prompts a strong response from the homeroom teacher as a result. Occasionally there may be some overdrinking of sake, perhaps on student outings, which is dealt with sternly. There is no drug use in school, period, because few drugs come into the country—period. On the whole their behavior is generally good, not because adults constantly monitor and intervene, but because the peer group pressure is very strong."

We walked out the main entryway, past the gymnasium, and across the athletic field.

"Plus, we have parent-teacher meetings at frequent intervals," Yoshimine went on, "which stress our teaching methods, of course, but also deal with behavior to the extent necessary. Japanese parents are very involved. We meet with them frequently, almost every month, by class, arranged by the homeroom teacher. Communication and cooperation are key."

We stood near the back gate and watched a group of Japanese boys running wind sprints as a relay team. Their faces reflected only serious intent. When they stopped to catch their breath, I chatted briefly with them, and they broke out into broad grins when they heard the familiar sounds of their own language. "*Gambare,*" I said, using the imperative form of the most frequently heard word in Japanese—persevere. Then I turned to my host, and we bowed our respectful good-byes.

Although Westerners have been preoccupied with the weaknesses of the Japanese educational system, Japanese leaders, too, in recent years, have begun to sense the necessity for change. (In a recent poll 70 percent of Japanese mothers said they would like to see the *juku*, and the attendant competitive examination system, changed.) In 1984 then–prime minister Nakasone created a national council to look into the problems and to recommend necessary changes.

The National Council on Educational Reform was comprised of forty-five members, twenty-five generalists and twenty specialists, drawn from a variety of sources in both the public and private sectors: business, finance, private foundations, primary and secondary schools, labor unions, metropolitan governments, the national bureaucracy, the press, science and technology associations, think tanks, and universities.

The council met, in committee and in subcommittee, for nearly three years, compiled 592 pages in four substantive interim reports, and submitted its recommendations in late 1987. America's own reform commission, which wrote the famous report *A Nation at Risk* in 1983, had just eighteen members, only one of whom—Bill Baker, the retired chairman of Bell Laboratories—came from outside the education profession. It met for about six months and produced only the single thirty-one-page report.

"Today, our formal education is at a grave crisis," the council reported. "During the course of 'catching up' since the Meiji Restoration, Japan has experienced a number of excesses [and] mistakes. Generally speaking, [while] formal education has fulfilled a great social mission, and [while] schools and teachers have been regarded as worthy of trust and respect by children, parents, and the public, in recent years public confidence in our schools and in our teachers has degenerated, and there has been increasing public criticism of our educational system. For the sake of our children's future, we must cooperate in planning and implementing reforms of our schools."

In order to "help remedy the evil effects of competition for university admission," the council proposed that a new "Common Test" replace the old university entrance examination, that it pose higher-quality (i.e., more essay-type) questions, and that it comprise only a part of the entrance requirements, rather than having test results be the sole determinant. It also recommended putting more emphasis on individuality in the classroom; developing creativity, thinking ability, and the power of self-expression; cultivating more analytical exercises that utilize the application of basic fundamentals; humanizing the environment by reexamining the competitive conditions under which students work; internationalizing the curriculum and making it less insular; and making the system more relevant to the needs of the new information age and the changing demands of the twenty-first century.

"Sometimes I think the requirements of our current educational system could be taken over by robots," Naohiro Amaya, the former vice minister of MITI and himself a member of the prime minister's council, remarked jokingly during our long interview. "But now we have to ask ourselves what kind of education is best for our people in the coming information-intensive age. What do we need to do with our educational system to create more Picassos and Newtons in the future?" And, presumably, more Thomas Edisons.

This point was echoed by Takashi Hosomi, a former high-ranking official in the Ministry of Finance and previously governor of the Overseas Economic Cooperation Fund, the agency that implements Japan's foreign aid. He is now adviser to Nippon Life, Japan's (and the world's) largest insurance company. As a member of the reform council, he chaired the committee on higher education.

"We have created excellent officers up to the class of major," Hosomi said to me, "but we need more generals and admirals now. We have to revitalize our higher education, to make it more individualistic and imaginative. Our elementary and secondary school systems have been very efficient in creating the soldiers we needed during the catch-up phase of our economic growth. But the students mostly follow what they have been taught. They lack creativity and originality, especially at the university level. We need more foreign researchers and teachers, and we'll get them over time. I am confident we can make the necessary adjustments and changes."

One measure of the importance of the national council's recommendations, and of education as a national priority, is the growing friction between central government bureaucracies. So far, the most significant turf battles have been between MITI and the Ministry of Education, the Mombusho. Until recently, the Mombusho, as with the postal ministry, has had to deal with a popular reputation as a "second-class" ministry, since MITI and MOF get the cream of Todai graduates. But after the council's three-year effort, that too is changing.

"MITI proposed creating an experimental information school," Hiroshi Kaneoka, director of the policy section of the Education Minister's Secretariat, told me. "And we turned them down, which many people said was just Mombusho's traditional stubbornness and resistance to change. But we are looking at the possibility of creating designated schools for educational reform in every prefecture throughout Japan, to implement as many of the council's recommendations as we can. MITI is a strong supporter of the council's focus on the technological needs of the next century and is studying how we should adapt to the changing requirements of the information age."

Kaneoka is a young, enthusiastic official who seemed to relish the prospect of locking horns with MITI. Naturally he is a product of Tokyo University.

"Our public school graduates have been excellent government servants and the highest-quality factory workers in industry, up to now," he went on, "but we have to look ahead, not back. Other significant issues for Mombusho include the use of computers in the classroom. During the next several years we will put computers into all middle and high school math and science courses, as part of regular classroom instruction. We will also be putting more emphasis on moral education in the future, emphasizing the joint responsibility of school and family together, stressing student dedication to learning, loyalty, obligation, proper duty, and so on. Our schools devote an hour a week to this now, and it will be increased."

While there is a broad consensus on future priorities, not everyone is optimistic regarding implementation. One who is not is Ikuo Amano, a prominent professor of educational sociology at Tokyo University and the only person who declined the prime minister's invitation to join the reform commission, citing the pressure of professional obligations. Amano did his graduate work at Yale, visits the U.S. at regular intervals, and has written extensively on Japanese education.

"Education is a conservative institution in any country, and Japan is no exception," he told me recently as we met in Tokyo over tea. "The present Japanese system is in its mature phase now, and equal opportunity—a genuine meritocracy—has been achieved. The system has been so successful, and the established standards so high, that pressure for change comes not from industry, as in your country, but primarily from parents and students. The big problem in Japanese society, as you know, is that creativity and independent thinking are not as widely respected, so real leaders don't stand out; they blend in. It's the old 'deru kugi' problem—strong social pressure creates conformity."

I asked him about the common misperception that university students in Japan are "lazy."

In America, graduating seniors at colleges and universities throughout the country take exams to get *out* of school, whereas in Japan all the pressure for years earlier is on getting *into* school, whether high school or university.

"Conventional wisdom says that Japanese university education is too relaxed and not rigorous enough," Amano said, nodding. "But the fact is, university education in Japan is quite rigorous, especially for the students in science and engineering, who make up more than half the total undergraduate population at our leading universities. The key question remains: what do Japanese students study for? And the answer is: for exams. But our exams—the ones used by the best universities, at least—are not just fill-in-the-blank or multiple-choice tests; they are content-oriented and essay-type questions that are designed to elicit knowledge in a compact form. Believe me, there's no playing around in the best science or engineering departments."

We talked for a while about reforms in higher education.

"We need to experiment, and we probably will," he said, "with a system of research units and put our best researchers into them. People forget that at our national universities humanities departments were established only after the war, so their primary focus remains on science, medicine, and engineering. But because Japanese society places such a high value on group cooperation and interdependence, efforts to move toward a more individual orientation will not be easy. I don't think the national council debated this point enough, and its conclusions may be somewhat unrealistic. America has the reverse problem in trying to encourage more group collaboration. But because your society puts so much emphasis on the individual, you won't have an easy time changing that either. There are two areas in which Japan has a decided advantage for the future: one is our highly developed level of human resources, which will be key to successful implementation of an information-intensive era. Our leading universities and industries already excel here. The other is our superior social stability, through the family, which provides such a strong emotional base for our students. America has some real problems there."

These sentiments were echoed by Nobutaka Machimura, an old friend and former MITI official in Amaya's era, now a Diet member and vice chairman of the LDP's Education Reform Committee.

"We used to have a saying in Japan," he told me, "which went '*Sanpo sagatte, shi no kage o fumazu.*' 'Walk three paces behind your teacher and never dare even to step on his shadow.' The current version goes something like '*Sanpo chikazuite, sensei o naguru.*' 'Take three steps toward your teacher and punch him.' So we have to be careful, I think, when we talk about educational reforms that put more emphasis on the individual, not to lose this fundamental element of respect for the teacher in our system."

Machimura is widely thought to be one of Japan's future leaders and is mentioned as a potential prime minister for the early years of the next century. He is concerned that Japan adapt its education successfully to the demands of the information age.

"We want to make sure our educational reforms track the changes in our society," he said, "and shift to fill the needs of the future. We need to enable our system to make the adjustments to a longer lifetime of education, to deal with the current problems of bad behavior and examination pressures, and to respond to the major trends occurring in Japan."

Professor Amano may be correct about the difficulty of implementing required changes, but over the years, it seems to me, perhaps because of their underlying humility, the Japanese have consistently underestimated their strengths and overestimated their weaknesses. The systematic ability of the Japanese to rally around a national priority and create the consensus necessary to force change is impressive. It is also disarming to most foreigners.

"One suspects that Japan's more conservative leaders, though they are prepared to shake their heads over the system with those who deplore it, are secretly well satisfied," Ronald Dore, a prominent British Japanologist, recently wrote in *Flexible Rigidities*. "Examination hell sorts the sheep from the goats; a man who can't take the psychological strain would be of no use anyway. And as long as you can keep adolescents in those crucial years, when they might otherwise be learning to enjoy themselves, glued to their textbooks from seven in the morning to eleven at night, the society should manage to stave off for quite a long while yet that hedonism which, as everybody knows, destroyed the Roman empire, knocked the stuffing out of Britain, and is currently spreading v.d. through the body politic of the U.S. At least one rather suspects that must be what they are thinking."

Today Japan has the highest literacy rate in the world, the highest graduation rates from secondary school, and consistently the highest marks on international academic and achievement tests. Not only have its best students shown their ability, under considerable pressure, to master large quantities of fundamental data, but its average students know how to gather and use basic information, how to work diligently, how to perform tasks well in teams, how to do a quick study of voluminous material, and how to develop a feeling for or grasp key points in new material. And despite media contentions to the contrary, it is America, not Japan, that has the higher statistical rate of teenage suicide.

"There is a profound lesson to be learned from the challenge of America to Japan of the last century," the scholar Benjamin Duke wrote in *The Japanese School: Lessons for Industrial America*. "And that lesson is that a nation's industrial competitiveness cannot be measured merely in terms of factory output, rates of productivity, or day-to-day management practices. The overall competitiveness of a nation's factories derives from the effectiveness of its entire social infrastructure; basic to that is the school system. In other words, the challenge to industrial America from Japan lies primarily in the classroom rather than in the factory."

Confucius has a word of advice for Japanese students. He said, "He who learns but does not think is lost." Yet the sage also had some wisdom for Americans when he said, "He who thinks but does not learn is in great danger," reflecting a chaos that arises from opinions not anchored in learning.

"Both Japan and America have traditionally valued efficiency," Thomas Rohlen wrote in *Japan's High Schools*, "but clearly the Japanese have surpassed us in their achievement of efficient schooling. This is a sobering fact, given the shrinking world of economic competition. Technological literacy is going to be a distinct advantage to Japan in the evolving competition. Japan produces more than twice as many engineers per capita as the United States, and the average Japanese worker has learned much more math and science in school. In the rapidly evolving, expanding areas of an economy, a shortage of skills is a predictable barrier to growth. This barrier is significantly lower in Japan due to education."

The higher skill levels and work habits developed by the average Japanese worker are as important as academic achievement alone. The ability to learn new equipment better and faster, the greater precision and attention to detail, the organizational discipline, and, not least, the capacity of small groups, built early in the schools, to foster motivation, implement change, and raise productivity rates to consistently higher levels are all significant factors positively impacting Japan's competitiveness.

That America is failing in these respects is recognized increasingly by a business establishment that spends an estimated $30 billion a year on private remedial education efforts. Japanese worker education and training is simple and effective because it is organically related to what goes on in the classroom. American worker education and training is complicated and ineffectual; it has to compensate for the many failures of the nation's public schools and develop the very foundations those schools should have provided.

New and higher international standards have been set quietly by the Japanese in an age when access to technology, capital, and natural resources has become increasingly equal. America's basic problem in failing to better develop its *human* resources is its failure to acknowledge education as the nation's highest priority.

The challenge to America is to meet, if not exceed, these new international standards. There may not be much soul in Japanese education, but there is no denying its accomplishments. The first order of business for American education now, as with American industry more than a decade ago, is to recognize that these higher standards exist and that they are being set not by America, but by Japan.

11
EXCELLENCE IN THE
LITTLE DRAGONS

Given the human attributes of a given population, and the training, skills, knowledge, education, and discipline of a people, it is left to the one to two percent of the population who are in positions of leadership to make the population give its best.

This means organizational coherence, and a spirit of keenness which is necessary for high performance. When the leadership is completely committed to the whole community, to share in their successes and failures, in their triumphs or defeats, then and only then will this leadership have that moral strength to arouse in their people that enthusiasm and drive to excel and to achieve.

Lee Kuan Yew, prime minister of Singapore

SINGAPORE: ON THE CUTTING EDGE

"Learning is like rowing upstream," Confucius once wrote. "Not to advance is to drop back." Anyone who visits an average high school in Singapore, as I recently did, would find it difficult not to be both impressed and inspired. I found the environment neat, clean, and orderly; the students well behaved, highly motivated, and polite; and the teachers bright, respected, and well paid. Education is a national priority in Singapore, as it is in Japan.

I toured the Nan Hua High School with its young principal, Ah Ching, and her Malay assistant, Sidney Tan, on a warm, sultry day late in January. Nan Hua, located not far from the national university in the southeastern part of Singapore near the industrial estate of Jurong, is a small high school by Asian standards, with only 1,000 students, who were assembling in the courtyard after lunch. The girls wore white cotton skirts and blouses, the boys white shorts and shirts, all with a navy blue stripe across the breast pocket. Nan Hua runs two "shifts" every day, Saturdays included, from 7:30 A.M. until 1:00 P.M. for the morning group and then from 1:05 to 6:30.

Suddenly all grew still as the students stood, all eyes on their monitor, the day's ceremonial leader, who was perched on a small raised platform facing them. Like a conductor, she raised her hands, and 500 voices began singing the Singapore national anthem. When they finished, they recited, in unison, the Singapore pledge, their voices calm but serious: "We, the citizens of Singapore, pledge ourselves as one united people, regardless of race, language, or religion, to build a democratic society based on justice and equality so as to achieve happiness, prosperity, and progress for our nation."

Then they were dismissed for class and dispersed, not shotgunlike, as one might expect of American youngsters, but neatly, row by row, until they had filed out of the courtyard. A dozen students, an equal number of boys and girls, remained behind to receive brooms and dustpans and began cleaning the courtyard, the walkways, and the grassy interior.

"You see," Ching said, gesturing toward the cleaning team as we descended the stairs toward the classrooms, "it's not really a complete cleaning the teams do, just enough to remove any visible trash. Their classes are divided into smaller teams, too, and they are responsible for cleaning the classrooms every day. It helps them build a sense of duty."

As we walked by a classroom, I saw students nattering informally, as students everywhere do, nodding deferentially to their principal as we passed, occasionally saying, "Good afternoon, sir," to the obvious guest. A broom and a dustpan, fashioned from what had been a ten-gallon cooking oil canister cut diagonally from top to bottom, stood in a corner.

"Last year," Ching explained, "we scored just above the national average of 82.6 in the secondary testing for O levels. In the past there was a rather high dropout rate, you see, so the government had to figure out a way to change that, because the students were all put together and the slow ones couldn't keep up. They were simply lost at the more advanced levels. Now they are streamed, and the system works much better."

For more than a century, education in Singapore emulated the British system, and testing today continues at both the O (for ordinary) and A (for advanced) levels, as in England. At the end of their third primary year, roughly age nine, Singapore students sit for school-based examinations; if they pass, they are "streamed" to what is called the normal bilingual, or N, course. (Streaming is a British term for tracking.) If they fail, they are streamed to an extended bilingual, or E, course, assuming they have passed the second grade satisfactorily. If not, they must later pass an achievement test given by the Ministry of Education, when they then enter the E course; if they fail again, they are streamed to a vocationally oriented monolingual, or M, course. Bilingual education is standard for all students except the Ms; classes are conducted in English, but a second language (generally Chinese, Malay, or Tamil, following Singapore's cultural composition) is required.

"This is the teachers' room," Ching said as we stopped by a large anteroom in which the desks had been arranged in clusters of four, face to face. "The teachers sit together by department, in small groups—mathematics, science, English, and so on—to facilitate communication and cooperation. When they are not in their classes, as they are now, they are here, and the students come freely for guidance or help." The desks were small, and there was not much space between them.

We stopped by several classrooms and watched. First we observed a Chinese language drill, which brought back memories of response patterns and character drills I had done in Japanese years ago. Next was a chemistry lecture, with successive rows of students on slightly raised levels, so all could see the blackboards in front. Then we stopped at a home economics class, where we watched students preparing ingredients for a delicious-looking Malaysian curry called *sari*, and a shop class, where some boys were making practical objects of metal and wood. Finally we saw the library, where several teams of students were busy stacking books and painting bookshelves in what was a more thorough exercise in maintenance than the normal routine of daily cleaning. A few looked up and smiled or waved. We waved back.

As we settled into Ching's office, she arranged for tea to be served, and I asked her if it was true, as I had read, that caning was still practiced in Singapore. She smiled and nodded as she dabbed beads of perspiration from her forehead.

"We cane students only when they are really naughty, you see," she said, "when they leave school without permission, or if they're lazy and don't do their homework. We cane them privately, only on the buttocks, and with just one or two strokes. We do it only if the parents agree, and sometimes they want us to cane their kids for things they do at home, and we have to say no. But we also praise the students when they do well, so we tell the parents, 'Praise your children and let them know you are doing things for them, sacrificing on *their* behalf.' Because, you see, if you get the support of the parents, then 99 percent of the work is done."

When she mentioned parents, I asked about the school's parent-teacher association. Tan reemerged, bearing our tea.

"Seventy percent of the parents participate in our parent-teacher meetings," she said. "We have no formal PTA as such, but the teachers communicate closely with parents on requirements, expectations, regulations, curriculum, rules, and so on. There is lots of room for feedback on our report cards, which go out weekly. Parents are the real issue, you see, because many have two careers and some have very limited financial resources, so it's important to bring the students' successes and failures to their attention, to get them *involved*. They cooperate pretty well."

I asked Ching if she had any sample report cards at hand, and she dispatched Tan across the hall. Moments later he returned with a handful of notebooks and handed them to her.

"Parents put a lot of pressure on kids," she said, flipping through the small books. "They want them to achieve, to do better than they did themselves, to have a better chance. Here."

I glanced at the notebooks, which had a page for each week, with ample room for written comments, rather than the single-card format used solely for grades in most American schools. Many of the scores were in the eighties, some lower but few higher.

"You must work harder!" a teacher had written for one student who had just squeaked by, at 51.9, in English. "Remember that courtesy begets courtesy!" wrote another. "Good work! Keep it up." "Put more effort on English—such an important subject. Try to do extra work during the holiday."

On one notebook a parent had written some remarks for the teacher, and I asked Ching about this as I handed the books back.

"Most parents call or come in for a conference," she said, "but many communicate with the teachers by writing, as this one did. They often criticize their children more than we do."

Hua Nan, as all secondary schools in Singapore, must follow the Ministry of Education's guidelines for curriculum, which concentrates on eight core subjects: English, literature, geography, history, a second language, math, general science, and a technical course, such as shop or home economics. Electives, such as art, drama, and music, are widely available.

"Another thing," Ching said, stacking the notebooks neatly on her desk. "If the students don't pass English, they can't go on, you see, even if they pass all their other subjects. So out of eight core courses, totaling 800, they must score at least 400 to pass. And Confucian ethics is required for everybody. That's twice a week during their last two years."

Singapore, as Japan, has a massive national commitment to education, living proof of another Confucian adage: "It is only when the cold season comes that we know the pine and cypress to be evergreens." The all-important strategic alliance among teachers, students, and parents seemed alive and well and thriving. The concept of "streaming" young children as early as the third grade would, I felt sure, meet with resistance in America, but safeguards also seemed built in, through the subsequent retesting hurdles. In a society built on capitalistic Darwinism, which stresses survival of the fittest in an increasingly competitive world, Singapore wants its very best at the top, and it is getting them.

HONG KONG: A STEP BEHIND

In Hong Kong, by contrast, I came away with the distinct impression that while the colony was doing an adequate job of educating its children for essentially commercial purposes—preparation for careers in light industry and manufacturing—something was missing. Hong Kong seemed to lack the drive, the momentum, and the energy of Japan or Singapore, lagging behind the intellectual cutting edge of both those countries.

Forty years ago Hong Kong's population was only a tenth its current size. It had a flood of refugees between 1949, when Mao took over, and 1953, when the U.S. banned trade with China, so the government took a wait-and-see attitude, not only toward education but also toward housing, letting people live, for the most part, in squatter's shacks. Then, in 1953, a huge fire on Christmas Day burned out an enormous squatter area, forcing the government to create resettlement blocks and to build housing estates, which today house more than half of Hong Kong's 5.5 million people. As the colony moved increasingly into light manufacturing, textiles, and shipping, it lured in foreign investors and decided on a systematic approach to education, level by level, also initially using a two-shift system because of overcrowding. The government experimented with putting schools on high-rise rooftops, then on the ground floor, then detached from the housing estates, in separate buildings, as tax revenues grew. By the early 1970s new goals of universal and compulsory primary education were set through age twelve; later they were expanded to early secondary education, through age fifteen.

With the help of Y. T. Li, Hong Kong's secretary of education, I arranged to spend some time in an early secondary school, Lui Ming Choi, equivalent to an American junior high school, at the Lek Yuen housing estate in Shatin, in the New Territories, about an hour's drive from Hong Kong Island.

A completely separate and detached L-shaped three-story building, the school sits, mushroomlike, among the tall apartment towers of the housing estate, home to more than a quarter million Hong Kong residents. It has thirty classes averaging forty students each, for a total student body of 1,200.

Rather than testing students on their readiness to leave primary school as in Singapore, Hong Kong requires them to take a secondary school entrance exam. Hong Kong divides its primary school leavers into five bands—percentiles, really—based on scholastic performance and an academic aptitude test, which adjusts different marks from different schools.

A few so-called "prestigious schools," or popular schools, like Lui Ming Choi, get the lion's share of applicants. Parents can choose any lower secondary school within their district, and they usually get one of their first three choices. Lui Ming Choi's students come from the top 20 percent of their primary classes.

The school colors are blue and gray; the girls wear blue jackets and gray skirts, with a white, open-necked blouse, and the boys blue blazers and gray trousers with white shirts and navy ties. Stitched into the jacket breast pocket is the school emblem, a small crest in gold, with the characters Lui Ming Choi in Chinese across the top, below which is an open book with the characters for teaching, knowledge, clarity, and morality.

For all the fuss Americans make over public school uniforms, saying they are too regimented and discourage individuality of expression, the Asian experience tends to indicate otherwise; they promote a sense of belonging and a feeling of community, which are important for the students' self-esteem; they create an environment of neatness and order, which certainly supports the learning process; and they save parents a small fortune in clothing expenses, always a problem in any culture and no minor concern in America, where preoccupation with the latest fashions can often take precedence over academic rigor.

Classes meet Monday through Friday from 8:15 to 3:15, though most students stick around until 5:00 or 5:30, working on extracurricular projects or sports. On Saturdays classes meet for half a day, mostly for informal club activities. Like all schools, Lui Ming Choi has a student handbook, which has a page for each week in the school year, with ample space for assignments, test scores, teachers' comments, and parents' feedback. Every day two students from each class clean the blackboards, but there is no organized team cleaning as in Japan or Singapore.

Drugs and alcohol apparently are not a problem at government schools, but they are at the expatriate schools. One of the colony's biggest problems is latchkey kids. As more and more two-career families move into the housing estates like Lek Yuen, extended families get left behind. So when many students go home, they have to fend for themselves or stay with neighbors, which is one reason they don't mind staying late at school to study with their friends.

The Hong Kong system of education is patterned after both British and Chinese models, so it can be rather confusing when officials talk about forms, O levels, A levels, certificates, and matriculation. Basically Hong Kong uses a six-three-three system, with standard instruction in the Chinese language through the first six primary grades, which keeps core subjects in the mother tongue. All primary schools are double-shift, with morning and afternoon sessions, because of space limitations.

The two major types of upper secondary schools are Anglo-Chinese schools, where English is the language of instruction, and Chinese middle schools, like Lui Ming Choi, where instruction is in Chinese and English is taught as a second language. There are two public universities, Hong Kong University and the Chinese University of Hong Kong, which together absorb only about 5 percent of the colony's secondary school graduates. Another 5 percent go overseas, mostly to Britain, the U.S., and Canada. The government is constructing a third university, scheduled to open in the early 1990s. Hong Kong graduates just under 80 percent of all secondary school students.

As 1997 approaches, pressure from China to change the curriculum could mount. One thing, however, seems certain. Given the upward spiral of emigration, Hong Kong should have plenty of classroom space for some time to come.

KOREA: MAKING THE JAPANESE LOOK LAZY

In Korea I visited the Ehwa Girls' High School in central Seoul, one of the country's leading secondary schools. Ehwa was founded in 1886 by the Methodist Episcopal Church as the first high school for Korean women, and its reputation for outstanding education has more than stood the test of time. Although chartered as a private school, Ehwa is supervised by the Seoul Metropolitan Board of Education under the direct responsibility of the Ministry of Education.

A pert, bouncy sixteen-year-old Korean named Glenda had recently returned to Ehwa for her junior year and was assigned to show me around the school. Her father was a senior executive for one of the large Korean multinational corporations, she told me, and she had spent the last several years in Los Angeles. After she graduated, she said, she very much wanted to go back to the United States to attend UCLA, because her sister was there, majoring in French. Another sister lived in New Jersey.

As at most Asian upper secondary schools, Ehwa's dress code is fairly strict, and the curriculum is geared toward college. Classes begin at 8:20 in the morning and run until 5:00 P.M. every day, including Saturday. Many students spend evenings there, too, normally from 6:00 until about 10:00, working on assignments. Students are not required to stay in the evenings, Glenda said, but peer pressure keeps most of them there. "Hunger is cured by food," Confucius said; "ignorance by study."

Ehwa has a first-rate physical plant, complete with athletic grounds, a fully equipped gymnasium, a large library and study hall, and an enormous outdoor amphitheater, with stone steps that looked as if it had been transplanted from Greece. Weeping cherry trees that give the campus a soft, delicate touch are everywhere in bloom.

The school has three classroom buildings, one for each grade—sophomore, junior, and senior—with about 1,200 students in each grade, so there are nearly 3,600 students in all. Class size averages about sixty. Although the classes are large, Ehwa also employs a *toban* system so all students get experience in class leadership, and each class is subdivided into small teams that take responsibility for group projects, research reports, and classroom cleaning. Seating is rotated once a week, so everybody gets a chance to sit up front. The students stay in one room; the teachers move around.

Ehwa employs 110 teachers, forty-five women and sixty-five men; most of the women are alumnae. The annual salary of Ehwa's principal, translated from won, the local currency, into dollars, would be about $15,000, or five times the average per-capita Korean income of nearly $3,000. By contrast, a well-paid American high school principal might earn $60,000, only about three times the U.S. per-capita average. Teachers are paid a monthly salary, plus a bonus equivalent to about seven months' salary a year. The principal gets paid some 20 percent more than the teachers, but other than two vice principals, a chaplain, and nine other staff members, Ehwa's administration, considering a student body of 3,600, is lean. In Korea, as elsewhere throughout East Asia, money is spent where it counts—on teachers, on the curriculum, in the classroom.

The school's principal, Shim Chi-sun, served some traditional ginseng tea as we talked about Ehwa's extracurricular activities. Since its founding the school has emphasized what it calls "whole person" education, so the students have created ten academic clubs (such as writing, poetry, and drama, in both Korean and English), fourteen artistic clubs (drawing, sculpture, flower arranging, calligraphy, chorus, chamber music, and so on), six athletic clubs, and fourteen "mission" clubs (which organize student volunteers to participate in social work in rural communities during vacation breaks).

Ehwa's academic curriculum compared very favorably with other leading Korean public schools, I learned later, when I visited with Dr. Cho Sun-jae, director general of the Ministry of Education. Cho had studied at the University of Minnesota years ago, before completing his doctorate at Korea's most elite institution, Seoul National University.

Ehwa is one of about four or five high schools in Seoul that compete for the best middle school graduates, he was saying in his office overlooking both the National Museum and, symbolically, the American Embassy. Entry-level teacher salaries are now very competitive relative to the private sector, and starting teachers in public high schools earn more than entry-level government bureaucrats. The public teachers' association is voluntary, and teachers, along with all other governmental officials, do not have the right under Korean law to form a union, so they can't appeal salary disputes. But Korea has a National Teacher's Day every year on May 15, a public holiday that gives them national recognition.

From Dr. Cho I learned that about two-thirds of all Korean children are now enrolled in preschool, and the government plans to increase the number of preschools by half. Korea now spends just over 20 percent of its annual budget on education, the second-largest budget category after national defense, which is about 4 percent of GNP.

Undergraduate education in Korea, as in Japan, centers around a handful of elite institutions, such as Seoul National, Yonsei, and Korea universities. Competition is tough, channeled through a standard entrance examination, although the Korean schools, again as in Japan, are now moving toward individual exams for each university and acceptance criteria that are broader than raw exam scores—including high school grades, leadership in extracurricular activities, and teachers' recommendations. The ministry has set out specifically to enhance the quality of public education. But by Cho's own admission, it has a long way to go before it will develop a level of graduate education equivalent to that in the advanced industrial countries.

About 30,000 Korean students are currently studying overseas, and while the government used to be concerned about the brain drain, it is less so today. Increasing numbers of students now return home to take productive places in Korea's dynamic economy. In education, as with commerce, Korea's focus remains external, and Japan is the country's chief competitive rival. Korea will stay vigilant in the years ahead, it seems to me, preoccupied with excellence and achievement and high standards, just a half-step behind its aggressive neighbor.

TAIWAN: THE VITAL TRIANGLE

"We have a National Teacher's Day, too," Michael Lee was telling me. "Teachers are one of the three legs in what for us is the vital triangle of teachers, children, and parents. Our elementary and middle school teachers pay no tax on their salaries, and extra teaching earns them bonus pay, tax-free."

Lee is director of the Bureau of International Cultural and Educational Relations in Taiwan's Ministry of Education and has what he calls an "MIT" education: made in Taiwan.

"We Chinese like to be scholarly, so there is a strong tradition of respect for learning. Confucius said it takes ten years to raise a tree and a hundred years to educate a nation. It's still a lifelong job."

We were sitting in his office across from the massive Chiang Kai-shek memorial in central Taipei, talking about public education and competitiveness in Taiwan.

"For us there is no other answer but education," he said. "Taiwan has no natural resources, so we *have* to develop our human resources. You can see the trade figures quarterly and evaluate business results every year, but results in education take longer and are less visible, not unlike a building, where the foundation is most important, even though you may be able to see a beautiful exterior. Our students have too much homework, even from junior high, and we're trying to ease that somewhat, but the parents push and push hard. There are currently more than a thousand supplementary schools here, like Japan's *juku,* where the kids can take extra work or cram for university exams. We spend nearly 6 percent of our GNP on education now. Our public schools have more prestige than our private schools do. We graduate nearly 80 percent of our students from high school, somewhat higher than the U.S. but considerably below Korea and Japan, where the comparable rate is nearly 90 percent."

That Chinese parents push their students to study hard is anecdotal lore of the first quality and has come to be synonymous with Confucianism, although Confucius probably never faced the kind of cutthroat competition that young students in Taiwan do today. Bo Yang, a prolific and highly respected Taiwanese literary figure who spent many years under house arrest during Chiang's time because of his caustic essays, wrote an exaggerated piece not long ago about life and education in Taiwan, where all schoolchildren wear glasses for myopia and where in order to cope with the pressures of schoolwork they turn their backs on family and friends. He tells of a young student's mother who faints and collapses, but when the boy goes to help her, she cries out to him, "Let me die! Don't bother with me. Do your homework! Do your homework!"

Taiwan sends 7,000 university graduates to study overseas every year. About 95 percent of them go to the U.S., where they pursue doctorates in science and engineering and where Taiwan has sixteen sister universities. About 25,000 students altogether are studying overseas today, with more Taiwanese students in America than from any other country.

Taiwan used to have a so-called twenty-twenty rule: 20 percent of its graduates went to the U.S. each year, and 20 percent of them came back to Taiwan with advanced degrees. But that is changing. Now more than 30 percent come back, because of political liberalization, greater job opportunities in engineering, new government subsidies to encourage their return, and a new science and industrial park at Hsinchu where they can do more research.

With Dr. Lee's assistance, I arranged to visit Taipei's leading junior high school, Nan Men, a short taxi ride from the center of town. Nan Men is a large public school by any standard, with 6,000 students in grades seven, eight, and nine and an average class size of forty-five. It is a well-known school by virtue of its position at the top of about every parent's list of desirable middle schools, and admission is gained by way of a highly competitive, Taipei-wide entrance exam.

As I climbed the front steps, past a bronze memorial to the late generalissimo, heading for the assistant principal's office, I watched the now-familiar student teams engaged in mid-afternoon classroom cleaning. They were so busy washing blackboards, sweeping halls, sponging windows, and mopping floors that they hardly noticed the foreigner walk by. I stopped for a moment and marveled again at this philosophically simple but pedagogically effective means of building cooperation among young people. One red-cheeked youngster looked up and smiled shyly. I mouthed what few words of Mandarin I knew, and her smile broadened. An unintelligible stream of Chinese came back.

Upstairs, the assistant principal, Chin Huan-teh, welcomed me, and we sat for a while in his small but uncluttered office, drinking lapsang tea and talking about Taipei's famous school. An older man, and serious, with many years of experience at Nan Men, Chin had attended school during the Japanese occupation of Taiwan, so we spoke in Japanese.

"Our purpose is to get *everybody* into high school from here," he said, "and there is considerable competition for the best high schools, to enhance their chances for getting into the best universities. Our school year begins September 1 and ends July 31, with vacation in August. Classes meet Monday through Friday from 8:20 until 4:20, and we are here half-days on Saturday, from 8:20 to 1:00. Each class is divided into smaller teams, under the *toban* system, and we spend twenty to thirty minutes near the end of each school day cleaning the rooms. We also use the small teams for class-by-class competition, to see which is the best in chemistry, or Chinese, or intramural sports."

Nan Men has a very strong reputation in music, Chin told me, and anyone who has not learned how to swim is not allowed to graduate. The school consistently wins athletic competitions and has been singled out by the education ministry for excellence in swimming. Nan Men also places a strong emphasis on moral education, centering on Confucian ethics, which is taught as part of social studies.

Teachers communicate with parents by means of the familiar student handbooks, and collective meetings are held at least once a semester, if not more frequently. The students average only about an hour of homework a night, perhaps because they are not dismissed from school until late in the afternoon.

"The Ministry of Education decides the overall curriculum," Chin said, "and the schools implement it. But there is considerable latitude, in the older years, for electives. We watch developments in Korea and Japan very closely, to track their reform efforts, and we'll probably revise our own examination system in the near future. Since Nan Men has a top ranking, we would like to continue to be number one, and our objective is never to drop below number three. But come; we don't have much time. The children will gather shortly for the closing ceremony, which I don't want you to miss."

We walked briskly down the hall and went up one flight to get a better view of the closing assembly just as the three classes were forming their ranks. The Nan Men building was a typical multistory square structure that embraced a huge open courtyard of packed sandy clay, perhaps three football fields in size. The seventh-graders were dressed in red jackets and white trousers or skirts; beyond them, the eighth-graders, all in forest green; and in the distance, the "seniors," in navy blue. Four inspirational calligraphic posters, in Chinese, hung from the top of the building. *Kokka,* read one, "the nation is most important"; *sekinin,* read another, "take responsibility"; *meiyo,* "earn respect and honor"; *fukumu,* "duty for the sake of society."

I pressed close to the edge of the balcony as the school band, comprised of second-year students, marched down the running track around the edge of the courtyard playing "Semper Fidelis," and all the students closed ranks behind their monitor. Then the band stopped and, from memory, with no music clipped to the instruments, struck up "Anchors Aweigh," full blast, as everyone across the huge courtyard stood shoulder to shoulder in impeccable order. Finally, all grew quiet.

Slowly and somberly, the band played the national anthem, and hands folded instinctively across hearts as the 6,000 Nan Men students sang proudly with one voice. Three preschool siblings, playing in the side yard below us, stopped and stood at attention. Then there was a pause, and the band played the flag-lowering song as the national flag, the city flag, and the school flag were lowered simultaneously, all eyes riveted forward. A team of third-year students came to the front, held the flags vertically aloft, and then slowly walked ahead until they cleared the courtyard, where they stopped, folded the flags, and stood at attention until the band stopped.

The head teacher, a Miss Yu, stepped up to the microphone and said a few words of encouragement and praise to the students. Then she dismissed them. Again, as with a single voice, they sang their school song as the band struck up the familiar tune.

> In this magnificent school building,
> Our beloved teachers care for us,
> Teaching us patiently,
> Helping us to be somebody.
> We cultivate conduct, studies,
>   sports, and teamwork,
> Making us the best citizens.
> Never shall we forget our beloved teachers;
> From dawn to dusk,
> We enjoy our times at school.

I watched the multitude of Nan Men students leave the courtyard through the huge gates, in clusters of two and three and four. In minutes they were gone, and the courtyard was ghostly still.

Human resources, indeed, I thought. These Taiwanese students possessed a degree of enthusiasm, energy, and spirit unknown today in the West. The closing ceremony, so precise, so spine-tingling, so uplifting at the end of a school day, said volumes about cooperation and teamwork. It also said volumes about commitment and competitiveness.

THE PHILIPPINES: IN AMERICA'S SHADOW

If one country in Asia stands out as uniquely insensitive to shame, it is the Philippines. "Our public schools are diploma mills," a friend told me. "They're like the U.S., but a hundred times worse."

America brought public schools to the Philippines, following annexation in 1898, and that is one of the problems. Philippine schools reflect American, not Asian, traditions, and the Confucian spirit, else-where so stout, is markedly absent. There is little rigor in the curric-ulum and little order in the schools. Teachers are not well paid and do not occupy a position of respect in society; government spending on education is low. Parents are, for the most part, not involved in the education of their children. There is no emphasis on cooperative learn-ing in the classroom through student teams, and school spirit appears nonexistent. That "vital triangle" linking parent, teacher, and child is, like much else of significance, weak.

Anyone who observes a public school in Manila, as I did on a recent trip to the Philippines, when I visited three of them, cannot help coming away with a feeling of despondence and despair. No doubt the children of the Philippine oligarchy can, by attending one of the many private or parochial schools, obtain an education that is in most respects equiv-alent to good private schooling in America. But that is not the point. It is a nation's *public* education system that reflects the priorities of its people; where there is good education, Confucius said, there is no distinction of class. Education in the Philippines is a weak sister of an American system that finds itself in serious decline.

The Manuel L. Quezon Senior High School is located in the Tondo section of western Manila, one of the city's several urban slums, with row after row of corrugated tin squatter's shacks jammed between run-down retail stores and small repair shops. Nearby, clusters of young boys, hordes of them, perhaps six or seven years old, bathe themselves in muddy streetwater, which had collected in large potholes, using old tin cans as makeshift scoops, their naked bodies glistening under the hot sun. In any other East Asian country they would have been in school, but not in the Philippines, where two-thirds of the population is less than fifteen years old.

The Manuel L. Quezon school is named for the first president of the commonwealth of the Philippines, who was elected in 1935. It has a total enrollment of 3,786 students in four grades, nine through twelve, and is situated on the third floor of a large, noisy three-story building. On the ground floor is a crowded meat market, swarming with flies, and on the second floor a police station. A gate on the concrete steps between the second and third floors is manned by a policeman who sits amid a collection of litter and half-eaten fruit, feeding more flies. Classes for juniors and seniors are conducted on the third floor, but freshmen and sophomores attend class in an annex building not far away. Class size averages thirty, maybe thirty-five.

In a science class, perhaps only half the students present paid attention, while the others either dozed, slumped back in their chairs, or gazed out the window, waiting for the bell to ring. Outside the rear of the school children played around a pile of trash in front of the familiar tin shacks. Down the hall, in the library, where there appeared to be many more magazines than books, some students had a study period. Several laid their heads on the tables; others flipped through magazines. The students were, however, wearing uniforms, which in Manila were brown khaki skirts and blouses for the girls, the same in shorts and T-shirts for the boys. An illusion of order in the midst of educational chaos.

I had not seen a single male teacher in any of the classrooms or offices that day, and I later found out why. Manila has thirty-nine school districts. There are seventy-three elementary schools with 180,000 students and 8,093 primary teachers, of whom 7,554 are women and only 539 men. The city has thirty secondary schools with about 100,000 students and 5,793 high school teachers, of whom 4,822 are women and only 971 men. Teachers are not unionized, but belong to the Secondary School Teachers Association.

Despite being surrounded in Asia by superior educational systems, public education in the Philippines remains practically if not culturally insulated from potential improvement. While this may come as no surprise in a country whose oligarchic leadership is, for the most part, educated abroad, and consequently maintains no strategic commitment to public education as a national priority, it spells further disaster, it seems to me, for a country whose economic fortunes are tied to exploiting a natural resource base rather than to developing its human resources.

The Philippines has lived in the cultural shadows of America, and before it, Spain, for far too long. As with its inability to emulate the successful models of capitalist economic development so prevalent now throughout East Asia, the Philippines has also ignored one of the most fundamental building blocks of those models—a highly competitive, rigorous, no-nonsense, egalitarian educational system. And because performance in America's own public schools has lagged of late, with a negative impact on the nation's competitiveness, it is the American system, and recent efforts to reform it, to which we turn next.

12

FLAWS AND FAILURES IN AMERICAN EDUCATION

Our Nation is at risk. Our once unchallenged pre-eminence in commerce, industry, science, and technological innovation is being overtaken by competitors throughout the world.... [T]he educational foundations of our society are presently being eroded by a rising tide of mediocrity that threatens our very future as a Nation and a people. What was unimaginable a generation ago has begun to occur—others are matching and surpassing our educational attainments.

If an unfriendly foreign power had attempted to impose on America the mediocre educational performance that exists today, we might well have viewed it as an act of war. We live [now] among determined, well-educated, and strongly motivated competitors....

Each generation of Americans has outstripped its parents in education, in literacy, and in economic attainment. For the first time in the history of our country, the educational skills of one generation will not surpass, will not equal, will not even approach, those of their parents.

National Commission on Excellence in Education,
A Nation at Risk, 1983

Six years ago, when the National Commission on Excellence in Education published its now-famous report, Americans were only vaguely aware that current standards of educational achievement were not as high as they had been in the past. But *A Nation at Risk* struck a responsive chord and was the first of several major reports calling for extensive reform of public education. In 1986 the Carnegie Foundation issued *A Nation Prepared,* which argued for significant changes in the ways American teachers were educated, certified, compensated, and trained and offered a vision of how schools could be organized for the twenty-first century.

In 1987 *Time for Results,* published by the National Governors Association, said if local school districts weren't going to take the initiative in implementing reforms, then states would step in and take control. The American public was beginning to realize just how poorly its children were faring, when measured both against past performance and against the increasingly higher standards of educational performance of America's international competitors.

By 1988 Americans had learned that the Scholastic Aptitude Test scores and American College Testing results of high school–aged children were far lower than they had been years before: between 1963 and 1980 combined average SAT scores plunged ninety points before leveling off at around 900. They learned that America's eighth-graders were placing twelfth out of fourteen among industrialized countries taking international mathematics tests. Japan was placing first.

They learned that the top 5 percent of American twelfth-graders were placing *last* out of twelve major countries taking advanced algebra and calculus exams. Japan, again, was first. They learned that seventeen-year-olds got barely half the answers right on a national history assessment and scored only 51.8 percent correct on literature, when 60 percent was the minimum passing score. They learned that average reading scores for nine-, thirteen-, and seventeen-year-olds were inversely related to the number of hours students spent watching television. They learned that two-thirds of all eleventh-graders did less than an hour of homework a night. They learned that only about two-thirds of American children were graduating from high school; more than 40 percent were dropouts in the state of Florida, nearly 50 percent in Louisiana, and 50 percent in the city of Los Angeles alone.

They learned that classroom teachers as a proportion of public school staff had dropped to about half the total, compared to nearly two-thirds in 1960, and they wondered where all the money for higher teaching salaries was going: teacher compensation had nearly tripled since 1972, to a national average of $25,000, but that seemed to be having little impact on productivity or performance. Engineers, scientists, accountants, and other white-collar workers were all earning more than teachers; only blue-collar production workers earned less.

In 1972 the average pupil/teacher ratio nationwide was twenty-two; by 1988 it had improved to less than eighteen, but the student/adult ratio was now six to one. Money was going into the bureaucracy, not into the classroom. Leadership, staff cooperation, student behavior, teacher control, and morale were all higher in America's private schools, despite the fact that average teaching salaries were lower.

Coursework in math, science, English, and social studies required for public high school graduation was far below levels recommended by the national commission in 1983 and well below private school levels. Only twenty-two hours a week were being spent by America's children on classroom activities in 1988, out of thirty hours a week in school. Teachers were spending only half their time teaching and the rest on school-related activities either inside or outside of school. America's typical school year was only 185 days, five days a week, six hours a day, compared to an academic year of 225 days common in East Asia and in Europe, 5½ to six days a week, seven to eight hours a day.

Nearly two out of every three American high school students in 1988 consumed alcohol regularly each month, and nearly a third said they used drugs. The rate of cocaine use among high school seniors had more than tripled since 1975. Students themselves complained that their textbooks were dull and unimaginative, yet increasing numbers of them could not add up a typical restaurant bill and calculate the correct change, or read a bus schedule, or get their geography right. On one international test a majority of American students thought Shanghai was the capital of Japan, could not identify that country on a map of the world, and placed seventh out of nine countries overall; only Italy and Mexico scored worse. Teachers complained that their biggest problem was lack of parental involvement; parents complained that their biggest problem was lack of classroom discipline.

In 1987 two books that dealt with America's educational shortcomings made the *New York Times* best-seller list. One was *The Closing of the American Mind* by Allan Bloom, a University of Chicago professor of classics, whose polemic cut American higher education down to size. The other was a critique of curriculum content called *Cultural Literacy: What Every American Needs to Know* by E. D. Hirsch, Jr., of the University of Virginia. These books were not easy reads. Both were more descriptive than prescriptive. But what they did, as had not been done before, was to rivet the nation's consciousness on the pressing need for reform.

Before reviewing recent efforts at educational reform, however, it might be worthwhile to take a look at how the system evolved, because an understanding of origins is helpful in clarifying future goals, and the origins are not well understood. More importantly, perhaps, the

American public has yet to come to grips with the issue of how the system *itself* may be a serious impediment to effective reform.

"Indeed, one of the chief reasons for the failures of educational reforms of the past," David Tyack wrote in his perceptive account of American schools called *The One Best System*, "has been that they called for a change of philosophy on the part of the individual school employee rather than systemic change. The search for the one best system has ill-served the pluralistic character of American society. Increasing bureaucratization of urban schools has resulted in a displacement of goals, perpetuating positions and outworn practices, rather than serving the clients, the children to be taught."

Schooling in mid-nineteenth-century rural America was just one part of a child's overall education, organically intertwined with family, church, and farm work. Teachers in those days knew to whom they were accountable: to the parents who entrusted their children to them and to the children themselves, whose respect and admiration they wanted to win. This organic interrelationship began to change in growing cities like New York, Chicago, and Philadelphia, where student performance faltered as population growth outstripped the schools' capacity to cope.

Famous reformers of the day such as Horace Mann, secretary of the Massachusetts Board of Education, and his colleague, Samuel Gridley Howe, evaluated test results in Boston, where poor performance persuaded them to call for the employment of a full-time superintendent. Their efforts were applauded by educators like William Harris, superintendent in St. Louis and later U.S. commissioner of education, who argued that the first requisite of American schools was to establish order. They sought a stable, predictable, and reliable *structure* in which their own roles as educational managers would be visible and secure, so they created a bureaucracy that provided a suitable hierarchy for the teacher.

In the mid-1890s the National Education Association, created by teachers in 1857, recommended consolidating schools, transporting pupils, and empowering superintendents, who would each be respon sible for a separate district and report to a separate school board. Educators were eager to create a bureaucratic system because it mirrored the growing demand for order and efficiency by American business for the emerging industrial era. Important in this new electromechanical age was mass production, and most important was the assembly line process, whereby components were standardized, production runs were strictly scheduled, and factory workers became cogs in the process. Workers performed best, managers thought, if they obeyed orders and did what they were told; they would learn to take orders and follow rules if taught to do so by the schools.

"The division of labor in the factory, the punctuality of the railroad, and the chain of command and coordination of modern businesses," Tyack wrote, "aroused a sense of wonder and excitement in men and women seeking to systematize the schools. Efficiency, rationality, and precision became watchwords of the consolidators. In short, they created a more bureaucratic system."

Schools soon began to emulate the army, the post office, and, eventually, the large corporate bureaucracy. One famous educator, John Philbrick, designed the "egg-crate" school, a multigrade, multistory building that replaced the one-room schoolhouse (which declined from more than 200,000 in 1910 to fewer than 20,000 by 1960). Military precision was required in the maneuvering of classes; teachers emphasized punctuality, attention, and silence, because these standards were valued by industry. The popular expression "to toe the line" originated in these new schools: when students had to demonstrate their skills, they were required to stand motionless, fully erect, with knees and feet together, the tips of their shoes touching the edge of a board in the floor. Control, not content, was the watchword.

Helen Todd, a school inspector in Chicago in the early 1900s, was concerned that immigrant children, who then comprised two-thirds of all students, spend their time in school and not in a factory. She thought the classroom was preferable to the alternative of industry exploiting child labor, but she was not prepared for the answers she got when she interviewed young truants. "The teachers hits ya if ya whisper," one boy tearfully told her, "and they hits ya if yer late, and they hits ya if ya ferget the page."

By the turn of the century the system had fostered subordination and a top-down autocratic structure controlled by men. By 1905 only 2 percent of America's teachers were male, though a generation earlier more than a third of them had been. Some 94 percent of all superintendents and principals were men, and they were paid on average 50 percent more than teachers, sometimes twice as much. But teachers (then as now) thought administrators simply gave them useless things to do; being required to write unnecessary reports and gather meaningless statistics, they found they had less time to teach. "The kind of man who is willing to supervise such a petty system," one teacher noted, "is mediocre by definition." The feminist Mary Abigail Dodge, a former teacher herself, deplored the factory analogy and argued that teachers should run the schools autonomously.

It also became apparent to administrators that laymen on school boards possessed the kind of power most of them sought. School boards were configured then in about as many ways as they are today: some were appointed, as in Chicago and New York; some were elected, as in Detroit; some were nominated by judges, as in Philadelphia. But the process had become politicized, much as it is now; there was such diffusion of responsibility from district to district that short-term decisions, such as where to put a new school and who should pay for it, became contentious and adversarial. Local politicians often sacrificed the schools to the needs of the political machine. Teacher allegiances, accordingly, took a rapid and understandable volte-face: school politics demanded that a teacher's loyalty be to the school board that appointed her, to the superintendent who confirmed her appointment, and to the principal who supervised her work, instead of to her students and their parents.

At the turn of the century 484 American cities reported an average of only four supervisors per city, but by 1920 all that had changed. According to one observer, there was now "a whole galaxy of principals, assistant principals, supervisors of special subjects, directors of vocational education, guidance counselors, deans, attendance officers, and clerks, who do no teaching but are concerned with keeping the system going." Problems in American education were being solved not by looking at its structure, but by adding layers to the bureaucracy. Teachers were positioned at the bottom of increasingly rigid, top-heavy, vertical hierarchies. The NEA itself opposed democratization of the process and was initially against equal pay for women.

The kinds of changes that have been taking place in American public education in recent years have been those that are possible to implement *without* systemic change—lengthening the school year by a few days, paying the teachers a little more, doing more testing, stiffening high school graduation requirements, or trying to broaden the talent pool from which teachers are recruited. These changes, while not unimportant, are all elements that a Washington friend, Robert Leestma, who directed the education department's informative and insightful study on Japanese education, calls the "easily measurables." The reform efforts have yet to evaluate the "not-so-easily measurables," which are of greater importance.

Even the clarion call of *A Nation at Risk* issued recommendations that were careful not to threaten the structure: raising standards of curriculum content, strengthening college admission requirements, raising teacher salaries, and lengthening the school day. But despite these efforts, the overall results have not impressed, and the net effect represents just a little nibbling around the edges of a problem that is far more structural in nature than most Americans realize.

"We're now coming to the end of the first phase of reforms," Dr. Harold Hodgkinson, director of the Institute for Educational Leadership in Washington, recently told me. "So far, we've focused on trying to raise standards, increase teacher compensation, set higher certification requirements and requirements for graduation. But it is amazing how little has changed in terms of classroom behavior. There is a 'filter' that keeps change out, and it's pretty strong."

I asked him about the next phase of reforms.

"The second phase will be restructuring," he said. "It will be more expensive and will take much longer to achieve. We're now in a hiatus, a very ambiguous period, waiting for things to happen. There are isolated examples of restructuring occurring now, in pockets around the country, but there is no real thrust in this direction yet. Some people say we have a decade in which to restructure; otherwise, Americans will push for vouchers and tuition tax credits so they will have more choice. A decade may be optimistic."

Compared to Asia, American parents tend to be less involved in the education of their children, and when I asked Dr. Hodgkinson about this, he said, "Half our kids are now being raised by single parents, and the single parent is usually a woman, and that woman has to work, so lack of parental involvement comes as no surprise. There is more American companies can do through flexwork and flextime arrangements, as well as providing better on-site child-care facilities. America is clearly behind in terms of education and child care for our preschool youngsters."

Demographics is destiny, in education as well as in politics.

"The white suburban middle-class birthrate is coming way down, and so is the black and Hispanic middle-class rate," he went on. "But the rate in the underclasses is escalating rather dramatically, which creates a disproportionate number of poor children for our public systems to educate, a trend that is exploding with the power of compound interest. In California today 56 percent of school-aged kids are already non-Anglo; in Texas 49 percent of them are. These trends raise some fundamental questions about how public education will reach larger numbers of precisely those segments of our population it has had the most difficulty educating in the past. These are all reasons why the business community has become more concerned."

John Akers, chairman of IBM, recently wrote that American business spends an estimated $30 billion a year on remedial education, reteaching high school graduates how to read and write effectively and how to perform simple arithmetic calculations, in order to raise their skill levels to a standard acceptable on the factory floor. David Kearns, chairman of Xerox, has said that public education puts America at a competitive disadvantage and that reforms are so far just "tinkering at the margins"; if American companies had a product reject rate as high as that of education, they'd go out of business, and teaching new workers basic skills is essentially doing the schools' product recall work for them. Brad Butler, retired chairman of Procter & Gamble, has been active in persuading communities of the need to raise more money for teachers' salaries, textbooks, and preschool programs for at-risk youngsters.

When I asked Dr. Hodgkinson about the role of school boards in the reform process, his response was not unexpected.

"I think we'll have to reinvent them," he said, "to get more efficiency into the system. It's a highly centralized bureaucracy today, and we need more percolation from the bottom up. Education does tend to emulate other sectors, but with a sizable lag."

Chester E. Finn, Jr., would agree. Dr. Finn, known to colleagues and friends as Checker, is professor of education and public policy at Vanderbilt and was, until recently, assistant secretary of education for educational research and improvement. Educated at Harvard and a former staff aide to Senator Pat Moynihan, Dr. Finn coauthored *What Do Our 17-Year-Olds Know?*

"We know that educational output is not directly related to financial input," he was saying as we sat in his Washington office in early 1988. "We also know outputs could be far higher, because for thirty years, to about 1980, inputs tripled, yet output has sagged. Achievement levels tend to vary more within schools than between schools, and there is no systematic relationship between resources and results. So more money is not necessarily the answer."

We talked for a while about money—where it goes or doesn't go— and why the system resists change.

"In 1985," he said, "average per-pupil expenditures in the U.S. were about $3,400. That meant about $100,000 available for an average class of thirty kids, taught by one teacher. But average teacher salaries were up to only $25,000, so where was the other $75,000 going? Into the bureaucratic apparatus, not into the classroom. Local school boards, which sit on top of this whole process, are gradually becoming obsolete. They are the dinosaurs, and district administrators are, too—they feel threatened by the process of structural change, so they tend to oppose it."

I asked him about the findings in his recent book.

"We tested 8,000 students nationwide," he said, "statistically weighted by region, sex, and race to resemble the population as a whole. We asked 141 questions on history and 121 on literature, choosing these two because testing for math and science had already been undertaken by the National Assessment of Educational Progress since 1969 and because requirements for history and literature were decreasing. The average results were appalling: 51.8 percent on the literature section and 54.5 percent on history, when sixty was passing. A majority could not answer simple questions about major works and authors."

When I read Finn's book, I was intrigued by his chapter "Behind the Scores," which analyzed the ethnic backgrounds and family structures of respondents and which, he admitted to me, had been pretty much ignored by reviewers.

Students whose parents had a college education naturally received higher scores; parents with the most education typically provided their children with the most literate home environment. Students from families with both parents present scored better in every instance, even if one or both parents worked. Students who had attended preschool scored higher than those who had not. White and Asian students scored higher than blacks, Hispanics, and Native Americans.

Asian students attending nonpublic schools performed better on both sections than any other group, dispelling the notion that Asians were inclined to do well in math and science but not in the English-based skills of history and literature. Asian-Americans take more SAT-related achievement tests, score higher, do more homework, and generate more admissions to elite universities than whites. (All eleven of New York's Westinghouse science semifinalists in 1988 were Asian-American, as is the current U.S. spelling bee champion.)

Students, regardless of race or sex, who attended private schools scored better than those who attended public schools, and those who did relatively more homework and watched less TV confirmed the conventional wisdom that successful students, whether wealthy or poor, really do work harder.

"We have ignored cultural literacy in thinking about education," Hirsch wrote in his 1987 best-seller, "precisely because it was something we have been able to take for granted. Only when we run into cultural illiteracy are we shocked into recognizing the importance of the information that we had unconsciously assumed."

Hirsch drew attention not only to falling SAT scores and poor test results but also to the fact that poor reading texts had replaced the classical stories that previous generations had read. The process was further diluted by the content-neutral ideas of earlier educators. Basal readers like *Dick and Jane* and *Run, Snail, Run* taught early reading skills as a simple technical process of "recoding and decoding," without imparting important cultural values, such as could be done by using simple versions of *Aesop's Fables* or Thorndike and Baker's *Everyday Classics*, which were popular in American elementary schools years ago.

"Facts and skills are inseparable," Hirsch concluded. "In future our debates about the extensive curriculum must keep clearly in view the high stakes involved: breaking the cycle of illiteracy for deprived children; raising the living standard of families who have been illiterate; making our country more competitive in international markets; achieving greater social justice; enabling all citizens to participate in the political process—in short, achieving fundamental goals of the Founders at the birth of the republic."

Finn's and Hirsch's works both touched on one failure of American education that has garnered little attention, and that is the difference preschool programs make in the lives of students, especially those in America's at-risk groups. In 1964 the High/Scope Educational Research Foundation began a twenty-year longitudinal study to track 123 disadvantaged children from preschool to age nineteen, comparing the performance of an experimental group of fifty-eight children against a control group of sixty-five children with no exposure to preschool. It was called the Perry Preschool Program, named after a dentist and local school board official in Ypsilanti, Michigan. The experimental group was comprised of children aged three and four who attended high-quality preschool classes prior to their enrollment in kindergarten, and the study's eventual results were published in 1984 in an extensive report called *Changed Lives.*

All 123 children had been born to poor families, about half of which received welfare assistance and were single-parent families, and only 21 percent of the mothers and 11 percent of the fathers had graduated from high school. Children in the study were assigned randomly to either the experimental group or the control group. Those in the experimental group attented preschool for 2½ hours a morning, five days a week, for one year at age four or for two years from age three. The curriculum focused on active learning through play, problem solving, and both adult and small-group interaction with peers. Teachers also visited the families for ninety minutes once a week to stimulate their interest and curiosity so they could improve the levels of instruction and interaction at home.

The results of the study were striking. Two out of three students from the preschool group graduated from high school, compared to one of two from the nonpreschool control group. Functional competence testing for the preschool group averaged 61 percent, compared with 38 percent for the control group; nearly 40 percent of the preschoolers enrolled in postsecondary school, compared to only 21 percent for the others; and only 15 percent were classified as "mentally retarded," compared to 35 percent for the others. The experimental group had a 31 percent detention and arrest rate in later years, compared to 51 percent for those with no preschool; the teenage pregnancy rate was sixty-four per one hundred females for the preschool group, compared to one hundred and seventeen per one hundred for the control group; at age nineteen, half the preschool group was employed, compared to only 19 percent of the others; and only 18 percent of the preschoolers were receiving welfare, compared to more than a third of the control group.

When I spoke with Dr. David Weikart, president of the High/Scope Educational Research Foundation, in the spring of 1988, he said, "Many people think our findings are overstated, which is simply not the case if you apply the results to similar environmental circumstances. If anything, we have been accused by public policy officials of understating the data. But if you consider the lower economic costs and the longer-

term social benefits of our preschool programs for at-risk youngsters
and compare them against the higher economic costs and shorter-term
holding action of building more prisons, which cost $75,000 a bed,
you begin to see some rather major differences in terms of public policy
implications."

The Perry findings were instructive in other, broader ways as well.
Economic benefits attained by the experimental group at the end of
high school, both predicted and actual, in terms of either higher-earning
jobs or entry into college, more than justified the cost of their preschool
education. The benefits to society, in terms of decreased social costs,
such as lower crime and arrest rates and lower rates of welfare assistance, were equally apparent.

The results have also been instrumental in persuading companies like
Texas Instruments to underwrite preschool education for disadvantaged
children in Dallas and individuals like Chicago philanthropist Irving
Harris to finance pediatric care and preschool expenses for at-risk children before they enter the Beethoven Elementary School on Chicago's
depressed South Side. Shorter-term measures, such as building more
prisons and beefing up police forces, are politically more palatable because politicians can point to tangible evidence of progress, like a new
building or more cops. It is, however, the longer-term structural benefits, which may not be evident until long after Election Day, that are
likely to be of greater benefit to society.

Private corporations, such as General Foods, and private philanthropic funds, such as the Ford Foundation and the New York Times
Foundation, support High/Scope's programs strongly—they, and others,
have contributed $8 million to the project's ongoing efforts. Weikart
and his colleagues in Ypsilanti now train 2,000 early-education specialists annually for hundreds of school districts around the nation. The
Los Angeles, Chicago, and New York elementary schools regularly send
their own early elementary teachers there to be trained.

When I saw Mark Shepherd, Jr., the former chairman of Texas
Instruments, in Dallas, he was not sanguine about America's ability to
solve its education problems over the short term.

"Education is the biggest problem we have," he said during our long
interview. "The family unit is essential for formal education systems
to work—systems that were designed with the father working and the
mother at home. But the systems today aren't responding to the changed
environment. In Japan mothers are incredibly involved in their chil-

dren's education, but that solution won't work here when fewer and fewer of our children come from traditional family-unit homes. Preschool is certainly one part of the solution, but another thing we need to consider is schoolfare—finding ways to keep kids from dropping out of school. It's analogous to our manufacturing problem. Everybody says robots and computers are the issue. Well, robots and computers are *not* the issue; lower operating costs and higher productivity are. Same thing in education. You have to look beyond the superficial to the real."

Schoolfare—paying kids to stay in school—is a controversial subject, and motivation is not something schools spend a lot of time worrying about. Some experiments with schoolfare have succeeded; others have failed. Some less affluent school districts in the Northeast have paid students $5 a day to stay in school, using direct financial rewards as an incentive. The kindest critics will say this is not enough to motivate the kids when they can earn multiples of that amount in a fraction of the time selling drugs. Harsher critics simply call them bribes.

Dr. Bradley Bucher, a behavioral psychologist with decades of experience in treating autistic children and children with learning disabilities, disagrees. Dr. Bucher has not one, but two, PhDs—in mathematics and in psychology. He taught at UCLA and is the author of numerous books and articles on behavior.

"Bribes are illegal payments for immoral behavior," he was saying one day as we discussed the whole issue of motivation. "But positive reinforcement should in no way be considered a bribe. You want to isolate the desirable behavior and reinforce it. For some kids $5 may work, whereas with others it may have to be something else. The same reward won't work for all kids, just as the same rewards don't work for all adults in the real world. It all comes down to motivation, but schools don't believe motivation is their problem. They steadfastly believe it should be internal on the part of each student, that students should love learning for its own sake or that the curriculum should turn them on. Therefore, schools oppose using anything external—like a reward—that they think may interfere with this love of learning, which I think most of us would agree the schools don't have a lot of success inculcating in the first place."

There are two sides to this coin: behavior you want and behavior you don't want. Schools or, more accurately, teachers tend to use punishment in their attempts to extinguish undesirable behavior, so somehow it seems odd that they should oppose the use of rewards for desirable behavior. But if they refuse to use rewards for reinforcement, they are forced to depend on punishment. And when rewards are viewed erroneously as bribes, the incentive for positive reinforcement is reduced correspondingly.

"Educators who think positive reinforcers are bribes," Bucher went on, "find themselves trying to solve a big problem—attendance, say, or motivation—but they balk at a solution because it has, for them, a minor cost. Reinforcers are not bribes, but even if they *were*, teachers still refuse to come to grips with the bigger problem. Years ago there was a well-documented case in the literature about an inner-city kid who came chronically late to school and then never stayed. The school arranged for a guidance counselor to meet with him when he was tardy, but he still came late. They didn't realize they were reinforcing him for coming late by giving him something he needed and wanted: time with an adult he respected and liked. They finally figured out they had it backwards. If he came to school on time, they told him, and stayed the day, *then* they would reward him by giving him time with his counselor. When they turned it around, it worked."

One educator who has come to symbolize control in the schools is Joe Clark, principal of embattled Eastside High School, a predominantly black and Hispanic school in Paterson, New Jersey. Clark patrols his hallways with a baseball bat and a bullhorn. He became a national folk hero when former secretary of education William Bennett praised his efforts to cleanse Eastside of drugs and violence by summarily expelling several hundred troublemakers over a period of years and padlocking the front door to keep them out. When the school board threatened to fire him, the White House offered him a job. But Clark had strong support from his students (and their parents), many of whom felt they had little at home to motivate them, so they looked up to him as a role model. When the school board issued its ultimatum, a majority of his students rallied around him and said, "If he goes, we go." (Clark attained even further notoriety through a riveting movie filmed at Eastside, appropriately called *Lean on Me*, which dramatized his experiences at the school.)

New Jersey officials had included Paterson on a short list of nine school districts that were near educational bankruptcy and candidates for takeover by the state. Per-pupil spending in Paterson in 1987 was under $2,700—ranking it number 572 out of 591 districts in the state—considerably below the national average of $3,750 and barely half the state average of $5,400. Fewer than half of Eastside's 3,000 students could pass proficiency exams in math and writing, and barely half passed reading. In 1987, 620 troublemakers were forced out by Clark, and more than 600 had left in each of the prior two years as well. Clark could eventually show how Eastside's average SAT scores had increased as a result of his efforts, though critics would note that averages always rise when poor performance is eliminated. The key issue was one of choice: does the state or the local community control the school?

I raised this issue recently with a friend who is the principal of a small suburban high school, predominantly black, just outside New York City.

"You're talking to a cynic now," he reminded me. "Schools and their districts typically form committees to study where things need to be changed. Hell, if you don't *know* where things need to be changed, you're an idiot. The major complaint teachers have is that they are supervised by people who haven't been in a classroom for twenty years. You have to be *in* the classroom, working by example, not by command. I agree the parents need to be more involved, but when they're all working, who's got the time? And the principal shouldn't run everything; otherwise the teachers get even more discouraged. But the bureaucracy isn't ready to give the teachers more power, because what the teachers gain the bureaucrats see themselves losing."

American public education produces teachers who become discouraged and demoralized because they are at the bottom of a top-heavy pyramid. Though they resent being treated like blue-collar workers, they use blue-collar tactics in the way they are unionized, compensated, and trained. The system also produces a bifurcated class of students, divided unintentionally into an academic track, which is college-bound with exaggerated employment prospects, and a vocational track, which is factory-bound and characterized by low self-esteem.

While America's claim to superior higher education may be valid when talking about its elite universities—the Ivy League schools and a handful of private and public institutions around the country—it is more difficult to justify for the average undergraduate school. During the course of the past two decades college students have become preoccupied with early specialization, particularly in business, medicine, and the law. What were once core curricula, which concentrated on humanities as the nucleus of a liberal education, have gradually given way to trends and fads, such as black studies, feminism, and business.

Business and law are the two most popular career choices in America today. In 1988 law school applications jumped 15 percent to nearly 80,000 nationwide, and law students admit they are interested in little more than making a lot of money. Average starting salaries for first-year law associates nationwide is almost $50,000, nearly $70,000 in New York City alone. But business runs a close second. Nearly 20 percent of all American undergradutes now study economics as a pre-business major. Starting salaries in investment banking and consulting, the two most popular professions of MBAs, are over $50,000, and commercial banking is not far behind, at $37,500.

Nearly two-thirds of the graduates of Harvard Business School now enter investment banking and consulting as careers, and 96 percent of its law school graduates go into corporate practice, rejecting public interest work and government jobs because of the disparate gap in compensation. At Columbia University nearly half of whose entering classes now major in either economics or business as undergraduates, investment and commercial banking are the two most popular careers chosen, attracting about half of the 1987 graduating class, whose average starting salaries were $47,500. Nationwide, the average starting salary for college graduates was $24,100, the most popular career choice, accounting.

"A great disaster has occurred," Allan Bloom wrote. "It is the establishment of the MBA as the moral equivalent of the MD degree, meaning a way of insuring a lucrative living by the mere fact of a diploma that is not a mark of scholarly achievement. It is a general rule that the students who have any chance of getting a liberal education are those who do not have a fixed career goal, or at least those for whom the university is not merely a training ground for a profession. The effect of the MBA is to corral a horde of students who want to get into business school and to put blinders on them, to legislate an illiberal, officially approved undergraduate program for them at the outset. Both the goal and the way of getting to it are fixed so that nothing can distract them. Getting into those elite professional schools is an obsessive concern that tethers their minds."

By late 1987 nearly 80 percent of America's college freshmen, a record number, felt that being financially well off was either an "essential" or a "very important" goal, according to questionnaires completed by more than 200,000 entering freshmen. More than 70 percent said that the primary reason for attending college was to make more money, and business continues to be the preferred career. Fewer than 10 percent indicated any desire to enter the field of teaching as a career.

"Economics overwhelms the rest of the social sciences and skews the students' perception of them," Bloom concluded. "A premed who takes much biology does not, by comparison, lose sight of the status of physics. None of this is so for the prebusiness economics major, who not only does not take an interest in sociology, anthropology, or political science, but is also persuaded that what he is learning can handle all that belongs to those studies. Moreover, he is not motivated by love of the science of economics but by love of what it is concerned with—money."

The fact that fewer than 10 percent of America's college graduates plan to teach has serious implications for public school teachers, nearly 40 percent of whom will retire within the next six years. Traditionally, America has sourced its teachers from the bottom quartile of graduating seniors: average SAT scores of those who teach for a while and then leave the profession are nearly 100 points higher than scores for those who stay, and teachers' average SAT scores are the lowest of any profession. To replace these retirees, let alone hire net additions, the system would need to employ about half of all university graduates between now and 1995, clearly an unrealistic proposition. An alternative is to broaden the talent pool by attracting people from other professions into teaching. Yet that is opposed by the bureaucracy, from state departments of education, which specify certification requirements, to local school boards, which feel uncomfortable hiring from a nontraditional labor pool, to superintendents and principals, who may feel threatened by more self-confident and competent professionals.

The yawning compensation gap is another deterrent. And for a society as money-motivated as America, this is not just an issue of inadequate teacher income, but also a problem of excessive corporate compensation. An equally important starting point for addressing the issue is not just in the collective bargaining sessions of America's teaching unions, but in the boardrooms of America's corporations. For if American business is serious about improving the quality of public education, it must also seriously address the issues of compensation and status by examining the extent to which its management may be overpaid. In Japan average compensation of senior executives across industry lines is about five times the average pay of production workers; in the United States, senior management receives, on average, *fifteen* times what average production workers are paid.

In a system that has kept teachers at or near the bottom of the professional pyramid, their social standing cannot be ameliorated overnight. First they must be rescued from the bottom of the pyramid, which means a significant restructuring of the bureaucracy. This is potentially threatening to local bureaucrats lodged in those fat middle layers—the superintendents, assistant superintendents, learning consultants, curriculum advisers, principals, and assistant principals who are much higher up, in both salary and status, than teachers. Restructuring represents a radical departure from a system most Americans have known for generations, but it may well represent the nation's best hope for the kinds of reforms that it has so far tried and failed to achieve.

The flaws and failures of American public education stand out in graphic relief when set against competitive systems in East Asia. Teacher status is just one comparative standard. The dynamics of small group interaction is another. The vital triangle of teacher, parent, and child is often missing in the American model, too, and without that strategic alliance, reform may be difficult and restructuring virtually impossible. The cry for higher achievement scores in America is often met with widespread and vocal opposition to testing. But testing is merely a subset of competition: how are we doing today compared to how we did yesterday, and how is our team doing against the others? If Asians overstress competition, Americans tend to understress it. The global community in which we now live is intensely competitive and becoming more so.

The educational systems of Japan and East Asia are also grappling with reform—how they must adapt to the changing needs of a new era characterized not by the smokestack but by the computer, which will require more individual creativity and innovation in a workplace dominated by teamwork and cooperation.

Over the years I have been involved at different levels of the process: as a product of an exceptionally fine public system, years ago, in the *Sputnik* era, in Dallas; as a parent of children presently enrolled in public schools, in Princeton; and most recently, as an elected member of a local school board. But it was the school board experience that introduced me to the overwhelming rigidity characteristic of America's public school bureaucracies and persuaded me that this vertical hierarchy is, by its very nature, systemically resistant to change.

Perhaps school boards cannot help trivializing education through their time-consuming process of micromanagement. Agendas overflow with items of administrative inconsequence, from perfunctory approval of bills paid, to waging of turf battles with other municipal bodies, to establishment of bureaucratic policies that, when written up, fill loose-leaf binders four inches thick. As a consequence there is very little time to deal with the more substantive issues of long-term planning, innovation, research and development, school autonomy, teacher accountability, or standards. Local boards are supplanted by county boards, by an association of local boards at the state level, and by the National School Boards Association nationwide. Public education has become a three-dimensional bureaucracy.

Parents avoid school board meetings, except for annual budget debates, in droves, and little wonder: they tend to be conducted with a degree of formality and stiffness not unlike a College of Cardinals. It is no secret, and no wonder, that voter turnout for school board elections averages far less than 10 percent of those registered to vote. This lack of parental involvement, also characterized by low attendance at parent-teacher meetings, is partially driven by economic necessity, when both parents in a two-parent family must work, and partially by irrelevance. Teachers are more loyal to their political bosses than they are responsive to parents, but their underlying allegiance, it seems to me, is still strongly to their students. They are the critical agents of change, and they are America's hope for the twenty-first century.

The new century will be dominated by the information-intensive era now emerging, and business will have needs quite different from those of the electromechanical age. Greater emphasis will be placed on small group interaction and shared data in the workplace; corporations will be structured more horizontally than vertically, a process already well under way; and marketable skills will depend less on what one knows than on how one is able to organize, manipulate, analyze, assess, or interpret that knowledge. American companies confronted directly by the commercial challenge from East Asia are already making their organizations leaner and flatter, more like partnerships.

The hope is that America's public education system will recognize the need to restructure, too, from a vertical, centralized bureaucracy in which administrators and local school board officials exercise control to a more flexible, decentralized system that is controlled, at the autonomous school level, by a strategic partnership among teachers, parents, and students. The threshold of educational change on which America stands today is every bit as important for the next century as the threshold the nation crossed a hundred years ago, when it moved from the traditional one-room schoolhouse to a multigrade, integrated bureaucracy. That bureaucracy is becoming as irrelevant today as the one-room schoolhouse became a century ago.

For if a system that resists reform cannot be restructured, the prospect of strengthening America's industrial competitiveness, by having to use inferior workers against better-prepared competitors in Japan and East Asia, is very discouraging indeed. But as a *result* of structural change, America may stand a better chance both of raising its standards of academic performance *and* of unleashing that collective dynamism and energy that characterize the very essence of its unique and creative entrepreneurialism, which will be much more crucial to America's competitive survival in the twenty-first century.

13
RESTRUCTURING AMERICAN
EDUCATION: REDEFINING CONTROL

In recent years, educational politics has centered on the quality of the public schools. Long-simmering discontent about declining test scores, loose academic standards and lax discipline, fueled by a series of national studies, have provoked a widespread reaction against the 'rising tide of mediocrity.'

Much the same is true within educational research. Studies of school effectiveness have focused directly on the schools, asking about those aspects of organization and immediate environment that explain school performance, such as clear school goals, rigorous academic requirements, an orderly climate, strong instructional leadership, teacher participation in decision making, cooperative principal-teacher relations, active parental involvement, and high expectations.

But it is the institutional system itself, accepted by one and all, that tells us how these desirable features are to be transmitted to the schools: they are to be imposed from above. For many objectives—tougher academic requirements, say—reform simply calls for new legislative or district policy. Not coincidentally, these have been among the more popular reforms. Other objectives are less amenable to formal imposition, but whether the means are formal or professional, the rationale of democratic control is to 'make' schools more effective by imposing desirable traits on them.

These reforms are likely to fail.

John Chubb and Terry Moe,
"Politics, Markets, and the Organization of Schools"

Perhaps no one has been more visibly identified with the issue of restructuring in American education than Albert Shanker, once the militant head of New York City's confrontational United Federation of Teachers, now the statesmanlike president of its national parent, the

280

American Federation of Teachers (AFT). Born in New York of immigrant parents and educated at Columbia University, Shanker taught for many years in the city's schools before becoming head of the AFT's New York affiliate in 1964, just as the issues of teacher organization and compensation were coming to a head.

The next several years were a period of turmoil in American public education. Teachers went on strike and formed picket lines as the bureaucratic system proved resistant to substantive change. My wife, who at that time was teaching high school in Granite City, Illinois, an AFT target, remembers those years well, and they were not pleasant ones. In 1968, as a graduate student in Tokyo, I recall reading the *New York Times* accounts of Shanker's adversarial tactics and remarking to a friend who had lived in New York just prior to coming to Japan, "Well, I guess we're seeing democracy at work." "No," she said rather sternly. "Not democracy. Chaos."

Twenty years later Shanker has moved from militancy to thoughtful advocacy. He has tried to position the AFT, which represents some 680,000 of America's 2.5 million teachers, predominantly those in urban schools, as innovative and supportive of change. He speaks frequently and eloquently on the issue of restructuring and writes an insightful weekly column called "Where We Stand" in which he shares with the public his thoughts on innovation and change.

When I met with Shanker in early 1988 at the AFT's new headquarters building overlooking the Capitol, I asked him about the second phase of educational reform and why the system remained impervious to change. A tall man in his early sixties, with soft gray hair and rimless glasses, he is imposing but friendly. His office is unadorned, with a pair of contemporary chairs facing a loaded desk.

"The structure of American schools is essentially custodial," he said, the familiar baritone voice carrying only a soft trace of his New York accent. "Structure does not resist change as much as it is a comfort factor. Most people are comfortable with how school was structured for them, and many parents are uncomfortable with experimentation. Traditionally, we've used the silver bullet approach to reforming education. One silver bullet: pay the teachers more. Another silver bullet: lengthen the school year. Or require more homework, raise graduation requirements, whatever. But we've successfully educated only about 20, maybe 25, percent of our young people over time, and that 25 percent is the group that is naturally motivated—they come from higher socio-economic levels, there is strong parental involvement in their early education, they have a rich home environment, they are all exposed to a good preschool experience, and so on. But we can't be looking for more silver bullets. We need to be looking at what we can do for the *other* 75 percent now, because we want to get them closer to where that desire burns inside so they can't *wait* to get to the next book."

He stooped down, snapped one briefcase shut, and opened another. "Now, how do we get from here to there?" he asked. "That's the real issue. One thing I'm proposing is that teachers be allowed to set up autonomous units within their schools so that we have an alternative, flexible structure running parallel to the existing bureaucratic one. The units would encourage the process of learning in small groups within each class; teachers would function as teams with differentiated status—head teachers, assistant teachers, and so on. The teams would utilize different ways of learning and at different rates; they would be integrative, both in terms of subject material and ways of thinking, the logical and the creative. They would maximize the use of technology as teaching and learning tools in the classroom. They would maximize exposure to out-of-school experience, to apply the learning in the real world, and they would reward performance by recognizing achievement in different ways. But the focus, in my view, needs to be on developing a team spirit, through team teaching and team learning."

I asked him if he thought teachers and, more importantly, parents, would support the kind of innovation he was recommending.

"I think the public is certainly aware of the need," he said. "But parents are used to the traditional school structure and may be uncomfortable with experimentation. So we need to set up the mechanism in parallel and experiment—see what works and what doesn't. That will take time, because teaching materials have to be reworked. Take time zones, for example. Normally a fourth grade teacher unrolls a projection map of the world and shows the kids the time zones. 'When it's two o'clock in New York, it's eleven o'clock in California'; that sort of thing. The kids memorize the twenty-four time zones and spit them back on a test. Now, what if that material were organized differently? What if, instead of just doing the rote learning, the kids integrated the data as teams and were encouraged to ask questions? When were time zones invented? Why do we need them? What if there were only two time zones in the world? One? Four? How would our lives be different? The demands of the future, in an information-intensive world, necessitate a much different approach to learning. We need to integrate all that much better."

In a recent article called "The Making of a Profession," Shanker had written about management structure in schools. "Putting teachers in charge of instructional decisions will lead to experimentation with new kinds of management in schools," he wrote. "Different models will emerge, but they will all be marked by a movement away from authoritarian, hierarchical structures. If there is one principle on which all the studies of effective schools—and effective businesses—agree, it is that top-down management does not work. Neither does top-down reform. Reform can only come from the mind and hands of a creative and sensitive teacher."

I asked Shanker about the traditional vertical structure of America's educational bureaucracy, and my question evoked an anecdotal response.

"If we ran our businesses the way we run our schools," he said, "we'd be bankrupt in forty-eight hours. Think about it for a minute. When we hire our education managers—our teachers—we tell them, 'We want you to spend forty-five minutes at this desk with this group of people, and then we'll ring a bell, and we want you to go to another room with another desk to work with another group of people for forty-five minutes, and we want you to do this six or seven times a day. In addition, we won't give you a telephone or an assistant or a secretary to help you, so you'll have to do it all yourself, and we can't pay you a competitive wage, but we expect your performance to meet the highest standards.' Is that how American business attracts the best and the brightest? Is that how *any* professional group attracts the best and the brightest?"

He ran a hand through his hair.

"Would we tolerate the same approach in medicine or science that we tolerate in our schools?" he went on. "But if our schools were *structured* differently, you'd have a qualitatively different approach. There are three levels. One, systematic and progressive inquiry. Two, continuous and rigorous experimentation. Three, admit the failures and build on the successes. Our current attitude says all educational experience is doomed to succeed, because we don't differentiate. If schools were organized to deal experimentally with their problems, like scientists try to deal with cancer or with the common cold, they would be qualitatively different. Try *A*, and see what happens against a control group. Better? Worse? No change? Then try *B,* run it in parallel with *A,* compare the differences. Keep detailed records. Encourage data sharing among experimenters. See what works and build on the successes. But the experimentation can't realistically proceed, in my view, *until and unless we deal with the issue of structure,* of working more in teams, as I indicated earlier. So don't worry about the silver bullets. Worry about restructuring."

A good example of what Shanker was talking about was occurring in Cologne, in West Germany, at the Holweide Comprehensive School, which started as an experiment in 1975 with grades five through twelve. It has more than 2,000 students and considerable diversity among them, not unlike American schools. Students at Holweide are assigned, in large groups of mixed abilities numbering about 120, to a team of six or eight teachers. The teaching team then makes the important decisions: How will the students be grouped? Which teachers will be assigned to which students? Which teachers will teach German, math, science, history? How many subjects should the students be taught at any given time? Students are then formed into smaller subgroups or teams of five or six, peer teaching is emphasized, and there is a minimum of lecturing, a maximum of active participation. The team of teachers remains with the same students for a full six years. They have turned the usual bureaucratic German school into an innovative, experimental one. Today, fifteen years after the experiment began, only 1 percent of its students drop out, compared to a national average of 14 percent, and 60 percent of Holweide's students do well enough on their exit exams to enter a German university, compared to 27 percent nationally.

I suggested to Shanker that, based on the Asian experience, parental involvement is key and asked whether he thought school boards are becoming irrelevant.

"I agree wholeheartedly that parental involvement is crucial to student performance," he said, "but it can't be done with the current structure. Besides, with an increase in the number of working parents and single-parent families, not to mention a majority of mothers now in the work force, available time becomes the critical factor. And I would say that while school boards aren't exactly irrelevant, they could be better organized. Instead of meeting once a week or twice a month, the way they do now, they ought to meet once or twice a year, say, for a week, in more of an oversight function, to review performance and help set goals. As it is, boards get too involved in day-to-day administration, which again is due to structure."

Were examples of innovative restructuring taking place in American schools?

"Look at Miami," he said. "Or Rochester. And Hammond, Indiana. They're all experimenting now, doing things differently, organizing around more flexible structures. Where there is strong teacher leadership, they have the confidence to change. Where there isn't, the boards won't let the teachers experiment. But my sense is the American public isn't going to tolerate many more failures. Our public schools have about a decade, maybe less, in which to show what they can do, how they can change and improve. Otherwise the pressure for vouchers and tuition tax credits will be unavoidable."

I looked into some of the examples Shanker had mentioned, where the seeds of restructuring were being sown. In Miami an experiment in shared decision making was intended to minimize the bureaucracy and create a new managerial model called *school-based management*. It began when the Dade County public school system, America's fourth-largest, with 260 schools and 255,000 students, recently turned over thirty-two schools to teams of teachers and parents who will be accountable for performance and decision making over a three-year term, with results to be published in late 1990.

Teachers are being trained so that their performance is evaluated by peers, who work in the classroom, rather than by principals, who do not. The position of assistant principal has been eliminated at four schools, and the money saved is being allocated by the management teams to pay for additional classroom materials, teaching supplies, and aides. Teams at other schools decide on curriculum revision, teaching schedules, budgets, and hiring. The single most important benefit, participants say, is that teachers now have *control* over what they are doing, and morale, after only a short time, has increased dramatically.

In Illinois the state legislature recently passed a bill intending to restructure Chicago's public schools, widely acknowledged as an example of "educational meltdown," putting the power to run the schools in the hands of parents. The eleven-member central board of education has been dissolved and replaced by fifteen people screened by a citizens' and parents' committee. Nearly 600 local school councils, each consisting of a principal, six parents, two neighborhood residents, and two teachers, will hire principals and set each school's budget. Principals will lose lifetime tenure and be rehired under three-year contracts. Teachers are enthusiastic, because they now have a greater say in how the schools are run.

In Rochester, New York, teachers are restructuring pay scales and performance criteria, eliminating seniority as the sole criterion of salary increases, implementing career ladders and a bonus system, creating new concepts such as a master teacher and a head teacher, who will be highly compensated, and implementing teams of teachers within the schools.

In Syracuse, New York, parents now have an all-choice school system, and teachers run the schools. In Indianapolis eight teachers persuaded the district administration to let them run their own elementary school, under a team-teaching concept based partly on theories of Howard Gardner, a Harvard psychologist, who is serving as an adviser to the team. The school is now a public magnet school.

In Minnesota a new law permits parents anywhere in the state to choose the school they want their children to attend, eliminating district residence requirements and forcing schools to compete. State aid of $3,600 accompanies each student to his or her new school, and the forsaken school loses the money. In Montgomery County, Maryland, local officials plan to implement an experimental school-based management program, not unlike Miami's. Cambridge, Massachusetts, is experimenting successfully with public magnet schools, which permit parental choice, and now nearly 10 percent of all students attend schools of choice. Brookline, a suburb of Boston, has put a "professional practice school" into place. And the state of New Jersey, under the leadership of Governor Tom Kean, has initiated public hearings to study the issue of parental choice.

As a monopoly, America's public schools have no incentive to change. The only alternative parents can exercise is private or parochial schooling, a choice normally available only at higher socioeconomic levels. But if parents and teachers are somehow able to generate conditions *conducive* to competition, they can isolate the losers and force change. Choice fosters competition, and these pockets of experimentation should improve teaching and learning as well as make the schools more competitive. Magnet schools, parental choice, and school-based management are all seeds of change in the formative process of restructuring American public education.

"Significant improvement will result only if we are clear about education's bottom line," Checker Finn wrote in a *Harvard Business Review* article called "Make the Schools Compete" not long ago. "Since the outputs of the education system bear no discernible relation to the financial inputs, the outputs could be far higher. The educational delivery system is virtually immune to large productivity gains. Without radical changes in governance arrangements and incentive structures, a pathological situation will persist."

Finn has argued that the incentives and discipline of the marketplace are necessary to bring about both greater competitiveness in education and the desired restructuring required to achieve it. Research on effective schools, whether public or private, rich or poor, he says, has confirmed a consistent pattern: they have a clear sense of purpose, high expectations for students, a coherent curriculum, adroit leadership, meticulous focusing of class time and other resources on priorities, an orderly (but not somber) environment, a full measure of parental involvement, and a keen sense of team spirit among staff.

He has proposed a list of ten guidelines for restructuring: (1) Focus public regulation on ends, not means, by prescribing standards but not how they are to be achieved. (2) Install a feedback and accountability system so parents and taxpayers can better track performance. (3) Let the schools manage themselves, the way school-based management systems, led by faculty teams, are capable of doing. (4) Promote more imaginative school leadership by opening the field to individuals with proven executive experience. (5) Open the teaching profession to more and varied people to broaden the talent pool. (6) Reward good performance and punish bad by establishing career ladders, incentive bonus systems, and penalties for failure. (7) Make better use of technology in the classroom. (8) Vary the school schedule and calendar to create more options and build in flexibility. (9) Bring the results of research into the classroom quicker and more effectively. (10) Engage parents better to make them more involved partners in the process.

"If research teaches us anything," Finn said when we met in early 1988 in Washington, "it is that schools need to function as a team, not like a post office bureaucracy run by the civil service, where everybody opens at the same time, closes at the same time, and delivers the mail equally slowly. What you teach, how you teach, and in what sequence you teach it should be school-determined, not imposed from above like a military command. Teachers are the ones who know best how they ought to organize themselves, and if we're serious about treating them as professionals, we have to let them do it."

I asked him about local school boards.

He said, "School boards as we know them are gradually becoming extinct. They're dinosaurs, and local school district bureaucracies—with all those middle-layer administrators—are becoming obsolete, too. What we ought to be looking at are advisory or community boards for individual schools that involve parents working with teachers. Japan has a highly centralized educational system, but at the individual school level parents are incredibly involved. The level of personal contact between home and school, in the way they exchange notebooks and personal visits, is impressive."

Checker Finn is also very knowledgeable about teacher politics and how the NEA and the AFT operate. It is no accident that Shanker's AFT is more progressive than the NEA.

"The NEA," Finn wrote in a *Commentary* article called "Teacher Politics," "consistently takes positions which discredit the evidence of qualitative deterioration in education and the means of acquiring such evidence; savage the critics of school quality; mount elaborate campaigns to persuade the public that American education is basically fine, and that any minor problems would be solved by the application of more money; steadfastly refuse to let teachers be rewarded (or penalized) on the basis of performance; and skillfully employ the rhetoric of educational quality and excellence in advocating policies that would achieve nothing of the sort."

What really distinguishes the two professional associations, Finn suggested, is that the AFT has come to be identified with innovation, whereas the NEA is preoccupied primarily with political goals. As a result, the NEA has dressed itself in the vestments of a special interest group and advocates strong positions on racial integration, bilingual education, national defense, nuclear arms reduction, and foreign policy—issues that have very little to do with education.

The NEA has also opposed testing in the schools, saying test results are used to differentiate rather than to measure performance. The AFT, on the other hand, strongly supports testing, and in response to the NEA's opposition Shanker replied, "We believe tests tell us things that are important for students, parents, teachers, colleges, government, and the society at large to know. We also believe the public unquestionably has a right to know what we are doing in the schools—how well or how badly."

When the first phase of educational reforms was evaluated by teachers nationally, the NEA took the negative position that schools had made little progress and blamed Washington—a political charge—for decreasing budgets but said nothing about its own resistance to change, such as opposing merit pay incentives for teachers. The AFT, however, emphasized the positive by pointing out how educational reforms to date have had no impact on teacher autonomy—only 21 percent of the nation's teachers said they had more freedom from nonteaching duties—and used the evaluation to show how restructuring could bring teachers out from under the pyramid.

The long-term strength of American public education, Finn concluded, depends on its success in imparting skills, knowledge, and fundamental values to children without allowing politics to intrude on the classroom. The AFT's value structure has emerged remarkably strong and resilient after a period in which so many of our major social and cultural institutions—and the elected officials who respond to them—have allowed their own values to soften and bend.

Gary Watts is the only person worth talking to at the NEA, friends in Washington told me, and when I met him in mid-1988, I found out why. The NEA's deputy executive director has an abundance of facts at his fingertips and is atypically nonbureaucratic. He is a tall man with thinning hair and an easy smile.

"Restructuring starts with the teachers," he agreed, "and moves from a vertical structure to a more horizontal plane. There are two major forces in America today driving structural reform in education. One is changing demographics. A majority of our public school kids will soon be predominantly black and Hispanic, disadvantaged, at risk, the underclass—the very students we have traditionally been unable to educate. The second is the process of globalization and international competition. In the past we wanted hubcap fitters and cog workers, people who would do what they were told and follow orders; today we need flexible workers, analysts, people who know how to manipulate facts and information, not just remember it. I think we will continue to grow poorer as a nation if our public education remains based on the traditional assembly line method of the past. Most people simply don't realize that basic classroom education hasn't changed in a hundred years."

And if the public schools can't restructure and produce results?

"Then we'll have to go the route of vouchers and tuition tax credits," he said. "We would have no other choice. And if we do, then our private and parochial schools will become princely, and our public schools will be the paupers. The threat of destroying our public school system is very real, and there are a lot of people out there who would not be disappointed to see it happen."

I asked him about the perceived differences between the AFT and the NEA, and he flashed a smile.

"Al Shanker's organization is lean and light, like a racehorse," he said, ducking the issue of politics. "It can move quickly in any direction. The NEA is like a team of Clydesdales by comparison. It takes a long time to get them organized, lined up, and hooked to the wagon, but when they get moving, boy, can they haul cargo."

The question, of course, is whether the NEA can get moving to support the key issues of school restructuring and choice. My experience with local affiliates of both unions has been that, while teachers as individuals may be enthusiastic about the prospect of greater autonomy, team teaching, and experimentation, collectively they are still more interested in the issues of the past—compensation, fringe benefits, and collective bargaining.

John Chubb, a researcher at the Brookings Institution in Washington, and Terry Moe, a political scientist at Stanford, have addressed the issue of school competitiveness in an *American Political Science Review* article entitled "Politics, Money, and the Organization of Schools."

"How can we study institutional effects if there is only one, all-encompassing institution?" they asked. "An instructive way to proceed, we believe, is to compare public schools to those that fall outside the hierarchy of democratic control: private schools. Private schools provide services in exchange for payment, and they must please their consumers—parents and students—if they are to prosper. In the private sector, educational choice is founded on what is called the exit option. The exit option not only promotes harmony and responsiveness, it also promotes school autonomy."

Chubb and Moe acknowledged a major disincentive to choosing private education, which is that public schools, being local monopolies, are free, while private schools are not. In the public sector exit is an obstacle to control.

"The drive to restrict autonomy is built into the incentive structures of politicians and bureaucrats," they concluded. "Politicians seek political support by responding to various constituency groups, particularly those that are well organized and active. These include teachers' unions and associations of administrators, but also a vast array of groups representing specialized interests—minorities, the handicapped, bilingual education, schools of education, and book publishers, among others. Bureaucrats play both sides of the governmental fence. Their power rests on the fact that bureaucracy is essential to direct democratic control. Control requires rules and regulations, monitoring, and other means of ensuring that those engaged in the educational process behave as they are supposed to behave. It requires a bureaucracy and bureaucrats who are a powerful special interest—an interest dedicated to hierarchical control. The system, in short, is inherently destructive of autonomy."

Private schools, Chubb and Moe found, tend to behave more like partnerships. Their teachers have better working relationships with principals, they are more involved in decision making, interact more productively with colleagues, and feel more positively about their jobs. It is no secret that private schools are rarely unionized, while public schools almost always are, despite the fact that private school teachers are paid, on average, *less* than their public school counterparts. Private school teachers trade economic compensation and formal job security for superior working conditions, professional autonomy, and personal fulfillment. Public school teachers do exactly the opposite.

This led the authors to conclude, correctly, I think, that the key to improving America's schools is not top-down reform, but *institutional* change, which implies restructuring, autonomy, and choice. This is very threatening to established interests—local school board officials, district bureaucrats, and school administrators—which is why it is proceeding slowly. But restructuring, Chubb and Moe agree, may be the only reform that ultimately makes all the other reforms possible, which forced them to conclude pessimistically that the other reforms may just not be possible.

When I saw Terry Moe at Stanford in the early spring of 1988, his conclusions had yet to appear publicly in book form. I felt that when they did, they would have the effect of telling the emperor he had no clothes. Moe is young and articulate, with a short, brush moustache and pool-clear eyes.

"Parents and students know what's best," he said as we sat in his office overlooking the campus, "because they're the closest to what's going on. Accountability and choice put more responsibility on the teachers and the principal, who know what works best educationally. We simply have to ask ourselves, what is it we want our schools to do? If parents and students are satisfied with current performance, then the schools are okay. But liberals *impose* goals and standards on the system, and the states, whether through school boards or commissioners of education, also implement a top-down approach—both from a very strict standpoint of political control. What's needed, I think, is a power shift from boards and superintendents to teachers and parents."

I asked him why he thought the system resists change when the idea of restructuring seems such a sensible one.

"Schools and school districts are not motivated by good ideas," he said, "but by political power. They're controlled from the inside, and insiders are interested in power, not in ideas. Restructuring dilutes that power; it doesn't enhance it. We all *know* what the characteristics of effective schools are. The teachers are autonomous, the principals lead, parents are more involved, standards are more rigorous, there is more homework, school goals are clear, and there are high expectations for student performance. But if a child is in a public school that's *not* effective, the parents generally have no choice. That's why exit options are good—they promote competitiveness. But you can't have them without autonomy, and you can't have autonomy without institutional reform."

Charles Murray, a social scientist at the Manhattan Institute for Policy Research, reached a similar conclusion and published his thoughts in an imaginative and stimulating book called *In Pursuit of Happiness and Good Government*, which addressed a host of public policy issues, including education.

If human beings *really are* making their own decisions, he wrote, and if they *really are* reliant on their own resources, their behavior will be guided importantly by that reality. The specific driving force is the relationship of parents to their children. Parents naturally want good things for their children. In a society where education means the opportunity to get ahead, one of those good things is education. Therefore, what parents in a free society want most intensely for their children is a good education.

"Give parents control over the education of their children," Murray concluded, "and you will unleash enormous energy and imagination, all tending toward the excellent end of educated children. The more natural the dynamics that produce good results, the more robust they will be under difficult circumstances. All that is really needed to accomplish this is that parents, teachers, and schools have freedom of choice. Three generic solutions accommodate this indispensable condition: One is to decentralize the public school system so that each school operates autonomously. Another is a voucher system that gives each parent a chit worth an amount sufficient to pay for an adequate education. And the third is a tuition tax-credit system that maintains a public system but permits parents to deduct part of the cost of private tuition from their taxes. [But] these solutions have little to do with political realities."

The federal government knows what the characteristics of effective schools are. The education department publishes, at regular intervals, a collection of its own research findings called *What Works*. If Washington did nothing else, its role as the primary research and development arm of American education would be enough.

Competitive firms in the private sector typically spend, on average, 6 to 8 percent of revenues on R&D each year. The federal government spends about $30 billion a year on education, in current dollars, which is either 3 percent of total federal spending of about $1 trillion or less than 1 percent of GNP, but only a fraction of that involves research. Total spending on education in America, including federal, state, and local funding, averages about 5 percent of GNP, though almost all of this too is for current operating budgets and little, if any, goes for research.

Political considerations aside, the argument needs to be made that more research funding is critical to the eventual success of efforts at restructuring, particularly if more experimentation is to be done and greater freedom of choice encouraged, as many believe should occur. To the extent that institutional reform can be achieved, it could potentially free up billions of dollars now spent on maintaining the bureaucratic structure that could otherwise be applied directly to classroom teaching, without raising taxes to generate the necessary funds.

Some of this additional money would need to be spent on technology, most experts agree. While many public school districts have purchased elaborate record-keeping software and new systems for administrative purposes, which benefit bureaucrats and administrators, very little technology has gone into the classroom. The result is that teachers still do many of the things computers can do better, like administering and grading achievement tests or teaching rote drills for fundamental mastery.

"Education systems of the next century will be drastically different from those of today," Lewis Perelman wrote in *Technology and Transformation of Schools*, an extensive 1988 study that tied educational productivity to economic competitiveness. "Whether Americans will lead the world in this educational transformation, or play catch-up with more enterprising cultures, will do much to determine whether the United States will continue its international leadership role in the ever more competitive world of the 21st century."

Perelman is a Harvard-trained specialist in strategic planning. He too argues that public education must become more productive but that school productivity cannot be enhanced unless the American public eliminates the bureaucratic barriers to innovation through a process of deregulation, decentralization, and decontrol—in a word, restructuring. He contends that the essential characteristics of market-based systems that the technology of public education needs to embrace are choice and competition.

"There are some valuable lessons school management can, and should, learn from corporate management," Perelman concluded. "Education officials should be studying the processes through which U.S. companies are working to transform their organizations and managements to meet the challenges of technological innovation and global competition."

There are numerous examples of American corporate reorganization in basic industries, like automobiles and steel, that have been exposed visibly to international competition during the past two decades. They too tend to suggest a trend toward more horizontal management structures, away from the top-down, armylike bureaucratic systems of the past.

In one case, in the late 1970s, the Ford Motor Company was about to scrap its Flat Rock, Michigan, auto assembly plant, one of its least productive facilities, when the corporation's senior management, taking a positive cue from the Japanese competition, decided to put the issue straight to the production workers—all members of the UAW—and let *them* decide whether, and how, the plant could be improved. The workers determined that their flagging productivity was tied to onerous work rules decided levels above them in endless negotiations between management and labor, that their low morale was a function of their inability to have any control over what they did or to change it, and that their hostile attitudes toward management were more a result of organizational structure than of conventional factors such as work hours or pay. They decided they could eliminate the cumbersome work rules if they could somehow be given more control over how their own jobs should be defined and how their work was to be carried out. So Ford let them do it, and the Flat Rock plant became one of its most productive facilities.

In another case an Alcoa plant in Arkansas had been characterized by adversarial management-labor relations for over forty years when workers of the United Steelworkers Union, which staffed the plant, redefined jobs and redesigned work methods. Autonomous work teams replaced individual assignments in every department on the production floor and practically eliminated the need for vertical shop floor management. Instead of eighteen job classifications, they wound up with no more than three. The teams designed their own jobs based on what they knew would work, and craftsmen moved to multicraft assignments. But it was the *workers* who decided how the groupings would be made and what the new jobs would be, not people several layers above them. The results were predictable. Morale went up exponentially and downtime was reduced, by half in the first three months, then by half again three months later. Workers were helping each other and discovering the hidden benefits of teamwork instead of relying on the old compartmentalized individual system.

"Schools today ought to look like the smartest high-tech companies," David Kearns, chairman of Xerox Corporation, recently wrote in a monograph called "Education Recovery." "Today's smart companies push decision-making down into the organization. Professionals and managers are trusted with the authority to get their jobs done—and they're held accountable for performing. Today, our public education system is a failed monopoly bureaucratic, rigid, and in unsteady control of dissatisfied captive markets. Competition for students and dollars would break that monopoly and invigorate the schools. States would fund students, not schools, and students could attend any public school they wanted to. For the first time, schools would have to compete."

American business is gradually learning that the American worker is not the problem. *Structure* is the problem. When customers abandon American products, they bring the only kind of pressure on management that matters. And since public education lags behind the business world, the system is only now beginning to realize that American teachers are not the problem but the solution. However, the system's customers, the parents, have to bring pressure on management—local school boards, district bureaucracies, and school administrators—to allow restructuring to occur. And that can be achieved only if the market forces of competition and choice are unleashed.

Focus on teamwork and small group interaction is also increasing in isolated pockets around the country. The Developmental Studies Center, a nonprofit, nonpartisan corporation founded in 1981 and headquartered in San Ramon, California, is attempting to develop school-based programs designed to help teachers and parents nurture in children qualities such as helpfulness, fairness, and cooperation. Within the existing structure of elementary classrooms in many California schools, the center's Child Development Project attempts to innovate small cooperative group activities, peer tutoring functions, student participation in home and classroom chores, and, through carefully selected literature and films, curriculum materials that stress children helping and taking collective responsibility—all designed to enable children to see themselves as part of a broader community.

William Streshly, superintendent of the San Ramon Valley unified school district, which has 15,000 students and ranks academically in the top 10 percent, has implemented the Child Development Project.

"Since the traditional structure of the family has become fragmented, and the influence of our religious institutions has declined," Streshly said in a 1987 speech, "schools have a major impact on ethical and moral development, whether they intend to or not. Six of our thirteen elementary schools were chosen five years ago to participate in this project, based on the strong interest of their principals, teachers, and parents. Each year as this cohort of children has progressed through the grades, they and their teachers have been regularly observed and interviewed, individually and in small groups. Students in the program have been observed to be significantly more friendly, supportive, helpful, and spontaneously pro-social in their behavior. They have also become significantly more skilled in dealing with conflict resolution and interpersonal problem solving."

Teachers, parents, and students. The strategic partnership, or the "vital triangle," as Michael Lee called it in Taipei. Some time ago, as chairman of the executive board of the Cherry Hill Nursery School, where my two children were enrolled, I participated in an active, flourishing strategic partnership.

Cherry Hill is, by charter, a cooperative preschool. Its parents voluntarily serve on the board, hire and evaluate teachers, prepare and implement a budget, organize fund-raising activities, and clean, maintain, and repair the school's six classrooms and its playground equipment. But they are required, under the school's bylaws, to participate in the classroom on a rotating basis as helping parents, by assisting the teachers with their curricular activities, monitoring behavior on the playground, and providing a healthful snack. In about half the school's families both parents work.

Over time this required participation creates in parents a deep sense of commitment to and involvement in the education of their children. Initially, the first year, with the two-year-olds, who meet twice a week, rotating participation is less frequent; but the following year the classes meet three times a week, and finally, for the multiage and four-year-old classes, daily. Importantly, the process begins early. Uncomfortably for some, it is required. But it builds a habit that becomes almost unconscious, it reinforces parent-child interaction at home, and it lays the groundwork for future involvement in the critical elementary and secondary years.

Cooperative preschools, because of their very nature, achieve both the degree and the kind of parental involvement that is associated with the best Japanese and East Asian early education programs. Cherry Hill, without formally emulating the Japanese concepts of class leadership or small groups, seats the children at worktables in groups of five, where they work on collaborative as well as individual projects. Every day a different child (generally, the child of the helping parent) is the "locomotive" for the class "train" and leads the class in singing, in moving from activity to activity, in bringing the children in from the playground and taking them out again. The teachers, while maintaining a close supervisory and pedagogical role, do not always intervene when there are problems between peers, but often let them attempt to sort out difficulties on their own first.

There is no reason why many of these cooperative features cannot be replicated in public schools, using parents as volunteers in the classroom, utilizing their skills as teachers' aides, and nurturing the process of parental involvement. With a more flexible structure, PTAs could play more valuable roles instead of the usual social functions—they too have the potential to become working partnerships.

Structural reform is a tall order for public education, but a necessary one. What teachers in our public schools are beginning to sense, it seems to me, is that they can have enormous power if they just organize themselves more effectively to wield it, just as American workers on the factory floor have recently found, *provided* management has the vision to allow them more flexibility. We know that, as financial inputs into the system have risen, measurable outputs—test scores, graduation rates, American performance on competitive international examinations—have all declined. Taken alone, cost is not the problem, and simply throwing more money at the current structure is not the solution. Criticizing teachers as the problem means missing the point; America's teachers are not the problem, just as America's workers are not the problem. *Structure* is the problem, and once the consumers of education begin to realize this, more pressure can be brought on boards and district administrations and school staffs to change. Miami and Rochester and Indiana and Illinois, in their own ways, are all visions of the future.

Pedagogically, too, Japan and East Asia emphasize small group dynamics in their educational systems not only because they believe in their inherent benefits as part of the educational process, but also because group interaction is a fundamental aspect of social organization and development, as natural to those cultures as rice and chopsticks. Similarly, American schools do not focus on the individual solely because of any inherent pedagogical benefits, but because American society stresses the uniqueness of each individual in it, a social characteristic as fundamental to the United States as the group is to Japan. So implementing more small group interaction will be no easy accomplishment for Americans—all the more reason to begin with early education in kindergarten at the latest, but preferably in preschool.

David Pearce Snyder is a professional forecaster and editor of *The Futurist* magazine. He studies social adaption to change and specializes in what he calls "techno-economic innovation."

"Education is the number one industry of the future in terms of teaching youngsters and retraining teachers and older workers," he was saying to me over lunch in early 1989, "which will entail enormous social disruption. So the only way to survive a revolution is to plan for it. This will require diligence, discipline, and effort—strengths more prevalent in Asia today than in America. Most of the educational reform movements so far have had zero impact on performance, because control has not really been affected. The key factors in learning are the intensity of the learning experience and involvement with the outside environment, which are not dependent on cost. Another key factor, we know, is parental involvement, but demographics will argue that is a declining possibility for Americans, so our performance may continue to dwindle and lag. And because great things do not happen overnight, there could be loss of heart and possibly loss of will."

Snyder views himself as a realist, not a pessimist, so I asked him what demographics were telling him about the future.

"In 1970," he said, "40 percent of all married couples worked. By 1987, 55 percent were working. By the mid-1990s between two-thirds and three-fourths of all married couples will require two full-time incomes just to maintain middle-class lifestyles. Today a majority of American mothers are working outside the home, either full- or part-time. By the early 1990s two-thirds of them will be, and half of all American households will have at least one child at home under the age of eighteen with no parental care or supervision. We have ten years of relative decline ahead of us, so we have the reverse of the emperor's new clothes. Today the emperor refuses to tell the people *they* have no clothes."

A century ago, when American public education embraced the changes that led to greater bureaucratization of the system and a factory-like atmosphere in the school, education was geared toward satisfying the needs of industry in an electromechanical age. Countries rich in natural resources, like the United States, benefited because the industrial system required those resources for the manufacturing process. Human resources were secondary. Countries not so well endowed, like Japan, were put at a competitive disadvantage.

But today the world sits on the threshold of a new era, an information-intensive age for which human resources are primary and in which a more cooperative workplace will be the norm. Natural resources are no longer as relevant. Countries rich in human resources, like Japan and Korea and Singapore, will find themselves positioned advantageously for the new age, while countries rich in natural resources but with underdeveloped human systems will now be at a competitive disadvantage. The new industrial era will put a premium on cooperation, collaboration, and the dynamics of small group interaction—precisely those characteristics that are so strong in East Asian schools.

Throughout history, there has never been a major technological transition during which the dominant nation prior to that transition remained preeminent afterward. Somehow the past successes of dominant enterprises fatally reduce their propensity to innovate. Research into human decision making also demonstrates that, rather than incurring the costs and uncertainties of taking innovative action, most people will pursue habitual patterns of behavior, especially if such behavior has been successful in the past.

If America cannot restructure its public schools, the time for vouchers (federal certificates issued to parents and valid at either public or private schools) and tuition tax credits (which provide relief for double taxation imposed on those who pay private tuition in addition to local school taxes) will almost certainly have arrived. Change would be better initiated from the bottom up, autonomously, than imposed from the top down. But either way, it must come, and when it does, it can mean a bright new future for American education.

While the process of restructuring cannot be achieved without the leadership of teachers, it also cannot be achieved without the involvement of parents, which raises worrisome questions about the deterioration of the American family, given the high divorce rate, the expanding number of single-parent families, and the nation's growing underclass.

When I met recently with Hisashi Kobayashi, dean of Princeton University's engineering school, we talked at length about manufacturing skills, human resources, and education. Dr. Kobayashi is a graduate of Tokyo University, received his PhD in electrical engineering from Princeton, and spent twenty-five years working for IBM and its Japanese affiliate.

I told him I was writing a section on the family and social stability.

"The family," he said, nodding. "That's key."

PART IV
THE FAMILY AS SOCIETY'S FORTRESS

14
SOCIAL STABILITY IN EAST ASIA:
WITHSTANDING THE WINDS OF
CHANGE

"What did one look like before one's mother and father were born?" This Zen question is daunting, but since human existence is ultimately dependent on the parents, it is not possible to eliminate the father and mother, however much one may achieve enlightenment. A Zen priest once said that satori *could be summed up in the words* filial piety. *Suzuki points out that the ways of thinking of the Westerner stem from the father, while the mother lies at the basis of Oriental nature. The mother enfolds everything in unconditional love. There is no question of right or wrong. Everything is accepted without questioning. Love in the East is all-embracing. It is open to all sides. One can enter from any direction.*

Takeo Doi, *The Anatomy of Dependence*

In the minds of Westerners, Confucius is identified predominantly with scholarship, and many of his anecdotes lend credence to that model. In the *Analects,* he wrote that there were two principal elements of benevolent rule: that the people be made well off and that they be educated. The former was in any case necessary for the efficiency of the latter.

When Confucius passed through Wei with Yen Yu, the story goes, he was struck by the populousness of the state.

"Since the people are so numerous," his disciple said, "what more should be done for them?"

"Enrich them," was Confucius's reply.

"And when they be enriched," Yen Yu asked, "what shall be done for them?"

"Teach them," the Master replied.

But Confucius's overwhelming concern was with human relationships, not education. Everything in life stemmed from the Five Basic

303

Relationships: father and son, which built trust; sovereign and subject, which stressed loyalty; husband and wife, which implied distinction; older and younger, which observed precedence; and friends, which encouraged fidelity.

Three of these primary relationships involve the family, which is the core of Confucian life and ethics; the other two use the family as a paradigm. Filial piety is the most important Confucian virtue, because all other relationships in life flow from it. Confucian relationships can be viewed best as a series of concentric circles, with the family at the center and the circles expanding outward to the local community, the village, the prefecture, the nation, and finally the world. These relationships are organic and interrelated, not linear as is more common in the West, where the individual is the focus of attention and personal relationships flow outward from the self, like the spokes of a wheel.

Confucius's concept of the Five Basic Relationships also emphasized a distinct hierarchy; the only horizontal relationship among the five is that between friends, and even there seniority is given precedence. Confucius was emphatic in saying that the relationship between husband and wife most closely resembled that of ruler and subject. The Master put great emphasis on duty, or *obligation,* as an outgrowth of the loyalty one naturally felt from filial piety; social values thus stressed obligation to the group and one's natural place in it, rather than individual rights and behavior.

Confucius lived in the sixth century B.C. He was a contemporary of Buddha and Lao-tzu, whose philosophies also flourished at the time. His legacy is contained in three books, but the *Analects* contain his more pithy and famous sayings. He was a philosophical mentor to Mencius, who lived several centuries later, a contemporary of Plato and Aristotle. Mencius upheld Confucius's hierarchical view of human relationships but said the ensuing responsibilities were not just top-down but mutual and reciprocal. Thus, while a subject owes loyalty to his ruler, and a child affection to his parents, the sovereign is expected to care for his subjects and the parents for their children. Mencius also stressed the family as a paradigm for social behavior. Society is, by extension, one big family: within the four seas, he said, all men are brothers.

Catholic missionaries never had much success converting the family-based Chinese to the individualistic beliefs of Christianity. In the sixteenth century Matteo Ricci, one of the first Jesuits to evangelize the

Central Kingdom, threw himself into the study of Confucianism in an attempt to penetrate the Chinese mind. He thought he had stumbled onto a number of references to a "supreme being" in the Master's texts (T'ien, for Heaven, and Shen, for Spirit), but the Chinese saw them merely as part of a universal force rather than as theologically endowed.

Ricci's successor, a rather enterprising Jesuit named Nicholas Longobardi, tossed out the Chinese terms because of their seemingly ambiguous (and non-Christian) meanings and introduced Deus as the quintessential reference to God. His subordinate in Japan, Francis Xavier, met with a typically cunning Japanese response. A native religious scholar, Hakuseki Arai, argued that the concept of Deus was incompatible with Confucian teachings, and he opposed Christianity because he felt it imitated Buddhism (which also taught absurd doctrines such as Heaven and Hell). So he fashioned a large bronze tablet and inscribed on it the phonetic ideographs for Deus, which in Japanese read "Dai Uso," or the Big Lie.

"The relationship between society and the family is like a big river and all its tributaries," Benjamin Schwartz, a former Chinese scholar at Harvard told me. "When the tributaries are full and flowing, then the big river is also full. But when the little rivers are polluted, then the big river is poisoned as well."

With thinning gray hair, a thick moustache, and bushy eyebrows, Dr. Schwartz bears a striking resemblance to Albert Einstein.

"Family relations are a paradigm of society as a whole," he said. "Families are inherently hierarchical and undemocratic, held together by strong emotional cement, as true in the West as it is in Asia. The family mirrors in miniature what happens in society, so if the family crumbles, what will happen to the rest of society?"

I asked him about the stronger dichotomy between the individual and society in the West, and he said, "Hierarchy, status, position, authority, power—everybody gets some degree of satisfaction out of playing his proper role, and those with smaller roles do not necessarily resent those playing larger ones. The aim is to promote harmony, which has its own beauty, so the social system carries with it a certain order and generates a kind of ceremonial beatitude. But it's also true that most people handle authority rather badly."

Hierarchy suggested more or less definitive roles, both within the family and in society at large, which seemed to be contradicted in the West.

"Role differentiation is a necessary part of a well-run society," Dr. Schwartz said. "Which is one reason the family in Asia shows evidence of much greater stability. But in America today there is widespread role confusion. The need for reciprocity in relationships, such as between husband and wife or between parent and child, doesn't necessarily contradict hierarchy, but in the United States, I think, there is not only contradiction but denial."

Role differentiation today is perhaps nowhere stronger in Asia than in Japan. This is reflected both in the family, since rates of divorce are much lower than in America, and in society, where interdependence is practically a household word. Japan exhibits probably the most extreme case of mutual dependency between mother and child, too. A Japanese mother regards the birth of her child as an event of sudden and shocking independence, and she spends an inordinate amount of time reestablishing the dependence that existed when the child was a fetus in her womb. Thus she will spend hours on end playing, bathing, and sleeping with her child.

In America, on the other hand, a child is encouraged to seek independence from its mother almost from birth, to be strong and to "stand on its own two feet." Despite all the popular literature on bonding, an American mother spends much less contact time with her child, who sleeps in its own crib from the day it comes home, a child-rearing practice most Asians regard as rather peculiar. (Cribs are called "cages" by Japanese mothers, who less by constraints of physical space than by historical tradition sleep on the same bedding with their children until the children are about ten.)

A decade ago two American sociologists, William Caudill and Helen Weinstein, conducted a longitudinal study of thirty Japanese infants and thirty American infants and how they interacted with their mothers. On the basis of their previous work they predicted that Japanese mothers would spend more time with their babies, favor physical contact over verbal interaction, and have as their goal a passive but contented baby. They also predicted that American mothers would spend less time with their infants, stress the verbal over the physical, and desire an active and assertive baby.

Actual results bore out their predictions: whether feeding, bathing, diapering, looking at, talking to, or playing with their babies, Japanese mothers physically held them rather than simply performing the necessary function at arm's length, as Americans tended to do. (Most Japanese mothers also keep their newborn child's umbilical cord after birth, treasured as a keepsake and a symbol of their mutual dependence.) As any casual foreign observer of the Japanese can attest, Japanese mothers constantly carry their infants about in "baby slings," which promote a close sense of "skinship" between mother and child, rather than pushing them around in prams or strollers, as most American mothers still do. Though many American mothers often use a "Snugli" in which to carry their infants, the Japanese custom has a long cultural tradition and is extended for a much greater period of time in the child's early life. The point to be made is that a practice that is merely popular (or trendy) in America is *pervasive* in Japan.

This strong distinction between dependence and independence was observed by a Japanese psychologist, Takeo Doi, during his first visits to the United States more than thirty years ago. The Japanese word for dependence is *amaeru,* which means to presume upon another's love or to avail oneself of another's kindness. (The adjective, *amai,* which means sweet or sugary, is used to suggest personal flattery as well as taste.) As a guest in American homes, Dr. Doi was often asked if he was hungry, a gesture that left him uncomfortable, since the Japanese would *presume* a guest was hungry and offer something to eat or drink without asking. Upon being served, he would be told, "Please help yourself," a command that suggested rather coldly that nobody else would.

The relationship between any two people in society was thus an extension of the relationship between mother and child. "In Japan," Dr. Doi noted in *The Anatomy of Dependence,* "there is a tendency to regard the parent-child relationship as an ideal, and to use it as a yardstick in judging all other relationships. Any relationship becomes deeper the closer it approaches the warmth of parent and child." This ideal relationship is hierarchical, a characteristic of all significant relationships in Japan. At school, children in different grades establish *sempaikohai* relationships, which distinguish senior from junior.

In organizations, older managers form mentor relationships with younger workers, a process called *oyabun-kobun* (literally, parent-child). Similarly, masters impart needed skills to apprentices not by impersonal training manuals but by direct, personal experience, a relationship known as *sensei-deshi,* or master-disciple. My own Japanese *oyabun,* now deceased, was invaluable to me during the years I worked in Japan, not only within the organization but externally as well, where his network of contacts and acquaintances proved crucial to forging new business and personal ties.

"Motherhood captures the depth of complexity inherent in a woman's self-fulfillment," the eminent anthropologist Takie Sugiyama Lebra recently wrote in *Japanese Women: Constraint and Fulfillment*. "On the one hand, it is mothering itself that constitutes *ikigai* [purposefulness] for her; it is the child's growth and achievement that fulfills her life's goal. On the other, it is as a mother that she loses her autonomy, enslaved by the tyranny of her child, who seeks her attention and care insatiably; motherhood is thus identical to sacrifice and selflessness."

Being a mother is no easy job anywhere, and it is especially tough in Japan, where husbands delegate the primary caretaking function to their wives. The operant proverb is "Good husbands are wise and frequently absent." Westerners generally overlook the extent to which Japanese mothers dominate and control a household; in working-class families it is common for the male wage earner to turn his monthly pay over to his wife, who then gives him an allowance, which is often squandered boorishly and insensitively. A British author, a longtime resident of Japan, dedicated one of his books thus: "To the gentle, self-effacing, and long-suffering mothers of the cruellest, most arrogant, and treacherous sons who walk this earth—the women of Japan—who will, as always, reap the richest harvest of suffering as their reward." And the analogy between Japanese mothers and Jewish mothers is often humorously drawn. In America mothers may threaten their children, saying, "If you don't do your homework, I'll kill you!" In Japan, mothers turn it around: "If you don't do your homework, I'll kill *myself!*"

Unlike Westerners, neither Japanese women nor Japanese men have ever regarded marriage as a prime source of individual happiness. Marriage is viewed rather as an institution for continuing a valuable social tradition, the family, without which society cannot prosper. Consequently, Japanese husbands and wives tend to view their children, rather than each other, as the true object of marriage, doubtless a factor in the low divorce rate: lower personal expectations generate a higher tolerance for frustration and disappointment. Honoring this traditional view of role differentiation has contributed to Japan's rapid industrialization, enhanced its competitiveness, and helped preserve a stable society. After all, someone must look after the most important investments in society's future—its children—and the Japanese woman plays the role of primary caretaker brilliantly. So we ought to be clear about one thing: the unsung hero of Japan's postwar economic miracle is none other than the Japanese woman. There has been little role confusion in Japan.

Western observers often criticize Japanese women because they are more passive than and do not enjoy equality with Japanese men. "If women are second-class citizens in most industrial countries," wrote one, "then they are third-class ones in Japan." But such views, conventional though they may be, tend to miss the broader point. Western society pays an enormous social price for the presumed benefits of job equality and dual careers: they may have their benefits in terms of self-fulfillment, but they also have their costs in terms of social instability and the disintegration of the family. In America, where half of all marriages still end in divorce, the divorce rate is about 5.2 per 1,000 of population, highest in the industrialized world; the rate in Japan is only 1.3, the lowest. In California, America's trend-setting state, 60 percent of all marriages now fail.

Families headed by a single parent now comprise more than 20 percent of all families in America, but only 6 percent in Japan. Half of all children born in America since 1980 are now expected to live with a single parent for at least part of their childhood lives; such a trend in Japan is statistically insignificant. In a recent poll 37 percent of Japanese women said marriage was unnecessary, and 56 percent said they can support themselves, but 52 percent indicated wives should not divorce their husbands under any circumstances (although 48 percent said divorce *might* be justified).

Because Japanese families are more stable, child care is not the urgent social issue in Japan that it is in America. Since extended families are closer in Japan, Japanese working mothers utilize a close network of kinship ties, through their mothers and mothers-in-law, but formal child-care facilities (the *hoikuen*, which operate twelve hours a day under strict government standards) are available, too.

According to the Fusae Ichikawa Memorial Association, a research group established in Tokyo in 1946 to commemorate universal suffrage, women in the Japanese work force outnumbered full-time housewives by about 500,000 by 1987. Women now comprise nearly 40 percent of the work force in Japan; women working part-time, defined as fewer than thirty-five hours a week, numbered 3.5 million, about 70 percent of all part-time Japanese workers. By 1988, 956 women had been elected to office throughout Japan; though the Japanese Parliament is 98.6 percent male, the head of Japan's Socialist party, Takako Doi, is a woman, and the country recently appointed its first female high court judge. Customs enforcement at Tokyo's Narita International Airport is now managed by a woman, as is the international operations center of the Bank of Tokyo. More than 80,000 Japanese companies, most of them admittedly small, are now headed by women, and average pay for women in Japan, as in America, is two-thirds that for men.

Japanese women have traditionally dominated the part-time labor market. When they work full-time, they typically stay until they become pregnant and then leave, bear children, and return on a part-time basis. Unlike the United States, Japan has a law mandating a national pregnancy leave, available to all women, an entitlement legitimized in only a few American states. Young Japanese women also dominate the hospitality and entertainment business in Japan (a world whose customers, needless to say, are mostly men), and older women have proven especially adept at selling insurance and taking deposits, jobs that entail lots of personal contact with other women as potential customers. Conflicts still arise, more with children than with husbands, and Japanese mothers often quit their jobs when they think their children's lives start to suffer or school performance begins to flag. There is little opposition to Japanese women in the official bureaucracy, which is by law and in practice sex-blind.

Young Japanese women, like American women, now tend to defer both marriage and childbearing to a later age. My former assistant, a university-educated Japanese woman who did graduate work in London, quit her job at the age of twenty-seven to marry and start a family. For her, as for many Japanese women, it was not a choice of either-or. "I will go back to work again," she told me, "but I want to be with my children while they are young." The old Japanese proverb expresses her sentiment well. *Tamuru nara wakagi no uchi:* if you would train a tree, do so while it is young.

Japanese women are better educated today than ever before, and their careers reflect it: television newscasts are now normally co-hosted by women, and it is common to find articles by women critics and commentators in leading Japanese journals. Dozens of magazines now target the working woman, such as *Nikkei Woman, Shufu no Onna,* and *Hanako,* the total monthly circulation of which approaches 25 million in a country of 120 million people. Japanese women are also becoming more prominent in university teaching; one of the nation's most famous sociologists, Professor Chie Nakane, recently retired as department head from Tokyo University, and a young, Yale-educated political scientist, Dr. Kuniko Inoguchi, author of a recent best-seller, teaches at Sophia nearby.

American women tend to live their lives as individuals, whereas Japanese women, whether or not they work, frame their lives within the group. While Westerners may view Japanese women as exploited, confined to domestic drudgery, and deprived of status, they often project their own cultural values onto the Japanese social system and fail to see women as exalted, as people who below the surface of society dominate men, who have almost dictatorial control over household affairs, and who enjoy considerable autonomy.

"American individualism and egalitarianism expose women's sex identity," Lebra concluded, "whereas Japanese rank-order sensitivity neutralizes women's sexuality in the eyes of males and females alike. There are many Japanese men who despise women and look down upon their wives, but the same men may be unrestrained admirers of their mothers and motherhood in general. Japanese women as mothers could thus be promoted to what amounts to an object of religious worship."

As, indeed, they are. Throughout Japanese mythology, and certainly in the folklore of Japan's native Shinto religion, women have what amounts to an awesome power over men. Amaterasu Ohmikami, the mythical creator of the Japanese archipelago, was a woman. The vagina is worshiped as an icon, much as the phallus has been in other cultures, perhaps because the de facto power of Japanese women is somewhat mysterious and therefore feared. The fearsome side of Japanese women is almost legendary; there are stories about clamlike vaginas that snip off male genitals like steel traps.

This preoccupation with female genitalia—at least with the magic if not the mystery of it—can be observed in any Japanese striptease parlor in the entertainment districts of major Japanese cities. One of the best is the Omiya Gekijo, in Kyoto, appropriately named the Great Temple Theatre; Kyoto is Japan's cultural capital. As the dancers complete their routines, they unwrap layer after layer of sheer, kimonolike undergarments, thereby prolonging the mystical moment of revelation. Then they squat at the edge of the stage and walk, ducklike, in front of popeyed customers, keeping one extremely thin garment in play. Finally they spread their legs slowly, and wide, as heads in the front rows bend forward for a full view of the revered organ. The more enterprising customers bring flashlights (not infrequently supplied by the maidens) so as not to be denied; as a woman passes by, they slump back in their chairs, exhausted, mopping sweat from their brows, salvation assured. The magic icon has been viewed.

I recall one incident with particular vividness. As a young graduate student I had traveled far into the northern reaches of Japan with a colleague one cold and blustery winter, across the Tsugaru Strait to the tiny village of Higashi Muroran on the island of Hokkaido, where the snow had buried our train. After a few inquiries we found a small inn with a hot-springs bath, so we bathed and took a short walk, lobster-red and steaming, in traditional robes and *geta*, the familiar elevated wooden clogs. We spied the local Omiya Gekijo. A performance was about to begin. We entered.

Just as the first dancer began her gyrations, we found two vacant seats facing the runway. More customers straggled in until the tiny hall was nearly full. The dancer squatted into her duck walk, stopping before each front-row patron, watching the flashlights, obviously enjoying the men enjoying her. Then she saw the two foreigners, padded our way, and threw open her remaining underwrap to give us an unobscured view. Perspiring heavily now, as much from the hot bath as from this mystical experience, we opened our own robes and let the Western phallus rise to greet the Asian icon. Silence. Then a surprised gasp. Then a scream, as she fainted and the hall exploded with laughter. Shouts of encouragement for an encore ensued; a second dancer nervously began as two assistants quickly revived the first and escorted her offstage.

Male and female, husband and wife, light and dark, day and night, ruler and ruled. Hierarchy. Place. Functional differentiation. These are the realities of *yin* and *yang*, the alternating rhythms of life, as old as recorded history. The sun knows its proper role and does not try to usurp the moon; nor does man attempt to take woman's place or woman man's. The ancient *yin-yang* symbol, a circle divided in half by an S-shaped curve, forms two equal, tear-shaped sides, representing the dualism of the universe in perfect balance.

In Korea this symbol is called the *taeguk*, and it is the dominant feature of the Korean national flag, in red and blue on a white background. The *taeguk* suggests a constant circular motion within the sphere of infinity; while the opposing forces—*yin* above and *yang* below—are in essential harmony, they exist in a state of perpetual dualism, symbolizing a kind of Sisyphean struggle for domination that neither side can ever win. Interaction between the two defines life, is its sustaining force, its organic *being*. Hence, ultimate acceptance and no role confusion. In the beginning there was man *and* woman.

On a recent trip to Korea in mid-1988 I visited with Dr. Lee Kwang-kyu, a renowned anthropologist who teaches at Seoul National University. He did graduate work in Vienna and had taught for several years in the United States; his Korean wife had a PhD in atomic physics and also was teaching.

"There is even stronger kinship solidarity in Korea than in Japan," Dr. Lee was telling me as we walked across campus to his office that warm spring afternoon. "Ancestor worship is still very strong here, and the Korean family, of course, is very hierarchical as far as role differentiation is concerned. Some sociologists say modernization is destroying older traditions and creating a new society based on wealth or education as Korea moves from an agrarian to an industrial economy. But I think Korean society is still based on the family, strongly anchored in the local community."

The caustic odor of pepper gas from a recent student riot still hung heavily in the air, so we hurried along, holding handkerchiefs over our mouths and noses. Dr. Lee told me that the major stem families in Korea—those with familiar names like Kim, Park, and Lee—each had an organized society of relatives nationwide, with an administrative system in each province. They were used to great effect during the recent National Assembly elections, he said, which was one reason the vote followed regional patterns.

"The point is," he said as we settled into his office, where the air was better, "social organizations in Korea are based on family, and kinship is key. Korean women are very active in society and are more visible here; unlike in Japan, their power is more apparent. Twenty percent of Seoul National students are women; you won't find numbers that high at Tokyo University. Our divorce rate, while increasing, is still low, about the same as in Japan and far lower than America, about a fifth of yours. But there is an enormous stigma attached to divorce in Korea. Normally children are left with their fathers, who may remarry; divorced women rarely do, so they wind up at the bottom of the pyramid. In that regard it's very tough for women."

Dr. Lee stressed that family continuity was very important in Korea. Americans have "achieved status," he said, based on wealth or education. Japan reached this stage more than a century ago, during the Tokugawa period. Koreans, however, like the Chinese, have "ascribed status," whereby the first son must be the lineal successor; even if the second son is brighter or more capable, he cannot head the family. Since the big Korean *chaebol*, like Samsung and Hyundai, are dominated by their founding families, the founder must hand over the company to his eldest son and damn the consequences, because blood ties and lineage are most important.

"Take the case of a man and woman who have three sons and a daughter, and the family owns twelve acres of land," Lee said, sketching out a small diagram. "In China, where the stem family is dominant, the three sons will each inherit four acres, and the daughter gets nothing, because it is assumed she will marry into another family. In Japan, where the system of primogeniture prevails, the eldest son gets all twelve acres; the other two sons and the daughter receive nothing. But in Korea the eldest son receives six acres and the other two sons three acres each. Yet the Korean daughter, too, gets nothing."

Korea's rapid industrialization has meant that Korean society flip-flopped from 80 percent rural and 20 percent urban to just the reverse in one generation, without significantly altering social traditions. Korean women moved from the countryside to the cities, especially to metropolitan Seoul, where about half the population of 40 million now lives.

As in Japan, Korean women dominate the ranks of part-time workers; they receive, on average, two-thirds the pay of men. At major firms young single women live in dormitories, segregated from their male colleagues; when they marry, they quit their jobs while their husbands continue to work. Role differentiation in Korea, as in Japan, is distinguished clearly and applied traditionally, on the job as well as at home. Unlike in Japan, however, abortion is not a widely accepted social practice; infants born out of wedlock are frequently wrapped in swaddling clothes and placed, late at night, at police boxes or on the steps of hospital entrances, with prayers pinned to their blankets expressing the hope the children will find love and happiness in a good family.

I took Seoul's spanking-new subway across town to see Chun Byung-hoon, president of the Social Welfare Society. SWS, as it is known, was formed in 1954 to place Korean war orphans and counsel unmarried mothers. Today it operates out of a modern six-story hospital building, with several field offices throughout Korea that administer foster homes, work with handicapped children, and run baby clinics for inoculations and pediatric treatment. Since both of my adopted Korean children had been "born" through SWS, I had kept in contact with Chun and his staff over the years.

"As in America not so long ago," he was telling me in his office at the Han Suh hospital, "there is still a stigma attached to unwed Korean mothers. They cannot keep their babies as single parents. Rare domestic adoptions that do occur are normally kept secret; they are not entered on official birth or family registers. The news media have been critical of adoption agencies placing Korean infants with foreign families, saying Korea is now an advanced industrial country and should stop doing that. But we have just emerged from a successful Olympics, so everything Korea does comes under more scrutiny."

One of the leading Korean dailies, *Chosun Ilbo*, had an editorial that very day criticizing "exports" of babies from Korea, which now totaled about 5,000 a year. But a society has very little choice, it seems to me, when its culture forbids or constrains both abortion and adoption and when potential parents in other societies are involuntarily childless.

The Korean government recently instituted a new policy whereby the younger adoptive parent must be no more than forty years older than the adopted Korean child. I thought about this as I sat directly across the hall from the room where I first held our infant daughter, Claire, exactly five years ago to the month, and our infant son, Peter, a year and a half after that. If the new rules had been in effect then, we would have just squeaked by.

I asked Chun about the role of Korean women today.

"Well," he said, "the Japanese say, if anyone is left in the middle of a desert with no food and no water, if she is a Korean, she'll survive. We call Korean mothers the 'Minister of Finance and Education.' Wives execute real power; fathers are by comparison just puppets. It was the Korean woman, after all, who upheld Korean traditions during the Japanese occupation."

Chun's comment about the Japanese was revealing, because on the surface Koreans will say they think they are inferior to the Japanese. But deep down they want to beat them in every respect. Other Korean friends had said they were overjoyed when Korea won more medals than Japan at the 1986 Asian Games held in Seoul's new Olympic stadium. Korea won 224 medals, finishing first overall, ahead of China, which placed second with 222, and Japan, which was third with 211.

At least Japanese and Koreans do not kill their daughters if they are firstborn children, as is often the case in China today. For years now Beijing has tried to limit the growth of the nation's population—well into its second billion now—mostly without success, and its heavy-handed bureaucratic methods have resulted in widespread female infanticide. Chinese parents are driven more by tradition than by ideology, and tradition says that families with a firstborn male are favored. In Japan the preferred proverb is *ichi hime, ni taro,* "firstborn a daughter, second a son."

"The Chinese people today are much worse off than they were a century ago," Bo Yang, the Taiwanese essayist, recently wrote in a clever and witty essay called "The Ugly Chinaman." "The most upsetting thing is that over the last century most of their hopes have vanished into thin air. Whenever a new hope appears on the horizon promising some improvement in their life, it inevitably ends up causing great disappointment and only makes the situation worse. How much hope can anyone have in one lifetime? Does the future hold promise, or is it paved with disappointment? People need inspiration and encouragement; I've been receiving it ever since I was a child. When I was five or six, grown-ups would tell me, 'The future of China is in your hands,' though at the time I felt this was too great a burden for me to bear all by myself. Later I told my son, 'The future of China is in the hands of your generation.' Now my son is telling his son, 'The future of China is in your hands.' How many more generations will this go on for?"

Some observers note how efficiently the smaller overseas Chinese communities function: business is competitive, the educational systems are first-rate, and the social fabric is strong and resilient. Yet the masses in China still encounter enormous problems in making their own society work, and many wonder why this is so. One obvious factor is size. Twenty million people in Taiwan, 5.5 million in Hong Kong, a little more than 2 million in Singapore—all reasonable multiples to work with and insignificant fractions of the billion-plus population on the mainland. China, if it grows any larger, may develop social gridlock. Another, less obvious factor is that while traditional Chinese society has a strong family base, the individual, not the group, is the focal point of social attention.

According to Bo Yang, Chinese culture is infected with "a virus of neurotic anxiety," which has been passed down from generation to generation. This huge country, with a quarter of the world's population, has created a legacy of problems for itself.

"Three good examples are filth, disorder, and noise," he wrote. "They once tried to carry out a campaign against filth and disorder, but it lasted only a few days. Our kitchens and our homes are always in a mess. In many places, when the Chinese move in, everyone else moves out. And Chinese voices must be the loudest on earth. A popular joke makes the point. When two Cantonese people are having a simple conversation, an American thinks they're fighting and calls the police. The police arrive and ask them what they're doing. 'We're just whispering' is their reply. Our sense of insecurity makes us feel that the louder we shout, the more right we are."

By contrast with China, it is often said that one Japanese alone is no better off than a pig, but three Japanese together make a dragon. Empirically verifiable evidence of this can be seen in personal negotiations, public or private, as any American, much to his dismay, will readily admit. Japanese organizational ability, starting with the family, reinforced by the schools, and continued in business and government, has convinced them they are practically invincible; the Chinese cannot begin to compare.

"If three Japanese people are in similar businesses, they will take turns making sales to protect their shares," Bo Yang admits. "But every Chinese is a dragon in his or her own right. With three Chinese businessmen, if the first sells something for $50, the second will sell it for $30 and the third for $20. Chinese can give the clearest, most logical explanations for anything. Put a Chinese to work in a research institute where no interpersonal relationships are required, and he can produce brilliant results. But put three of them together, and it can be disastrous. This is because of our addiction to quarreling. We squabble incessantly. There is an old Chinese saying that goes, 'One monk carries his water on his back; two monks carry their water between them on a pole; three monks have no water at all to drink.' The Chinese are simply unable to appreciate the importance of cooperation. But if you tell them that, they will write a book called *The Importance of Cooperation* for your benefit."

When they take control of Hong Kong in 1997, the Chinese will need cooperation more than ever if they want the former British colony to continue functioning and retain the middle-class professionals necessary to run it. Socially much is already changing, with the outflux of émigrés whose perception is that Beijing's cooperation will be tailored to Alice in Wonderland's definition: it means exactly what the Chinese intend it to mean, nothing less, nothing more. So many of Hong Kong's best and brightest are voting with their exit permits.

Cooperation will also help Beijing implement the many other changes that will be necessary after July 1, 1997. Street names, for example, and identity cards and passports and postage stamps, to name just a few. The status of one rather permanent institution, the Royal Hong Kong Jockey Club, is, as far as I could tell on a visit in early 1988, at best uncertain. It combines the finest of British social entertaining with the raw Chinese addiction to gambling. It is located in Happy Valley, another place name that will become much less poetic after 1997, replaced by something like Zhao's Square or the People's Park.

I was sitting at the private table of the chief steward of the Royal Hong Kong Jockey Club one evening to watch the races from his private box. The position of chief steward, by tradition, is held by the chairman and chief executive officer of the Hong Kong and Shanghai Banking Corporation. That is Willie Purves, an old friend who was the bank's chief accountant years ago when I lived in the colony. The room was thick with Chinese attendants offering a steady stream of aperitifs, canapés, and cigars. Of the twenty or so people gathered there that night, perhaps half of them were from the bank; the rest were influential British and Chinese guests, young and old.

To my left an elderly Chinese man, a real estate kingpin, clicked false teeth like castanets as he refuted the more spirited arguments of Martin Lee. "Some people think democracy is what Hong Kong wants," he said in his impeccable British accent, "but I don't think that's what the majority really want at all." To my right a senior manager of the bank gestured dramatically, spinning his hands in small circles as he recounted a recent divestiture for the benefit of a young, pin-striped Chinese nearby—"brightest lad in the whole government," I was later told. "We're really farting against thunder," he said in clipped tones, "if we think we can find a buyer without putting the assets under belts and braces first."

A soft baritone announced the first race, in Cantonese and English. I am a terrible gambler, by both ideology and instinct. For me picking winners is an art that borders on the mystical. A combination of the horse's number, the square root of the sum of its recent wins, the colors of the jockey's jersey, and coin flips was just some of the friendly advice I was given. Disregarding all advice, I picked Highway Patrol in the first race. The letters *HP* also stood for Hewlett-Packard, a strong competitor in Far Eastern markets. Also, HP times itself was HP squared; two letters thus became four, and the Japanese character for four was synonymous with death, ordinarily a bad omen but one that seemed neutralized by a footnote symbol resembling a grave marker explaining that Highway Patrol was a fifth-class horse running in a fourth-class race. My hunch was that the two death signs would cancel out (they did), and the horse would try harder, by virtue of its promotion, to win (it did), thereby moving up a class and simultaneously justifying both my faith in the future of Hong Kong and my genius at geomancy. (I bet HK$10, about $1.50, and cleared five times that amount.)

Between races, I pulled Willie Purves aside to talk a little about the changes he thought might be forthcoming after 1997. Nearly sixty, with silver hair that framed his features in a soft halo, he was still as fit and trim as I had remembered him. He spoke of the confidence factor having fallen but said that Japan was investing aggressively in Hong Kong and that America ought to be doing the same, because Hong Kong would be an effective point of entry into China in the future.

"There's an object lesson here for your countrymen," he said quietly. "They can't always expect to be in places where the outcome is guaranteed."

Willie, of course, had lived in Hong Kong at the time of the civil riots in 1966 and 1967, on the heels of Mao's Cultural Revolution, and I thought about that chapter in Hong Kong's history as I flew out the next day for Singapore, another city-state whose recent history included severe social unrest, strikes, and political riots. But unlike Hong Kong, Singapore's future seemed confidently assured, given its independence, the high quality of its political leadership, and its strong social cohesiveness.

Airborne, I picked up a copy of the *Straits Times,* Singapore's leading English daily, and saw an article about the Central Provident Fund. More than 10,000 people had funded retirement accounts, not for themselves but for their *parents.* During 1987 sons and daughters in Singapore had added more than $100 million under a scheme that permitted such tax-deductible contributions. Later, during a lull on the long Singapore Airlines flight, I asked the purser whether he had been a contributor.

"No, I wasn't, but my sister was," he said. "We all talked about it—I have a brother and a sister—and we decided she would contribute now, based on her higher income."

They all lived together, he said, with their parents, in one government-owned flat. Tall for a Chinese, he spoke three languages—English, which he used at home, he said; Chinese (the Hakka dialect, the prime minister's native tongue); and Malay. He said his father used to be in the timber business, a lucrative trade in resource-rich Southeast Asia, but had retired and now drove a taxi part-time.

I asked him whether his family observed the Confucian tradition of filial piety.

"Not really," he said. "But whenever we have problems or need to make a decision, we always include our parents and ask for their advice. We may not follow it—they expect us to be mature and use our own judgment—but we would never think of not consulting them."

He excused himself momentarily, then promptly returned.

"We've applied for a larger flat," he went on, "with five rooms. You get on the list, they show you three possibilities. We looked at one. If you decline all three, you go back to the end of the queue. My father and I will use part of our CPF funds to create the down payment, and I will pay the monthly maintenance. When he passes away, the flat reverts to me. He wanted it that way."

"What about the CPF beneficiary?" I asked.

"My parents. If they predecease me, which is likely, then I have to pick a new beneficiary. Under Singapore law your spouse is the beneficiary unless you choose another."

Having noticed the loose frame on my eyeglasses, he disappeared again and soon returned with a pocket-sized kit containing some miniature screwdrivers. He chose one, tried it, picked another, and tightened the tiny screw.

"Here you are," he said, handing my glasses back.

The concept of service in Asia is something most Americans would find difficult to comprehend. The very thought of such attention to detail on an American airline is simply preposterous.

Singapore, like Japan and Korea, has very stable families, with an extremely low rate of divorce. In 1986 there were 1,485 divorces out of a population of 2.5 million, a rate of 0.59 per 1,000, compared to 1.3 in Japan and Korea and 5.2 in the U.S. The rate in America is nearly ten times as high.

Singapore's social stability is due in part to the government's creative use of tax and other policy incentives; stabilization of the population was one result. In 1957 the population growth rate was 5.4 percent, one of the highest in Asia; since 1983 it has been increasing at 1.1 percent, the lowest. The government offered specific tax relief to families who had fewer children, creating a disaggregated tax structure favoring smaller families. In order to slow the growth of the poor, the government offered outright cash grants if couples stopped at two children, paying $10,000 into their CPF accounts.

Today Singapore has a rate slightly lower than zero growth (about 1.5 children per woman of childbearing age), which has persuaded the government to reverse its policy. The popular slogan "Stop at two" has now been replaced by "Have three or four if you can afford it." Since 1984 young couples have been given tax incentives to bear more children. Professional women and women with graduate degrees with at least three children qualify for premium housing, and they can register their children for primary school with top priority.

Women now comprise 48 percent of Singapore's work force, up from only 30 percent as recently as 1970, although average pay is only about half that for men. This development is not entirely attributable to government policy but is also an outgrowth of other socioeconomic trends such as higher levels of education for women and their decision to postpone marriage and children. In the late 1970s the government located light industrial projects within public housing estates, again through the artful use of tax and other incentives, to provide jobs for women near their homes.

Work force participation rates by women fall off rather precipitously after age twenty-three, reflecting the dominance of social over economic concerns. Nearly 80 percent of Singapore's women work at age twenty-two, for example, but by age twenty-seven the rate is closer to 60 percent and by age thirty-two less than 50 percent. About 90 percent of all single women between the ages of twenty and twenty-nine work, whereas only about 40 percent of married women from that age group are in the work force.

While child-care facilities in Singapore have not expanded fully to meet demand, some innovative approaches have been taken. The Singapore police run a boys' club that cares for sons of working mothers after school hours, and most larger employers provide on-site child-care facilities. The National Productivity Board has recommended job sharing as another alternative, whereby two partners share one job and take mutual responsibility for child care. Singapore's position at the leading edge of the high-technology learning curve suggests that the Lion City will continue to devise other innovative techniques too.

The Philippines is a Catholic country, which in itself says volumes about its inability to implement the kinds of family planning and population control incentives Singapore has used so successfully. A hand-painted sign hangs in the lobby of the Department of Agriculture in Manila; it summarizes a key difference between this backward culture and its more successful Asian neighbors. "It is by grace you are saved, through faith," it reads, "and not by yourselves; it is the gift of God, not by works, so that no one can boast." The Little Dragons boast not of gifts but of works.

If Singapore has the lowest population growth rate in Asia, then by all accounts the Philippines has the highest. Exploding at 3 percent a year, population growth exceeds economic growth, which has meant a steadily deteriorating per-capita income for Filipinos. People flood into Manila from the countryside, creating a huge demand for social services that the government can ill afford.

Masses of illiterate, unemployed Filipinos—15,000 of them according to a recent estimate I saw on my last visit in early 1988—live at the foot of a sprawling garbage dump in the northwest section of Manila called Smokey Mountain. Rows of squatter's shacks sit at the base of tall mountains of raw garbage, and when the Manila trucks dump out loads of fetid trash, scavengers ranging from the very young to the very old claw their way through the refuse as yellow bulldozers plow ahead of them. Plastic bags and tin cans can be recycled. Bones can be crushed to make fertilizer or animal feed. Children no older than nine or ten pick with experienced if diseased hands. Smoke steams from the garbage, created by spontaneous combustion, giving the landmark its name. The stench is overwhelming.

"I have been going to the dump site for more than ten years now," Father Benigno Beltran, a Dominican priest, said in late 1987, "and I still have not gotten used to the smell. It becomes infested with millions of flies that often get into the chalice when I say Mass. The smell makes you deaf."

There is not one Smokey Mountain in Manila, but *seven*. Down the road some teenagers play a game of basketball in a small area cleared of garbage. A makeshift hoop, fashioned from an old five-gallon paint can, is stuck to the side of their shack. The smoke is ubiquitous, following the soft currents of the wind; it sticks to your clothing as a constant reminder: you are in purgatory.

I was overwhelmed by conflicting feelings of anger and dread as I waded through the filth, stumbling over rotten fruit, discarded medical waste, and empty tins, holding a handkerchief over my face to stifle the urge to gag. That any living being, human or animal, could be permitted to live in such conditions, never mind working in them, was simply inconceivable.

When I later described my feelings to Renato Constantino, a well-known and respected historian at the University of the Philippines, he nodded understandingly. During the Marcos years he had published a clandestine column called "Marcos Watch," now called "Aquino Watch." He is an elegant man, soft-spoken and thoughtful.

"The Church is an obstacle," he said quietly, "but there is an underground church, operating mainly in the rural areas, distributing cash as well as condoms, all against official Church policy. The Church blocks the Department of Social Welfare from distributing prophylactics, of course, but the underground bishops are making progress."

I asked why the government didn't take more forceful action against such outrageous social conditions as Smokey Mountain. He simply shrugged his shoulders.

"After typhoon Sisang, when so many people died," he said, "boxes were placed near elevators in Makati office buildings, soliciting contributions for the families. Instead of throwing money into the bins, people used them as wastebaskets. Some changes have occurred on the surface, but the quicksand below remains."

Half a city away, by contrast, Forbes Park adjoins the glittering Makati business section. Manila's elite—oligarch and expatriate alike—live behind heavily fortified walls in elegant houses that could exist in a luxury neighborhood anywhere in America. BMWs are as prevalent in Forbes Park as handmade wooden wagons at Smokey Mountain; manicured lawns are tended by armies of gardeners, and each home comes with its own cook, housemaid, and driver. But there are armed guards at all of its entrance gates, so precarious is its security.

Jaime Cardinal Sin is the highest-ranking prelate in the Philippines, chief spokesman for Church policy, member of the College of Cardinals. He sits in what many call the "catbird seat" of Philippines politics, enjoying great privilege, a massive constituency, and unlimited term of office. His former press aide, Felix Bautista, had spent forty years in journalism, thirteen of them close to the cardinal. A Catholic himself, he was currently press spokesman for Senator Jovito Salonga, president of the Philippine Senate, when I called on him at his Manila office during my visit to Manila in early 1988.

I asked Bautista about Smokey Mountain.

"Every time we relocate or resettle them," he said with a shrug of his large shoulders, "they keep going back. Scavenging is their way of life. One multinational corporation wants to turn Smokey Mountain into a fertilizer factory as a means of dealing with the urban poor. But the scavengers earn fifty pesos a day. That is their livelihood. What else would they do?"

Fifty pesos a day was the equivalent of about $3 at current rates of exchange. Three dollars a day, times 240 working days, was more than $700 dollars a year, about 20 percent higher than the average per-capita income. Bautista's numbers were not faulty; that figure had been cited in local press accounts, along with the common lore that you couldn't relocate the scavengers because they would simply return, like lemmings, to the dumps. Were people so gullible as to believe that a sub-human class forced to live like foraging animals could earn more than an average wage?

Bautista is a portly man, and rotund, with a moon-shaped face that perspired profusely. He had twelve children. I asked him about the population explosion.

"This is a big, big problem," he admitted. "But you have to remember, we are a strongly Catholic country, and Catholicism is opposed to birth control. The Church is implacable on this point. You must also realize that children are regarded as wealth in the Philippines, so the more you have, the wealthier you are perceived to be."

When I asked Bautista for his assistance in arranging an interview with Cardinal Sin, he readily agreed. On the night before my audience with His Eminence, I watched him deliver a eulogy to Don Juan Bosco, a Jesuit who had established Catholic schools all over the world.

"We exhort our young people to be loyal to Christ," he intoned in his televised speech, resplendent in yellow robes as he stood before an audience of thousands. "Sacrifice yourselves for Christian principles, not for secular values. For Jesus is the Lord of the twenty-first century and the hope of our youth. There is no country in the world which has been blessed more than ours."

As he spoke, a banner unfurled across the bottom of the screen: sponsored by the San Miguel Corporation, the Philippines' finest beer.

Jaime Cardinal Sin was the second-youngest of sixteen children, the first nine of whom died shortly after childbirth. Not a brilliant scholar, he never finished college until pressed by the Jesuits to do so. He was the youngest bishop ever to join the College of Cardinals.

I called on him at dawn the next morning at his heavily guarded estate, Villa San Miguel, where a dozen gardeners were busy edging flower beds and trimming plants. He was dressed in his familiar yellow robes and cap and sat, smiling seraphically, behind a wooden desk. At that very moment, back in America, separated by two centuries and thirteen time zones, the Washington Redskins were playing the Denver Broncos in Super Bowl XXIII.

I asked Cardinal Sin about Smokey Mountain.

"The politicians have tried to resettle the scavengers or move them back to their original provinces," he said in his high-pitched voice, "but they always come back to the garbage. People don't understand; this is their *livelihood*. The government bought an incinerator, but the scavengers destroyed it. They make fifty pesos a day! We can't rob these people by taking away their incomes. We are a young country, very young. And when America was a young country, it had problems, too, fighting a terrible civil war and persecuting the Indians. We need your understanding."

He lifted his arms as if in supplication and smiled, tilting his head to one side.

I mentioned the population rate, which was outstripping Philippine economic growth and forcing real income to decline. The cardinal with the ironic name slowly shook his head.

"You know the position of the Church," he said, his face pimply now with perspiration. "You may plan the size of your family providing your methodology follows natural law. Abortive action is not permitted, nor is the Pill. Singapore is planning big families again, but we are a poor country, yet rich in children. We will know how to limit our children when we educate the poor. They need electricity, not condoms. When it is dark, what else are they going to do?"

I pressed him on education.

"You know," he said, smiling, "more than 98 percent of our people know how to read and write, 60 percent have finished high school, and 40 percent have been educated at the college level. The Catholic Church alone has created seventeen universities in the Philippines, 900 elementary schools, 900 high schools, and 900 colleges."

As he played with his rosary, it occurred to me that it must have had 900 beads. His answers to questions on land reform and politics seemed equally hypocritical.

"There is no need for land reform legislation," he said, wagging a finger now, "because being a Christian is having a commitment to share what you have with others. But before our lands can be distributed to the landless, the tenants must be educated, because they may not be able to manage it. They need training centers so they can till the land properly and credit cooperatives so they can get fertilizer and markets for their crops. Otherwise the tenants will simply sell their land and stay put."

The cardinal concluded with a poem he had written for Cory Aquino.

"Justice without mercy is tyranny," he said, "mercy without justice is weakness, justice without love is socialism, and love without justice is baloney."

Then he arched his head back and shook with laughter, a belly laugh that somehow seemed strangely out of place.

I thanked Cardinal Sin for his time and was escorted back down the red-carpeted staircase to the front door, past a shiny new Toyota sedan, pristine white with smoked windows, its engine idling as it waited to take His Eminence in air-conditioned comfort downtown to Quiapo Chapel for a morning service.

His platitudes, the moral judgment, the hokey sayings, all seemed to fit a bankrupt country that was living increasingly on borrowed time. Hypocrisy in official circles, both political and religious, fed a process that kept the Philippines in an unalterable condition of social apartheid.

In stark contrast, I recalled the words of a longtime Filipino friend who had told me, "The underground Church is working against all the 'isms' now: communism, feudalism, colonialism, cronyism, and paternalism. We need economic growth and political stability, but we can't have the former until we create the latter. The bishops hate Cardinal Sin. Why didn't he intervene to topple Marcos sooner or to prevent Ninoy—Cory's husband—from being assassinated? He's nothing more than a reactionary now and irrelevant."

As I left Villa San Miguel and walked across Shaw Boulevard, thick with early-morning traffic, to flag an empty cab, the familiar but sad Jeepneys belched by in the opposite direction, their cryptic signboards a constant appeal to an unreal optimism in a land without hope, a country where the Crucifixion seems to have been converted into a plastic dashboard Jesus. Turbo City. Ring Ring. Queen of Rock.

And as I finally headed back downtown, I could see people begin to emerge from their makeshift corrugated metal shacks, aimlessly tossing bucketsful of trash into the clogged gutters, to be picked up and transported days later to one of the seven Smokey Mountains.

I was reminded of another country, half a world away, that was also borrowing from its future as it experienced its own version of social meltdown. America, with the highest divorce rate in the civilized world, was becoming a society of single parents, endangering the emotional and economic lives of its children, sacrificing its future at the altar of self-fulfillment. The disintegrating American family was being plagued by role confusion, the triangular relationship of work, home, and school dangerously out of balance. If social stability is another key to East Asian competitiveness, through a family system that protects the emotional well-being of society's children, then America may have more to worry about than just budget and trade deficits, poor product quality, and falling educational performance.

It may have to worry about survival.

15

AMERICA'S MOST PRECIOUS NATURAL RESOURCE: THE MINDS OF ITS CHILDREN

Children may be told over and over again that their parents have a right to their own lives, that they will enjoy quality time instead of quantity time, that they are really loved by their parents even after divorce, but children do not believe any of this. They think they have a right to total attention and believe their parents must live for them. There is no explaining otherwise to them, and anything less inevitably produces indignation and an inextirpable sense of injustice. To children, the voluntary separation of parents seems worse than their death precisely because it is voluntary.

Children learn a fear of enslavement to the wills of others, along with a need to dominate those wills, in the context of the family, the one place where they are supposed to learn the opposite. Of course, many families are unhappy. But that is irrelevant. The important lesson that the family taught was the existence of the only unbreakable bond, for better or for worse, between human beings.

The decomposition of this bond is surely America's most urgent social problem.

Allan Bloom, *The Closing of the American Mind*

The concept of living in harmony with nature never had much in common with the American tradition of rugged individualism. Nature was man's formidable opponent; it had to be mastered if not enslaved. In Asia, by contrast, the operative concept of human relationships is recognizing one's place in nature. Asians respect nature. Americans want to change it.

When, in the early 1960s, Rachel Carson wrote *Silent Spring*, which documented the tragic aftereffects of inorganic chemicals on American

328

wildlife, the very use of those chemicals was thought to be a step forward. Science had created a way for the American farmer to achieve mastery over nature, to achieve greater crop yields and generate higher profit margins while simultaneously eliminating almost everything that stood in the way of both.

But farmers have seen crop yields fall, economic costs rise, and farm profits vanish. Soil erosion, polluted groundwater, and new mutations of pesticide-resistant bugs have all combined to take their toll on both farm output and natural wildlife. The miracle of inorganic chemistry has not brought nature to her knees; it has created an environmental nightmare of sorcerer's apprentice proportions. The American farmer has somehow forgotten the cardinal principle of regenerative farming, that nature must be man's partner, not his slave.

And, like the soil that has been bleached of nutriments by the cumulative effects of modern chemistry, so it is with the American family, parched of value by the cumulative effect of divorce. Because it has disintegrated, the family is no longer the social resource it once was and cannot be relied on to transmit a generation's worth of values to America's children—values such as commitment and sacrifice and deferred gratification—because those values have been eroded and are no longer in evidence.

The American family may well be on the verge of extinction, as measured by any contemporary social yardstick: the highest divorce rate in the industrialized world; the largest ratio of single parents to traditional two-parent families; the escalating number of latchkey children; the percentage of children in poverty; and the substitution of strangers as primary caretakers through the institutionalization of child care. If the family is nature's traditional means of enabling society to invest in its future, is there any question why America's future may be increasingly at risk?

By 1970 about 1 million American children a year under the age of eighteen were experiencing the divorce of their parents and the consequent deterioration of stable family life. By 1980 one out of every two existing American marriages had experienced the emotional trauma of divorce. By 1981 female-headed families totaled nearly 20 percent of all families with children under eighteen, and an estimated 30 percent of American children were suffering the consequences of divorce. California was the trendsetter, with the highest divorce rate—six per thousand of population compared to about five per thousand for the rest of the country. Today 40 percent of all children in America will experience the trauma of divorce, and 20 percent of America's children will live through *two* divorces before they reach the age of eighteen.

"Morality seems to be squarely on the side of selfishness," Allan Bloom wrote. "Or, to put it otherwise, the concern with self-development and self-expression has gradually revealed itself to be inimical to society. A young person's conditional attachment to divorced parents merely reciprocates what he necessarily sees as their conditional attachment to him, and is entirely different from the classic problems of loyalty to families, or other institutions, which were clearly dedicated to their members. In the past, such breaking away was sometimes necessary but always morally problematic. Today it is normal."

Virtually all social and psychological studies of divorce have focused on divorcing adults as the objects of pathological attention. But Judith Wallerstein, a social scientist working at Stanford's Center for Advanced Study in the Behavioral Sciences, recently completed the first-ever longitudinal study of the effects of divorce on children, a ten-year effort that studied sixty divorcing California families with 131 children between the ages of three and eighteen at separation, called *Surviving the Breakup: How Children and Parents Cope with Divorce*. (Her updated sequel, *Men, Women, and Children a Decade after Divorce*, followed in early 1989.)

"The history of marriage and divorce in our society is replete with examples of the many unwarranted assumptions that adults have made about children," Dr. Wallerstein concluded, "simply because such assumptions were congenial to the adults' needs or wishes at the time. Thus the conventional wisdom of yesteryear was that unhappily married people should remain married 'for the good of the children.' Today's conventional wisdom holds, with equal vigor, that a marriage that is unhappy for the adults is unhappy for the children, and that a divorce that promotes the happiness of the adults will inevitably benefit the children as well. This presumed commonality of interests and perceptions between adults and children, along with the companion notion that the experience of the children can be subsumed under the experience of the adults, was called into sharp question by our young subjects."

In reading through Wallerstein's interviews, case studies, and analytical findings, I was impressed by how *long* the psychological effects of divorce remained, creating emotional scar tissue that would be years in healing, if it healed at all.

The preschoolers, aged three through five, experienced anger, generalized fear, regression, macabre fantasy, fear of hunger, anxiety about lack of protection, bewilderment, fear of abandonment, disruption of play, an increase in aggression, inhibition, and guilt. The children aged six through twelve exhibited deprivation, a strong yearning for the departed parent, anger at the custodial parent, loyalty conflict, camouflaged feelings, simultaneous denial and distress, transfer of pain and unhappiness into the pleasure of achievement, a shaken sense of identity, and parental betrayal. Adolescents in the study, aged thirteen through eighteen, displayed severe loneliness, generalized fear and anxiety, isolation, sexual competition with their parents, anger at parental selfishness, and a felt need to be around strong and stable adults who were reliable and supportive; they had severe feelings of worry, panic, anger, resentment, withdrawal, failure to cope, regression, and insomnia.

"We were surprised at first to find that many marriages that had been unhappy for the adults had been reasonably comfortable, even gratifying for the children," Wallerstein wrote, "and that very few of the children concurred with their parents' decision or experienced relief at the time of the separation. Five years after the separation, most of the adults approved the divorce decision and only one-fifth of them felt strongly that it had been ill-advised. Among the children, however, over one-half did not regard the divorced family as an improvement over their predivorce family."

The study found that what was poor parenting to begin with remained poor parenting afterward and that the separated father's psychological importance to his children did not decline. Open rejection, even abandonment, on the part of a parent neither dimmed a child's awareness of that parent nor diminished his or her sense of longing. Custody posed serious logistical problems, and both custodial and visiting parent experienced severe disruption of the parenting function from social, psychological, and economic points of view.

The study questioned neither the moral legitimacy of divorce nor the longer-term social and cultural consequences of rising divorce rates; divorce was simply assumed to be a normal event, and the study generated additional ways of helping those affected to cope with the future.

But it was clear that, for the children involved, divorce remained the *central* event of their lives for years afterward.

Unavoidably, many children of divorce undergo therapy. They have been told how to feel and what to think about themselves by therapists who are paid to make everything work out as painlessly as possible for the parents. Divorce means big bucks for therapists, since divorcé(e)s are eager to get back to their own lives, pursuing personal growth and self-fulfillment.

Psychologists also provide the ideology justifying divorce—that it is worse for kids to stay in stressful homes, which provides further incentives for adults to make it as unpleasant as possible there instead of counseling couples toward a reconciliation of their relationship or encouraging the revitalization of their marriage. They naturally become the sworn enemies of guilt. And they create an artificial language for the artificial feelings with which they try to equip children, but they're not really helping the children much at all.

If a third of America's children are now the sons and daughters of divorced parents, then it follows that divorce and resulting family instability are at least one reason behind their falling academic performance in school. In Wallerstein's study, younger children of divorce complained of an inability to concentrate and seemed most vulnerable to the disorganizing effects of family disruption. Frequently teachers were themselves divorced parents and knew the signs of trouble but were often incapable of helping, so preoccupied were they with their own problems. In instances of questionable student behavior, teachers suspected parental difficulties but felt it inappropriate to interfere or even inquire.

James Coleman, a University of Chicago sociologist, noted in his seminal book *High School Achievement* that parents of school-aged children were having less reason to regard raising a family as the central focus of their adult lives. Child rearing, as he observed it in his sample families, had changed and had become merely a brief phase that quickly allowed parents to resume the leisure activities they enjoyed before they had children. This change had dramatic consequences. If studies of school achievement show one thing, it is the importance of the family to student achievement. So if early withdrawal of family attention and involvement is becoming the fate of an increasing fraction of America's youth, it can be expected to have serious social consequences.

In 1980 the National Association of Elementary School Principals published a longitudinal study of the school needs of one-parent families. They found that single-parent children showed lower achievement than their two-parent peers, with only 1 percent ranked as high achievers compared to 30 percent of children from traditional families. Fully 40 percent of single-parent children were ranked as low achievers. Their absence rate was higher, and they were more likely to be subject to disciplinary action. Single-parent children were also more than twice as likely to give up on school entirely. In 1960, 76.3 percent of all students were graduating from high school, but by 1980 only 73.6 percent were.

In 1988 the American Council for Drug Education reported that 100,000 American elementary school children get drunk on a weekly basis. In New York state 16 percent of students in a recent survey said they had tasted liquor before their ninth birthday. A study by the University of Michigan indicated two-thirds of high school seniors had had a drink in the month before the survey, and more than a third had been drunk in the preceding two weeks.

Results of such studies are all the more disquieting considering that American students still proclaim parents to be their primary role models. What this portends for the future of a nation whose social fabric is being ripped apart by family instability may be unclear to American policymakers who now calmly accept as morally legitimate what was considered socially unthinkable a generation ago.

Proclamations about human rights also tend to ring hollow when nearly two-thirds of all American children born in 1984 were expected to be in a one-parent home by their eighteenth birthday; nine out of ten would be in a female-headed household with no father present. It was estimated that one-third of America's white youth and two-thirds of its black children then aged seventeen had spent time during their childhood in a broken family. Projections indicate that by the early 1990s those proportions would rise to 46 percent for whites and 87 percent for blacks.

Every year sixty out of 1,000 American women under eighteen have abortions; in Canada only eighteen do. Fully 40 percent of all American teenage pregnancies end in abortion, by any yardstick a traumatic experience and all the more so for an adolescent. By 1985 the rate of teenage pregnancy in America was ninety-six per thousand of population, highest in the industrialized world. America is the only developed country where the rates of teenage pregnancy have been *increasing.*

In half the states, illegitimate births to women under twenty comprise more than 50 percent of all births. In New Jersey the rate is 71 percent. In Washington, D.C., it is 88 percent. The ideology of freedom and human rights means very little to children who have neither the emotional security nor the family stability on which to build later, healthy lives. The foundation of economic livelihood for America's children is being constructed on quicksand.

In an era when the issues of intergenerational equity loom ever larger, the influence of children, who have neither the ability to organize nor the right to vote, is far outweighed by that of older adults, who have both. Between 1970 and 1983, 65 percent of the increase in the number of children living in poverty in America occurred in single-parent households. Only 38 percent of voters live with a child; put another way, nearly two-thirds of American voters now live with no child in the home, so political issues are more likely to favor the elderly than the young. With increasing numbers of Americans living in childless households, childlessness has replaced the traditional two-parent family as the contemporary version of the American dream: tomorrow is being sacrificed for today.

According to a recent paper by demographer Samuel Preston of the University of Pennsylvania, America's population aged sixty-five or over grew by 54 percent between 1960 and 1980. While federal spending totaled just under $10,000 per capita for the elderly in 1983, the per-capita figure for children was only one-tenth that amount. Fewer than a third of America's divorced children are supported by payments from their biological fathers, which puts tremendous economic stress on the single-parent female. Intensification of marital discord means increasing emotional disturbance of children, Preston concluded, mirroring Wallerstein's findings. And single-parent homes, overwhelmingly headed by females, means patriarchal abdication of responsibility for America's young: deterioration of the nuclear family reflects society's evasion of joint responsibility for its children.

America's antichild ethic, in addition to destroying the family, has also poisoned the American dream of upward mobility. In the past the homeless in America were statistically insignificant and mostly male— itinerant panhandlers, loafers, and bums who clustered around bus stations in large cities looking for handouts and asking for change. But today the chilling fact is that families with small children have become the fastest-growing segment of America's homeless. Nationwide their 1988 numbers total about 2 million, according to the Department of Health and Human Services.

If children of households headed by single female parents account for a third of all children currently being reared in America, they make up about half of all children in poverty. Because two-thirds of divorced fathers contribute nothing toward the economic support of their children, the income of single-parent mothers is deflated by about 70 percent on average. Barely half of all divorced women are awarded any child support, and of the 5 million single mothers who are legally due child support payments, fewer than a third actually receive them.

The breakdown of the family may also be one of the most enduring and irreversible acts of the baby boom generation. According to Landon Jones, author of *Great Expectations,* baby boomers see themselves as free-choosing and self-defining, but the rest of the world sees them merely as a demographic group. By the year 2000 they will comprise nearly 40 percent of America's total population. Jones suggested that a combination of education and affluence would make them a superclass, but the baby boomers grew up with unrealistic and unachievable expectations instead.

"They did not experience the corrective lessons of the past," he wrote. "Isolated by age and education, abetted by television, they were whipsawed between high aspirations and low motivation. They wanted, but were kept by their own numbers from reaching. They had little appreciation for the role of sacrifice and commitment in life. The hope of the sixties, when the generation thought that it just might change the world, turned into a generational malaise of frustration and anxiety. They had expected to be masters of change, but now change had mastered them. The plague of the baby boom was uncertainty."

In less than a generation America's cultural values have changed from a focus on the future to a preoccupation with the present; from the child as priority to the adult as individually self-fulfilled; from a concern for community to love of self; from sacrifice to narcissistic indulgence; from investment saving to consumption spending. Americans can pine over the loss of past values and ask why. But one might better ask how. How can these culturally defeating trends toward divorce, single parenthood, childlessness, family breakdown, and social instability be arrested?

"A considerable part of the new attitudes can be laid at the foot of an ancient capitalist dilemma," Karl Zinsmeister, policy analyst at the American Enterprise Institute, recently wrote in a thoughtful article called "The Family's Tie to the American Dream." "How to absorb the materialistic indulgence capitalism allows, even requires, without extinguishing the forbearing values (like deferral of gratification, investment in the future, and good neighborliness) that made the plenty possible in the first place. One of the traits of the Anglo-Saxons, who gave us capitalism and much of the rest of our culture, was their substitution of the nuclear family for the clan and kinship groups of their predecessors. Now we are seeing further shrinkage of the family universe to the conjugal pair in many instances, to just the self in others. It is not only children that have slipped out of the American dream, but also the attachment to family, kin, and extended social groups."

Child care in America today has become another victim of altered cultural values. In 1950 fewer than 12 percent of American mothers with children under the age of six worked; by 1987 nearly 57 percent of them did. More strikingly, in 1976 only 31 percent of mothers with children under the age of one were in the labor force; by 1988, 51 percent of them were. Today 53 percent of mothers with toddlers and infants work, as do 72 percent of all mothers with preschoolers. As with divorce, what was once unthinkable has become the cultural norm: most women work, not because they want to, but because they have to. Child support payments accrue to only a third of America's single-parent mothers; the average payment is only $2,500 a year. Women have gone to work to maintain two-parent family incomes since only one job in four pays enough to support a family of four comfortably. In 1973 mortgage payments consumed 21 percent of average take-home pay, but by 1984 they took 44 percent. Divorce and a declining living standard have pushed women into the work force.

There are four generally recognized categories of child care. The first and by far the most preferred is known as "family care" and accounts for about 40 percent of all children cared for outside the home. This typically involves a woman in the neighborhood who cares for several children simultaneously in her own home. Perhaps 10 percent of these women are licensed, and standards vary widely. Costs range to about $75 per week per child. "Formal child-care centers," generally licensed by local municipalities, provide another 10 percent of child care required by working mothers. Many of these centers are subsi-

dized; perhaps half of them service poor, single mothers, and the remaining half are private, profit-making institutions that cater to an
upper-middle-class customer base and charge from $100 to $200 per
week per child. Standards, again, are uneven.

A third option for working women is the full-time baby-sitter or
nanny, an alternative that can run $300 per week per child or more
and is out of the reach of all but the professional class. The final category
is called "multiple informal arrangements," whereby working mothers
create a patchwork quilt of help from relatives, neighbors, and paid
sitters. Although nearly half of all child care in America today is arranged in this way, it provides neither a dependable standard nor a
reliable pattern for working mothers, who undergo considerable stress
trying to make the system work. It is not difficult to draw the conclusion
that America's children are being compromised by inadequate child care.

There have been three "waves" of child-care research in America.
The first was in the late 1970s, when researchers studied children under
six years of age in university-related, high-quality programs. They were
curious to see why some children did well and others didn't. The second
wave occurred in the early 1980s, when researchers studied children
less than three years old to examine the same factors. In both age-group
studies, most researchers agreed that children exposed to not more than
twenty hours of high-quality, enduring, nonmaternal child care a week,
with a caretaker/child ratio not exceeding five or six, benefited from
such arrangements. But most agreed that such arrangements constituted
the exception rather than the rule.

More recently the focus of child-care research has shifted to infants,
and the evidence is far from persuasive that infant care is beneficial.
Jay Belsky, professor of human development at Penn State, has highlighted a number of disturbing signs that raise questions about the
advisability of child care for infants.

His review of numerous studies in 1986 showed evidence of insecure
avoidance-attachment patterns among infants subjected to three times
as much nonmaternal child care as their more securely attached counterparts, indicating that avoidance of mothers may be a factor associated
with early substitute child care. But other researchers viewed the results
differently, suggesting that such patterns might be evidence of preco-
cious maturity, since children tend to exhibit independence (or parental
avoidance) as they age anyway.

The uncertainty in interpreting the data forced Belsky to examine further studies about the later behavior of children who had been exposed to extensive infant care, and those results were also not positive. Follow-up studies of preschoolers with prior nonmaternal infant care showed them to be much more physically and verbally aggressive, less cooperative with adults, and less tolerant of frustration. They also displayed significantly less enthusiasm in confronting a challenging task and tended to be less compliant in following their mothers' instructions. Further, those with infant care were more likely to hit, kick, and push than children with no infant care, and they displayed a greater tendency to swear, threaten, and argue.

It is clear that a persuasive *circumstantial* case can be made that early care *may* be associated with increased avoidance, Belsky suggested, possibly to the point of greater insecurity in the attachment relationship, and that such care *may* also be associated with diminished compliance and cooperation with adults, increased aggressiveness, and greater social maladjustment in the preschool and early school-age years. The studies that Belsky reviewed led him to conclude that child care in the first year of life was clearly a "risk factor" for the development of insecure-avoidant attachments in infancy and heightened aggressiveness, non-compliance, and withdrawal later on.

One is tempted to ask whether the practice of infant child care justifies such a potentially serious risk.

I put that question to Belsky when we met in New York recently, and he said, "We simply don't know. We need to do more analysis of the evidence, to see which is clean and which is contestable. Since there may be a potentially higher risk associated with more than twenty hours a week of nonmaternal infant child care, we at least ought to try to find out."

I asked him about the conventional wisdom that suggests that young children are immune to the harmful effects of negative experience.

"We've gone from a view that the child is vulnerable to a view that the child is resilient," he explained. "And that even if something is harmful to the child, such as divorce, it builds character. It's like freedom and responsibility—where's the balance? They're both right, both necessary, and both insufficient in the extreme."

I spoke of the intensive dependence on extended-family relatives in Asia—grandmothers, mothers, and mothers-in-law—for the child-care needs of working mothers, and asked Belsky whether he thought that was a preferable alternative to institutionalizing young children.

"I see no movement in this direction at all in America," he said. "In Asia, and also in Scandinavia and parts of Europe, caretakers are enduring people, not strangers, and there is a high probability of a bloodline relationship. We may ultimately wind up with extended parental leave policies, as Sweden is doing, or moving to flexwork arrangements, with more part-time work options, because one thing we are learning is that women who once worked full-time do not necessarily want to work full-time again after they have children."

I mentioned the Japanese literature that demonstrated mutual dependence as a desired interpersonal goal.

"Americans foster independence," Belsky said, "almost innately. We cut our eyeteeth on independence and individuality. We may have paid a very small psychological penalty for social change in the past, but we may have a cross to bear as social engineers in the future. There are no more oceans to sail, no more motherlands to leave, no more frontiers to tame or conquer. We are now being forced, for virtually the first time in our history, to focus on development *in place*, without moving away from our roots. The future represents a new challenge for us."

How did he view the ongoing debate over child care versus traditional maternal care?

"I don't have any confidence—and I'm an optimist at heart—that we're getting closer to any answers," he said. "We are strikingly avoidant of the key issues. Most child-care arrangements are family day-care homes, too often underground, understaffed, and unlicensed, so we need to foster more child-care networks. Look at it as one spoke of a wheel. It is a system that dramatically needs rewiring, to build in the commitment and the devotion and the *enduring* nature of the adult-child relationship. But part of the problem is ideological—Democrats against Republicans, liberals against conservatives, feminists against traditionalists. We spend more time arguing over our differences than we do trying to find consensus on areas where we agree. This process needs to be transcended, because child care and family stability are national, not ideological, issues."

Edward Zigler is perhaps American's foremost child-care expert. Well into his sixties now, he helped create the Head Start program and currently teaches at Yale.

"The child-care crisis is now nearly twenty years old," he was telling me recently, "and really began in 1971 when President Nixon vetoed the comprehensive Child Development Act. At that time child care was viewed as a welfare mother's problem, not as a mainstream issue, though a third of America's preschoolers had mothers in the work force even then. Today few people realize that the quality of job creation in America has much to do with the issue of child care; the nation has to find a way to create more high-tech jobs and fewer 'hamburger' jobs, which can never support the traditional two-parent family. Socioeconomic status is the underlying issue here."

We talked for a while about the deterioration of the family, and Zigler spoke about the negative implications for children as he saw them.

"There is a growing concern that basic standards of safety in child-care institutions have yet to be defined," he said. "Today, after a decade of debate, America still has no national child-care safety requirements, and that is inexcusable. An increase in child abuse is another problem stemming from family instability. More than 2,000 children die of child abuse every year in this country. And with the number of latchkey children rising—it's over 5 million now—accidents at home have become the number one killer of children. The United States has the highest rate of any country for accidental death due to firearms for children between the ages of five and fourteen, for example, and it is estimated that two-thirds of all fires at home are started by unsupervised children playing with matches. These are not healthy developments for the future of our society."

As we spoke, Congress was debating two bills that had framed the federal response to child care, each crystallizing around partisan politics. One was a $2.5 billion measure called the Alliance for Better Child Care, known as the "ABC Bill," sponsored by Senator Christopher Dodd of Connecticut and Representative Dale Kildee of Michigan, both Democrats. It would increase federal spending for low- and moderate-income families, set child-care regulations and standards, and create a social services bureaucracy to monitor compliance. The other was a $250 million proposal called the Hatch/Johnson Bill, named for Senator Orrin Hatch of Utah and Representative Nancy Johnson of Connecticut, both Republicans, which would channel block grants to states and create tax credits for employers that set up their own facilities.

"We have all the knowledge necessary to provide absolutely first-class child care in this country," Zigler said. "What's missing is the political commitment and the national will. The American people have to be convinced that child care is not just a baby-sitting service, but a social environment in which their children will develop for a significant proportion of their young lives. For a child, child care is an everyday, year-long phenomenon. But no country can solve a social problem of this magnitude unless there is a widespread consensus that the problem exists. Demographics drive social policy, and politics has yet to catch up with demographics."

While few would begrudge women the gains they have made in the past two decades, many observers have criticized the feminist movement as being part of the problem rather than part of the solution. "The feminists made one gigantic mistake," Sylvia Hewlett wrote in a perceptive account of the woman's liberation movement called *A Lesser Life*. "They assumed that modern women wanted nothing to do with children. As a result, they have consistently failed to incorporate the bearing and rearing of children into their vision of a liberated life."

The only exception to the continued trend of motherhood, Hewlett noted, was a statistically insignificant fraction of American women, the "elite professionals," quintessential Yuppies who became bankers and accountants and lawyers and symbolized the unisex role, with a media impact far exceeding their numbers or their importance. (Twenty percent of them remain childless, but even those with children find that their careers have become bifurcated: the traditional "fast track" to vice president or partner for men and childless women, the "mommy track" with lower pay and slower advancement for mothers.)

"The real victims of our lack of public child care and job-protected maternity leave," Sylvia Hewlett concluded, "are working-class women and their children. A vice president of the Chase Manhattan Bank might have a rough time when she attempts to breast-feed without missing a beat at work, but Chase has a decent maternity policy (by American standards), and the odds are she can afford to pay market rates for a full-time baby-sitter. But for fast-food waitresses, secretaries, or retail clerks, the consequences of our lack of support policies are more severe. Most of them have no rights to maternity leave, and they can't afford adequate child care. Tell them that America is a nation that venerates mothers and children, and they will tell you a different tale."

Dual professional careers for America's elite point out another problem, however, and that is the negligence of fatherhood. If both mother and father increasingly work full-time, sixty hours a week or more, who is looking after the children? Nannies and baby-sitters, to be sure, but even when working professionals can afford high-quality full-time child care, does society stop to ask whether this is right for the child, whose time with parents is limited to precious minutes in the evening and catch-as-catch-can on weekends? Instead of being slaves to their family, today's parents have become slaves to their employers.

So "quality time" has become the modern equivalent of snake oil. Any parent knows, intuitively and deep down, that it is the *quantity* of time he or she spends with a child and the variety of different moods and temperaments and rhythms of that time that are most important. Children bear the brunt of being accommodating in all these arrangements. They say good night to Mom and Dad on the phone instead of having books read, getting hugs, and being tucked in. They eat dinner with the nanny instead of with their parents. They tell their school stories to the baby-sitter.

Parenting is a two-person job; it entails a strong process of role modeling for the children. The lessons learned by the children of America's dual-career professional elites, who work because they want to, are that a son or a daughter is not the most important person in the world, that it's *okay* to be a part-time parent, that neglect is normal. For the children of America's two-income working-class couples, who work because they have to, the lessons learned are that their choices will be few; therefore their expectations are uncommonly low. Either way, is this pattern for America's future children one that society would consciously condone?

"The inharmoniousness of final ends finds its most concrete expression in the female career, which is now the same as the male career," Allan Bloom wrote. "There are two equal careers in almost every household composed of educated persons under thirty-five. And those careers are not mere means to family ends, they are personal fulfillments. The result is that both marriage and career are devalued. The feminist response that justice requires equal sharing of all domestic responsibility by men and women is not a solution, but only a compromise, an attenuation of men's dedication to their careers and of women's to family, with arguably an enrichment in diversity of both parties but just as arguably a fragmentation of their lives. Moreover, this compromise does not decide anything about the care of the children. Previously, children at least had the unqualified dedication of one person, the woman, for whom their care was the most important thing in life. Is half the attention of two the same as the whole attention of one? And is this not a formula for neglect?"

In recent years Americans have been fascinated by the phenomenon of hardworking Asian immigrant groups. They bring valuable professional and entrepreneurial skills to America, and their children score well on tests of academic achievement and aptitude. They have become known as America's perfect minority. But recent studies suggest that those social and economic pressures in the American environment that have contributed to a deterioration of the American family have resulted in a breakdown of the traditional Asian family too. The plant does not always survive the transplanting.

For the first time in nearly a century legal immigration to the United States during the decade of the 1980s will equal or exceed the record of 8.7 million immigrants who settled in America between 1901 and 1910. Then, about 85 percent of all legal immigrants came from Europe; today 85 percent come from Asia and Latin America, with Asians the single largest subgroup, more than half the total. Six states have gained sixteen congressional seats strictly due to immigration; since 1950 California alone has added six, Florida two. Two-thirds of all immigrants tend to settle in or around one of four major American cities: New York, Los Angeles, Chicago, and Miami.

In Los Angeles, sociologist Eui-young Yu recently documented a case involving eighty-six Korean adolescents aged twelve to twenty-one, all of whom had problems in school that led to delinquent behavior and violent gang activity. These children, as with so many of their American counterparts, had become victims of dysfunctional, pathological family lives. They had also experienced a severe conflict of values, given the excessive work patterns of their parents.

In New York, Queens College sociologist Pyong-gap Min recently highlighted the problems of Korean immigrant entrepreneurs in a study of 557 self-employed Korean businessmen. Nearly all were engaged in small businesses; most had achieved what the American media would define as success: survival, modest growth, and a decent living. One reason for their success was their long workweeks averaging sixty hours. They suffered from boredom, depression, lack of sleep, and overwork. They were often in physical danger because their shops are located in low-income areas where robberies and shoplifting are recurrent problems and subject to boycotts by minority customers because of their strong business orientation and high energy levels. They were also subject to discrimination by their landlords, who raised rents sharply when they saw the Koreans' business begin to thrive, and subject to harassment by suppliers, who often delayed deliveries and engaged in price-gouging. The children of these Korean immigrant entrepreneurs consequently experienced many of the same problems other Americans do: parental neglect, severely disrupted families, stressful homes.

Won-moo Hurh, a thoughtful, soft-spoken sociologist who teaches at Southern Illinois, did a comparable study of 622 Korean immigrants in 1987 in Chicago and came up with similar findings. When I spoke with him about this, he said, "We found that a majority of the working wives still performed ordinary household tasks and that fewer than 10 percent of the immigrant men did. But we also found that these tasks had been shifted increasingly to children rather than to husbands."

Hurh, who is married to an American woman, said that the traditional Korean family structure obligated the wife to seek temporary work but not long-term employment. His study found that the additional income justified neither the extra work involved nor its negative impact on children.

"I told my mother, years ago, that I intended to marry an American," he said laughingly. "She said if I did, I would no longer be a son of hers and would pollute our ancestral blood. Needless to say, her views have changed. But the longer-term problem I see in assimilating Korean children into American society is that they may adopt the worst characteristics of each culture: the male chauvinism of Korean men and the full-time career orientation of American women."

If increased rates of divorce, parental neglect, homelessness, working mothers, infant care, child care, and child stress have come to characterize a deterioration of the traditional two-parent American family, which has put the nation's children at risk, then the rising use of illegal drugs may well be a barometer of even broader social instability. Drugs are an acid that is slowly eating away the infrastructure of American society, a catalyst that simultaneously accelerates the rates of crime, violence, and social unrest. Historically we know that increased rates of drug use by an ever-larger percentage of a nation's population lead, over time, to gradual decreases in productivity, life expectancy, and health, all culminating eventually in systemic decline.

In the Moslem world, in the fifteenth century, when prohibitions against cannabis were repealed, a large number of people from all levels of society soon reached a state of constant intoxication. In Peru, following conquest by the Spanish in the sixteenth century, the Incas became addicted to coca leaves, which they chewed daily, and remained in continuous states of low-grade intoxication, as they do to this day. In China, in the mid-nineteenth century, Britain forced opium use on the Chinese; by the turn of the century more than 90 million were addicted, and it would take the Chinese a good fifty years to curtail the practice. In England, in the mid-twentieth century, heroin use was legalized, a practice that seemed to work well as long as the number of addicts was small, but by 1985 they had mushroomed to an estimated 85,000.

Only in East Asia today does one find widespread, unilateral constraints against illicit drug use, coupled with harsh penalties, strict interdiction, and unyielding enforcement—legitimized and, one might argue, successful because of the more authoritarian political systems. In a recent poll roughly half of all Americans questioned believed supply to be the principal problem, and the other half demand; combined, they were both right. In another poll a near majority identified drug trafficking as America's primary international problem, way ahead of arms control, terrorism, and unrest in the Middle East or Central America. But the nation has yet to use the one harsh tactic that outshadows all the rest in terms of its success rate, and that is the death penalty upon conviction for either dealing or possession.

Federal spending on drug enforcement techniques has trebled since 1981 under the government's "zero tolerance" program, but with little end effect: corruption of law enforcement officials has become part of the problem, so prevalent and so generous are the payoffs. Eradication of coca plants in Latin America (notably, Colombia, Bolivia, and Peru) has resulted in destruction of less than 5 percent of total acreage; production continues to rise, peaking at nearly 250,000 tons in 1988. Drug traffickers are richer, better armed, and control larger armies than the national governments in which the drugs are grown.

Nearly two-thirds of all cocaine enters the United States by air, by far the easiest means of penetration. Only a tiny fraction of total supply is ever interdicted; in 1987 a "mere" thirty tons. But an estimated 6 million Americans need illicit drugs and are willing to pay $140 billion a year to support a habit that cannot be controlled—nearly three times the cost of the nation's imported oil. The current drug of choice, cocaine, is an invisible import into an insatiable market.

Cocaine and its especially caustic derivative, crack, are further corroding America's poor and working-class families, whose fathers are already absent, whose mothers quit their poor-paying jobs to disappear into the streets, where they can earn $3,000 a day instead of $12,000 a year, and whose children stretch an already overburdened public foster-care system. The lives of all of them have been reduced to a threshold of vanishing expectations—the role model has simply become inoperative. The disease has come full circle, to the point where the virus infects the working-class poor and poisons the lives of the rich and the famous, creating conditions of social and cultural apartheid.

It bears repeating, but if Americans continue to regard divorce as morally legitimate, except perhaps in instances of proven emotional instability, physical abuse, or drug and alcohol addiction, then both child-care reforms and workplace innovations will represent only temporary solutions to the nation's urgent social problem of family deterioration. Indeed a fresh look at marriage and incentives to keep two-parent families together, including ways of coping with supposed incompatibility, may be necessary to cure the social disease of divorce; this may necessitate coming back, in culturally acceptable ways, to a workable concept of role differentiation between the sexes and away from the more destructive role confusion of the recent past.

Equally important are incentives that build greater flexibility into the workplace so parents are not forced to make a simple either-or decision between working full-time and parenting full-time, a decision that discriminates against working women if they are forced to abandon their children to institutional child-care arrangements or to abandon their jobs entirely when they have children. For most women, given the incidence of divorce and single parenthood in America, job abandonment is a distinct impossibility.

Still, America has become progressively antichild and increasingly antifamily. Margaret Mead perhaps put it best of all when she said, "As the family goes, so goes the nation."

16
THE VIRTUALLY EXTINCT AMERICAN FAMILY: CAN IT BE REVITALIZED?

The most important moral and legal rule concerning the physiological side of kinship is that no child should be brought into the world without a man—and one man, at that—assuming the role of sociological father; that is, guardian and protector, the male link between the child and the rest of the community. This generalization amounts to a universal sociological law, and as such I have called it the principle of legitimacy. The form which it assumes varies according to the laxity or stringency which obtains regarding prenuptial intercourse; the value set upon virginity or the contempt for it; and above all, whether the child is a burden or an asset to its parents.

Yet through all these variations, the father is indispensable for the full sociological status of the child as well as of its mother: the group consisting solely of a woman and her offspring is sociologically incomplete and illegitimate. The father, in other words, is necessary for the full legal status of the family.

Bronislaw Malinowski, *Sex, Culture, and Myth*

"In the early nineteenth century," Bonnie Maslin said to me, "when life expectancy was short, it was not unreasonable for the marriage vow to say, 'till death do us part.' But today, the vow has more frequently become, 'till divorce do us part.' "

Bonnie Maslin is a nationally known marital therapist and the author of *Not Quite Paradise*, a recent book about "marital gridlock" that shows couples how to identify and be comfortable with different languages of love. We were sitting in her Park Avenue office talking about the state of American marriage.

"It's not that marriages suffer from too little, but from too much," she said. "We expect too much from one person. We want our spouse

347

to be lover, confidant, friend, household manager, provider, parent, and career adviser, all rolled into one. It's unreasonable. The man still expects and needs more from the woman, and for him the wife is usually his *only* intimate relationship. We have to realize there are different styles between men and women, and they need to recognize and understand those differences."

Years earlier, Celia Halas had written an incisive account of these fundamental differences called *Why Can't a Woman Be More Like a Man?* In it she analyzed quite brilliantly the twenty or so questions men most frequently ask about women in an attempt to help men understand why women *can't* be more like men. Clinging, Halas noted, is a perennial problem men have with women.

"I explain to everyone who will listen," she wrote, "that the elements of a healthy relationship include three distinct yet overlapping parts: one is the life I lead that is independent of you, another is your life that is independent of me, and the third is the life that we share with each other. When each one of us has a productive life in his or her own area, we bring fresh experiences and self-esteem to the part of our lives that we share. If we live together constantly and develop no identities away from each other, we have little to share and soon feel stale when we are together."

I asked Bonnie Maslin what, in her view, made it so difficult for American men and women to accept different styles in each other.

"In America the mother is viewed as all-providing," she said, "and the early years are spent weaning a child from its mother's omnipotence, pushing it into independence practically from birth. Love in our culture is about getting *back* to that material bliss, to wanting everything from that one person, and that creates problems. In part that's also because American culture is very individualistic in nature. Our materialism, our consumerism, our narcissism force us to separate early from our families. Having been cast out, we learn to be self-sufficient, disconnected, separate. As a consequence, it is very hard for us to build a sense of interdependence."

We talked for a while about interdependence, and then I asked how she viewed the issue of child care as it related to children of divorce.

"The one-income family is a luxury of the past," she said. "Two-income families have become a necessity in this country. This creates a whole series of problems. A third of all kids under the age of eighteen will live with a single parent, and two-thirds of all divorced fathers pay little or no alimony. And if children have very little advocacy in America, poor children have none. So the price we pay for all this individual, self-centered pleasure is virtual punishment for the neglect of our kids."

We talked about divorce, and I asked whether, in her experience, divorce created more problems than it solved. Did America make it too easy for couples to divorce?

"Margaret Mead used to say that instead of making divorce more difficult, we ought to make getting married more difficult. Divorce was previously seen as a solution to marital difficulties, but now I think it's seen as part of the problem. Singlehood had a halo around it for a long time. But the *tendency* to divorce is still a problem, and there is no question that divorce leaves an indelible mark on children and becomes the central emotional event of their lives. Americans rarely view divorce and marital stress from a child's point of view. Child advocacy is not a cultural priority in America—we're not a child-centered culture. Where Asian societies tend to protect their children, we tend to make them vulnerable."

The rising incidence of divorce in America has produced an entire industry of professionals who specialize in terminating relationships, from psychologists who help separating adults justify the termination to lawyers who make it all legal. One person who began to study the beginnings of relationships was Maggie Scarf, a well-known writer on psychology and the author of *Intimate Partners*. It bothered her that "there was so much attention being given to the *endings* of attachments, and less to the important questions of how they form and how to go about maintaining them." Since most divorces statistically occur within two years of marriage, the reasonable conclusion was that marriages might be better off if the partners knew more about each other *before* they tied the knot.

In conducting her research, Scarf made use of an interviewing device known as a genogram, a very detailed chart that diagrams the important emotional attachments in the lives of each marital partner: parents, grandparents, stepparents, and siblings. Interaction among generations is charted carefully to gain fuller knowledge of the emotional setting within which a husband and a wife learn the rules, the expectations, and the assumptions about their interpersonal behavior. "Genograms provide a systematic way of looking at the family subculture in which each partner was reared," Scarf wrote, "and discerning those repetitive patterns of behavior which have been brought forward from the past and resurrected in the marriage of the present."

Scarf found that American marriages tended to be overwhelmingly *love-object*–centered, rather than goal-centered: the spouse as an individual was the focus of attention, rather than children who extend a marriage into a family by enriching past traditions or continuing a family line. She found many emotional themes and sequences present in earlier generations that tended to repeat in later ones: patterns of dominance and submission, pain and pleasure, projective identification, role playing, and birth order (when two first children marry, for example, it is almost a surefire formula for conflict). These are repetitive themes and patterns that need to be better understood before people marry.

In addition to helping couples understand more about where they are coming from, Scarf also shed valuable light on where they are in the present and where the marital relationship may go in the future. She outlined a number of purposeful tasks couples can undertake, such as "talking and listening," whereby one partner talks, uninterrupted, for thirty minutes about what is on his or her mind and the other simply listens, and "odd day, even day," whereby couples share control on alternate days rather than continually fighting every day about who is in charge. She looked at sexual problems as well as emotional problems; she included a long discussion of the child-launching years and their impact on marriage; and she analyzed the five basic levels on which couples relate.

At the Olympian level of integration, autonomy and intimacy are experienced as integrated aspects of each partner's personhood and of the relationship that the two of them share; autonomy and intimacy are perceived as states of being, not as linear positions of distance. The relationship becomes mutually self-supporting.

A primary resource for Scarf was Stuart Johnson, the former director of family therapy at the Yale Psychiatric Institute in New Haven. Today Johnson runs an active private practice and is considered one of the best marital therapists in the area. He is a rotund, pipe-smoking man in his early fifties and avuncular, with a distinctly open and friendly manner.

"Major shifts in marriage and family stability occur primarily during and after wars," he told me. "Genealogical research tells us that men were married on average between two and four times in their lives from the seventeenth through the nineteenth centuries, because of the high mortality rate of women after childbirth. Regional differences also played a role. But in the old marriages role differentiation was clearly fixed. Our culture has put a premium on upward social and economic movement, and there can be real tyranny in that model."

On the back of his office door Johnson has a sign in full view of his patients. "I know you believe you understand what you think I said," it reads, "but I am not sure you realize that what you heard is not what I meant."

Since Johnson had mentioned social movement in America, we talked for a while about mobility as a factor in marital breakdown.

"The interesting thing," he said, "is that there are striking numbers of adult kids now living at home with their parents. This reflects not only housing costs and job quality, but is also a reaction to mobility. America has been built on mobility, from the Pilgrims to the westward expansion to the tremendous transience evident in corporate transfers today. This is especially hard on young children, who are pushed early into highly structured and organized lives—every minute is filled with some kind of activity, and there is less and less time for simple play. But now America has no more frontiers; we're being confronted with a major challenge, which other cultures have had to face far longer, and that is development in place."

The phrase was the exact one Belsky had used earlier, a striking coincidence. I asked Johnson if he saw a declining trend toward divorce.

"I think we're beginning to move beyond easy divorce as a solution," he said, refilling an old pipe. "More people are recognizing that divorce is part of the problem now, because they re-create old patterns with a new mate without having learned how to resolve them first. We're also learning that couples therapy is better than individual therapy; when just one spouse is in treatment, it puts more stress on the marriage and the relationship shifts. Married people need to look at their relationship periodically and retool it, or remodel it, if it isn't working. Otherwise chronic conflict sets in, and that's never good."

Anger, which is often driven by unresolved conflict in marriage, is an emotion most American couples have major problems with, and the inability to resolve conflict constructively leads, in many instances, to irreconcilable differences. American women are taught by their culture not to display anger overtly, because it is thought to be unladylike; when women become angry, they tend to cry, in part due to cultural constraints on their ability to vent anger more directly. But American men are taught from birth that it is quite all right to show anger, and they grow up doing just that: swearing and shouting, pounding fists, and slamming rackets, doors, or tools. From time immemorial man and woman have had a difficult time relating to each other, which is one reason our classical literature is full of stories about men and women quarreling. But the contemporary American couple seems somehow unable to honor the marital vow of commitment, sacrifice, and resolution.

These differences are taught in very subtle ways. In popular children's stories, for example, men are always shown getting angry, but women rarely are. The gods in fairy tales rage and thunder, men shout and stomp and fume, but goddesses tend to pine or sigh, and women just cry. A wonderful book by Ann McGovern, *Too Much Noise*, makes this point tellingly. In it, a man named Peter lives by himself in a quiet little house with a bed that squeaks, a floor that creaks, and a teakettle that whistles on the stove. (My four-year-old, Peter, has a special fondness for this tale.) Because of the noise, the old man can't sleep, so he makes numerous visits to the village elder, who tells him to get a cow, a sheep, a donkey, a chicken, a dog, and a cat, in that order.

Page by page, and animal by additional animal, Peter is driven slowly crazy as the noise level escalates. Finally the old boy *gets angry*. He goes back to the village elder, pounds his fist on the wise man's desk, and shouts for the eighth time that there is too much noise. The wise man shrewdly counsels him to get rid of all the animals now, and the house suddenly becomes quiet again. A story about relative noise tolerance on the conscious level teaches quite another lesson about emotions—and their ability to control people—on the preconscious level.

Men who feel extremely uncomfortable with the expression of emotion in women often say they allow the expression of emotion—especially tears—to control them. Women are often accused of using tears to manipulate, although in my experience that's generally not true. Tears result from women's frustration or anger, which is the emotion most frequently expressed, most commonly felt, and has the greatest impact on controlling others. But women express anger far less frequently than men, who are reasonably careless about the problems it causes for others.

Sex is another major source of conflict, leading often to irreconcilability. While tomes have been written about this subject, and quite famous ones too, intimate *intra*marital sex is something many Americans still have difficulty achieving, despite the fact that America is by any standard the most sexually permissive society in the world. Deep down, however, American society is also hypocritical, a characteristic that stems in part from its Puritanical origins. America's continued resistance to legalizing prostitution, for example, means an unavoidable continuation of uncontrolled crime and sexually transmitted disease (all the more dangerous with a new epidemic, AIDS). And extramarital affairs, though quite the cultural norm, reinforce a dangerous process of marital deception and mistrust. Unconstrained by Christianity, Asian cultures have a more tolerant view of sex than America does; again, marital expectations are lower and the frustrations fewer, but appropriately controlled outlets are condoned and strictly monitored, from Turkish baths to love hotels. And mistresses, an established practice in old Europe, are still a favored tradition in Japan.

Jane Wagner, the author of *The Search for Signs of Intelligent Life in the Universe*, a masterful theatrical commentary on contemporary American life (and played to perfection on Broadway by Lily Tomlin), offered one tongue-in-cheek solution to the problem of sex in America.

> I wanted to improve the sex lives of suburban housewives. You'd never suspect I was a semi-nonorgasmic woman. Meaning, it's possible to have an orgasm but highly unlikely. And then along came *Good Vibrations*. Now I'm a regular Cat on a Hot Tin Roof.
>
> As a love object it surpasses my husband Harold by a country mile. But this is no threat to the family unit. Think of it as a kind of Hamburger Helper for the boudoir.
>
> Can you afford one, you say? Can you afford *not* to have one, I say. The time it saves alone is worth the price. I'd rank it up there with Minute Rice, Reddi-Wip, & Pop-Tarts. Ladies, it simply takes the guesswork out of making love.
>
> But doesn't it kill romance, you ask? What doesn't, I say. So what'll it be, the deluxe model or this handy purse-sized model for the lady on the go? It fits anywhere, and comes with a silencer to avoid curious onlookers.
>
> What about guilt, you ask? That did cross my mind. I used to feel guilty using a cake mix instead of baking from scratch. I learned to live with that, and I can learn to live with this.

In the past, when marital problems arose, *individuals* were treated, but the problems remained. Then family therapy evolved, as therapists realized that problems had to be looked at *systemically* within the marriage and the family itself. In short, the marriage became the patient. A number of important and fascinating discoveries were made along the way, each of which contributed to a better understanding of what makes strong, healthy families.

A pioneer in family research was Herbert Otto, a psychologist at the University of Utah in the early 1960s. He devised programs that enabled families to develop essential strengths already present, rather than to focus on pathological problems. His research isolated several key items essential to developing a network of family strengths; among them were shared values, common purpose and goals, and love and happiness of children. The ability of a family to grow *with and through children* was a frequently recurring theme.

Some years later, Robert Hill, director of research for the National Urban League, published a report called *The Strengths of Black Families*, based in part on the research pioneered by Otto. This was the first systematic, empirical refutation of commonly held misperceptions about black families—namely, that they were characterized by instability, criminality, delinquency, and drug addiction. He isolated the core strengths in black families that were functional in their survival, development, and stability: strong kinship bonds, a strong work orientation, a strong achievement orientation, and firm religious beliefs.

In the mid-1970s Nick Stinnett and his colleagues at Oklahoma State University evaluated the responses of 180 families in seventy-seven Oklahoma counties. From their analysis they found six characteristics that accounted for the success, happiness, and stability of these families: appreciation, spending time together, good communication patterns, commitment, closeness to children, and an ability to deal with crises in a positive manner. One of the most amazing things about his research was that these six qualities were mentioned time and time again. Not every family mentioned all six, but the pattern became apparent. Of the variables, the most frequently mentioned, with a response rate of 88.9 percent, was closeness to children.

Researchers David Kantor and William Lehr at the Cambridge Family Institute began asking basic questions about healthy family systems, but instead of sending out questionnaires, they actually went into the homes of twenty-nine urban and suburban Boston families. They placed microphones in every room to record verbal communication among family members, conducted three sets of interviews, and administered thematic apperception tests for all family members. They isolated six dimensions of a strong family process that created cooperative as opposed to competitive conditions: three were physical (space, time, and energy) and three emotional (intimacy and nurturance; power, or the ability to achieve what the family wants; and shared values and goals).

Another major study of healthy families, which exemplified the shift from individual to family therapy, was completed by Jerry Lewis and Robert Beavers at the Timberlawn Foundation in Dallas. The Timberlawn team focused on "family interactional variables" through both individual observations and self-reports. The study was conducted with a pilot sample of twelve "patient" families and a control group of eleven "nonpatient" families. A series of videotaped family interactions was evaluated by clinical professionals who did not know which families belonged to which subgroup. Their findings showed that healthy families were more likely to demonstrate a structure of shared leadership, and the parental coalition was clear. Closeness was obvious. They demonstrated skill in effective negotiation, were clear in their expressions of thoughts and feelings, accepted responsibility for their actions, and were openly expressive.

Importantly, the Lewis and Beavers study showed that children from the two groups of families were *more alike than different*. With rare exception, they appeared psychologically healthy, were mastering age-appropriate developmental tasks, developing significant interpersonal skills, and accomplishing academic goals. This finding alone had major implications for the conventional wisdom that children of nonoptimal or unhappy families were better off if their parents divorced than if they remained married.

A final contribution to healthy family research was made by David Olson and Hamilton McCubbin at the University of Minnesota. They studied normal families in all stages of development and structured their research around five themes: family types, family resources, stress and change, family coping, and family satisfaction. They sampled 1,140 families with a goal of having at least a hundred families in each of seven "stages of development": just married, no children; families with preschool children; families with school-age children; families with adolescents; launching families (children leaving home); empty nest families; and families in retirement. Two major internal "coping strategies" emerged as characteristic of the healthy families: reframing, defined as the ability to regard stressor events as a challenge that can be overcome; and passive appraisal, a strategy whereby a stressor event is regarded as something that will take care of itself over time. One key, Olson and McCubbin found, was that healthy families used different coping strategies at different stages of the family cycle; another was the fact that healthy families always had a *variety* of strategies to use, were aware (though not always consciously) of what they were, and used them.

What these various research studies of American families all clearly showed, it seemed to me, was that in order for families to remain strong and healthy they had to have incentives to *stay together;* in most instances, those incentives revolved around children.

Arguably the most significant piece of legislation ever enacted in the United States was the tax code stemming from the Sixteenth Amendment to the Constitution that made interest payments on money borrowed to purchase a home tax-deductible. Home ownership was determined to be a desirable national priority for all Americans, so the government created a disaggregated incentive to make this possible. That incentive became a primary ingredient for the fulfillment of the American dream.

Families are, or should be, a similarly desirable national priority for America. And similarly, the government can create more incentives to help them stay together. It once did.

In 1948 the median income for an American family of four was $3,468, and the threshold for federal income taxes that year was $2,667 (the $600 personal exemption, times four, plus the $267 standard deduction). The ultimate effect of this incentive was that *more than three-fourths* of the median family income was exempt from federal tax. This was, in effect, a powerful national family policy.

It costs a lot of money to raise a family—an average of about $85,000 per child through age eighteen—so *in the past* the federal government did not tax most of the income necessary to support a family. But in 1983 the median income for a family of four was $29,184, and the federal income tax threshold had risen to only $8,783, which meant that *less than a third* of median family income was now exempt from tax.

The central point here is that if the personal exemption today were the equivalent of what it was in 1948, it would be close to $6,000 rather than the $1,900 it is now. Tax policy does not normally treat such questions, because children are considered a consumption good, not an investment in the nation's future. To the extent that such thinking is reflected in *tax* policy, it becomes a part of the government's *family* policy.

"We do not know the processes of social change well enough to be able confidently to predict them, far less to affect them," Senator Pat Moynihan wrote in *Family and Nation.* "What we do know is what we generally value as a society and what we generally think is conducive to the things we value. We value self-sufficiency. We are offended by poverty. It follows that we should not tax individuals, much less families, to the point where they are officially poor and potentially dependent. We now do that. Would recent trends in family structure change if we stopped doing it, or if we did it to a lesser degree? We don't know. But it is not necessary to know. We can agree that we are not so much changing things as restoring what was once in place, remembering answers we once thought obvious."

We now know, from considerable social science research, that divorce in America is creating larger numbers of single-parent families; that it creates incalculable emotional problems for children; that more than half the children born in the 1970s and after may spend much of their youth in female-headed households; that the burden of American poverty is borne disproportionately by women and children; that only 10 percent of divorced fathers make alimony payments to their former wives; and that the standard of living of divorced fathers rises on average 42 percent after divorce, while that of divorced mothers falls on average 73 percent.

A disaggregated tax code that provided incentives to families to encourage them to stay together, in the form of targeted tax exemptions and higher levels of personal deductions, and simultaneously imposed *dis*incentives on divorced fathers—whether by levying a national "divorce" tax on their income or requiring a fixed percentage of their income to be withheld at source and paid into an escrow account on behalf of their children—could be a powerful social policy tool with enormous benefits for the American family, to keep it intact rather than letting it continue to disintegrate. For until America can establish the kind of national commitment to healthy family life that is characteristic of Asian cultures because of their longer historical and cultural traditions, tax policy may have to play a larger role.

New legislation proposed by Senator Moynihan, called the Family Security Act, was passed by Congress in 1988. It replaced the fifty-year-old Aid to Families with Dependent Children (AFDC) program.

Under the new act absent parents required to pay child support after the bill becomes law will have child support payments withheld automatically from their paychecks. Any absent parent who must pay child support under conditions imposed prior to enactment of the new law and who falls behind by more than thirty days will also be subject to the new withholding requirement. The new bill also requires that all recipients of cash assistance with children three years old or older participate in a job program.

"Simply put," Moynihan said at the time the new legislation was passed, "this bill turns the present family welfare system on its head. Rather than beginning with a public assistance payment that is supplemented by sporadic child support payments and occasional earned income, the bill places responsibility for supporting children where it has always belonged: with parents. *Both* parents."

Half a century ago, when AFDC started, one or both parents of half the children receiving assistance were dead. By the early 1940s the ratio had dropped to below one-quarter. Today only a handful of welfare families are needy because of a deceased husband; in nearly half of all welfare families there has never been a husband to begin with. According to projections by the Bureau of the Census, of a net 13 million families to be added during the last two decades of this century, *fewer than half* will be traditional two-parent families. Put another way, female-headed families are increasing at more than five times the rate of husband-wife families. In less than two generations single-parent families will have doubled.

"The central conservative truth is that culture, not politics, determines the success of a society," Moynihan wrote in *Family and Nation*. "The central liberal truth is that politics can change a culture and save it from itself. Nothing warrants optimism. The larger social system will not work without important inputs from the family; if all individuals calculate only what is best for each person, then the integration of society will falter."

Conventional political rhetoric has it that the quality of a civilization may be measured by how it cares for its elderly. But just as surely, the future of a society may be forecast by how it cares for its young.

The positive elements of tax disaggregation that attempt to restore dual parental responsibility in welfare reform have been lacking in current attempts at child-care reform. Washington's leading child-care proposal, the Dodd/Kildee ABC Bill, called "designer label" legislation because of its expensive price tag of $2.5 billion, merely expands the federal bureaucracy's involvement in child care as opposed to offering a system of tax credits disaggregated by either family status or income.

Washington already spends $7 billion directly for child-care activities, through Title XX, Head Start, child nutrition programs, and AFDC. Only a minor portion of the ABC funds would support development of national child-care standards; most of its funding is intended to subsidize state bureaucracies within narrowly prescribed federal rules. Estimates of the bill's eventual annual cost when fully implemented range from $75 billion to $100 billion.

In an era of shrinking tax revenues and a spendthrift Congress, America has to ask how it can afford to fund such an extravagant bill. It also has to ask whether further expansion of an already oversized and inefficient federal bureaucracy is a desirable social goal. Asian countries tend not to be so top-heavy, despite their reputation for large central governments. With only half the population of America, Japan uses just *one-tenth* the number of people to administer its health, education, and human services bureaucracy.

Ideally tax disaggregation as a tool of social policy can be used to reverse the trend toward single-parent families and prevent more two-parent families from being taxed into the work force. But if, as a culture, America treats single-parent families as the rule rather than the exception, high-quality child care must somehow be regarded as a social priority. As with public education, a system that emphasizes *incentives and choice*, rather than simply adding more layers to an already over-layered bureaucracy, ought to be the system of preference for America's policymakers.

Some experts, notably Lawrence Lindsey at Harvard, have proposed a system of child-care tax credits that targets single-parent and low-income families as beneficiaries by further disaggregating the dependent care tax credit already in existence. This tax credit keeps the vital child-care choice directly with parents, not with bureaucrats; it wastes no money in administrative costs; and it can be targeted to those most in need. Lindsey has estimated that in 1988, 43 percent of this credit went to families making more than $50,000 and only 23 percent to families earning less than $20,000.

He suggests three changes: that the tax credit be made refundable, since it is currently worthless unless a family has taxable income, which discriminates against most low-income families; that the aggregate be increased; and that single-parent families be targeted. Implementing these three changes, according to his calculations, would not only cost the government less than the ABC Bill; it would also disaggregate the money where it is most needed: families earning less than $30,000 would receive 88 percent of the funds and single-parent families 76 percent.

"There is simply no way the ABC Bill, with its monstrous administrative overhead and complex regulations," Lindsey has said, "can match these support levels or this degree of distributional equity."

The crucial question of who will care for America's children and who should decide on that care—parents or the state—is an ideological issue separating liberals and conservatives of both parties. It is also a fundamental concern of both working and nonworking parents and directly impacts choice.

"We have to be careful that any legislation intended to address America's child-care needs does not penalize the mother who stays at home," Gerry Regier, former president of the Family Research Council, told me. The council is a nonprofit, bipartisan Washington-based research group.

"Despite increases in maternal employment," he said, "the number of children cared for at home by their mothers remains surprisingly high—more than 50 percent under the age of five, according to recent census data. Economic circumstances permitting, I think most Americans would prefer to keep child care in the family. While some research suggests many parents would enroll their children in group care if it were more affordable, other data show that more working mothers would prefer to stay at home with their children if it weren't for severe economic constraints. In other words, alleviating financial pressures on families with children would undoubtedly spur some movement in both directions, which is why it is important to provide stay-at-home mothers with any tax credits to be legislated."

Legislation that strengthens federal control over social issues should be treated as a powerful drug; not used at all, if possible, and no more than absolutely necessary otherwise. This point was made in a brilliant book called *Losing Ground* by Charles Murray, a social scientist at the Manhattan Institute for Policy Research. Murray formulated three "laws" that he suggested characterized most federal transfer programs. The Law of Imperfect Selection held that any objective rule defining eligibility for a social transfer program will irrationally exclude some persons. The Law of Unintended Rewards said that any federal social transfer increases the net value of being in the condition that prompts the transfer. And the Law of Net Harm stated that the less likely unwanted behavior will change voluntarily, the more likely a program to induce change will cause net harm.

Theoretically, Murray wrote, any federal program that mounts an intervention with sufficient rewards to sustain participation will generate so much of the unwanted behavior (in order for the participant to become eligible for the program's rewards) that the net effect will be to *increase* the incidence of the unwanted behavior. In reality the programs that deal with the most intractable behavior problems have included a package of rewards large enough to induce participation, but not large enough to produce the desired result. Could we expect it to be any different for federal child care?

A similar argument was made by Harvard's Nathan Glazer in an insightful account of failed federal programs called *The Limits of Social Policy*. Glazer, like Murray, showed how, despite rising welfare outlays at the national level, the number of welfare recipients was increasing. Conditions seemed to deteriorate as social policies *expanded*. A generation ago, incentives favored marriage and work; today, it pays to stay unmarried (or get divorced) and go on welfare.

"When there are large differences in a population," Glazer wrote, "differences of race and ethnicity related to differences of income, productivity, culture, and values, the introduction of a uniform national system is difficult. The present mood in America does not favor a fully developed federal system of social policy."

Yale's Ed Zigler has created an approach to child care that would emphasize parental choice, help restructure the child-care system, and downplay the role of the federal bureaucracy.

"We know that two-thirds of American mothers with school-age children are in the work force," he told me. "And our best projection is that by the end of the century 75 percent of all two-parent families will have both parents working. What does this imply for their children? There will be 2 million infants, 9 million children between one and five, 7 million children between six and nine, and 8 million between the ages of ten and fourteen. That's 26 million kids—fully *half* of the nation's children—with either one or both parents working. How are we going to provide for their care?"

He lifted a sheaf of charts off his desk.

"Today in America," he went on, "hundreds of thousands of children are subjected to child-care environments that compromise their development. Child/adult ratios are too large. Care is minimal or barely adequate, especially for the poor. I don't think we ought to waste our energy pursuing federal solutions. So our child-care system ought to be primarily state-based and tied to a major institution in order to become a part of the structure of our society."

Like an image coming into focus, what he had in mind became clear.

"The public schools," he said, "are the only system America has that can adapt the varying needs of families and children. Leaving aside the issues of infant care and parental leave, look at what we could do for child care in a school-based program. Elementary school buildings could open two hours before school begins and stay open two hours after school ends, to permit before- and after-school care for kids aged six to twelve. For preschoolers we could create a child-care facility within the school itself, with kindergartners in school the first half of the day, in child care the other half. In short, you're looking at the school of the twenty-first century."

I asked Zigler who would staff the programs, since most teachers are overworked if not underpaid, and how the effort would be funded.

"Staffing is a problem," he admitted. "More than three-quarters of all American adults caring for children today make less than the minimum wage. On average we pay the caretakers of our next generation less than we pay zookeepers. The program should be headed by an early-education specialist who would supervise a staff of trained child-development associates qualified to work with kids. By the early part of the next century, when the critical mass of women are in the work force, the costs could be absorbed primarily through property taxes, as education is funded today. In the meantime a fee system would probably work, based on a sliding scale and ability to pay. Business won't fund it all, and government can't. We've got pilot projects now under way in Missouri and Connecticut to provide the basis for more research. But the child-care problem in America is so massive, and has been ignored for so long, that the Band-Aid cures being proposed just won't work."

I asked him about parental leave and infant care, two aspects that would not be covered by his school-based approach.

"You know," he said, "the United States is alone among the industrialized nations in not having a statutory maternity leave law. The average length of *paid* leaves in seventy-five other countries is more than four months, and benefits average over two-thirds of the mother's working wage. In America women have no nationally guaranteed right to leave work for newborn care, they get no income when they do, and no job protection when they come back. Employers argue that infant care leave is too costly, but the alternative—infant day care—is prohibitively expensive, of questionable quality, and the consequences for later development risky. So a system of paid parental leave would be less costly to society, in the long run, than institutionalized infant-care programs. A minimum standard would be six months, with three months paid at 75 percent of salary."

Zigler's innovative use of the public schools, coupled with Lindsey's disaggregated expansion of child-care tax credits to put decision-making power—and choice—in the hands of America's parents rather than in the federal bureaucracy in Washington, could well represent the kinds of informed, cost-effective solutions to a national problem that would provide parents with quality choices and at the same time encourage the family unit to remain intact. National legislation for parental leave, for both new mothers and new fathers, while inherently commonsensible, needs to be crafted with care to retain the important advantages of flexibility and choice. The option clearly needs to be there, especially for mothers and in the critical first year of life; today it is not, except in a handful of states.

In a sense these issues too can be viewed as a combination of accident and historical circumstance. We are like the prehistoric animals with fins when the globe was covered with water. Now the water is beginning to dry up, and the question is, what shall we do with these fins? In the nineteenth and early twentieth centuries America had the advantage of accident and circumstance, endowed with abundant natural resources, which it used to build an enormous industrial base. Now, on the threshold of the information-intensive era, those nations with abundant and well-trained human resources will be the ones to profit.

Penn State's Jay Belsky sees a tremendous change coming in America's human resources infrastructure.

"Look at it this way," he said to me. "What we're seeing now is a total restructuring of the work-parent-child relationship, similar to what we went through when we altered our physical infrastructure earlier in this century to accommodate cars as we moved out of the horse-and-buggy era. The transition is very painful. The question is, does our society have the will to invest in a new kind of social infrastructure? As Zigler says, we need a creative strategy, and we need to be experimental. And I agree that some kind of mandatory parental leave policy is imperative. Furthermore, based on my own research, because fewer and fewer mothers want to return to the work force on a full-time basis after they have a child, and because extensive infant day care is a potential developmental risk, mothers need the option of working part-time during their infant's first years with guarantees of full-time job protection after that. But neither of these options currently exists."

Part-time jobs typically carry no full-time benefits, so part-time employees are usually second-class citizens. In the past, when American firms were organized around the techniques of mass production and a centralized factory system, an employee's physical presence was required during a standard eight-hour manufacturing shift; otherwise the system could not function. Today business organizations are becoming leaner and flatter; production is more often organized around batch processing; decentralization is the norm, with decisions made closer to the factory floor; speed and communication are more important than physical presence because markets are now global.

Consequently the old Monday-to-Friday, nine-to-five collective work format is gradually being supplemented by more flexible systems, since employees can often work more productively at home, in personal offices, undistracted, with a personal computer, telephone, facsimile, and modem. The process is called telecommuting. But employers, with one foot in the old world, resist the transition, and employees can't be comfortable if their employers aren't. And since most people will want to spend a part of their workweek with colleagues, in meetings or for social reasons, the new system will never completely dominate the old, although America's smaller, more entrepreneurial companies are more comfortable with it than larger corporations.

But the key to retaining women who want to combine career and family is to provide the flexibility and family supports they need in order to function responsibly as working adults and as serious parents. Working mothers still take primary responsibility for child care, and this causes considerable distraction, anxiety, and absenteeism in the workplace, in addition to the inescapable feeling of guilt.

So flexibility also means the ability to take more time off *when it is needed* or to combine work at home with work in an office, and telecommuting—through modern communications technology—makes this increasingly possible. Such flexibility is not limited to working mothers, either. Many fathers too want more time with their children, in order not to miss the marker events of their children's formative years. Flexibility also means splitting one job between two people—job sharing—which Singapore has used so successfully and which enhances continuity as well as customer contact.

Some critics have contended that the process of building this kind of flexibility into the workplace necessarily results in the creation of prejudicial "mommy tracks" in corporate organizations, to the detriment of women who aspire to senior management but who may be penalized by their decision to spend more time with their young children. But if, as a society, we are beginning to recognize that our children need and deserve more of our time as parents—mother and father alike—then the track has been inappropriately named. Perhaps it should more properly be called a "parent track" in recognition of both working mothers *and* working fathers who share a mutual commitment to job and family.

However, these trends do mean that flextime and flexwork patterns will be more supportive of the kinds of family, parenting, and child-care concerns that have become national priorities. Recently major American corporations, both manufacturers and service companies, have been moving away from the concept of institutionalized on-site day care for employees to more flexible systems that provide parents with the option of spending more time with their children in their natural environment, at home. Such systems may in the long run be less costly to society, and since increasing numbers of professional women do not want to return to the workplace full-time, employers are faced with a Hobson's choice: either require working mothers to come back full-time and risk losing them (and the extensive investment in their training) or give them more flexibility. Such flexible systems cannot avoid treating mothers differently from fathers, which may also mean a return to somewhat clearer role differentiation in American society and will give many feminists problems. But as most experts would agree, the benefits to family and society will be much greater.

Recently two major American corporations have demonstrated how important these more flexibile approaches are to our national competitiveness. When Arthur Andersen & Co., one of the nation's top accounting and auditing firms, learned that more and more of its female partners and staff were preferring to stay at home with their newborn children and work only part-time thereafter, the firm was faced with a major problem: either require the new mothers to return to work full-time to retain the firm's substantial investment in their training or force them to give up their jobs entirely. The firm thus began experimenting with more flexible approaches that encompassed a spectrum of patterns, and it soon realized the benefits of greater openness by enabling these new mothers to maintain a major commitment to the responsibilities of parenting as well as to continuing their careers.

Similarly, when American Telephone & Telegraph reached agreement with its principal unions in mid-1989 regarding maternal leave, family care leave, and reimbursement of adoption expenses, another milestone was reached. AT&T granted 160,000 affiliated employees of the Communications Workers of America and the International Brotherhood of Electrical Workers a major extension of unpaid parental leave from six months to one year, guaranteeing reinstatement to an equivalent job upon return from leave. Employees can utilize what AT&T calls "flexible hours," under which they can take an "excused workday" in successive two-hour increments. And for the first time, AT&T agreed to reimburse employees up to $2,000 for expenses incurred in connection with the adoption of a minor child, including court costs, medical costs, and agency fees.

As with our trade and investment policies, so with our social and family policies: we cannot emulate the Japanese; we must find our own flexible solutions to these problems. Flexibility and adaptation are inherent American strengths. Unlike Japan, America does not have the benefit of centuries of historical traditions that have nurtured a strong family ethic. Nor can America turn the clock back to an earlier era when only men were in the workplace and women stayed in the home with sole responsibility for rearing children; today's demographics coupled with the emergence of greater choice for women have rendered that impossible. Incentives that encourage more flexible systems are the American way.

"Two fundamental benefits that were unattainable in the past are now within our reach," wrote Felice Schwartz, president of Catalyst, Inc., in a recent *Harvard Business Review* article called "Management Women and the New Facts of Life." "For the individual, freedom of choice—in this case the freedom to choose career, family, or a combination of the two. For the corporation, access to the most gifted individuals in the country. These benefits are neither self-indulgent nor insubstantial. Freedom of choice and self-realization are too deeply American to be cast aside for some wistful vision of the past. And access to our most talented human resources is not a luxury in this age of explosive international competition but rather the barest minimum that prudence and national self-preservation require."

Corporate career interruptions, plateauing, and turnover are expensive, and much more so for women than for men, as recent studies have confirmed. But the biological fact of maternity reinforces a permanent and immutable difference between men and women. One result of this gender difference has been to persuade some corporate executives that women are not CEO material if they have to interrupt their careers to bear children. Another result is to reinforce the old black-and-white "work-or-parent" decision that relegates women either full-time to the workplace or full-time to the home. But America can do better than limit itself to such inflexible options, especially since 80 percent of new entrants to the work force for the remainder of this century will be women, minorities, and immigrants. And the nation will need the very best of them to retain its competitive edge in an era characterized by intense global competition.

"The majority of women," Schwartz concluded, "are what I call career-and-family women, women who want to pursue serious careers while participating actively in the rearing of children. [They] are willing to work part-time while [their] children are young, if only [their] employer will give [them] the opportunity. There are two rewards for companies responsive to this need: higher retention of their best people and greatly improved performance and satisfaction in their middle management."

When I spoke with Schwartz, in mid-1989, I asked her whether she saw flexible workplace options representing a national trend.

"I see it happening at an accelerating pace," she said, "and when I say 'it,' I mean the awareness that women are an enormous resource for America now, given both the demographics and the investment by corporations in their training and experience. Many corporations are finally beginning to realize that it makes good business sense to keep their talented women in the firm, that it positively impacts their bottom line. Maybe twenty companies are taking the lead on this now, with the vast majority somewhere in the middle."

I asked her if national parental leave legislation would act as a spur, since the U.S. is practically alone among major industrialized nations in not having a nationally mandated parental leave law. Her response was measured.

"Not necessarily," she said. "In our free-enterprise system, for better or for worse, American CEOs value their economic freedom, and they are often antagonistic toward legislation that constrains their flexibility. On the other hand, I also think that legislation can be good because it often forces companies to confront issues they might otherwise disregard."

Current efforts, of course, stress flexible options for women, since as mothers they still bear the primary responsibility for child care in American society. But what about men and their more involved roles as fathers?

"I think there is a much greater sense on the part of men of wanting to participate more actively in the family—a great deal more than a generation before—which I think is great for women when they can share the child-rearing responsibilities with their husbands. This enables them *both* to function at much higher levels, at home and at work. And I think there is a nascent awareness now that women's productivity is being greatly enhanced as a result of broader participation by men in American family life."

France's former president Charles de Gaulle once said that women should get the same benefits and respect accorded to men in military duty, because they are both performing the ultimate service to the nation. We pay a double price for our failure to provide adequate support structures for today's families. We sacrifice efficiency, and we sacrifice our future as a nation.

Religion too, so long a fundamental part of the social fabric in America, has seemingly failed to address larger social issues in a constructive way. As the elite Protestant denominations in America have become secularized, they have become little more than social clubs and demand little of their members. Conservative denominations and new sects thus expand to fill the spiritual gap, aquiring a power base in socially disadvantaged groups and then moving slowly into the mainstream. Today the liberal church is in decline and the conservative fundamentalist movement is expanding to take its place. Half the population of America is estimated to belong to one of the major religious denominations; Catholics are the most numerous, at nearly 50 million, followed by Southern Baptists with almost 20 million.

James McCord, former head of the Princeton Theological Seminary, is retired but still active as director of the Center for Theological Study and Inquiry. When I met with him in late 1987, his mood was somber. "There are two recurring weaknesses in America," he said to me. "One is anti-intellectualism, the other isolationism. We're experiencing them both again now. Divorce is a dehumanizing process, and we should not let our children be reared by surrogate parents. Man is the only creature that can make a promise, and if we cannot keep that promise, then we are less than human beings."

I asked him about the perceived decline of religion in America. He smiled as he smoothed a hand over his balding head. "St. Paul said it best," he replied. "The strong despise the weak, and the weak hate the strong. But we also have to be aware of more powerful forces at work. As the Mediterranean region was the fountain of learning for the ancient world, and the Atlantic the source of inspiration for the modern world, I think the Pacific will be the primary source for the new world. Then perhaps America can begin its ascent again."

When I left McCord's office and threaded my way back through the snow-covered campus, I wondered if the divisive forces in America would continue to prevail over the more innovative efforts to achieve social change. The issues of marital stability, family unity, child care, and parental leave should not be so narrowly defined as to be preempted by either Democrat or Republican, conservative or liberal, male or female, culture or politics. These are *national* issues, yet the strange mutation of special interest politics in the country now seems singularly incapable of achieving consensus on issues of such vital significance.

I think America knows what the building blocks are for its future; the question is whether the will can be found to put them in place. When a nation no longer cherishes its young, it ceases to qualify as the standard-bearer, a model worthy of emulation, in the global arena of social equity. America's ideology remains strong, but the substance has become weak. By default, the nation could lose its claim to global leadership.

"For several centuries, we have been embarked on a great effort to increase our freedom, wealth, and power," Robert Bellah wrote in *Habits of the Heart*. "Our achievements have been enormous. Yet we seem to be hovering on the brink of disaster from the internal incoherence of our own society. What has gone wrong? How can we reverse the slide? We have put our own good as individuals ahead of the common good. Livy's words about ancient Rome also apply to us: We have reached the point where we cannot bear either our vices or their cure. But the time may be approaching when we will either reform our republic or fall into the hands of despotism, as many republics before us have done."

PART V
RETHINKING AMERICA'S
NATIONAL SECURITY

17

REGIONAL SECURITY IN A MULTIPOLAR WORLD

A dilemma is a situation that requires a choice among unpleasant alternatives. The first horn of the contemporary Japanese defense dilemma refers to the fears—real, pretended, and imagined—of the citizens of Japan, the United States, the USSR, and the nations Japan invaded during World War II, that Japanese rearmament is imminent and will lead to "revived Japanese militarism."

The other horn of the dilemma is the persistent charge that Japan is taking a "free ride" on the backs of the Americans, the Koreans, the Taiwanese, and all the other people of the Pacific Basin who take seriously their responsibilities to maintain a stable and secure environment. This free ride is doubly galling since no nation profits more from international political and military security than Japan. Certainly, if one views national defense expenditures without taking into account military threats, the geopolitical aspects of strategy, or possible non-defense budget contributions Japan does not seem to be carrying its share of the burden.

Chalmers Johnson,
"Reflections on the Dilemma of Japanese Defense"

Some years ago, when I was living and working in Tokyo, a Japanese colleague and I were entertained one evening by Japanese friends who worked for a core company of the Mitsubishi *keiretsu*, a conglomerate with major interests in just about every industry sector. After an informal dinner in Shimbashi, we repaired to the home of one of them— Mr. Yamamoto, say—for a nightcap of sake. As must be common knowledge now to even the most casual observers of Japan, being invited to the home of a Japanese is a rare event.

A pair of shiny black sedans (Mitsubishi, of course) ferried us there, and Mr. Yamamoto escorted us into a modestly appointed den, where a chilled bottle of sake and six tiny cups waited on a small lacquerware platter. We had been in a celebratory mood all evening, having just renewed a major agreement, and the atmosphere was still convivial as we downed the thimblesful of sake. One bottle turned into two, as I recall. We soon linked arms and sang traditional Japanese folk songs, and there was considerable good-natured laughter at the plight of a slightly inebriated foreigner who created some nonexistent lyrics when the first stanzas gave out.

But the laughter subsided quite abruptly when Mr. Yamamoto, weaving his way unevenly to the phonograph, put an LP on the turntable to produce a stream of music and lyrics that brought everyone, my Japanese colleague included, to ramrod-straight attention. Everyone started singing loudly now, and with feeling, as I stood quietly by and watched, unfamiliar with this particular battery of songs. One had a frequent refrain: "Getsu, Getsu, Ka, Sui, Moku, Kin, Kin," which had been adopted by Japanese industry as its typical workweek—Monday, Monday, Tuesday, Wednesday, Thursday, Friday, Friday. Suddenly, leaning his head back, Mr. Yamamoto closed his eyes, and I watched as tears streamed down his cheeks.

"Is he all right?" I asked my colleague.

"Of course," he told me, his voice choked with emotion. "We always get this way when we sing the old imperial navy marching songs."

The coin dropped as soon as he mentioned the Japanese navy, because the Mitsubishi group had been prime contractor for the Japanese fleet, both before and during the war. There had always been a close relationship between Mitsubishi and the government, going back to the Meiji era. Consequently, when the war ended, many demilitarized naval officers found their way into one of the Mitsubishi companies.

This vivid experience comes to mind when skilled observers of Japan, such as Chalmers Johnson, speak about the fears, real or imagined, of revived Japanese militarism. It was spooky, not least because two of the Mitsubishi guests were too young to have served in the war but knew most of the lyrics to the marching songs *anyway*. One problem, of course, is that governments and public institutions, in Japan and the United States as well as East Asia, are still run by people who either were directly involved in the war or are contemporaries of someone who was. Hence the comment of Singapore's foreign minister Wong Kan Seng, who, when given the analogy of Japan as an economic giant, a political pygmy, and a military rodent, could say to me, only half-joking, as he did recently, "We would prefer Japan remained a military rodent forever!"

But perceptions change. And the passage of time may have much to do with changing perceptions of Japan's military capabilities. Also, the more vivid fears of a revived Japanese militarism are based on what happened half a century ago and assume the Japanese have not learned from their mistakes. The younger generation of political leadership in Asia knows only too well that, as Korekiyo Takahashi, a former minister of finance, said in 1936, "It is much harder to nullify the results of an economic conquest than those of war."

The economic goals of the old Greater East Asia Co-Prosperity Sphere, based in part on Japan's hostile military dominance, have long since been exceeded by a purely economic postwar strategy, the United States providing security but with benevolence rather than belligerence. Still, Japan cannot be considered a global superpower without political and military influence commensurate with its economic strength, so it may be only a matter of time before the Japanese political pygmy becomes a giant and the military rodent turns into what might more reasonably resemble a *Tyrannosaurus rex.*

Critics of Japan's "free ride" point out that Japan spends only 1 percent of its GNP on defense, compared to higher levels in Western Europe, where averages of 3 to 5 percent pertain, or the United States, where defense spending is between 6 and 7 percent of GNP. In 1987 the Pentagon's budget was $282 billion, or 6.4 percent of America's $4.4 trillion GNP that year; in 1988, $285 billion was budgeted, or 6.3 percent of a $4.5 trillion GNP.

As a percentage of GNP, Japan budgets the least of any nation in Asia for defense. Taiwan spends over 8 percent, South Korea and Singapore just over 5 percent, and the People's Republic of China just under 2 percent. The Soviet Union, of course, tops out regularly at 13 to 15 percent of GNP, not the least because it is *the* quintessential military-industrial complex.

But translated into absolute dollars, Japan's defense spending is not as minuscule as critics might otherwise imply. As of 1988 Japan was spending *more* in absolute terms than any other country in the free world outside the United States, a situation that hardly warranted being called a "free ride." For fiscal year 1989, which began April 1, the Japanese government approved a 5.2 percent increase in its defense budget to ¥3.9 trillion, or just about $30 billion—more than the United

Kingdom or France or West Germany will spend. (Japan is also now the largest foreign aid donor in the world, with an annual budget of about $10 billion, and nine of its ten largest recipients are in Asia.) Since 1980 Japan has steadily increased its spending on defense, in real terms, by an average of 5 percent a year.

These facts are all the more astounding considering that Tokyo has, since 1983, imposed a "minus ceiling" rule on all discretionary government spending. Total budget outlays have been cut 5 percent across the board every year, *except* for defense and official development assistance (foreign aid). The mystery is not that the Japanese spend such a small amount of GNP on defense, but that Americans spend such a large amount—*ten times* as much as Japan. And when Congress votes, as it did in 1987 by a lopsided margin of 415 to one, to recommend that Japan commit 3 percent of its GNP (or $100 billion) annually on defense, it is hard to imagine *any* country in the region, Japan included, that would accept such a staggering outlay. A defense budget of that magnitude would truly signal a revival of Japanese militarism.

"Since the late 1970s the Japanese have increased defense expenditures step by step," a senior Western diplomat in Tokyo told me during a visit in late 1988, "beginning in 1979, when they funded construction of replacement facilities at American bases. Then, in 1983, Tokyo funded some support for local base workers and in 1988 began footing 50 percent of their total wage bill. Once the yen started rising against the dollar, it didn't take long before it was costing Washington twice as much to maintain its forces in Japan."

We talked about the bilateral security treaty, under which the U.S. pledges to defend Japan (but which does not mutually obligate the Japanese in any way). The agreement is popularly known as Japan's nuclear umbrella, because it obviates the necessity for Japan to develop, produce, or use its own nuclear weapons. Drafted in 1952, and renewed in 1970 for perpetuity, it can be revoked by either side with a year's notice, but there are no provisions for amendment or revision. In a recent cross-border opinion poll, 79 percent of Americans questioned said they thought the U.S. would defend Japan if it were attacked. But only 42 percent of the Japanese polled said that, and 54 percent said explicitly they did not believe America would defend Japan under any circumstances.

"There has been discussion in the Japanese Diet about Japan's Self-Defense Forces assisting American forces," my informant, a military officer with considerable experience in Japan, went on. "But it's not clear what this would mean. The SDF has wide latitude for tactical response. Its air force routinely intercepts Russian bombers that penetrate Japanese airspace, and Japanese warships can protect commercial shipping as far afield as the Persian Gulf."

The maritime SDF can also return fire. Japan probably has the most capable navy in the Far East after the United States; it has more Orion PC-3 search and reconnaissance aircraft and a greater number of tactical jet fighters—about the number the U.S. has in Japan, Korea, and the Philippines *combined*. What's more, although Japan has only a quarter of a million men under arms, they are almost all officer-quality personnel, so in an emergency the nation could easily mobilize.

There are roughly 150,000 men in the Japanese army, called the Ground Self-Defense Force, with thirteen divisions and more than 1,000 tanks and peripheral equipment; about 90,000 men in the navy, which commands fifteen submarines, thirty-six destroyers, and eighteen frigates operating out of five naval bases in Japan; and a 90,000-man air force, whose six combat air wings fly nearly 500 aircraft, including the F-15, America's most advanced tactical fighter.

When Japan adopted its postwar constitution in 1947, Article 9 specifically renounced the nation's use of war, specifying the use of military forces strictly for defense. And in 1981, under Prime Minister Suzuki, Japan began patrolling its own sea-lanes out to 1,000 nautical miles from Tokyo, taking over responsibility (and expense) for this function from the U.S. So when these levels are all taken into account, coupled with Tokyo's higher outlays for U.S. facilities and forces, Japan's Far East defense spending can no longer be regarded as negligible.

I recently put the question of rearmament to my godfather, a senior corporate executive at one of Japan's major *keiretsu*. Could the government, I asked, ultimately revoke Article 9 to pave the way for a broader expansion of military power?

"*Zettai nai*," was his abrupt response. "Absolutely not. Besides, there is no reason for us to have to do that, given the flexibility the SDF has, as well as the higher absolute levels of defense spending being approved by the Diet. Short of an all-out, aggressive attack on another country, there is a wide latitude in what the SDF can actually do. I would be more concerned about upgrading our sophisticated air defense systems than I would worry about Japanese troops tromping ashore somewhere in Southeast Asia."

A similar point was made by Hisahiko Okazaki, a senior Ministry of Foreign Affairs official and until recently Japan's ambassador to Saudi Arabia. He said that air superiority would be the decisive factor in any war involving Japan. "When the government's 1986–1990 Five Year Plan is implemented," he recently wrote in an article called "Japanese Defense Policy," "Japan will have 163 F-15s in addition to 130 remodelled F-4s. The F-15 may be the best fighter built in this century. It has at least a three-to-one edge over the MiG-23. In addition, the new Five Year Plan will introduce 180 Patriot surface-to-air missiles (SAMs) into Japan. There are some 945 Soviet fighter and attack aircraft deployed in the Far East. Japan's fighters and SAMs together have the strength to intercept the invasion of about 800 of them."

Because Japan has stepped up its spending on defense, the issue of whether to "buy or build" now dominates bilateral discussions in Tokyo and Washington. As America's own defense procurement becomes subject to higher levels of foreign componentry, its trade deficit with Japan of course refuses to narrow. And as Japanese protection of its own sophisticated technology becomes an increasing irritant, American negotiators have to choose between exporting a greater volume of high-technology American weaponry and having major Japanese defense contractors, such as Mitsubishi and Kawasaki, develop Japan's own home-grown military technology. This has given rise to a new irritant called *techno-nationalism*, as we shall see when we consider the recent sale of military technology to the USSR by Toshiba and Japan's procurement of the next generation of tactical jet fighters called the FSX.

A short three-hour flight across the Sea of Japan, another significant defense saga is unfolding, this on the Korean Peninsula, arguably the most strategic piece of real estate in the Far East. Since partition into Communist North and democratic South in 1945, the peninsula has been plagued by instability: the Korean War was fought there between 1950 and 1953; the U.S. has had two divisions (about 45,000 men) stationed there since the armistice was signed at Panmunjom; and North Korea has been singularly responsible for numerous acts of terrorism against the South, further isolating a nation long regarded as irrational if not paranoid. North Korea tacitly admitted assassinating several members of President Chun's cabinet in Rangoon in 1986 and planted a bomb at Kimpo Airport that killed many people on the eve of the Asian Games in Seoul later that year. In 1987 Pyongyang was also implicated in the downing of a Korean Airlines jet that disappeared from radar screens over Burmese airspace.

In 1979, during the Carter administration, the U.S. attempted to withdraw one of its two divisions in Korea, but the move met with such widespread opposition in the region that it was quickly abandoned. A successful Olympiad in Seoul in 1988, combined with renewed efforts between Pyongyang and Seoul to discuss eventual reunification, long a political reverie on both sides of the Demilitarized Zone, have most recently helped to stabilize the situation somewhat. But the South's emerging democratic process, as evidenced by recent presidential and National Assembly elections, suggests that the country's political constituency is now domestic and no longer foreign (meaning American). Hence there is growing anti-American sentiment in South Korea as Washington pressures Seoul to import more U.S. beef and tobacco, angering Korean farmers and consumers. The Pentagon has also asked the Korean government to contribute to America's peacekeeping efforts in the Middle East.

"If the United States continues to pursue its policies of the past," Dr. Kwon Moon-sool was telling me in mid-1988, "then there will definitely be more anti-American feelings here. American foreign policy is essentially business style: businessmen want to make short-term profits without thinking about long-term strategy, and Washington asks for too much too fast. American pressure on Korea to reform its democratic system may also be contradictory to the issue of strong national security. The government party under President Roh can't do anything now without consulting the opposition. In the long run, democracy will be good for Korea, but it all takes time."

Dr. Kwon is deputy director of the Institute for National Security Affairs at the National Defense University in Seoul. The institute has some 500 students, two-thirds of whom are active military officers and a third Korean government officials.

"But I don't think the U.S. will ever withdraw its troops from Korea," he went on. "Because if the U.S. pulls out, then Korea may be confronted with the necessity of having to develop its own nuclear weapons, to maintain the balance of power. Also, as Washington learned in 1979, if America does not maintain its security commitment to Korea, few in Asia will believe in America's commitment to the Far East, including, most importantly, Japan, and *they* would probably go nuclear in due course, too. America trades more with Asia than it does with Europe, so it needs a forward defense strategy now more than ever."

I asked Kwon about North Korea's intentions, and his response echoed sentiments I heard from most military observers in Seoul.

"The North has 60 percent of its forces within ten kilometers of the Demilitarized Zone, less than an hour from Seoul," he said. "Seoul has a third of our population and two-thirds of our wealth. We discovered three tunnels the North had dug under the DMZ, wide enough to drive armored vehicles through, and we think there may be more. We know the North wanted to prevent the Olympic Games from taking place and that they seem to want to provoke instability down here. And everybody asks why. Well, terrorism glosses over their domestic problems by serving as a distraction, and it reminds Beijing and Moscow that Pyongyang exists. Reunification is a dream of our young people, as far as I'm concerned; it won't happen in my lifetime."

Armed forces in the North somewhat outnumber those in the South according to recent data, but when U.S. forces and firepower are included, they are about equal. North Korea maintains standing forces of about 850,000 men, with a half million in reserves, and 840 combat aircraft, mostly older model MiG fighters supplied by Russia. The South has just under 650,000 men in arms, with reserves of more than 3 million, and about 500 combat aircraft, centered primarily around F-5A and F-4D tactical fighters. Each country spends about a third of its national budget on defense, but because the GNP differential is so large, only 5.2 percent of South Korea's GNP goes for defense, compared to 23.8 percent of GNP in the North. Neither country is a member of the UN. The Demilitarized Zone, which separates the two countries, is a diplomatic oxymoron: it is one of the most strongly fortified, heavily armed, and dangerous areas in the world.

Recently a suggestion has surfaced that Tokyo intermediate between Seoul and Pyongyang to help negotiate an accord of some sort between these two ideologically separated capitals.

"My sense is that neither Pyongyang nor Seoul wants the Japanese to speak for its interests," a senior American diplomat told me. "The Japanese are terrific about representing their own interests, but lousy at representing others. We run a number of joint maneuvers with the Koreans, and many with the Japanese, but there are no joint Korean-Japanese maneuvers as yet, and none including all three of us."

I asked him if he felt the North was militarily superior to the South.

"Maybe in bullets and beans," he said, "but not in generalship or morale. South Korean forces are tough and very efficient; the air force has good pilots; and the U.S. assists in all sorts of indirect ways such as training, logistical support, and intelligence. The North may have an ideological edge, but only because of its fierce indoctrination; they are regularly taught that the South has only dirt roads and beggars. But I say, forget about the bad guys in the North. We've got to negotiate a whole host of issues just between ourselves and Seoul. We'll probably work a division down in due course, a battalion at a time, and maybe shift it to Okinawa so it can participate in regional surveillance."

Mutual force reduction on the Korean peninsula is an effort that is long overdue, but it is also subject to mutual suspicion and distrust between North and South. Disarmament cannot be achieved without the direct participation of Washington and Moscow, since Pyongyang and Seoul are both pawns in the larger superpower game. Still, the thaw in the Soviet-American cold war, if it is a longer-term trend, could lead to a more stable situation on the peninsula, if not to reunification eventually, and that could contribute even more to regional stability. But that implies a less direct American presence in Korea, not likely anytime soon.

"America has given up its policy of indiscriminate anti-communism," the political scientist Kang Sung-hack wrote recently in an article called "America's Foreign Policy Toward East Asia for the 1990s." "It now expects to maintain the East Asian balance with a greater role played by Japan, thereby decreasing the U.S. defense burden. In the light of this changed mood, it could be inferred that the U.S. will continue to cut back in Asia during the 1990s, transforming itself from Godfather to de facto military outsider on the eve of the 21st century."

Kang teaches at Korea University, located atop a craggy hillside not far from central Seoul.

"I like my coffee sweet because life is so bitter," he said as we sat down to lunch in the spartan faculty club.

"American cultural values dominate the formulation of its foreign policy," he was saying. "Your country fluctuates back and forth between moralism and pragmatism, optimism and pessimism, introversion and extroversion, to the point where we don't know what your policy is anymore. It lacks consistency. My fear is that America may be going into a period of protracted introversion, despite its rhetoric to the contrary. It is not a comfortable feeling."

Concern about strategic disengagement raised, for him as for others, the question of a stronger Japanese presence in the region.

"Any American withdrawal would almost surely push the Japanese to rearm," he said. "And is it reasonable to assume that Japan would stop without achieving the ultimate symbol of sovereignty in the nuclear age? Even so, is it desirable for America to provide a security umbrella for Japan without determining the mutual circumstances under which that protection is viable? Remember, the Japanese always prefer policy to be made in Tokyo."

A situation not unlike the historical hostility between North and South Korea has persisted between China and Taiwan ever since the Nationalists fled the mainland in 1949. The two countries were continually in a state of war and remain so today; throughout the 1950s each country vowed it would recapture the other, a somewhat comic threat from the generalissimo, considering the disparity in numbers between his armed forces and those of Chairman Mao. In 1979 the United States, and later Japan, officially recognized the People's Republic as the legitimate government of China, and since then the China-Taiwan relationship has become noticeably less belligerent.

Beijing never abandoned the concept that Taiwan would eventually be reunited with China, because Taiwan was considered to be China's sacred territory. In 1982 Beijing suggested a "special administrative zone" for Taiwan. In 1984, on the heels of the Sino-British Accord for Hong Kong, Deng Xiaoping also proposed extending the "one country, two systems" concept to Taiwan, although the political leadership in Taiwan saw through that Trojan horse in pretty short order.

Subjecting Taiwan to outright attack would cause the United States, Europe, and Japan to reassess their own relationships with China, which could have serious implications for Beijing's expanding trade and technology needs. Then, too, an attack might not succeed, in which case Beijing would suffer humiliation as well as defeat. And any attack would leave the Taiwan economy in ruins, hardly desirable since an entrepreneurial Taiwan could be critical to Beijing's own long-term success in modernizing its state-run economy.

Considering armed forces alone, various estimates confirm that forty armored divisions would be necessary to invade Taiwan successfully. In 1979 the Senate Foreign Relations Committee disclosed that 300,000 American troops would have been required to dislodge the 32,000

Japanese ground forces occupying Taiwan in 1945—a differential of ten to one. Although the People's Liberation Army outnumbers Taiwan's troops by 2.9 million to 290,000, the concentration of Chinese troops near the Formosa Straits about equal Taiwanese forces in the battle zone. But it would take the *entire* PLA to invade Taiwan successfully, if U.S. estimates are to be believed, and any movement that massive would be noticed well in advance by American intelligence.

China's naval and air forces considerably outnumber those of Taiwan, however, giving the PRC a clear tactical advantage. China has forty submarines in its East China Sea fleet, to Taiwan's two; its coastal craft outnumber Taiwan's 290 to twenty-eight; it has ninety missile-armed ships to Taiwan's thirty-three; and its navy totals 340,000 men to Taiwan's 77,000. China is also a nuclear power, with more than a hundred medium-range ballistics missiles; Taiwan, of course, has none. China also has a fleet of nearly 1,000 tactical bombers, and again, Taiwan has none; the PRC's combat aircraft, including tactical jet fighters and interceptors, total more than 5,000, to just over 500 for Taiwan. On water and in the air, China is clearly dominant.

"The Chinese threat is still there," Thomas Lee was telling me during a visit to Taipei in late 1988, "but the level of confrontation has deescalated considerably. The contacts between Taiwan and the PRC, through our exchange of family visits, are people to people, not government to government. Because they have been so successful, they may reduce alertness among Taiwanese, so we have to stay on guard. Peking is still using the same tactics in trying to isolate us in the international community—at the Asian Development Bank, for example—but we have been keeping a distinct image and reputation for ourselves. We may soon apply for membership in the General Agreement on Tariffs and Trade in our own name."

Lee is secretary general of the Society for Strategic Studies in Taipei, at Tamkang University. The SSS conducts research in comprehensive security and analyzes mainland China affairs, focusing on psychological warfare and propaganda.

I asked him about the "one country, two systems" issue, and he said, "We think the PRC is using Hong Kong as a stepping-stone toward its ultimate objective of recapturing Taiwan, which is why we're unanimously opposed to it. Peking will never allow a separate and independent system to function under its political leadership. It will gradually impose more rigid rules on Hong Kong; Peking's noose will tighten around Hong Kong's neck, and the West will be helpless to do anything but stand by and watch it happen. Hong Kong is too vulnerable—for one thing, it depends on China for all its food and water. Besides, if the PRC turns Shanghai into a trade and financial center, too, then the significance of Hong Kong will be lessened anyway."

Just how friendly China will remain toward America (and how peaceful toward Taiwan) may depend, to some degree, on whether the U.S. was serious or just bluffing when it sent a team of specialists to Taipei in early 1988 to consider alternative sites for its bases in the Philippines at Clark Air Base and Subic Bay Naval Station, whose leases expire in 1991. The two military bases are the jewels in America's Far East regional security crown, the oldest and largest and arguably the most important U.S. facilities anywhere in the world.

Subic Bay, a deep natural harbor northwest of Manila, has been a major repair, training, and logistics center for the U.S. navy ever since Admiral Dewey defeated the Spanish fleet in 1898. Carrier-borne aircraft of the Seventh Fleet are regularly serviced there, because it is the only facility outside the United States where flip-wing aircraft can be lifted directly from carrier decks and placed in repair hangars. Subic can support training in almost every kind of naval and amphibious warfare: it has fields for tank maneuvers, protected bays where Marines regularly practice amphibious landings, and thick jungles nearby for simulated survival skills. Subic is home to nearly 8,000 American sailors and Marines and 10,000 dependents; it is key to American defense efforts in the western Pacific.

Clark Air Base, north of Manila, is headquarters of the U.S. Thirteenth Air Force. It serves as a staging point for strategic airlifts to the Indian Ocean; it permits constant and easy surveillance of what the military calls "choke points" in the region (the Malacca, Sunda, and Lombok straits, in and around Indonesia, through which most of Japan's and about half of the region's oil steams on its way from the Middle East); and its long runways can handle just about every type of aircraft from helicopters to tactical jet fighters to strategic bombers. Clark is also the site of the Crow Valley weapons range, the only fully computerized bombing-practice range outside the U.S. There are some 12,000 American servicemen at Clark and 15,000 dependents; the base is key to American security efforts in Southeast Asia as well as to defense of the Philippines.

If a dilemma is a choice between two equally unsatisfactory alternatives, then the U.S. has a dilemma with regard to Clark and Subic. It can either renew the Military Base Agreement, known as the MBA, which expires in 1991, for some predetermined future period to be negotiated with the Aquino government; or it can move the bases somewhere else. The reason each alternative is unsatisfactory is a function of cost and benefit. The 1947 MBA was renegotiated in 1966 for a fixed twenty-five-year term that gave title to the Philippines and use privilege to the U.S. But the payments are negotiated for five-year periods. The final five years, through 1991, cost Washington $180 million a year, and Manila has demanded more for a single year than the U.S. is paying over five years now—$1.2 billion. That is expensive, but so is the cost of moving the bases to other locations, which has been estimated at between $5 billion and $10 billion. (In late 1988 the U.S. agreed to pay Manila $962 million in political and economic aid in 1990 and 1991, the last two years under the current agreement.)

Beyond their obvious strategic importance, local benefits of the bases are more complicated to calculate. In addition to the annual rent, the U.S. spends an additional $500 million *a year* in the Philippines through indirect expenditures necessary to support the bases. By 1988 Clark and Subic employed nearly 70,000 Filipinos, at an annual cost to the American taxpayer of $96 million—the second-largest payroll in the Philippines after the Philippine government itself. But Clark and Subic also spend more than $400 million a year on service contracts with Philippine companies, on utilities and rents for personnel and dependents, on entertainment at nearby clubs, and in shops, markets, and restaurants. A sack of rice costing 350 pesos can feed an average Filipino family of six for a month. A million dollars (20 million pesos) buys enough rice to feed 5,000 Filipino families for a year. Five hundred million dollars can feed 2.5 million families—15 million Filipinos, or a fourth of the total population—for an entire *year*.

Moving the bases to alternative sites not only means losing skilled Filipino workers and established supply points, but distancing reconnaissance and patrol operations considerably farther from their targets. If Clark Air Base were shifted to Guam, and Subic's facilities were replicated in Okinawa, the Thirteenth Air Force and the Seventh Fleet would be several hundred miles (and several hours) removed from their theaters of operation in Southeast Asia and the Indian Ocean. Taiwan cannot be a serious contender as an alternative site; Beijing would never tolerate a U.S. military facility there. Singapore, which offers some ship repair facilities for use by American naval vessels, is too small to be of any significance. The sultanate of Brunei, located nearby, is also too small. And Tinian, Saipan, and Palau, in Micronesia, all have the same geographic disadvantages as Okinawa and Guam.

Not moving the bases, however, leaves the U.S. open to two further concerns. One is the perennial problem of "blackmail" by Manila, as successive Philippine governments could ratchet up future rents, thus holding America hostage to its own strategic interests in the Pacific. The other, equally serious, is that the bases are obvious targets of anti-American sentiment by the nationalist right and anti-American attacks and harassment by the Communist left. Three American servicemen were shot and killed outside Clark Air Base in late 1987; then in April 1989 Col. James Rowe, a U.S. Army officer who spent five years as a prisoner in Vietnam before escaping in 1968, was assassinated in his car as he was being driven to work at the Joint United States Military Advisor Group in Quezon City, just outside Manila. The New People's Army took immediate responsibility for these shootings and urged the populace to support withdrawal of the bases from Philippine soil.

"We probably ought to start phasing out a withdrawal now, in stages, and move some of the operations to Palau," one knowledgeable American in Manila recently told me. "It would mean more up-front money— *lots* more. But it's a big problem, any way you look at it. Another complicating factor is that all the ASEAN military attachés say they want the bases to stay, because they're a prime factor in keeping Southeast Asia quiet. But we're not using our leverage on the Filipinos; we're letting them use *their* leverage on us. It's not clear at this stage what will happen, but when you come down to it, it's really none of the Philippines' goddamn business *what* we do with the bases."

I asked him about the New People's Army and the threat to internal security. He said, "Their force level has peaked at about 25,000 now. Arrayed against them are a quarter of a million Armed Forces of the Philippines personnel. But because the AFP is so poorly paid, they turn to stealing and forcing the villagers to pay 'taxes.' This creates more sympathy for the NPA, though they have trouble attracting new recruits and their candidates in local elections have been soundly defeated. They haven't been successful in staging urban strikes, and some of their leaders have been captured, along with computer disks that detailed a lot of their debates on strategy. But their random violence has created a backlash, so who knows what tactics they may try next."

The NPA is the most recent insurgent movement in the Philippines. Based on the principles and discipline code of China's Red Army, it was founded in 1969 by José Maria Sison, a tense, brilliant, and energetic Filipino who had earlier started the Kabataang Makabayan, the nationalist youth movement. The landless peasants were pleased with early NPA help. They were called the "Nice People Around" in those days. Then an upwardly mobile guerrilla named Satur Ocampo rode his reputation as a gunslinger to power during the anti-Marcos years of the 1970s. Today, at forty, he is the ruthless leader of what is arguably the most brutal Communist insurgency in the world. The NPA's strategy was pure Chinese, right from the legends of Mao: start in the poor rural areas and encircle the cities, which would ultimately fall like ripe plums. By 1979, when the second oil shock hit the Philippine economy hard, Romulo Kintanar, who had been dispatched to Mindanao in the South, tactically succeeded in killing Filipino soldiers to procure more guns for the NPA's hit squads, called "sparrow units." He set off such an escalation in violence that some observers have nominated the NPA as the new Khmer Rouge.

"We are a country with two distinct societies," the Filipino historian Renato Constantino wrote years ago. "The masses who struggle more and more fiercely for change, and the beneficiaries of the system who fight back with violence and repression to preserve the status quo."

Unfortunately, instead of passing crucial land reform legislation that would help landless tenants by eliminating the primary source of their discontent and the rallying cause of the insurgents, the Philippine government has chosen direct, armed confrontation with the NPA in antiguerrilla action reminiscent of the U.S. involvement in Vietnam, with comparable results. Unlawful and deliberate killings by the government have become a serious human rights problem in the Philippines.

"Yes, abuses and human rights violations by the AFP may be up," a disaffected, high-ranking officer of the Philippine armed forces admitted to me in Manila in early 1988. "But only under the bad commanders. Management is the basic problem, and the AFP is poorly paid. People don't realize that Filipino soldiers eat out of empty ammo boxes and have to buy their own underwear and food. And half the Aquino government's total military budget is dependent on Washington."

When I asked him about the bases, he said, "The sovereignty issue has already been decided. The Philippines own the land, and the U.S. operates the bases. It's our land, but regional security is your business, not ours."

He was also not terribly sanguine about the NPA. "The more difficult question is structural change," he said. "Philippine business leadership and the landowners will continue to conspire to derail any land reform plans. But without structural change, there may be no way out for the Philippines. The Marxist bug has already bitten, and it's only a matter of time before the virus spreads."

Cardinal Sin, in my interview with him, expressed disappointment about the lack of progress on the bases.

"A large majority of Filipinos still favor retention," he said, "because we realize they are not just for us, but for Asia. But why does your country give $5 billion to Israel without discussion, while Filipinos gave their lives and their loyalty to the United States? Even under the Marshall Plan, you gave billions of dollars to former enemies, and the Philippines are forgotten. Filipinos have no hatred for America, just a little pain and bitterness."

The Soviet Union, which now owns and operates the former American military bases at Cam Ranh Bay and Da Nang in Vietnam, finally has a warm-water facility for its navy in the Pacific. But its presence could still be offset if the American bases were moved to Guam and Okinawa. In any case, the bankrupt Vietnamese economy costs the Soviets $3 million to $5 million a day in foreign aid, which Moscow can ill afford given its own domestic problems with *perestroika*. The likelihood that the Soviet Union would attempt an attack on the Philippines if the U.S. moved out is not only small but negligible. With its quicksand economy, the Philippines hardly represents an attractive takeover candidate for a failing Communist ideology.

As the Philippine population continues to grow and the economy to stagnate, it becomes increasingly clear that, for better or for worse, Manila must somehow free itself of its economic dependence on America. There is probably no better symbolic action Washington can take than unilateral withdrawal. Neither alternative, staying or leaving, is very good, but leaving is the lesser of the two evils. God, Cardinal Sin would probably argue, helps those who help themselves.

"The underlying basis for growth since World War II, especially in Asia, has been the stability and security provided by the United States,"

Singapore's prime minister Lee Kuan Yew said in a speech in late 1987. "For several decades to come there is no other power that can balance the increasing presence of the Soviet navy and air force in the Far East. The most terrifying thought for me is a fundamental shift in the belief of the Japanese that the world they have known since 1945 is at an end and that they have to either defend themselves or come to some understanding with China or the Soviet Union. Then there is a joker in the pack."

The United States spends a total of nearly $50 billion a year in American taxpayers' money on regional security in the Far East. There is no reason why Japan, Korea, Taiwan, and the Association of Southeast Asian Nations cannot be required to contribute more to the region's security and assume a greater share of the total cost currently now borne entirely by the U.S. Everyone understandably prefers the status quo. But America can no longer afford the status quo. Clark and Subic may be the first to go. And perhaps forces should be shifted from Korea to Okinawa, or a step farther, to Hawaii, or to Guam; if the U.S. does not take the initiative, the Koreans may, which could be nasty given rising anti-Americanism there. The patchwork quilt of regional defenses is rather tightly sewn together, bound with strong American thread. The removal of any one patch will leave an obvious gap, to be filled either by a destabilizing force, such as the Soviet Union or China, or by a stabilizing one, represented by more generous contributions from those nations in East Asia whose prosperity in large part depends on a continued American military presence in the region.

"Singapore clearly would like the bases to stay where they are," Second Minister for Defense (B.G.) Lee Hsien Loong, the prime minister's son, told me in early 1988. "There is simply no substitute for America's presence, given the Russian positions in Vietnam, which are much better for them than Vladivostok. There is also a confidence factor for the region, not just from the Seventh Fleet's occasional patrols, but from the *knowledge* that their presence is there. Russia's preoccupation with domestic economic concerns will not prevent them from playing geopolitical games. And if the Chinese are not preoccupied with modernization of their own economy, then opportunities for them to support insurgent forces in the region are not negligible."

The alternative to a dominant America in the region could be a dominant Japan, which brought us full circle to the issue of revived Japanese militarism.

"It's all right for Japan's military to remain defense-oriented," the B.G. said, "but any aggressive buildup by them or any increase beyond their thousand-mile sea-lanes would not be desired by the region, and I think the Japanese realize this."

When I saw him in Washington a year later, he talked about the concept of burden-sharing.

"With a tight federal budget and a persistent trade deficit," he was saying, "the mood today in the U.S., especially in Congress, is for more burden-sharing. Whether funding the Philippines aid plan or deploying military forces in Japan and Korea, America is looking for allies to share the cost. While the principle is not wrong, the practice will prove difficult. Which countries will share the burden? If Japan, will it do so by disbursing foreign aid, by compensating the U.S. for its own military expenses, or by building up its self-defense forces to take over operational duties from American forces? Each possibility presents its own problems."

As we enter the last decade of the twentieth century, the United States still maintains essentially the same military network and regional security structure that was in place in the Far East at the end of World War II. But in no way does America today have the same security *burden* that it did nearly half a century ago, when Korea was being ravaged by war, when Japan was struggling to rise from the ashes of defeat, when Singapore was emerging from a crucible of Communist-inspired strikes and riots, and when China and the USSR were thought by Washington to control a monolithic Communism bent on world domination, the only salvation from which was a massive American commitment to defend freedom and democracy anywhere in the world.

So the world has changed, and the region has changed, too. Japan is now the economic giant of East Asia. Singapore is a beacon of stability in Southeast Asia. Beijing and Washington have become allied tactically against Moscow. The Soviet Union has become preoccupied internally with *perestroika*. China is struggling with its own reforms, economic and political, and Hong Kong's reversion is imminent. Vietnam is history. Korea, Taiwan, and the nations of ASEAN—the emerging NICs of the 1990s—are all standing proud, in large part because of America's past protection. And the future will undoubtedly bring more change, including changes in the factors affecting regional security, which may mean a possible restructuring of alliances—and an unavoidable redistribution of burden-sharing—if stability in the region is to be preserved.

18
RESTRUCTURING ALLIANCES:
BURDEN-SHARING IN AN ERA OF
COMPREHENSIVE SECURITY

To say that every age seeks a view of history suitable for its needs is not to say that it will find one. Instead, political elites may cling to a view of the past quite unfitted to the present situation. Historical interpretations, like all ideas, take on a life of their own; they may easily outlive the circumstances that made them appropriate. An idea, adopted by one generation for its convenience, may come to possess the next generation and drive it to ruin.

If the hegemonic view of world history suited America's position very well in 1945, and justified the role the United States was about to assume, it may equally well prove inappropriate to the American position at the end of the twentieth century. Clearly, a view of the past that sees no options between the hegemony of a single power and systemic chaos is unlikely to prove constructive in any period when the world balance of forces makes hegemony increasingly unsustainable.

In short, the same historical view that justified creating a hegemonic system becomes increasingly inconvenient as the hegemony matures. For, as a hegemony matures, it also declines.

David Calleo, *Beyond American Hegemony*

There is a sense in which Rudolf Bing had something in common with Washington, Tokyo, Moscow, and Beijing. Bing was the famed general manager of the Metropolitan Opera at a time when labor relations with its union of singers, musicians, and stagehands were not the most harmonious. On one occasion the union leader turned to the powerful impresario and said, "Mr. Bing, you are displaying contempt for me." To which the indefatigable Bing reportedly replied, "On the contrary. I am trying to conceal it."

391

Something not unlike this attitude tends to characterize relationships of great powers with client or second-tier states from time to time, given the disparities in relative size, power, and influence. And no doubt the relationships between Moscow and Pyongyang, Tokyo and Seoul, or Washington and Manila have occasionally reflected this sentiment, because security alliances in the Far East lack the unanimous threat perception that prescribes great power relationships in Europe.

The Soviet Union's role as a Far Eastern power is one that to me has always seemed deceptive if not misplaced. It is driven by the paranoia that characterizes the USSR's foreign affairs in general and by a historical if not fanatic preoccupation with the desire for an ice-free, warm-water port in the Pacific (a desire that was finally realized in 1974 when the U.S. was forced out of Vietnam). Vladivostok, at the southern tip of Siberia, is Russia's only continental access to the Pacific and hardly qualifies as ice-free. But it does give Soviet leaders the perception that their country is a Far Eastern power, despite the fact that most of the USSR's own commercial trade, perceived military threat, and intellectual traditions are with, from, and in Europe. In fact, were it not for Moscow's own threat to stability in the Far East, the United States would arguably have less need to be so concerned with projections of its own power in that part of the world.

But the Soviet military buildup in Asia has been expanding, and hardly in response to increases in American military forces, since they have either declined or remained fairly stable. The Soviet Union now has nearly a hundred Backfire bombers in its Far East command, compared with none a decade ago; fifty-seven Soviet Army divisions (up from fifteen); some 2,400 tactical combat aircraft, including sophisticated MiG-23s, MiG-27 Floggers, and MiG-31 Foxhounds; 400 tactical surface-to-surface missiles (although SS-20s will be removed under the latest arms control agreements); two aircraft carriers; ninety-eight submarines; and nearly 200 combatant ships such as frigates and destroyers.

This military buildup may be viewed as a result of three factors: one was the deterioration of the USSR's relationship with China, which led to serious border disputes (and bloodshed) through the early 1970s; a second was the escalation of America's involvement in Vietnam, which the Soviets countered by aiding Hanoi; and the third, and most recent, has been Japan's real increases in military spending since 1980, viewed by Moscow as extending U.S. power in the Pacific. "Russian fears about external dangers," former ambassador to Moscow and containment architect George Kennan wrote in his memoirs, "were continually expressed with a histrionic vehemence which throws doubt on their sincerity."

So in late 1986, in a speech in Vladivostok, Mikhail Gorbachev proclaimed that "the Soviet Union is also an Asian and Pacific country." By this time Gorbachev's policies of *glasnost* (openness) and *perestroika* (economic restructuring) were becoming household words, and the Soviet Union's predominant concerns had become economic, not strategic. Moscow, well aware of the gains achieved by Japan and the Little Dragons, calculated that these nations might have increasing problems with America, given protectionist trends, and thought it could acquire valuable technology from Asia that it could not get from the United States. The Soviet Union's political leadership, notably Alexander Yokolev, a former secretary of the Central Committee's propaganda department and now, as a member of the Politburo, regarded by many as the second most influential man in Moscow, sensed that these turbocharged economies, with their external orientation, might be interested in closer economic relations with the socialist states.

This would be especially true if two things happened: if Japan and the NICs began to distance themselves from America, to seek greater economic independence, and if the Soviet economy became more "open" relative to its "closed" past. Siberia was rich in natural resources, Moscow reasoned, so the Soviet Union could offer raw materials, rare minerals, timber, and fuel in exchange for access to advanced products and technology from Asia that would enable the Russians to position themselves advantageously as a high-tech power on the eve of the twenty-first century.

Prior to *glasnost* and well before *perestroika*, in 1975, when I was still living and working in Tokyo, I spent several weeks in Moscow and Leningrad. I wrote in advance to the Institute of Mathematical Economics, a well-known Moscow think tank at the Academy of Sciences that specialized in the Soviet economy, requesting an interview with its director, Nikolai Fedorenko. Dr. Fedorenko never responded to my letter, but the phone in my hotel room rang one morning, and a gruff voice commanded me to be in the lobby in an hour. At the appointed time a nervous young man drove up in a black Volga and whisked me out to the academy. Fedorenko was tied up in meetings at the Presidium all day, I was told, but the institute's deputy director, Vasily Shatalin, would see me.

Shatalin was a small man, and bald, with a sinister-looking scar in the middle of his scalp. His only remaining hair was on the sides, which he was in the habit of constantly smoothing back with his hands. After a brief introduction we talked about planning, distribution, and pricing in the Soviet economy.

"Westerners wonder what there is to be proud of," Shatalin said through a translator, "but Westerners are not remembering the conditions before the Revolution. We have plans at the lower level, plans at the middle level, and plans at the top, all shifting back and forth. There is no concept of supply and demand in our economy, but there will be in the future. This lack is most evident now by our overcoat problem. There is a surplus of overcoats in central Russia, where it is very warm, and a scarcity in Moscow, where they are desperately needed. They are symbolic of problems we have with distribution everywhere in a centrally planned economy."

He laughed. I had not expected such candor. The overcoat imbalance was only one of many such problems the Soviet Union had at the time, and still has, stemming from inadequate intermediation in the economy. Consequently, a whole service sector called *tolkach*, agents whose job it is to know where bottlenecks are and to move sufficient supply to satisfy demand by circumventing the system, has evolved. The *tolkach* comprised a pool of management talent that Wassily Leontief, the Harvard economist, considers the best entrepreneurs in Russia. They are no doubt in great demand in the automotive sector.

There was a story, popular at the time, about a man who visited his local Volga distributorship and placed a 100 percent down payment on a black sedan.

"When can I expect delivery?" he asked the salesman.

"Well, since you've made the down payment," he said, flipping through his calendar, "I can promise you delivery ten years from Friday."

"Morning or afternoon?" the customer asked.

"In ten years, what difference does it make?" the salesman replied.

"It makes a lot of difference," the customer insisted. "The plumber is coming that morning."

We turned our attention to agriculture.

"The state sets prices," Shatalin went on, "and as a result we have no inflation. The price of bread has not changed since 1937, and prices for dairy products were last set in 1962. The price of wheat may rise and fall on world markets, but the price of bread to the Russian consumer never changes."

I asked Shatalin whether private farms would ever replace the *kolkhoz,* or state farms, given well-publicized differences in productivity, and he said, not without some agitation, "They are not private, they are personal. There is no such thing as private property in the Soviet Union. And they are not farms, they are small plots, and they exist solely for people to grow their own vegetables."

The shocking statistic about Soviet agriculture is that today, more than seventy years after the Revolution, it still employs nearly 50 million people—about 20 percent of the work force, compared to 4 percent in the U.S.—and yet its per-capita output is *less* than it was in 1913. Russia, in short, cannot feed its own people. Waste is rampant; central planning practices cause some 70 percent of the country's annual production of timber to be lost. Between 20 and 30 percent of its crops rot in transport, and spoilage ruins more than half of all harvested fruits and vegetables.

As a result the Soviet people have an estimated 40 percent vitamin deficiency, and the Soviet Union is the only country in the world where life expectancy for males is actually *declining.* Less than a third of all housing is constructed with amenities such as plumbing or central heat. About a fourth of all construction in progress was started over twenty-five years ago. Since enterprises are rewarded by incentives encouraging them to take on new projects specified by Gosplan, the central planning agency, projects are rarely finished. Soviet workers are motivated neither by personal gain, as in America, nor by institutional pride, as in Japan. The Soviet economy is, in the words of economist Ed Hewlett of the Brookings Institution, "a system that eats resources."

It was difficult to grasp the essential reality that the Soviet Union had been, until recently overtaken by Japan, the second-largest economy in the world, with a world-class space program and titanium-hulled submarines that speed faster and dive deeper than any other. But 80 percent of the system's production is in heavy industrial equipment and defense, with little in the way of consumption goods for the average Soviet consumer. This is evident not only in the inevitable lines that form at most shops and stores but also in the paucity of products that cause those lines in the first place.

In the evenings and on weekends, as I strolled around the Kremlin or rode the vaunted, squeaky-clean Moscow subway, I would frequently be approached by Russians, young and old, offering to buy my blue jeans or asking if I had any Western cigarettes, chocolate, or soap. My overwhelming impressions of day-to-day realities in this supposed superpower were that *economically* the Soviet Union was an underdeveloped Third World country.

Anyone who has visited the Soviet Union and spent some time there, as I have, cannot help being struck by rather dramatic differences between the Russian people, who may be the most dour and sullen in the world, and the Japanese, no doubt the world's most purposeful and intent. Red Square is typically jammed, with queues of Russians waiting patiently to see Lenin's tomb and parading through picturesque St. Basil's Cathedral or the government-owned department store, GUM, nearby. *Babushkas,* brightly colored kerchiefs tied about their heads, offer a stark contrast to the Russian men, whose hard, chiseled faces reflect the seriousness of Soviet life if not the shortcomings of its economy. Older women, stout and stern, proudly wear hero badges and posthumous military medals, evidence still of the sacrifices their husbands made in the great war.

One senior American I spoke with in Moscow at the time said that corruption was a major problem and getting worse. Payment for services was rarely in rubles but in vodka, he said; to get one's car repaired on time requires an additional bottle. This may well be an unavoidable consequence of a system based on mistrust, suspicion, and fear, all national traits of the country.

Alcoholism has more recently reached epidemic proportions in Soviet cities, producing a crackdown on illicit payments and limits on individual consumption such that the hours of operation for retail liquor stores have been greatly reduced. These developments have produced a certain grumbling about Mikhail Gorbachev in their own right. A currently popular story is told about two men, waiting endlessly in line at their local vodka shop.

"I'm sick and tired of standing around in these lines," the first man said.

"What are you going to do about it?" asked the second.

"Well, I think I'll just go over to Gorby's place and shoot the bastard. Save my place."

Several hours later the man returned and found his friend had hardly moved forward.

"Well, how'd it go?" his friend asked. "Were you successful?"

"No," the first man replied. "The line over there was even longer than it is here."

Mikhail Gorbachev is by no means the first Soviet leader to attempt serious reforms in his country's poorly performing economic system; he is simply the first to publicize those reforms and slap the *perestroika* label on them. When I was last in Moscow, Aleksey Kosygin had just announced four of his own economic reforms in an attempt to revive the system. He proposed scrapping the *sovnarkhoz*, the regional economic councils, recommending that they be recentralized in Moscow. He tried to abolish the excessive regulations of industry to create more bank loans and to enable enterprises to retain some of their earnings. He established eight targets, or success indicators, from volume and type of goods produced to the amount of profits retained. And he overhauled the jerry-built system of wholesale prices in an attempt to eliminate bottlenecks.

But Kosygin's reforms all failed, and I think Gorbachev's reforms will ultimately fail, too. The system is simply not geared to shift with changes in incentives or to respond to the cultivation of competitive markets. Gorbachev wants to modify the central planning process, require self-financing of industrial projects, institute price reforms, encourage entrepreneurial "freedom," and "democratize" management. But if that all happens, which seems doubtful, the system is no longer Communist but capitalist.

"Whether Gorbachev can effectively reform the system *without* abandoning the fundamentals of the Communist ideology is extremely doubtful," Yale historian Paul Kennedy recently wrote in a thoughtful *Atlantic* article. "The evidence of the past seventy years of Party rule suggests that the real problem is the Leninist system of government and the economy itself. If they remain, fundamental reform is impossible; if they go, the USSR will no longer be a 'Soviet' and 'Socialist' republic. No amount of partial or cosmetic change will allow Gorbachev and his Party to escape this basic contradiction."

Faced with erosion of power, central ministries will reassert control where they can, and the bureaucracy, used to the perquisites of power, will not let it erode. Based on recent trials, Russian courts are deciding cases in favor of laid-off workers and against the system. Corruption will unavoidably increase as new incentives fail to displace the old. Inequality of income distribution will grow, which could create widespread resentment if the *tolkach*, those agents of entrepreneurial intermediation, increase in number and influence. And important export markets will prove difficult to penetrate, given the strategic technological advantages and superior product quality of goods from Japan and the Little Dragons.

"Democratic communism is an oxymoron," Zbigniew Brzezinski recently wrote in a brilliant book, *The Grand Failure*. "Successful pluralization of the Soviet Union is less likely than ... a protracted and inconclusive systemic crisis which might eventually subside into a renewed period of stagnation, punctuated by outbreaks of social turbulence by economically dissatisfied urban masses and politically more restless non-Russian peoples. [This] would further deepen the general crisis of communism ... and accelerate the process of ideological dissolution. Gorbachev has unintentionally placed on history's agenda the possibility of the actual dismantling of the Soviet Union."

Communism is less an economic system than an ideology. The message to the rest of the world as a result of Gorbachev's attempted reforms is clear: the Soviet ideology is dead. Communism *has* no further demonstration effect for the nonaligned countries of the world. It was a system invented by a politician, a European friend once told me. If it had been invented by a scientist, it would have been tried on laboratory mice first.

In China, if one looks at recent economic reforms through Chairman Deng Xiaoping's Four Modernizations, one comes to very much the same conclusion as with Gorbachev's *perestroika:* they too are doomed to fail. Conventional wisdom holds that China is Asia's next economic giant; indeed, many contend that China will soon be on center stage because its huge population, long an object of fascination, will be the single largest moving force in determining the future. But if the past hundred years of history and experience can be used as a guide, it is difficult *not* to subscribe to the unconventional wisdom, which says that China's overtaking Japan as Asia's economic superpower is simply not in the cards.

"There are certain innate cultural factors about China," T. L. Tsim, director of the Chinese University Press, once told me. "It is antidevelopmental, antichange, and antiprogress."

The clues to China's future are very much in its past. The Manchu dynasty clung to power after the opium wars with Britain, then was stung by the Tai P'ing rebellion and suffered a humiliating dismemberment at the hands of the Western powers, who carved up the defenseless Central Kingdom mercilessly. In 1895 China was defeated by an aggressive, expansionist Japan and lost Taiwan. In 1901 the Boxer rebellion occurred, and in 1911 the Manchu dynasty collapsed, having long since lost the mandate of heaven. The Chinese achieved some semblance of unity under Sun Yat-sen and his newly emerging Nationalist party, but soon lost it through internal squabbling as Chiang Kai-shek came to power. The nation was weakened further by civil war with the communists under Mao Zedong and then collapsed totally under the force of the Japanese invasion. Then came World War II, followed by more war with the Communists, followed by independence as the People's Republic in 1949, followed in succession by the Great Leap Forward, the Five Antis, the Hundred Flowers, the Cultural Revolution, Mao's death, and finally the current Four Modernizations. And the whole process almost came unglued again in late spring 1989 when 1 million students massed in Tiananmen Square to demonstrate for democracy.

This historical pattern, briefly, is the basis on which contemporary analysts would have us believe China is Asia's next giant. I am underimpressed. Compared to Japan's achievements in the last century, and the strong cultural roots that fed them, China's record more nearly resembles a scattergram than a rising curve of accomplishments. The Central Kingdom's claim to fame, simply put, is Confucius; everything else is hidden in small print and buried in footnotes.

The early postwar Chinese economy was based on the Soviet industrial model, though Mao was continually at odds with his counterparts in Moscow because his revolution had been agrarian, not proletarian, in nature. When the Great Leap Forward collapsed in 1960, China struggled for years, trying to balance a Soviet-style central-command economy with a program of mass mobilization in the rural areas, and achieved an anemic annual economic growth rate of only 4 percent through the 1970s. Rural incomes barely kept even with increases in population, which was expanding at more than 2 percent a year.

Enter the new chairman with a radically new idea.

"I don't care whether the cat is black or white," Deng Xiaoping said, "as long as it catches mice."

In 1979 the Chinese began to favor economic sectors that used less energy. They explored for oil offshore, sent their students in large numbers to the United States to study science and advanced technology, joined the United Nations, became members of the International Monetary Fund and the World Bank, set up export processing zones, paid more attention to marketing, gave their managers more accountability, imported new and necessary technology, established joint ventures with the Western capitalists, encouraged their farmers to sell "above-quota" items on the free market, and even toyed with the idea of setting up a fledgling stock market in Shanghai.

As the cat began to catch some mice, people began to ask what color it was. Economic systems based on the concepts of supply and demand, freely fluctuating prices, profit incentives, sophisticated macroeconomic controls, and vigorously competitive markets were notably *not* communist.

Despite export growth that has risen 22 percent a year since 1980, although admittedly from a tiny base, reports of success in the Chinese economy have been exaggerated. Individuals and enterprises still make their way through a veritable mine field of contradictory rules and regulations; despite lip service paid to market decentralization, the economy is still centrally run by Beijing. True, larger numbers of Chinese workers are being drawn from the ricefields to the factories, especially in export processing zones such as Shenzhen, and the process of urbanization is finally under way—a necessary stage in liberating the economy from its agrarian past. But is this enough to enable the country to *triple* its per-capita income from an estimated $400 in 1985 to $1,200 by the year 2000, as many Sinologists are projecting?

Such optimism seems seriously overdrawn and inadequately cognizant of those forces on the dark side that always tend to accompany unencumbered growth in capitalist economies.

If China were to replicate the economic growth of Japan or the Little Dragons during the next decade, there would be a *massive* shift from the countryside to the cities, which would double the urban population from 300 million to 600 million in a very short time. Such a dramatic shift would put immense strain on the urban infrastructure and create a set of problems that Beijing, through inexperience, is totally unprepared to deal with: air and water pollution, sanitation demands, a population explosion, abortion, divorce, unemployment, transportation bottlenecks, crime, corruption, and homelessness. Japan, Korea, and Taiwan went from a 40 percent urban population, on average, to a 60 percent urban population—a 50 percent increase—but over a thirty-year time frame. China wants to double the rate in less than half the time.

It is one thing for a Chinese Communist government to eliminate rural disease and poverty in an agrarian population over a period of two generations, but it is something else again to cope with the huge increases in urban slums and squatters that would naturally accompany such rapid economic growth.

Something approximating these conditions is, however, already beginning to occur. In discussions with Chinese friends I have been told that as income inequality has risen, corruption has, too, with predictable results. Bureaucrats in Shenzhen are being bribed to accelerate approvals for new construction projects or to look the other way when defective or substandard materials have been used, or to ignore falsified tax returns. The faulty construction of the Daiya Bay nuclear power project, in Guangdong, is another example. In Shanghai early last year, raw sewage severely polluted local rivers feeding into the harbor, causing the worst outbreak of hepatitis ever. Inflation has soared uncontrollably. Add the impact of rising consumer expectations to growing income inequality, and you create the groundwork for *another* revolution—a capitalist revolution—with profound implications for Chinese Marxist politics.

"Modern Chinese have become increasingly narrow-minded and closed off," the essayist Bo Yang has written, "through an habitual inability to admit mistakes and a predilection for bragging, lying, and slander. Due to their inveterate arrogance, even the slightest success is overwhelming. It is all right if a few people behave in this manner, but if a majority behaves this way, it spells disaster for the nation. Generations of despots and tyrannical officials have rubbed their hands in glee at the thought of the Chinese masses acting wisely and playing it safe."

Overlaid against these developments, of course, is the sequence of events in late spring 1989, when Chinese students spontaneously occupied Tiananmen Square in Beijing to commemorate the death of Hu Yaobang, one of the architects of China's economic modernization policy. When a million demonstrators converged on the central square, martial law was declared by aging chairman Deng Xiaoping (who applied Mao's dictum that political power grows from the barrel of a gun), but the army, seemingly sympathetic to the students, appeared hesitant. A fierce power struggle thus ensued in the Communist party between the factions of premier Li Peng, a hard-liner, and general secretary Zhao Ziyang, a moderate who had earlier supported the trend toward democratic liberalization. Throughout late May, the internal debate raged, with Li the apparent victor; Zhao was stripped of his party power (but not his post) and dropped from sight.

So in early June—"June 4, China's day of shame," as it was called in Hong Kong—the People's Liberation Army moved to take control of the square and suppress the students, rolling its tanks and armored vehicles over bicycles, tents, and, in many cases, bodies. Firing indiscriminately, the PLA killed several hundred civilians who had emerged to join the students. It was the first time the Chinese government had used hostile force against its own people, an event likely not only to remain etched in the popular memory but also to render further economic and political reforms difficult if not unattainable. Deng Xiaoping had risen to power by rescuing China from anarchy at the time of the Cultural Revolution and had breathed fresh life into the Chinese political economy, but he risked it all (possibly including a counterrevolution and another civil war) on that fateful weekend in June.

One of China's leading intellectuals, the poet Shao Yanxiang, had said just prior to these tragic events that if the blood of the students were spilled, it would mean the final self-destruction of the Communist party in China was imminent. Another prominent dissident, the filmmaker Chen Kaige, noted that the dominance of China's political leadership by Maoist ideas had been like a giant magnet that fixed the order of all the independent iron filings. Now, with the big magnet jolted, the iron filings would be scattered everywhere.

The success or failure of domestic economic restructuring in the Soviet Union and China also has security implications. If Gorbachev is successful, either relatively or absolutely, the future of Soviet socialism may not be clear, but the perceived Russian threat to Western Europe's security may be diminished considerably. Yet that raises questions about the future of Eastern Bloc countries, which may feel encouraged by Moscow's economic successes (in fact, they are already) such that further liberalization occurs, with predictable pressures for greater nationalism and independence. And *that* implies a totally different kind of security threat to Western Europe, possibly throwing the continent back into its traditional state of perpetual cross-border conflict and war. If Gorbachev fails, as is more likely, chances are good a downsized version of the cold war could return as Soviet leadership seeks external means of distracting its people from the consequences of economic failure.

In China, even if Deng continues to succeed with the Four Modernizations, highly doubtful in the aftermath of the June massacre, the country could be totally preoccupied with institutional restructuring and the immense difficulty of fulfilling the expectations of its 1.2 billion people. If Deng fails, which is more likely, domestic political turbulence will increase, Hong Kong may be at even greater risk, Taiwan may be under renewed pressure, and the cycle will lurch two steps back, in sync with past patterns. Either way, success or failure does not *eliminate* security concerns; it merely makes the potential scenarios—and the necessary responses to them—different.

Again, Brzezinski, from *The Grand Failure*: "It does not follow that setbacks in China's economic programs would somehow revitalize or relegitimate the ideology. On the contrary, any such failure is likely to be viewed by many Chinese as further proof that economic success is not possible in a quasi-communist setting and can be achieved only by a comprehensive abandonment of all traditional Marxist-Leninist restraints on political freedom. China is almost inevitably fated to experience intensifying political tensions."

As we enter the final decade of the twentieth century with the two Communist superpowers engaged in historical efforts at domestic economic and political reform, a strange sort of strategic lull has settled over the Far East, with neither the Soviet Union nor China a current threat to stability in the region. The Soviet Union is no longer the evil empire and America's international enemy number one; it has, somehow, become a friend. China no longer underwrites insurgencies overseas or exports arms to Iran; it, too, has become a friend. The demonstration effect of turbocharged capitalism, as evidenced by the successes of Japan and the Little Dragons, has stood Communism on its head.

These two recent and simultaneous experiments in domestic economic reform explain, in part, the Soviet decision to withdraw from Afghanistan; the arms control agreement between Moscow and Washington; signals from Moscow that the long-standing border dispute with China can be resolved; intercession by China to end the Vietnamese occupation of Kampuchea; quiet steps between Beijing and London to bring about the reversion of Hong Kong; informal feelers from Taipei to permit personal visits from Taiwan to China; and signals from the Soviets to the Japanese that Moscow may be prepared to return the

Kuriles. In sum, Moscow and Beijing can attempt serious economic reform only if the external environment is at peace.

For what purpose, then, in an emerging era of multipolar relationships, will the United States maintain a Far Eastern security network consisting of the Seventh Fleet and its more than seventy ships with 250 carrier-based aircraft; naval and air bases in Japan and Okinawa, with 50,000 troops and 200 tactical aircraft stationed there; air bases in Korea with 100 aircraft and two divisions totaling 43,000 men; Clark Air Base and Subic Bay Naval Station in the Philippines with another 25,000 men—all costing the Pentagon $50 billion a year to maintain?

Or, half a world away, a NATO security alliance consisting of complex command interrelationships with America's European allies and costing *$150 billion* a year to maintain? Americans know only too well the fallacy of predicting a permanent trend based on short-term evidence. If the enemy of my enemy can so quickly become my friend, then he can just as quickly become my enemy again. Lord Palmerston said it best, recall, more than a century ago: Nations do not have permanent allies, nor do they have permanent enemies. They have only permanent interests.

These questions of deployment focus increasingly on cost, not on strategy, and cost to the American taxpayer in an era of $150 billion global trade and federal budget deficits every year has become a matter of understandable concern. Is the nation getting its money's worth, and by extension, are the nation's traditional friends, such as Europe and Japan, paying their fair share?

As we have seen, America spends about 6 percent of GNP on defense, the European countries average 3.7 percent, and Japan little more than 1 percent. The United States accounts for less than half the combined GNP of the NATO countries plus Japan plus the United States itself, yet it pays *two-thirds* of NATO's total defense costs. NATO members have about 40 percent of the combined wealth but account for less than a third of NATO's costs. Japan, with some 16 percent of the combined wealth, provides only about 4 percent of total allied defense spending.

Still, America's European allies provide 53 percent of all NATO tanks, 46 percent of its artillery, 54 percent of its combat aircraft, 83 percent of its combat naval ships, 58 percent of its active-duty military personnel, and 80 percent of all reserves. Yet Britain has *reduced* its military spending by 5 percent over the past two years, and Japan now pays half the support costs necessary to keep U.S. troops stationed in that country. Tokyo will, over time, move to absorb them all. But those costs relate primarily to the defense of Japan; regional security costs are borne entirely by the United States.

In an era of changing superpower relationships it is necessary to address two aspects of the comprehensive security problem. One is the question of burden-sharing, viewed from three strategic perspectives—NATO, Northeast Asia, and Southeast Asia. The other is whether traditional alliances are in any danger of being realigned or restructured. The broader question of whether America is getting its money's worth involves a more extensive domestic cost-benefit analysis, including examination of the unacceptably high levels of waste involved in Pentagon spending, fraudulent practices by American defense contractors, substandard equipment produced by those contractors, and expensive military retirement pensions.

Those domestic considerations are important. America spends $300 billion a year on defense. If a football field, including both end zones, were covered with $20 bills stacked tightly side by side, it would create a pile thirty-three feet high weighing 15,000 tons. A third of this amount—$100 billion—is considered excessive and could be pared from the budget. The estimated annual increase in cost from fraudulent practices, shoddy workmanship, cost overruns, and poor product quality alone is half of that, about $50 billion.

Poor product quality is not limited to American automobiles and consumer electronic goods, nor is it a recent phenomenon in military procurement. Many defense contractors allow random inspections of products prior to shipment but then substitute defective parts in already approved shipments. Others purposefully mislabel substandard goods with chemicals that foil the inspection process. Inflated labor billing and faked time cards are frequent offenses. Pentagon employees are often bribed by contractors to provide them with inside information used to strengthen bids or to defeat a competitor.

Spare parts are egregiously overpriced. In recent years the navy paid $436 for a hammer that retails for $7 in any hardware store. The legally billed difference represented $102 for overhead, $93 for engineering and assembly time, $37 for administrative costs, and a $56 finder's fee. The Pentagon has also paid $110 for a 4¢ diode, $44 for a 17¢ lamp, and $122 for a $2 microchip.

In February 1988, Robert Costello, the Pentagon's top procurement official, went on record as saying that DOD wastes about 25¢ out of every $1 it spends on procurement—or about $50 billion a year. The practice of reinforcing failure is largely at fault; lack of competition and choice in weapons procurement means higher cost overruns and lower quality. (Of the top ten defense contractors in 1963, eight were still in the top ten in 1988; many fail when they venture into the competitive commercial market.) The goal is a return to what former assistant secretary of defense (and Hewlett-Packard chairman) David Packard calls "competitive prototyping"—a "fly before you buy" approach that tests weapons in prototype (not just on paper) before they are bought by the Pentagon. Two of the most successful weapons systems in America—the F-16 and the A-10—were produced in this way.

Because of poor product quality and price-gouging, the Department of Defense has shifted to foreign suppliers for more reliable (and cheaper) componentry and equipment. Another reason is the limited ability of American manufacturers to get a product from design to market. These developments have resulted in a dangerous degree of dependence on foreign sources for defense technology, a trend that is most pronounced in the "dual-use" sector— high-technology industries that manufacture primarily for the commercial market but also make important components for defense systems. The Pentagon became so concerned about increasing reliance on foreign suppliers that it asked the Office of Technology Assessment to look into the problem.

The OTA report found that high-technology products were increasingly manufactured outside the United States and that the ability to design at the leading edge followed manufacturing overseas, reducing DOD's access to the technology it needs. Other nations have national policies to attract, nurture, and protect high-technology industries, it said, contributing to the continuing deterioration of U.S.-based manufacturers.

NATO represents America's biggest chunk of spending on defense ($150 billion), its largest overseas concentration of troops (328,000), and the greatest need for a more equitable sharing of burdens. NATO was put in place when the perceived threat to European security was considerably different than it is today and when the United States had the world's strongest and most fiscally sound economy, an Atlas that shouldered the free world's defense burdens.

In 1950 the United States had 150,000 troops stationed at its bases in Europe. By 1981, after one round of detente and two rounds of

SALT talks, the U.S. had more than twice that number. Today, with a depreciated currency, every 10 percent decline in the dollar costs the Pentagon about $500 million more to house, feed, and train those troops overseas. Given America's economic problems and its cumulative trade and budget deficits, maintaining those levels of troop concentration is no longer feasible.

The obvious solution is to bring some of them home, perhaps upward of five divisions—100,000 men—but that raises other questions. Will the U.S. then be perceived to be "soft" on defense of Europe? Can the Europeans make up the difference, given declining birthrates? Should such a move be made unilaterally without requiring a similar pullback by Soviet troops from Warsaw Pact countries?

An immediate objective, both to reduce spending and to lessen tensions, should be to negotiate troop withdrawals on both sides and demobilize them, with the Soviets to bring their troops back from Eastern Europe and American forces to return home from Germany.

"Wars are not caused by nations having armies," international relations specialist Dr. Christopher Layne remarked recently. "Wars are caused by political conflicts that create crises that spin out of control. Now, the Soviets are not going to wake up one morning and say, 'Let's invade Europe today.' But their being in Eastern Europe prevents the national political evolution of the Eastern European countries. Thus political tensions within those countries fester—they have no safety valve. Sooner or later, under these conditions, an explosion will happen; popular unrest will break out. What will the Soviets do then? Will they sit back and watch their empire disintegrate, or will they be tempted to launch a war against the West to save the empire?"

America pays $150 billion to defend Europe, where education, health care, and child care are all free. Europeans put their taxes into benefits for their people because we put our taxes into defending them. The savings realized through demobilization can be put to work in America and applied to American priorities, to help reduce the federal deficit and restore a higher level of private savings necessary to fight the battles of the future, more likely to be economic than military in nature anyway.

As a result, the issue of burden-sharing has become a major preoccupation among NATO members. When a new military base has to be constructed in a member country, who pays what share of the cost? The host country bears no small burden when it removes land from its tax rolls for the purposes of collective defense. When a new gen-

eration of equipment becomes necessary, how should the costs be allocated? When a new tactical jet fighter is developed, shouldn't NATO
allies fund a portion of the R&D costs as well as import it from the
United States?

Burden-sharing—who pays, how much, and for what—is likely to
dominate the European alliance for the remainder of this century. The
alternative—devolution, or transferring responsibility for NATO to the
European community itself—is not yet an acceptable political concept,
either on the Continent or in Washington.

Still, President Bush took a giant step toward devolution at the NATO
Summit in Brussels in June 1989 when he proposed a unilateral 20
percent reduction in American combat forces stationed in Europe, and
set an interim ceiling of 275,000, with the forces withdrawn to be
completely demobilized, all by 1992. He encouraged the Soviets to
reduce their combat manpower level in the European theater to an
equal number (though that would mean a cut of 325,000 men from
their present total of about 600,000, or elimination of more than 50
percent). The American proposal sought an agreement on common
numerical ceilings for military hardware in Europe, as well, in response
to Gorbachev's earlier call for a mutual reduction in short-range nuclear
missiles. In the same policy statement, Bush also called for free elections
and greater political pluralism in Eastern Europe and demolition of the
Berlin Wall.

"Logically, the United States should serve its own and the general
interest by learning how to make use of the strengths and interests of
others," the security specialist David Calleo wrote in *Beyond American
Hegemony*. "Given America's present and predictable degree of overextension, something beyond traditional burden-sharing is required. An
intelligent policy of geopolitical devolution seems an urgent necessity.
And given the significance of the NATO commitment in our fiscal
overextension, NATO seems the logical place for devolution to be
employed, an ideal way to adapt to and, indeed, take advantage of the
global pluralization of power. If devolution cannot succeed in Europe,
it seems unlikely to succeed elsewhere."

But even if devolution works in Europe, the source of America's
intellectual and cultural traditions, its success in the Far East, where
economic ties are strong but cultural heritage is weak, seems less likely.
In Northeast Asia, security on the Korean Peninsula is still the primary
concern. Prospects for reunification between North and South Korea

may be stronger than most observers acknowledge, especially as South Korea expands strategic trade and investment relationships with China.

Yet until and unless the security issue is addressed, bilateral trade and economic ties between the two Koreas are unlikely to form. The time seems ripe for four-power disengagement talks on the peninsula involving Moscow, Beijing, Washington, and Tokyo. There is widespread consensus that one of America's two divisions in South Korea could be moved out, preferably before anti-American pressure builds in Seoul to force it out; to avoid repeating past mistakes, its withdrawal should be undertaken neither unilaterally nor overnight. Mutual disengagement is the answer, starting with a joint pullback from the Demilitarized Zone. Washington could agree to withdraw a division, possibly to Okinawa, if Beijing removed the equivalent from its territory north of the Yalu and Moscow made appropriate reductions in its Far East forces, including withdrawal from the Kuriles north of Japan.

"Of the four powers operating in northeast Asia," the political scientist Harold Hinton wrote in a thoughtful essay called "The Impact of Korea on U.S. Western Pacific Strategy," "the only one with a libertarian tradition is the United States. America has no interest in regional expansion there, and is not a neighbor of the Korean peninsula. For these reasons, the United States is the only one of the four that has never displayed interest in dominating the peninsula, but has demonstrated a real interest in Korea and Koreans for their own sake."

Korea would not likely permit Japan to intermediate any reunification talks. Nor would Korea seek a bilateral security treaty with Japan were the U.S. to withdraw from the Korean peninsula entirely. But by the sheer size of its giant economy, Japan dominates Northeast Asia. Given traditional animosities and historical conflict between Japan and Korea, China, and Russia, what can Japan do other than represent the leading edge of American power in the region?

Behind the lack of receptivity to a regional defense role for Japan is the question of its reliability. As far back as 1979 the Toshiba Machine Company, a subsidiary of Toshiba Electric, Japan's second-largest electronics manufacturer, began selling the Soviet Union numerically controlled propeller milling machines that help ship propulsion systems run more quietly. Soviet submarine propellers were noisy, which made tracking them by sophisticated American sonar systems relatively easy, until U.S. specialists began noticing a demonstrable reduction in noise. In early 1987 the Pentagon discovered the Toshiba infractions and pressed the Japanese government to take appropriate action. The Senate exploded in anger, denounced Japan, and voted to bar Toshiba exports to the U.S. for two to five years. American congressmen took sledge-hammers to a Toshiba stereo, creating an unforgettable photo oppor-tunity on Capitol Hill, the results of which caused a furor in Tokyo.

Not long thereafter, ASEAN protested Japanese exports to socialist Vietnam, and four Japanese were arrested in Tokyo for stealing secrets relating to the F-16 tactical jet fighter and selling them to a member of the Soviet trade office. Then MITI suspended exports of heavy Japanese trucks to North Korea after learning that Pyongyang was converting them to mobile missile launchers. And the manager of Tokyo Aircraft Instruments Company was arrested for selling diagrams of a Boeing 767 altitude control system to a Soviet trade representative. Japan, it seemed, had become a veritable paradise for spies.

The upshot of all these developments was to reveal the Soviet strategy of trying to move Japan away from its security dependence on the United States. Moscow *had* to do so if it was to gain access to Japanese technology and to the expanding Pacific economy on its own terms. Previously the USSR had approached Japan only with a stick. Gor-bachev was ready to offer some carrots—trade, certainly, and perhaps even the Kuriles. Contradictions in Japan's relationship with the U.S. gave Moscow good opportunities to push the idea of neutrality further into Japanese domestic politics.

But the Soviet Union is on its way to becoming less communist, or so Gorbachev would have us believe, which has prompted American firms to visit Moscow in droves. A security distinction can clearly be drawn between selling the Soviets Pepsi and providing them with so-phisticated ship propulsion systems, but the point many Japanese make is twofold. First, American foreign policy has a tendency to vacillate between the Soviet Union as being evil one year and benign the next, so if the Japanese constrain development of commercial relationships with the USSR, they fear their American competitors may have an unfair advantage. Therefore, Japan maintains an aggressive commercial strategy. Second, American incidents of espionage and treasonous be-havior, not to mention exports of sensitive equipment, far exceed those of Japan. Over a decade ago Caterpillar Tractor signed an agreement to build a major truck manufacturing plant on the Kama River, with the proviso of a Soviet promise to restrict output of the facility to commercial vehicles. It was a promise Moscow did not keep. The

Soviets will develop a security application from practically any product or process technology they buy from the West.

Other strains in the Japanese-American relationship have occurred over selection of the next generation of tactical jet fighters for the Japanese Air Self-Defense Forces, designated the FSX, using the American F-16 as the developmental model. Both MITI and Japan's leading defense contractor, Mitsubishi Heavy Industries, wanted to manufacture the new fighter indigenously in Japan. The Congress wanted to export the F-16, since selling aircraft and weapons is one of the few ways the United States can try to offset its negative trade balance with Japan and the F-16 can literally be sold "off the shelf." While criticizing Japan for being a "free rider" on defense, Washington also did not want Tokyo to adopt an independent defense policy by embarking on domestic production of the FSX, but the Department of Commerce argued in favor of linking defense with trade issues, something the Pentagon has long opposed. The Pentagon favored co-development and co-production.

The Japanese argued that domestic production had advantages in terms of quality, lower development costs, and enhanced performance, even though the total product cost would be greater. Japan was also in a position to apply new advances in commercial semiconductor technology to weapons development, the mirror image of American capabilities, which gave Washington pause. (National security had been a factor in an earlier decision, correct in my view, to prevent Fujitsu, a leading Japanese semiconductor manufacturer, from acquiring America's Fairchild Semiconductors in 1987.) In the end a difficult compromise was reached whereby the Japanese agreed to develop the FSX under sixty-forty joint production and development with the U.S. rather than develop a totally new aircraft on their own, even though Tokyo could have acquired twice as many F-16s off the shelf at half the cost.

But the debate over the FSX in Washington in early 1989 had been acrid. Senator Jack Danforth of Missouri (where McDonnell-Douglas is headquartered and General Dynamics has a large presence) favored outright exports of the American F-16 to help trim the trade deficit. Congress challenged commerce secretary Bob Mosbacher and U.S. Trade Representative Carla Hills in their confirmation hearings to justify the FSX co-development project on trade grounds. Senator Jeff Bingaman of New Mexico, who had long been concerned about the decline of America's defense industrial base, wrote the White House opposing co-production, as did Jesse Helms of North Carolina, who requested a complete review of the administration's memorandum of understanding with Tokyo. Senator Alan Dixon of Illinois introduced legislation disallowing *any* transfer of F-16 technology to Japan, and Congressman Mel Levine of California followed suit in the House.

In May 1989 the Senate finally approved the memorandum of understanding, but not before tacking on a resolution proposed by Senator Robert Byrd of West Virginia that imposes strict conditions guaranteeing American manufacturers (principally General Dynamics and its domestic components subcontractors) 40 percent of the $6 billion in production contracts, as stipulated in side-letter agreements; delineating the specific work shares to be split between Japan and the U.S. throughout the project; and guarding against the transfer of critical engine technologies to Japan.

The political compromise over the FSX suggests some truths about Japan–U.S. cooperation in defense, over and above the inability of American agencies to coordinate a unified policy toward Japan. That the United States needs to keep Japan's defense policy, including weapons development, under its own control is clear. The U.S. also realizes that the Japanese arms industry has become capable of developing next-generation fighter aircraft by producing major weapons under U.S. license.

By the late 1980s Japan's self-confidence toward indigenous fighter production was very high. Japanese industry had earlier designed and produced the supersonic XT-4 jet trainer on its own, and quite successfully. This was the first Japanese aircraft to use carbon-fiber composites on a large scale as well as a domestically developed aluminum aircraft skin. The XT-4 was also Japan's first defense project for the Japan Defense Agency based on comprehensive use of computer-aided design and manufacturing equipment (CAD/CAM). It had replicated in miniature all aspects of an FSX program but with considerably less demanding technology.

So to check the transfer of weapons technology to Japan and retain control over Japanese defense policy, the U.S. ought to sell only the finished products, a policy that unavoidably weaves nationalism into technology. Allowing the Japanese to develop the FSX jointly with the U.S. not only dilutes control; it also helps Japan achieve its stated goal of becoming a world-class competitor in producing commercial jet aircraft.

In an insightful working paper called "Defense Production and Industrial Development: The Case of Japanese Aircraft," MIT analysts Dick Samuels and Ben Whipple perceptively predicted in late 1988 the Japanese commitment to develop their own commercial jet aviation and aerospace technology.

"Convinced that aerospace can help revitalize the troubled heavy industrial sector and spread high technology benefits throughout the economy, frustrated in attempts to develop commercial aircraft, anxious to capitalize on new opportunities to exploit domestic technology, and continually pressured by the U.S. to rearm more vigorously," they wrote, "Japanese policy makers in the 1980s have turned to military spending as [another] mechanism for industrial development."

Hiroshi Morikawa, executive director of the Defense Production Committee at Keidanren, put it more bluntly.

"We have no alternative but to pin our hopes on the FSX," he said, "given the current lack of progress in plans to jointly develop civilian aircraft with the U.S. and Europe."

The process is called *techno-nationalism*, and it represents the next stage in Japan–U.S. competition. Techno-nationalism stands in the way of America's exporting two Aegis systems to Japan—the same sophisticated phased-array radar system that shot down an Iranian Airlines passenger jet over the Persian Gulf in 1988. Each Aegis system costs about $1 billion and represents the best of America's proprietary technology. But with Japanese reliability at risk, many congressmen fear Japan may leak that technology to the Soviets and have balked at approving the export.

"One of the things I listen to when people talk about technology," Fred Bucy, former president and chief operating officer of Texas Instruments, recently told me, "is whether they *understand* it. Now technology is not product, and it is not science; it's know-how. It's the 10,000 or 100,000 detailed steps needed to convert science into a workable product."

I had asked Bucy about reverse technology flows, and he said, "We seem to let foreign governments use more leverage over our companies than our government is prepared to use over theirs. Where was Washington when the Japanese pressured Boeing into cooperating on the 757 and 767 commercial jet aircraft systems? Where we have proprietary technology, we need to hold on to it. If the Japanese government owns a patent, they say it can't be licensed outside Japan because it's against government policy. We gain more than we lose by keeping scientific channels open, but the Japanese don't always march to the same tune."

A few years ago Bucy wrote a thoughtful article called "Linking Defense, Trade, and Economic Interests with Japan." In it he argued that Japan should build up its defense capability by buying military equipment outright from the U.S., rather than licensing American technology so Japanese firms can produce it with higher costs (and with smaller production runs) through co-production. The issue is all the more nettlesome because the U.S. alone funds *all* the R&D to develop the underlying technology.

Since development of world-class commercial jet aircraft is a targeted priority of Japanese industrial policy planners, Boeing's creation of joint ventures with Japan has encountered more than its share of critics. Fred Bucy is one of them.

"We have friendly competitors, and we have enemies," he said. "But when I talk about competitors, I mean *all* competitors. I wouldn't give my competitor across the street technology that would put me down and help him up, so why should I give it to these folks in East Asia? Technology is our lifeblood. The Japanese understand this very well. They use every bit of leverage they can to get technology and forestall buying the product, whatever it is. But their people are learning our commercial jet aircraft technology from Boeing, and they'll take it home with them, and one day we'll wonder, now how in the world did they do that? There's not a more natural business for Japan to be in, outside the computer business, because the amount of material it takes to make a jet airplane is pretty small. The avionic, high-tech componentry is where you get all the value added. And they're damned easy to export too. Just fire 'em up and fly 'em out."

There is one aspect of comprehensive security that seems tailor-made for Japan, and that is the Strategic Defense Initiative. With nearly 200 Soviet intermediate-range nuclear missiles in Siberia and twenty-five Soviet submarines equipped with sea-launched ballistic missiles in the Far East, Japan is especially vulnerable to nuclear attack. Development of an SDI shield to enhance air defenses would not only allay the fears of Japan's Asian neighbors about "massive Japanese rearmament"; it would also be compatible with Japan's constitution. The so-called "boost phase" component of SDI, consisting of nonnuclear armed satellites orbiting the Soviet Union, would be particularly advantageous to Japan, as would a weapon called ERIS—an Exoatmospheric Reentry Intercept System—which could protect Japan against tactical missiles. And given Japan's technological leadership in industrial ceramics and in certain applied phases of telecommunications and semiconductor technology, American interest in Japanese research for SDI should be strong.

In Southeast Asia traditional differences in the perception of threats to regional security, geographical distances, and differing cultural traditions among diverse members make the creation of a regional security alliance for ASEAN much more difficult. The Philippines, consisting of 7,000 islands, has an internal insurgency fed by rural poverty and by lack of any meaningful land reform. Malaysia and Indonesia have had problems with the Chinese going back to the 1950s, when they defeated Communist insurgencies soundly. Thailand is preoccupied with an aggressive neighbor, Vietnam, and its occupation of neighboring Kampuchea. Singapore has more problems with Moscow as an adversary than with Beijing, and its leaders view China as more benign than belligerent; it has an Israeli-trained, 55,000-man military guarding its strategic position at the tip of the Malay Peninsula. At present, defense of the ASEAN region is paid for entirely by the United States, and there is little opportunity for a mutual security pact among its members, although a Zone of Peace, Freedom, and Neutrality—called ZOPFAN—has been considered.

Given the diversity of interests and needs in Southeast Asia, a sensible approach could be to calculate the percentage of America's regional defense costs for ASEAN pro rata by GNP and allocate an appropriate portion to each member. These costs should be kept separate and distinct from U.S. military assistance programs, nearly 90 percent of which are U.S. exports, not grants or aid. Human rights violations are often cited as a reason to restrain or prohibit the export of American arms. But American arms are not the *cause* of human rights violations in other countries, and the absence of sophisticated American weapons will not deter them. So future emphasis should be on mutual contributions in an attempt to develop a more equitable regional security alliance.

Given its economic dominance of East Asia, its industrial and financial power, and its growing technological leadership, how can Japan contribute more equitably to regional defense needs in Asia? The primary issue for Washington is cost; under no circumstances should the

U.S. relinquish *control* over regional security, and that will be a major issue for Japan.

Given the Toshiba and FSX cases, the issue of control is vital and one that will surface repeatedly in the waning years of this century. If Korea will not accept Japanese control over regional security in Northeast Asia, and if ASEAN is not prepared to accept Japanese control over regional security in Southeast Asia, the United States must be prepared to retain control over both, but at a price commensurate with its ability—and the growing ability of its allies, principally Japan—to pay.

Much has been made of the coming of a "Europe without frontiers" in 1992, when the European community is scheduled to achieve the common unity intended thirty years ago. Contrarian to the end, I remain skeptical about Europe's ability to close ranks around common goals. In a multipolar world, especially one marked by the decline of bipolarized power between the Soviet Union and America, the risk of destabilization in Western Europe may be greater than the prospect for harmony. Historical patterns of nationalism may work as much against a unified Europe in 1992 as they have in the recent past, especially now that pressure for greater freedom, more democratic institutions, and even elections is growing rapidly in Eastern Europe.

The recent democratic stirrings in Eastern Europe have produced a mixture of cautious optimism combined with fear of possible Soviet repression. Memories of Budapest in 1956, East Berlin in 1961, Prague in 1968, and Warsaw in 1980 are still quite fresh. At present Moscow cannot risk intervention; the cost in terms of the fragility of its own domestic political reforms is far too high. But when *glasnost* and *perestroika* fail, what can Eastern Europeans expect but a further tightening of the noose around their necks? So the potential ripple effect on Western Europe—whether Eastern Europe becomes freer or reverts to stricter Soviet control—is considerable, and portends relatively more uncertainty and instability either way.

The recently concluded free trade agreement with Canada is but an extension of a close historical relationship between two countries separated by a practically invisible border. Any replication with Japan is doomed for political reasons relating to agriculture and domestic politics in Japan and to defense and domestic politics in America. The evolution of a common market in Asia tends to ignore the same issues of underlying differences in cultural traditions, economic conditions, geographic distances, and threat perceptions that characterize regional relationships as a whole.

But what if the relationship between Japan and America continues to deteriorate? If the United States were to adopt more protectionist policies in the years ahead, or if Washington put a price on market access that was linked to specific Japanese contributions to help underwrite the costs of regional security, Japan might be forced to further diversify external markets by focusing more intently on its Asian relationships. Japan could retaliate against U.S. products, develop a regional economic zone in which the yen would be the marker currency, and possibly even revoke its security treaty with the U.S.

The Soviets would see any of these developments as a golden political opportunity and would make overtures to Tokyo about returning the Kuriles as part of a mutual treaty of commercial trade and economic aid. Such a strategy of seeking Japanese technological assistance would be all the more important for the Soviets if *perestroika* were failing. Japan would in effect become a neutral country, isolated and vulnerable, and could dramatically escalate its spending on defense. Article 9 could be amended. The prospect of developing its own nuclear weapons would loom large, and the potential for regional if not global conflict would become unavoidable.

The creation of a Tokyo-Beijing axis has been theorized by some as a means of uniting the two most powerful countries in Asia against their perceived enemies. China has natural resources (and, more importantly, food) to offer Japan, and Japan can provide China with all the technological assistance it could now or ever need. The two, linked together by common racial and historical ties, could unite Asia in a self-sufficient trading bloc and exist independently of the West. Such a scenario, however, implies unanimity of purpose in Beijing and Tokyo, something the two have never shared and, in my view, never will.

The Chinese regard the Japanese with a deep underlying sense of suspicion and distrust, not least because of Japan's egoistic tendency to whitewash history by eliminating references to its barbaric behavior in China during the Pacific war. The Chinese also view the Japanese as cultural thieves who have bastardized elements of their own culture, such as language and religion. While the rest of Asia may view China as nonexpansionist and benign, and Japan as potentially exploitative, the suggestion that the two countries could work *together* in a system of shared power not only seems vacuous on its merits but also would be opposed vociferously by practically all other Asian nations.

Is there a chance Moscow and Beijing might return to an earlier era of close ideological cooperation? In one sense, yes; and that is if both fail to fulfill desired expectations from current attempts at economic reform. Should that happen, it is not inconceivable that China and the Soviet Union could become outwardly belligerent again, seeking to cause disruptions in the external environment to distract from internal failures. Restoration of the Moscow-Beijing axis could also put pressure on Tokyo and Washington, irrespective of their own competitive differences, to cooperate more closely for both economic and mutual security purposes.

But negative scenarios such as these could evolve, it seems to me, only if the United States were to lose control of Far East security—if Pax Americana falters and fails. America has for nearly half a century borne the lion's share of defense in the Far East to keep the region stable. But as America's relative shares of global manufacturing and trade have declined, and as its budget and trade deficits continue to put unsustainable strains on its economy, it can no longer bear that burden alone. By all accounts, America should continue to be the dominant global power in the next century. But the nation's future role must be commensurate with the changing mix of economic and political relationships in East Asia and in Europe if it is to retain control as *primus inter pares* in an emerging multipolar world.

Part of the problem today is America's reluctance to recognize that its absolute power has ebbed. Part of the problem is also the reluctance of America's allies to share more of the cost of defending the free world. The final part is the difficulty of finding an appropriate substitute for American hegemony in a multipolar world. Japan is increasingly challenging America's economic and political leadership now, and this challenge brings a more urgent meaning to the end of the twentieth century.

19

THE DECLINE OF AMERICAN
HEGEMONY AND THE RISE OF JAPAN

The depression of 1929–39 was so wide, so deep, and so prolonged because the world economic system was in transition from British to American leadership. Britain could not provide the public good of international economic stability. From 1929 to 1939, the United States refused to do so. A decade later it was forced to, and the transition was complete. The world returned to economic stability.

A study of history suggests that the collapse of American leadership in the economic system will not be followed by a system of altruism. The system will limp along until it produces in evolutionary Darwinian fashion a new system in which the rules of the game, however devised and promulgated, are asymmetrically enforced and their costs asymmetrically shared. No obvious candidate for leader exists, whether a unified Europe, a rich and growing Germany or Japan, or a revitalized United States. The transition to the choice of such a leader, made implicitly rather than by an election process, will be dangerous. The present restraint will be constantly jeopardized by thrusting short-run maximizers or the spread of free-riding.

Charles Kindleberger,
"Systems of International Economic Organization"

"Before we look ahead to the next fifty years," Yale historian Paul Kennedy was telling me, "it's probably not a bad idea to look back fifty years, just to see how flawed and precarious the international system really was half a century ago."

Kennedy and I were talking in mid-1988 about the forces that cause certain nations to rise on the world stage, accumulate power, and then decline, a pattern of global leadership almost seasonal in its rhythms.

He had recently written a best-seller, *The Rise and Fall of the Great Powers.*

"Remember, in the late 1930s," he continued in his soft British accent, "the world was still controlled by European imperial powers. Britain, France, and the Netherlands dominated their colonial empires, but they were beginning to lose control. The Soviet Union was industrializing with a fury, and Stalin was consolidating his grip of terror. The international trade system had collapsed, and the major industrial nations were languishing in depression. Fascist dictatorships were coming to power on the continent. Despair was endemic all over the world."

Kennedy paused to collect his thoughts. Bearded, with angular features and clear blue eyes, he looked more like a Shakespearean actor than a historian.

"The Western democracies responded meekly to the challenge of the extremists," he explained, "not just because of their policies of appeasement, but also because of fundamental economic weaknesses. Their currencies were weak, their balance of trade was overextended, they relied too heavily on imports, and there were too few trained craftsmen, especially engineers. In contrast, the American economy, off to one side, though also hurt by the Depression, had tremendous strengths: higher productivity rates, a strong education system, greater numbers of craftsmen and engineers, lots of spare manufacturing capacity, and a bigger GNP than all the continental powers combined."

Half a century into the international order known as Pax Americana, the United States is faltering, too, for reasons related to what Kennedy calls "imperial overstretch"—underwriting a global network of alliances that are a drain on its treasury. I asked him whether he thought America would suffer inevitable decline as the great powers before it had.

"America has a strong tradition of commitment to certain ideals and principles," he said, "such as democracy, freedom, liberty, and justice. But the United States today is subject to much greater international competition than ever before. The result is that it has a much lower share of world manufacturing output, its productivity growth has slowed, it no longer has all the engineers it needs, its technological leadership has lagged, its public school students perform poorly on international achievement tests, it is running these enormous budget and trade deficits, and its foreign debt is now the highest in the world. So if America is to lead the world into the twenty-first century, then just being strong in ideals and principles will not be enough if the country is *also* not strong in productivity, wealth creation, science and technology, and public education—and if it is not solvent as a nation."

When asked if any nation sliding downhill has ever reversed itself without tremendous dislocation, he said he couldn't think of any but that we could learn from history.

History, as recounted in *The Rise and Fall of the Great Powers,* shows that the Spanish refused to tax themselves to pay for their own growing empire. That France became unable to support its increasingly expensive armed forces. That Britain could no longer underwrite the control and protection of her colonial empire. That Germany failed to achieve manifest destiny, leading the continent into two world wars. And that the United States too has found itself in the position of those other great powers, seemingly repeating the historical pattern. Power, Kennedy argued, can be maintained only by a prudent balance between a country's creation of wealth and its military expenditure. Great powers in decline nearly always hasten their demise by shifting more from the former to the latter.

"It was as clear to a Renaissance prince as it is to the Pentagon today," Kennedy wrote, "that military power rests upon adequate supplies of wealth, which in turn derive from a flourishing productive base, from healthy finances, and from superior technology. The assumption [is plausible] that these broad trends of the past five centuries are likely to continue."

Critics have dismissed Kennedy's Cassandralike forebodings, which suggest that the United States must inevitably suffer the same fate as its predecessors.

Jeane Kirkpatrick, former ambassador to the United Nations, has argued there is no connection among defense expenditure, economic growth, and national decline; retrenchment, in her view, is more often a symptom of decline than a cure. Pat Moynihan suggested that America's decline was caused by a foolish domestic strategy that has failed and is now having foreign policy consequences.

George Will suggested that America is not imperial Rome; its body politic has a head as well as a mind, and politics is all about choosing a destiny, not just adjusting to one. Norman Podhoretz, editor of *Commentary,* said America is neither outstretched nor spending too much on defense. As he saw it, America's problem was loss of national will. And Bill Bradley suggested it was possible to make a few changes, raise revenues, and reduce spending, and years from now people would say, "Decline?"

"Until conditions were ripe for a new leader," David Calleo wrote in *Beyond American Hegemony,* "the world suffered decades of political and economic conflict, culminating in two massively destructive wars. The lesson seems clear: without an effective hegemony, the world system breaks down into chaos. The lesson of the postwar era seems equally clear: Pax Americana followed with four decades of stability."

Hegemony is not a word that occurs with regularity in everyday, ordinary discourse. *Webster's* defines *hegemon* as a nation with "preponderant influence or authority." Pax Romana. Pax Britannica. Pax Americana. What makes many so nervous about the *relative* decline in American power is that the alternative to stable control by one dominant nation in a more pluralistic world—based on the historical examples—seems to be instability, chaos, and even war.

"Geopolitical theory does, however, provide a major alternative," Calleo suggested, "a pluralist, or balance-of-power, model of international order that comes complete with a different set of historical interpretations. The basic idea of this model is simple: unchecked power corrupts its holder and leads to overextension and instability. By contrast, a system of several closely integrated states remains orderly and peaceful so long as power is distributed evenly enough so that no single state or coalition is tempted to dominate or can succeed when it tries."

This pluralist interpretation in effect stands the hegemonic theory on its head, arguing that it is hegemonic systems *themselves* that are inherently unstable. The international system thus collapses not because unbalanced or aggressive new powers try to dominate their neighbors, but because declining old powers try to become more exploitative. Unfortunately, neither the League of Nations nor the United Nations offers much optimism as a role model for a pluralistic system.

"The decline of hegemonic powers appears to have a certain inevitability," Calleo wrote. "This is not merely because exercising hegemony weakens the leader absolutely, though it may well do so, but because the success of a liberal hegemonic system tends to strengthen the other members relative to the leader. Hegemony then deteriorates into the means for exploiting the international system for national ends rather than managing it in the general interest."

David Calleo is director of European studies at the Johns Hopkins School of Advanced International Studies in Washington. When I spoke with him in mid-1988, I asked if there was a certain inevitability to international instability without one dominant nation to stabilize the system and run it.

"I remain an agnostic on that subject," he said. "I think if you live in an era with a global hegemon, and it is beneficent as America certainly has been, I think you're lucky and you should just relax and enjoy it. But the world is clearly emerging as more pluralistic—a natural development after forty years of American domination. We have to find a way to work in a more pluralistic world, and so far we haven't been able to do that."

I asked him where he thought Japan fit into this changing global system.

"On the issue of national security," he said, "I don't sense the same degree of urgency that exists in the European case, where we maintain several hundred thousand troops. In Japan our tactical weapons are a big navy and a big air force. Second, I think there is a major problem in urging Japan to spend 2 percent or more of its GNP on defense. We have to ask, what is their proper military role in Asia and how would China react? We would look foolish if we drove the Chinese back to the Russians by insisting that the Japanese rearm. And third, if we don't get the European situation in hand, Japan is probably the most vulnerable if the global financial and economic systems really begin to unravel."

We talked for a while about the everyday implications of living in a world *not* dominated by a single power.

"In a more pluralistic world," he said, "everybody is your friend *and* your rival at the same time, or can be. I think there's more sensitivity to this now, in a foreign policy sense. The real question is, how do we manage it? Does change have to be sudden and violent, or can it be brought about by logical forethought and gradual evolution? America's biggest problem is fiscal, and we first have to figure out a way to pay for the size of government we've created for ourselves."

The well-known MIT economist Charles Kindleberger suggests there are five basic systems of international economic organization. There is the altruistic system, in which no unit has absolute power and self-interest works to the good of all, but altruism is unsatisfactory for a global system. Second, there is enlightened self-interest, where the good is the enemy of the necessary. Then there is the international economic system managed by rules, a pluralistic system consisting of global organizations like the UN, the IMF, the World Bank, the OECD, and so on. Its main problem is coordination, and it is subject to inherent frustration: in the absence of one dominant country to push for particular action, nothing much is likely to happen.

Fourth, there are regional blocs, which yield a stronger sense of participation and less insecurity, but they are primarily vehicles for expressing the views of the bloc leader. Finally there is what Kindleberger calls the leadership system, which can only come from dominance and persuasion, hence hegemony, which ultimately declines because of either war or inner decay.

"There is evidence," he wrote in a perceptive article called "Systems of International Economic Organization," "far from conclusive, that the United States, too, has aged and slowed down. Even if the rest of the world wanted the United States to play the role of leader, and it were willing, its capacity for discharging the responsibilities of leadership may have declined. This view assumes that leadership has economic costs on balance, rather than benefits. But whether or not the leader is destroyed in taking up his role, the *stability* of the system is threatened by the absence of a leader prepared to provide [that] stability."

Robert Keohane, a political scientist at Harvard, sees the world as divided into two opposing groups, which he calls institutionalists and realists.

The institutionalists argue that cooperation may not always prevail, but since interests are malleable, interdependence creates an interest in cooperation. Realists on the other hand hold that international politics is a kind of competition that knows no restraints other than those imposed by the changing necessities of the game and the shallow conveniences of the players. They say that the postwar international system was constructed on the basis of principles espoused by the United States and that American power was essential for its continuation and maintenance.

Realists, such as Charles Kindleberger, believe a hegemon is necessary to provide global stability; institutionalists, such as Keohane, do not.

A hegemonic power must possess just enough military power to be able to protect the international political economy from incursions by hostile adversaries, Keohane wrote, but it need not be militarily dominant worldwide. Kindleberger suggests that danger to the system comes not from too *much* power vesting in the global political economy, but too little.

If we look back about twenty-five years, we can see how America has provided what Kindleberger calls the public good of global stability. In the early 1960s the United States was far and away the most powerful nation in the world, viewed from any perspective—military, political, industrial, financial, economic. The Pentagon kept America ready at all times to fight two-and-a-half wars: major simultaneous confrontations with the Soviet Union and China and a half-war (which turned out to be Vietnam) anywhere else. Politically, America controlled the world's only consultative body, the United Nations, and defined the principles of the free world's ideology, articulating the goals of freedom, liberty, and justice through a system of representative democracy, defending them against the evils of totalitarianism.

But it was America's economic, industrial, and financial strengths that dominated the global system, underpinning the invisible infrastructure of exchange rates, international trade, and foreign lending. This invisible infrastructure was codified in the late 1940s. The Bretton Woods system pegged foreign currencies at fixed rates of exchange. The General Agreement on Tariffs and Trade set the rules for free trade. The International Monetary Fund, the World Bank, and the Bank for International Settlements supervised an innovative system of credits. All these systems—the invisible public goods—were America's charges, and America controlled them not just for its own benefit but for the good of the world.

But by 1971 the dollar had come unhinged, Washington had abandoned the gold standard, and floating currencies had replaced fixed rates under the Smithsonian Agreement. The yen had become the marker currency. The World Bank had become mired in lending to stagnant Third World nations, the IMF preoccupied with an international "debt overhang" that seemed intractable. Free trade, as Bismarck predicted a century before, had become the hypocrisy of strong exporting countries. GATT was languishing in meaningless, tariff-reducing sideshows as *negotiated trade* and *managed trade* became the new buzzwords. With America generating $150 billion annual trade deficits, Japan was now the marker merchant power. America, still strong and still the single largest economy, was still quarterback, but the players were rejecting America's game plan. Then, on October 19, 1987, Wall Street crashed.

It was this dissipating loss of *control* that prompted thoughtful observers to question whether the stability of this invisible infrastructure of public goods could be maintained. If American power was in decline, they asked, who was going to provide the global economic and political stability necessary for continued growth and prosperity?

Stability and prosperity need more than just military might; they require an effectively functioning international financial system anchored by one dominant industrial nation whose currency is strong and commands respect. During the last 150 years there have been only two periods of these circumstances. One was Pax Britannica, in the mid–nineteenth century, when England ruled the world and the pound sterling was supreme. The other was Pax Americana, when America ran the world and the dollar was supreme.

But the periods of decline, from 1873 to about 1913 for England, and since the early 1970s for America, have been characterized by low growth and instability. In the interhegemonic period, between 1913 and 1946, when nobody dominated the global system, not only was economic growth minuscule, but two totally destructive world wars occurred. It is the pattern of the past century and a half, therefore, that leads many to conclude that a system dominated by one nation produces stability and prosperity, whereas the absence of control leads to conflict, chaos, and war.

"The process of uneven growth stimulates political conflict because it undermines the international political status quo," Princeton political scientist Robert Gilpin recently wrote in *The Political Economy of International Relations*. "This redistribution of power accentuates the conflict between rising and declining states. If the conflict is not resolved, it can lead to a 'hegemonic war' whose ultimate result is to determine which state or states will be dominant in the new international hierarchy."

The most significant redistribution of economic power during the past three decades has clearly been the transfer from the United States to Japan. Japan is now the world's number one creditor nation, while America has overtaken Mexico and Brazil as the world's leading debtor. Japan's high rates of personal saving and capital formation have created a pool of surplus capital that cannot be absorbed by the Japanese economy alone, but must be exported, primarily to the United States. By 1986, Japan was exporting capital at the rate of $100 billion a year to America, most of which went toward the purchase of Treasury bonds:

Japan was effectively underwriting nearly half of Washington's annual budget deficits. In the early 1950s America's share of gross world production was nearly 45 percent; by 1980 it had fallen to close to 20 percent. Meanwhile, Japan's share of global output had almost tripled, to 12 percent.

Japan is now the free world's leading producer of automobiles and steel and has overtaken the U.S. in output of computer memory chips, machine tools, and consumer electronic products. While the United States is generating record merchandise trade deficits, Japan is generating record surpluses. American productivity has slowed, while productivity growth in Japan is now the highest in the industrial world. Japan is now the largest contributor to the Asian Development Bank, is tied with the U.S. as the largest shareholder in the IMF and the World Bank, and is the second-largest contributor to the UN.

The top ten banks in the world, measured by their dollar capitalization, are now Japanese. The Tokyo Stock Exchange, in terms of market capitalization, is now the world's biggest, and Osaka's exchange is now even larger than New York's. The yen has become the marker currency in East Asia, and Tokyo is the region's international financial center. Japan has replaced the United States as the world's largest contributor of foreign aid and leads in the research, development, and funding of critical high technologies for the next century, including industrial ceramics, biotechnology, superconductivity, hypersonic jet aircraft, and undersea construction.

This redistribution of economic power has brought about the now-familiar strains in the U.S.–Japan bilateral relationship. Washington politicians regularly engage in "Japan bashing." The introduction of strongly protectionist legislation, increasingly targeted at Japan, has become commonplace on Capitol Hill. Fears of a "trade war" between America and Japan are now expressed more openly, despite the fact that the two nations have been waging a trade war for more than thirty years. Mercantilistic conflict, as Princeton's Robert Gilpin has observed, is a precursor to hegemonic war.

Yoshio Suzuki, an official at the Bank of Japan, agrees. "History teaches that whenever a newly risen, asset rich nation refuses to open its markets to other countries or fails to effectively channel its financial resources to the development of the world economy," he wrote recently, "the result is growing conflict between the old order and the new. Today's intensifying international economic frictions and mounting protectionism in the United States are both warning signs that the world is once again faced with just such a crisis."

Because the two economies have become so financially interdependent, it has become fashionable to refer to them jointly as the *Nichibei* economy, as if they were somehow no longer separated by diametrically opposed cultural values, centuries of historical difference, an insuperable language barrier, conflicting strategic industrial and trade policies, and more than 5,000 miles of geographic distance across the largest ocean in the world. The problem with this "Nichibei" economy, however, as Americans increasingly realize and the Japanese are reluctantly forced to admit, is that it is making Japan a prince while turning America into a pauper.

But the prospect of even more troublesome contentiousness and dispute between the world's newest and fastest-growing industrial power and the world's "most spectacularly declining older one" (quoting Heilbroner) has prompted political leadership in both countries to view their nations as mutually dependent—Japan in security terms for Washington and America in economic terms for Tokyo—out of mutual fears that America could lose its most important strategic ally in Asia and that Japan could lose its most important global market.

"By the mid-1980s," Robert Gilpin wrote, "Japan had replaced West Germany as America's principal economic ally, and was the financial backer of the continued economic and political hegemony of the United States. Japanese investment supported the dollar, helped finance the defense buildup, and contributed to American prosperity. More importantly, it masked America's relative economic decline. Thus, the world monetary and financial system had become largely underwritten by Japanese capital."

This shift in economic power is not without its folklore. One popular story has it that George Bush suffered a stroke shortly after his inauguration, making Dan Quayle acting president.

When Bush recovered, three years later, Quayle was at his side.

"How's the federal deficit doing?" Bush asked groggily.

"With help from the Japanese, it has been reduced significantly," Quayle replied. "Inflation and interest rates are way down, too."

"Wonderful," the president said with a sigh. "And the trade deficit?"

"Again, thanks to Tokyo, we are now running a small surplus," Quayle said.

Bush frowned.

"And the price of milk at the corner grocer?"

"Two hundred yen a quart."

It is easy to see why the Japanese have been willing to invest their savings and surplus capital in the United States. If American power is indeed in decline, could Japanese financial backing possibly put off its ultimate demise? Japan's political leaders are well aware of the practical consequences, and they worry, as well they should, about a world that America can no longer control.

But as we leave the twentieth century and enter the twenty-first, there seems to be no alternative to American dominance. Japan is by no means ready to assume the role of global hegemon, nor is the world prepared to trust a system of Japanese hegemonic leadership—a Pax Nipponica, if you will—that would require political and military power commensurate with Japan's financial and industrial strength.

"Realistically speaking, I think we have no alternative but to have some form of shared power with Japan," Chalmers Johnson, the University of California political economist, recently told me. "The only really viable option we have is joint hegemony, and the economic foundations for it have already been established in the Nichibei relationship. All that's missing is the political vision and leadership necessary to implement it, and in that sense the Japanese have been considerably ahead of the Americans in understanding this."

But a joint hegemonic system would necessitate rewriting the U.S.-Japan security treaty, which at present is a one-way street.

"Some form of genuine bilateral alliance should be negotiated," Johnson said, "similar to our NATO agreement, which spells out the precise responsibilities and obligations of each country, the conditions for consultation, and the mutual costs. It would stop short of completely rearming Japan, but it would clarify what the Japanese have to contribute. But the mere fact of negotiating such an alliance would be a clear signal that the American era of hegemony—in the Pacific, at least—was over. It would also be a signal to the Japanese that they would not be any more welcome as economic conquerors of Asia than they were as military conquerors half a century ago. It would reassure the rest of Asia that Japan could play a larger role in regional security, but not alone. And it would reassure the Japanese people that they will not be isolated and vulnerable again, which they fear more than anything else."

On the surface the concept of shared power, or joint hegemony, is attractive. It combines the strengths of both countries—America's dominant political position and its unparalleled military strength with Japan's manufacturing-based industrial and financial power. But on reflection, would such an arrangement be practical? Historical precedent is lacking, except perhaps in the medieval case of Portugal and Spain dividing up the world between them, the legacy of which is not altogether inspiring.

There is an old Japanese adage that has come to characterize Japan's dominance of the U.S. market and the simultaneous impenetrability of its own, which provides a hint of the Japanese attitude toward control. It says, "What's mine is mine, and what's yours is half mine." Japan has no underlying principles other than those that bring the greatest benefit to itself at the lowest possible cost. Japanese cultural values center on loyalty, conformity, hierarchy, obedience, and duty—quite divergent from America's primary values of freedom, liberty, and justice. So the necessary ingredients seem to be in place for *more* bilateral conflict, not less.

When I put this apparent dichotomy to Johnson, he did not budge.

"I think joint hegemony is the only viable alternative for Japan and the United States," he reiterated. "What's required is the leadership to educate the publics of both countries as to its logic and need. Unfortunately, leadership is in short supply on both sides. I don't think there is anything conceptually difficult about imagining a true alliance. The problem is selling it politically."

The more I thought about the inherent dichotomy, though, the more skeptical I became. There *were* a number of inherent conceptual difficulties, it seemed to me, and if a system of joint hegemony couldn't be worked out conceptually, it could never be sold politically, for at least three reasons.

First, there is the problem of control. The United States is used to being in a position of control—its influence if not its dominance has run global systems for the past fifty years. Japan, as we have seen, in instances ranging from development of new technology to opening its domestic market, does not like to be controlled. The seeds of intense conflict rest right there. If the trade relationship between Japan and America is any indication—characterized by contentious, adversarial, and suspicious behavior on both sides—imagine how much more difficult it would be to achieve bilateral consensus on issues of political substance.

Second, the Japanese would find it nearly impossible to tolerate the kind of profligate economic behavior and social disorder that has prevailed in the United States for the past generation. America would find it equally impossible to be told by Japan how it ought to put its fiscal and political houses in order. A wide divergence of national and domestic political interests exists between the two countries with respect to trade and economic policy, intellectual property rights, patent protection, access to technology, sharing of research and development efforts, capital formation and savings rates, fiscal management, and market access. In short, the prospects are strong for even more conflict.

Third, the whole security issue is murky. Assume a bilateral treaty were renegotiated along truly mutual lines such that Japan would also assist the United States if America came under attack. The question remains, with what? To the extent that Japan has no nuclear capability or long-range power-projection capabilities, mutual assistance provisions would be meaningless. And in the case of conventional warfare, Japanese national interest would almost always outweigh any imputed treaty obligations. For example, would Japan send its own armed forces to another Asian country in support of American strategic objectives? Vietnam provides a hint: Japan practically disowned its political relationship with America and distanced itself considerably from American security aims in Indochina while profiting enormously from the war. So the prospect of joint hegemony, while not only politically difficult, may also be conceptually flawed.

There are those on both sides of the Pacific, of course, who favor a continuation of the status quo. The Japanese public and the mainstream Liberal Democratic Party, along with the Ministry of Foreign Affairs and the U.S. Department of State, would doubtless prefer to see things continue as they are.

Advocates of such a policy base their thinking on extension of the Yoshida Doctrine, named for Japan's first postwar prime minister. When forming his first cabinet in 1946, he remarked that history provides examples of winning by diplomacy after losing in war and saw advantage accruing to Japan from the emerging cold war hostility between the Soviet Union and the U.S. He based Japan's diplomatic position on the premise that economic rehabilitation was primary (and that political cooperation with the U.S. would be necessary to achieve it), that the nation should be armed for defensive purposes only (to free capital, manpower, and energy for economic rebuilding), and that the country would provide military bases for the U.S. in exchange for a guarantee for its own security.

This status quo posture has produced a kind of omnidirectional Japanese foreign policy that is essentially value-free, avoids ideological conflict by trying to separate economics from politics, and seeks friendship from all countries. The problem with the status quo is that it too becomes increasingly unrealistic as the world changes, and sooner or later something has to give—moving a division of U.S. troops out of Korea or solving the cost-sharing problem of regional security. Keeping the status quo might be workable if Japan were not now an economic superpower.

So the status quo option, it seems to me, would not be workable either. Nor would the alternative of a Pax Nipponica replacing Pax Americana, which would be seen by Washington, Beijing, and Moscow as threatening the balance of power in East Asia and raising political tensions unacceptably. But the Pax Nipponica debate has fueled a strong neonationalist revival in Japan and has a certain force of domestic momentum behind it.

A third option is what Yale-educated political scientist Kuniko Inoguchi calls "Pax Consortis," a multilateral system of shared power. Dr. Inoguchi rejects the hegemonic order and favors decentralized cooperation among nations based on policy coordination and continuous micromanagement of mutual interests. Her recent book, *Post-Hegemonic Systems and Japan's Options,* became a Tokyo best-seller and a topic of almost constant discussion in Japan.

Dr. Inoguchi's concept relies on international agreements to set the rules for the invisible infrastructure of public goods, like the recent Plaza and Louvre accords, which attempted to realign major currencies and stabilize exchange rate behavior.

When I saw her on a recent visit to Tokyo, we talked about her concept.

"Since one country can no longer control everything," she told me, "the idea of a global hegemon is dying out. Military protection, financial stability, commercial trading rules, international credits—this vast, enormous system of international public goods is proving to be too much for one nation, even America, to control. I think it will eventually shift to a shared system whereby the rules will be set and administered by a consortium of countries. It should be possible for a group of mutual national interests to converge, especially now that economic rather than military solutions are becoming a more important means of conflict resolution."

But a Pax Consortis would seem to sow the seeds of its own impracticality within the global system, because agreements like the Plaza Accord are more limited in scope and restricted in power. And even considering the Pax Consortis concept as a "team" approach rather than an individual country effort, the question of who *leads* again becomes paramount: as an orchestra cannot make good music without a conductor, no team can play without a coach. What, then, becomes of conflicting national interests in the absence of a strong leader to resolve them?

"I think the whole system of incentives will change," Inoguchi said, "from one that favors individual or nationalistic games to more of a communal approach. I also see a shift from a preoccupation with national territorial issues to a new kind of shared nationalism based on international trade. But Japanese leaders are very worried about America's relative industrial decline, and they want her to recover to continue to be a major player."

It is perhaps fitting that this concept of shared multilateral power should have as its innovator a Japanese. Japan is a group-oriented culture in everything from domestic politics to education to the family and social policy. Mutual dependence rather than independence is a major underlying force. And Japanese society is controlled by an enormous amount of peer pressure, so it is not surprising that some Japanese might be drawn to a consortium-type arrangement. Japan may also function more effectively in a pluralistic system in which every nation is both friend and foe, because the Japanese culture accepts the co-existence of conflicting forces, like good and evil, as opposed to Western dualism, which treats them as adversaries.

But other countries don't behave as Japan does—most, in fact, do not. This makes Japanese commercial self-interest in an emerging age of interdependence even more ironic. So a Pax Consortis could well be an extension of the Japanese domestic political system, which lacks a center of accountability: a rudderless boat that somehow tries to get its crew to cooperate without a captain. While that may be possible for Japan to accomplish domestically (and even that is arguable), it remains conceptually difficult to see the *international* system working that way.

Another problem with the Pax Consortis concept is its inherent idealism, something a realist like Naohiro Amaya, the former MITI minister, has serious difficulties with. Amaya is a severe critic of Inoguchi's shared-power concept and believes it is not anchored in a realistic assessment of great power relations. In one of his writings he embraced the supermercantilist role for Japan, seeing the world divided into distinct classes, much as Tokugawa Japan was defined hierarchically by the four strata of *samurai,* peasant, artisan, and merchant.

Amaya thought the United States and the Soviet Union would be the world's *samurai* states, with Japan the quintessential merchant power and the Third World nations the peasants. The world of international relations was a real jungle, he argued, and it was therefore necessary for a merchant power to act with circumspection. He concluded that if Japan's efforts as a merchant country could not guarantee its security, the time would have arrived for Japan to become a *samurai* nation itself. But Amaya felt Japan lacked the ability, shrewdness, and self-discipline of its sixteenth-century merchant leaders, whose skillful and clever maneuvers in a society dominated by *samurai* allowed them to prosper.

The intellectual leader of the mercantilists is Kyoto University political scientist Masataka Kosaka. Kosaka has argued that Japan should always be a middleman, taking advantage of commercial relationships and avoiding involvements in international politics. "A trading nation does not go to war," he once wrote; "neither does it make supreme efforts to bring peace. It simply takes advantage of the situation created by stronger nations." Kosaka believes that a mercantilist role suits Japan best and that it prospered during the 1960s and 1970s precisely because it had played that role so well.

Amaya was enough of a realist to back away from his earlier mercantilist position once he saw how much external conditions had changed. He had lost considerable face in having to apologize to Washington for Japan's purchase of Iranian oil during the hostage crisis, for example. In addition, the U.S. had become increasingly critical of a Japan looking out only for its own selfish interests.

When I saw Amaya recently in Tokyo, he was more openly critical of Japan's previous role as a mercantilist country, in part because external criticism had become so sharp.

"Mercantilism is defensible if you are poor and needy," he told me, "but impractical and indefensible as you grow wealthier. The problem for Japan now is an overwhelming absence of *values* for its society, having embraced the mercantilist role so aggressively. Therefore, it simply doesn't make sense for Japan to increase its military power before setting its value system right. The world won't accept us, and that's partly what happened fifty years ago."

I mentioned my discussion with Dr. Inoguchi and asked him what he thought about Pax Consortis.

"The challenge to Japan is to embrace the rational, not the ideal," he said. "We will be rational if we accept a primary role in the global system. The ideal of our continuing a merchant nationalism cannot be maintained. There must be one hegemon in the free world in order to make the system work. A Pax Consortis won't work, because we know that in the end the IMF and the UN don't work either without the underlying strength of a single, dominant power. The key is to somehow form a political partnership between the United States and Japan, such that the U.S. controls political and military affairs and Japan the economic and financial."

Iwao Nakatani earned his doctorate in economics at Harvard and teaches political economy at Osaka University. He is another leading Japanese intellectual concerned about a shift in power from the United States to Japan. In a recent article he wrote, "The world is moving steadily toward economic disaster despite the deliberately optimistic statements of American and Japanese authorities. Unless the United States is prepared to undertake an immediate and radical policy shift, the world economy will inevitably be plunged into crisis, and we [Japanese] will be forced to start exploring ways and means of constructing a new economic system."

One way the Japanese have started exploring ways and means of constructing a new system is through an expression of neonationalism, which has in recent years become quite strong. Its resurgence has unavoidably helped to rekindle memories of a more militaristic Japan. The neonationalists' point of departure is the realists' belief that competition between strong national interests within an international environment constantly verging on anarchy is the only practical way of understanding global politics. They do not share a community of interests and values with the Western democracies that would compel them to cooperate in a genuine alliance, and they support the mercantilists' hard-line position on economic nationalism.

One of their most articulate spokesmen, the late Ikutaro Shimizu, has written, "On the one hand, Japan must encourage friendly relations with America and the Soviet Union, but at the same time we must not forget for an instant that Japan is alone. In the end, we can only rely on Japan and the Japanese. If Japan acquired military power commensurate with its economic power, countries that fully appreciate the meaning of military power would not overlook this. They would defer; they would act with caution; and in time they would show respect."

Shimizu has come out in favor of point-blank nuclear rearmament for Japan, saying that even if the nuclear superpowers do not use their weapons, they are able to instill fear in those countries that do not have them. A country like Japan that does not possess nuclear weapons and is afraid of them will be easy game for the nuclear powers.

The neonationalists have touched sensitive nerves in Japan, stirring emotions that are at once contradictory and dangerous as well as nationalistic and proud. Shimizu was a respected intellectual. He was a leading postwar political theoretician, and his writings have served as a barometer of changing political opinion. The nationalist right has been a fringe element ever since the war, the most visible evidence of it being a white sound truck emblazoned with the imperial Japanese rising sun flag, which perambulates central Tokyo daily, blaring harsh messages of restoration and rearmament, and is ignored by resident foreigner and native Japanese alike. Shimizu was not associated with them, nor with the radicals formerly led by the ultranationalist writer Yukio Mishima, who commited ritual suicide in his commanding general's office at the self-defense headquarters in Tokyo nearly two decades ago, calling on the nation to recapture its historic *samurai* strengths.

But while Shimizu's writings may reflect an intellectually respectable venue for an otherwise taboo subject, more events, occurring at the grass roots level, are stoking Japan's neonationalist fires. On August 15 every year, commemorating the end of the Pacific war, Japanese political leaders pay homage to the war dead whose souls are enshrined at Yasukuni Shrine in downtown Tokyo. When former prime minister Nakasone made that visit official several years ago, Asian nations unanimously voiced their objection to this presumed reconnection of present politics with past militarism.

In late 1986, Minister of Education Masayuki Fujio was dismissed for publicly stating that Japanese textbooks were not sufficiently patriotic, that the prime minister was soft on foreigners, that Japan had done nothing to be ashamed of during the war, and that "the core of Japanese education should be to make our children Japanese again."

Fujio meant recapturing what the Japanese have lost, namely, the "pure Japanese spirit" of its *samurai* past.

"When national soul becomes a tool of political propaganda in Japan," Ian Buruma, former cultural affairs editor for the *Far Eastern Economic Review,* recently noted, "it is time for the rest of the world to take note, especially when steadily worsening trade conflicts and American threats of protectionism could easily provoke an emotional swing of the old Japanese pendulum, from emulation to rejection of the West. The more extremist ideals of right-wing nationalism may not be widespread, but the notion of Japanese uniqueness and the feeling of Japan being misunderstood and unfairly treated by the rest of the world are widely held."

In 1987 former prime minister Nakasone dedicated ¥20 million to build the Institute of Japanology, saying, "Now is the time to establish the Japanese identity once again." The institute, still in its infancy, is headed by Takeshi Umehara, a fundamentalist scholar whose study of history has led him to conclude that the decline of Western civilization is like a virus threatening the health of the modern world. "The only cure," he has said, "is to be found in Oriental culture—especially Japanese culture."

Umehara and his colleagues are preoccupied with fundamental questions concerning the Japanese soul and national identity, a process that has become known as Yamatoism, based on the original name for the Japanese nation. Feeling increasingly rejected and ignored by the West, the Yamatoists are racial purists, imbued with the historical spirit of ancient Japan, and unabashed supporters of revision of Article 9 of Japan's constitution, which would pave the way for eventual nuclear rearmament. The danger of the Yamatoists is not their numbers, which are relatively small, but that their brand of irrational national mysticism could eventually lead to greater political authoritarianism at home and wider conflict abroad.

"Because it is determined to avoid following Western models," the perceptive political scientist Ronald Morse recently observed in an article called "Japan's Drive to Pre-Eminence," "Japan's problem, as seen internally, is how to bring its culture and behavior, which have existed in isolation of recent economic successes, into line with its new global responsibilities. The Japanese style of rule in the 21st century is likely to reflect the ways the country has fostered a centrally controlled trading empire based on its domestic cultural and social needs."

How the world copes as America moves from an era of Pax Americana to an era in which America is barely keeping control raises the ultimate concern as to whether American global leadership can be reinvigorated or whether an unsustainable system of joint hegemony with Japan may temporarily emerge, followed ultimately by a world under Japanese dominance and control.

The realists would seem to have the weight of history in this evolving debate; namely, that the global system cannot be maintained without a single, dominant power to control it. While the American hegemony may be weakening, it is far from clear that it can be replaced by a shared-power arrangement with Japan. The real question then, it seems to me, is whether America can revitalize itself to extend Pax Americana into the next century—an accomplishment of heretofore historically unthinkable proportions—or will be replaced eventually by a Pax Nipponica whose cultural values of hierarchy, conformity, and loyalty will vanquish the American ideology of freedom, liberty, and justice.

20

PAX NIPPONICA: THE ERA OF
JAPAN'S MAJESTIC DOMINANCE?

Lacking a vision for a new world trade regime, Japanese are still uncomfortable thinking of themselves as the dominant economic power, let alone as capable of imposing a Pax Nipponica over world trade. But the combination of their superior competitiveness, their dominance in financial markets as the world's leading creditor, their superior information networks, and the dependence of others on Japanese products and technology creates great de facto power. This power will enable Japan to dominate world trade and use that power to serve its national interests. . . .

The prospects for the next few years, therefore, are for a pattern of limited and uneven Pax Nipponica, led by a country of modest military strength and of limited ability to attract a foreign following, but of great economic leverage. It is surely in the interests of Japan, as well as the United States and Europe, to work toward the expansion of partnerships in the Pacific basin and elsewhere. [But] no matter how extensive this intertwining, the economic leverage of Japan is likely to grow and to be used in pursuit of neomercantilist objectives.

Ezra Vogel, "Pax Nipponica?"

Former prime minister Yasuhiro Nakasone is still the only Japanese postwar prime minister who previously served as director general of the Japanese Defense Agency. Despite his reputation as an internationalist, he has always been recognized at home as a hawk, with a strong following from both the conservative wing of his own party and right-wing nationalists. One of his loyal supporters is a leading conservative intellectual named Jun Etoh, who recently wrote a book that was very popular in Tokyo called *Nichibei Senso wa Owatteinai (The War Between Japan and America Is Not Over).*

In 1985, in a speech to the Defense Academy graduating class, Nakasone reminded the young military officers that it was his calligraphy that hung in the academy's great inner hall. The aphorism, consisting of six characters, reads *fuu shinzan garyoh*. Literally translated, this means, "Amid wind and rain, hidden deep in the mountains, there lies a reclining dragon." Nakasone explained that the phrase meant the Self-Defense Forces were always prepared for any emergency, not unlike the "Semper Fidelis" of the U.S. Marines. That explanation, of course, was pure *tatemae*—ceremonial principle, or pretense—for which the Japanese are famous.

There is a more ominous meaning concealed behind the maxim's literal *kanji,* however, and Japan's domestic conservatives are not the only ones to detect it. A more realistic interpretation would suggest that "amid wind and rain" implies a Japan under criticism and attack from the hostile Western powers. "Hidden deep in the mountains" conveys an image of Japan rearming beyond the knowledge of the outside world. The "reclining dragon" is, in fact, nothing less than a militarily rearmed Japan. This rendition is *honne*—the real, underlying motive or actual intent. As with any Japanese public utterance, true intent can never be stated openly.

In addition to the image of concealed strength and covert rearmament, the aphorism conveys a sense of being devious or clever, traits the Japanese are both fond of and expert in. In Japanese this is known as *zurui,* being sly or cunning, which has a negative connotation of slickness and dishonesty. These innuendos, like so much of Japan's homogeneous culture, can be communicated between Japanese with but a knowing glance, a wink of the eye, a nod of the head. But it is this very cultural homogeneity that gives the nation its dark side, that most stands in the way of Japan's ever achieving a global Pax Nipponica, because the very culture that is so rich and so dynamic for its own people remains closed and off-limits to the rest of the world. In a word, Japan is monoracial.

Not long ago former prime minister Nakasone praised the cultural homogeneity of Japan in a setting he thought was private. He was therefore open and completely candid with his audience, a small seminar of senior Liberal Democratic Party politicians. There was no need for pretense; he was among trusted friends. So *honne,* his true feelings, could be revealed.

The prime minister was full of pride for the postwar economic achievements of Japan, which reflected the accomplishments of the Japanese as a high-level information society, rich in knowledge. "There is no other country in the world that puts such diverse information so accurately into the minds of its people," he stated. "It has become a very intelligent society. Against the likes of America, it is by far so, when seen from averages. In America there are many blacks, Puerto Ricans, and Mexicans, so seen on the average, America's per-capita level of intelligence, as gained through education and the mass media, is still extremely low. But because Japan is such a vibrant society and highly educated, a society in which people are so *dynamic,* we must continually progress to suit the people's appetite for more knowledge and information and intelligence."

Honne. Actual intent.

Needless to say, Nakasone was shocked to learn afterward that his comments had been conveyed to Washington via the public press. America was outraged. Congress protested. Consumer groups threatened to boycott Japanese products unless a formal apology was made.

Shortly thereafter, it was. *Tatemae*—pretense—was not long in coming. The prime minister humbly apologized, suggesting his remarks had somehow been taken out of context and misapplied.

More recently, Michio Watanabe, a former trade and finance minister who is now chairman of the LDP's Policy Research Council and is considered a future candidate for prime minister, made a similar breach when he addressed a party conference.

"Americans use a lot of credit cards," he said at the time. "They have no savings, so they go bankrupt. If Japanese risk bankruptcy, they think it serious enough to escape into the night or commit family suicide. But among the Americans are so many blacks and so on, who would think nonchalantly, 'We're bankrupt, but from tomorrow we don't have to pay anything back. We just can't use credit cards anymore.'"

Honne.

Watanabe's remarks were reprinted in the Japanese press. When it became apparent that his audience was much wider than he had intended, he apologized immediately.

"I made misleading and inadvertent remarks," he said humbly, "though in no sense did I ever imply any racial discrimination. I very much regret that my remarks may have hurt the feelings of American friends, and I withdraw those words with apologies."

Tatemae.

Because their country is culturally homogeneous, resulting from centuries of isolation on a narrow, overcrowded island, the Japanese people have absolutely no innate sense of *sharedness* with other cultures. There is little awareness of commonality, no sense of shared fate. Until very recently, foreigners arriving at Tokyo's Narita International Airport were required to queue behind signs marked "Alien," as if they were somehow extraterrestrial beings. *Gaijin,* the Japanese word for foreigner, literally means "outside person."

Yet this feeling of exclusion is not directed solely at foreign countries; it is also applied to domestic minorities within Japan, such as resident Koreans and the *burakumin,* social outcasts who are restricted to meat-handling and leather-tanning trades. Half a century ago, after the great Kanto earthquake in 1923, resident Koreans in Tokyo were thought to be responsible for the disaster, so they were unanimously targeted as scapegoats. Anti-Korean sentiment was encouraged by the Japanese government and became so strong that Tokyo police were given carte blanche to kill any Korean on sight. The result was a bloody massacre that still stains the pages of Japanese history.

Prejudice against Koreans and the *burakumin* remains indelible. Official family registers, called *koseki,* are required for all Japanese. They are annotated at birth with the blemish of race. They follow a person throughout his life and comprise part of the official documentation used for admission requirements by Japanese universities and in employment procedures by Japanese government ministries and corporations. They can be, and have frequently been, used to deny acceptance on the exclusive grounds of nationality or race.

The *burakumin* are sarcastically called *yotsu* by the Japanese. Literally this means four-legged animal and is the cruelest taunt of all, for only the bare feet of animals touch the ground. With no sense of belonging that all mainstream Japanese otherwise share, young *burakumin* outcasts are prime recruits for the *yakuza,* Japan's criminal underground, which controls the nation's gambling, prostitution, and entertainment trades.

Racial discrimination is the dark side of the Japanese culture, a deep shadow at the base of the nation's otherwise bright and impressive achievements.

It is the postwar period of extraordinary growth and economic success that has led so many Japanese to credit their country as being exceptional, special, and unique. But this sense of cultural uniqueness is nothing new. It goes back centuries in Japanese history, to the myths that substantiate the nation's own creation. These myths have always set Japan apart from other nations. In the beginning the deities Izanami and Izanagi created the nation of Yamato. One of their offspring danced before the Heavenly Cave to lure out their daughter, Amaterasu the Sun Goddess, who had shut herself in. When she emerged, she bestowed her blessings on the Japanese people and in so doing gave Yamato its name, Land of the Rising Sun.

The British Japanologist Peter Dale, in *The Myth of Japanese Uniqueness,* has shown how Japan is still strongly transfixed by its mythical past.

Japanese trade negotiators, for example, are careful to explain to their Western counterparts that Japanese stomachs are different from Western stomachs. Since they are "uniquely" smaller and cannot therefore digest the quantities of food that Westerners eat, it would be impractical for Japan to increase quotas of imported beef.

MITI bureaucrats publicly proclaim that Japanese snow is unique, so that only Japanese-made skis can adequately navigate the slopes; foreign skis thus cannot be allowed in.

A Japanese physician, a neurologist, suggests that the Japanese brain processes certain sounds differently from any other brain; it must, therefore, be exceptional. His book, *The Japanese Brain,* was a best-seller in Tokyo.

A Japanese entomologist distinguishes behavioral differences between Japanese and Western honeybees, which he says correspond precisely to cultural differences between the Japanese and Westerners. Western bees colonize discarded Japanese hives without discrimination, but Japanese bees refuse to inhabit Western hives; they must destroy them first and then construct new ones.

A well-known Japanese linguist argues that the declining success of Japanese athletes in postwar global competition is due to the damage their neurological reflexes suffer from the forced study of foreign languages. Foreign languages, being consonantal, confuse the uniquely vowel-wired Japanese brains.

"This obsessive self-analysis is like a national neurosis," Ian Buruma wrote in a recent *New York Times* article, "and like most neuroses, it is frequently irrational. The trade disputes so much in the news raise a larger, and deeper, question: How long can an increasingly interdependent world live with a developed nation that still clings to such ancient ideals of national purity?"

Buruma is a Dutchman who went to Japan to study Japanese film-making and now lives in Hong Kong. He wrote a highly perceptive analysis of Japanese character called *A Japanese Mirror*, which analyzed heroes and villains in Japanese mythology, literature, and film. When I met with him in early 1988, he talked about the inherent narrowness of the Japanese culture.

"Only in Japan do people refer to themselves as *Nihon minzoku*, the Japanese race," Buruma said, "a notion that is scientifically absurd."

Minzoku, which means race, is something like the Nazi use of the word "Volk" and implies an identical sense of exclusiveness and superiority.

"It is the kind of national mysticism that appeals to people who are still deeply anxious about their place in the world," he went on, "and who periodically seek to retreat from modern confusion into the security of the monoracial state."

Many Japanese are convinced that their nation is blessed with a uniquely peaceful disposition, I suggested, a feeling that may have its roots in Japan's historical embrace of Zen Buddhism. But this feeling is contradicted by Japan's equally strong embrace of martial arts and the *samurai* ethic. Japan is, therefore, naturally chauvinistic, feeling itself threatened only by hostile foreigners.

"What is disturbing about Japanese chauvinism," Buruma noted, "is that it is racist. What is more disturbing is that only a very few Japanese are conscious of it."

When Buruma later wrote about the phenomenon in an article called "A New Japanese Nationalism," a stunned Japanese diplomat remarked, "We are not Nazis." Of course not, Buruma replied. But Japan's strong sense of nationalism does come awfully close. An old Japanese proverb conveys this sentiment of superiority and exclusion well. It is *tabi no haji wa, kakisutete;* when you travel, shame stays at home. Peer pressure may work within the narrow confines of Japanese culture, but not on Bataan or in Shanghai.

This feeling of Japan's uniqueness and superiority has led to a sense of arrogance among many Japanese. They now feel that their country has not only caught up with but bettered the West. In a recent poll conducted by the Economic Planning Agency, 90 percent of the Japanese companies surveyed believed they had surpassed the technological capacity of American firms. Similarly, the *Asahi Shimbun* reports that a majority of the Japanese people now regard themselves as superior to Westerners.

Foreign criticism of Japan over many years—of closed markets, patent infringements, adversarial trade—has produced a kind of siege mentality in Tokyo that generates a strong feeling of pride in national accomplishment but also of resentment toward the critical Westerners who are believed to be so inferior. Japan has followed international rules for the most part, the Japanese will argue, and has won the game of international competition by producing higher-quality goods at lower prices. Other countries have sacrificed imports on the altar of national strategy, so why should Japan be singled out because it has done so more successfully? The Japanese believe they have mastered the Western rules and have beaten the West at its own game, while the West is now in decline. In fact, the Japanese word for economic decline is *Eikoku byo*, the English disease. Now the Americans have caught it, most Japanese believe; perish the thought it should travel across the Pacific to infect Japan.

I have seen this attitude expressed in a number of personal ways. Most Japanese bureaucrats now insist that foreigners converse with them in Japanese. Speaking the host country's language is by no means an unreasonable attitude in any country, but it does rather dramatically highlight how the tables have turned in Japan. Years ago Japanese bureaucrats and businessmen were outwardly pleased to converse with foreigners who had made the exasperating effort to master their language. Today they expect it. Many Americans are now paying for their linguistic laziness in Tokyo.

Masao Kunihiro is an adviser to former prime minister Takeo Miki and a highly regarded Japanese sociologist I have known for many years. He is the author of numerous books and articles about the Japanese character. In his mid-sixties now, he says the overwhelming sense of superiority many Japanese feel has produced a widespread embrace of henotheism—the worship of one god without denying the existence of others. This has put the Japanese into what he calls a "suspender-snapping" mood.

"In times of crisis," Kunihiro said to me, "polytheistic Japan becomes monotheistic, and the one god, which surfaces and dominates, is Japan itself. Overseas we are becoming known as the 'ugly Japanese.'"

Racism, insularity, arrogance, narrowness, and resentment. The dark side of Japan. In some ways Japan on the threshold of the next century is not unlike the United States at the beginning of this one. America too was poised advantageously to benefit from historical accident: its great endowment in natural resources. It was an inward-looking nation, staunchly isolationist, preoccupied with domestic expansion, investment, the railroads. Inexperienced in international affairs, America had only begun to look back across the Atlantic to tap European investment capital for its domestic needs. But America too had a blemish on its national character: slavery.

There are, the political scientist George Modelski tells us, four essential tests for global hegemonic leadership, based on his theory of long cycles in global politics. One is a favorable geography, preferably insular. The second is a cohesive and hardworking society. The third is a lead economy. And the fourth is a geopolitical strategy of global reach. England has a perfect score. So does the United States. Japan, he concluded, has passed the first three tests, but it fails the fourth.

But Modelski may have been a bit premature in his judgment. While Japan's external political influence has not yet grown to match its economic power, Japanese leaders are now moving quickly and strategically to redress that perceived imbalance. With a greatly strengthened external political presence to complement its industrial and technological power, growing financial influence, and a healthy military capability, the seeds of a future Pax Nipponica are already being sown. Perhaps it remains for Japan's future leaders to reap the harvest.

Former prime minister Nakasone recognized earlier than any other Japanese politician that Japan would in the future be a leader nation and no longer just a follower. As a hawk on defense issues, he has maintained close ties to the right wing. At the young age of thirty-two, as a representative in the Japanese Diet in the final year of the American occupation, he submitted a 7,000-word petition to General MacArthur arguing for constitutional revision and creation of an independent defense establishment. MacArthur angrily rejected his petition, so Nakasone conspicuously absented himself when the Diet voted to approve the treaty. Wondering what might have happened if Japan had made a different decision at the time, he made it one of his goals to try to transcend what he calls the "treaty system."

"The first necessity is to change our thinking," he wrote when he became prime minister in 1981. "Having caught up with the West, we must now expect others to try to catch up with us. We must seek out a new path for ourselves, and open it up ourselves. We are destined to become the world's economic, scientific, and technological leaders in the next century. Japan is destined by its unique economic, scientific, and cultural skills to become the pioneer of a new stage of technology, and this will project Japan into a role of global leadership. This may take 20 or even 30 years to realize, but we should not let the long time span deter us."

The prime minister knew only too well, from his study of history, that leadership of a technological revolution also brings leadership of the international system. He sensed the inevitability of Japan's rise to prominence. In the nineteenth century Britain's pioneering role in creating the steam engine and steel technology, and their subsequent application to rail and ocean transportation, paved the way for a Pax Britannica. Similarly, in the twentieth century America's innovations of the internal combustion engine and the technology of mass production, and their application to the automobile and air transportation, laid the foundation for a Pax Americana.

"In the past," Nakasone wrote, "the country which held the overwhelming advantage in a specific industry or technology that was a paradigm for the world's economic development in a given era became the leader of international society and took the initiative in forming the new international order of that era."

In a word, the basis for a Pax Nipponica will be technology.

Recognizing this, the prime minister set in motion during his seven-year term numerous national reforms that would strengthen Japan where it was perceived to be weak. His economic reforms and leadership in efforts to privatize government functions rekindled domestic demand in a country previously perceived to be export-driven. His education reforms targeted the system of rote learning and put more emphasis on individual initiative and creativity. And his political reforms eliminated historical barriers to defense spending and stressed the importance of eventual constitutional revision to eliminate Article 9.

"Approaching the 21st century," Nakasone said presciently in a recent speech, "the Japanese state and the Japanese race can walk proudly in the world, for on the one hand Japan must become more international, but at the same time it is important to reestablish Japan's own identity."

It would be left to Nakasone's successor as prime minister, Noboru Takeshita, wealthy scion of one of Japan's most successful sake brewers and a veteran of thirty years of LDP politics, to quietly lead Japan's effort at reestablishing that identity after he took office in late 1987. Despite the negative effects of a domestic political scandal that began earlier but widened after he assumed office, Takeshita's external initiatives demonstrated the deep strength of Japan's bureaucracy and reinforced his reputation as a talented leader with a painstaking devotion to detail.

In 1988, during the first year of his administration, Takeshita made eight overseas trips to thirteen countries and produced a number of firsts for Japan.

A Japanese observer was named to the United Nations team monitoring the Soviet withdrawal from Afghanistan. Japan's foreign minister, Sosuke Uno, visited Israel for the first time ever. A Japanese scientist was appointed head of the World Health Organization. During a visit to Canberra, the prime minister proposed a "Pacific League of Parliamentarians," a regular summit of Asian nations. The Ministry of Foreign Affairs advanced an innovative plan to fund a peacekeeping force in Kampuchea, supervised by a Japanese observer. And the Japanese Defense Agency director, Tsutomu Kawara, toured Southeast Asia to reassure regional leaders that Japan would never again dominate the region militarily. This was the first such visit by the head of Japan's defense establishment since the war.

During Takeshita's watch Japan replaced the United States as the largest shareholder in the Asian Development Bank. Tokyo courted the IMF assiduously, becoming the second-largest shareholder after Washington. It was at the 1988 Toronto summit, however, where the prime minister surprised Western leaders by taking the diplomatic initiative. Armed with statistics showing a dramatic turnaround in the domestic Japanese economy, Takeshita introduced a new credit allocation proposal for Third World debt through the IMF and announced financial commitments totaling $50 billion over five years that have now made Japan the world's leading donor of foreign aid. The prime minister had begun to lay the vital *political* groundwork for eventual creation of a Pax Nipponica.

Takeshita's successor as prime minister, Sosuke Uno, resigned following the LDP's loss of its majority in the Upper House elections. Whether his successor will be able to build on that important groundwork himself will be unavoidably sidetracked by the domestic political fallout of the Recruit scandal that forced both Takeshita and Uno from office in 1989 remains to be seen. Given the preponderant strength of the Japanese bureaucracy, however—the locus of political power in Japan—the institutional momentum toward Pax Nipponica could well carry forward.

With Japan's emergence as a political force in global affairs, the West is beginning to have a glimpse of what a world under Pax Nipponica would be like. It will be based on Japan's three pillars of strength: economic (industrial), technological, and financial. Because of Japan's position as the world's leading financial power, Japanese dominance of the international political system will eventually evolve. And Japan's military power will gradually expand to match its economic and political power, including the eventual possession of nuclear weapons.

First of all, since Japan does not subscribe to the principles of free trade, the operative concept of Pax Nipponica will be managed trade —*strategic* trade. Based on the experience of the past century, we know Japan will feel obligated to run a trade surplus with virtually every nation in the world. Product cartels will be established specifying which countries will supply Japan with imports of what raw materials and which intermediate goods and in what quantity and which countries will be markets for exports of Japanese finished products, by what sector and in what market shares.

Because of the Japanese cultural predilection for dominance and control, as reflected in its hierarchical view of the world, every country will have a fixed position in the trade hierarchy and will be expected to stay in place. Japan will, of course, sit atop the global pyramid; the second tier will in all likelihood not be the consumption economies of America and Europe but the producer nations of Japan's natural neighborhood, East Asia, linked by technology agreements to the mother country's lead. The U.S. and Europe will represent an industrialized third tier, followed at the bottom by the Third World, Latin America, and Africa. From each according to its loyalty, to each according to its respect. Pax Nipponica, in short, will attempt to make the entire world a vast economic co-prosperity sphere for Japan.

Economically Japan will continue its strategic industrial policies and sectoral targeting for the domestic economy. It will ensure that it stays at the forefront of technological leadership by creating relevant incentives for the targeted sectors, by funding its own as well as American research and development aggressively, and by covertly protecting its home market from meaningful foreign competition. It will expand its own generous funding for domestic research and development in the strategic industries so that Japan's technological capabilities remain the world's marker skills. Personal savings and capital formation rates will remain high relative to the rest of the world, despite its own tax reforms, to protect and strengthen its position as the world's leading creditor.

Pax Nipponica will position Japan as the economic locomotive, and East Asia will be its fuel tender. The yen, which is already the marker currency in the Pacific region, will become the dominant currency in the world, to underwrite Pax Nipponica as the dollar underwrote Pax Americana before it. Under Japanese leadership the international financial system will return to a framework of fixed foreign exchange rates and abandon the Smithsonian system of floating rates. Most likely Japan will implement a global extension of the European currency snake, which permits foreign currencies to change value only within narrowly defined bands.

The demonstration effect of Japan's turbocharged capitalism, arguably the most powerful force for economic change in the world today, will become the global role model under Pax Nipponica, replacing the neoclassical economic model of the West. The world will see a rapid growth of technological advancements, stemming from the superior system of government-business cooperation that the Japanese have developed, gradually replacing the more contentious and adversarial public-private sector relationships that predominate in the West.

"Unlike Western societies, which are based on the individual," a recent Japan Economic Institute report concluded, "Japanese culture values the relationship *between* persons. This basic characteristic permeates, and serves as the foundation for, the Japanese economic system. Rather than encouraging intense competition between individuals, with each wholly responsible for his actions, the Japanese economy relies on collegial groups that are based on various relationships created within and between companies. In some instances, such relationships can be detrimental to 'freedom' and 'competition' and contain many undesirable aspects. But the Japanese economy is the very model which Western societies are now beginning to emulate."

Mexico and Brazil will be logical next targets for Japan to demonstrate the superiority of its strategic industrial policies and capitalist development theories, replacing America's free trade ideology and neoclassical economic theory. These two countries alone comprise more than 50 percent of the Third World's accumulated external debt. Teams of elite Japanese bureaucrats will work side by side with technocrats in the Mexican government to restructure its official bureacracy, reform and strengthen public education, implement economic incentives to stimulate the growth of strategic industries, eliminate low value-added goods from production, and orchestrate a system of import restrictions and currency controls to create the national sacrifice necessary to achieve a level of future growth for the long-term economic health of the country.

Civil liberties and personal freedoms will be curtailed, of course; this is part of the price of an economic system dominated by a more authoritarian government. But personal savings rates and individual incomes will rise dramatically. Over time, under Japanese tutelage, Mexico will surely cease exporting cheap handicrafts, shoddy merchandise, and low-quality products to become a force in intermediate manufactured goods and electronics. It will also no longer be a poor neighbor of the United States. Mexico's new president, Carlos Salinas, is taking no chances; he is already sending his children to Japanese schools.

Japan's economic, industrial, and trade policies, on which Pax Nipponica will be based, are already beginning to redefine the way in which the world works: strategic trade, product cartels, negotiated export quotas, managed currency rates, strategic incentives, unparalleled product quality, the highest standards in manufacturing technology and public education, and effective public-private sector collaboration. Similarly, Japan's political system, rudderless though it may be and lacking a center of accountability, may well come to dominate the process of international affairs.

The Japanese style of communication and interaction, as we have seen, is less adversarial, confrontational, or contentious. It tends toward vagueness; being collaborative, it seeks consensus and harmony; it is slow and values persistence; process is accorded as much value as performance; it is low-key, quiet, and unobtrusive. In a world dominated by Pax Nipponica small teams of Japanese diplomats will be continuously at work *defusing* potentially explosive situations to preserve overall harmony. The "Lone Ranger" approach to international diplomacy will disappear. Expectations will be kept reasonable to minimize failure and loss of face. Responsibility will be delegated to multilateral teams headed by Japanese "captains" to work on systemic issues such as terrorism, Palestinian rights, and regional security. Befitting Japan's underlying strengths, complex economic measures rather than simple military solutions will be applied as a means of resolving conflict.

In the United States, of course, Japan will work to protect the strategic investments in its most important overseas colony. Those strategic investments are already well under way today, from prime commercial real estate in America's major metropolitan centers to key acquisitions of both industrial and financial institutions. Japan's high savings rates will continue to throw off surplus capital. Unable to absorb it all in the domestic Japanese economy, Tokyo will remit the balance to Washington, investing in Treasury obligations, underwriting the federal deficit, acquiring sufficient leverage to hold Washington hostage should the American government sponsor policies unacceptable to Tokyo. With insufficient capital of its own, America will then lose control over its own destiny.

In Europe Japan will continue to play off one continental government against another, as it has so successfully in the past. The coming of "fortress Europe" in 1992 will be a meaningless event. In the past five years major Japanese corporations have doubled their direct investments in the European community, focusing primarily on low-labor countries like Spain and Portugal. Japan now produces more in Europe than it exports to Europe, and that trend will continue. Europe will be a major source of capital earnings for Japan, while Europe will seethe with frustration at its inability to penetrate the Japanese market. It will be powerless to retaliate; the balance of political power will have swung to Japan.

But will Japan's style of diplomacy benefit the world or just Japan?

In Southeast Asia Japan is now the largest shareholder of the Asian Development Bank in Manila. Tokyo seconds its chief executive and funds more than 90 percent of its soft loan portfolio. Prior to stepping down as prime minister in 1987, Nakasone announced a coordinated Japanese package of development credits to promote private industry in the ASEAN countries. With $50 billion in foreign aid commitments over the next five years, Japan has replaced America as the world's leading donor; needless to say, nine of the top ten recipient countries are in Asia.

"I have a vision of a new Asia," former prime minister Nakasone said in Bangkok in 1987. "It is an Asia which turns its diversity into a source of vitality, where conflict and poverty are overcome. Asia as a whole will become a region in the limelight of world attention and wield an influence all its own."

In the Middle East, which supplies two-thirds of Japan's crude oil, Japan has worked quietly in support of Palestinian self-determination and pushed for Israel's withdrawal from the occupied territories. Japan has long thought that American policy in the Middle East has been too one-sided to be effective, its approach too confrontational.

In Africa Japan's Ministry of Foreign Affairs has been engaged in a quiet turf war with MITI and has successfully pulled Japan back from its position as South Africa's leading trade partner. The MFA recently invited the head of the African National Congress to Tokyo, and the Japanese government hosted the visit of Nobel Prize winner Bishop Tutu, organizing an official showing of the antiapartheid film *Cry Freedom*. The Ministry of Foreign Affairs is also studying the possibility of subsidizing African embassies in Tokyo because of the extremely high operating costs there. Rather than playing off the black African nations one against the other, Japan is treating them as a valued block of clients. The Japanese objective: sufficient votes to gain a seat on the Security Council at the United Nations.

Today the United States funds 25 percent of the UN's annual $4 billion operating budget. But Japan is now the second-largest contributor. The U.S. today is powerless to influence the UN's agenda, with 159 member nations, most of them Third World countries ideologically opposed to American leadership and continuously critical of U.S. policy, particularly its tilt toward Israel. The General Assembly now votes as the U.S. does only 18 percent of the time. Under Pax Nipponica, especially with Asia as the dominant region in the world, it will not be surprising to see the UN move its headquarters to Tokyo.

The stickiest point of all, without question, will be Japan's rearmament. But Japan's political leaders will be averse to accepting dominant economic and political power in the world without commensurate military power to back it up. Such is the nature of global superpower status. But being the most sensitive issue, a gradual, thirty-year time horizon for a full scale military buildup would not seem unreasonable. By the year 2020 Pax Nipponica will have enabled the Japanese constitution to be revised, with Article 9 either removed or substantially amended so as to permit the production of offensive military weapons, including world-class aircraft carriers, ballistic missiles, long-range bombers, and attack submarines. By then Japan will also have achieved its own nuclear capability.

Under Pax Nipponica Japan's three "no-nuclear" principles will have been abandoned, perhaps early in the next century, in a speech by the prime minister at the UN General Assembly meeting in Tokyo, announcing Japan's guarantees for global security. Japan would hardly send its own troops alone to resolve armed conflict elsewhere in the world, but rather will work through multilateral teams, relying more on economic strength and financial leverage to achieve a solution—paying the bill without risking the visible presence.

"The Great Gamble has been launched," British writer and longtime resident of Japan Robert Standish wrote in *The Three Bamboos*. "Such is the nature of these people that I do not believe them now capable of steering a middle course. By which I mean that they will either achieve their dream of world domination, or they will go down to such appalling destruction as the world has not seen since the fall of ancient Carthage."

Standish wrote those words in early 1942. Despite Japan's aggressive military tactics and the atrocities committed while occupying other Asian countries during the Pacific war, the Japanese have long felt themselves to be the victims of that war because of Hiroshima and Nagasaki. They were the *gisei*, the sacrifice, the first and only nation in the world to have suffered a nuclear attack. That memory has been etched into the nation's consciousness as firmly as the myth of its unique creation by the Sun Goddess, Amaterasu; it will never die.

Regardless of how the Japan–U.S. relationship evolves over the next two decades, whether toward greater interdependence or more bilateral conflict and tension, Japan could conceivably be drawn into using its future arsenal against the United States, partly in retaliation for 1945, partly out of revenge for America's postwar condescension.

The Japanese can be prone to emotional backlash; they are strongly motivated by pride, by nationalism, and by "downright irrationality," typified by their kamikaze spirit and a "fight to the last man" mentality. Former undersecretary of state George Ball once observed, "You never know when the Japanese will go ape." Harold Brown, secretary of defense in the Carter administration, put it somewhat more diplomatically: "The Japanese, as their economic activities show, never do things by halves." They would of course risk destroying many of their own assets and productive investments by the madness of such an attack, which logic and practicality would suggest they should avoid doing, but not for nothing have they become known as the world's foremost rebuilders.

"There are a few who love the Japanese," Standish concluded, "and many who fear and hate them. But there is none who can afford to ignore them."

Still, the wisdom of Sun-tzu might pull Japan back from the brink. It was he who said that to win a hundred victories in a hundred battles is not the acme of skill. To subdue the enemy without fighting is the acme of skill. And perhaps that skill, above all others, will characterize Pax Nipponica. Two earlier periods of Japanese industrial dominance and political strength—the anti-Westernism of the early Meiji era in the 1870s and the Japanese rule by the sword in the 1930s—displayed more of Japan's negative traits than positive ones. But the Japanese have learned from their mistakes, or they say they have. Today they are infinitely more sophisticated, more skillful, more cunning and clever.

"I am convinced," the elder statesman Masayoshi Hotta wrote on the eve of the Meiji Restoration more than a century ago, "that our policy should be to stake everything on the present opportunity, to conclude friendly alliances, to send ships to foreign countries everywhere and conduct trade, to copy the foreigners where they are at their best and so repair our own shortcomings, to foster our national strength and complete our armaments, and so gradually subject the foreigners to our influence until in the end all the countries of the world know the blessings of perfect tranquility and our hegemony is acknowledged throughout the world."

That Japan has emerged as a global power is undeniable: Tokyo today is the economic, financial, industrial, and technological capital of the world. Tokyo Bay is Japan's last frontier, and more than forty large-scale development projects are now planned to conquer that frontier with new landfill islands, highways, bridges, and tunnels. The master plan will concentrate Japan's high-technology industries in Kawasaki, on the Tokyo side, and in Kisarazu, on the Chiba side, linking them both by means of a cross-bay tunnel and bridge. The Ministry of Transport will build a 180-acre artificial island in the center of the bay. The Ministry of Posts and Telecommunications has designed a baywide telecommunications and information network called Marinet, linking Tokyo, Kawasaki, and Chiba by an optical fiber loop.

As the population of Tokyo continues to increase, its land prices rise, and increasing numbers of world-class Japanese companies compete to establish headquarters there, the Tokyo Bay project will mean more space for housing and offices. Japanese government ministries will eventually move to that artificial island in the center of the bay, fifteen minutes from downtown Tokyo by high-speed levitation rail, the product of Japan's commercialized breakthroughs in superconductivity. Tokyo fifty years from now will little resemble the Tokyo of today, reflecting the sentiment of a Japanese proverb that says, "If you want to lead, then you must *appear* to lead."

"The publication of a book entitled *Shorai no Nihon* (*The Future of Japan*) by a brilliant young journalist has electrified the Japanese reading public," political scientist Kenneth Pyle recently wrote in "Japan, the World, and the 21st Century," "by its description of the changes that will transform Japan and the world in the approaching new century. The author foresees a world dominated by a new economic system, increasing interdependence and free trade, the decline of nationalism and military spending, and the emergence of a peaceful world order."

The year was 1886. The author was Tokutomi Soho.

History has a way of surprising us with change. Not long ago I was asked to write an article about the demise of Emperor Hirohito—he was then eighty-eight and not well—and the implications for Japan under his successor, Crown Prince Akihito. Hirohito's ensuing death, I wrote, brought to an end the longest reign of Japan's 124 emperors; he ruled for more than sixty-two years. Emperor Akihito now continues the world's oldest functioning imperial system; his reign name is the Heisei era, the age of achieving universal peace.

Reign names go back more than a millennium. The modern period began in 1868 with the Meiji Restoration, when the emperor was restored to power under the age of enlightened rule. It was followed by the era of great righteousness, the Taisho Jidai, and finally, in 1926, when Hirohito ascended the throne, by Showa, the age of harmony and peace.

Despite the linguistic palliatives, these three contemporary periods have been anything but free of unrest and violence. It was during Meiji that Japan defeated China, annexed Taiwan, colonized Korea, and eliminated Russia as an adversary. During Taisho, Japan was more than an innocent bystander in the First World War, benefiting substantially as a great power from reconfiguration of the world's navies.

Showa, of course, produced Shanghai, Nanking, Bataan, Iwo Jima, Hiroshima, Nagasaki, and the firebombing of Tokyo, not to mention the unparalleled postwar aggressiveness of Japanese industrial policy, culminating in its predatory commercial behavior as a mercantilist mercenary throughout the world.

Before the Heisei name was chosen as successor to Showa, I engaged in a little speculation as to what the new era might be called. Perhaps the Hansei Jidai, I thought; but in retrospect I knew "anti-Western" might be a bit too direct for the understated Japanese style, despite the growing sense of superiority and arrogance. Tohkoh Jidai, then. The Rise of the East. That seemed better; at least it contained a hint of the West's undeniable though relative decline.

Then it clicked. The Iwa Jidai: the era of Japan's Majestic Dominance. For the enabling Japanese characters—*odosu* and *wa*—contain the elements of both dignity and majesty as well as a sense of dominance and threat, thus permitting the Japanese to contribute both pretense and true intent to the coming era they would so like to dominate and control.

That Japan today has the ingredients necessary for global hegemonic leadership is becoming increasingly clear. But whether Japan can use those ingredients thoughtfully, to positive effect for nations other than itself, in a spirit of benevolence rather than belligerence, remains to be seen. And whether America can recover its own historic strengths and create the strategic policies necessary to retain the reins of global leadership also remains to be seen.

The major unanswered question is how the world will get from here to there. Will chaos and uncertainty, perhaps even another major war, prevail, as geopolitical theorists of hegemonic stability warn? Will Japan, with unknowable consequences, successfully create a Pax Nipponica, despite its insularity, its authoritarianism, and its monoracial homogeneity? Or can the United States implement the necessary domestic reforms that will enable it to project a revitalized Pax Americana into the future, appropriate to the new age?

EPILOGUE

21

REINVIGORATING PAX AMERICANA

American strength derives not from the law of complexity, but from the law of the microcosm. Unlike oil, a material extracted from sand, semiconductor circuitry is written on sand and its substance is ideas. To say that huge conglomerates will dominate the world information industry because they have the most efficient chip factories is like saying Canada will dominate world literature because they have the tallest trees.

The drive to predict the demise of chronic entrepreneurialism continues strong in intellectual circles. The system often gives economic dominance to people who came to our shores as immigrants with little knowledge of English, to all the nerds and wonks disdained at the senior prom or the Ivied cotillion. But the entrepreneur remains the driving force of economic growth in all vibrant economies, including the U.S. economy, the most vibrant of all.

George Gilder, "The Law of the Microcosm"

"A greatly revitalized America can be nurtured by policies that exploit the special complementarity of American and Japanese interests," former national security adviser Zbigniew Brzezinski wrote recently in *Foreign Affairs*. "It is really quite striking how much the two countries' needs and interests match: the strengths of one compensate for the weaknesses of the other. Only through the deliberate fostering of a more cooperative, politically more intimate, and economically more organic relationship can these two major countries not only avoid a debilitating collision but also ensure that America continues to play the role the world system requires."

Brzezinski, a brilliant European strategist, sees the U.S.–Japan relationship as characterized increasingly by mutual Japanese and Amer-

461

ican participation at the board level in multinational corporations, by cross-border mergers of leading firms, by an expanded exchange of scientific talent, and by greater collaboration in high technology.

But we know from experience that the Japanese are driven primarily by *control:* their cultural roots demand it, their domination of commercial joint ventures proves it, and their aggressive trade and investment policies sustain it. Therefore, if some form of shared power between Japan and America emerges as an outgrowth of Pax Americana, it may make sense only as an interregnum to buy time for an American renewal—assuming the Japanese give us that luxury. Perhaps it will last a generation, maybe as long as two. But America needs to see such a period of joint leadership, if it ensues, as a gift of time, because it is almost certain that the Japanese will use it to their own advantage, irrespective of what America does.

Japan has always played the game that suits its own national interests and objectives best. But Japan's initiatives and responses are nearly always the result of external pressure, selfishly tailored to benefit itself, with strings attached, rather than being internally driven by a desire, either benign or beneficent, to see global harmony prevail.

A global system of shared power may also be justifiable only if America is the dominant or senior partner, in order for benevolence to remain the underlying force in world affairs. Otherwise, with an increasingly aggressive and self-confident Japan in control, its narrower national and cultural interests are more likely to surface as the defining factors. Above all, Japan appears most interested in maximizing comparative advantage so it can continue to dominate if not control its competitors. Its neomercantilist successes have followed on the heels of that strategy. The primary issue in any shared-power arrangement must inevitably boil down to *whose* power will prevail.

"History suggests that the optimistic American view of mutually beneficial interdependence with Japan may be unrealistic," the political scientist Ronald Morse observed recently in an insightful essay called "Japan's Drive to Pre-Eminence." "It seems almost inevitable that Japan at some point will assume positions on economic policy and on political and strategic issues that conflict with those preferred by the United States. Then deeper questioning about the relationship will begin. There will be rising uncertainty in the United States over how far Japan can be trusted to assume a benign leadership role for an open and fair trading and political relationship. And there will be growing uncertainty in Japan over America's capacity to manage its own economy and accept its new place in the world. Beneath the present rhetoric of cooperation, both sides are already observing each other with restraint and caution as they sort out their own national interests."

Lord Palmerston's advice bears repeating: Nations have neither permanent friends nor permanent enemies. They have only permanent interests. Half a century ago, Britain's economic decline and loss of world power came less from external pressure than from internal decay. Its entrepreneurship had floundered and become flabby. Strategic industries and new technology were not pursued with adequate vigor. Science and technical education lagged. And the relationship between business and government became mutually suspicious rather than mutually supportive. These are precisely the ingredients in America's recent relative decline, but unlike Britain, the United States need not face the future as a second-rate power. If it finds the will, it has the power to reinvigorate itself.

Restoration and renewal in America, then, must be a priority of the first magnitude in order to revitalize Pax Americana. America's strengths are extraordinary: An uncompromising ideological commitment to representative democracy and individual freedom and liberty. An incredibly diverse and resilient society capable of unmatched entrepreneurial energy, vitality, and skill. A market second to none in responsiveness, flexibility, and size. An unparalleled inventiveness. A dynamic, ethnic heterogeneity. A vibrant multiracial society. And the ability, because of all these, to attract the very best people—regardless of nationality, irrespective of class and religion and race—from all over the world.

Most of America's newest immigrants, well over half, now come from Asia. They bring with them the kinds of personal and professional skills America vitally needs in order to succeed in the next century, America's Pacific century: A strong commitment to education. The willingness to sacrifice and work hard. Unswerving devotion to family and children. The discipline to avoid excessive consumption. An ability to save and invest for the future. The strength to defer gratification from today to tomorrow. These are not uniquely Asian characteristics. They are American as well and were the vital ingredients that helped make this country great.

"No country has an entitlement to prosperity," Denmark's former economics minister Staffan Linder wrote in 1986 in *The Pacific Century*.

"No region has special privileges. There must be adjustment without tears, and Asian-Pacific competition now underscores this reality. It demonstrates dramatically that staleness is not tolerable. The virtue of the demonstration effect of Pacific dynamism is that it exposes the need for vitality and the necessity to look for what can be *achieved* rather than for what can be maintained."

Japan and East Asia have exposed America's weaknesses, but they have by no means rendered the nation incapable of generating the kinds of imaginative and innovative solutions that enabled Americans to create an exciting new nation two centuries ago. To carve the world's most productive economy out of raw wilderness. To abolish slavery and work toward eliminating racial prejudice. To win two world wars. To educate generations of immigrant children from all over the world. To create the technology and harness the resources that powered the industrial age. To invent the basic technology that has created the information age. And to form the ideology for a principle—freedom—that may be valued rhetorically everywhere but is given primary substance in the United States.

Japan and East Asia have also spurred a competitive response in this country. American product quality today is improved by orders of magnitude over a decade ago. Automation has begun to bring jobs back from overseas. Corporate organizations are leaner and stronger now than before. Management of both human and material resources is smarter. Inflation is down and employment is up, with the number of days lost in labor disputes now the lowest since the immediate postwar years. The responsiveness of the private sector is quicker and more flexible, which by extension gives rise to optimism in the public sector too.

But America is dangerously in debt. Cumulative federal deficits reaching $3 trillion, annual trade deficits of $150 billion, and an unenviable ranking as the world's leading debtor are worrisome indicators of the nation's increasing tendency to live beyond its means. Incentives to rebuild America's pool of savings and restore its capital self-sufficiency must be found before the country finds itself hostage to foreign creditors.

In 1957 the U.S. waged war on sterling during the Suez crisis in order to force Britain to acquiesce with America's Middle East policy; England's retreat was a result. In 1979 Germany's refusal to support the dollar was a major factor in forcing the United States to adopt a tighter monetary policy; double-digit inflation and the highest interest rates in the nation's history were the results. In 1995, if not before, Japan could threaten to pull the plug on America by refusing to renew its Treasury bond investments, precipitating another market panic and leaving Washington with a crisis of unthinkable proportions.

America has paid an expensive price for its proud rise from the malaise of a decade ago: it has become financially spendthrift and seems spiritually exhausted, far less prepared than a superpower should be to make the kinds of sacrifices that will be necessary during the next generation to preserve its global leadership, its prosperity, and its freedom. The nation has a new administration now, governed by more traditional New England values than its predecessors, which could lay the foundation for America's future in a world more intensely competitive than any known in the past.

America needs to devise incentives that can increase federal tax revenues without further penalizing the individual American taxpayer, without tempting a spendthrift Congress to increase the federal deficit, and without constraining the tremendous entrepreneurial spirit that gives the American economy its dynamism and its drive. Those incentives should be designed to spur both productivity and economic growth in the nation's strategic sectors, but they must also include a combination of consumption and special use taxes to help achieve fiscal soundness—especially a more realistic energy policy, where America lags behind both Europe and Japan.

America may also have to modify its free trade rhetoric by coming to the realization that trade in the new era is strategic. Neither free nor fair, trade (especially with Japan) is *managed* now, and the nation's substantial leverage must be brought to bear in negotiating stronger positions for itself, based on its own national interests in maintaining the lead in the higher value-added technologies. The nation's trade policies must also be linked more strategically to political and defense issues, which means a greater premium on national policy *coordination* in the future than has been the case in the past. But protectionism is not the answer. Strategy is. The Japanese, by their own admission, recognize that if America shifts to more strategic trade policies, the days of their easy victories are over.

Does Japan want to keep 25 percent of the largest automotive market in the world? Then that market share may carry a price tag: it will cost Tokyo more to share with Washington the burden of the free world's regional security responsibilities. Does Japan wish to retain control of half the American market for numerically controlled machine tools? Then the price Tokyo may have to pay is outright purchase of sophisticated American weapons rather than licensing U.S. technology to enhance Japan's own advanced manufacturing base in the strategic industries. And does Japan want the benefit of continued access to America's high-technology markets? Then the cost may be *quid pro quo* access by American manufacturers to Japan's markets coupled with the tough-minded imposition of temporary tariffs until that access has been achieved.

These tactics are not protectionist. They are *strategic*. Strategy is the only language the Japanese understand, and negotiating *quid pro quo* agreements through linkage may be the only way that language can be communicated effectively to Tokyo.

Devised incentives must also enable American corporations to recapture their position of world-class leadership in manufacturing, for manufacturing is the source of the nation's higher value-added services and its better-paying jobs. Short-term financial gain may have been sufficient as a barometer of American corporate performance in the past, but it is inappropriate as a benchmark for the future. Market share and industry leadership, both measured on a global basis, have become the new standards. Disaggregated tax incentives, more aggressive investment tax credits, and accelerated depreciation benefits must be developed, without increasing the corporate income tax rate, to maintain America's lead in the strategic industries of the future—incentives that benefit production, not consumption.

Vital in any shift from consumption to production will be *massive* financial incentives to cure America's anemic savings rate. American savings as a percentage of net disposable income are the lowest in the industrialized world. Without a stronger capital base and higher rates of capital formation, the nation not only makes its deficits harder to reduce; it also runs the risk of placing its destiny in the hands of foreign powers.

Except for Britain, America today has the highest capital gains taxes in the industrialized world. They must be reduced significantly, if not eliminated altogether. Tax rates also need to be staggered to favor longer-term holdings and penalize short-term churning. America is also the only industrial country that imposes a double tax on dividends, and that too must be rectified.

Most importantly, America needs dramatic new incentives to encourage the average saver to put money away, to reinvest rather than spend. That means exempting from tax all earned interest income on a rather large principal base in approved accounts, providing it is reinvested. It also means imposing penalties on all money borrowed for purposes other than financing the purchase of a primary residence. Incentives to save cannot be effective if existing incentives to spend remain in place.

America is gradually learning that it cannot compete as a world-class competitor without world-class workers in its factories. Public education at the preschool, primary, and secondary levels must be strengthened dramatically. The first step that needs to be taken is to restructure public education by depoliticizing the process; in short, by redefining control. School boards and centralized district bureaucracies must eventually be dismantled and power returned to individual schools through parent-teacher advisory boards to reinforce that vital triangle among parent, teacher, and child. Large educational bureaucracies, structured around a rigid, vertical hierarchy of political power, may well have suited America's needs during the industrial age. But that age is gone. America's public schools must now become more like its private schools, based on the principles of autonomy, teacher accountability, and higher standards, if the nation is to respond adequately to the challenges and demands of the information age.

Schools of *choice* will become the driving force in American public education in the last decade of this century. Magnet schools, interdistrict choice, and intradistrict choice are all gathering momentum now and will be the new agents of change. A primary virtue of free choice is that it permits parents to put their children into schools that are run according to their own higher personal standards of achievement.

It is widely recognized now that the school day and the school year both need to be extended to at least the average of the industrialized world: seven-hour days, five-and-a-half-day weeks, 225-day years. Average class size must be *increased,* not reduced, to encourage more creative experimentation with collaborative teaching, cooperative learning, and peer group dynamics, all of which more accurately reflect the new reality of the workplace, where success depends on small group interaction. Personal effort must be stressed over innate ability. Parents must be involved and share more of the burden, especially if curricula are to be made more rigorous; the education of our children is far too important to be left just to the schools. And the unions will have to be partners in the process. Teachers will never achieve white-collar status by using outdated blue-collar organizational tactics.

But all American schools must share some common goals: that the curriculum be far more rigorous; that standards of performance begin to *exceed* the higher international standards now being set by East Asian schools; that teachers be accountable to their clients, the parents, and not to the bureaucracy; that superior teaching be rewarded and inferior teaching no longer tolerated; that economic barriers to education be eliminated by making public education from preschool through university entirely free and based on choice; and that tax credits be devised that will enable parents to send their children to any school to which they can gain admittance. The greatest change will occur in our urban schools; the least in America's small towns, where the public school systems are already more responsive to parental pressures and where public schools already operate as if they were private.

In at least one province—higher education—America still leads the world. Yet that has created an ancillary problem: a tidal wave of foreign students. More than 300,000 foreigners are enrolled at American universities, nearly two-thirds of them in technical and scientific fields. According to statistics collected by the National Science Foundation from 1963 to 1983, the percentage of foreign-born PhDs in industrial engineering in America grew from 7 to 68 percent, in electrical engineering from 23 to 55 percent, in chemical engineering from 22 to 52 percent, and in civil engineering from 37 to 63 percent.

As of 1987, foreign students comprised nearly *half* of all doctoral candidates in cognitive science, artificial intelligence and computerized expert systems, software engineering, and nonlinear mathematics. As these capable and hardworking foreigners increasingly return home, they produce a "negative brain drain" and deprive America of their valuable talents and skills (though their native countries benefit, as well they should). The problem is not that America has too many foreigners mastering these technical subjects, but too few Americans, so incentives need to be devised to attract more.

"The United States is the world's university," Jean-Jacques Servan-Schreiber, author of the best-seller *The American Challenge*, recently wrote. "But it needs to enroll more American graduate students. Their pride is on the line, [and] they will not easily accept being surpassed by those who work with extra energy because they are immigrants.

But a striking sign of America's natural generosity and courage in competition is that the excellence of foreigners here breeds none of the anti-foreign sentiments observed in so many other parts of the world."

The most vital unit in any society is the family. America desperately needs to devise new incentives to encourage families to stay together. Tax policy itself can be the driving force, beginning with higher and more realistic personal deductions for families with children, to make it economically advantageous for married couples not only to bear children but to stay together with them as a family unit, to slow the socially disabling rate of divorce and single parenthood.

With a majority of American mothers now in the work force, workable incentives for adequate child care and paid parental leave must also be found. But those incentives must be designed carefully around tax credits that put decision-making power and choice in the hands of individual parents, not to expand further the size and power of the federal bureaucracy. America's tax policies, as with savings, investment, and federal revenue enhancement, must be more innovative and need to decentralize power, not concentrate it.

America's corporations, too, must experiment more with flextime and flexwork procedures to enable parents—fathers and mothers alike—to spend more time together with their children, particularly in the first five years of life but especially in the critical year following childbirth. The United States is the only industrialized country with no national parental leave law. Flexibility, in terms of freedom to choose from a menu of applicable corporate benefits, is becoming the watchword and is an American strength.

The information age is eliminating the necessity for all employees to work at one central location during the same core hours of the day. Increasing numbers of America's working parents are finding institutional child care insufficient to meet their needs. As with our schools, incentives must emphasize choice. Public schools are empty, by and large, in early morning and late afternoon. They can be used more innovatively for child-care activities both before and after classes. Much more work can be done at home, and more productively, enabling both mothers and fathers to be closer to their children. Child-care benefits should not penalize them, and America's corporations must respond flexibly to their needs.

"To be attached to the subdivision, to love the little platoon we belong to in society, is the first principle of public affections," Edmund Burke wrote in *Reflections on the French Revolution.* "It is the first link in the series by which we proceed towards a love to our country, and to mankind."

America too often chooses to organize itself through a federal bureaucracy when it ought to be decentralized, as with poverty programs and welfare assistance. Sufficient evidence has been accumulated to show federal welfare and social legislation now tax America's poor into poverty and could be scrapped. This would force the individual beneficiary to rely on public or privately funded sources in the local community for support and eventually to strive for self-sufficiency. Arguably the most justifiable benefits go to the much larger population of individuals who have tried to do things correctly but have been penalized because they refuse to turn themselves into wards of the state. Abolishing urban rent-control laws, for example, and encouraging more private-public partnerships will do more to make affordable housing available (and reduce the numbers of America's homeless) than simply relying on increased federal spending and control.

"Socioeconomic mobility has been America's stock in trade," the social scientist Charles Murray wrote in *Losing Ground.* "Immigrants arrive penniless and work their way up. The sharecropper's son becomes an assembly-line worker and his granddaughter goes to college. The immigrant who speaks no English has a son who goes to night school for nine years and finally gets a law degree. These are the personal triumphs that constitute the American ethic."

Sacrifice, self-sufficiency, commitment, deferral of gratification. Not for nothing have these been America's traditional building blocks. But incentives and rewards are necessary to sustain these efforts over the long haul.

"There is no shortage of institutions to provide the rewards," Murray noted. "Our schools know how to educate students who want to be educated. Our industries know how to find productive people and reward them. Our philanthropic institutions know how to multiply the effectiveness of people who are already trying to help themselves. In short, America is very good at reinforcing the investment of an individual in himself."

While decentralization is preferable in areas such as welfare assistance and education, America also often delegates power to the individual states when it ought to be more centrally focused, as with foreign investment. Foreign countries (especially Japan) tend to play one American state off against another in competing for the most advantageous terms and conditions under which to make their corporate acquisitions or to site their manufacturing plants. As a result there is no centralized monitoring process, regional growth is unbalanced, and control of policy is lost. No other industrialized country in the world permits direct foreign investment without a review or approval process at the national level. For America this does not mean increasing the size of its federal bureaucracy, but it does mean improving the means by which policy is coordinated, statistics are collected, and monitoring is done.

Whether this process will necessitate creating a cabinet-level competitiveness council, or merging relevant Department of Commerce divisions into the office of the U.S. Trade Representative, or establishing a strategically focused department within the National Security Council—all of which have been proposed—it is clear that better policy coordination at the national level will be essential to blunt the growing Japanese challenge. Longer congressional terms of office, coupled with a single six-year term for the presidency and public funding for campaigns for national office, all constitutionally empowered, will help slow the dangerous dependence on narrow special interest groups and return political power to the American people through a more effective process of representative democracy. The objective is to reverse the focus from short-term to long-term.

In national defense too America's strategies need more innovation and flexibility and less reliance on the status quo. Three hundred billion dollars is a heavy burden for this nation to bear. Even if it is historically not out of line as a percentage of GNP, dramatic growth in federal social spending has made these two components of the national budget the largest. The defense burden could be reduced by a third without sacrificing America's security, through better procurement management, a more flexible weapons strategy, more productive private efforts to move weapons from design to market, and more cost-effective and equitable burden-sharing with both NATO and Japan, including a delegation of regional security functions under direct American cognizance and control. The United States must be more selective and strategic in determining where its vital interests lie and how it chooses to defend them. But the world must know that America can and will use its strengths to defend those interests and those of its friends.

America need not decline, but it does have to *change* to meet the needs of a changed world. The nation has to strengthen the foundations on which Pax Americana has worked in the past and adapt them to fit a world that America no longer dominates as it once did.

Because of the magnitude of the investments necessary to reinforce those foundations—to generate new tax revenues, to rebuild capital and savings dramatically, to restore the nation's world-class manufacturing base, to strengthen its public education, to create more cohesive social policies for its families and its children—a recession may be inevitable. But the nation must be told by its leaders, truthfully, why investments to strengthen the nation's future cannot be made unless some sacrifices are also made, and shared, in the present. If we can no longer bear our vices, then we must be prepared to bear their cure.

Pax Americana can be revived, revitalized, and restored. It must be. Because the alternatives, whether an unpredictable dominance and control by Japan under Pax Nipponica or chaos and uncertainty resulting from a world with no dominant single power at all, are both less tolerable.

"Is there a third power on the horizon?" the historian John Lewis Gaddis asked in a recent *Atlantic* article. "What seems most likely is not that some new rival will emerge, capable of challenging the superpowers militarily, but rather that the standards by which we measure power will evolve, with forms other than military—economic, technological, cultural—becoming more important. To some extent this is already happening: one superpower, the Soviet Union, has already been eclipsed by a third power, Japan, in gross national product; another, China, has demonstrated what the Soviet Union has not, which is how a socialist economy can become agriculturally self-sufficient. Nor should Americans be so complacent as to consider themselves exempt from such trends, particularly if we persist in transforming our economy from its traditional industrial base into one geared chiefly toward the provision and consumption of services."

Pax Americana, Pax Nipponica, no pax.

Those appear to be the choices at the threshold of the twenty-first century. There is, unavoidably, a price to be paid for each. America's primary values are freedom, liberty, and justice. Under Pax Americana its social cohesiveness, its national policy coordination, its once-high educational standards, and its fiscal solvency have all been sacrificed at the altar of freedom. There are no guarantees that America can restore the balance.

Japan's historical values are loyalty, duty, conformity, and obedience. Under Pax Nipponica individual freedoms would be sacrificed to the group under a more hierarchical, authoritarian political system that would seek to gain the benefits of strong industry, cutting-edge technology, and a more equitable distribution of wealth—a system that works well in a homogeneous culture but breaks down and provokes resistance when it tries to dominate or control others. America has tried to act in ways that would benefit the world; Japan, on the other hand, acts primarily in ways that benefit itself.

Japan is still a one-dimensional power; its economic, industrial, and financial strengths are now well known. It lacks global political influence and military might, but its leaders are working to increase both. The Japanese are seeking greater dominance of multilateral bodies such as the UN and the IMF to achieve a level of political influence commensurate with their economic power. Japan's defense spending has risen to the second-highest absolute level in the free world after the United States.

The rest of Asia is, however, rooting for America, not for Japan. Japan's model has always been the flying geese format, with Japan as the head goose, but Asians don't want to fly in that formation. Japanese society is closed to outsiders and impossible to penetrate; it cannot serve as a beacon for others. That, in a nutshell, is the nation's dilemma: being closed is its greatest weakness. Japan has narrowed the gap with America. Now the real race begins.

With no pax, of course, anarchy may rule. Continental Europe has, in this century, twice rejected Germany's attempts at hegemonic control. America and Asia have each rejected Japan's earlier attempts at dominance and control. For Americans, is there really a choice?

In a more pluralistic world, which is replacing the postwar bipolar system and where America's friends may also be its foes, the road to stability and prosperity is neither as straight nor as well marked as it once was. Economic competition will prevail over traditional military disputes, which makes the trade war between America and Japan that much more significant.

No other nation is presently ready to replace the United States in its role as the "wisdom of last resort." But precisely because the world is now more interdependent, America can less afford a retreat to a fortress of isolationism. "Do we pay more to preserve a free and open world?" former Federal Reserve Bank chairman Paul Volcker recently asked. "Yes. Do we pay more than it's worth? Absolutely not."

Europe's own future remains clouded at best. The Continent contains all the great powers of Western history, a market of 325 million people with a combined GNP larger than America's and more than twice the size of Japan's. Europe possesses a cultural and historical heritage in common with America, world-class standards in education, and high standards of living. But it is preoccupied with its past, too, and seemingly incapable of mapping a unified future. Despite its push to reassert itself as a borderless economy in 1992, Europe remains a collective of clashing interests, with a dozen independent nations and as many currencies and languages. These people have warred against each other for centuries, divided by their differences and united only by a common fear—of Soviet military power, of Japanese industrial power, of American dominance. The most critical global relationship for America now is with Japan, not Europe.

Japan's challenge to America is becoming clear. What of the other nations in East Asia?

Insatiably competitive and driven by a historical hostility toward Japan, Korea will remain a powerful industrial force in East Asia, the second-largest GNP after Japan, and a showcase for the ongoing struggle between authoritarianism and democracy. Tension between the nation's economic planners, who want continued growth, and its political leaders, who wish to see more equitable progress, will increase. That tension will produce uncertainty and tenuous change. But the Koreans should not be underestimated. They are survivors. That a renewed effort at reunification comes in the afterglow of Korea's democratic reforms is another hopeful sign.

As for Taiwan, it is difficult not to be optimistic about the likelihood of eventual independence for this resilient island nation. If China's economic reforms do fail, as is likely, and the Central Kingdom turns inward once again, Taiwan will be drawn inexorably toward independence, separating itself from the mother country by a common language and culture. Its hardworking, entrepreneurial business class should continue to demonstrate the kind of flexibility and adaptiveness in the future that has brought the country such profound success in the past.

Hong Kong's fate, regrettably, seems inexorably sealed, both now and after the magic year of 1997. The very nature of China's bureaucratic, central command system cannot help impacting the former colony, and its quality of life, negatively. At the rate at which its skilled, middle-class professionals are leaving, the Fragrant Harbor will soon be a ghost town. China's loss will be the world's gain, as hundreds of thousands of talented people leave their birthplace for new and more promising futures. So when the Union Jack is lowered less than a decade from now, and the Red Star of China takes its place, one of the most colorful and dynamic chapters in human history will have come to a close.

At the opposite end of Asia, Singapore's star should continue to shine brightly. Its second generation of political leadership—astute, experienced, well educated—seems poised to guide the Lion City prosperously into the new century. Singapore is likely to continue to have an influence in regional and world affairs far beyond its size, and well it should, as its strategic location, its communications infrastructure, its highly educated work force, and its successful experimentation with innovative social policies have earned the republic a place in the Pacific sun.

The Philippines remains Asia's most heartbreaking disappointment, socially, politically, and economically. Irrelevantly rich in natural resources, it has failed all the tests that the rest of East Asia has passed so successfully. On the threshold of the information age, the Philippines seems irretrievably locked into its past. The United States must be prepared to abandon its bases there, for it can and will find alternatives. The security issue is overdrawn; the Philippine economy represents damaged goods, and no external power can afford to assume that burden now. The Philippines must be allowed to get out of America's shadow and begin to emulate its more successful neighbors.

Conventional wisdom holds that China will emerge as Asia's new giant, replacing and eventually dominating Japan. While the West may continue to be mesmerized by the lure of China's size, a preoccupation with the Central Kingdom seems misplaced. Its economic reforms are more likely to fail than to succeed, because its primary asset, its population, is also its chief liability. China does not need territory, and it is not inherently an expansionist power; its strategic needs are, and will remain, primarily defensive in nature.

All China has to show for its efforts at economic reform during the past decade are rampant inflation, a resurgence of corruption, erratic industrialization, urban pollution, and a sizable increase in an already unmanageable population. In addition, Beijing must now deal with an increasingly impatient intellectual and managerial class whose expectations have been raised to new heights. The stage is set for further domestic unrest, possibly more violence, perhaps instability, conceivably a counterrevolution if not another civil war. China is far from becoming a superpower of the twenty-first century. The events at Tiananmen square in Beijing in mid-1989 offer further confirmation of this.

The Soviet Union, as Winston Churchill once observed, remains a riddle wrapped in a mystery inside an enigma. After Japan, it is the second joker in the pack. That *perestroika* is doomed to fail is becoming increasingly apparent, faster than even the skeptics had predicted. The USSR's Eastern European allies are already showing an eagerness to break loose from Moscow's hold. Should that trend continue, Russia would be forced to preoccupy itself with its western front, and East Asia may be spared for a time. But so long as that paranoid nation remains a one-dimensional superpower, defined solely by military strength, a force counterbalancing its projection of power in East Asia will be necessary. Better that force be American than Japanese. The world now knows what America has long contended: that Communism is dead and Marxism is a failed ideology.

The Soviet leaders are faced with the daunting task of bringing their people out from under the heavy weight of political serfdom. But they have created a vicious circle for themselves: they cannot achieve results without breaking the inertia, and yet they cannot break the inertia without showing some results. The prospects for either circumventing an entrenched central bureaucracy or winning over a labor force that remains unconvinced and largely unmotivated are not only poor, it seems to me, but hopeless.

From now into the next century, the ideological challenge to America will not be Communism, from either the Soviet Union or China, but a softer brand of authoritarianism from Japan shrouded in the guise of its capitalist developmental economics called turbocharged capitalism. Japan may well be the locomotive of global economic growth in the future and East Asia its fuel tender. America must learn to understand better what makes this political and industrial adversary tick and develop the necessary strategy and tactics to deal with it. New global standards of product quality, of advanced technology, of manufacturing productivity, of political organization, of education, of social cohesiveness, of the quality of human resources are all being set now by Japan. America has its own unique skills, strengths, and talents. It need not—in fact, cannot—emulate the Japanese model. But it does have to meet the challenge.

There has been a recent tendency to sell America short. Pessimism about America's future is now clearly in vogue. The doomsayers have taken the upper hand; their gloom-and-doom scenarios dominate the national media. America's political leadership often seems to be the most pessimistic of all; its business leaders may be somewhat more cautiously upbeat. But it is the average citizens, out in the heartland, who refuse to snuff out the flame of optimism, who know that America's demise is not inevitable. Only change is.

"Introducing basic change is never easy," Harvard's Ezra Vogel wrote in *Japan as Number One* a decade ago. "But to expect Americans, who are accustomed to thinking of their nation as number one, to acknowledge that in many areas its supremacy has been lost to an Asian nation and to learn from that nation, is to ask a good deal. Americans are peculiarly receptive to any explanation of Japan's economic performance which avoids acknowledging Japan's superior competitiveness. It is not clear that Americans are ready to respond to the challenge now posed by Japan's success and that will soon be posed by the success of Korea and other Asian nations. The Japanese have become the masters of change rather than its victims. Other countries were devastated by foreign influence, but Japan was invigorated. America, like Japan, can master the new challenges; it can respond with foresight rather than hindsight, with planning rather than crisis management, sooner rather than later."

While Japan works assiduously at maintaining its homogeneity and racial purity by keeping its society closed to outsiders, America continually restores and revitalizes itself through the waves of immigrants that stream toward "the shining city on a hill." More than half a million of them come to America legally every year, and more than half of those are from Asia. They all invigorate America's national energy, bring new skills and talents, and regenerate the American dream.

The evolving competition between America and Japan is not a zero-sum game, wherein only one winner will emerge. But it *is* a competition with extremely high stakes, with numerous contests and frequent wins and losses. Japan has to date realized this far better than America. Japanese strategy has roots deep in its cultural history; its persistence and perseverance are legendary. America's new strategies must be similarly derived from its own cultural legacy, not to emulate Japan but to become even more like America.

The story of America is the story of a competitive nation rising to meet a challenge, any challenge, to guard its freedom, to protect its independence, and to ensure a continually rising standard of living for its people. It is a story of a nation competing and a nation winning. The will to win and the will to excel are the things that endure.

The Japanese have been winning because they have managed to transplant a dynamic concept that is uniquely American: that ordinary people can be inspired to work together to achieve extraordinary things. Doubtless, America can do it again. But new strategies are required.

The first fifty years of this century, with no dominant global power, were characterized by two world wars separated by a depression; the following fifty years, under Pax Americana, were shaped by relative peace and prosperity. What will the next fifty years look like?

America, an Atlantic power, has led the past half century. America, also a Pacific power, can lead the next. If war comes to America again— a major war, one that threatens its survival—Americans will respond, as they have done before, in defense of freedom and liberty. War creates the kind of shared sacrifice and common commitment that enable the American system of representative democracy to pull together as one. No foreign power, friend or foe, should ever forget that. The most precious experiment in human history is far too valuable to lose.

But the problem for any representative democracy, and especially for America, is that war is often the only means of galvanizing a national consciousness. In the late 1950s the Soviet *Sputnik* spurred America from complacency to educational reform, technological achievement, and greater vigilance. In the early 1990s Japan's continued commercial and industrial challenge should be a comparable competitive spur. America has so far been slow to perceive the nature of that challenge.

By the mid-1990s, if Tokyo chooses to boycott a Treasury bond issue or sells its substantial dollar holdings to precipitate another market panic, or when Japan launches its own hypersonic jet aircraft that could do to Boeing and McDonnell-Douglas—long America's strongest exporters—what Toyota and Honda have done to Detroit, perhaps the nature of the next *Sputnik* may be clear. Without a galvanized national consciousness, it will be considerably more difficult for America to achieve the kind of consensus it needs for revitalization, restoration, and reform.

At the beginning of this century America was remarkably endowed with all the advantages it needed for success in the industrial age, and Japan had to struggle against all odds to compete. On the threshold of the next century Japan now has the natural endowments for success in the information age, and America will have to struggle to compete.

Natural resources and a self-contained market no longer count for what they did. *Human* resources are now the key, and America lacks no shortage of talented and innovative people. But the trick will be to educate more of them, to get them to work together harder and more productively in order to compete with a Japan now endowed by accident and historical circumstance.

It was so once. It can be so again. The American century, as we know it, may be over. But America's decline is not absolute. The future is ours to create. A *new* American century is well within our capabilities to achieve.

"America is the most vital nation in the West, and will remain so," former West German chancellor Helmut Schmidt recently said. "It is a nation of vitality and optimism, and that helps a lot even if it sometimes blinds wisdom."

As the curtain lifts on the last decade of this century, America is becoming preoccupied with domestic concerns. Reducing the federal budget deficit. Rebuilding its world-class manufacturing base. Strengthening public education. Battling poverty and homelessness. Winning the war against drugs. Coping with hazardous waste. Creating affordable public housing. Finding innovative solutions for child care. Reviving the two-parent family. Restoring public faith in its political system. Resolving inequities between its elderly and its children. Containing the costs of health care.

The temptation will be to turn inward and become isolationist again, a real danger now that the external world is at relative peace. The Soviet Union has withdrawn from Afghanistan, preoccupied with *perestroika*. China is absorbed with its own domestic problems. The two Koreas are tiptoeing toward reunification. Iran and Iraq have stopped fighting. Israel and Palestine have begun to talk.

America now has a window of opportunity. Not to take advantage of it may be to miss the best chance this nation has had in a generation to put its own house in order in anticipation of the greater challenges to come. In a sense America's domestic problems are at their apogee now—they can't get much worse. So the trend lines of international competitiveness need to be viewed in terms of American "lows" against Japanese "highs." These lines are now beginning to converge: American competitive performance will get better because it can't get much worse.

But the Japanese are by no means standing still. Even if you are on the right track, Will Rogers used to say, you will get run over if you just sit there. So American performance cannot improve solely through benign neglect. It must be enhanced by the kinds of incentives proposed throughout this book.

The world does not have the privilege of voting for a dominant leader. That leader emerges (or not), over time, in response to changing external conditions. The only way America can lose its role of global leadership to a third power, like Japan, is by default.

"The twentieth century was the American century," Seizaburo Sato, foreign policy adviser to former prime minister Nakasone, said recently. "I think the twenty-first century will be the American century, too."

What Mr. Sato no doubt intended as *tatemae,* or pretense, may turn out to be *honne,* or actual intent.

But not automatically, and certainly not without a lot of hard work, based in large part on the kinds of incentives we have been examining.

At issue is whether the United States is prepared to face its future as a second-rate power. In my view, it is not. In time, America must find ways to galvanize the national consciousness, to bring its commitment to the new age into white-hot focus. If the nation can do that, then America will be able to lead the coming century as a *primus inter pares* with every bit as much optimism and confidence as it has in the past.

But if it can't, then the doomsayers will have their day, and America will ultimately and inevitably traverse the downward spiral of decline like all the great powers before it that failed to reverse their slide toward oblivion and that failed to plant the vital seeds of renewal, of adaptation, and of change.

It is a question of leadership and of national will. All the danger signs—and the incentives necessary to avoid them—are there. Can America find the collective strength to heed them?

SOURCES

ACKNOWLEDGMENTS

Scores of people, both in America and in Asia, have helped in countless ways to shape this book from its early conceptualization to its finished form. I want to acknowledge their extensive contributions and thank them for their assistance.

I am indebted to the many business leaders, government officials, educators, economists, and working parents on both sides of the Pacific who shared their time, their convictions, and their thoughts with me. They are reflected (and named) in the many interviews that follow; space limitations prevent listing them here, but they alone can take credit for making the text so human and lively. They all know they have my heartfelt thanks and gratitude, for without their participation and effort this book could not have come alive.

To Chalmers Johnson of the University of California and Marius Jansen at Princeton, who commented thoughtfully on early manuscript drafts and provided helpful suggestions, I extend my deepest appreciation; their intellectual, historical, and practical knowledge of Japan and East Asia is without equal on either side of the Pacific. It has been a pleasure as well as a privilege to count them both as friends.

I also wish to acknowledge the help of the following individuals for their invaluable assistance in opening doors, providing introductions, suggesting sources, arranging interviews, extending encouragement, or serving as sounding boards throughout the life of this project: in Dallas, Norman Neureiter and Vladi Catto at Texas Instruments, and Bill and John Richardson; in Palo Alto, Bob Weeks; in Wilmington, Delaware, Bill Whipple and Stephanie Hood at DuPont; in New York, Sandy Burton and Hugh Patrick at Columbia University, Peter Randall and Ian Brett of the Hong Kong Consulate, David Dyche at Arthur D.

Little, Ambassador Ro-myung Gong and Consul Kyong-bo Choi at the Korean Consulate, Eddie Tsai of the Coordination Council for North American Affairs, Peter Burnim and David Martin at Citibank, Nicholas Lakas of the U.S.–Korea Society, Susan Heinz of the Asia Society, John Wheeler of the Japan Society, and former ambassador Hidetoshi Ukawa and Hisao Yamaguchi of the Japanese Consulate; in Detroit, Mike Morrison at Chrysler; in Grand Rapids, Steve Channer and Steve Nobel of the Business & Institutional Furniture Manufacturers' Association, John Klein at Steelcase, and the late Alan Keith of Haworth; in Muscatine, Iowa, Stanley Howe, chairman of Hon Industries; in Cambridge, Ezra Vogel at Harvard University, Amitai Etzioni at the Harvard Business School, and Dick Samuels at MIT; in Boston, Merry White at Boston University; in Stamford, Connecticut, Joe Cahalan at Xerox; in Basking Ridge, New Jersey, John Hinds, president of AT&T International; in Trenton, Carl Golden, press secretary for Governor Tom Kean; and in Princeton, Bob Gilpin, Hisashi Kobayashi, Kent Calder, Martin Collcutt, Sheldon Garon, Dennis Helms, Harry Levine, Marge Smith, Tsuneyoshi Takai, and Terry Wilson.

In Washington, Robert Leestma at the Department of Education; Bella Rosenberg at the American Federation of Teachers; Gary Watts at the National Education Association; Congressman Frank Wolf, Congresswoman Marcy Kaptur, and Congresswoman Helen Bentley; Ira Wolf, legislative assistant to Senator John D. Rockefeller IV; Jeremy Karpatkin, legislative aide to Senator Paul Simon; Jo Ellen Urban, press secretary for Congressman Richard Gephardt; Greg Tucker, press assistant to Congresswoman Marcy Kaptur; Pat Wait, press aide to Congresswoman Helen Bentley; Rikki Baum, legislative aide to Senator Daniel Patrick Moynihan; Sheila Ward, press secretary for Congressman Newt Gingrich; Steve Hilton, press secretary for Senator Jack Danforth; Jack DeVore, press secretary for Senator Lloyd Bentsen; Yoke-kwang Lee of the Singapore Embassy; Tae-ik Chung of the Korean Embassy; Adolfo Paglinawan of the Philippine Embassy; Ke-Sheng Sheu, director of the Economic Division, and Shuang Jeff Yao, director of the Information Division of the Coordination Council for North American Affairs; Joe Kyle at the Washington office of the American Institute in Taiwan; Ron Morse at the Library of Congress; Gerald Lowrie of AT&T; Bill Peterson of the Construction Industry Manufacturers' Association; Nathaniel Thayer of the School of Advanced International Studies at Johns Hopkins University; Gerry Regier of the Family Research Council; Ed Lincoln at the Brookings Institution; Tom Robinson and Michael Novak of the American Enterprise Institute (which sponsored an outstanding conference on democracy and development in East Asia in spring 1988); Roger Brooks at the Heritage Foundation; John Bennett of the Korea Economic Institute of America; Fred Brown, Paul Kreisberg, and Clyde Prestowitz at the Carnegie Endowment for International Peace; Stephen Marris and Dr. Soon Cho (now deputy prime minister of the Republic of Korea) at the Institute for International Economics; and Karl Jackson and Jim Auer at the Pentagon.

In Tokyo, Tomomitsu Ohba, Masao Kunihiro, Katsuhiro Nakagawa, Takenori Ishikawa, Dick Rabinowitz, Frank Gniffke, Andy Knox, Kiyoshi Nishitani, Masaya Miyoshi, Peter Fuchs, Kiyoshi Nagata, Mike Mochizuki, Akira Ogata, Keith Bovetti, Katsuhiko Sakuma, Rieko Suzuki, Naoto Wada, and Taisei Yamada; in Seoul, Kang Young-suk, Chang Dong-chul, Hyun Oh-seok, Shin Doo-byong, Shin Jong-ick, Han Sung-joo, Steve Tsitouris, Mark Clifford, and Sam Kidder; in Taipei, Paul Chu, Paul Kung, Yang Jyh-Shoung, Chu Chi-hung, Liu Tai-ying, C. P. Hu, Chung Cheng-hung, Steve Craven, Chen Yu-chu, Chang Liang-zen, and Paul Tsai of Tsar & Tsai; in Hong Kong, Leo Goodstadt, Julia Wen, George Hicks, Liu Tzong-biau, T. L. Tsim, Denny Lane, Ian Buruma, Jay Branegan, and Jeffrey Henderson; in Singapore, Michael Choo, Sum Soon-lim, Pin Lim, Fock Siew-wah, Lim Han-soon, and Yuan Tsao Lee; in Manila, Steve Lohr, now in London, Joan Orendain, and Victor Tuazon.

To the research staff at the Social Science Research Institute of Princeton University's Firestone Library, and to the reference librarians at the Princeton Public Library, notably Jane Clinton and Eric Greenfeldt, special thanks for special help.

To my agent, Dominick Abel, who had faith from the start that a modest proposal would grow into a finished book; to my editor, Bernard Shir-Cliff, editor-in-chief at Contemporary Books, who provided invaluable feedback, inspiration, and support as the manuscript worked its way toward completion; and to my manuscript editors, Christine M. Benton and Elliott Sanger, who fashioned a more focused effort from somewhat scattered beginnings—grateful appreciation and a deep bow.

Lastly, heartfelt thanks to those closest of all who sacrificed their time and energy, showered me with understanding and love, and protected me from external distractions of every kind: my wife, Marty, whose flexibility, commitment, and openness are unmatched; our children, Claire and Peter, who bring form and meaning and an untold dimension to our lives; and Brad Bucher and Robbie Griffith, friends in the truest (and only) meaning of the word.

Despite the generous assistance, advice, and guidance I have received from one and all, including those who preferred to remain anonymous, I am solely responsible for the interpretations, opinions, and judgments reflected throughout the text; any errors resulting therefrom are my own.

Princeton, New Jersey,
and Singapore
June 1989

NOTES

(Complete citations appear in the Bibliography that follows.)

Prologue

Chapter 1: Looking Back from the Year 2001: Resolutions for the New Century
P. 3. A dollar's worth of government. From George Will, *The New Season*, 1987.
P. 4. Trade figures: see U.S. Department of Commerce, Bureau of the Census, Foreign Trade Division, "Highlights of U.S. Export and Import Trade," FT-990, December 1987.
P. 4. U.S. trade figures across the Atlantic and Pacific: see Chalmers Johnson, "The Pacific Basin's Challenge to America: Myth and Reality," *USA Today*, March 1987.
P. 5. U.S. and Japan net foreign capital positions: see Peter Peterson, "The Morning After," *Atlantic*, October 1987.
P. 5. Figures on national debt and federal budget deficits: see Peterson, *op. cit.*
P. 6. Reference to exchange rate and monetary policy deliberations: see Robert Heilbroner, "Hard Times," *The New Yorker*, September 14, 1987.
P. 8. Japanese defense expenditures: from personal interviews with Pentagon officials, Washington, D.C., January 1988.
P. 9. Reference to 1980 *Asahi Shimbun* newspaper poll: see Kenneth Pyle, "Japan, the World, and the 21st Century," in Okimoto & Inoguchi, eds., *The Political Economy of Japan, Vol. 2; The Changing International Context*, 1988.
P. 14. For a full, conventional description of China's modernization policies: see Dwight Perkins, *China: Asia's Next Economic Giant?*, 1987.
P. 16. References to entitlement benefits: see Peterson, *op. cit.*
P. 18. American family and social policy data: from personal interview with Gerry Regier, President, Family Research Council, Washington, D.C., March 11, 1988.

Part I: The Visible Hand of the Market: Policies and Incentives for Growth

Chapter 2: Turbocharged Capitalism: The Dynamics of Japanese Economic Development
P. 23. Opening quote: 1945 portion from Russell Braddon, *Japan Against the World*, 1983, pp. 69, 90, 129; 1985 portion from discussion with Swiss official, Tokyo, March 1985.
P. 23. U.S. Atlantic and Pacific trade comparisons: see Chalmers Johnson, "The Pacific Basin's Challenge to America."

P. 24. U.S. merchandise trade deficits: see U.S. Department of Commerce, Bureau of the Census, Foreign Trade Division, "Highlights of U.S. Export and Import Trade," FT-990, December 1987.

P. 26. Strategic industries: see E. Herbert Norman, *Origins of the Modern Japanese State*, 1975 ed., especially Chapter 4, "Early Industrialization," pp. 211–242, for an excellent account of the development of the strategic industries concept in Japan and discussion of that nation's initial modernization efforts.

P. 27. Historical background on MITI: see Chalmers Johnson, *MITI and the Japanese Miracle*, 1982, especially Chapter 1, "The Japanese Miracle," pp. 3–34, and Chapter 3, "The Rise of Industrial Policy," pp. 83–115. Dr. Johnson is far and away the leading American expert on Japan's industrial policy, and his book is a lucid account of the Japanese model.

P. 31. Personal interview with Chalmers Johnson, San Francisco, March 26, 1988.

P. 34. Personal interview with Naohiro Amaya, Tokyo, April 20, 1988.

P. 37. Personal interview with Akira Nambara, Tokyo, April 20, 1988.

P. 39. Personal interview with Haruo Mayekawa, Tokyo, October 14, 1988.

P. 40. "Americans Talk Security" poll: see *Boston Globe*, March 7, 1988.

P. 40. Japanese plant and equipment investment: see Peterson, *op. cit.*

P. 41. For a detailed discussion of U.S. public policy formulation in trade negotiations with Japan, see Clyde Prestowitz, *Trading Places: How We Allowed Japan to Take the Lead*, 1988.

P. 42. The Battle of Poitiers is described in fuller detail in my 1984 book, *Trade War*, pp. 99–100.

P. 42. "Super 301": See *1989 National Trade Estimate Report on Foreign Trade Barriers*, pp. 97–114, and front-page news accounts in *New York Times* and *Wall Street Journal*, June 1 and 2, 1989.

Chapter 3: Clones of the Capitalist Developmental State: Korea, Taiwan, Singapore, and Hong Kong

P. 44. Opening quote by Lee Kuan Yew from James Minchin, *No Man Is an Island*, 1986.

P. 45. Korean statistics: see Chalmers Johnson, "Political Institutions and Economic Performance: the Government-Business Relationship in Japan, South Korea, and Taiwan," in Frederic C. Deyo, ed., *The Political Economy of the New Asian Industrialism*, 1987.

P. 47. See Hagen Koo, "The Interplay of State, Social Class, and World System in East Asian Development: the Cases of South Korea and Taiwan," in Deyo, *op. cit.*, 1987.

P. 49. Personal interview with S. H. Jang, Seoul, April 29, 1988.

P. 49. Personal interview with Roger Mathus, Seoul, April 30, 1988.

P. 50. See Suh Sang-mok, "Challenge for the Future: Industrial Restructuring and Policy Response," *Korea Business World*, April 1988.

P. 51. See Danny Leipziger, "Industrial Restructuring in Korea," in the World Bank's *Korea: Transition to Maturity*, 1988.

P. 52. See Bruce Cummings, "The Origins and Development of the Northeast Asian Political Economy: Industrial Sectors, Product Cycles, and Political Consequences," in Deyo, *op. cit.* See also Chalmers Johnson and Koo articles, *op. cit.*

P. 53. Trade and currency figures: see China External Trade Development Council (CETDC), *Economic and Trade Indicators*, 1987.

P. 54. Discussion with Jim Klein, General Instruments, during a working breakfast for members of the Business and Institutional Furniture Manufacturers Association (BIFMA) trade mission, presented by the American Chamber of Commerce in Taiwan, Taipei, September 24, 1987.

P. 55. Personal interview with Morris Chang, Taipei, November 29, 1988.

P. 56. Personal interview with Y. T. Chang, Taipei, April 26, 1988.

P. 57. Personal interview with Shirley W. Y. Kuo, Taipei, April 27, 1988.

P. 57. Background on Singapore from *Singapore 1988,* published by the Ministry of Communications and Information, Singapore government, pp. 23–32, and from James Minchin, *No Man Is an Island.*

P. 59. Comparative Singapore GNP growth rates from Tan Han Hoe, ed., *Singapore 1987,* pp. 240–241.

P. 59. Personal interview with Daniel Selvaratnam, Singapore, January 26, 1988.

P. 60. Personal interview with Dr. Richard Hu, Singapore, January 25, 1988.

P. 60. Personal interview with Dr. Teh Kok Peng, Singapore, January 26, 1988.

P. 61. Personal interview with Fock Siew-wah, Singapore, January 27, 1988.

P. 62. Background on Hong Kong from Aladin Ismail, ed., *Hong Kong 1988,* Government Information Services, Hong Kong government, 1988.

P. 62. Personal interview with Francis Leung, Hong Kong, February 3, 1988.

P. 63. Personal interview with Tony Miller, Hong Kong, February 3, 1988.

P. 64. Background on the Philippines from Richard Kessler, *U.S. Policy Toward the Philippines After Marcos,* 1986; "Philippines Background Notes," U.S. Department of State, 1986; and A. James Gregor, *The U.S. and the Philippines: A Challenge to a Special Relationship,* 1983.

P. 66. Land reform measures: see Roy Prosterman, *Land Reform and Democratic Development,* 1987, arguably the best single-volume source on this subject.

P. 68. Personal interview with Carlos Dominguez, Manila, January 30, 1988.

P. 69. Personal interviews with senior American diplomats, American Embassy, Manila, January 29, 1988.

Chapter 4: Why American Policy Mechanisms Have Failed

P. 71. Opening quote by Raymond Vernon from Koo, *op cit.*

P. 74. Cigarettes: see *New York Times,* June 19, 1988.

P. 74. Japanese consumers and rice: see *New York Times,* June 18, 1988.

P. 75. Market share figures, derived from internal Texas Instruments data, February 1988.

P. 77. Neoclassical economic theory: see Robert Kuttner, "The Poverty of Economics," *Atlantic,* February 1985.

P. 78. Development of a more strategic orientation to U.S. trade policy: see Paul Krugman, ed., *Strategic Trade Policy and the New International Economics,* 1987.

P. 80. A full account of Japan's complex industrial structure is contained in Daniel Okimoto, "Outsider Trading: Coping with Japanese Industrial Organization," *Journal of Japanese Studies,* summer 1987.

P. 83. Governors' trips to Asia: see *USA Today,* June 13, 1988.

P. 83. Quotes are from Sun-tzu, *The Art of War,* 1963 ed., pp. 76–77.

P. 86. C. Fred Bergsten and William R. Cline, *The United States–Japan Economic Problem,* 1987, p. 46.

P. 88. See Heilbroner, "Hard Times," *op. cit.*

P. 88. See Peterson, *op cit*

P. 90. See Staffan Burenstam Linder, *The Pacific Century: Economic and Political Consequences of Asian-Pacific Dynamism,* 1986.

Chapter 5: American's Return to World-Class Manufacturing

P. 91. Opening quote from Masaaki Imai, *Kaizen,* 1987, Chapter XI, "Creating the Kaizen Culture."

P. 92. Personal interview with Mark Shepherd, Dallas, February 22, 1988, and reference to internal documents prepared at Texas Instruments.

P. 94. See Stephen S. Cohen and John Zysman, *Manufacturing Matters*, 1987, pp. xiii–xiv; linkages, p. 19; services, p. 29; scales of competitiveness, p. 61; quality of service sector jobs, p. 55. Though written for a more specialized audience, this book deserves a wider readership; it is concise, well written, and timely.

P. 95. For full Bureau of Labor Statistics data, see David Pearce Snyder, *Future Forces*, 1987.

P. 96. Data from *Washington Post*, national weekly edition, June 13–19, 1988, p. 6.

P. 96. See Office of Technology Assessment, *International Competition in Services*, 1987.

P. 97. Personal interview with John Alic, Washington, D.C., December 14, 1987.

P. 98. For full tax data, see Rudiger Dornbusch et al., "The Case for Manufacturing in America's Future," 1988, especially Section I, "Manufacturing and the American Economy," pp. 8–14, and Section II, "Fiscal Policies and U.S. Manufacturing," pp. 15–20. This monograph is a lucid account of the impact of tax and savings incentives on business growth and sectoral development and deserves a wider audience.

P. 100. Personal interview with Mark Shepherd, Dallas, February 22, 1988.

P. 101. Robot statistics from "Japan 1988," published by Keizai Koho Center, 1989, the Japan Institute for Social and Economic Affairs, pp. 25, 27.

P. 102. Machine tools, see Prestowitz, *op. cit.*

P. 103. From Ramchandran Jaikumar, "Postindustrial Manufacturing," *Harvard Business Review*, November-December 1986.

P. 104. See Imai, *op. cit.* p. 14. This book is about the best description of the Japanese approach to creativity and innovation that is available.

P. 106. See Richard Schonberger, *Japanese Manufacturing Techniques: Nine Hidden Lessons in Simplicity*, 1982, pp. 211, 215, 218.

P. 107. Personal discussions with Ichak Adizes, New York and Santa Monica, August 1986 and January 1988.

P. 110. See C. K. Prahalad, "Strategic Partnerships: The Challenge of Competitive Collaboration," 1986, and Daniel Okimoto's insightful article on Japanese industrial organization, *op. cit.*, for fuller treatment of the competitive aspects of collaboration with Japanese firms.

P. 111. Boeing: Correspondence between the author and the Boeing Company in late summer 1989, which occurred after the manuscript had gone to press and too late to permit substantive revisions, elaborated on the company's experience with its Japanese suppliers and denied the allegations in the text. "The critical structures, systems, equipment and materials [of the 767 and to a lesser extent the 757 aircraft] are predominantly developed, designed, and manufactured by either Boeing or U.S. manufacturers," Boeing said. Boeing also said that they were not aware of any rumor of the alleged government interference as indicated and that "a better example of dominant commercial airplane industry alignments would be the European partners of Airbus Industrie."

P. 112. LBOs: see testimony dated May 17, 1989, by Louis Lowenstein, Columbia University professor of law, before the U.S. House of Representatives, Committee on Ways and Means, pp. 5–6, 8, 15–16, and 23–25. See also a statement to the same committee of the same date by Margaret Cox Sullivan, president of the Stockholders of America, Inc., pp. 2–3.

Part II: Political Affairs: East Asia's Authoritarian Systems and the Future of Representative Democracy

Chapter 6: Authoritarianism on the Soft Shell

P. 119. Opening quote from Karel van Wolferen, "The Japan Problem," *Foreign Affairs*, winter 1987, p. 289.

P. 120. The Japanese bureaucracy: see Chalmers Johnson, "Japan: Who Governs?," *Journal of Japanese Studies,* winter 1975, pp. 1–3. See also Chalmers Johnson, "Studies of the Japanese Political Economy," unpublished paper, winter 1988.

P. 121. See Chalmers Johnson, "Japan: Who Governs?," p. 11.

P. 121. See T. J. Pempel, "The Unbundling of 'Japan, Inc.,'" *Journal of Japanese Studies,* summer 1987, p. 286.

P. 122. See Chalmers Johnson, *MITI and the Japanese Miracle,* Chapter 3, "The Economic Bureaucracy," pp. 35–82.

P. 122. Chopping off the apex of the pyramid: from *Japan Times,* December 13, 1971.

P. 122. Quote from van Wolferen, *op. cit.,* pp. 290–291.

P. 123. Personal interview with Karel van Wolferen, Tokyo, April 26, 1988.

P. 123. Reference to Sahashi: see Chalmers Johnson, *MITI and the Japanese Miracle,* pp. 65, 74.

P. 124. Reference to Etsusaburo Shiina: see Chalmers Johnson, *MITI and the Japanese Miracle,* p. 55.

P. 125. Elite in Japanese bureaucracy: see Chalmers Johnson, *MITI and the Japanese Miracle,* p. 61, and B. C. Koh, "Recruitment of Higher Civil Servants in Japan," *Asian Survey,* March 1985, p. 292.

P. 126. American specialists in Japanese bureaucracy: see Ronald Morse, "Japan's Bureaucratic Edge," *Foreign Policy,* fall 1983.

P. 128. MITI, "say good-bye" and "write white papers": see Pempel, *op. cit.*

P. 129. "Telecom wars": see Chalmers Johnson, "MITI, MPT, and the Telecom Wars," 1989, pp. 1–35. See also Michael Erony, "NTT: A Japanese Public Corporation's Experience with Privatization and Deregulation," unpublished paper, 1988, and Stephen Anderson, "Japan's Biotech Battles and Trade Wars," unpublished paper, 1988.

P. 129. Zoku: see Pempel, *op. cit.,* p. 289, and Chalmers Johnson, "MITI, MPT, and the Telecom Wars," pp. 1–35.

P. 130. Factions: see Nathaniel Thayer, *How the Conservatives Rule Japan,* 1969, pp. 1–58.

P. 131. Takeshita resignation and Uno succession: see *New York Times* and *Wall Street Journal* accounts, June 1 and 2, 1989.

P. 133. See Robert Bellah, *Tokugawa Religion,* 1957, pp. 178–197.

P. 133. Personal discussion with George Packard, Princeton, March 1988.

P. 134. See *Washington Post,* June 10, 1989.

P. 135. See Kenneth Pyle, "The Future of Japanese Nationality," *Journal of Japanese Studies,* winter 1982.

P. 136. *Asahi Shimbun* editorial referenced in the *Washington Post,* national weekly edition, June 13–19, 1988, p. 19.

P. 138. Background on the PM: see Alex Josey, *Lee Kuan Yew,* 1980, pp. 1–44; reference to the British and the Japanese from p. 41; reference to Harold Macmillan from p. 25.

P. 139. Background data from *Singapore 1988,* pp. 140ff.

P. 140. Personal interview with Goh Geok Ling, Singapore, January 27, 1988.

P. 140. See Robert Shaplen, *A Turning Wheel,* 1979, pp. 197–198.

P. 140. Lee Kuan Yew quote from Shaplen, *A Turning Wheel* pp. 197–198.

P. 141. Singapore port statistics from *Singapore 1987,* p. 130.

P. 142. Personal interview with Lee Hsien Loong, Singapore, January 26, 1988.

P. 142. B. G. Lee: statement made on the occasion of his visit to Washington, D.C., on May 16, 1989, during an Asia Society reception at the Hotel Madison.

P. 143. Personal interview with Wong Kan Seng, Singapore, January 26, 1988.

P. 143. Personal interviews with Prof. Kernial Sandhu, Singapore, January 25, 1988, and June 30, 1989.

P. 144. By far the best and most objective account of Singapore's tussles with the Western press is by Owen Harries, "Exporting Democracy—and Getting It Wrong," *The National Interest,* fall 1988, pp. 3–12.

P. 145. "Consumed by fear": see Ian Buruma, "Singapore," *New York Times Magazine,* June 12, 1988.

Chapter 7: The Delicate Seeds of Democracy

P. 147. Opening quote from Herbert Muller, *The Loom of History,* 1958, Chapter II, "The Beginnings," pp. 51–84.

P. 148. Hong Kong reference from the Sino-British Accord dated September 26, 1984, pp. 8, 15.

P. 148. Hong Kong land leases from *Hong Kong 1988,* published by the government of Hong Kong, 1989.

P. 149. Reference to certificates from William McGurn, ed., *Basic Law, Basic Questions,* 1988, p. 2.

P. 150. Personal interview with Barrie Wiggham, Hong Kong, February 2, 1988.

P. 152. Personal interview with Martin Lee, San Francisco, March 25, 1988.

P. 152. Personal interview with Frank Ching, Hong Kong, February 6, 1988.

P. 153. Reference to Margaret Ng from *South China Morning Post,* January 26, 1988.

P. 153. Personal interviews with George Hicks, Hong Kong, February 3 and February 5, 1988.

P. 154. Personal interview with T. L. Tsim, Hong Kong, February 4, 1988.

P. 154. Antidemocracy responses: see Perry Link, "The Chinese Intellectuals and Revolt," *New York Review of Books,* June 29, 1989.

P. 155. Personal interview with James So, Hong Kong, February 4, 1988.

P. 156. Personal interview with Leo Goodstadt, Hong Kong, February 5, 1988.

P. 157. Reference to Richard Hughes, *Hong Kong: Borrowed Place, Borrowed Time,* 1968, p. 170.

P. 158. Reference to Martin Lee: see *New York Times,* May 22, 1989.

P. 159. Korea background data from Chalmers Johnson, "The Democratization of South Korea," July 8–9, 1988, p. 10.

P. 160. Personal interview with B. S. Kang, Seoul, May 3, 1988.

P. 162. Reference to equity vs. growth from David Steinberg, "Sociopolitical Factors and Korea's Future Economic Success," *World Development,* January 1988, pp. 30–31.

P. 163. See also Chalmers Johnson, "The Democratization of South Korea," p. 21. Other thoughtful accounts are by Hagen Koo, *op. cit.*; Chalmers Johnson, "Political Institutions and Economic Performance: the Government-Business Relationship in Japan, South Korea, and Taiwan"; and Stephen Haggard and Tun-jen Cheng, "State and Foreign Capital in the East Asian NICs," in Deyo, *op. cit.* The danger in assessing government-business relationships in East Asia is twofold: either assuming it is overdrawn, which is not the case, as in Japan, or assuming it is understated, which is also not the case, as in Korean and Taiwan.

P. 163. For a fuller discussion of recent political events in Taiwan, see "Taiwan: Transition on Trial," *The Economist,* March 5, 1988, and Thomas Omestad, "Dateline Taiwan: A Dynasty Ends," *Foreign Policy,* summer 1988.

P. 165. Personal interview with Nicholas Kristof, Taipei, April 29, 1988.

P. 166. See Trong Chai, "The Future of Taiwan," *Asian Survey,* December 1986, pp. 1309–1323.

P. 168. Personal interview with Thomas Lee, Taipei, April 28, 1988.

P. 170. Philippines description from Shaplen, *A Turning Wheel,* pp. 203–228.

P. 172. From James Fallows, "A Damaged Culture," *Atlantic,* November 1987.

P. 172. Reference to political parties from David Rosenberg, "Socio-Cultural Developments in the Philippines," unpublished paper, May 18–19, 1988.

P. 173. See Ian Buruma, "Marcos and Morality," *New York Times Review of Books,* August 13, 1987, and "St. Cory and the Yellow Revolution," *New York Times Review of Books,* November 6, 1986; the quote by Father Edicio de la Torre is from the latter.

P. 173. From Seth Mydans, "The Embattled Mrs. Aquino," *New York Times Magazine,* November 15, 1987, p. 42.

P. 175. Quote from editorial by Rodolfo Romero, *Manila Bulletin,* February 2, 1988.

P. 175. Personal interview with Rolando Tinio, Manila, January 31, 1988.

P. 176. Personal interview with Blas Ople, Manila, February 1, 1988.

P. 177. Background data on Juan Ponce-Enrile from Raymond Bonner, *Waltzing with a Dictator,* 1987, pp. 326–328.

P. 177. Meeting with Juan Ponce-Enrile and visit to Philippine Senate, Manila, February 1, 1988.

P. 178. Quote from Lambertson statement to the House Committee on Foreign Affairs, December 1987.

Chapter 8: Flaws in the American Political Model

P. 180. Opening quote from Peter Peterson, *op. cit.,* p. 69.

P. 181. See Peterson, *op. cit.,* p. 46.

P. 182. Government spending breakdown from James Fallows, *National Defense,* 1982, pp. 4–9.

P. 184. Economic comparisons from Emma Rothschild, "The Reagan Economic Legacy," *New York Review of Books,* June 30, 1988, and July 21, 1988.

P. 185. See Elizabeth Drew, "Politics and Money," *The New Yorker,* December 6 and 13, 1982.

P. 186. From Philip Stern, *The Best Congress Money Can Buy,* 1988, pp. 194–195, 277–279.

P. 187. See "Chaotic Congress," *Wall Street Journal,* March 21, 1988.

P. 188. From Garry Wills, "New Votuhs," *New York Times Review of Books,* August 18, 1988.

P. 188. From Steven Smith, *Revolution in the House,* 1986.

P. 188. From David Broder, *Washington Post* columns, May 9 and June 1, 1988.

P. 188. Turnover figures from an op-ed article by Elliott Richardson, "Civil Servants: Why Not the Best?," *Wall Street Journal,* November 20, 1987.

P. 188. *Economist* quote from *Wall Street Journal* editorial, May 24, 1988.

P. 189. Personal interview with Mark Shepherd, Dallas, February 22, 1988.

P. 190. From personal discussions and correspondence with Vladi Catto, Texas Instruments, March 1988.

P. 191. See Robert Eisner, *How Real Is the Federal Deficit?,* 1986, especially Chapter 12, "Implications for Policy," pp. 145–164.

P. 192. For a more complete analysis of a gasoline tax, see *Newsweek,* November 9, 1987, and *New York Times,* November 22 and December 28, 1987

P. 192. For a more complete description of sin taxes, see Charles Phelps, "A Happy Hour for Alcohol Taxes," *Wall Street Journal,* January 12, 1988.

P. 193. Editorial on the capital gains tax, *Wall Street Journal,* March 5, 1988.

P. 194. Capital gains tax proposals: see United States Department of the Treasury, "General Explanation of the President's Budget Proposals Affecting Receipts," February 1989, pp. 1–16, and statement of Dennis E. Ross, acting assistant secretary (tax policy), before the Committee on Finance of the United States Senate, March 14, 1989, pp. 5, 9, and 11.

P. 195. See Benjamin R. Friedman, "What Is the 'Right' Amount of Saving," *National Review,* June 16, 1989.

P. 195. Reference to COLAs: see Peterson, *op. cit.,* p. 69.

P. 195. "Frontal lobotomy": quoted in *New York Times,* November 24, 1987.

P. 195. "Double jeopardy": see Peterson, *op. cit.,* p. 69.

P. 196. Grace Commission recommendations: see George Will, *The New Season,* 1987, pp. 72–73.

P. 196. Pensions: see Peterson, *op. cit.,* pp. 61–62.

P. 196. Reference to indexation, Medicare: see Peterson, *op. cit.,* pp. 63–64.

P. 197. See Daniel Patrick Moynihan, *Came the Revolution,* 1988.

P. 197. George Will, as quoted in Moynihan, *Came the Revolution,* p. 318.

P. 197. Python analogy: see Emma Rothschild, *New York Review of Books,* July 21, 1988, p. 35.

P. 198. From Heilbroner, "Hard Times."

P. 198. Christopher Columbus analogy from Peterson, *op. cit.,* p. 46.

P. 198. See *Economic Report of the President,* February 1989.

P. 198. Personal interview with Ambassador Ukawa, New York, February 1988.

P. 199. Quote from James Chace, *Solvency,* 1981, pp. 103–104.

Chapter 9: Reinvigorating American Democracy

P. 200. Opening quote from a longer citation referenced in George Will, *The New Season,* p. 13.

P. 200. From *Beyond the Fringe,* produced by Alexander H. Cohen. Los Angeles: Capital Records, 1964.

P. 201. Quote from Edward Vrdolyak, "Playing the Political Game," *Wall Street Journal,* July 7, 1988.

P. 202. Background data on Republicans from Will, *The New Season,* pp. 44ff and 59.

P. 203. Reference to Moynihan from Will, *The New Season,* p. 79.

P. 203. Reference to Republicans from Will, *The New Season,* p. 83.

P. 203. Reference to government intrusiveness from Will, *The New Season,* pp. 85, 89.

P. 203. Reference to political choice from Will, *The New Season.*

P. 204. Acheson quote from Will, *The New Season,* pp. 94–95.

P. 204. Electoral college lock, *New York Times,* July 8, 1988, and Will, *The New Season,* p. 125.

P. 204. Reference to Democrats from Will, *The New Season,* pp. 94ff.

P. 205. Personal interview with George Will, Orlando, November 17, 1987.

P. 206. Personal interview with Paul Hewitt, Washington, D.C., March 11, 1988.

P. 210. Demographic statistics from Americans for Generational Equity, internal memoranda.

P. 210. Reference to baby boomers, see also Landon Jones, *Great Expectations,* 1980, Chapter 1, "The Challenge of an Aging Society," pp. 1–26.

P. 213. See Michael Novak, "Old Values Made New Again," *Washington Times,* January 29, 1989.

P. 214. See Charles Murray, *Losing Ground,* 1984, pp. 217–239; Chapter 17, "Choosing a Future," is an especially thoughtful analysis of policy options.

P. 214. From Alexis de Tocqueville, *Democracy in America,* 1956 edition, p. 89.

P. 215. See Noboru Makino, *Decline and Prosperity,* 1987, p. 196.

P. 215. From Naohiro Amaya, *Where Is Japan Going?,* 1988, 121–123.

P. 215. See Will, *The New Season,* p. 200.

P. 216. Personal interview with Bruce Babbitt, Phoenix, December 9, 1988.

Part III: The Legacy of Confucius: Forging Educational Excellence

Chapter 10: Cooperative Learning in Japan: Parents, Teachers, and Children as the Vital Triangle

P. 219. Opening quote from John Hall, *Twelve Doors to Japan*, 1965, pp. 386 and 409.

P. 220. Japanese school year from Thomas Rohlen, *Japan's High Schools*, 1983, p. 160.

P. 220. Background data on Japanese education from Cynthia Hearn Dorfman, ed., *Japanese Education Today*, 1987, pp. 1–4; from Rohlen, *Japan's High Schools*, pp. 45–76; and from a four-part series on Japanese schools by Edward Fiske in *New York Times*, July 10–13, 1983.

P. 222. See Lois Peak, "Formal Pre-elementary education in Japan," March 25–27, 1988, p. 7.

P. 222. See Cathy Lewis, "Japanese Nursery Schools," p. 73.

P. 223. Reference to peer behavior from Lewis, *op. cit.*, pp. 78–79.

P. 223. Reference to John Dewey from Merry White, *The Japanese Educational Challenge*.

P. 224. Personal interview with Cathy Lewis, San Francisco, March 27, 1988.

P. 224. Reference to *toban* from Lewis, *op. cit.*, p. 80.

P. 225. Rice cooker anecdote from Lewis, "Observations," p. 13.

P. 226. Personal interview with Sarane Boocock, San Francisco, March 27, 1988. See also Boocock, "The Japanese Preschool System," and the chapter entitled "Classroom Organization and Management" in M. C. Wittrock, ed., *Handbook of Research on Teaching*, pp. 392–431.

P. 227. Peak, *op. cit.*, p. 74.

P. 228. Parental involvement, Dorfman, *op. cit.*, pp. 21–23.

P. 229. Textbooks and mothers: see Merry White, *The Japanese Educational Challenge*, 1987, p. 14.

P. 229. Reference to teaching profession from Dorfman, *op. cit.*, pp. 15–20, 25–28.

P. 231. Comments on curriculum: see Fiske, *op. cit.*, July 10, 1983.

P. 231. Comments on homework from Rohlen, *Japan's High Schools*, p. 277, and White, *The Japanese Educational Challenge*, p. 70.

P. 232. International test scores from William J. Bennett, *What Works: Research About Teaching and Learning*, 1986, pp. 28–30.

P. 232. See Rohlen, *op. cit.*

P. 232. Peer teaching: see Bennett, *What Works: Research About Teaching and Learning*, p. 36.

P. 233. Reference to hypertrophy: see Takie Sugiyama Lebra, *Japanese Women: Constraint and Fulfillment*, 1984, pp. 205–238.

P. 233. Personal visit to Hibiya High School and personal interviews, Tokyo, April 21, 1988.

P. 234. Reference to Sontoku Ninomiya from Merry White, *The Japanese Educational Challenge*, p. 51.

P. 236. References to education reform council interim reports: issued, in order, June 26, 1985; April 23, 1986; April 1, 1987; and August 7, 1987

P. 237. Personal interview with Naohiro Amaya, Tokyo, April 20, 1988.

P. 237. Personal interview with Takashi Hosomi, Tokyo, April 20, 1988.

P. 238. Personal interview with Hiroshi Kaneoka, Tokyo, April 21, 1988.

P. 239. Personal interview with Ikuo Amano, Princeton, May 6, 1988.

P. 240. Personal interview with Nobutaka Machimura, Tokyo, April 21, 1988.

P. 241. See Ronald Dore, *Flexible Rigidities*, 1986, p. 49.

P. 241. Benjamin Duke, *The Japanese School,* 1986, pp. 20–21, p. 220.

P. 242. Rohlen, *Japan's High Schools,* pp. 314–326.

Chapter 11: Excellence in the Little Dragons

P. 244. Opening chapter quote from Josey, *op. cit.,* p. 535.

P. 245. Personal interview with Ah Ching, principal, Nan Hua High School, Jurong, Singapore, January 27, 1988.

P. 249. Personal interview with Y. T. Li, Secretary of Education, Hong Kong, February 3, 1988.

P. 250. School data from personal interview with Joseph Cheng, acting principal, Lui Ming Choi Early Secondary School, Lek Yuen, Shatin, Hong Kong, February 5, 1988.

P. 252. Personal interview with Shim Chi-sun, principal, Ehwa Girls' High School, Seoul, May 2, 1988.

P. 252. Personal interview with Dr. Cho Sun-jae, director general, Ministry of Education, Seoul, May 2, 1988.

P. 253. Personal interview with Michael Lee, director, Bureau of International Cultural and Educational Relations, Ministry of Education, Taipei, April 27, 1988.

P. 255. Personal interview with Chin Huan-teh, principal, and Yu Tsong-chin, head teacher, at the Nan Men Middle School, Taipei, April 26, 1988.

P. 258. Personal visit to the Manuel L. Quezon Senior High School, Manila, and interview with Presentacion F. Guzman, principal, January 29, 1988.

Chapter 12: Flaws and Failures in American Education

P. 260. Opening quote from National Commission on Excellence in Education, *A Nation at Risk,* 1983, pp. 5, 6, 11.

P. 261. American performance statistics from National Commission on Excellence in Education, *op. cit.,* and Diane Ravitch and Chester E. Finn, Jr., *What Do Our 17-Year-Olds Know?,* 1987.

P. 262. The most comprehensive single source on the history and background of the U.S. educational establishment is *The One Best System,* 1974, by David Tyack. Historical references in this narrative are from pp. 10–11, 14–15, 16–18, 41–42, 44–45, 49–50, 55, 57, 59, 64, 72, 77, 82, 89, 100, 177–178, 185, 255, 259, 268, 278–279, 282–284, 287–289.

P. 266. Personal interview with Dr. Harold Hodgkinson, March 29, 1988.

P. 267. Personal interview with Dr. Chester E. Finn, Jr., Washington, D.C., January 15, 1988.

P. 268. Reference to Asian-Americans from *Time,* August 31, 1987.

P. 268. Reference to national history and literature exams from Ravitch and Finn, *op. cit.,* pp. 121–199.

P. 269. See E. D. Hirsch, Jr., *Cultural Literacy,* 1987, pp. 112–113; quote from p. 19; readers and reading, p. 131; concluding quote from pp. 133, 145.

P. 269. Reference to Perry High/Scope project from David Weikart, *Changed Lives,* 1984, pp. 1–18.

P. 270. Personal interview with Dr. David Weikart, July 29, 1988.

P. 271. Reference to preschool and business support from "The Education Crisis," *Fortune,* July 4, 1988.

P. 271. Personal interview with Mark Shepherd, Dallas, February 22, 1988.

P. 272. Personal interview with Dr. Bradley Bucher, Princeton, July 26, 1988.

P. 273. Reference to Joe Clark and Eastside High School, Paterson, New Jersey, from *New York Times,* January 14, 1988.

P. 274. Principal's perspective from confidential personal interview, March 14, 1988.

P. 274. Statistics on undergraduate education and careers from *New York Times,* June 10, 1988, and July 25, 1988; *USA Today,* June 13, 1988; and *Columbia Business School 1987,* pp. 20, 22.

P. 275. Quote from Allan Bloom, *The Closing of the American Mind,* 1987, pp. 369–370.

Chapter 13: Restructuring American Education: Redefining Control

P. 280. Opening quote from John Chubb and Terry Moe, *What Price Democracy? Politics, Markets, and America's Schools,* forthcoming.

P. 281. Personal interview with Albert Shanker, Washington, D.C., March 11, 1988.

P. 284. Background references from Albert Shanker, "Our Profession, Our Schools: The Case for Fundamental Reform," *American Educator,* fall 1986, pp. 10–45, and from Albert Shanker, "The Making of a Profession," *American Educator,* fall 1985, pp. 10–48.

P. 285. References to various school system experiments from *New York Times:* Dade County, Miami, January 10, 1988; Chicago, July 13, 1988; Indianapolis, February 17, 1988; Massachusetts, July 11, 1988. Reference to Minneapolis from *Wall Street Journal,* May 14, 1988. Reference to Montgomery County, Maryland, from *Washington Post,* May 19, 1988. Reference to New Jersey from *Trenton Times,* January 17, 1988.

P. 287. Quote from Chester Finn, "Make the Schools Compete," *Harvard Business Review,* September-October 1987, p. 63.

P. 287. Personal interview with Chester Finn, Washington, D.C., January 15, 1988.

P. 288. Reference to NEA from Chester Finn, "Teacher Politics," *Commentary,* February 1983, p. 29.

P. 288. Shanker quote re testing and citation re teacher autonomy, from the Carnegie Forum report *A Nation Prepared,* 1986, pp. 45–51, 117–118.

P. 289. Finn, "Teacher Politics," p. 29.

P. 289. Personal interview with Gary Watts, Washington, D.C., January 15, 1988.

P. 290. Reference to Chubb and Moe from "Why the Current Wave of School Reform Will Fail," by John Chubb, *The Public Interest,* January 1988, pp. 28–49. The most salient conclusions and recommendations of the book by John Chubb and Terry Moe, *What Price Democracy? Politics, Markets, and America's Schools,* are contained in this shorter article by Chubb.

P. 292. Personal interview with Terry Moe, Palo Alto, March 25, 1988.

P. 292. Competition and choice, from Charles Murray, *In Pursuit of Happiness and Good Government,* 1988, pp. 246–248. This book should provoke thoughtful policy debate in a number of areas, not least education, and deserves to be widely read. Of particular interest is Part III, "Toward the Best of All Possible Worlds," especially Chapters 9–13.

P. 294. From Lewis Perelman, *Technology and Transformation of Schools,* 1987, pp. 1–16.

P. 295. Reference to Alcoa from Shanker, "Our Profession, Our Schools," p. 15.

P. 295. Quote from David Kearns, "Education Recovery," October 26, 1987, p. 4–5.

P. 296. Streshly quote from William Streshly and Eric Schaps, "A Character Education Program That Works," The Development Studies Center, undated, pp. 3–5.

P. 298. Personal interviews with David Pearce Snyder, Princeton, February 16, 1988, and Washington, D.C., January 19, 1989.

P. 300. Personal interview with Hisashi Kobayashi, Princeton, December 22, 1987.

Part IV. The Family as Society's Fortress

Chapter 14: Social Stability in East Asia: Withstanding the Winds of Change

P. 303. Opening quote from Takeo Doi, *Amae,* 1973, p. 77.

P. 303. References to Confucius from Julia Ching, *Confucianism and Christianity,* 1977, pp. 96–99; James Legge, *The Works of Mencius,* 1984, pp. 38–49; Archie J. Bahm, *The Heart of Confucius,* 1969, p. 98.

P. 305. Personal interview with Benjamin Schwartz, Princeton, April 6, 1988.

P. 306. References to maternal dependence from Takie Sugiyama Lebra, *Japanese Culture and Behavior*, 1987, p. 202–238.

P. 306. Reference to Caudill and Weinstein study from Lebra, *ibid.*

P. 307. References to Takeo Doi from *Amae*, pp. 11–13, 33–36.

P. 308. See Lebra, *Japanese Women: Constraint and Fulfillment*, p. 216.

P. 309. Careers of Japanese women, see *The Economist*, May 14, 1988, pp. 19–22, and the Fusae Ichikawa Memorial Association, "Report," March 1988.

P. 311. See Lebra, *Japanese Women*, pp. 224–245.

P. 311. See Buruma, *Behind the Mask*, pp. 6–8.

P. 313. Personal interview with Dr. Lee Kwang-kyu, Seoul, April 30, 1988.

P. 315. Personal interview with Chun Byung-hoon, Seoul, April 28, 1988.

P. 316. Quote from Bo Yang, "The Ugly Chinaman," *Renditions*, spring 1985, pp. 87–88, 93–94.

P. 319. Personal interview with Willie Purves, Hong Kong, February 3, 1988.

P. 320. See *Statistics on Marriages and Divorces*, Singapore Department of Statistics, March 1986, pp. 31–44.

P. 321. See Linda Low, "Strengthening of Employers' Initiatives," unpublished paper prepared for the Singapore National Employers Federation conference, March 6, 1987.

P. 322. Personal visit to Smokey Mountain slum, Tondo, Manila, January 29, 1988.

P. 322. Beltran quote from James Fallows, "A Damaged Culture," p. 54.

P. 323. Personal interview with Renato Constantino, Manila, February 1, 1988.

P. 324. Personal interview with Felix Bautista, Manila, January 31, 1988.

P. 325. Personal interview with Jaime Cardinal Sin, Manila, February 1, 1988.

Chapter 15: America's Most Precious Natural Resource: The Minds of Its Children

P. 328. Opening quote from Bloom, *op. cit.*, p. 119.

P. 330. See Bloom, *op. cit.*, pp. 118–119.

P. 330. Statistics on the long-term emotional impact of divorce on children from Judith S. Wallerstein, and Joan Berlin Kelly, *Surviving the Breakup*, 1980, pp. 3–31.

P. 331. See Wallerstein and Kelly, *op. cit.*, pp. 55–95.

P. 331. Quote from Wallerstein and Kelly, *op. cit.*, p. 305.

P. 331. See Wallerstein and Kelly, *op. cit.*, pp. 307–308.

P. 332. Reference to divorce therapy from Bloom, *op. cit.*, pp. 120–121.

P. 332. Reference to students from Wallerstein and Kelly, *op. cit.*, pp. 264–284.

P. 332. Reference to school and family from James Coleman, *High School Achievement*, 1982, pp. 190–191, and as quoted in Moynihan, *Family and Nation*, p. 193.

P. 333. NAESP results from Moynihan, *Family and Nation*, pp. 92–93.

P. 333. Reference to ACDE and consumption of alcohol by children from *New York Times*, August 7, 1988.

P. 333. Statistics on children in poverty and teenage pregnancies from Moynihan, *Family and Nation*, pp. 48, 53, 89–91, 100–101, 167–171.

P. 334. Reference to federal spending on the elderly and on children: see Samuel Preston, "Children and the Elderly in the U.S," *Scientific American*, December 1984.

P. 334. Reference to single-parent homes and patriarchal abdication: see Karl Zinsmeister, "The Family's Tie to the American Dream," *Public Opinion*, September/October 1986.

P. 335. Reference to the growing population of homeless in America: see Jonathan Kozol, "The Homeless and Their Children," *The New Yorker*, January 25, 1988, p. 71.

P. 335. Reference to financial support from fathers: see Sylvia Hewlett, *A Lesser Life*, 1986, p. 115.

P. 335. Reference to custodial mothers: see Hewlett, *op. cit.*, p. 62.
P. 335. Reference to baby boomers: see Landon Jones, *op. cit.*, p. 389.
P. 336. Zinsmeister quote from "The Family's Tie to the American Dream."
P. 336. Reference to mothers in the workforce: see *New York Times*, May 1, 1988, and June 17, 1988.
P. 336. Reference to categories of child care: see Hewlett, *op. cit.*, pp. 118–121.
P. 337. Reference to the three waves of child-care research and infant child care: see Jay Belsky, *Infant Day Care: A Cause for Concern?*, 1986.
P. 338. Personal interview with Dr. Jay Belsky, New York, May 20, 1988.
P. 339. Personal interview with Dr. Edward Zigler, New Haven, May 8, 1988.
P. 341. Quote from Hewlett, *op. cit.*, p. 284.
P. 341. Reference to elite professionals: see Hewlett, *op. cit.*, pp. 177–179, 281–284.
P. 341. Reference to dual professional careers: see Deborah Fallows, *A Mother's Work*, 1985, p. 22.
P. 342. Quote from Bloom, *op. cit.*, pp. 127–128.
P. 343. Reference to Los Angeles Asian gangs: see Eui-young Yu, *Juvenile Delinquency in the Korean Community in Los Angeles*, 1986.
P. 343. Reference to Asian businesses in New York: see Pyong-gap Min, "Problems of Korean Immigrant Entrepreneurs," unpublished paper, March 26, 1988.
P. 344. Reference to Korean immigrants in Chicago: see Won-moo Hurh and Kwang-chung Kim, *Korean Immigrants in America*, 1984.
P. 344. Personal interview with Dr. Won-moo Hurh, Princeton, April 9, 1988.
P. 344. Reference to historical data on drug use from Gabriel Nakas, "The Decline of Drugged Nations," *Wall Street Journal*, July 11, 1988.
P. 345. Reference to rising drug use in America and related interdiction statistics: see *New York Times* three-part series on April 10–12, 1988.

Chapter 16: The Virtually Extinct American Family: Can It Be Revitalized?
P. 347. Opening quote from Moynihan, *Family and Nation*, p. 169–171.
P. 347. Personal interview with Bonnie Maslin, New York, May 20, 1988.
P. 348. Quote from Celia Halas, *Why Can't a Woman Be More Like a Man?*, 1981, p. 113.
P. 349. Reference to Maggie Scarf: see *Intimate Partners*, 1987, pp. 7–8, 40–41, 373.
P. 350. Personal interview with Dr. Stuart Johnson, New Haven, June 8, 1988.
P. 351. Reference to conflict and anger from Halas, *op. cit.*, pp. 143–145.
P. 353. Quote from Jane Wagner, *The Search for Signs of Intelligent Life in the Universe*, 1987.
P. 354. Reference to family research from Elizabeth Morgan, *Pioneer Research on Strong, Healthy Families*, 1987, pp. 1–24.
P. 356. Tax-deductibility of first mortgages from Will, *The New Season*, p. 134.
P. 357. See Moynihan, *Family and Nation*, pp. 159–160, 161–163.
P. 357. Reference to social science research: see Moynihan, *Family and Nation*, and Hewlett, *op. cit.*
P. 358. Moynihan quote from *New York Times*, July 21, 1987, and from the Family Security Act briefing package produced by the senator's Washington office.
P. 358. Reference to AFDC, see Moynihan, *Family and Nation*, pp. 13, 147.
P. 359. Lawrence Lindsey's child-care proposals: see "Better Childcare, Cheaper," *Wall Street Journal*, July 5, 1988.
P. 360. Personal interview with Gerry Regier, Washington, D.C., January 15, 1988.
P. 360. See Murray, *Losing Ground*, pp. 205–236, especially Chapter 16, "The Constraints

on Helping," and Chapter 17, "Choosing a Future." Murray's writing is a refreshing change from the (mostly) liberal orientation of American social science researchers and reporters; it represents what may well be a new point of departure for social science and public policy research in the United States. For those interested in the future direction of public social policy, *Losing Ground* is essential reading, as is his companion volume, *In Pursuit of Happiness and Good Government,* and a shorter article entitled "The Coming of Custodial Democracy," September 1988.

P. 361. See Nathan Glazer, *The Limits of Social Policy,* 1988, pp. 187, 192.

P. 361. Personal interview with Dr. Edward Zigler, New Haven, June 8, 1988. See also his unpublished papers, "A Solution to the Nation's Childcare Crisis," dated October 14, 1987, and "The Medical and Social Science Basis for a National Infant Care Leave Policy," accepted for publication in the *American Journal of Orthopsychiatry.*

P. 363. Personal interview with Dr. Jay Belsky, New York, May 20, 1988.

P. 364. See Hewlett, *op. cit.,* pp. 381–382.

P. 366. See AT&T *Bulletin* dated June 1, 1989: "New AT&T, CWA, IBEW Pact: More Details of a 'Vanguard' Agreement."

P. 366. See Felice N. Schwartz, "Management Women and the New Facts of Life," *Harvard Business Review,* January-February 1989, pp. 65–66, 68–69, 72–74, 76.

P. 367. Personal interview by telephone with Felice Schwartz, June 8, 1989.

P. 368. Reference to religion from *Free Inquiry,* "Is Belief in the Supernatural Inevitable?," spring 1988, and *New York Times,* August 11, 1988.

P. 369. Personal interview with Dr. James McCord, Princeton, December 7, 1987.

P. 369. Closing quote from Robert Bellah, *Habits of the Heart,* 1985, pp. 284, 294.

Part V: Rethinking America's National Security

Chapter 17: Regional Security in a Multipolar World

P. 373. Opening quote from Chalmers Johnson, "Reflections on the Dilemma of Japanese Defense," *Asian Survey,* May 1986, pp. 558–560.

P. 375. Personal interview with Foreign Minister Wong Kan Seng, Singapore, January 26, 1988.

P. 375. Takahashi quote from Masao Miyoshi, *As We Saw Them: The First Japanese Embassy to the United States, 1860,* as cited in Schlossstein, *Trade War,* p. 63.

P. 375. Defense spending figures from *Economic Report to the President,* February 1988; Far Eastern Economic Review *Asia 1988 Yearbook*; and *JEI Report,* July 29, 1988.

P. 376. Personal interview on background, Tokyo, April 18, 1988.

P. 376. Public opinion poll, cited in Chalmers Johnson, "Reflections," p. 571.

P. 377. Self-Defense Force levels, Far Eastern Economic Review, *Asia 1988 Yearbook,* p. 20.

P. 378. Hisahiko Okazaki, unpublished article, September 9, 1987.

P. 379. Personal interview with Dr. Kwon Moon-sool, Seoul, May 2, 1988.

P. 380. Statistical citations from Far Eastern Economic Review, *Asia 1988 Yearbook,* pp. 18–21.

P. 380. See Edward Olsen, "The Arms Race on the Korean Peninsula," *Asian Survey,* August 1986, p. 862.

P. 381. Sung-hack Kang, "America's Foreign Policy Toward East Asia," *Korea and World Affairs,* winter 1987, p. 707.

P. 382. U.S. Senate Foreign Relations Committee citations from Martin Lasater, *Taiwan: Facing Mounting Threats,* 1987, pp. 49–51.

P. 383. See Far Eastern Economic Review, *Asia 1988 Yearbook,* pp. 18–21.

P. 383. Personal interview with Thomas Lee, Taipei, November 29, 1988.

P. 384. From U.S. Department of Defense, "Background on the Bases," 2nd ed., December 1987.

P. 385. See James Fallows, "The Bases Dilemma," *Atlantic,* February 1988, p. 18.

P. 387. Reference to the NPA from Ross Munro, "The New Khmer Rouge," *Commentary,* December 1985, p. 18.

P. 387. Human rights violations, from Amnesty International, *The Philippines: Unlawful Killings by Military and Paramilitary Forces,* 1988.

P. 387. See Renato Constantino, *The Philippines,* 1978.

P. 388. Personal interview with Jaime Cardinal Sin, Manila, February 1, 1988.

P. 388. Lee Kuan Yew quote from a speech delivered in Singapore at a conference on the Pacific Century sponsored by the *International Herald-Tribune,* November 11, 1987.

P. 389. Personal interview with Brigadier General Lee Hsien Loong, Singapore, January 26, 1988.

P. 390. B. G. Lee: statement made on the occasion of his visit to Washington on May 16, 1989, during the Asia Society reception at the Hotel Madison.

Chapter 18: Restructuring Alliances: Burden-Sharing in an Era of Comprehensive Security

P. 391. Opening quote from David Calleo, *Beyond American Hegemony,* 1987, p. 131.

P. 391. Rudolf Bing anecdote from Harold Hinton, "The Impact of Korea on U.S. Western Pacific Strategy," in *Lectures, America's New Pacific Era,* April 19, 1984, p. 105.

P. 392. See "East Asian Security," *The Economist,* December 26, 1987, pp. 35–41.

P. 392. See George Perkovich, "Moscow Turns East," *Atlantic,* December 1987, p. 30.

P. 392. Soviet military force statistics from U.S. Department of Defense, *Soviet Military Power: An Assessment of the Threat,* 1988, p. 15.

P. 392. See George Kennan, *Memoirs: 1925–1950,* 1972, p. 268.

P. 394. Personal interview with Vasily Shatalin, Moscow, June 8, 1975.

P. 395. From Moynihan, *Came the Revolution,* p. 253.

P. 395. See Daniel Ford, "Rebirth of a Nation," *The New Yorker,* March 28, 1988, pp. 61–80.

P. 397. See Paul Kennedy, "What Gorbachev Is Up Against," *Atlantic,* June 1987, pp. 29–43.

P. 398. See Zbigniew Brzezinski, *The Grand Failure,* 1989, p. 245.

P. 398. Personal discussion with T. L. Tsim, Hong Kong, February 2, 1988.

P. 399. See Perkins, *op. cit.,* pp. 68–71, 67, 72–73.

P. 400. From Shaplen, A *Turning Wheel,* p. 368.

P. 400. See "East Asian Security," p. 40.

P. 401. From Bo Yang, "The Ugly Chinaman," pp. 96–99.

P. 401. China: see front-page news accounts from *New York Times* and *Wall Street Journal,* May 29–31 and June 1–5, 1989.

P. 402. Link, "The Chinese Intellectuals and Revolt," 1989.

P. 403. From Brzezinski, *The Grand Failure,* p. 250.

P. 404. See "About Burden Sharing," *New York Times,* May 2, 1988.

P. 405. $300 billion from Richard Halloran, *To Arm a Nation,* 1986, pp. 200–201, 242.

P. 405. See Richard A. Stubbing and Richard A. Mandel, "How to Save $50 Billion a Year," *Atlantic,* June 1989.

P. 406. See United States Congress, Office of Technology Assessment, *The Defense Technology Base,* 1988, pp. 3–6.

P. 407. Layne quote from Jack Beatty, "The Exorbitant Anachronism," *Atlantic*, June 1989.

P. 408. Reference to Bush and NATO from *New York Times*, June 1, 1989.

P. 408. From Calleo, *Beyond American Hegemony*, pp. 216, 233.

P. 408. *Ibid.*, pp. 217–218.

P. 409. See Hinton, *op. cit.*, p. 93.

P. 410. From Chalmers Johnson, "Japanese-Soviet Relations in the Early Gorbachev Era," *Asian Survey*, November 1987, pp. 1145–1160.

P. 411. See Robert Pear, "Confusion Is the Operative Word in U.S. Policy Toward Japan," *New York Times*, March 20, 1989.

P. 411. FSX: For a detailed summary of the FSX issue, see Barbara Wanner, "The FSX Project: Changing the Nature of Defense Technology Transfers," *JEI Report*, May 26, 1989.

P. 412. See Shinji Otsuki, "Battle over the FSX Fighter: Who Won?," *Japan Quarterly*, April–June 1988, pp. 139–145.

P. 413. See Richard J. Samuels and Benjamin C. Whipple, "Defense Production and Industrial Development: The Case of Japanese Aircraft," Massachusetts Institute of Technology Japan Science and Technology Program, working paper #88-09, 1988.

P. 413. Personal interview with J. Fred Bucy, February 11, 1988.

P. 414. Bucy reference from an internal Texas Instruments memorandum, undated but written in 1986.

P. 414. From Guy Pauker, "Security Assistance to Southeast Asia," in *America's New Pacific Era*, Heritage Foundation *Lectures*, June 7, 1984, p. 120.

Chapter 19: The Decline of American Hegemony and the Rise of Japan

P. 419. Opening quote from Charles Kindleberger, "Systems of International Economic Organization," in David Calleo, *Money and the Coming World Order*, 1976, pp. 35–36.

P. 419. Personal interview with Paul Kennedy, New Haven, June 8, 1988.

P. 421. See Paul Kennedy, *The Rise and Fall of the Great Powers*, 1988, pp. 515ff. See also Michael Howard, "Imperial Cycles: Bucks, Bullets, and Bust," *New York Times Review of Books*, January 10, 1988, p. 1. Also of interest: Peter Schmeisser, "Is America in Decline?," *New York Times Magazine*, April 17, 1988, p. 24; and Pat Moynihan and James Schlesinger, "Debunking the Myth of Decline," *New York Times Magazine*, June 19, 1988, p. 34.

P. 421. From Kennedy, *The Rise and Fall of the Great Powers*, pp. 439–440.

P. 422. See Calleo, *Beyond American Hegemony*, pp. 137, 142–143.

P. 424. From Kindleberger, "Systems of International Economic Organization," p. 34.

P. 424. See Robert Keohane, *After Hegemony*, 1984, pp. 8–9.

P. 426. From Robert Gilpin, *The Political Economy of International Relations*, 1987, pp. 343–352.

P. 426. As quoted in Heilbroner, "Hard Times," pp. 96–109.

P. 427. Gilpin, as quoted in Heilbroner, "Hard Times," p. 107.

P. 427. Suzuki quote from Chalmers Johnson, "The End of American Hegemony and the Future of U.S.-Japanese Relations," unpublished paper, April 1988.

P. 428. Heilbroner, "Hard Times," p. 106.

P. 428. Gilpin, *The Political Economy of International Relations*, pp. 54–55, 92.

P. 429. Personal interview with Chalmers Johnson, San Francisco, March 26, 1988.

P. 432. From Kenneth Pyle, "Japan, the World, and the 21st Century," pp. 453–455.

P. 432. Personal interview with Kuniko Inoguchi, Tokyo, April 2, 1988.

P. 434. From Kenneth Pyle, "Japanese Nationality: The Rising Debate," in Okimoto and Rohlen, eds., *Inside the Japanese System*, 1988, pp. 235–242.

P. 434. Personal interview with Naohiro Amaya, Tokyo, April 20, 1988.

P. 435. See Iwao Nakatani, "Can Japan Support the World Economy?," winter 1987, as quoted in Johnson, "The End of American Hegemony," p. 5.

P. 435. References to neo-nationalism from Pyle, "Japanese Nationality," pp. 240–242.

P. 435. Shimizu quote from Pyle, *ibid.*

P. 437. See Ian Buruma, "A New Japanese Nationalism," *New York Times Magazine*, April 12, 1987.

P. 437. From Ronald Morse, "Japan's Drive to Pre-Eminence," *Foreign Policy*, winter 1987–88, pp. 3–21.

Chapter 20: Pax Nipponica: The Era of Japan's Majestic Dominance?

P. 439. Opening quote from Ezra Vogel, "Pax Nipponica?," *Foreign Affairs*, spring 1986, pp. 762, 767.

P. 440. As cited in Chalmers Johnson, "Reflections on the Dilemma of Japanese Defense," p. 557.

P. 440. Nakasone's gaffes as quoted in Kenneth Pyle, "In Pursuit of a Grand Design," summer 1987, pp. 243–270.

P. 441. Watanabe, as quoted in *New York Times*, July 26, 1988.

P. 441. Watanabe, as quoted in *New York Times*, July 31, 1988.

P. 442. References to Korean and *burakumin* minorities, as cited in Schlossstein, *Yakuza*, forthcoming.

P. 443. Examples of "Japanese uniqueness" from Peter Dale, *The Myth of Japanese Uniqueness*, 1986, pp. 188–200, especially pp. 189–191.

P. 443. "Obsessive self-analysis," from Buruma, "A New Japanese Nationalism."

P. 444. Personal interview with Ian Buruma, Hong Kong, February 1, 1988.

P. 444. Polls, as cited in Pyle, "In Pursuit of a Grand Design," p. 252.

P. 445. Personal interview with Masao Kunihiro, Tokyo, April 20, 1988.

P. 446. Modelski model as cited in Pyle, "Japan, the World, and the 21st Century," p. 450.

P. 446. Reference to Pax Nipponica from Vogel, "Pax Nipponica?," p. 760.

P. 446. Nakasone background and quotes from Pyle, "In Pursuit of a Grand Design," pp. 254–256.

P. 448. Takeshita references and overseas initiatives from *Far Eastern Economic Review*, August 25, 1988, 20–23.

P. 450. As cited in the *JEI Report*, Number 30-A, August 5, 1988, pp. 4–5.

P. 451. Japanese communication styles from Ellen Frost, *For Richer, For Poorer*, 1987, pp. 85ff.

P. 452. Nakasone speech in Bangkok, as quoted in *Japan Times*, September 27, 1987.

P. 453. References to the Middle East and Africa from *JEI Report*, Number 9-A, March 4, 1988, "Japan and the Middle East."

P. 453. Reference to Africa from "Can Japan Lead?," *Business Tokyo*, April 1988.

P. 454. Standish quote from Robert Standish, *The Three Bamboos*, 1942, author's introduction.

P. 454. George Ball and Harold Brown quotes from Pyle, "In Pursuit of a Grand Design," p. 248.

P. 455. Standish, *op. cit.*

P. 455. Hotta quote, as cited in Schlossstein, *Trade War*, p. 104.

P. 455. Reference to Tokyo Bay from Yasoi Yasuda, "Tokyo on and under the Bay," *Japan Quarterly*, April–June 1988, pp. 118–126.

P. 456. Tokutomi quote from Pyle, "Japan, the World, and the 21st Century," p. 446.

P. 456. Reign names, as cited in Schlossstein, "The Coming Era of Japan's Majestic Dominance?," *Business Tokyo*, March 1989, and an unpublished memorandum, "What's in a (Reign) Name?," November 15, 1988.

Epilogue

Chapter 21: Reinvigorating Pax Americana

P. 461. Opening quote from George Gilder, "The Revitalization of Everything: The Law of the Microcosm," *Harvard Business Review*, March/April 1988.

P. 461. See Zbigniew Brzezinski, "America's New Geostrategy," *Foreign Affairs*, spring 1988, pp. 680–699.

P. 462. See Morse, "Japan's Drive to Pre-Eminence," pp. 3–21.

P. 463. Linder quote from *The Pacific Century*, p. 118.

P. 464. Suez crisis and German refusal to support the dollar from Heilbroner, quoting Gilpin, in "Hard Times," p. 106.

P. 465. Reference to New England values in the new administration from *The Economist*, January 21, 1989, pp. 13–14.

P. 468. See Jean-Jacques Servan-Schreiber, "America Must Remain the World's University," *Washington Post*, November 15, 1987.

P. 469. Burke quote as cited in Murray, *In Pursuit of Happiness*, p. 260.

P. 470. Charles Murray quotes from *Losing Ground*, pp. 221–233.

P. 472. Gaddis quote from "How the Cold War Might End," November 1987, p. 100.

P. 473. Wisdom of last resort and Volcker quote from *Wall Street Journal*, February 21, 1989. In early 1989, the *Journal* ran a most insightful, highly detailed, and thoroughly researched five-part series by Karen House on the challenges to America's global leadership called "The Second Century: The 1990s and Beyond," which ran on January 23, January 30, February 6, February 13, and February 21.

P. 474. Reference to Europe and 1992, *ibid.*, February 13, 1989.

P. 474. Reference to China's problems, *ibid.*, February 6, 1989.

P. 476. Reference to Soviet failures, *ibid.*, February 6, 1989. See also Radek Sikorski, "The Coming Crack-Up of Communism," *National Review*, January 27, 1989, pp. 28–30, and Brzezinski, *The Grand Failure*.

P. 477. Vogel quote from *Japan as Number One*, 1979, pp. 255–256.

P. 477. Immigration and invigoration of America's open society: see Samuel Huntington, "The U.S.: Decline or Renewal?," *Foreign Affairs*, winter 1988–89, p. 90.

P. 477. For a thoughtful contribution to the growing debate about American decline and renewal, see James Fallows, *More Like Us: Making America Great Again*, 1989.

P. 479. Helmut Schmidt quote from *Wall Street Journal* series, February 21, 1989.

P. 480. Will Rogers quote from C. Jackson Grayson, *American Business: The Two-Minute Warning*, 1988, p. 332.

P. 480. Satoh quote from "Now the World Is Japan's Co-Prosperity Sphere," *The Economist*, August 13, 1988, pp. 27–30.

BIBLIOGRAPHY

Books

Abegglen, James C., and George Stalk, Jr. *Kaisha: The Japanese Corporation.* New York: Basic Books, 1985.

Adizes, Ichak. *How to Solve the Mismanagement Crisis.* New York: Dow Jones-Irwin, 1979.

Aikman, David. *The Pacific Rim: Area of Change, Area of Opportunity.* Boston: Little, Brown, 1986.

Akimoto, Hideo. *Japan Bashing.* Tokyo: Nimi Shobo, 1987.

Alston, Jon P. *The American Samurai: Blending American and Japanese Managerial Practices.* New York: DeGruyter, 1986.

Amano, Ikuo. *Kyoiku kaikaku o kangaeru. (Thinking About Educational Reform.)* Tokyo: University of Tokyo Press, 1985.

Amaya, Naohiro. *Nihon Kabushiki Kaisha: Nokosareta Sentaku. (Japan, Inc.: Remaining Options.)* Tokyo: PHP Press, 1982.

Amaya, Naohiro. *Nihon wa doko e iku no ka? (Where Is Japan Going?)* Tokyo: PHP Press, 1988.

Amaya, Naohiro. *Saka no ue no kumo to saka no shita no kubo. (The Clouds at the Top of the Mountain and the Swamp Below.)* Tokyo: Tsushosangyokai, 1985.

American Chamber of Commerce in Japan. *United States–Japan Trade: White Paper: 1987 Review and Update.* Tokyo: ACCJ, 1987.

Amnesty International. *The Philippines: Unlawful Killings by Military and Paramilitary Forces.* New York: Amnesty International, 1988.

Auer, James E., and Karl D. Jackson. *The Future of the U.S. Role in Northeast Asia.* Unpublished monograph, 1987.

Baerwald, Hans H. *Party Politics in Japan.* Winchester, Mass.: Allen & Unwin, 1986.

Bahm, Archie J. *The Heart of Confucius.* New York: Walker-Weatherhill, 1969.

Barone, Michael, and Grant Ujifusa. *The Almanac of American Politics.* Washington: National Journal, 1985.

Batra, Ravi. *The Great Depression of 1990.* New York: Simon & Schuster, 1987.

Bauer, Gary L. *The Family: Preserving America's Future.* Washington: U.S. Department of Education, 1986.

Bautista, Felix. *Cardinal Sin and the Miracle of Asia.* Manila: Vera-Reyes, 1987.

Bayard, Thomas O., and Young Soo-Gil, eds. *Economic Relations Between the United States and Korea: Conflict or Cooperation.* Washington: Institute for International Economics, 1988.

Bellah, Robert J. *Habits of the Heart.* Berkeley: University of California Press, 1985.

Bellah, Robert J. *Tokugawa Religion: Values of Pre-Industrial Japan.* Glencoe, Ill.: The Free Press, 1957.

Belsky, Jay. *Infant Day Care: A Cause for Concern?* Washington: Family Research Council, 1986.

Bennett, William J. *American Education: Making It Work.* Washington: U.S. Department of Education, 1988.

Bennett, William J. *Schools That Work: Educating Disadvantaged Children.* Washington: U.S. Department of Education, 1987.

Bennett, William J. *What Works: Research About Teaching and Learning.* Washington: U.S. Department of Education, 1986.

Bennett, William J. *What Works: Schools Without Drugs.* Washington: U.S. Department of Education, 1986.

Bergsten, C. Fred, et al. *Resolving the Global Economic Crisis: After Wall Street.* Washington: Institute for International Economics, 1987.

Bergsten, C. Fred, and William R. Cline. *The United States–Japan Economic Problem.* Washington: Institute for International Economics, 1987.

Bloom, Allan. *The Closing of the American Mind.* New York: Simon & Schuster, 1987.

Bo Yang. *Secrets.* Translated and with an introduction by David Deterding. Boston: Cheng & Tsui Company, 1985.

Bonner, Raymond. *Waltzing with a Dictator.* New York: Times Books, 1987.

Boocock, Sarane, and Walter Wallace. *Nursery School Education in Japan.* Princeton: Princeton University Press, 1985.

Booz, Allen & Hamilton, Inc. *Direct Foreign Investment in Japan: The Challenge for Foreign Firms.* Tokyo: Booz, Allen, 1987.

Braddon, Russell. *Japan Against the World, 1941–2041: The 100-Year War for Supremacy.* New York: Stein & Day, 1983.

Bresnan, John, ed. *Crisis in the Philippines.* Princeton: Princeton University Press, 1986.

Brzezinski, Zbigniew. *The Grand Failure: The Birth and Death of Communism in the 20th Century.* New York: Charles Scribner's Sons, 1989.

Brzezinski, Zbigniew. *Strategic Zones and Global Security: Implications for Japan and the U.S.* New York: Columbia University, 1982.

Buchanan, Daniel Crump. *Japanese Proverbs and Sayings.* Norman, Oklahoma: University of Oklahoma Press, 1965.

Bunge, Frederick M., ed. *Philippines: A Country Study.* Washington: Government Printing Office, 1984.

Buruma, Ian. *Behind the Mask.* New York: Pantheon Books, 1984.

Calleo, David P. *Beyond American Hegemony.* New York: Basic Books, 1987.

Calleo, David P. *The Imperious Economy.* Cambridge, Mass.: Harvard University Press, 1982.

Calleo, David P. *Money and the Coming World Order.* New York: Lehrman Institute/NYU Press, 1976.

Carnegie Forum on Education and the Economy. *A Nation Prepared: Teachers for the 21st Century.* Washington: Carnegie Forum, 1986.

Chace, James. *Solvency: The Price of Survival.* New York: Random House, 1981.

Chamberlain, Basil Hall. *Things Japanese.* Tokyo: Charles Tuttle & Co., 1905.

Chapman, J. W. M. *Japan's Quest for Comprehensive Security: Defence, Diplomacy, Dependence.* New York: St. Martin's Press, 1982.

Chapman, William. *Inside the Philippine Revolution.* New York: W. W. Norton, 1987.

China, Government of the People's Republic of, and Government of the United Kingdom of Great Britain. *The Sino-British Joint Declaration on the Future of Hong Kong.* Hong Kong: Hong Kong Government Press, 1984.

Ching, Julia. *Confucianism and Christianity: A Comparative Study.* Tokyo: Kodansha International, 1977.

Chiu, Hungdah, ed. *The Future of Hong Kong: 1997 and Beyond.* Westport, Conn.: Greenwood Press, 1987.

Chiu, Hungdah, ed. *Symposium on Hong Kong: 1997.* Baltimore: University of Maryland, 1985.

Choy, Jon K. T., ed. *Japan: Exploring New Paths.* Washington: Japan Economic Institute, 1988.

Christopher, Robert C. *Second to None: American Companies in Japan.* New York: Fawcett Columbine, 1986.

Chubb, John E., and Terry M. Moe. *What Price Democracy? Politics, Markets, and America's Schools.* Washington: The Brookings Institution, forthcoming.

Cohen, Stephen S., and John Zysman. *Manufacturing Matters: The Myth of the Post-Industrial Economy.* New York: Basic Books, 1987.

Coleman, James S. *High School Achievement.* New York: Basic Books, 1982.

Constantino, Renato. *The Philippines: The Continuing Past.* Manila: Foundation for Nationalist Studies, 1978.

Council on Foreign Relations. *Korea at the Crossroads.* New York: COFR, 1987.

Crane, Paul S. *Korean Patterns.* Seoul: Kwangjin Publishing, 1978.

Cummings, William K. *Education and Equality in Japan.* Princeton: Princeton University Press, 1980.

Curran, Dolores. *Traits of a Healthy Family.* Minneapolis: Winston Press, 1983.

Dale, Peter N. *The Myth of Japanese Uniqueness.* New York: St. Martin's Press, 1986.

Denison, Edward F., and William K. Chung. *How Japan's Economy Grew So Fast.* Washington: The Brookings Institution, 1976.

Destler, I. M., and John S. Odell. *Anti-Protection: Changing Forces in United States Trade Politics.* Washington: Institute for International Economics, 1987.

DeVos, George, ed. *Heritage of Endurance: Family Patterns and Delinquency Formation in Urban Japan.* Berkeley: University of California Press, 1984.

DeVos, George, and Chang-Soo Lee. *Koreans in Japan: Ethnic Conflict and Accommodation.* Berkeley: University of California Press, 1984.

Deyo, Frederic C. *The Political Economy of the New Asian Industrialism.* Ithaca, N.Y.: Cornell University Press, 1987.

Doi, Takeo. *Amae. (The Anatomy of Dependence.)* Tokyo: Kodansha International, 1973.

Dore, Ronald P. *Education in Tokugawa Japan.* Ann Arbor, Mich.: University of Michigan Press, 1984.

Dore, Ronald P. *Flexible Rigidities: Industrial Policy and Structural Adjustment in the Japanese Economy.* Stanford: Stanford University Press, 1986.

Dore, Ronald P. *Taking Japan Seriously.* Stanford: Stanford University Press, 1987.

Dorfman, Cynthia Hearn, ed. *Japanese Education Today.* Washington: U.S. Department of Education, 1987.

Drifte, Reinhard. *Arms Production in Japan: The Military Applications of Civilian Technology.* Boulder, Colo.: Westview Press, 1986.

Duke, Benjamin. *The Japanese School: Lessons for Industrial America.* New York: Praeger, 1986.

Economist Intelligence Unit. *Country Profile: Singapore.* London: The Economist, 1986.

Eisner, Robert. *How Real Is the Federal Deficit?* New York: The Free Press, 1986.

Etoh, Jun. *Nichibei senso wa owatteinai. (The War Between Japan and America Is Not Over.)* Tokyo: Bungei Shunju, 1986.

Fallows, Deborah. *A Mother's Work.* Boston: Houghton Mifflin, 1985.

Fallows, James. *More Like Us: Making America Great Again.* New York: Houghton Mifflin, 1989.

Fallows, James. *National Defense.* New York: Vintage Books, 1982.

Far Eastern Economic Review. *Asia 1988 Yearbook.* Hong Kong: Review Publishing, 1988.

Feigenbaum, Edward A., and Pamela McCorduck. *The Fifth Generation: Artificial Intelligence and Japan's Computer Challenge to the World.* Reading, Mass.: Adison-Wesley, 1983.

Fodella, Gianni. *Social Structures and Economic Dynamics in Japan to 1980.* Milan: Institute of Economic and Social Studies for East Asia, 1982.

Foster, Richard. *Innovation: The Attacker's Advantage.* New York: Summit Books, 1986.

Frost, Ellen L. *For Richer, For Poorer: The New U.S.–Japan Relationship.* Tokyo: Charles E. Tuttle Co., 1987.

Fukukawa, Shinji. *21 seiki sangyo shakai no kihan koso. (The Basic Concept of Industrial Society for the 21st Century.)* Tokyo: Tsusho Sangyo Sho (MITI), 1986.

Fukutake, Tadashi. *Japanese Social Structure.* Translated and with an introduction by Ronald P. Dore. Tokyo: University of Tokyo Press, 1982.

Fukutake, Tadashi. *Japanese Society Today.* Tokyo: University of Tokyo Press, 1981.

Futtrell, Mary Hatwood, ed. *Teachers for Tomorrow.* Washington: National Education Association, 1987.

Gardner, Howard. *Art, Mind, and Brain: A Cognitive Approach to Creativity.* New York: Basic Books, 1982.

Gardner, Howard. *Frames of Mind: The Theory of Multiple Intelligences.* New York: Basic Books, 1985.

George, T. J. S. *Lee Kuan Yew's Singapore.* Singapore: Eastern Universities Press, Ltd., 1973.

Gilder, George. *Wealth and Poverty.* New York: Basic Books, 1981.

Gilpin, Robert. *The Political Economy of International Relations.* Princeton: Princeton University Press, 1987.

Glazer, Nathan. *The Limits of Social Policy.* Cambridge, Mass.: Harvard University Press, 1988.

Gold, Thomas B. *State and Society in the Taiwan Miracle.* New York: M. E. Sharpe, Inc., 1986.

Gramich, Edward M. *Educational Achievement: Explanations and Implications of Recent Trends.* Washington: Congressional Budget Office, 1987.

Grayson, C. Jackson. *American Business: The Two-Minute Warning.* New York: Free Press, 1988.

Gregor, A. James. *The U.S. and the Philippines: A Challenge to a Special Relationship.* Washington: The Heritage Foundation, 1983.

Grilli, Susan. *Preschool in the Suzuki Spirit.* New York: Harcourt Brace Jovanovich, 1988.

Hahn, Andrew, et al. *Dropouts in America.* Washington: Institute for Educational Leadership, 1987.

Halas, Celia. *Why Can't a Woman Be More Like a Man?* New York: Macmillan, 1981.

Hall, John Whitney. *Twelve Doors to Japan.* New York: McGraw-Hill, 1965.

Halloran, Richard. *To Arm a Nation: Rebuilding America's Endangered Defenses.* New York: Macmillan, 1986.

Harrington, Joseph. *Understanding the Manufacturing Process: Key to Successful CAD/CAM Implementation.* New York: M. Dekker, 1984.

Harrison, Selig. *The Security of Korea: U.S. and Japanese Perspectives in the 1980s.* Boulder, Colo.: Westview Press, 1980.

Heilbroner, Robert L., and Lester Thurow. *Five Economic Challenges.* Englewood Cliffs, N.J.: Prentice-Hall, Inc., 1981.

Hendry, Joy. *Becoming Japanese: The World of the Preschool Child.* Honolulu: University of Hawaii Press, 1986.

Heritage Foundation, The. *U.S.–China Relations: Challenge to American Policymakers.* Washington: The Heritage Foundation, 1984.

Hewlett, Sylvia Ann. *A Lesser Life: The Myth of Women's Liberation in America.* New York: William Morrow, 1986.

Hirsch, E. D., Jr. *Cultural Literacy.* Boston: Houghton-Mifflin, 1987.

Hobson, John A. *Imperialism: A Study.* London: Allen-Unwin, 1902.

Hofheinz, Roy, and Kent Calder. *The East Asia Edge.* New York: Basic Books, 1982.

Hong Kong Government. *Green Paper: The 1987 Review of Developments in Representative Government.* Hong Kong: Hong Kong Government Press, 1987.

Hong Kong Government. *Hong Kong 1988.* Hong Kong, 1989.

Hong Kong Government. *White Paper: The Development of Representative Government.* Hong Kong: Hong Kong Government Press, 1988.

Hosomi, Takashi. *Economic Aid and Japan's Security.* New York: Columbia University, East Asian Institute, 1983.

Hoyt, Edwin P. *Japan's War.* New York: McGraw-Hill, 1986.

Hughes, Richard. *Hong Kong: Borrowed Place, Borrowed Time.* London: Andre Deutsch, 1968.

Hurh, Won-moo, and Kwang-chung Kim. *Korean Immigrants in America.* Cranbury, N.J.: Associated University Presses, 1984.

Iga, Mamoru. *The Thorn in the Chrysanthemum: Suicide and Economic Success in Modern Japan.* Berkeley: University of California Press, 1986.

Igarashi, Koichi, ed. *Statistical Abstract of Education, Science, and Culture.* Tokyo: Ministry of Education, 1985.

Iizuka, Koji. *Ajia no naka no Nihon. (Japan in the Midst of Asia.)* Tokyo: Heibonsha, 1975.

Imai, Masaaki. *Kaizen: The Key to Japan's Competitive Success.* Cambridge: Productivity Press, 1987.

Inoguchi, Kuniko. *Posuto-Haken Shisutemu to Nihon no Sentaku. (Post-Hegemonic Systems and Japan's Options.)* Tokyo: Chikuma Shobo, 1987.

Inoguchi, Takashi, and Tomoaki Iwai. *Zoku giin no kenkyu. (The Study of Zoku Dietmembers.)* Tokyo: Nihon Keizai Shimbunsha, 1987.

Inoki, Masamichi. *Asian Security.* Tokyo: Research Institute for Peace and Security, 1981.

Ishida, Takeshi, ed. *The 21st Century: The Asian Century.* Berlin: Express Editions, 1985.

Ishinomori, Shotaro. *Manga: Nihon Keizai Nyumon. (Introduction to the Japanese Economy: The Comic Book.)* Tokyo: Nihon Keizai Shimbunsha, 1986.

Ismail, Aladin, ed. *Hong Kong 1988.* Hong Kong: Government Information Services, 1988.

Jackson, Karl D., and M. Hadi Soesastro. *ASEAN Security and Economic Development.* Berkeley: University of California Press, 1984.

Jacobson, Gary. *Xerox, American Samurai.* New York: Macmillan, 1986.

Japan Economic Journal *The Restructuring of Japan's Economy.* Tokyo: Nihon Keizai Shimbunsha, 1988.

Johnson, Chalmers. *The Industrial Policy Debate.* San Francisco: ICS Press, 1984.

Johnson, Chalmers. *Japan's Public Policy Companies.* Washington, D.C.: American Enterprise Institute, 1978.

Johnson, Chalmers. *MITI and the Japanese Miracle.* Stanford: Stanford University Press, 1982.

Johnson, Chalmers. *MITI, MPT, and the Telecom Wars: How Japan Makes Policy for High Technology.* Berkeley: Berkeley Roundtable on the International Economy (BRIE), 1986.

Johnson, William B., and Arnold E. Packer. *Workforce 2000: Work and Workers for the 21st Century.* Indianapolis, Ind.: Hudson Institute, 1987.

Jones, Landon. *Great Expectations: America and the Baby Boom Generation.* New York: Coward, McCann, and Geoghegan, 1980.

Josey, Alex. *Lee Kuan Yew.* Singapore: Times Books International, 1980.

Joya, Mock. *Things Japanese.* Tokyo: Tokyo News Service, Ltd., 1960.

Kago, Saburo, et al., eds. *Kotowaza kojiten. (Dictionary of Japanese Proverbs.)* Tokyo: Fukushi Kanshoten, 1968.

Kahn, Herman. *The Japanese Challenge: The Success and Failure of Economic Success.* Tokyo: Charles E. Tuttle Co., 1978.

Kaneko, Taizo, ed. *21 seiki to kan taiheiyo ken e no tembo. (Looking Toward the 21st Century and the Pacific Region.)* Tokyo: Tokyodo Shuppan, 1986.

Kennan, George F. *Memoirs: 1925–1950.* Boston: Little, Brown, 1972.

Kennedy, Paul. *The Realities Behind Diplomacy: Background Influences on British External Policy, 1965–1980.* New York: Allen-Unwin, 1981.

Kennedy, Paul. *The Rise and Fall of the Great Powers: Economic Change and Military Conflict, 1500–2000.* New York: Random House, 1988.

Kennedy, Paul. *Strategy and Diplomacy: 1870–1945.* New York: Allen-Unwin, 1983.

Keohane, Robert. *After Hegemony.* Princeton: Princeton University Press, 1984.

Kessler, Richard J. *U.S. Policy Toward the Philippines After Marcos.* Muscatine, Ia.: The Stanley Foundation, 1986.

Kim, W. Chan, and Philip K. Y. Young. *The Pacific Challenge in International Business.* Ann Arbor, Mich.: UMI Research Press, 1987.

Kirby, Stuart. *Toward the Pacific Century: Economic Development in the Pacific Basin.* London: Economist Intelligence Unit, 1983.

Kojima, Shinji. *Ajia kara mita kindai Nippon. (Modern Japan as Viewed from Asia.)* Tokyo: Aki Press, 1978.

Kosaka, Masataka. *Bunmei ga suiboh. (The Collapse of Civilization.)* Tokyo: Shinseyusho, 1981.

Krause, Lawrence. *The Pacific Community Concept: Japan and the United States.* New York: Columbia University, 1981.

Krause, Lawrence. *Singapore's Economy Reconsidered.* Singapore: Institute for Southeast Asian Studies, 1987.

Krauss, Ellis S., et al., ed. *Conflict in Japan.* Honolulu: University of Hawaii Press, 1984.

Krugman, Paul R., ed. *Strategic Trade Policy and the New International Economics.* Cambridge, Mass.: MIT Press, 1987.

Kunii, Toshiyasu. *Pax Japonica.* Tokyo: President Publishing Co., 1988.

Kuroyanagi, Tetsuko. *Madogiwa no Totto-chan. (Totto Chan: The Little Girl at the Window.)* Tokyo: Kodansha, 1984.

Lasater, Martin. *Taiwan: Facing Mounting Threats.* Washington: The Heritage Foundation, 1987.

Lebra, Takie Sugiyama. *Japanese Culture and Behavior.* Honolulu: University of Hawaii Press, 1987.

Lebra, Takie Sugiyama. *Japanese Patterns of Behavior.* Honolulu: University of Hawaii Press, 1976.

Lebra, Takie Sugiyama. *Japanese Women: Constraint and Fulfillment.* Honolulu: University of Hawaii Press, 1984.

Lee, Kyu-uck. *The Concentration of Economic Power in Korea: Causes, Consequences, and Policy.* Seoul: Korea Development Institute, 1986.

Legge, James. *The Works of Mencius.* New York: Dover Publications, 1984.

Lewis, Hunter, and Donald Allison. *The Real World War: the Coming Battle for the New Global Economy and Why We Are in Danger of Losing.* New York: Coward, McCann & Geoghegan, 1982.

Lewis, W. Arthur. *Growth and Fluctuations, 1870–1913.* New York: Allen-Unwin, 1977.

Lewis, W. Arthur. *Perspectives on Economic Development.* Barbados: University Press of America, 1982.

Li, Fei Kan. *The Family.* Peking: Foreign Languages Press, 1958.

Lim, Chong-Yah, ed. *Singapore: Resources and Growth.* New York: Oxford University Press, 1986.

Lin, Yutang. *The Wisdom of Confucius.* New York: Random House, 1938.

Lin, Yutang. *The Wisdom of Laotse.* New York: Random House, 1948.

Lincoln, Edward J. *Japan: Facing Economic Maturity.* Washington: The Brookings Institution, 1988.

Lincoln, Edward J. *Japan's Economic Role in Northeast Asia.* Lanham, Md.: University Press of America, 1987.

Linder, Staffan Burenstam. *The Pacific Century: Economic and Political Consequences of Asian-Pacific Dynamism.* Stanford: Stanford University Press, 1986.

Lippit, Noriko Mizuta, ed. *Stories by Japanese Women Writers.* New York: M. E. Sharpe, Inc., 1982.

Lu, Martin. *Confucianism: Its Relevance to Modern Society.* Singapore: Federal Publications, Ltd., 1983.

Luns, Joseph M. A. H. *The Western Alliance: Its Future and Its Implications for Asia.* Singapore: Institute for Southeast Asian Studies, 1985.

MacKnight, Susan. *Japan's Expanding U.S. Manufacturing Presence.* Washington: Japan Economic Institute, 1987.

Makino, Noboru. *Decline and Prosperity: Corporate Innovation in Japan.* Tokyo: Kodansha International, 1987.

Marris, Stephen. *Deficits and the Dollar: The World Economy at Risk.* Washington: Institute for International Economics, 1987.

Maslin, Bonnie. *Not Quite Paradise.* New York: Dolphin Doubleday, 1987.

McCormack, Gavan, and Yoshio Sugimoto. *Democracy in Contemporary Japan.* New York: M. E. Sharpe, Inc., 1986.

McCraw, Thomas K. *America vs. Japan.* Boston: Harvard Business School Press, 1986.

McGovern, Ann. *Too Much Noise.* Boston: Houghton Mifflin Company, 1967.

McGurn, William. *Basic Law, Basic Questions.* Hong Kong: Review Publishing, 1988.

Minchin, James. *No Man Is an Island: A Study of Singapore's Lee Kuan Yew.* London: Allen & Unwin, 1986.

Ministry of Education, Government of Korea. *Education in Korea.* Seoul: Government Printing Office, 1987.

Ministry of Education, Republic of China. *Education in the Republic of China: 1987.* Taipei: Government Information Office, 1987.

Ministry of International Trade and Industry (MITI). *Nihon no sentaku. (Japan's Options: Toward a New Globalism and Policy Alternatives in an Era of New Industrial and Cultural Nationalism.)* Tokyo: Tsusho Sangyo Sho, 1988.

Ministry of International Trade and Industry (MITI). *2000 nen no joho sangyo bijion. (Information Industries Vision for the Year 2000.)* Tokyo: Tsusho Sangyo Sho, 1987.

Morgan, Elizabeth A. *Pioneer Research on Strong, Healthy Families.* Washington: Family Research Council, 1987.

Morley, James W. *The Pacific Basin Movement and Japan.* New York: East Asian Institute, 1987.

Morse, Ronald A., and Richard J. Samuels. *Getting America Ready for Japanese Science and Technology.* Washington: Woodrow Wilson International Center, 1985.

Moynihan, Daniel Patrick. *Came the Revolution.* New York: Harcourt Brace Jovanovich, 1988.

Moynihan, Daniel Patrick. *Family and Nation.* New York: Harcourt Brace Jovanovich, 1986.

Muller, Herbert J. *The Loom of History.* New York: New American Library, 1958.

Muller, Herbert J. *The Uses of the Past.* New York: New American Library, 1952.

Murray, Charles. *In Pursuit of Happiness and Good Government.* New York: Simon and Schuster, 1988.

Murray, Charles. *Losing Ground: American Social Policy, 1950–1980.* New York: Basic Books, 1984.

Nakagawa, Yatsuhiro. *Nippon: choh-senshinkoku. (Japan: The Ultra-Advanced Industrial Country.)* Tokyo: Kodansha, 1980.

Nakane, Chie. *Tate shakai no ningen kankei. (Japanese Society.)* London: Penguin Books, 1973.

National Academy of Engineering. *Strengthening U.S. Engineering through International Cooperation.* Washington: NAE, 1987.

National Commission on Excellence in Education. *A Nation at Risk.* Washington: U.S. Department of Education, 1983.

National Governors Association. *Time for Results: The Governors 1991 Report on Education.* Washington: NGA Center for Policy Research and Analysis, 1986.

Nihonjin Kenkyukai. *Changing Values in Modern Japan.* Tokyo: Nihonjin Kenkyukai, 1976.

Noguchi, Yukio. *Nijuisseiki no Nihon. (21st-Century Japan.)* Tokyo: Toyo Keizai Shinposha, 1968.

Norman, E. Herbert. *Origins of the Modern Japanese State.* Edited and with an introduction by John W. Dower. New York: Random House, 1975. (Reprint of the 1940 edition.)

Ohkawa, Kazushi, and Henry Rosovsky. *Japanese Economic Growth: Trend Acceleration in the 20th Century.* Stanford: Stanford University Press, 1973.

Okimoto, Daniel, ed. *Japan's Economy: Coping with Change in the International Environment.* Boulder, Colo.: Westview Press, 1982.

Okimoto, Daniel, and Takashi Inoguchi, eds. *The Political Economy of Japan: Vol. 2: The Changing International Context.* Stanford: Stanford University Press, 1988.

Okimoto, Daniel, and Thomas Rohlen, eds. *Inside the Japanese System.* Stanford: Stanford University Press, 1988.

Patrick, Hugh, ed. *Japan's High Technology Industries.* Seattle: University of Washington Press, 1986.

Pepper, Thomas, et al. *The Competition: Dealing with Japan.* New York: Praeger, 1985.

Perelman, Lewis J. *Technology and Transformation of Schools.* Alexandria, Va.: National School Boards Association, 1987.

Perkins, Dwight. *China: Asia's Next Economic Giant?* Seattle: Washington University Press, 1987.

Porter, Michael. *Competitive Strategy: Techniques for Analyzing Industries and Competitors.* New York: The Free Press, 1980.

Prestowitz, Clyde. *Trading Places: How We Allowed Japan to Take the Lead.* New York: Basic Books, 1988.

Prosterman, Roy. *Land Reform and Democratic Development.* Baltimore: Johns Hopkins, 1987.

Pugel, Thomas A., et al., eds. *Fragile Independence: Economic Issues in U.S.–Japanese Trade and Investment.* Lexington, Mass.: Lexington Books, 1986.

Pyle, Keneth B., ed. *The Trade Crisis: How Will America Respond?* Seattle: Journal of Japanese Studies, 1987.

Ravitch, Diane, and Chester E. Finn, Jr. *What Do Our 17-Year-Olds Know?* New York: Harper & Row, 1987.

Regier, Gerald P. *Cultural Trends and the American Family.* Washington: Family Research Council, 1987.

Reischauer, Haru Matsukata. *Samurai and Silk.* Tokyo: Tuttle Books, 1987.

Republic of Singapore. *Singapore 1987.* Singapore: Ministry of Communications and Information, 1988.

Republic of Singapore. *Singapore 1988.* Singapore Ministry of Communications and Information, 1989.

Riser, Sarah Dawn. *Family Demographics Fact Sheet.* Washington: Family Research Council, 1987.

Robins-Mowry, Dorothy. *The Hidden Sun: Women of Modern Japan.* Boulder, Colo.: Westview Press, 1983.

Rohlen, Thomas. *Japan's High Schools.* Berkeley: University of California Press, 1983.

Sako, Katsuro. *How Japan Can Do More to Defend Itself.* Washington: The Heritage Foundation, 1987.

Sandhu, K. S. *Institute for Southeast Asian Studies Annual Report: 1986–87.* Singapore: ISEAS, 1987.

Sato, Seizaburo, and Tetsuhisa Matsuzaki. *Jiminto Seiken. (The Liberal Democratic Party Regime.)* Tokyo: Chuo Koronsha, 1986.

Scalapino, Robert, and Sung-Joo Han, eds. *United States-Korea Relations.* Berkeley: University of California, 1986.

Scarf, Maggie. *Intimate Partners: Patterns in Love and Marriage.* New York: Random House, 1987.

Scarf, Maggie. *Unfinished Business: Pressure Points in the Lives of Women.* New York: Doubleday, 1980.

Schlossstein, Steven. *Kensei: The Sword Master.* New York: Congdon & Weed, 1983.

Schlossstein, Steven. *Trade War: Greed, Power, and Industrial Policy on Opposite Sides of the Pacific.* New York: Congdon & Weed, 1984.

Schmidt, Helmut. *A Grand Strategy for the West: the Anachronism of National Strategies in an Interdependent World.* New Haven: Yale University Press, 1985.

Schmidt, Helmut. *The Soviet Union: Challenges and Responses as Seen from the European Point of View.* Singapore: Institute for Southeast Asian Studies, 1984.

Schonberger, Richard. *Japanese Manufacturing Techniques: Nine Hidden Lessons in Simplicity.* New York: Free Press, 1982.

Schonberger, Richard. *World Class Manufacturing: The Lessons of Simplicity Applied.* New York: Free Press, 1986.

Scott, Bruce R. *U.S. Competitiveness in the World Economy: An Update.* Boston: Harvard Business School Press, 1987.

Servan-Schreiber, Jean-Jacques. *The American Challenge.* New York: Avon Books, 1967.

Sha, Seiki. *America no Choraku. (America's Decline.)* Tokyo: Tokuma Books, 1988.

Shannon, Richard. *The Crisis of Imperialism.* New York: Paladin, 1976.

Shaplen, Robert. *A Turning Wheel.* New York: Random House, 1979.

Shimazaki, Toson. *The Family.* Tokyo: University of Tokyo Press, 1976.

Shimer, Dorothy Blair. *Rice Bowl Women.* New York: New American Library, 1982.

Sicker, Martin. *Soviet Strategy in Asia*. Washington: The Heritage Foundation, 1987.

Simon, Sheldon W., et al. *America's New Pacific Era*. Washington: The Heritage Foundation, 1985.

Singapore Department of Statistics. *Statistics on Marriages and Divorces*. Singapore: Government Printing Office, 1986.

Singapore Ministry of Education. *Towards Excellence in Schools*. Singapore: Government Printing Office, 1987.

Singer, Kurt. *Mirror, Sword, and Jewel: The Geometry of Japanese Life*. Tokyo: Kodansha International, 1973.

Smith, Steven S. *Revolution in the House*. Washington: The Brookings Institution, 1986.

Snyder, David Pearce. *Future Forces*. Baltimore: The Futurist, 1987.

Standish, Robert. *The Three Bamboos*. London: Peter Davies, 1942.

Stern, Philip M. *The Best Congress Money Can Buy*. New York: Pantheon, 1988.

Sugimoto, Yoshio, et al., eds. *Democracy in Contemporary Japan*. New York: M. E. Sharpe, Inc., 1986.

Suhr, Myong-Won. *Education in Korea, 1987–88*. Seoul: Ministry of Education, 1988.

Sun-tzu. *The Art of War*. Translated and with an introduction by Samuel B. Griffith. Oxford: Oxford University Press, 1963.

Tan, Han Hoe, ed. *Singapore 1987*. Singapore: Ministry of Communications and Information, 1987.

Tanabe, T. *Ajia kara mita dai toa kyoeiken*. (*The Greater East-Asia Co-Prosperity Sphere Viewed from Asia*.) Tokyo: JCA Press, 1983.

Tanaka, Yukiko, ed. *This Kind of Woman: Ten Stories by Japanese Women, 1960–1976*. Stanford: Stanford University Press, 1982.

Thayer, Nathaniel. *How the Conservatives Rule Japan*. Princeton: Princeton University Press, 1969.

Timmons, Thomas J. *The U.S. and Asia: A Statistical Handbook, 1987*. Washington: The Heritage Foundation, 1987.

Tocqueville, Alexis de. *Democracy in America*. Edited and abridged by Richard D. Heffner. New York: New American Library, 1956.

Tsurumi, E. Patricia, ed. *The Other Japan*. New York: M. E. Sharpe, Inc., 1988.

Tu, Wei Ming. *Confucian Ethics Today*. Singapore: Federal Publications Ltd., 1982.

Tyack, David. *The One Best System*. Cambridge; Mass.: Harvard University Press, 1974.

United States Congress, Office of Technology Assessment. *Commercializing High-Temperature Superconductivity*. Washington: Government Printing Office, 1988.

United States Congress, Office of Technology Assessment. *The Defense Technology Base*. Washington: Government Printing Office, 1988.

United States Congress, Office of Technology Assessment. *International Competition in Services*. Washington: Government Printing Office, 1987.

United States Department of Defense. *Soviet Military Power: An Assessment of the Threat, 1988*. Washington: Government Printing Office, 1988.

United States Department of State. *China: Background Notes*. Washington: U.S. Government Printing Office, 1987.

United States House of Representatives, Committee on Ways and Means. *Managing U.S.-Korean Trade Conflict*. Washington: Government Printing Office, 1987.

Utsunomiya, Tokuma. *Ajia ni tatsu*. (*Perspectives from Asia*.) Tokyo: Hodansha, 1978.

Vogel, Ezra F. *Comeback*. New York: Simon & Schuster, 1985.

Vogel, Ezra F. *Japan as Number One*. Tokyo: Charles E. Tuttle Co, 1979.

Vogel, Ezra F., and George Lodge, eds. *Ideology and Competition: An Analysis of Nine Countries.* Boston: Harvard Business School Press, 1987.

Wagner, Jane. *The Search for Signs of Intelligent Life in the Universe.* New York: Harper & Row, 1987.

Wallerstein, Judith S., and Sandra Blakeslee. *Men, Women, and Children a Decade After Divorce.* New York: Ticknor & Fields, 1989.

Wallerstein, Judith S., and Joan Berlin Kelly. *Surviving the Breakup: How Children and Parents Cope with Divorce.* New York: Basic Books, 1980.

Watanabe, Fujio. *Education in Japan.* Tokyo: Ministry of Education, Science and Culture, 1986.

Weikart, David P. *Changed Lives: The Effects of the Perry Preschool Program on Youths Through Age 19.* Ypsilanti, Mich.: High/Scope Educational Research Foundation, 1984.

Wheeler, Jimmy W., and Perry L. Wood. *Beyond Recrimination: Perspectives on U.S.–Taiwan Trade Tensions.* Indianapolis, Ind.: Hudson Institute, 1987.

White, Merry. *The Japanese Educational Challenge: A Commitment to Children.* New York: The Free Press, 1987.

Will, George F. *The New Season.* New York: Simon and Schuster, 1987.

Wittrock, Merlin C. *Handbook of Research on Teaching.* New York: Macmillan, 1986.

The World Bank. *Korea: Transition to Maturity.* Washington, D.C.: The International Bank for Reconstruction and Development (IBRD), 1988.

Yamamura, Kozo. *Economic Policy in Postwar Japan.* Berkeley: University of California Press, 1967.

Yamamura, Kozo, and Yasukichi Yasuba. *The Political Economy of Japan: Vol. 1, The Domestic Transformation.* Stanford: Stanford University Press, 1987.

Yankelovich, Daniel. *New Rules: Searching for Self-Fulfillment in a World Turned Upside Down.* New York: Random House, 1981.

Yankelovich, Daniel, and Sidney Harman. *Starting with the People.* Boston: Houghton Mifflin Company, 1988.

Yasutomo, Dennis T. *The Manner of Giving: Strategic Aid and Japanese Foreign Policy.* Lexington, Mass.: Lexington Books, 1986.

Yoffie, David B. *Power and Protectionism: Strategies of the Newly Industrializing Countries.* New York: Columbia University Press, 1983.

Young, John A. *Global Competition and the New Reality.* Washington: Report of the President's Commission on Industrial Competitiveness, 1985.

Yu, Carver. *Being and Relation: An Eastern Critique of Western Dualism.* Wolfeboro, N.H.: Longwood Publishing Group, 1987.

Yu, Eui-young. *Juvenile Delinquency in the Korean Community in Los Angeles.* Los Angeles: The Korea Times, 1986.

Zigler, Edward F., et al., eds. *Children, Families and Government: Perspectives on American Social Policy.* Cambridge, Mass.: Cambridge University Press, 1983.

Zigler, Edward F., and Maryl Frank, eds. *The Parental Leave Crisis: Toward a National Policy.* New Haven: Yale University Press, 1988.

Articles

Ahn, Byung-joon. "Korea's International Environment." Unpublished paper presented at the American Enterprise Institute Conference on Development and Democracy in East Asia, Washington, May 18–19, 1988.

Alic, John A. "The Federal Role in Commercial Technology Development," *Technovation,* winter 1986.

Alic, John A. "Industrial Policy: Politics and Economics." Unpublished paper presented to the Electronic Show & Convention, Boston, May 15–17, 1984.

Alic, John A. "Japanese R&D and U.S. Technology Policy." Washington: Office of Technology Assessment working paper, 1986.

Alic, John A. "Technology and Economics in a Shrinking World." Statement before the Task Force on Technology Policy, Committee on Science, Space and Technology, U.S. House of Representatives, October 22, 1987.

Amano, Ikuo. "The Dilemma of Japanese Education Today," *Japan Update*, number 3, winter 1987.

Anderson, Stephen J. "Japan's Biotech Battles and Trade Wars: State Capacities and Negotiated Protectionism in Japanese Foreign Economic Relations." Unpublished paper presented at the annual meeting of the Association for Asian Studies, San Francisco, March 25, 1988.

Andrews, John. "Taiwan." *The Economist*, March 5, 1988.

AT&T. "New AT&T, CWA, IBEW Pact: More Details of a 'Vanguard' Agreement," *Bulletin* dated June 1, 1989.

Awanohara, Susumu. "Look East: The Japan Model," *Asian-Pacific Economic Literature*, May 1987.

Azumi, Koya. "Creativity of Japanese Companies." The Japan Foundation, *Newsletter*, Volume 14, number 4, 1986.

Beatty, Jack. "The Exorbitant Anachronism." *Atlantic*, June 1989.

Bell, Daniel. "The World and the United States in 2013," *Daedalus*, summer 1987.

Bennett, John. "Economic Developments in the Republic of Korea." Unpublished paper presented at the American Enterprise Institute Conference on Development and Democracy in East Asia, Washington, May 18–19, 1988.

Berlin, Gordon, and Andrew Sum. "Toward a More Perfect Union: Basic Skills, Poor Families, and our Economic Future." New York: Ford Foundation, Project on Social Welfare and the American Future, Occasional Paper number 3, February 1988.

Billington, David P. "In Defense of Engineers." *The Bridge*, National Academy of Engineering, summer 1986.

Boocock, Sarane. "The Japanese Preschool System." Unpublished paper presented at the annual meeting of the Association for Asian Studies, San Francisco, March 25–27, 1988.

Bo Yang. "The Ugly Chinaman," *Renditions*, spring 1985.

Branscomb, Lewis M. "National and Corporate Technology Strategies in an Interdependent World Economy." *The Bridge*, National Academy of Engineering, fall 1986.

Brick, Andrew B. "The Case for Taipei's Membership in International Economic Organizations." The Heritage Foundation, *Backgrounder*, number 82, October 27, 1988.

Brimelow, Peter. "Are We Spending Too Much on Education?" *Forbes*, December 29, 1986.

Brooks, Roger A., ed. "The U.S.–Republic of China Trade Relationship: Time for a New Strategy." The Heritage Foundation, *Lectures*, April 18, 1988.

Brzezinski, Zbigniew. "America's New Geostrategy." *Foreign Affairs*, spring 1988.

Bucy, J. Fred. "Linking Defense, Trade, and Economic Interests with Japan." Unpublished memorandum, 1986.

Buruma, Ian. "Marcos and Morality." *New York Review of Books*, August 13, 1987.

Buruma, Ian. "A New Japanese Nationalism." *New York Times Magazine*, April 12, 1987.

Buruma, Ian. "St. Cory and the Yellow Revolution." *New York Review of Books*, November 6, 1986.

Buruma, Ian. "Singapore." *New York Times Magazine*, June 12, 1988.

Buruma, Ian. "We Japanese." *New York Review of Books*, March 3, 1988.

Buruma, Ian. "What Keeps the Japanese Going?" *New York Review of Books,* March 17, 1988.

Business Tokyo. "Can Japan Lead?" April 1988.

Calder, Kent E. "The North Pacific Triangle: Sources of Economic and Political Transformation." Unpublished paper presented at the Conference on Coordinating Policies in the Asia-Pacific Region in the 1990s and Beyond, Oiso, Japan, December 9–11, 1988.

Calleo, David. "NATO's Middle Course." *Foreign Policy,* winter 1987–88.

Catto, Vladi. "Declining U.S. Competitiveness: Causes and Remedies." Speech to the French-American Chamber of Commerce, Dallas, by the chief economist of Texas Instruments Incorporated, November 6, 1987.

Chace, James. "A New Grand Strategy." *Foreign Policy,* spring 1988.

Chai, Trong R. "The Future of Taiwan." *Asian Survey,* volume XXVI, number 12, December 1986.

Chan, Heng Chee. "Singapore in 1985: Managing Political Transition and Economic Recession." *Asian Survey,* volume XXVI, number 2, February 1986.

Chen, Edward K. Y. "The Economics and Non-Economics of Asia's Four Little Dragons." Inaugural lecture, University of Hong Kong, Hong Kong, January 26, 1988.

Cheng, Chu-Yuan. "U.S.–Taiwan Economic Relations: Trade and Investment." *Columbia Journal of World Business,* volume 21, number 1, spring 1986.

China External Trade Development Council. "Economic and Trade Indicators, 1987." Taipei: CETDC, 1987.

Chinworth, Michael W. "Responding to the Japanese Competitive Challenge." Japan Economic Institute, *JEI Report,* number 1A, January 8, 1988.

Chinworth, Michael W. "The Trade-Defense Linkage." Japan Economic Institute, *JEI Report,* number 35A, September 18, 1987.

Chinworth, Michael W. "What Ever Happened to Defense Technology Transfers?" Japan Economic Institute, *JEI Report,* number 30A, August 7, 1987.

Choy, Jon. "The Changing Pattern of Japanese Trade." Japan Economic Institute, *JEI Report,* number 16A, April 22, 1988.

Choy, Jon. "Japanese Equity Markets: An Overview." Japan Economic Institute, *JEI Report,* number 38A, October 9, 1987.

Choy, Jon. "The Mayekawa Reports: Reality or Rhetoric?" Japan Economic Institute, *JEI Report,* number 39A, October 14, 1988.

Chubb, John E. "Why the Current Wave of School Reform Will Fail." *The Public Interest,* January 1988.

Clinton, Bill. "The Next Educational Reform." *Issues in Science and Technology,* summer 1987.

Colbert, Evelyn. "Japan and the Republic of Korea: Yesterday, Today, and Tomorrow." *Asian Survey,* volume XXVI, number 3, March 1986.

Cummings, Bruce. "The Origins and Development of the Northeast Asian Political Economy: Industrial Sectors, Product Cycles, and Political Consequences," in Frederic C. Deyo, ed., *The Political Economy of the New Asian Industrialism.* Ithaca: Cornell University Press, 1987.

Cutler, Robert S. "Japanese Science and Technology: The Changing Institutional Framework." Presentation to the annual meeting of the American Association for the Advancement of Science, Chicago, February 16, 1987.

Davis, Winston. "Japan as 'Paradigm': Imitation vs. Insight." *Christianity in Crisis,* September 20, 1982.

Davis, Winston. "Religion and Development: Weber and the East Asian Experience," in Myron Weiner and Samuel P. Huntington, eds., *Understanding Political Development.* Boston: Little, Brown, 1987.

Doherty, Eileen Marie. "Japan's Foreign Aid Policy." Japan Economic Institute, *JEI Report*, number 41A, October 30, 1987.

Doherty, Eileen Marie. "Japan's Role in Multilateral Aid Organizations." Japan Economic Institute, *JEI Report*, number 20A, May 20, 1988.

Dornbusch, Rudiger, James Poterba, and Lawrence Summers. "The Case for Manufacturing in America's Future." Monograph underwritten by the Eastman Kodak Company, Rochester, N.Y., 1988.

Drew, Elizabeth. "Politics and Money." *The New Yorker*, December 6 and 13, 1982.

Drucker, Peter F. "Japan's Choices." *Foreign Affairs*, summer 1987.

Economic Planning Board, Republic of Korea. "Korean Economic Indicators." Seoul: Government Printing Office, 1988.

The Economist. "East Asian Security." December 26, 1987.

The Economist. "Now the World Is Japan's Co-Prosperity Sphere." August 13, 1988.

The Economist. "The Philippines: A Question of Faith." May 7, 1988.

The Economist. "South Korea: Foursquare to the Future." May 21, 1988.

The Economist. "Taiwan: Transition on Trial." March 5, 1988.

Erony, Michael. "NTT: A Japanese Public Corporation's Experience with Privatization and Deregulation." Unpublished paper presented at the Association for Asian Studies annual meeting, San Francisco, March 25, 1988.

Fallows, James. "The Bases Dilemma." *Atlantic*, February 1988.

Fallows, James. "Containing Japan." *Atlantic*, May 1989.

Fallows, James. "A Damaged Culture: A New Philippines?" *Atlantic*, November 1987.

Fallows, James. "Playing by Different Rules." *Atlantic*, September 1987.

Feldstein, Martin. "Budget Card Tricks and Dollar Levitation." *Wall Street Journal*, December 1, 1987.

Feldstein, Martin. "Correcting the Trade Deficit." *Foreign Affairs*, spring 1987.

Ferguson, Charles H. "The Competitive Decline of the U.S. Semiconductor Industry." Massachusetts Institute of Technology, VLSI Memo 87–366, March 1987.

Ferguson, Charles H. "From the People Who Brought You Voodoo Economics: Beyond Entrepreneurialism to U.S. Competitiveness." *Harvard Business Review*, volume 66, number 3, May/June 1988.

Ferguson, Charles H. "Technological Development, Strategic Behavior and Government Policy in Information Technology Industries." Massachusetts Institute of Technology, VLSI Memo 88–446, March 1988.

Finn, Chester E., Jr. "Make the Schools Compete." *Harvard Business Review*, September-October 1987.

Finn, Chester E., Jr. "Teacher Politics." *Commentary*, February 1983.

Fiske, Edward B. "Education in Japan: Lessons for America." *New York Times*, July 10–13, 1983.

Ford, Daniel. "Rebirth of a Nation." *The New Yorker*, March 28, 1988.

Frey, Donald N. "Science and Commercial Enterprise: Policies to Match National Needs." *The Bridge*, National Academy of Engineering, fall 1986.

Friedman, Benjamin R. "What Is the 'Right' Amount of Saving?" *National Review*, June 16, 1989.

Fuchs, Peter. "High Tech Trade Wars: Japan in the Next Decade." *Business Tokyo*, October 1987.

Fukui, Haruhiro. "The Policy Research Council of Japan's Liberal Democratic Party." *Asian Thought and Society*, volume 12, number 34, March 1987.

Fusae Ichikawa Memorial Association. "Report." March 1988.

Gaddis, John Lewis. "How the Cold War Might End." *Atlantic,* November 1987.

Gilder, George. "The Revitalization of Everything: The Law of the Microcosm." *Harvard Business Review,* volume 66, number 2, March/April 1988.

Gilpin, Robert. "American Policy in the Post-Reagan Era." *Daedalus,* summer 1987.

Grayson, Lawrence P. "Assessing the Frontiers of Technology in Japan." *Engineering Education,* April/May 1987.

Green, Gretchen. "Japan's Foreign Aid Policy: 1988 Update." Japan Economic Institute, *JEI Report,* number 43A, November 11, 1988.

Haberman, Clyde. "The Presumed Uniqueness of Japan." *New York Times Magazine,* August 28, 1988.

Haggard, Stephen, and Tun-jen Cheng. "State and Foreign Capital in the East Asian NICs." In Frederic C. Deyo, ed., *The Political Economy of the New Asian Industrialism,* Ithaca, N.Y.: Cornell University Press, 1987.

Haley, John O. "Sheathing the Sword of Justice in Japan: An Essay on Law Without Sanctions." *Journal of Japanese Studies,* volume VIII, number 2, fall 1982.

Hamada, Tomoko. "Corporation, Culture, and Environment: The Japanese Model." *Asian Survey,* December 1985.

Hamel, Gary, Yves Doz, and C. K. Prahalad. "Strategic Partnerships: Success or Surrender?" Unpublished paper presented at the 1986 Conference on Cooperative Strategies in International Business, Philadelphia, October 1986.

Han, Sung-joo. "South Korea in 1987: The Politics of Democratization." *Asian Survey,* volume XXVIII, number 1, January 1988.

Harries, Owen. "Exporting Democracy—and Getting It Wrong." *The National Interest,* fall 1988.

Harris, Martha Caldwell. "The Internationalization of Japanese Science and Technology." Paper presented to a symposium of the 153rd annual meeting of the American Association for the Advancement of Science, Chicago, February 16, 1987.

Harrison, Selig S. "Dateline South Korea: A Divided Seoul." *Foreign Policy,* summer 1987.

Hartle, Terry W. "Education Reform: We Have a Lot to Learn." *Public Opinion,* volume 10, number 3, September/October, 1987.

Hayashi, Kiichiro. "The Internationalization of Japanese-Style Management." *Japan Update,* number 5, 1987.

Heckert, Richard E. "Competitiveness and the Quality of the American Workforce." Testimony by the chief executive officer of E. I. duPont de Nemours and Company to the Subcommittee on Education and Health of the Joint Economic Committee of the United States Congress, Washington, December 3, 1987.

Heckert, Richard E. "Education's Role in the Technological Revolution." Speech by the chief executive officer of E. I. duPont de Nemours and Company to the NAACP Life Membership Luncheon, New York, July 8, 1987.

Heilbroner, Robert. "Hard Times." *The New Yorker,* September 14, 1987.

Hernandez, Carolina G. "Political Developments in the Philippines." Unpublished paper presented at the American Enterprise Institute Conference on Development and Democracy in East Asia, Washington, May 18–19, 1988.

Hicks, George. "Explaining the Success of the Four Little Dragons: A Survey." Unpublished paper presented at the Convention of the East Asian Economic Association, Kyoto, Japan, October 29–30, 1988.

Hinton, Harold C. "The Impact of Korea on U.S. Western Pacific Strategy." In the Heritage Foundation Lectures, *America's New Pacific Era,* Washington, D.C., April 19, 1984.

Hiraoka, Leslie S. "A History of Assimilation: Japan's Technology Trade." *Speaking of Japan,* November 1986.

Ho, Samuel P. S. "Economics, Economic Bureaucracy, and Taiwan's Economic Development." *Pacific Affairs,* volume 60, number 2, summer 1987.

Holbrooke, Richard. "East Asia: The Next Challenge." *Foreign Affairs,* spring 1986.

Hooley, Richard. "Economic Developments in the Philippines." Unpublished paper presented at the American Enterprise Institute Conference on Development and Democracy in East Asia, Washington, May 18–19, 1988.

House, Karen Eliot. "The Second Century: The 1990s and Beyond." *Wall Street Journal,* January 23, January 30, February 6, February 13, and February 21, 1989.

Hu, Richard. "Singapore and the Asian NICs: Similarities and Contrasts." Speech delivered by the Minister of Finance, Republic of Singapore, to the Oxford and Cambridge Society of Singapore, December 10, 1987.

Huntington, Samuel P. "The U.S.: Decline or Renewal?" *Foreign Affairs,* winter 1988–89.

Hurh, Won-moo. "Korean Immigrants' Mental Health: A Sociological Analysis." Unpublished paper presented at the Association for Asian Studies annual meeting, San Francisco, March 26, 1988.

Hurh, Won-moo, et al. "Asian-Americans and the 'Success' Image: A Critique." *Proceedings of the American Association for Mental Health Research Council,* volume V, numbers 1–2, January/April 1986.

Hyoung, Lho-joo. "Korea's High-Tech Challenge." *Korea Business World,* November 1988.

Iida, Tsuneo. *"Dare mo sutoppu dekinai America no tenraku."* ("Decline of the American Superpower.") *Shukan Toyo Keizai,* May 9, 1987.

Ishida, Hideto. "Anticompetitive Practices in the Distribution of Goods and Services in Japan: The Problem of Distribution Keiretsu." *Journal of Japanese Studies,* volume 9, number 2, spring 1983.

Ishikawa, Yukinori, et al. "The Golden Age." *Time,* September 21, 1987.

Jaikumar, Ramchandran. "Japanese Flexible Manufacturing Systems: Impact on the United States." Working Paper #28, presented at the New York University symposium on Financial Investment in the United States and Japan, New York, April 27–28, 1987.

Jaikumar, Ramchandran. "Postindustrial Manufacturing." *Harvard Business Review,* November-December 1986.

Johnson, Chalmers. "The Democratization of South Korea: What Role Does Economic Development Play?" Paper presented at the 2nd Ilhae-Carnegie Conference on Democracy and Political Institutions, The Ilhae Institute, Seoul, July 8–9, 1988.

Johnson, Chalmers. "The End of American Hegemony and the Future of Japanese-American Relations." Unpublished paper, April 1988.

Johnson, Chalmers. "How to Think about Economic Competition from Japan." *Journal of Japanese Studies,* summer 1987.

Johnson, Chalmers. "Japan and the North Asian NICs: Implications for World Trade." *Venture Japan,* volume I, number 1, spring 1988.

Johnson, Chalmers. "Japan: Who Governs? An Essay on Official Bureaucracy." *Journal of Japanese Studies,* winter 1975.

Johnson, Chalmers. "Japanese-Soviet Relations in the Early Gorbachev Era." *Asian Survey,* volume XXVII, number 11, November 1987.

Johnson, Chalmers. "Japanese-Style Management in America." *California Management Review,* volume 30, number 4, summer 1988.

Johnson, Chalmers. "MITI, MPT, and the Telecom Wars: How Japan Makes Policy for High Technology." From *Creating Advantage: American and Japanese Strategies for Ad-*

justing to Change in a New World Economy, to be published in 1989 by the University of California, Berkeley Roundtable on the International Economy (BRIE).

Johnson, Chalmers. "The Pacific Basin's Challenge to America: Myth and Reality." *USA Today,* March 1987.

Johnson, Chalmers. "Political Institutions and Economic Performance: the Government-Business Relationship in Japan, South Korea, and Taiwan." In Frederic C. Deyo, ed., *The Political Economy of the New Asian Industrialism.* Ithaca, N.Y.: Cornell University Press, 1987.

Johnson, Chalmers. "Reflections on the Dilemma of Japanese Defense." *Asian Survey,* volume XXVI, number 5, May 1986.

Johnson, Chalmers. "Studies of the Japanese Political Economy: A Crisis in Theory." Unpublished paper, winter 1988.

Johnson, Paul. "The English Disease: 1945–1979." *The Wilson Quarterly,* autumn 1987.

Johnstone, Bob. "The Robot Generation." *Far Eastern Economic Review,* November 19, 1987.

Jones, Randall. "Economic Restructuring in Japan." Japan Economic Institute, *JEI Report,* number 37A, October 2, 1987.

Junkins, Jerry R. "Winning in Global Markets." Presentation to the New York Society of Security Analysts by the Chief Executive Officer of Texas Instruments, November 7, 1986.

Kang, Sung-hack. "America's Foreign Policy Toward East Asia for the 1990s: From Godfather to Outsider." *Korea and World Affairs,* volume XI, number 4, winter 1987.

Karatsu, Hajime. "Costly Defects: U.S. Semiconductor Industry from a Japanese Perspective." *Speaking of Japan,* November 1986.

Kasman, Bruce. "Japan's Growth Performance over the Last Decade." Federal Reserve Bank of New York, *Quarterly Review,* summer 1987.

Kawai, Motoyoshi. "High-Tech War Heats Up." *Business Tokyo,* October 1987.

Kearns, David T. "Education Recovery: Business Must Set the Agenda." Speech by the Chief Executive Officer of the Xerox Corporation to the Economic Club of Detroit, Detroit, October 26, 1987.

Keizai Koho Center. "Japan 1988." Published by the Japan Institute for Social and Economic Affairs, Tokyo, Japan, 1989.

Kennedy, Paul M. "The (Relative) Decline of America." *Atlantic,* August 1987.

Kennedy, Paul M. "What Gorbachev Is Up Against." *Atlantic,* June 1987.

Kennedy, Paul M., et al. "Lessons from the Fall and Rise of Nations: The Future for America." Washington: Woodrow Wilson International Center for Scholars, 1987.

Kindleberger, Charles P. "International Economic Organizations." In David Calleo, ed., *Money and the Coming World Order.* New York: The Lehrman Institute/NYU Press, 1976.

Kindleberger, Charles P. "On the Rise and Decline of Nations." *International Studies Quarterly,* volume 27, number 1, March 1983.

Kobayashi, Hisashi. "Creativity in Research and Development." Unpublished paper presented at the 7th New Energy Industrial Symposium, Tokyo, Japan, October 20–21, 1987.

Kobayashi, Hisashi. "Scientific Creativity and Engineering Innovation in Japan." In Robert S. Cutler, ed., *Japanese Science and Technology: The Changing Institutional Framework.* Washington: National Academy of Engineering, 1987

Kodama, Fumio. "Technological Diversification of Japanese Industry." *Science,* July 18, 1986.

Koh, B. C. "Recruitment of Higher Civil Servants in Japan." *Asian Survey,* March 1985.

Komiya, Ryutaro. "Industrial Policy's Generation Gap." *Economic Eye,* volume 7, number 1, March 1986.

Komiya, Ryutaro. "Japan's Industrial Policy: Perspective and Reassessment of the Policy Debate." *Nihon Keizai Shimbun,* November 18–23, 1985.

Koo, Hagen. "The Interplay of State, Social Class, and World System in East Asian Development: the Cases of South Korea and Taiwan." In Frederic C. Deyo, ed., *The Political Economy of the New Asian Industrialism*. Ithaca, N.Y.: Cornell University Press, 1987.

Kosaka, Masataka. "Nihon no kiki wa doko kara kuru ka?" ("Where Will Japan's Crisis Come From?") *Bungei Shunju*, January 1986.

Koyama, Kenichi. "Rethinking Education." *Look Japan*, December 1987.

Kozol, Jonathan. "The Homeless and Their Children." *The New Yorker*, January 25 and February 1, 1988.

Kristof, Nicholas D. "In China, the Buck Starts Here." *New York Times*, December 20, 1987.

Kuttner, Robert. "The Poverty of Economics." *Atlantic*, February 1985.

La Brecque, Ron. "Something More than Calculus." *Education Life*, supplement of *New York Times*, November 6, 1988.

Lasater, Martin. "Taiwan's International Environment." Unpublished paper presented at the American Enterprise Institute Conference on Development and Democracy in East Asia, Washington, May 18–19, 1988.

Lawless, Richard P., and Therese Shaheen. "Airplanes and Airports: The Subtle Skill of Japanese Protectionism." *SAIS Review*, volume 8, number 1, spring 1988.

Lee Kuan Yew. "The Asia-Pacific Region: Present Trends, Future Consequences." Speech delivered by the prime minister of Singapore to the International Herald Tribune conference, "Pacific 2000: Global Challenge," November 11, 1987.

Lee, Martin C. M. "The Basic Law for Hong Kong: Will It Bring About 'One Country, Two Systems?'" Unpublished paper presented at the Association for Asian Studies annual meeting, San Francisco, March 26, 1988.

Lee, Martin C. M., et al. "Position Paper of the Delegation for Democracy in Hong Kong." Hong Kong, January, 1988.

Leipziger, Danny M. "Industrial Restructuring in Korea." In *Korea: Transition to Maturity*. London: Pergamon Press, 1988.

Levy, Brian, and Wen-Jeng Kuo. "Investment Requirements and the Participation of Korean and Taiwanese Firms in Technology-Intensive Industries." Seoul: Korea Development Institute, 1987.

Lewis, Cathy. "Japanese Nursery Schools." Paper presented at the annual meeting of the Association for Asian Studies, San Francisco, March 25–27, 1988.

Lin, Tzong-Biau. "International Competition: A Challenge from the Asian-Pacific Rim." Innsbruck, Austria: Hans Martin Schleyer Stiftung Congress, May 21–23, 1986.

Lindsey, Lawrence. "Better Childcare, Cheaper." *Wall Street Journal*, July 5, 1988.

Link, Perry. "The Chinese Intellectuals and Revolt," *New York Review of Books*, June 29, 1989.

Lohr, Steve. "Inside the Philippine Insurgency." *New York Times*, November 3, 1985.

Low, Linda. "Strengthening of Employers' Initiatives in Favor of a Better Integration of Women in Economic and Social Development." Unpublished paper presented at the International Labor Organization and Singapore National Employers Federation joint conference, Bangkok, Thailand, March 6, 1987.

Lowenstein, Louis. Statement before the U.S. House of Representatives, Committee on Ways and Means, May 17, 1989.

Lu, Ya-Li. "Political Developments in the Republic of China." Unpublished paper presented at the American Enterprise Institute Conference on Development and Democracy in East Asia, Washington, May 18–19, 1988.

Lynn, Leonard. "Japanese Research and Technology Policy." *Science*, July 18, 1986.

MacKnight, Susan. "The Appreciating Yen and Japanese Export Pricing." Japan Economic Journal, *JEI Report,* number 10A, March 11, 1988.

MacKnight, Susan. "The Debate over Japanese Investment in the United States." Japan Economic Institute, *JEI Report,* number 21A, May 27, 1988.

MacKnight, Susan. "Japan's Expanding U.S. Manufacturing Presence." Japan Economic Institute, *JEI Report,* number 47A, December 18, 1987.

Main, Jeremy. "Trying to Bend Managers' Minds." *Fortune,* November 23, 1987.

Makino, Noboru. "Understanding the War of the Chips." *Japan Echo,* volume 14, number 3, 1987.

McAbee, Michael. "The Changing Face of Foreign Direct Investment in Japan." *East Asian Executive Reports,* October 15, 1987.

Melloan, George. "Companies Team Up to Develop Better Tools." *Wall Street Journal,* December 1, 1987.

Min, Pyong-gap. "Problems of Korean Immigrant Entrepreneurs." Unpublished paper presented at the Association for Asian Studies annual meeting, San Francisco, March 26, 1988.

Minabe, Shigeo. "Japanese Competitiveness and Japanese Management." *Science,* July 18, 1986.

Modelski, George. "The Long Cycle of Global Politics and the Nation-State." Discussion paper presented at the Tenth World Congress of the International Political Science Association, Edinburgh, Scotland, August 21, 1976.

Moore, Stephen. "Privatization Lessons for Washington, Part II: Improving Human Services." The Heritage Foundation, *Backgrounder,* number 674, September 28, 1988.

Moore, Stephen. "Why America Does Not Need More Taxes." The Heritage Foundation, *Backgrounder,* number 680, November 22, 1988.

Morse, Ronald. "Japan's Bureaucratic Edge." *Foreign Policy,* fall 1983.

Morse, Ronald. "Japan's Drive to Pre-Eminence," *Foreign Policy,* winter 1987–88.

Morse, Ronald. "Policy Coordination Memo." Unpublished monograph, spring 1988.

Munro, Ross H. "The New Khmer Rouge." *Commentary,* December 1985.

Muramatsu, Michio. "In Search of National Identity: The Politics and Policies of the Nakasone Administration." *Journal of Japanese Studies,* volume 13, number 2, summer 1987.

Murray, Charles. "The Coming of Custodial Democracy." *Commentary,* September 1988.

Mydans, Seth. "The Embattled Mrs. Aquino." *New York Times Magazine,* November 15, 1987.

Nakas, Gabriel. "The Decline of Drugged Nations." *Wall Street Journal,* July 11, 1988.

Nakatani, Iwao. "Pakkusu Konsoruchisu Jidai no Torai." ("The Advent of Pax Consortis.") *Keizai Seminaa,* July 1986.

National Academy of Engineering. "Strengthening U.S. Engineering Through International Cooperation: Some Recommendations for Action." Washington: NAE, 1987.

Neureiter, Norman. "The Challenge of Asia." Speech delivered to the Business and Institutional Furniture Manufacturers' Association annual meeting, Newport Beach, November 19, 1987.

Njoroge, Lawrence M. "The Japan-Soviet Territorial Dispute." *Asian Survey,* volume XXV, number 5, May 1985.

Novak, Michael. "Old Values Made New Again." *Washington Times,* January 29, 1989.

Office of the U.S. Trade Representative. "1989 National Trade Estimate Report on Foreign Trade Barriers," Washington, D.C., April 12, 1989.

Ogbu, John. "Black Students and the Burden of Acting White." *The Urban Review,* volume 18, number 3, 1986.

Okazaki, Hisahiko. "Japanese Defense Policy." Unpublished memorandum, 1987.

Okimoto, Daniel I. "Outsider Trading: Coping with Japanese Industrial Organization." *Journal of Japanese Studies*, volume 13, number 2, summer 1987.

Olsen, Edward A. "The Arms Race on the Korean Peninsula." *Asian Survey*, volume XXVI, number 8, August 1986.

Omestad, Thomas. "Dateline Taiwan: A Dynasty Ends." *Foreign Policy*, summer 1988.

Ostrom, Douglas. "The Changing Nature of Japanese Manufacturing." Japan Economic Institute, *JEI Report*, number 23A, June 17, 1988.

Ostrom, Douglas. "Japan's Imports of Manufactured Goods." Japan Economic Institute, *JEI Report*, number 14A, April 8, 1988.

Ostrom, Douglas. "Japan's Role as an International Creditor." Japan Economic Institute, *JEI Report*, number 35A, September 16, 1988.

Otsuki, Shinji. "Battle over the FSX Fighter: Who Won?" *Japan Quarterly*, volume 35, number 2, April–June 1988.

Packard, George. "The Coming U.S.–Japan Crisis." *Foreign Affairs*, winter 1988.

Park, Yong-ok. "ROK-US Security Relations in the 1990s." *Korea and World Affairs*, volume 11, number 4, winter 1987.

Patrick, Hugh. "Japanese High Technology Industrial Policy in Comparative Context." Unpublished memorandum, Columbia University Seminar on Modern Japan, December 13, 1985.

Pauker, Guy. "Security Assistance to Southeast Asia." *America's New Pacific Era*, Heritage Foundation *Lectures*, June 7, 1984.

Peak, Lois. "Formal Pre-elementary Education in Japan." Paper presented at the Association for Asian Studies annual meeting, San Francisco, March 25–27, 1988.

Pempel, T. J. "The Unbundling of 'Japan, Inc.': The Changing Dynamics of Japanese Policy Formation." *Journal of Japanese Studies*, volume 13, number 2, summer 1987.

Perkovich, George. "Moscow Turns East." *Atlantic*, December 1987.

Perry, Nancy J. "The Education Crisis: What Business Can Do." *Fortune*, July 4, 1988.

Perry, Nancy J. "Saving the Schools: How Business Can Help." *Fortune*, November 7, 1988.

Peterson, Peter G. "The Morning After." *Atlantic*, October 1987.

Phelps, Charles E. "A Happy Hour for Alcohol Taxes." *Wall Street Journal*, January 12, 1988.

Plunk, Daryl. "Political Developments in the Republic of Korea." Unpublished paper presented at the American Enterprise Institute Conference on Development and Democracy in East Asia, Washington, May 18–19, 1988.

Prahalad, C. K., et al. "Strategic Partnerships: The Challenge of Competitive Collaboration." Unpublished memorandum, University of Michigan, 1986.

Preston, Samuel H. "Children and the Elderly in the U.S." *Scientific American*, December 1984.

Pye, Lucian W. "Taiwan's Development and Its Implications for Beijing and Washington." *Asian Survey*, volume XXVI, number 6, June 1986.

Pyle, Kenneth. "The Future of Japanese Nationality: An Essay in Contemporary History." *Journal of Japanese Studies*, winter 1982.

Pyle, Kenneth. "In Pursuit of a Grand Design: Nakasone Betwixt the Past and the Future." *Journal of Japanese Studies*, summer 1987.

Pyle, Kenneth. "Japan, the World, and the 21st Century." In Okimoto & Inoguchi, eds., *The Political Economy of Japan, Vol. 2: The Changing International Context*. Stanford: Stanford University Press, 1988.

Reich, Robert. "Education and the Next Economy." Speech delivered to the National Education Association, Washington, April 1, 1988.

Richardson, Elliott. "Civil Servants: Why Not the Best?" *Wall Street Journal*, November 20, 1987.

Rohlen, Thomas P. "Why Japanese Education Works." *Harvard Business Review*, September-October 1987.

Rosenberg, David. "Socio-Cultural Developments in the Philippines." Unpublished paper presented at the Conference on Development and Democracy in East Asia, American Enterprise Institute, Washington, May 18–19, 1988.

Ross, Dennis E. Statement before the Committee on Finance of the United States Senate, Washington, D.C., March 14, 1989.

Rothschild, Emma. "The Reagan Economic Legacy." *New York Review of Books*, June 30, 1988, and July 21, 1988.

Samuels, Richard J., and Benjamin C. Whipple. "Defense Production and Industrial Development: The Case of Japanese Aircraft." Massachusetts Institute of Technology Japan Science and Technology Program working paper #88-09, 1988.

Samuels, Richard J. "Research Collaboration in Japan." Paper presented to a symposium at the 153rd annual meeting of the American Association for the Advancement of Science, Chicago, February 16, 1987.

Samuelson, Robert J. "Forget About Being Number One." *Washington Post* national weekly edition, volume 6, number 2, November 14–20, 1988.

Satoh, Hideo. "Aiding the Wounded Eagle." *This Is*, June 1987.

Schlossstein, Steven. "The Coming Era of Japan's Majestic Dominance?" *Business Tokyo*, March 1989.

Schlossstein, Steven. "Co-Opting America's Objectivity on Japan," *Washington Post*, June 10, 1989.

Schlossstein, Steven. "The Hundred Years' War." Speech delivered to the Construction Industry Manufacturers' Association annual meeting, Orlando, November 17, 1987.

Schlossstein, Steven. "What's in a (Reign) Name?" Unpublished memorandum, November 15, 1988.

Schram, Stuart. "Political Reform in China." International House of Japan *Bulletin*, volume 8, number 2, spring 1988.

Schwartz, Felice N. "Management Women and the New Facts of Life," *Harvard Business Review*, January–February 1989.

Scott, Bruce R. "U.S. Competitiveness in the World Economy: An Update." Unpublished memorandum, February 6, 1987.

Servan-Schreiber, Jean-Jacques, and Herbert Simon. "America Must Remain the World's University," *Washington Post*, November 15, 1987.

Shanker, Albert. "The Making of a Profession." *American Educator*, fall 1985.

Shanker, Albert. "Our Profession, Our Schools: The Case for Fundamental Reform." *American Educator*, fall 1986.

Shaplen, Robert. "The Thin Edge." *The New Yorker*, September 21 and 28, 1987.

Shaw, Yu-Ming. "An ROC View of the Hong Kong Issue." *Issues and Studies*, volume 22, number 6, June 1986.

Shaw, Yu-Ming. "A View from Taipei." *Foreign Affairs*, summer 1985.

Shepherd, Mark. "Current Challenges for American Industry." Speech delivered at the University of Utah, March 6, 1987.

Shepherd, Mark. "The Role of Technology in Manufacturing." Speech delivered to the International Industrial Engineering Conference, Dallas, May 13, 1986.

Sikorski, Radek. "The Coming Crack-Up of Communism." *National Review*, January 27, 1989.

Snyder, David Pearce. "Learning for Life in Revolutionary Times: Imperatives for Educators in a Deacade of Techno-Economic Change." *Journal of Studies in Technical Careers,* volume IX, number 2, spring 1987.

Steinberg, David I. "Sociopolitical Factors and Korea's Future Economic Success." *World Development,* volume 16, number 1, January 1988.

Streshly, William, and Eric Schaps. "A Character Education Program That Works." The Development Studies Center, San Ramon Valley, California, undated.

Stubbing, Richard A., and Richard A. Mandel. "How to Save $50 Billion a Year." *Atlantic,* June 1989.

Suh Sang-mok. "Challenge for the Future: Industrial Restructuring and Policy Response." *Korea Business World,* April 1988.

Sullivan, Margaret Cox. Statement before the U.S. House of Representatives, Committee on Ways and Means, May 17, 1989.

Sumney, Larry W., and Robert M. Burger. "Revitalizing the U.S. Semiconductor Industry." *Issues in Science and Technology,* summer 1987.

Sunley, Emil M. "Tax Policies for Reindustrialization." In Robert Thornton, ed., *Reindustrialization: Implications for U.S. Industrial Policy.* Greenwich, Conn.: JAI Press, 1984.

Thayer, Nathaniel B. "Race and Politics in Japan." *The Pacific Review,* volume I, number 1, 1988.

Thurow, Lester C. "A Weakness in Process Technology." *Science,* December 18, 1987.

Thurow, Lester C., and Laura D'Andrea Tyson. "The Economic Black Hole." *Foreign Policy,* winter 1987.

Trotter, Robert J. "Project Day Care." *Psychology Today,* December 1987.

Tsim, T. L. "One Country, Two Systems." Unpublished paper presented at the Association for Asian Studies annual meeting, San Francisco, March 26, 1988.

Uhlenberg, Peter. "Adolescents in American Society: Recent Trends and Proposed Responses." Paper presented to the Family Research Council Annual Resource Network Conference, Washington, June 12–14, 1986.

United States Department of Commerce, Bureau of the Census, Foreign Trade Division, "Highlights of U.S. Export and Import Trade," FT-990, December 1987, December 1988.

United States Department of Defense. "Background on the Bases," 2nd edition, December 1987.

United States Department of State. "Philippines Background Notes." Washington, D.C., 1986.

United States Department of the Treasury, "General Explanation of the President's Budget Proposals Affecting Receipts," Washington, D.C., February 1989.

Van Wolferen, Karel. "The Japan Problem." *Foreign Affairs,* winter 1987.

Vogel, Ezra F. "Pax Nipponica?" *Foreign Affairs,* spring 1986.

Wade, Robert. "East Asian Financial Systems as a Challenge to Economics: Lessons from Taiwan." *California Management Review,* volume 27, number 4, summer 1985.

Wallerstein, Judith S. "Children After Divorce: Wounds That Don't Heal." *New York Times Magazine,* January 22, 1989.

Wanner, Barbara. "The FSX Project: Changing the Nature of Defense Technology Transfers." Japan Economic Institute, *JEI Report,* number 21A, May 26, 1989.

Wanner, Barbara. "The Opposition Parties in Japanese Politics." Japan Economic Institute, *JEI Report,* number 41A, October 28, 1988.

Wanner, Barbara. "Sharing the Defense Burden with Japan: How Much Is Enough?" Japan Economic Institute, *JEI Report,* number 19A, May 13, 1988.

Watanabe, Toshio. "Asia: New Frontier of Growth." *Economic Eye,* March 1988.

Watanabe, Toshio, and Hitomi Kuwa. "Eastern Asia: Engine of Growth," in *Japan Echo,* spring 1988.

Weinstein, Else. "High School Teacher." *Education Life,* supplement of *New York Times,* November 6, 1988.

Welch, John F., Jr. "Balancing the Scale Between Innovation and Manufacturability." *The Bridge,* National Academy of Engineering, winter 1986.

White, Merry I. "The Virtue of Japanese Mothers: Cultural Definitions of Women's Lives." *Daedalus,* summer 1987.

White, Theodore. "The Danger from Japan." *New York Times Magazine,* July 28, 1985.

Will, George F. "Public Affairs, Public Policy, and American Society." Speech delivered at the Construction Industry Manufacturers' Association annual meeting, Orlando, November 17, 1987.

Wills, Gary. "New Votuhs." *New York Review of Books,* August 18, 1988.

Wu, Chung-Lih. "Economic Developments in the Republic of China." Unpublished paper presented at the American Enterprise Institute Conference on Development and Democracy in East Asia, Washington, May 18–19, 1988.

Wysocki, Bernard, Jr. "Technology: The Final Frontier" (with insert, "Japan Assaults the Last Bastion: America's Lead in Innovation"). *Wall Street Journal Reports,* November 14, 1988.

Yamamoto, Takayuki. "In Self Defense." *Business Tokyo,* February 1988.

Yamamura, Kozo. "Shedding the Shackles of Success: Saving Less for Japan's Future." *Journal of Japanese Studies,* summer 1987.

Yang, Charles Y. "Demystifying Japanese Management Practices." *Harvard Business Review,* November/December 1984.

Yasuda, Yasoi. "Tokyo on and under the Bay." *Japan Quarterly,* volume 35, number 2, April–June 1988.

Yoshikawa, Akihiro, and Brian Woodall. "The 'Venture Boom' and Japanese Industrial Policy: Promoting the Neglected Winners." *Asian Survey,* volume XXV, number 6, June 1985.

Zinsmeister, Karl. "The Family's Tie to the American Dream." *Public Opinion,* September/October 1986.

Zinsmeister, Karl, et al. "Having Children, Helping Children." Policy Conference on Family Issues, American Enterprise Institute, Washington, March 1988.

INDEX

529